GW01143853

How to do *just about* anything on the **INTERNET**

READER'S DIGEST

HOW TO ANYTHING

DO *just about* ON THE INTERNET

Reader's Digest Sydney

Contents

How to use this book............6

GETTING STARTED

Introduction
What is the Internet?..................10

Getting connected
Are you Net ready?......................14
Exploring Windows XP................16
Choose an ISP............................20
Set up your modem....................22
Make the connection..................24
Start browsing............................26

Using e-mail
What is e-mail?..........................30
Different e-mail programs...........32
Set up Outlook Express...............34
Explore Outlook Express..............36
Send and receive e-mail..............38
Build an address book................40
Manage your e-mail....................42
Send e-mail attachments.............46
Receive e-mail attachments.........48
Multiple e-mail accounts.............50

Safe and sound
Security on the Internet...............52
Shop safely on the Web...............54
Filter out unsavoury sites.............56
Avoid computer viruses...............58
Dealing with spam......................62

Have a go at searching
Search the Internet.....................64

Advanced browsing
Improve your browsing................76
Solve browsing problems.............82
Software on the Web..................84
Download from the Web..............86

Other options
Other ways to connect................88
Other ways to communicate.........92

Sharing interests
Take part in a newsgroup............96
Use a bulletin board..................100
Use a chatroom........................102

EXPLORE THE WEB

Advice and information
Learn something new.................110
Do some research......................113
Get the latest news on-line..........116
Find legal advice.......................120
Look for a job..........................122
Seek medical advice..................126
Improve your diet and fitness.......130
Solve computer problems...........133
Help your child to learn on-line.....136

Hobbies and leisure
Go into outer space...................142
Take a virtual tour.....................145
Tune into television...................148
Listen to the radio....................152
Explore the natural world...........156
Trace your family's past..............159
Access showbiz news.................164
Enjoy the literary world..............166
Make new friends.....................169
Explore painting.......................172
Keep the children entertained......174
Go motoring............................180

Improve your home	183
Play games on-line	186

Money and shopping
Do your weekly shop	192
File your tax return	196
Become a share trader	198
Buy a book, CD or video	201
Get a mortgage quotation	204
Support a good cause	206
Buy and sell at auction	208
Open an on-line bank account	212

Great days
Mark a special occasion	218
Find a fun night out	222
Enjoy the great outdoors	225
Book a perfect holiday	228
Plan your overseas trip	232
Get cooking	236
Live the sporting life	238
Plan a wedding	241

MAKING WEB SITES

Introduction
What is a Web site?	246
How are Web sites made?	248
Web site ingredients	250

Your first Web page
Web design basics	254
Build a Web page in Word	256
Upload your site	262

Building on your site
Add a picture to your page	264
Link to more pages	270
Add sound to your page	276
Add a video to your page	282

Other design tools
Design a Web page on-line	288
Other design programs	294
Advanced Web design tools	296

Getting professional
How e-commerce works	298
Set up a business site	300
Ensure your site is seen	306

DIRECTORY 312
An A–Z guide to the best of the Web

Index	344
Acknowledgments	351

How to use this book

Discover how to **make the most of the Internet**

How to do Just About Anything on the Internet will make the Internet more accessible to all. With easy-to-follow, clearly illustrated step-by-step procedures, we guide you through the basics of using the Internet, giving information of the benefits (and possible difficulties) you will encounter along the way. On virtually every page, you will find helpful tips on how to save time and solve problems, plus useful information that will help you to get the most out of the Internet. We show exactly what will appear on your screen at every stage, so that you can check your progress as you journey around the World Wide Web.

Finding your way around
The book is arranged in three main sections. They do not need to be read in order, but you will probably get more out of the Internet if you read the introductions to getting on-line and using e-mail, before starting out. If you are looking for something specific, try the Index on page 344.

Getting started
Here we explain how to set yourself up with an ISP (Internet Service Provider), how to send e-mail and begin browsing the Internet. You will also find information on how to protect your computer and family from the less savoury aspects of the Web.

Explore the Web
This is your tour guide to the best Web sites on a variety of subjects, from finding information to booking a flight or organising a wedding. It shows how you can use the Internet to make your life easier, and how to browse to best advantage.

Making Web sites
Use this section if you want to know how to design and set up your own Web site, then enhance it by adding extra features such as sounds, videos and pictures.

Directory
Find all the sites mentioned in the book and hundreds more in this handy, A-Z reference guide.

HOW THE PAGES WORK
Signposts, step-by-step guides and other features are designed to make the book clear and easy to use.

The best Web sites
The names and addresses of Web sites relating to the topic in question, as well as a brief description of why they are worth visiting. Web addresses are given in **bold type** so that you can identify them easily. You will also find many snapshots of what the Web sites look like.

Additional information
Other useful information relating to the subject, such as 'case studies' explaining how people have succeeded in using the Internet to find what they want.

Search it yourself
Use the tips in this box to find more sites that suit your particular needs.

Extra help
Here you will find useful DOs and DON'Ts, and other important points to remember.

Hints and tips
There are seven types of tip, each clearly marked with its own icon: 'Did You Know?', 'Time Saver!', 'Watch Out!', 'Problem Solver!', 'Money Saver!', 'Jargon Buster' and 'iMac'.

See also
Other sections of the book that deal with related topics.

What you need
This book assumes that readers are operating PCs that run Windows XP Home Edition, but users of Windows Millennium Edition (Me) and Windows 98 will be able to use the book without problems. Users of Apple Macs will also be able to follow the book – the screen shots will look different, but the principles are largely the same. Significant differences are pointed out in iMac boxes.

The browser shown in all screen snapshots is Internet Explorer 6 and the e-mail software is Outlook Express 6. Users of other programs will be able to follow all the principles shown.

To see whether you have all the hardware necessary for accessing the Internet, see *Are You Net Ready?*, page 14.

'How-to' step-by-steps
A brief introduction introduces each operation and provides key information.

Screen snapshots
Every step is illustrated with a snapshot or 'grab' of exactly how the screen will look as you proceed. Intermediate stages are illustrated with smaller inset images.

Clear instructions
Each step is fully explained and **bold type** is used to indicate each time you have to click on something with your mouse.

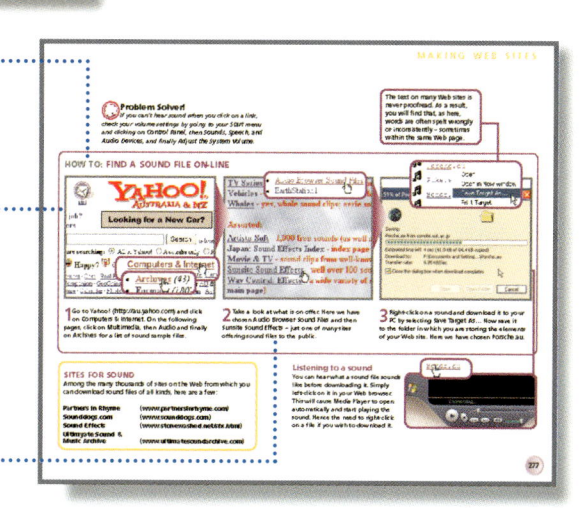

SECTION ONE
Getting started

Use your computer to access the Internet and send e-mail. Then discover the range of information available on the Web, and how you can find and use it.

INTRODUCTION

What is the Internet?

Discover the uses and potential of the Web

The word 'Internet' is a contraction of the words '*inter*connected' and '*net*work'. It refers to a vast, worldwide network of powerful computer servers that are constantly connected to each other via high-speed communication cables. When you connect to the Internet on your home or office PC, you establish a connection to just one of these servers, but it is able to give you access to all the files stored on all the other servers. Connecting to the Internet is also called 'going on-line' or 'dialling up'.

How it works
Imagine you had two computers in your house that were connected to each other with a cable. You could write a message on one and send it to the other over the cable. You could also use one computer to open a file on the other one.
This is exactly how the Internet began way back in the late 1960s.

Today's Internet works in the same way except that there are now millions of powerful computers called servers onnected together via a dedicated communication network.

As an individual computer user, you connect to one of these server computers, then use it as your gateway to the rest of the Internet.

GETTING STARTED

USES OF THE INTERNET

There are two main uses of the Internet – transferring electronic mail (e-mail) from computer to computer, and digital publishing on the World Wide Web (WWW or Web for short). Because the World Wide Web is the part of the Internet that you can see on your screen, people often use the terms 'Web' and 'Internet' interchangeably. But in fact the Web is only part of what the Internet has to offer.

The World Wide Web

This is a unique service offered by the Internet. It is a huge collection of 'pages' containing text, graphics and other media, which you can view via your computer's Web browser. Anyone with an Internet-connected computer can view Web pages – no matter where the pages originate from or where the viewer is in the world.

Web pages are also connected by 'hyperlinks' (also called 'links'). These are electronic connections between pages on the same or different Web sites, usually on similar or related subjects. This makes information on the Web more accessible.

Electronic mail

More commonly known as e-mail, electronic mail is the primary means of communicating over the Internet. E-mail can be text-only, or can include attached files – such as sounds or images. It is extremely fast, transferring information almost instantaneously (see *What is e-mail?*, page 30).

Newsgroups

Areas on the Net where people can read others' messages and leave their own, newsgroups are another useful aspect of the Internet. Many thousands of newsgroups can be found on every subject imaginable. In fact, newsgroups existed before the Web in a system called Usenet. They are a good example of a way in which the Internet unites people with shared interests (see *Take part in a newsgroup*, page 96).

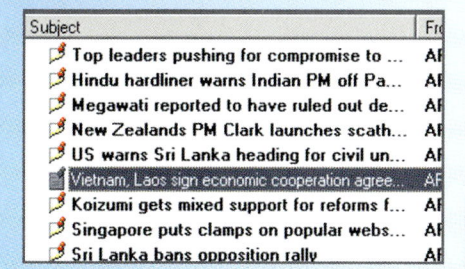

THE HISTORY OF THE NET

The Internet has its origins in a US Department of Defense (DOD) project dating from the 1960s. Called ARPANET (Advanced Research Projects Agency Network), this linked various DOD computers, and was designed to protect key data from nuclear attack.

Simultaneously, the US university sector started to link remote computers together as a means of sharing research papers between distant campuses. The network grew quickly and, in the early 1970s, spread to Europe, with England and Norway coming on board first.

In the mid 1980s, the National Science Foundation linked five supercomputers to form NSnet.

Other institutions took advantage of the power these provided, and this spurred more international growth.

But the Internet as we know it was still far from formed. It wasn't until 1989 that Tim Berners-Lee, a British physicist, devised a network in which data from any source could be accessed in a simple way using the same program, on any type of computer. This laid the foundations for what we know today as the World Wide Web.

Jargon Buster!

Web page
A document that is published on the Internet and can be viewed on a computer screen (see *What is a Web site?*, *page 246*).

Did You Know?

The Internet is increasingly popular as an alternative to telephoning, especially over long distances. You can also connect a tiny Web-cam that allows you to see the person you are talking to (see Other ways to communicate, *page 92).*

11

INTRODUCTION

PROS AND CONS OF THE INTERNET

The Internet has assets that set it apart from other sources of information and forms of communication. But it is by no means perfect and cannot fully replace other forms of media.

Speed
The Internet provides an amazingly quick way to access information and send messages – taking just seconds to send data around the world. On the other hand, the speed of the Internet depends on how many people are using it, and the speed of your connection.

At times, the Internet can be maddeningly slow – especially when a simple phonecall might provide all the information you need.

Economy
Except for the connection charges incurred while you are on-line, the Internet is mostly free. You can access information and then print it out or save it to your own computer to look at later. The Internet cannot replace books, newspapers and magazines, but it lets you access much of the same information – and a great deal more – in a different way.

Accessibility
All this is available if you have a phone line and a computer. Internet cafés and on-line services in public places such as libraries mean that you don't need to be at your own computer to access the Internet. However, the Internet can be impersonal, and sometimes it is easier to phone a person, rather than spend time searching on-line.

Breadth of information
The Internet contains detailed information on almost every subject you could possibly think of, and can offer specialised information that you might be unable to find elsewhere.

Multimedia
You can download pictures, text, video, sounds, software and many other things to enhance your computer and the time you spend using it.

Quality
Regrettably, a lot of information on the Web is inaccurate or out-of-date, and some of it may be pure propaganda, so you need to exercise your own critical judgment and common sense. Fortunately, search engines and the Web's link-based structure make it easy for you to move from one site to another to compare and check information.

Although many people worry that the Internet makes it easy to access pornography and other material that may be offensive, there are various steps you can take to block sites containing a range of contents that you might prefer your children not to see (see *Filter out unsavoury sites*, page 56).

WHO OWNS IT ALL?
No single organisation owns the Internet. Its technical infrastructure is maintained by a mix of commercial, government and academic institutions. Some of the information and services on the Internet are provided by and for commercial companies, some by clubs and organisations. Other material comes from or is used by schools, charities and government bodies. Still more is produced by individuals – themselves also Internet users. Literally anyone can be a part of the Internet, but nobody can claim to control it.

Despite the huge revenues it generates for some companies, the Internet itself runs on a non-profit-making basis. Several organisations are involved. The Internet Society (**www.isoc.org**) ratifies technical standards, and the World Wide Web Consortium (**www.w3.org**) considers the Web's future.

Did You Know?

There are many different indexing services for the Web. Called 'search engines', they index Web sites on your behalf, and can be searched by using keywords. For more on this, see Search the Internet, *page 64.*

Money Saver!

Sometimes goods are offered for sale on the Internet for a cheaper price than in stores. This is often because on-line stores have fewer overheads and they pass savings on to the customer.

GETTING STARTED

WHAT TO DO ON-LINE

Go shopping
You can save time by browsing through the catalogues of Internet stores and then placing an order on-line. From fresh food to videos, or a second-hand car, you can buy it on the Web (see pages 180, 192, and 201).

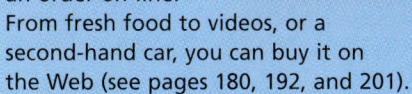

Find information
A range of Web sites and reference sources mean that you can find out almost anything on the Internet – and usually very quickly.

From information about academic or scientific matters, to news and weather, entertaining trivia or facts about your computer, the Internet can provide information updates faster than any newspaper or book.

Have a chat
Internet chatrooms make it easy for you to exchange views and information with other Internet users from all around the world, and to communicate with people you would never otherwise have been able to find (see *Use a chatroom*, page 102).

Send an e-mail
E-mail allows you to send and receive text, pictures and other media almost instantaneously around the world (see *Send and receive e-mail*, page 38).

Run a business
The Internet makes it easier than ever before to set up a business – provided you have something worthwhile to offer. Whether selling a product or a service, you can investigate the Internet as a possible way of generating income (see *Set up a business site*, page 300).

Follow the news
Many news Web sites provide as-it-happens updates. Follow a story as it evolves, rather than waiting for bulletins on TV or radio. You can also install an on-screen device to relay news updates to your computer while you work on other things (see *Get the latest news on-line*, page 116).

Listen to music
You can download music of all kinds from the Internet. You can also send and receive music files via e-mail. The laws regarding on-line music are currently under review and you may find that in future you have to pay for previously free downloads.

Have fun
All kinds of computer games can be played on-line or downloaded to your PC. Play against an opponent on the other side of the planet, or even against a 'virtual' opponent (see *Play games on-line*, page 186).

Learn something new
It is hard to rival the Internet as an extensive reference tool (see *Search the Internet*, page 64). You can trace a family member, look up a historical event, or follow technological discoveries (see *Learn something new*, page 110).

Help others
The Internet makes it easy to support your favourite charity or good cause. Many have a 'click-to-give' feature which allows you to help by simply clicking your mouse. You can also find out how to help in other ways (see *Support a good cause*, page 206).

Note on changing Web sites
The Internet is constantly evolving. Web site addresses and the contents of Web sites can change rapidly, and some sites may disappear without warning, regardless of whether they belong to large companies or individual enthusiasts.

However, even if certain sites change in content or appearance, or vanish altogether, the principles of using different types of Web sites, as demonstrated in this book, can still be applied.

Did You Know?
According to the United Nations, there are more than 360 million Internet users around the world, of whom around 109 million live in Europe, 96 million in the USA, some 6.6 million in Australia and 830,000 in New Zealand.

SEE ALSO
- Are you Net ready? – page 14
- What is e-mail? – page 30
- Security on the Internet – page 52
- Search the Internet – page 64

GETTING CONNECTED

Are you Net ready?

Discover what **hardware** and **software** you need to start **surfing the Web**

Most computers bought in the past five years will be equipped to access the Internet. Certainly, any home PC bought in the past two years will have sufficient memory, a modem and all the necessary software – and it will probably all be set up for you. But there are a few checks you should make to be sure (see right).

BASIC HARDWARE

When you buy a new computer, the hardware necessary to access the Internet should all be provided.

Computer

The ability of your computer to access the Internet depends on how quick its central processing unit (CPU) is and how much random access memory (RAM) it has installed.

The CPU is your computer's brain. Every time you ask your computer to do anything, you are issuing thousands of instructions. The speed of your CPU depends on how quickly it processes these instructions. This is given as the number of 'clock ticks' in each second (every instruction can take one or more clock ticks). A 400MHz chip is capable of 400,000,000 clock ticks each second – enough to keep up with most software.

Your computer's RAM is the amount of memory it has for storing and using software. All software – whether the Windows operating system or a program – is loaded into the computer's RAM from the hard disk when you open it. Memory, like hard disk space, is measured in terms of 'bits' and 'bytes'.

A bit is the smallest unit of computer storage. A combination of eight bits makes up a byte. A kilobyte (Kb) is 1024 bytes; a megabyte (Mb) is 1024Kb; and a gigabyte (Gb) is 1024Mb. A typical home PC running Windows XP should have around 128Mb of memory.

Modem

A modem is a device which connects your computer to the Internet and allows digital data to be sent through telephone lines. Most computers come with a modem as a standard accessory. However, if your computer does not have one, you can easily buy a modem and connect it yourself (see *Set up your modem*, page 22).

Modems operate at different speeds. The fastest transfer data at a rate of 56 kilobits a second (56K), but a speed of 33.6K is sufficient for accessing the Internet.

Sound card and speakers

Web sites can incorporate sounds, but you won't hear them unless you have a sound card to process the information and speakers to play it on. Most new computers are supplied with these features as standard.

If your PC plays a tune when you turn it on, then it has a sound card and speakers. If there is no sound, you may wish to have a sound card and speakers fitted, though they are not essential for accessing the Internet.

Monitor

A 17-inch monitor (measured diagonally across the screen) is more than large enough for viewing and browsing the Net. An even bigger monitor, however, will allow you to see more of any Web page at a time.

GETTING STARTED

THE BASIC SOFTWARE

To begin using the Internet you need two pieces of software: a Web browser and an e-mail program. If you have a new PC running Windows XP, you will have all the necessary software pre-installed. If not, your Internet Service Provider (ISP) should provide you with all you need when you sign up for access to the Internet.

Web browser
This is the software that your computer uses to display Web sites. Internet Explorer (which comes as standard with Windows XP) and Netscape Navigator are the most widely used browsers. Although there are important differences between them, most sites will display their information correctly through either one.

E-mail software
You'll need an e-mail program, such as Outlook Express, to send and receive mail using your computer. Again, this program is a standard component of Windows XP. For more information on using e-mail software, see *What is e-mail?*, page 30.

News reader
There are e-mail-based discussion forums on the Web, called newsgroups, that are free to join. To access them you need a news reader program. To start with, you can use Outlook Express as a news reader. For other programs, see *Software on the Web*, page 84. However, you can do without news reader software for most surfing purposes.

Check your software
To see what software is installed on your PC, go to the **Start** menu and click **Programs**. Check the list that comes up for programs such as Outlook Express and Internet Explorer.

OPERATING SYSTEMS

All computers require an 'operating system' (OS), a complex piece of software that handles their basic functions. Operating systems are changing all the time. Before December 2001, most PCs used Windows 95, Windows 98 or Windows Me. Any PC purchased after December 2001 would most likely come with Windows XP, which looks and operates quite differently from earlier forms of Windows.

To find out which OS is installed on your machine, click on the **Start** button on your menu bar and then right-click on the **My Computer** icon that appears in the pop-up window. This will show you exactly what OS you are using.

If you have an older version of Windows, you will be able to use this book and access the Internet without problems. If you have Windows XP, however, you have a number of powerful new tools, which are discussed overleaf (see *Exploring Windows XP*, page 16).

Extra software
As you become more proficient as an Internet user, you may find that you need additional software. This may include FTP software, which you can use to upload your own Web pages onto the Internet, Macromedia Flash, which allows you to view animations and RealOne Player, which allows you to listen to Internet radio and other sound files. Most additional software can be acquired over the Internet (see *Software on the Web*, page 84).

Did You Know?
You do not have to connect to the Internet via a modem. For other connection types, such as ADSL and cable, see Other ways to connect, *page 88.*

SEE ALSO
- Make the connection – *page 24*
- Start browsing – *page 26*
- Download from the Web – *page 86*

15

GETTING CONNECTED

Exploring Windows XP

Discover the features that make this operating system user-friendly

Microsoft designed Windows XP – its latest operating system – to provide users with a variety of interactive multimedia facilities, as well as quick and easy access to many of the most popular features of the Internet. As a result, Windows XP has a range of powerful tools that were not found in older operating systems, such as Windows Me or 98. In this section, we examine some of the ways in which XP is different, and show you how to set up your PC so that several members of your family can use it without affecting one another.

WINDOWS XP BASICS

Windows XP has three great features to help you to make the most of your computer: configuration wizards, unique user accounts and passwords.

Configuration wizards

All the main settings in Windows XP can be managed by means of easy-to-use mini-programs called 'wizards'. The most important wizards relating to the Internet are the Add Hardware wizard, for installing a modem, and the New Connection wizard for setting up an ISP account. Both are described in detail later in this book (see pages 23 and 25).

The User Accounts wizard, described in this section, is another powerful tool that allows you to define the access rights that different users have to your computer.

User accounts

In the past, if more than one person worked on a computer, they all had to share the same settings. With Windows XP, however, every user can log-on to the PC using a password and a distinct personal 'account'. They can then create their own settings without affecting anyone else's.

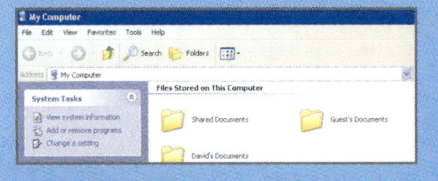

This means that when different users log-on, they'll find their own choice of wallpaper on the Desktop, their own list of 'Favorites' in Internet Explorer, and their own preferences in a range of programs. Their e-mail will also be delivered into their own Outlook Express Inbox, and any documents they create will be stored in a special folder reserved for them alone.

Passwords

When you set up an account for yourself, you can choose to protect your log-on rights with a password. The first and most important profile to set up is the one that comes labelled 'Owner'. You can change this name to whatever you want, and it would be wise to set up a password, especially if you'll be allowing your children to work on your PC.

With password-protection, no-one else will be able to see your e-mails or documents; nor will they be able to alter your settings. You, however, will be able to create settings that other users can't change – for example, blocking access to unsavoury sites on the Internet.

GETTING STARTED

HOW TO: SET UP THE OWNER ACCOUNT

When you install Windows XP, the program automatically creates two user accounts, called 'Owner' and 'Guest'. The Owner account has administrator rights, while the Guest account is allocated limited rights (see below). In either case, these rights determine what different users can access and change on the computer.

The first thing you should do is to set up a password on the Owner account, and perhaps rename it if you wish. This will give you control over the computer and over all other accounts.

1 Go to the **Start** menu at bottom left of your screen and click on **Control Panel**, then **User Accounts**. Under 'Pick a task', click **Change an account**.

2 Click on the **Owner** account and select **Create a password**. Then type in your chosen password, confirm it, and type in a hint in case you forget it. Click **Create Password**.

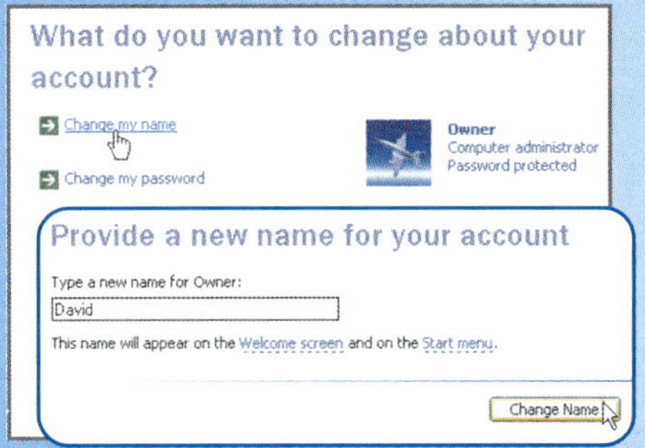

3 If you want to change the name of the account, click **Change my name**, and in the next window type in the name you'd prefer. Confirm your choice by clicking **Change Name**.

4 You will now see your account name in bold type, together with its main characteristics: 'Computer administrator' and 'Password protected'. You are now ready to set up more accounts.

TYPES OF ACCOUNTS

Every account must be either of the 'administrator' or 'limited' variety. You should ensure that there is at least one administrator account operational on your PC.

Administrator accounts
An administrator account has unlimited power to modify the computer, to view its contents, to install software and to alter the settings of all other accounts.

Limited accounts
By giving your children accounts with limited rights, they won't be able to change your settings, see your files or inadvertently delete important information.

Guest account
This account allows someone who is not a regular user of your PC to access its basic functions.

Watch Out!

If you alone have administrator rights and you forget your password, you will be locked out of the computer and no-one else will be able to help you. An obvious solution is to give someone else you trust administrator rights as well. Otherwise, write down your password and store it in a safe place in case of emergencies.

17

GETTING CONNECTED

Watch Out!

If you delete an account, you will also delete all files, documents and e-mails associated with that account. If any of these are important, transfer them manually into the 'Shared Documents' folder before deleting the account.

HOW TO: SET UP A NEW ACCOUNT

Once you have set up a password and all your preferences for the Owner account (or whatever you have decided to call it), you can proceed to create accounts for everyone else who will be using your PC.

If your children are young, you may wish to create a single account, with limited rights, for all your children, and call it, for example, 'Kids'. But if your children are older, and have their own e-mail accounts, it may be better to let them have separate, individual accounts. That way, they can receive their own e-mails, and create their own documents, without being able to spy on each other.

1 Go to the **Start** menu at the bottom left of your screen and click on **Control Panel**, then **User Accounts**. In the options under 'Pick a task', click **Create a new account**.

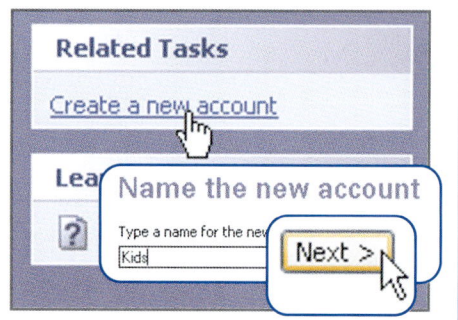

2 In the next window, click **Create a new account** and then give the account a name. Here, we have chosen the name 'Kids'. To confirm your choice, click **Next**.

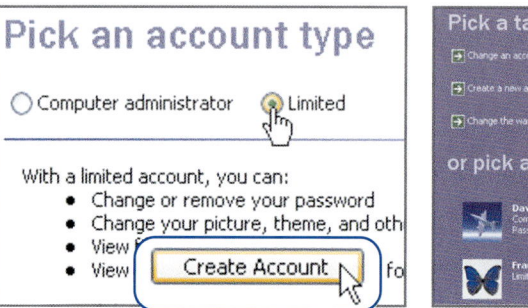

3 You will now be asked to select the type of account you want to set up – here, we have chosen 'Limited'. Then click **Create Account** to return to the 'User Accounts' window.

4 Repeat steps 1–3 for as many accounts as you wish to create. But beware of giving administrator rights to other users, as they could change your settings and lock you out of the PC.

ACTIVATING THE GUEST ACCOUNT

Although Windows XP automatically creates a Guest account with limited rights, this account is, by default, not turned on. To activate your Guest account, go to your **Start** menu and click on **Control Panel**, then **User Accounts**. You will see that the picture for the Guest account shows a suitcase in black and white, and has the label 'Guest account is off'.

Click on the account, and in the next window click on **Turn on Guest Account**. The account will be activated and its picture will change to something else in full colour. Unlike other accounts, the Guest account cannot be password protected, which makes it ideal for visitors who may need to use your PC.

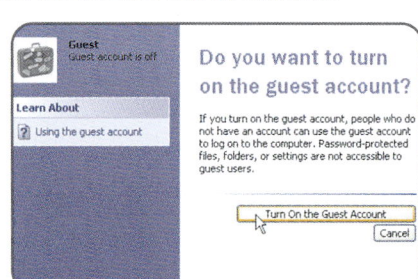

GETTING STARTED

HOW TO: MOVE BETWEEN ACCOUNTS

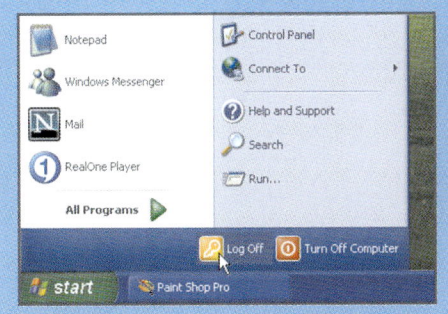

1 If you are switching users for a short while, save your documents and close them. Then click on your **Start** menu and choose **Log Off**.

2 In the 'Log Off Windows' panel, click on **Switch User**. The Welcome screen will then open, showing all available accounts. Another user can now log on.

3 The new user will be asked for a password (if the account has been set up to require one). They should type it in and then click on the button with a green arrow. The new account will start up with all associated preferences, such as Desktop wallpaper, Desktop layout and other settings.
When finished, the second user should repeat steps 1–2 to log off so that you (or someone else) can log on to the computer.

HOW TO: CHANGE YOUR ACCOUNT PICTURE

1 If you'd prefer a different picture on your account, go to **Control Panel**, then **User Accounts**. Choose your account and click **Change my picture**.

2 Now choose a picture from the selection that appears, or click **Browse for more pictures** to look for alternatives on your hard drive.

3 Make your selection and click **Change picture**. Your new picture will appear on the Welcome screen whenever you need to log on to the PC.

Resources
Beware of using up all your PC's resources when switching between user accounts. For example, if a program such as Word is running in three separate accounts, your computer will see it as three different programs, each using its own memory allocation. Be careful not to have too many programs open in this way, or you could crash your computer.

SEE ALSO
- Are you Net ready? – *page 14*
- Multiple e-mail accounts – *page 50*
- Filter out unsavoury sites – *page 56*

19

GETTING CONNECTED

Choose an ISP

Find out which **provider** is best for you

An Internet Service Provider (ISP) is a company which provides you with access to the Internet. With many ISPs to choose from, it is important to select the best one for you. ISPs vary in a range of respects, in order to cater for a wide variety of different needs – business, leisure or personal.

Before you choose an ISP you need to work out what your needs are, then do some research to see which ISPs meet them. It is quite usual for people to try out a few ISPs before they find the service that matches their requirements.

HOW ISPS DIFFER

There are three main ways in which ISPs differ from each other – content, which is the selection of services on offer, reliability and payment plan.

Content
The larger ISPs, such as OzEmail (http://au.ozemail.yahoo.com/home) or Quik Internet (www.quik.co.nz), offer benefits to their members, known as 'content'. OzEmail, for example, offers news, stock quotes, a racing services and a download centre, all accessed from its homepage. Most ISPs also offer members up to six free e-mail addresses, as well as Web space to store their own homepages.

Reliability
The reliability of an ISP is also very important – can you connect to the Internet first time, or is the line often busy? How quickly can you access Web pages once you are on-line? Unless you are willing to try out a number of ISPs, the only way to judge this is to read magazine or Web site reviews of the services that are being offered.

Payment
ISPs all offer a range of plans. Basic plans generally offer a set number of access hours per month for a set fee. Additional time on-line must be paid for at an agreed hourly rate. More attractive for those who spend a lot of time browsing are plans that offer unlimited access for a set fee. Often, you are able to get cheaper deals if

Plan Name	Monthly Fee	Includes	Additional Use
OzE3	$7.95	3 hours	$3.95 per hour
OzE10	$15.95	10 hours	$3.50 per hour

you are prepared to pay in advance for, say, three or four months of unlimited time on-line.

One feature to watch out for is a download charge. Some schemes offer a set fee for unlimited access, but with a limit on the amount of data that can be downloaded. Additional downloads must be paid for.

Because the deals on offer vary a lot, it can be hard to work out which is best. Establish your usage pattern before making any commitments.

WORTH A LOOK

- **Australian ISP List (www.cynosure.com.au/isp)**
Search for an ISP by territory or state, or enter your phone number in a search box to see those closest to you. The site also offers ratings, statistics and articles.
- **NetGuideWeb (www.netguide.com.au/useful_stuff/isp_watch)**
A monthly guide to the best ISP deals for serious Net users.
- **Wired Kiwis Web (www.wiredkiwis.co.nz/isps)**
Useful advice on choosing a service provider, as well as geographical and alphabetical listings of ISPs.
- **NetGuide Web (www.netguide.co.nz/isp_directory)**
A directory of New Zealand ISPs.

GETTING STARTED

CHOOSING AN ISP

Questions and answers

Do you require a lot of assistance with the Internet?
The major ISPs generally offer free help with setting up an account, as well as with simple day-to-day queries. In addition, they often provide articles on how to deal with common problems.

How much time will you spend on-line?
Until you find out how much you are going to use the Internet, it's difficult to know how much time you need to pay for. If you buy a set number of hours per month, and don't use them, the unused time is not credited to the next month. Don't sign a long-term contract until you know how much time you need.

Will you use the Internet outside normal office hours?
If so, you may need technical support to be available off peak and/or at weekends.

How fast should your connection be?
Standard modem connections operate at a maximum speed of 56Kbps. Other, faster options, which require special subscriptions, include ADSL (Asymmetrical Digital Subscriber Line) and cable from your cable TV provider. 56Kbps is usually fast enough for most people's needs.

How do you get help setting up an ISP on your computer?
Choose an ISP, such as OzEmail or AOL, that provides a CD which completes the set-up process automatically.

How many e-mail addresses will you get?
If several family members want to share the same computer, they each might like to have their own e-mail addresses. Many ISPs provide you with several e-mail accounts free of charge. However, you cannot keep the same e-mail address if you change ISP. The only way to do this is to sign up with a non-ISP e-mail service such as Yahoo! Mail (http://au.yahoo.com), but you will still need an ISP to connect to the Web.

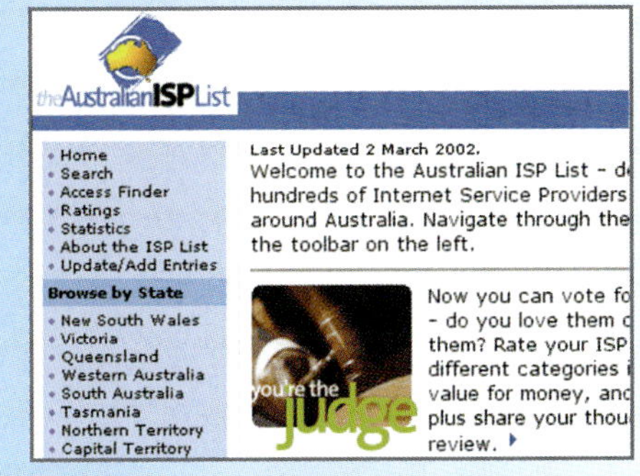

Will you want to run your own Web site?
Most ISPs will provide some free Web space for the publication of your site. Note that in some cases there may be a limit on the number of 'hits' the site can receive in a week.

FURTHER RESEARCH

As well as the checklist above, there are several other methods you can use to evaluate an ISP, including the following:
- Computer magazines regularly research ISPs, saving you time and effort. For Australian magazine links go to WebWombat (**www.webwombat.com.au/magazines/listings/computingau.htm**).
- It is well worth asking friends for recommendations, and learning as much as you can from their experiences.
- If you are already on-line, try typing terms such as 'isp list' and 'isp review' into a search engine, and limiting the search to Australia or New Zealand.

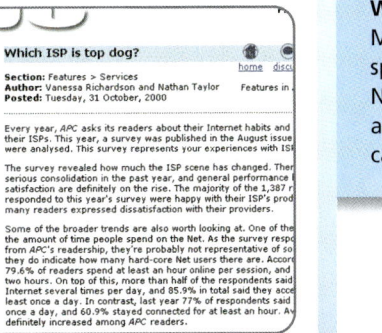

Did You Know?
The List of ISPs (http://thelist.internet.com) is an extensive guide to ISPs worldwide, and a useful source of links to information about the Internet.

Jargon Buster!
Broadband
A collective term for technologies that allow Internet connections which are faster than modems. ADSL, cable and satellite are all broadband types.

SEE ALSO
- Are you Net ready? – page 14
- Set up your modem – page 22
- Other ways to connect – page 88

21

GETTING CONNECTED

Set up your modem

Your modem **links** your computer to the Internet – it needs to be set up correctly for maximum **speed** and **efficiency**

A modem is the device that connects your PC to the Internet. It translates the digital data that your computer understands into a signal that can pass through the telephone network. It also works in reverse, converting the signal received through the telephone line back to a digital format that your PC can display on screen. Most new computers come either with a modem built in, or supplied as an external device. For older machines, you may need to buy and install the modem yourself.

CHOOSE A MODEM

The most important factor in choosing a modem is its speed. The faster your modem, the faster you can download Web pages, send e-mail and surf on the Internet. The fastest standard modems currently available are rated at 56K (kilobits of electronic data transferred a second). To use the Internet efficiently, you need at least a 33.6K modem.

Internal or external
Hardware modems come in two types, internal and external. Internal modems are cheaper to buy, but far more fiddly to fit and move between computers than external modems. For fitting an external modem, see opposite.

Hardware or software
Some newer PCs use software to perform all the tasks of a modem without the need for extra hardware. These 'software modems' are inexpensive and easy to upgrade.
However, they use your computer's central processor to a greater extent than hardware modems, and so can slow it down. The PC also still needs to have a telephone socket.

Extra features
Many modems include extra features, such as the facility to fax directly to and from your PC, or use it as a telephone answering machine. If you're interested in any of these capabilities, ask your local computer dealer.

Modems for portable PCs
There are special modems available for portable PCs. They are called PCMCIA (Personal Computer Memory Card International Association) modems. These credit card-sized devices fit in special slots on portable PCs. They are small and light, but will drain battery power when used for long periods, limiting their usefulness for Internet browsing on the move.

Upgrading your modem
The process for upgrading your modem is almost identical to installing a new one. Simply remove the old device and insert or connect the new one. When you then turn your PC on, it will recognise that a new modem has been installed and ask you to insert the CD-ROM that came with it.

Alternative connections
You do not need to have a modem to connect to the Internet. In fact you can get a speedier connection by paying for services such as ADSL (Asymmetrical Digital Subscriber Line) or cable modems. These are fitted by your cable TV or telephone company and use different technologies (see *Other ways to connect*, page 88).

Swann External Modem Installation
Contents
▶ Software Installation

GETTING STARTED

FITTING & STARTING UP

If you've opted for an external modem, connect it to your PC and install its drivers as shown on the right. Internal modems are explained below.

INTERNAL MODEMS

Many new computers come with an internal modem as a standard feature. In such cases, the modem's drivers will have been installed and configured by the company that manufactured the computer, or by the vendor. All you need to do is to plug a phone line into the modem port as shown below, and connect the other end to a phone wall socket.

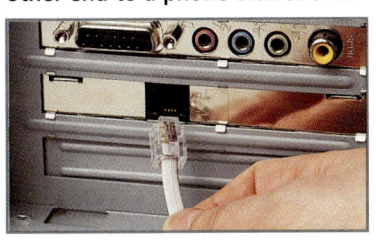

EXTERNAL MODEMS

1 Connect the modem according to the vendor's instructions and turn it on. Windows XP's Found New Hardware Wizard should start automatically.

2 If the Wizard does not start, click on **Start**, then **Control Panel**, then **Printers and Other Hardware** and finally choose **Add Hardware**.

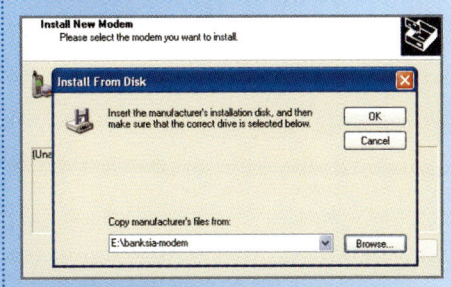

3 If the device drivers for your modem are not included with Windows XP, you will be told to select them from the vendor's installation disk.

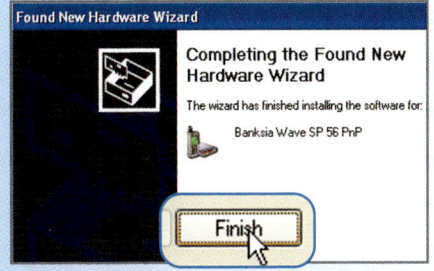

4 The Wizard will proceed to install the modem's drivers. Click **Finish** when the process is complete. You can now configure your modem (see below).

Configure your modem

Your PC needs to know how to use the new modem you have fitted.

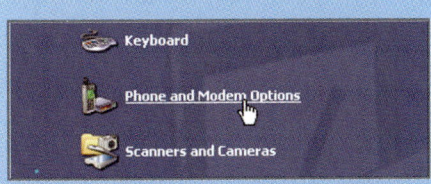

1 Go to the **Start** menu and click on **Control Panel**, then **Printers and Other Hardware** and finally **Phone and Modem Options**.

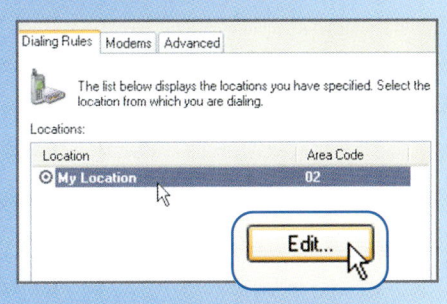

2 When the 'Phone and Modem Options' window opens, click on **Dialing Rules**, then highlight **My Location** and click **Edit**.

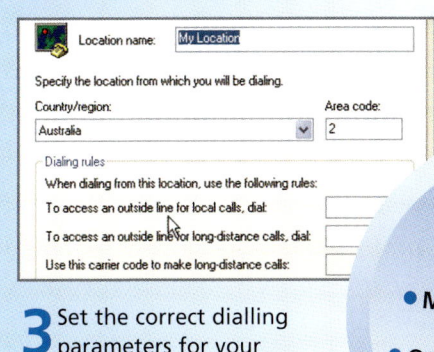

3 Set the correct dialling parameters for your location. Exit all menus and start using your modem.

Did You Know?

The speed rating of a modem is only its potential top speed. Factors such as the number of people on-line and the amount of static on your phone line can slow your modem down.

Watch Out!

Make sure you disable 'call waiting' if you use it (there is usually a button on your phone to do this). If someone calls you while you are on-line, the 'call waiting' signal will break your Web connection.

SEE ALSO
- **Choose an ISP** – page 20
- **Make the connection** – page 24
- **Other ways to connect** – page 88

23

GETTING CONNECTED

Make the connection

How to set up your computer to **access the Internet**

When you have chosen an Internet Service Provider, and are sure you have a modem installed (see page 22), you are ready to set up your computer to connect to the Internet for the first time. This is often referred to as 'configuring your ISP account' because it involves giving your computer the details of your ISP.

There are two ways to do this. Some ISPs provide you with a CD-ROM, which automatically sets up your computer (asking you for some personal details as it does so). Other ISPs give you information with which to set up your computer manually.

USE A CD-ROM TO SET UP AN ACCOUNT

This process will almost certainly involve going on-line so make sure your modem is connected to the phone line and then insert the installation CD-ROM. You will now be presented with a set of easy on-screen instructions. All you have to do is fill in your personal details as you go. When you have finished, you can then access the Internet (see *Testing your new connection*, opposite).

Before you insert the CD-ROM, it is a good idea to gather together all the information you are likely to need. The things you need to know are:

Your modem type

This information can usually be found on the packaging that came with the modem or on the modem itself (if it is an external type).

The details are also stored on your computer, once the modem's drivers have been installed (see page 23). To see what is recorded there, click on the **Start** menu followed by **Control Panel** and then **Phone and Modem Options**. Then choose the 'Modems' tab.

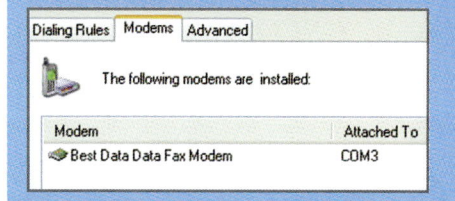

A username

As part of the installation process, your ISP will give you an e-mail address. To do this, it first asks you for a username, which will form the first part of the address. This can be your name, a nickname, a company name – whatever you like. It is worth having a couple of choices ready because many names will already have been taken by other users of your ISP.

One trick is to combine your name and house number (for example, susan34). This is unlikely to have been taken and is easy to remember.

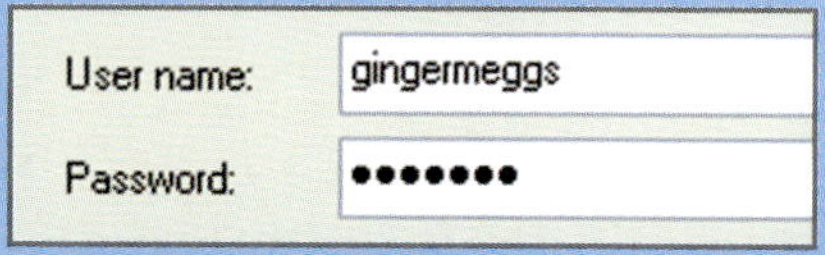

A password

Some ISPs require their users to enter a password every time they connect to the Web – to ensure that no one else can use your ISP account. A few ISPs generate a random password for you but many ask you to choose your own.

Be sure to read the ISP's guidelines on choosing a password. Some set a minimum and maximum length, or ask you not to use symbols such as '?' or '*'.

Try to think of something that only you can know and that would be hard to guess – such as your grandfather's middle name. You should also choose something easy to remember or – if you absolutely have to – write down the password and keep it somewhere safe.

GETTING STARTED

SET UP YOUR INTERNET CONNECTION MANUALLY

If your ISP does not provide you with an installation CD-ROM, you will instead receive various details that you need to enter into your computer.

The essentials are the telephone number you call to connect to your ISP, and your username and password. A few ISPs may also supply two DNS addresses. DNS stands for Domain Name Server. This is the computer that translates text addresses – such as www.google.com – into a numerical address.

DNS addresses are made up of four sets of numbers (each up to three figures long) divided by full stops, such as 192.168.52.4.

1 Go to the **Start** menu and select **Control Panel**, followed by **Network and Internet Connections**. Finally, click on **Set up or change your Internet connection**.

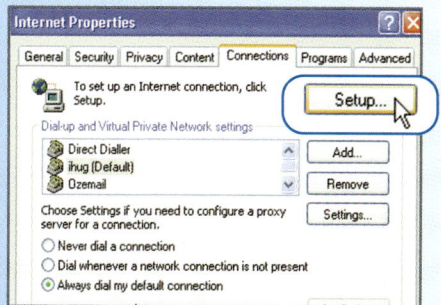

2 In the 'Internet Properties' box, choose the 'Connections' tab and then click **Setup**. This will launch the New Connection Wizard that will guide you through the entire process.

3 In the first few Wizard screens, choose 'Connect to the Internet', followed by 'Set up my connection manually' and 'Connect using a dial-up modem' (if that is what you are doing).

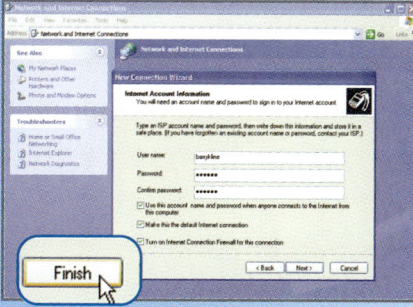

4 You will now be prompted to provide some details, including those supplied by your ISP. These include the ISP's name, phone number, and your username and password. When ready, click **Finish**.

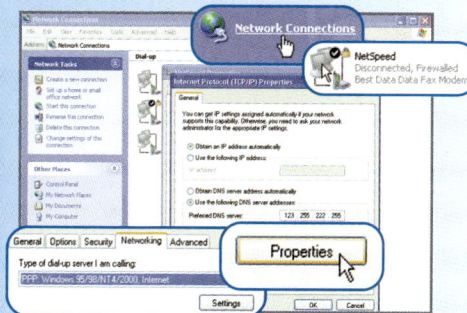

5 To enter DNS numbers, click on **Network Connections**, then double-click on the new ISP icon. Now choose **Properties**, **Networking**, then **Properties** again, and fill in the relevant numbers.

Testing your new connection

Go to the **Start** menu and click **Connect To** to see a list of available dial-up connections. Click on the connection you have just created and, when its window appears, click **Dial** to connect to it.

Your modem now begins to dial up your ISP and various on-screen messages relay its progress. When the connection has been made, you can launch Internet Explorer and start surfing the Web.

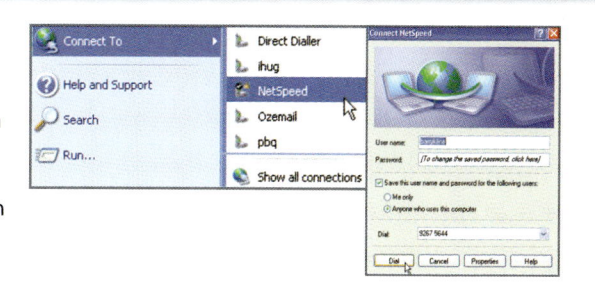

Problem Solver!

If you have an internal modem and you are not sure if it's working, click Start, Control Panel, Network and Internet Connection and then Phone and Modem Options. Choose the 'Modem' tab and if the modem is working it will be listed there.

Did you Know?

If you have trouble setting up your computer, you can call your ISP, and a technician will talk you through the process. This service is free with most, but not all, ISP accounts.

SEE ALSO
- Choose an ISP – *page 20*
- Set up your modem – *page 22*
- Set up Outlook Express – *page 34*

25

GETTING CONNECTED

Start browsing

Find out how to **move around** the **Internet**

Browsing simply means exploring the World Wide Web. It is also called 'surfing' – although surfing might better be defined as 'browsing without a specific purpose'. To move around the Web you need a piece of software called a browser. A browser is your window on the Web – it is the program that displays pages on your screen and takes you from one Web site to the next. The most widely used browser is Internet Explorer, produced by Microsoft, but there are others that you may want to try.

Internet Explorer and Netscape Navigator

Many people know only one Web browser – Internet Explorer, which often comes pre-installed on new computers and is a standard feature of Windows XP.

Others prefer Netscape Navigator, a versatile browser that offers some different features from Explorer. For example, Netscape's search tool gives you access to several search engines while Explorer provides only one.

You can download the Netscape browser (called Navigator) on its own, or an entire suite of programs – including e-mail, Internet chat and messaging – by selecting Netscape 6 at the Netscape site (**http://wp. netscape.com/download**).

Before doing so, check to see what software was provided by your ISP: you may already have the latest version of Netscape on CD.

GETTING STARTED

BROWSING COMMANDS

When you open your browser you will see a row of icons at the top of the screen. This is known as the 'toolbar'. Each icon represents a function of the browser, which will come in useful as you explore the Web. Shown here is the toolbar of Internet Explorer 6, but all browsers have essentially similar functions.

Search splits the screen into two parts to let you search for a particular term without losing the page you are viewing.

History opens a list of sites you have used recently on the left-hand side of the screen.

Edit allows you to save and edit the page you are viewing, usually as a Microsoft Word file.

Back returns you to the page that you visited last. Clicking on the arrow to the right will show a list of the last pages you visited.

Stop prevents a page from loading up. You can use this if a page is taking a long time to load, or if you typed in the wrong address.

Favorites opens up a list of Web sites which you have stored there previously so that you can revisit them more easily.

Print sends a copy of the page you are viewing to your printer.

Discuss allows you to type comments directly onto a Web page (usually only on a company server).

Forward takes you on to pages you visited after the one you are now viewing. This is particularly useful if you have clicked back several pages and now wish to return to where you were.

Home takes you to your homepage – generally your favourite page or the one you wish to begin on.

Refresh reloads the page you are currently viewing. If the page has been updated since you first loaded it (for instance, a news page), this ensures that you are viewing the most recent version.

Mail opens a list of e-mail options: for example, **Send a Link** opens a new mail message containing the address of the page you're viewing (if you want to send it to someone). **Send Page** e-mails the whole page.

Address Box displays the address of the site you are viewing or loading. This is where you type the address of any site you wish to view – click **Go** when you want to go to it.

Media takes you to Microsoft's media Web site, for on-line music and video clips.

Messenger launches Microsoft Messenger for real-time communication on the Web.

iMac

Internet Explorer looks different on an iMac. For example, the buttons for Search, Favorites and History all appear down the left side of the browser window. But the program still works in much the same way.

27

GETTING CONNECTED

✋ Watch Out!

Some parts of a Web address are case-sensitive. This means you need to type them with upper and lower case letters in the right place to access a site – www.hq.nasa.gov/office/pao/History for example.

HOW TO: START BROWSING

When you double-click on the browser icon in your Start menu, you are asked whether you want to connect to the Internet; click **Connect**. Your modem will then be activated and it will establish an Internet connection.

You can then begin to browse. Here's how you can access the site of a known address. (If you don't have a Web site address, you could try searching under the subject area – see *Search the Internet*, page 64).

Say you read in a magazine about a music site called Electric Blues (www.electricblues.com). Here's how to bring the site up on-screen, move around it and move on to other Web sites with similar themes.

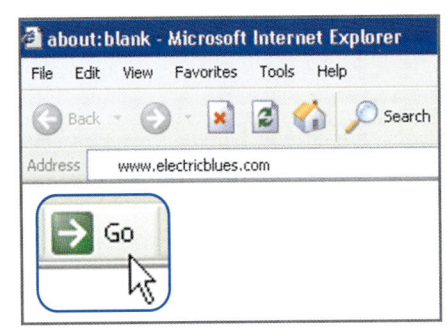

1 First, click in the Address Box and delete any text inside it. Then type in the Web address of the Electric Blues site (**www.electricblues.com**) and click **Go**.

2 Most Web sites consist of a number of pages. You can move between them by clicking on different 'links', which may look like buttons. Click on one to open up that part of the site.

3 As the new page opens you can see the address change in the address box. After viewing this page, click on the **Back** button to go to the previous page or click another link to continue.

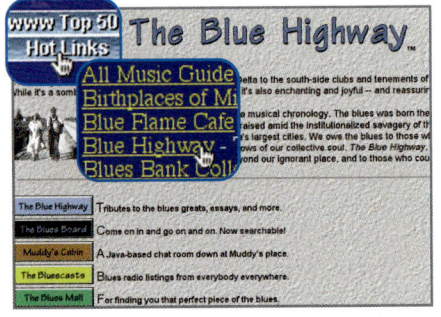

4 Most Web sites also have links that take you to other Web sites. Look for a section called 'Links' and click on it. Then click on one of the links provided to move to a different site.

WEB ADDRESSES

A Web address can be any combination of letters, numbers and symbols, which refer to the location of a Web site. Your Web browser uses these details to find the Web site's 'real' address, which actually consists of a series of numbers.

Web addresses are generally kept as simple as possible so that it is easier for people to remember them. They follow the same conventions for suffixes as e-mail, which help to indicate the type of organisation behind the Web site, and its location – for example, .com, .edu and .org. See *Send and receive e-mail*, page 38, for a list of these.

How to stop browsing

Close your browser window. Your computer should then ask if you want to disconnect from the Internet. Click **Disconnect Now**. If your computer does not ask you, double-click on the icon with two computers on it in the bottom right-hand corner of your screen. Then click **Disconnect**.

To ensure that your computer does ask you, right-click on your browser icon and select **Internet Properties**. Click on the **Connections** tab, then **Settings** and **Advanced**. Finally, check the box next to 'Disconnect when connection may not be needed'.

GETTING STARTED

HOW TO: SET YOUR HOMEPAGE

Every time you start up your browser, it begins at the same page, which was pre-set by the browser's manufacturer. This is called your homepage. You can change this to any Web site you want, allowing you to begin browsing at a Web page that is useful for you – for example, your favourite search engine.

To select a new homepage, identify the site you want to use (see below) and type its address into your brower to open it up.

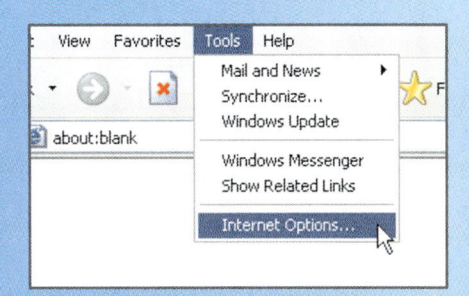

1 Go to the **Tools** menu at the top of the screen, then select **Internet Options** from the drop-down list.

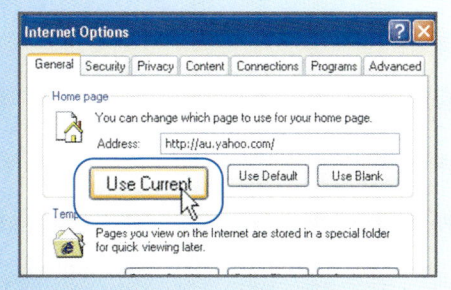

2 A new window will appear. In the 'Home page' section, click on the **Use Current** button and the address of the page you are currently viewing appears in the address box. Click **OK**.

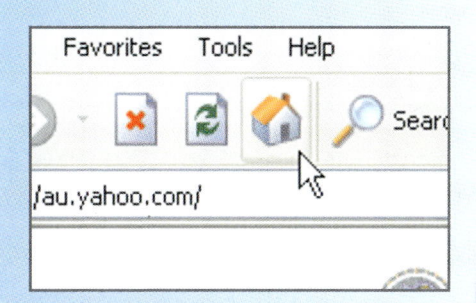

CHOOSING A HOMEPAGE

You should first consider whether there is a site that you often go on-line specifically to see. It may be worth making this your homepage to save you the bother of having to enter its address every time.

Many people choose a charity site as their homepage, where just clicking a button means that the site's corporate sponsors will make a small donation to the cause. This can be a good way to make a regular charity contribution. Sites such as The Hunger Site (**www.thehungersite.com**) are popular choices.

Or you might like to start browsing at a page that shows the latest news. In this case it would be best to choose a site that you can set up to show the type of news and other features that you want to see. Sites such as My Yahoo! (**http://au.my.yahoo.com**) allow you to customise a homepage to show breaking news updates, sports results, property listings, job advertisements and much more.

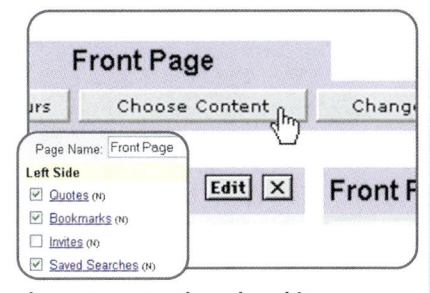

Once you have registered for a free personalised site at My Yahoo! (**http://au.my.yahoo.com**), you can click on the **Choose Content** and **Change Layout** options to add or remove items from your page. The **Colours** option allows you to alter the appearance of the page as well. Be sure to sign out once you've made all the changes you want.

3 Now, whenever you click the **Home** button or open Internet Explorer you will be taken directly to that Web site.

Did You Know?

Watch the cursor as you move it around a Web page. If it changes into the shape of a hand, the object you are hovering over is a link, and clicking on it will take you to another Web page.

SEE ALSO
- Security on the Internet – page 52
- Search the Internet – page 64
- Solve browsing problems – page 82

USING E-MAIL

What is e-mail?

Find out about e-mail and how to use it

Electronic mail (e-mail for short) is the system that allows you to send a message from one computer to another over the Internet. For many people e-mail is the most important aspect of the Internet. You can use it to transmit a message to any computer in a matter of seconds, for the cost of a local telephone call. You need only be connected to the Internet for as long as it takes to send and receive your messages. So the amount of time and money you spend on the phone line is kept to a minimum.

Software
To start using e-mail, you need two things: some software and an e-mail account. Your computer should come supplied with e-mail software already on it – usually a program called Outlook Express. There is more information on this and other e-mail programs overleaf.

E-mail accounts
You will get an e-mail account as part of your contract with an Internet Service Provider (ISP) – the company that gives you a connection to the Internet. They will give you an e-mail address (or let you choose one) and either set up your e-mail program or explain what details are needed so that you can do it yourself. To set up an e-mail account, see page 34.

Your e-mail address is, in effect, a mailbox kept by your ISP. When someone sends you an e-mail message, it is stored by your ISP until you connect to the Internet to check for mail.

GETTING STARTED

HOW E-MAIL WORKS

The process
There are five major steps involved in sending an e-mail. Imagine that there are two friends, Bob in Liverpool, England, and Emma in Sydney, Australia.

Message written and sent
In Liverpool, Bob opens up his e-mail program and – before he goes on-line – composes a message to Emma. He enters Emma's e-mail address at the top of the message and clicks the **Send** button.

Connection to the Net
Bob's e-mail program then connects to the Internet and transfers the message over the telephone line (via a modem) to the 'server' computer owned by his Internet Service Provider (ISP).

Address checked
The ISP's computer looks at the address on the message. This address shows whereabouts on the Internet one of the server computers owned by Emma's ISP is. It also specifies which of the ISP's customers the message is for. The message is then sent there.

Recipient connects
Emma decides to check for e-mail messages. She uses her e-mail program to connect to the Internet. The program then asks the ISP's computer if Emma has any messages.

Message received
The ISP's computer then sends the message to Emma's computer via her modem where it appears in the Inbox of her e-mail program.

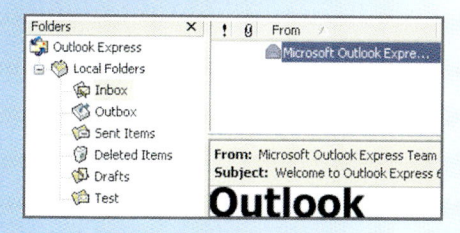

WHAT MAKES IT SO QUICK?
When you send an e-mail, your modem takes the electronic file and converts it into a form that can be sent over the telephone line. The message is also split into smaller packets of information because each part can travel more quickly over the Web via different routes than the whole message would via one route.

The parts are then reassembled at the other end before being deposited in your recipient's Inbox. Each part of the message is passed from one 'router' computer to another according to an automatic routing system. Each stage of the journey is the equivalent of a telephone call that is instantly answered, understood and passed on.

This makes the whole process only marginally slower than talking to your recipient over the phone – but the difference is that you can say as much as you like in just a couple of seconds.

Where it all began
The first e-mail was sent in 1971 by Ray Tomlinson, a computer engineer, working for the company hired by the United States Defense Department in 1968 to build ARPANET (Advanced Research Projects Agency Network) – the precursor to the Internet. The message was sent between two computers placed next to each other. The program was designed to allow programmers and researchers working in different parts of the Defense Department to leave messages for each other.

Did You Know?
In the year 2002, an average of 20 billion e-mails were sent every day. It is estimated that by 2005, this figure will have risen to 35 billion.

SEE ALSO
- Different e-mail programs – *page 32*
- Set up Outlook Express – *page 34*
- Send and receive e-mail – *page 38*

USING E-MAIL

Different e-mail programs

Select **the right software** to send your messages

Most computers come with some e-mail software – probably Outlook Express – already installed. But there are many other e-mail programs on the market, such as Netscape, Eudora and Pegasus, one of which may suit your needs better. It doesn't matter which one you choose – all the programs perform the basic e-mail functions equally well and you can use any one of them alongside any browser. It is largely a matter for personal choice – perhaps based on the look of the program or a particular feature that it offers.

Outlook Express

Outlook Express is the e-mail program that is used in this book. It is made by Microsoft, the company that also devised Internet Explorer, Windows and Word. The design of Outlook Express is similar to other Microsoft products, so if you are familiar with programs such as Word and Excel, you will find it easier to use.

Because Outlook Express (together with Internet Explorer) comes free with Windows XP, it is by far the most popular and widely used e-mail package. That means it's easy to find helpful tips on using the program from your friends, in books and magazines, and on the Internet.

Outlook Express is designed to integrate seamlessly with Internet Explorer and other Microsoft products, so it will automatically open a pre-addressed message window when you click on an e-mail link in a Web site or a Word document.

If you are not running Windows XP and have an earlier version of Outlook Express on your computer, you may wish to see if there are any updates available at the Microsoft Web site (**www.microsoft.com/downloads**).

GETTING STARTED

OTHER PROGRAMS

If you do not want to use Outlook Express, or would like to sample some alternatives, you can download and use other e-mail programs for free from the Web sites of their manufacturers.

Netscape
(http://wp.netscape.com/download)
The latest version of the Netscape Web browser comes with its own e-mail program built in. The program also has its own Internet chat, phone and instant messaging software, which make it very versatile to use.

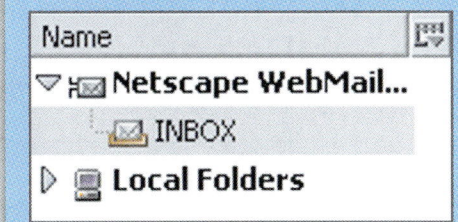

During the installation process, you are offered a range of options that allow you to choose the add-ons and features that will be most useful to your needs.

Eudora
(www.eudora.com)
This program looks different because it often uses icons in place of words. Unlike some other programs, it can be set up to leave e-mail on the server, even after you have read it. That's useful if you are accessing e-mail from a computer other than your own. Eudora also lets you view the last few links to Web pages that you received via e-mail. You can view any sites mentioned in e-mails – even if you can't recall who sent them to you.

Pegasus
(www.pmail.com)
Unlike the other programs mentioned here, Pegasus does not have a Mac version, but it has a number of excellent features, such as the option to download message headers before you download the whole message. This means you can look through the headers to choose which messages you most urgently wish to download – a useful time-saver if you are often sent large files.

Another advantage of Pegasus is that it takes up comparatively little of your computer's memory. Like some other programs, it also allows you to use multiple e-mail addresses. This is useful if, for example, several family members use the same computer to access their e-mail.

WEB-BASED E-MAIL

Providers such as Hotmail, Yahoo! and mBox offer free e-mail accounts that you can access from any computer worldwide with an Internet connection – particularly useful if you are on holiday.

You do have to be on-line to compose, read and send messages, which means connect time charges can mount up. Despite being stored on-line, your messages are private and secure – you are required to enter a password to view message folders.

The first part of the e-mail address can be personalised, making it easy for you and others to remember.

Nameplanet (**www.nameplanet.com**) encourages you to use your own name as an e-mail address. Popular addresses such as 'david@jones.net' are likely to be taken, but by adding a middle name or a number, you can still create a good personalised address.

iMac
Eudora, Netscape Messenger and Outlook Express are all available on the Mac. Each may look different to its PC equivalent but the functions remain the same.

Did You Know?
If you have a WAP phone, you can use it to access your e-mail messages.

SEE ALSO
- Make the connection – *page 24*
- What is e-mail? – *page 30*
- Set up Outlook Express – *page 34*

Set up Outlook Express

Let your e-mail program know your e-mail address

Before you can send and receive messages, you need to have an e-mail address. You are provided with an address when you register for an account with an Internet Service Provider (ISP) during the registration process. Your e-mail program will probably be set up to use this address automatically. But if not, you will be required to enter your address and other account details yourself.

Testing your program

First check whether your e-mail program has been set up for you. To do this, go to the **Start** menu and click on **E-mail Outlook Express**. When the program has opened, click on the button marked **Send/Recv**. A dialogue box will appear asking if you want to connect to the Internet. Click **Connect**.

If your program has been set up automatically, your modem should now dial up to the Internet and check to see if there are any messages for you. Normally, there is one from your ISP, welcoming you to their service. This will appear in the Outlook Express Inbox. You can click on the message icon to open it.

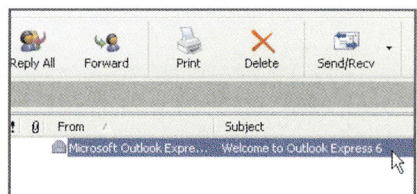

Do-it-yourself

If this process fails, you need to set up Outlook Express manually. To do this, you will need some information from your ISP, which should have been sent to you in the post. The set-up process is described opposite.

GETTING STARTED

HOW TO: SET UP YOUR PROGRAM MANUALLY

The process for setting up Outlook Express is similar to the one you used to set up Internet Explorer (see *Make the connection*, page 24). In fact, Outlook Express uses the same Internet connection as your Web browser. All you need to do is to let Outlook Express know what e-mail address to check and where to check it. To do this, you need to have some information to hand – see *The information you need* below.

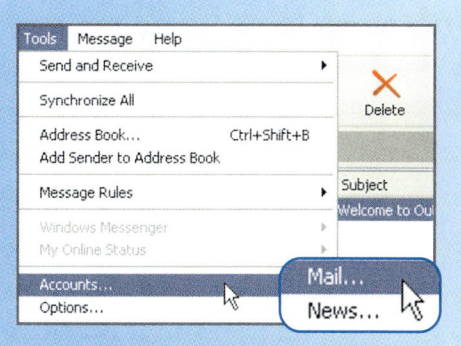

1 First go to the **Tools** menu and select **Accounts**. Then click on **Add** and then **Mail**.

2 This opens the Internet Connection Wizard, which first asks you to give your account a name. Enter your own name, then click **Next**.

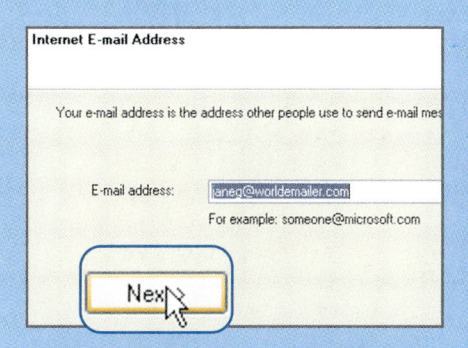

3 Now enter your e-mail address in the box labelled 'E-mail address'. Then click **Next**.

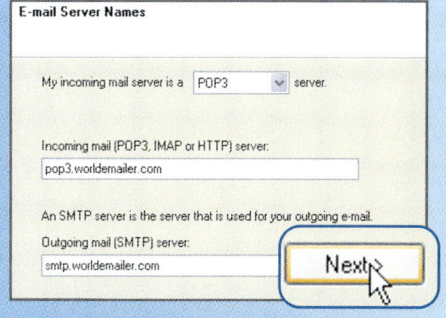

4 You now need to select the type of incoming mail server you'll be using (usually POP3) and enter its address. Also specify the address of the outgoing mail server. Then click **Next**.

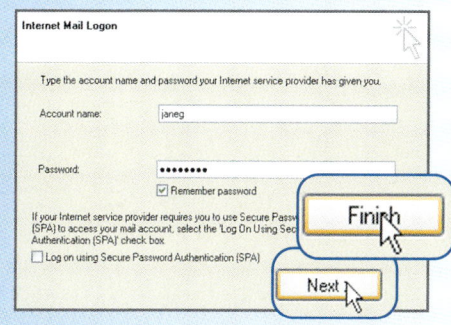

5 Enter your ISP account name and password and click **Next**. Click **Finish** to save your settings. Repeat the process shown opposite in *Testing your program* to check that your account is working.

The information you need

To set up your e-mail program manually, you need your e-mail address, an address for your 'incoming mail server', often referred to as a POP3 (Post Office Protocol) server, and another for your 'outgoing mail server' – often known as an SMTP (Simple Mail Transfer Protocol) server. These addresses should have been sent to you by your ISP. You also need your ISP account name and password. If you are in doubt about any of these details, call the ISP's support line.

Jargon Buster!

Mail server A large computer owned by an ISP which handles e-mail for the ISP's clients. An outgoing mail server handles messages sent by a client. An incoming mail server stores messages sent to the clients.

Did You Know?

Some people like to have more than one ISP and e-mail address (for example, to separate personal and business mail). You can use the process shown here to add new e-mail accounts, without affecting your original one.

SEE ALSO
- **What is e-mail?** – page 30
- **Explore Outlook Express** – page 36
- **Manage your e-mail** – page 42

35

USING E-MAIL

Explore Outlook Express

Open your **e-mail program** and see how it works

Outlook Express is an electronic postman, delivering all the messages you want to send and bringing in all the mail sent to you. It is also an efficient filing clerk, automatically storing all the messages you have sent or received, filing any documents enclosed with the messages, and keeping a record of all your e-mail contacts. All you need to do is give it a few simple commands.

Giving orders

Outlook Express works in a similar way to other Microsoft programs such as Word, Excel and Internet Explorer. You can enter commands by clicking on a drop-down menu and selecting an option, or you can click on an icon on the program's toolbar.

The toolbar contains the functions you are likely to need most regularly, such as creating a new message, sending and receiving mail, and opening your list of contacts. But all these functions can be found in the drop-down menus too.

Opening Outlook Express

To open the program, go to the **Start** menu and select **E-mail Outlook Express**. If you don't see the program there, look for it under **All Programs** in the **Start** menu. When the program has opened, you may be asked if you want to connect to the Internet. For the moment, click **Cancel**. You can explore the program without going on-line.

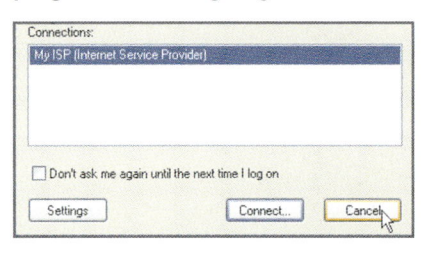

GETTING STARTED

TOOLBAR ICONS
The quickest way to get things done in Outlook Express is to use the icons provided on the program's toolbar. All the most commonly used functions can be accessed here.

Click on this to open up a blank message window, which you can use to compose a new e-mail. Click on the arrow next to 'Create Mail' to see a list of e-mail 'stationery'. These are colourful patterns which you can use as backgrounds to your message. Click on the one you want and a blank message window will open with the background in place.

These are the folders already set up in Outlook Express for storing your incoming and outgoing e-mail messages.

When you have read an incoming message, click this button to open up a pre-addressed message window ready for you to compose a reply.

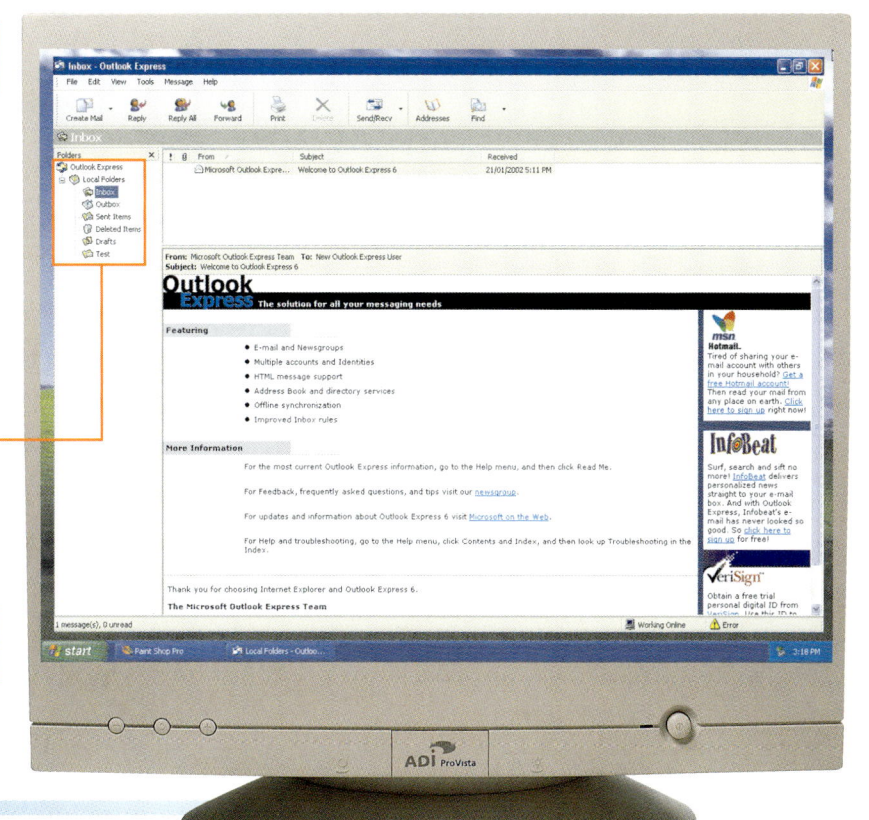

If a message was sent to several people including you, click **Reply All** to open a new message addressed to the sender and the other recipients.

If you want someone else to read an e-mail you have been sent, click on **Forward**. This opens a new message window with the text already inserted, ready for you to send on to your intended recipient. You just add the address.

To obtain a paper copy of an e-mail message, click **Print**.

To erase an unwanted message, click on it and click **Delete**. This moves it into the 'Deleted Items' folder, which Outlook Express empties at intervals of your choice.

Click here to connect to the Internet, to send any mail you have composed and to receive any waiting for you.

Click here to search for a particular e-mail message using criteria such as name of sender or the time it was sent.

OTHER BUTTONS
When you click on **Create Mail** to compose a new message, the toolbar will contain four more useful buttons.

Attach — Allows you to enclose a separate file with an outgoing message.

Spelling — Checks the spelling in your message.

Priority — Lets your recipient know the message is urgent or important.

Send — Puts your message in the Outbox, ready to be sent.

Addresses — To find an e-mail address, or to add a new address to your list of contacts, click on this icon.

37

USING E-MAIL

Send and receive e-mail

With **Outlook Express** it is easy to start e-mailing, using just a few simple commands

The two most basic functions of your e-mail program are sending messages and receiving them. Once you master these processes, you will know most of what you need to understand about e-mail. From beginning to end, sending a message should take as long as it takes to type your message and click on a couple of buttons.

E-MAIL ADDRESSES

Before you can send an e-mail to anyone, you will need their e-mail address. E-mail addresses usually take the form shown below, or a variation on this theme. The '@' symbol – read as 'at' – tells you that this is an e-mail address. Everything after the '@' symbol is known as the 'domain name'.

E-Mail Address	Business
annetteb@ozemail.com.au	
craigandrews@nbct.com.au	
David.Wilson@unsw.edu.au	
schon4535@bliss.co.nz	
Felicity@mailexpress.com.au	

The person's first name, nickname, account name or Web site name

The domain name: this is usually the company or organisation where the person works, or their ISP address

The type of site suffix (com = company; org = organisation). See below for more examples

firstname.surname@companyname.com.au

The dot is a programming code which separates different parts of an address. This can also be an underscore or omitted altogether

The country code for the physical location of the company or ISP – see below for more examples

UNDERSTANDING ADDRESSES

The domain name and country code in an e-mail address can often tell you what sort of organisation your correspondent works for or has an e-mail account with, and where in the world they live. Addresses which do not specify a country code are probably based in the USA (where the country code – us – is rarely used).

Domain types:
com	Company/commercial organisation (Aust.)
co	Company/commercial organisation (NZ)
edu	Educational institution
gov	Government site (Aust.)
govt	Government site (NZ)
net	Network (a major Internet server site)
org	Organisation (often non-profit)

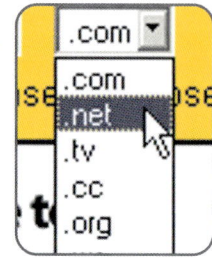

Country codes:
au	Australia	de	Germany	nz	New Zealand
ca	Canada	jp	Japan	uk	United Kingdom

GETTING STARTED

HOW TO: SEND E-MAIL

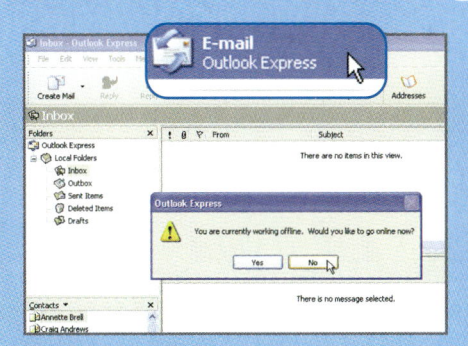

1 Open Outlook Express from the **Start** menu. A box will appear, asking if you want to go on-line. Click **No**. It's cheaper to connect only when you're ready to send your e-mail.

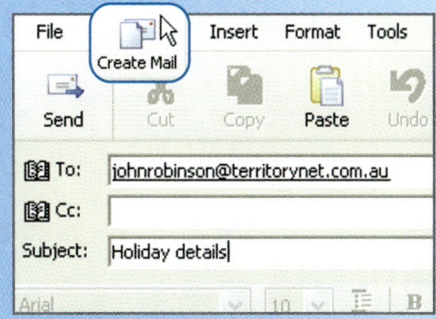

2 Click on **Create Mail**. A message window opens up. Type the address of your recipient in the 'To:' section, a subject in the 'Subject:' section, and then write your message in the main window.

3 When you have finished typing, click **Send** and the message will be stored in the Outbox, ready to send when you connect to the Internet. Write any more messages you want for this session.

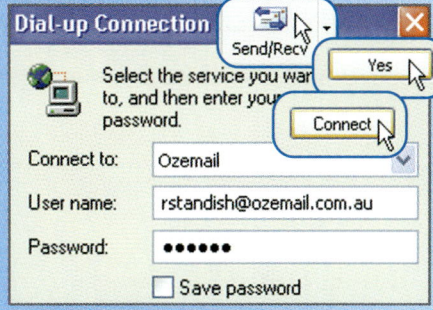

4 When you are ready to send all your messages, click **Send/Recv** and a box will appear, asking if you want to go on-line. Click **Yes**, then **Connect** when the dial-up connection window appears.

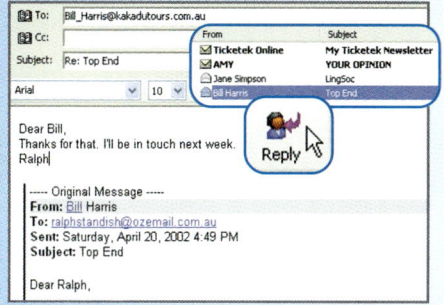

5 Outlook Express will now send your messages and collect new ones for you to read. To answer a message, click on it and then click the **Reply** button. Type your reply in the window that appears.

The Drafts folder

If you are working off-line, any e-mail message you compose will be stored in the Outbox, ready for dispatch as soon as you go on-line. However, if you are writing a message and would like to store it so that you can work on it a bit more before sending it, place it in the 'Drafts' folder instead.

To do this, simply click **File**, followed by **Save**, and a box will appear telling you that your message has been stored in the Drafts folder. Click **OK**.

To continue working on a message stored in this way, click on the Drafts folder icon, highlight the message in question and click **File**, followed by **Open**. To send a message from the Drafts folder, or to transfer it to the Outbox, simply double-click on it.

Sent or not?

When you send a message, Outlook Express first places it in the Outbox. Once it has been sent successfully, the message is moved into the 'Sent Items' folder. Click on the icon for either folder to see its contents.

Time Saver!

You can write as many messages as you want at a time, then send and receive all your e-mail in one go.

SEE ALSO
- What is e-mail? – page 30
- Manage your e-mail – page 42
- Send e-mail attachments – page 46

USING E-MAIL

Build an address book

Use your e-mail **address book** to keep track of friends, family and contacts around the world

As soon as you get an e-mail address of your own, you'll find that you quickly start collecting other people's. A dedicated e-mail address book will make it easy to handle these details. It also makes it quicker to send out e-mail messages because there is no need to keep entering those awkward long addresses every time. You can do this using Outlook Express, which allows you to store all sorts of useful information about your contacts and friends.

ADD A CONTACT

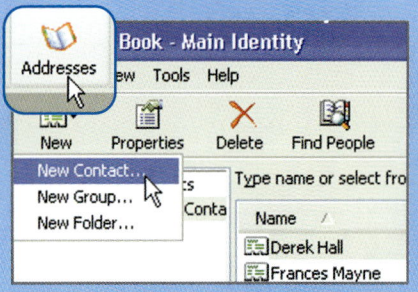

1 Open Outlook Express, then click on the **Addresses** button on the toolbar. Next click **New** and then select **New Contact**.

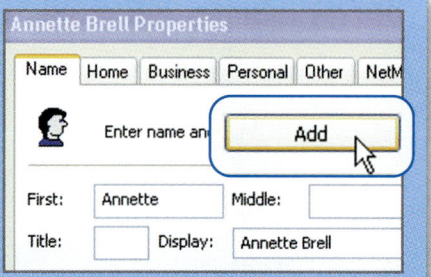

2 Type in the details in the form provided and click **Add**. Repeat this process for as many contacts as you have, then click **OK**.

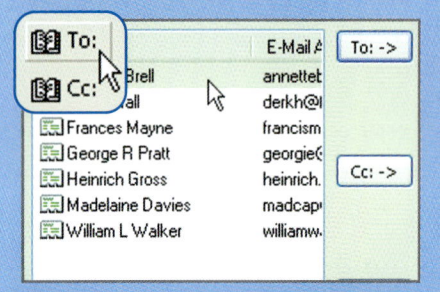

3 To send a message to one of your contacts, open a new message and click on the **To:** button. Next, double-click on the person you wish to e-mail. Their address will appear in the 'To:' box. Click **OK** to confirm.

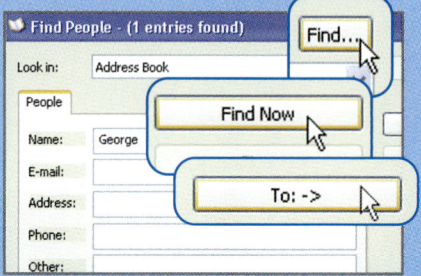

4 If you have a long list of contacts, you can quickly find a particular one by clicking the **Find** button. Type part of the person's name into the box provided and click **Find Now**. Select the correct name and click **To:**.

AUTOMATIC ENTRY

You can set up Outlook Express to add an e-mail address to your address book whenever you reply to an incoming e-mail. Click on the **Tools** menu and choose **Options**. Click on the **Send** tab, and then put a tick next to 'Automatically put people I reply to in my Address Book'. Then click **OK**.

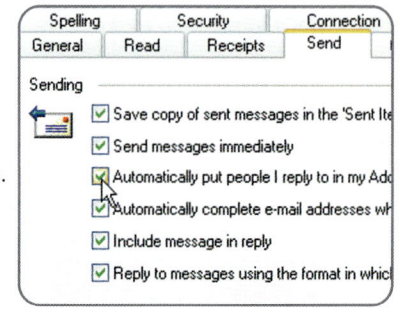

GETTING STARTED

HOW TO: SET UP GROUP E-MAILS

It's easy to set up groups of contacts in your Outlook Express address book. If you're sending e-mails containing the same information to several people it's a quick and easy way to communicate with them all at once. By entering the name of the group in the 'To:' dialogue box, you can make sure that you include all its members.

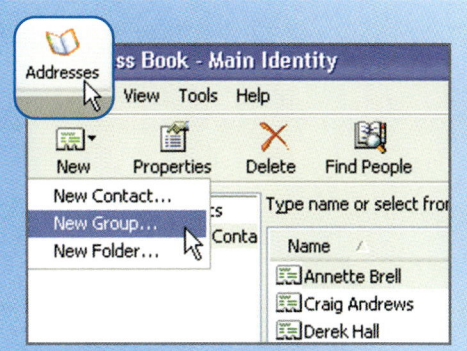

1 Click on **Addresses** in the toolbar, then click on the **New** button, and choose **New Group** from the list.

2 Enter a name for your group – such as 'My Family' or 'Club Members' – and click on the **Select Members** button.

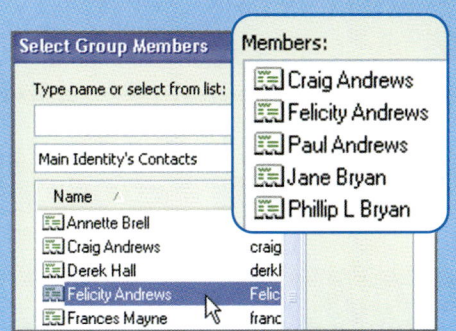

3 Double-click all the entries in the list on the left that you want to be part of your group. These names will then appear in the 'Members' box on the right of the window.

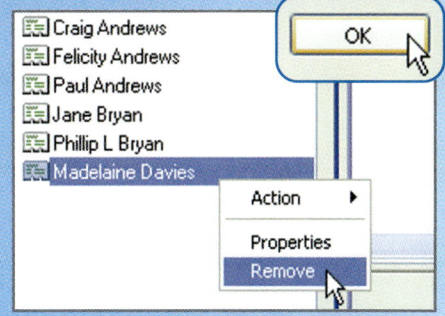

4 If you make a mistake, right-click the offending entry in the list on the right and choose **Remove**. When all are on the list, click **OK**, and then **OK** again to exit the group properties window.

5 To send a message to your new group, open a new e-mail message, click the **To:** button, and choose your group from the list you've made.

Utilise your address book

You can store more than e-mail addresses in your address book. By clicking on the **Addresses** button, selecting a **Contact** and then **Properties** you can add home, business, personal and conferencing details.

You can use your address book in other Windows applications, import contact details from Outlook Express into Excel and use the names and addresses for a Mail Merge in Word.

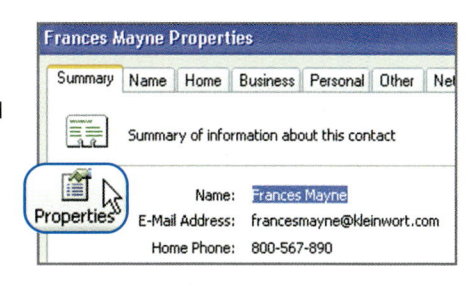

Did You Know?

You can print out your entire address book by opening it and clicking on Print in the menu bar.

Time Saver!

To delete a contact, open the address book, click on the name and then click the Delete button on the toolbar. Click Yes to confirm.

SEE ALSO
- Send and receive e-mail – page 38
- Manage your e-mail – page 42
- Multiple e-mail accounts – page 50

41

USING E-MAIL

Manage your e-mail

Organise your e-mail Inbox

Once you have an e-mail address, you'll be surprised how quickly your Inbox begins to fill up. Outlook Express is designed to make it easy for you to deal with your messages. It's a good idea to keep your Inbox tidy, because the more messages it contains, the longer it takes for Outlook Express to open. File the ones you need but try to weed out old messages.

Good housekeeping

Outlook Express can help to manage your e-mail in lots of different ways. You can forward messages to people at the press of a button, so there is no need for cutting and pasting. And you can instantly view your Inbox to see what messages you've received, and your 'Sent Items' folder for a record of what you've sent to other people.

Using folders

If you receive a lot of e-mails, you may want to create a range of folders to file messages under different headings – for example, 'Work' and 'Personal'. You can even set up Outlook Express to sort your messages into these different folders before you read them.

Deleting a message

An important part of managing your e-mails is deleting messages that you no longer need. When you delete a message in Outlook Express, it is first moved to the 'Deleted Items' folder within the program.

To make sure you don't delete any messages by mistake, Outlook Express will not empty its Deleted Items folder until you tell it to do so.

GETTING STARTED

HOW TO: FORWARD MESSAGES

You will often receive messages that you want other people to see, such as an e-mail from a family member on holiday, a business message from a client, or just a good joke. Outlook Express makes it easy to send on the message to lots of people – for example, if you're passing on good news, or if the original sender doesn't know a third party's e-mail address, and has asked you to forward a message on to them.

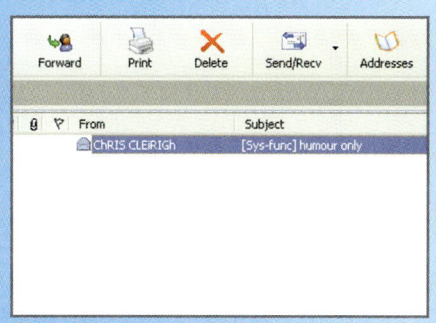

1 In your Outlook Express Inbox, click once on the message that you want to forward.

2 Now click the **Forward** button on the toolbar. A new message window will open, with the text and title of the first message already in place. Only the address section needs to be filled in.

3 To enter the addresses of your intended recipients, type in the address or click on the **To:** button and choose entries from your contacts list.

4 You can also add some words of your own at the top of the message, explaining why you are forwarding it. You simply type in text as you would for a normal message.

5 Finally click the **Send** button to despatch your message.

On-line petitions

Many petitions are circulated via e-mail in support of charities and aid organisations. These rely on recipients forwarding them, and are a way of promoting awareness for specific causes. However, they can also be annoying if they are unsolicited or worded unsympathetically. Don't forward a petition without reading it carefully.

CHECKLIST
- Deal with your incoming mail immediately
- Delete all unwanted messages
- Create a clear filing system
- Empty the Deleted Items folder regularly

Watch Out!
Only respond to petitions and chain letters from reliable sources. Many are not genuine and may be intended to clog up the Internet rather than help a cause.

USING E-MAIL

HOW TO: CREATE FOLDERS

Outlook Express comes with all the folders you will need to get started, including an Inbox folder, an Outbox folder, a Sent Items folder, a Deleted Items folder and a Drafts folder. However, it is possible to add as many new folders as you like to help you to organise your mail. You might like to try creating a folder for work-related mail, or one for mail from your friends.

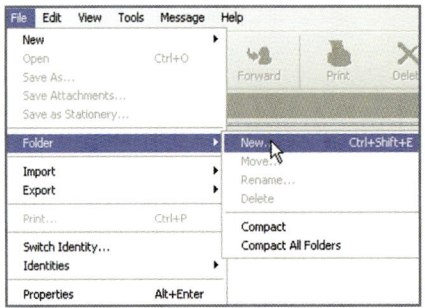

Did You Know?

To empty the Deleted Items folder every time you close Outlook Express, go to **Tools** and select **Options**. Click **Maintenance** and tick next to 'Empty messages from the Deleted Items folder on exit'.

1 To create a new folder, go to the **File** menu, select **Folder** and then **New**.

2 Your new folder can stand alongside the other folders in the list, or it can be a sub-folder within any of them. Select where you want the new folder to be created and enter a name. Click **OK**.

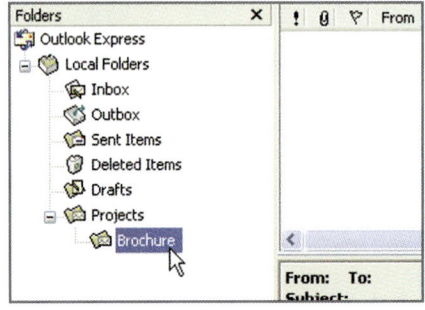

3 Your new folder will be displayed in the 'Folders' list on the left of the Outlook Express window. If you created it inside another folder, you will see it indented beneath that folder.

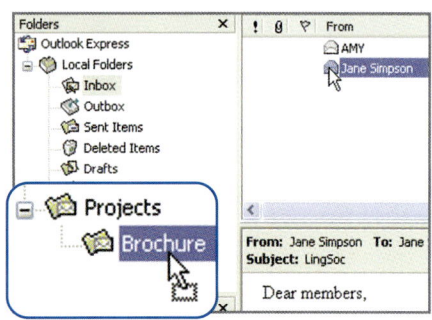

4 To file a message in your new folder, simply drag the message across from the main window and 'drop' it into the folder when it's highlighted. Click on any folder to see its contents.

DELETING MESSAGES

There are a number of ways to delete e-mail messages:

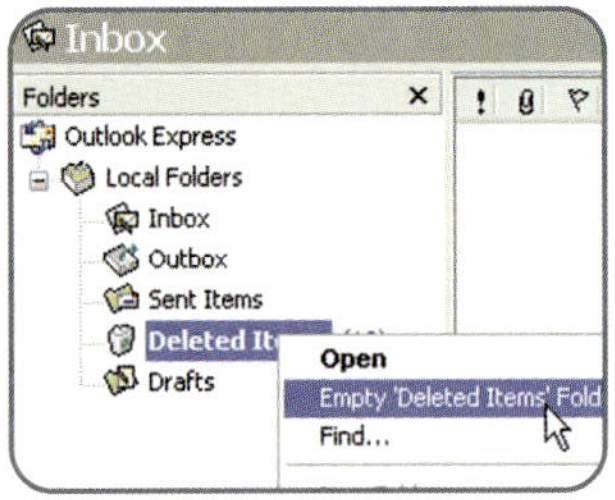

- Click on the message to be removed and press the **Delete** key on your keyboard.
- Drag the message to the Deleted Items folder which you can find under 'Folders' in the main Outlook Express window.
- Right-click on the message and choose **Delete** from the pop-up menu.
- Select the e-mail and click the **Delete** button on the toolbar.

All these methods place the messages in the 'Deleted Items' folder in Outlook Express. To delete the items for good, right-click on the **Deleted Items** folder and select **Empty folder** from the pop-up menu.

GETTING STARTED

HOW TO: ACCESS E-MAIL THROUGH THE WEB

1 Most ISPs will allow you to send and receive e-mails via their Web site, which is very useful for travellers. Log on to the site, and find the link that gives you access to e-mail.

2 The sign-in screen appears next, where you must enter your e-mail address and password – the same password you use to access your dial-up account from your home computer.

3 The next screen shows all the new messages in your Inbox, together with any that were not deleted on previous visits. To open a message, simply click on it.

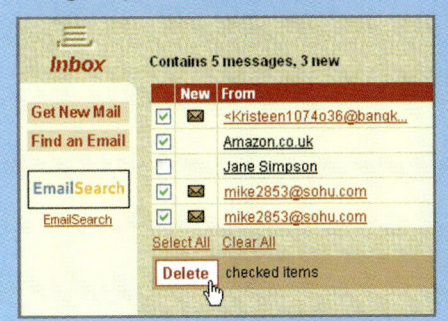

4 You can delete unwanted e-mails individually, or in a group if you wish. Undeleted e-mails will remain in your Inbox until you delete them or download them at home.

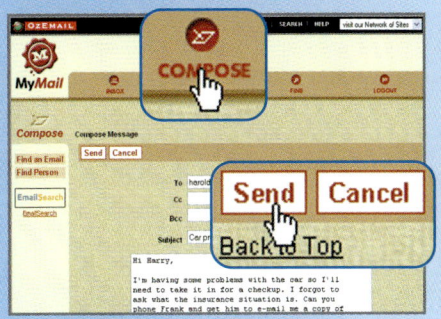

5 Compose new messages just as you would on your home computer. But remember that you will not have on-line access to your address book, so you will need to carry a list with you.

6 When you have finished reading your mail and sending replies, log off from the site. To ensure people can't use the 'Back' button to read your mail, shut down the browser as well.

Did You Know?

When you access your e-mail account via the Web, you do so using a Web browser such as Internet Explorer, rather than an e-mail program such as Outlook Express. This means that you need to be on-line to compose and read all your mail. It also means that your mail will not be downloaded to the machine you are using.

Why use Webmail?

There are many reasons for using your ISP's Webmail facility. If you are visiting friends and need to check your e-mail, you can use their computer to log on to the Web to gain access to your e-mail account. Or you may be travelling overseas, in which case you can use the facilities of an Internet café to monitor your e-mails and respond to any that are urgent.

SEE ALSO
- What is e-mail?
  – page 30
- Different e-mail programs
  – page 32
- Other ways to connect
  – page 88

USING E-MAIL

Send e-mail attachments

Use **Outlook Express** to **send** documents with your **e-mail messages**

You can enclose pictures, spreadsheets and lengthy documents with your e-mail messages. To do this, you attach them to a standard e-mail message, much like enclosing photographs or a cassette in a package along with a letter. Any file included with an e-mail is called an 'attachment'. Adding an attachment to an e-mail is simple, and – provided you follow a few rules – the recipient will also find it easy to open.

HOW TO: ATTACH A FILE TO A MESSAGE

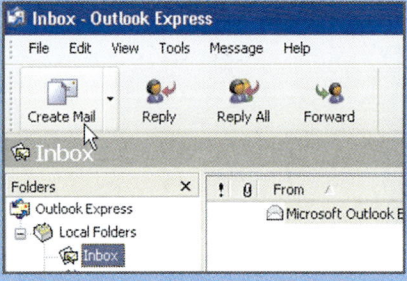

1 Make a note of the name and location of the file you want to attach to your e-mail message. Open Outlook Express and click **Create Mail**.

2 Draft your message in the normal way. When you are ready to attach the file, click on **Attach** or go to the **Insert** menu and click **File Attachment**.

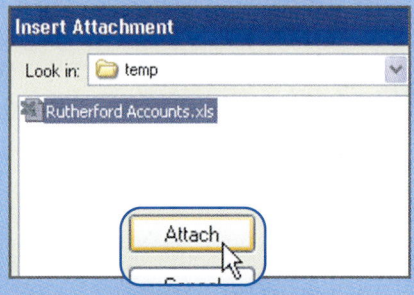

3 The 'Insert Attachment' window will open. Locate your file on your hard drive and click **Attach**.

4 The attached file will now be displayed next to 'Attach' in the message window. Click **Send** to place your message in the Outbox.

SENDING ATTACHMENTS

Before sending attachments, always bear the following points in mind:
- Explain in your message what the attachment is and why you are sending it.
- Use a virus-scanner to check that your attachment isn't infected with a virus.
- Don't send very large files (over 2Mb), even if they are compressed, without prior agreement.
- Make sure your correspondent can read your attachment. Don't send it unless they have the appropriate compression package, graphics or application software to decompress and open your file.

GETTING STARTED

HOW TO: COMPRESS AND SEND AN ATTACHMENT

If an attached file takes up a lot of space on your hard drive, it will take longer to send by e-mail. It will also be slower to download onto the recipient's computer. An attached Word document should take only seconds to send, whereas a minute-long home movie clip might take over an hour.

It is a good idea to reduce the size of large files by using the built-in capabilities of Windows XP (illustrated here) or a commercial program such as WinZip (**www.winzip.com**) or StuffIt (**www.stuffit.com**), which you can download from the Web.

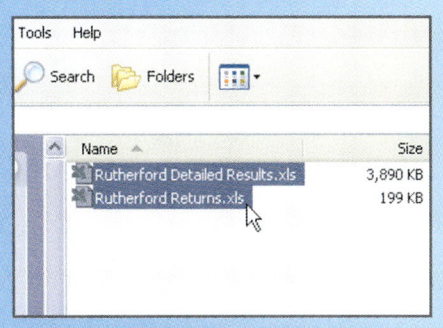

1 Open the folder containing the file or files you want to compress. Hold down the shift key and click on each of the files you want to select.

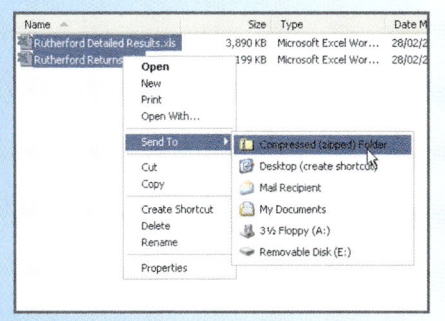

2 Next, right-click on your selected files and choose **Send to** and then **Compressed (zipped) Folder**.

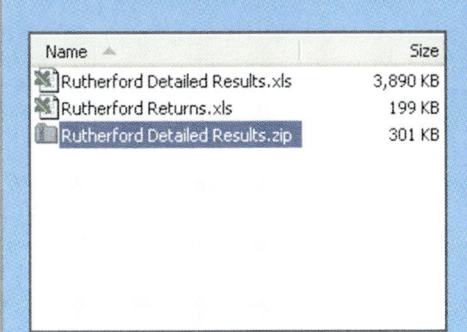

3 Windows will automatically create a compressed file (it looks like a folder with a zip on it) containing all the files your selected, and you can easily see how much smaller it is than the originals.

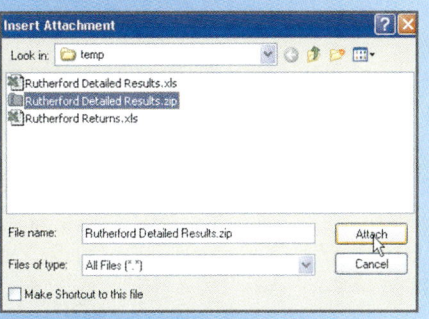

4 Return to Outlook Express, create your message, and attach the newly compressed 'zip' file. (This can be opened by anyone using Windows XP or a program such as WinZip or StuffIt.)

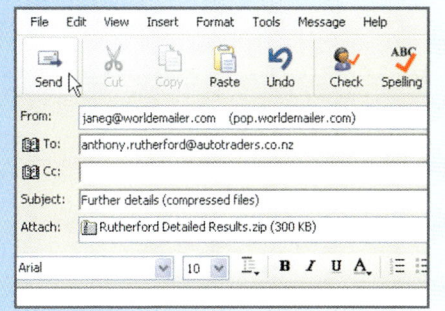

5 If you don't wish to attach further files, click **Send** to place the message in your Outbox, ready for transmission the next time you click **Send/Recv**.

E-etiquette

If you are forwarding a message you have received with an attachment, you should always check that it is what it says it is, and that it is virus-free. You should also only send on attachments you know will be appreciated by the recipient. Be particularly careful if their e-mail address is at their place of work.

Watch Out!

Compression software works better with some file formats than others. It is more effective on large Excel files, for example (reducing them by half), than on pictures.

Did You Know?

*You can check the size of a file by right-clicking on it and selecting **Properties**. You should compress any file over 500Kb (kilobytes) before sending.*

SEE ALSO
- Receive e-mail attachments – page 48
- Avoid computer viruses – page 58
- Download from the Web – page 86

47

USING E-MAIL

Receive e-mail attachments

Check whether a file has been enclosed with an **e-mail** message before opening it

Learning how to recognise and open e-mail attachments is very useful as it means you can be sent – and can make use of – documents, pictures, videos and spreadsheets. You will need specialist software in order to open some attachments. Others may contain unwanted viruses that you need to recognise and delete before they infect your computer.

DEALING WITH ATTACHMENTS

How do I know if I have received an e-mail attachment?

You will be able to recognise whether an e-mail message has an attachment or not by the presence of a paperclip icon next to the message in your Inbox window. This tells you that something extra has arrived along with the e-mail.

Should I open the attachment?

If you click on the message so that it opens in the Preview window below the Inbox window, you'll see a larger paperclip icon on the far right. Click on this to see what the attachment is. If it has a file extension which your PC is able to recognise (such as '.doc' for a Microsoft Word file), then the application's icon will be displayed.

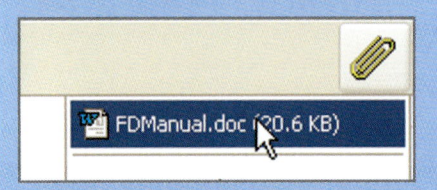

It is tempting to just double-click on the icon to open the attached file in the appropriate application, but you shouldn't do this immediately.

If the sender is not known to you, and the message is unsolicited and general (for example, with a name such as 'You must see this!'), then you should delete the entire e-mail and attachment immediately. They could well contain a virus (see *Avoid computer viruses*, page 58).

How do I open the attachment?

Take a moment to check that this attachment is from a trusted source, and that you know what it is likely to contain. Then click on the paperclip icon and select **Save As** to place the file in a folder on your hard drive.

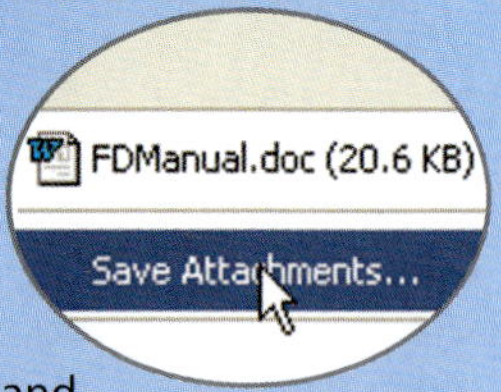

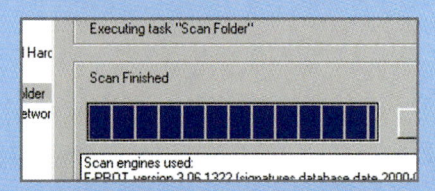

You should now use your anti-virus software to scan the file to make sure it is not infected with a virus. Even if you trust the person who sent it to you, the file could still have been accidentally contaminated.

Once you are sure that the file is virus-free, right-click on it and choose **Open** to view its contents.

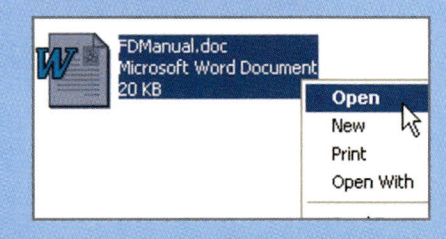

GETTING STARTED

WHAT IF YOU CAN'T OPEN AN ATTACHMENT?

If it is not immediately obvious what a file contains, or what application it should be opened with, read the accompanying message to see if the sender has provided any information to help you out. The file may not open because it has been compressed using software different from that on your computer, or the sender may have forgotten to add the appropriate extension to the file name.

File extensions

The file extension is the two- or three-letter suffix to the file name that identifies the application required to open the file. For instance, the extension '.doc' indicates that a file was made with Microsoft Word and should be opened with this program.

If the file has an unfamiliar extension, you can check the index at the ExtSearch Web site (**http://extsearch.com**). Type the file extension into the search box and the appropriate program will then be identified from the site's database.

Common application extensions are:

doc	Word document
xls	Excel spreadsheet
txt	Notepad text file
bmp	image file
gif	image file
jpg	image file
tif	image file
mov	video file
avi	video file
mpg	video file

Decompression packages

If the document has been compressed, the file extension will refer to the compression program used.

Attachments with the file extensions '.arc', '.arj', '.lha', '.sit', '.uue' and '.zip' are all compressed files. In order to open them, you will need to use decompression software – either the in-built package in Windows XP or a commercial program, such as StuffIt Expander, which can decompress files from many different programs, including the popular '.zip' format.

For more information on Windows XP compression, click on the **Start** menu, select **Help and Support**, and then search for 'compression'.

FILE YOUR ATTACHMENTS

You should always detach and file attachments away from the e-mail messages they arrived with. This allows you to scan all attached files for viruses before opening them.

Remember that some viruses are designed to use an e-mail address book to duplicate themselves over the Internet. So just because an attachment has come from a friend does not mean that it is virus-free.

It's a good idea to make a habit of saving all attachments into a specially prepared 'Downloads' folder for scanning. Once you are sure the file is virus-free, move it somewhere else, where you'll be able to find it easily in the future.

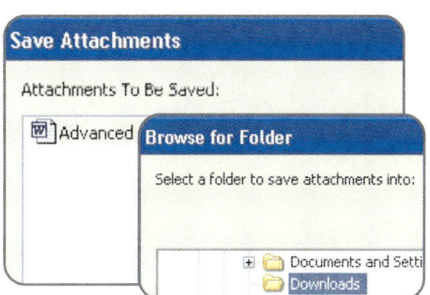

Problem Solver!

*You can download Stuffit Expander from Aladdin Systems, Inc. (**www.stuffit.com**). This free decompression utility works with most compressed files.*

SEE ALSO
- Manage your e-mail – page 42
- Avoid computer viruses – page 58
- Software on the Web – page 84

49

USING E-MAIL

Multiple e-mail accounts

Set up Outlook Express to send and receive e-mail from more than one account

Outlook Express has a useful feature that allows you to send and receive messages for more than one e-mail account using the same Windows XP log-in name. This means you can have several e-mail 'identities', which can be very handy if you operate a business from home. In Outlook, these separate identities function like individual letterboxes: the mail for each one arrives in its own Inbox, so there is no chance of getting your e-mails mixed up.

HOW TO: CHANGE THE MAIN IDENTITY

Unless it is told otherwise, Outlook Express assumes that you will be using only one account and one identity when sending and receiving e-mails. It therefore creates a pre-programmed setting called 'Main Identity', which is not assigned a specific username or password.

Before you create any new e-mail identities for yourself, it's a good idea to give this pre-set identity a name and password, to distinguish it from any others you may decide to set up.

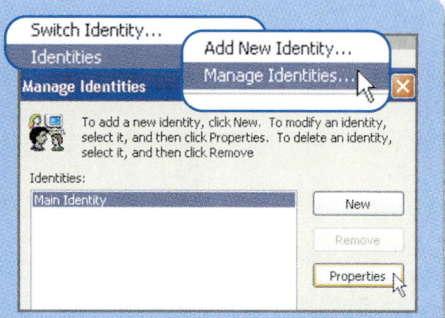

1 Open Outlook Express. Under the **File** menu, select **Identities**, then **Manage Identities**. Highlight 'Main Identity', then click on **Properties**.

2 Next, change the name in the 'Type your name' box and tick 'Require a password'. Enter a password and confirm it. Click **OK**.

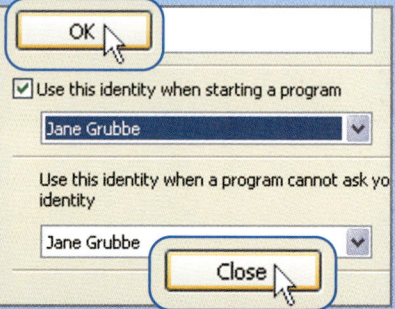

3 Click **OK** again, then make sure that the box next to 'Use this identity when starting a program' is ticked. Finally, click **Close**.

OTHER FAMILY MEMBERS

If you have created different log-in names for different family members in Windows XP (see pages 16–19), and your ISP allows you to have more than one e-mail address – one for each family member, say – Outlook Express will automatically route incoming messages to each person's Inbox, so that they can only be viewed by the person logged in under a particular name. What's more, each person using the computer can set up more than one identity in Outlook, which can end up becoming very complicated. As the computer 'administrator', you may want to limit the proliferation of e-mail identities on your PC.

GETTING STARTED

HOW TO: ADD A NEW IDENTITY

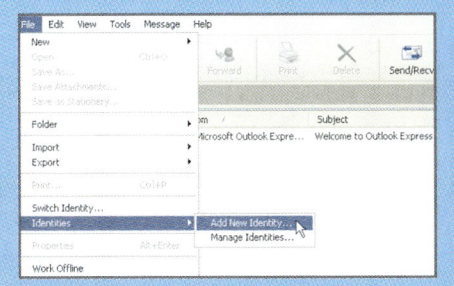

1 To add the first new identity, go to the **File** menu, select **Identities** and then **Add New Identity**.

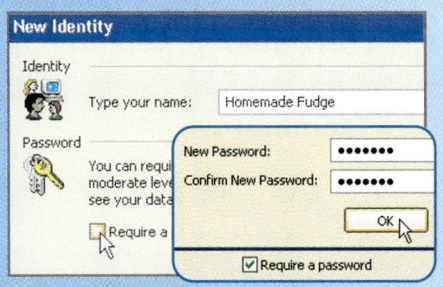

2 In the 'New Identity' window, choose a username for this identity. If you want, tick the 'Require a password' box and type in a password. Then click **OK**.

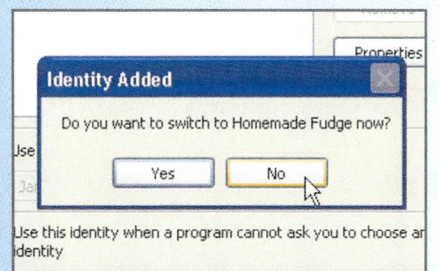

3 Outlook Express will then ask if you want to switch to the new identity. Choose either **Yes** or **No**, depending on which account you wish to use.

HOW TO: SWITCH BETWEEN IDENTITIES

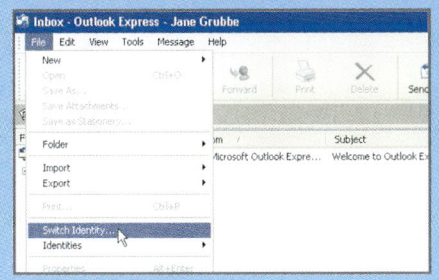

1 Open Outlook Express and click on the **File** menu, and then on **Switch Identity** near the bottom.

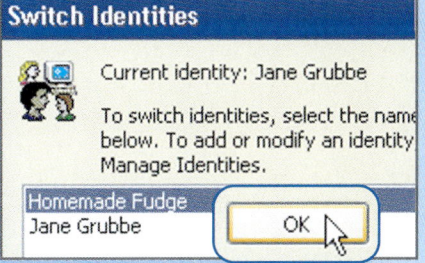

2 Select the identity you wish to use, enter your password and click **OK**. The Internet Connection Wizard starts up, so you can type in details of the new identity's e-mail account (see pages 34–5).

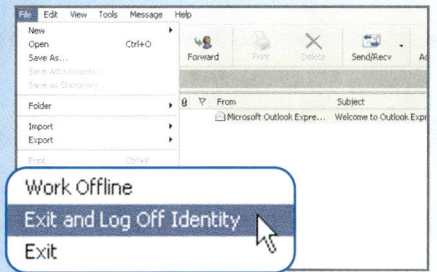

3 When you have finished with your e-mail and wish to reactivate your password protection, go to the **File** menu and click **Exit and Log Off Identity**.

Switching identities

If all your accounts are with the same ISP, you won't have to make a new Dial-Up Networking connection for every e-mail identity on your PC (see pages 24–5). You can simply switch identities without disconnecting from the Internet. However, if your business account, say, is with a different ISP from your personal account, you can tell Outlook Express to disconnect and reconnect to the new ISP automatically when switching identities.

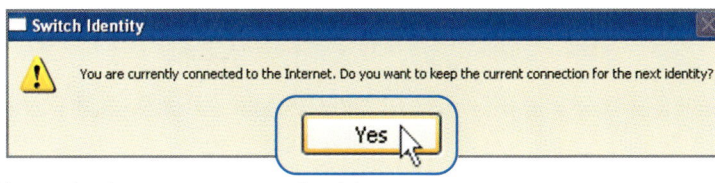

Watch Out!

Remember that Outlook Express stores all incoming e-mails on your computer hard disk, no matter whom they're addressed to. This means that your e-mails could be opened by anyone with sufficient knowledge of how Outlook works. If you are seriously worried about the confidentiality of your e-mails, think carefully about allowing anyone else to use your computer – ever!

SEE ALSO
- Windows XP – page 16
- Send and receive e-mail – page 38
- Manage your e-mail – page 42

SAFE AND SOUND

Security on the Internet

Take your **first steps** towards **browsing the Web safely**

Stories abound about the dangers of the Internet: hackers getting into your system, viruses bringing down companies, people having their credit card details stolen and, most commonly, the presence of unsuitable material that children might access. There are certainly people who use the Internet for unsavoury ends. However, you and your children will be able to make the most of the Internet perfectly safely if you take a few simple precautions.

The facts
You are extremely unlikely to be a victim of credit card fraud on the Internet, provided you use an up-to-date browser and make sure that you are logged on to a secure site (see pages 54–55) before typing in your credit card details.

Hackers and firewalls
Individual users are generally safe from hackers, unless you have a Broadband connection, such as Cable or ADSL. You can protect yourself, however, by using the built-in Windows XP Connection Firewall, or by buying a program such as Norton Internet Security.

Filtering software
It is well worth buying anti-virus software to protect your PC from infected files sent by e-mail (see page 58). And you may want to protect your children from certain material on the Internet by using a filtering program (see page 56).

GETTING STARTED

HOW TO: SET UP YOUR BROWSER'S DEFENCES

Internet Explorer's own filtering system allows you to choose the levels of language, nudity, sex and violence you think are acceptable. Each time you try to access a site, your browser will check it first and decide whether to show it. You can change these settings at any time – provided you use your password.

Internet Explorer's filtering system only works on sites whose authors have added a special rating file describing their site's contents. This means that any sites without these files are also blocked – even if their content is harmless. Other filtering programs may be more practical (see page 56).

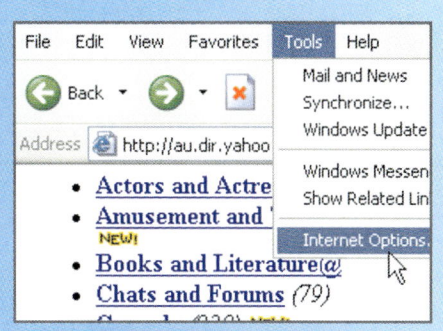

1 Open Internet Explorer. Go to the **Tools** menu and then select **Internet Options** from the drop-down menu.

2 In the dialogue box that appears, click on the tab marked **Content**. In the top half of this is a section marked 'Content Advisor'. Click on **Enable**.

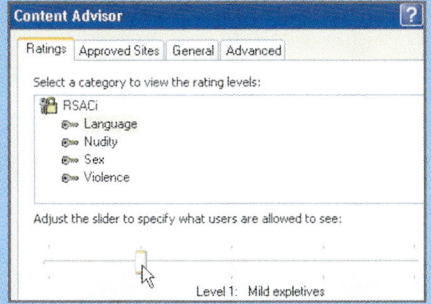

3 Set the levels of language, nudity, sex and violence you want to allow. Click on each category and adjust the slider from, in 'Language', for example, 'Mild expletives' to 'Explicit or crude language'.

4 To allow Web sites that don't have a rating file, click on the **General** tab and tick the box next to 'Users can see sites that have no rating'. Note that many unsavoury sites will still slip through.

5 Once you're happy with your settings, click **OK**. You will be asked to choose and confirm a password, then click **OK**. No one else will be able to change your settings if you keep the password secret.

Even greater protection

You can also set your browser to block any site you have not vetted personally. To do this, follow the procedure above but miss out step 4. This means that if a site has no rating (because you have not yet vetted it), your browser will not show it. As a consequence, you won't be able to visit any site you haven't already visited.

Jargon Buster!

Hacker A person who uses a computer to gain unauthorised access to data on another computer.

iMac

To access Internet Explorer's filtering system, go to the Edit menu, select Preferences and then Ratings.

SEE ALSO
- **Shop safely on the Web** – page 54
- **Avoid computer viruses** – page 58
- **Dealing with spam** – page 62

SAFE AND SOUND

Shop safely on the Web

Learn how to **go shopping** with **confidence** on the Internet

Many people worry about buying goods on the Internet, but the rules for shopping safely on-line are the same as those you would follow when shopping at your local mall or via mail order. You can protect yourself by using a reputable company, keeping your credit card details safe, and checking the company's customer service policy. Shopping over the Internet is at least as safe as giving your credit card details over the phone.

Secure sites
The most common concern with shopping over the Internet is that your credit card details might fall into the wrong hands. Reputable sites have worked to counter this fear by setting up a system that encrypts all the details that a shopper sends to them. These are known as 'secure' sites and can be used with confidence.

Encryption
When data is encrypted, it is translated into code that can only be deciphered by the recipient with the key to it – in this case, the shop you are buying from. This makes it almost impossible for a hacker to gain access to your credit card details or any other information you have supplied.

What to look for
Use the guidelines opposite to ensure that you are using a reputable, secure site. It is also a good idea, when dealing with a new company for the first time, always to look for a real street address (not a PO Box), along with a telephone number. If the company doesn't provide such information, it'll be more difficult for you to find them and obtain redress if things go wrong.

GETTING STARTED

HOW TO: SHOP SAFELY

When shopping on the Net, be sure you know who you are doing business with. Ask around – if someone else has had a good experience using a certain shop, the chances are that you will too.

Look for official approval
Reputable on-line businesses submit the security systems on their sites to be tested by impartial monitors, in the hope that they will gain an accreditation and so increase consumer confidence in their site.

Look for the logo of an international e-shopping monitor, such as VeriSign (www.verisign.com), eTick (www.etick.com) or TRUSTe (www.truste.com).

The logo normally acts as a link to the monitor's own Web site.

Check terms and conditions
A reputable shopping site should have a clearly marked section devoted to its terms and conditions and customer service policy. This should tell you how secure the site is and its refund and billing policy. It may also list frequently asked questions (FAQs) and allow you to monitor the progress of your order.

If you can't find this section, or are not satisfied with what it says, either contact the company or quit the site without buying. If you do decide to go ahead with your purchase, print out these terms and hold onto them. This can help if a site changes its terms after you have placed an order.

Look for the padlock
Once you've picked your 'shop', you should check that your credit card details are safe. You can do this by looking at the purchasing process.

When you are asked to submit your payment details, there should be a small padlock icon at the bottom of your browser window. The padlock shows that you are in a secure site. Depending on the way your browser is set up, a small box might also appear on screen, saying 'You are about to view pages over a secure connection'. This is also telling you that your credit card details will be safe. If the padlock does not appear, then you are not in a secure area. Contact the site to ask why.

Know your rights
Both the Australian Competition and Consumer Commission (www.accc.gov.au/ecomm/access1b.htm) and New Zealand's Ministry of Consumer Affairs (www.consumer-ministry.govt.nz/advice.html) offer useful advice to on-line shoppers. Both organisations collaborate with econsumer (www.econsumer.gov), an international site set up specifically to deal with cross-border e-commerce complaints.

Use common sense
Above all, use your common sense. If you see a deal that seems too good to be true, then it probably is just that.

Guard against fraud
All credit card companies offer protection against traditional types of fraud, but it is worth checking the exact terms of your bank's or card supplier's policy on Internet shopping.

If you suspect that you have been the victim of Internet credit card fraud, contact your card company immediately and give them as many details of your transactions as you can. It's a good idea to keep a written note of these.

CHECKLIST
- Ask friends to recommend reliable sites
- Check for a physical address
- Look for an accreditation
- Read the terms and conditions
- Look for the padlock sign
- Keep written details of all transactions
- Use your common sense
- If in doubt, don't proceed

Watch Out!
Never give out your credit card details via e-mail or in a chatroom. These are not secure areas.

SEE ALSO
- Do your weekly shop – page 192
- Buy a book, CD or video – page 201
- Buy and sell at auction – page 208

Filter out unsavoury sites

Use filtering software to control the sites your family can see

Filtering software is designed to help people who are worried about material they or their children will stumble across on the Internet. Also known as net nannies or censorware, filtering programs view and assess all the sites you wish to access. They judge the sites on criteria that you control, which means that you can choose which Web sites you and your children can or cannot view on the Internet.

FILTERING SOFTWARE

What it does
As well as blocking access to undesirable sites, filtering software lets you monitor any personal information being given out by you (or other users of your computer), and allows you to track on-line activity.

You can customise settings for different users, control the use of particular words and phrases, and prevent use of your browser at certain times of the day or night.

The drawbacks
Filtering software does have certain limitations. For instance, programs that block any site containing the word 'sex' might stop you viewing gardening sites that deal with the pollination of flowers.

Likewise, some filtering programs rely heavily on regularly updated lists of offensive sites. Although you can get frequent software updates containing these lists, it is impossible to keep a list of every offensive site on the Internet, when new ones are continually being created.

What software is available?
A number of filtering programs are available to buy or download from the Internet. They include Net Nanny (**www.netnanny.com**), CyberPatrol (**www.cyberpatrol.com**) and CYBERsitter (**www.cybersitter.com**).

When you purchase CyberPatrol, you receive a year's subscription to the program's CyberLISTS, including daily updates – called 'HotNOTS' – of inappropriate sites. You need to renew your subscription annually for a fee. In contrast, CYBERsitter and Net Nanny offer free updates, though you may periodically have to upgrade the software itself.

Most filtering software can also prevent children from divulging personal information over the Internet. This will help to protect them from giving out addresses, phone numbers or other contact details that might put them at risk.

Choosing your software
It is well worth downloading free trial versions of different filtering programs and trying them for a few days. You can then attempt to access a selection of sites in order to see how well the software works.

The program that you find most effective and easiest to set up – as well as least disruptive of your own use of the Internet – should be the one that you decide to buy.

GETTING STARTED

HOW TO: DOWNLOAD AND TEST FILTERING SOFTWARE

1 To download a trial version of CYBERsitter, go to **www.cybersitter.com** and click on the icon beside **Free Trial**. You should choose to save the installation program to your desktop.

2 Now double-click on the icon that appears on your desktop, and follow the on-screen instructions. Then double-click on the new icon that looks like an eye on your toolbar.

3 A control panel for CYBERsitter now opens. Click on the tabs and adjust the program settings. You should also create a password, though this is not possible with the trial version.

4 Once you have finished, click on **Done**. Now, if you attempt to access any site deemed unsuitable according to your criteria, you will be told that the page is not available.

Safety guidelines

- Try educating your children to use the Internet safely in the first place.
- The best method of monitoring Internet use is through supervision.
- Encourage children to search using search engines such as Yahooligans! (**www.yahooligans.com**), which list only sites suitable for young users.
- Teach children to search using categories, such as 'Science & Nature' or 'Sports & Recreation', not keywords. Sites found within categories will have already been approved by the search engine.
- If you cannot provide supervision, use a program, such as Internet Watcher (**www.internetwatcher.com**), which keeps a log file listing every Web site and page that has been visited by your computer, so you can find out exactly which Web pages have been viewed. 
- Remember: you cannot put all your trust in filtering software. Criteria used by programmers to sift Internet content may differ from your own, and may pass sites you would still consider harmful or block data you would actually wish to receive.

Watch Out!

Place the computer in a room used by all the family (not, for example, a bedroom), so that you or another adult can keep an eye on any sites that flash up on-screen.

SEE ALSO
- **Security on the Internet** – page 52
- **Search the Internet** – page 64
- **Improve your browsing** – page 76

57

SAFE AND SOUND

Avoid computer viruses

Protect your **computer** by **understanding** what viruses are, how they work and by installing **anti-virus software**

A virus is a computer program or piece of code designed to copy itself on as many computers as possible. Some are harmless, but others are designed to destroy programs or documents. While there are many viruses in existence, you can – with good practice, protective software and common sense – prevent your computer from being infected. The most important method of defence is to buy and use anti-virus software.

VIRUS QUESTIONS

Where do computer viruses come from?
Viruses are created, either accidentally or intentionally, by humans. Viruses can come from anywhere in the world, and are often designed by malicious programmers attempting to annoy other computer users.

The huge number of people using e-mail has made it easy for viruses attached to e-mail messages to be sent around the world at a remarkable speed.

How can you catch a virus?
One of the most common ways of 'catching' a virus is by opening an e-mail attachment that contains a virus. Other viruses can be transmitted when you load a floppy disk onto your computer or, much more rarely, through using a CD-ROM.

How likely are you to catch a virus?
This will depend on how often you use your computer, what you use it for and what precautions you take.

If you never use e-mail or borrow floppy disks, it is highly unlikely that your computer will contract a virus.

What will a virus do to your PC?
The most common viruses send e-mails with the virus attached to everyone in your PC's address book. Other types of virus infect programs instead of e-mails, causing PCs to crash unexpectedly. The more harmless viruses will simply cause a message to be displayed on your monitor.

About 75 per cent of viruses are known as 'macro' viruses. These are incorporated into pictures or documents such as Word files. Every time you open the 'infected' document, you will activate another copy of the virus, and so slowly infect your computer even further.

What can you do?
In most cases, you can find the source of the virus and search the Internet for a disinfecting program (a specific piece of anti-virus software) to solve the problem. Software manufacturers are constantly creating cures for the latest viruses. The best place to look for this software is at the Symantec site (**www.symantec.com**), one of the world leaders in anti-virus products. Click on **Search Virus Encyclopedia** for definitions of a vast range of viruses and advice on how to deal with them.

security response
downloads
about symantec
search

Virus Definition Updates
Virus Removal Tools
Renew Live Update Subscription

GETTING STARTED

DEALING WITH VIRUSES

Is there an attachment?
When an e-mail arrives, you should first look to see whether it has been sent with an attachment. Usually this is signalled by a paperclip symbol or something similar. If you were expecting the attached file and know what it is, there is no need to worry. But if you were not, the next step is to check who the sender is.

Who sent it?
If you do not recognise the sender, always treat the attachment with suspicion. And even if you *do* recognise the sender, you should always remain alert.

Some viruses send themselves on automatically from an infected computer. It is therefore possible for a virus to arrive from a personal friend or contact.

Read the cover message
Next you should read the cover message (remember: few viruses can be caught by opening and reading a basic e-mail message). The cover message should explain what the attachment is.

Most attachments are perfectly innocent – and if you are convinced of the sender's honesty, you should open it. But remember that the cover message with a virus is intended to encourage you to open the attachment. So do not be taken in by free offers.

Ask the sender
If you are still in doubt, write back to the sender before opening the file and ask for clarification. It is perfectly safe to do this via e-mail.

Scan the file
Most viruses can be detected using anti-virus software. Follow the instructions on page 60 in order to scan the suspect file.

Don't take risks
If the file still appears to be dubious, the safest thing to do is get rid of it. You can always have it re-sent if necessary.

Delete it
First right-click on the suspect message and select **Delete** from the pop-up menu. This places the file in the 'Deleted Items' folder.

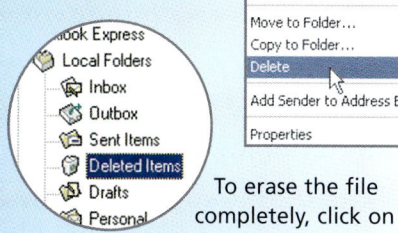

To erase the file completely, click on the **Deleted Items** folder icon. Then right-click on the suspect file again and click **Delete** again.

A window pops up asking you if you want to delete the file permanently. Click **Yes**. The file will now have been fully removed from your computer.

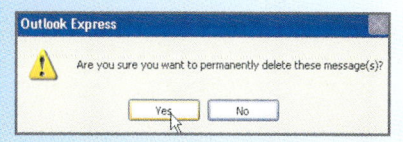

Hoaxes
You may receive messages alerting you to an e-mail with a name like 'Penpal Greetings'. Such warnings are usually hoax chain letters: there is no real virus.

These e-mails do no harm to your PC, but create a huge volume of mail when they are passed on, which slows or even clogs the Web.

Go to **www.vmyths.com** for more information on virus hoaxes.

Jargon Buster!
Attachment Any document sent with an e-mail. It is just like putting a photograph or newspaper cutting into an envelope along with a letter.

59

SAFE AND SOUND

iMac

There is an iMac version of Norton AntiVirus. You cannot download a free trial version of this, but you can buy it from the Symantec site.

Problem Solver!

To keep up-to-date with the latest reports on viruses, go to V-Buster (**www.v-buster.com**) and click on **Virus News**.

HOW TO: DOWNLOAD VIRUS PROTECTION

Anti-virus software works by looking at all potentially vulnerable files. Once these are identified, they are searched for particular 'signatures' (the recognisable markings of known viruses). The software contains details of more than 40,000 virus signatures. If it matches a signature with one in a suspect file, it will alert you, giving you the option of erasing the file, or restoring the original file from a back-up disk.

New viruses appear all the time, so it is important to update your software's list of virus signatures. Most software manufacturers offer a subscription to an update service. For a small cost, you can ensure that your software receives automatic updates on all the latest viruses. To do this, visit your software manufacturer's Web site.

A free trial version of Norton AntiVirus 2002, shown here, is available from the Symantec Web site (**www.symantec.com**). Note that the download process may take two hours over a modem connection.

1 Go to **www.symantec.com** and click on **downloads**. Scroll down the page and click on **Consumer Product Trialware**. Then click the link to the next page.

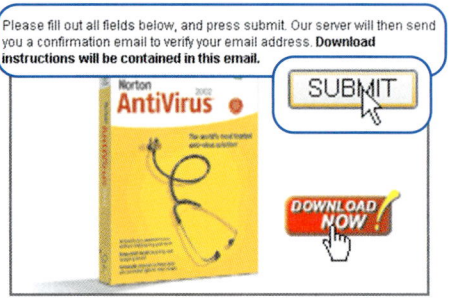

2 Click **Download Now!** for Norton AntiVirus, then enter your personal details, including e-mail address, on the next form and click **Submit**.

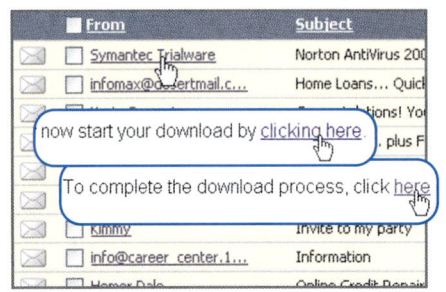

3 Check your e-mail for a message from Symantec. Open the message and click on the **Download** link, and again on the next one you are taken to.

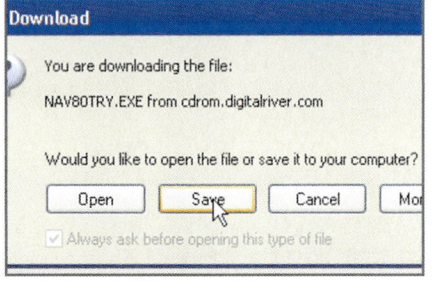

4 In the 'Download' window, choose to save the incoming file to your PC rather than opening it. Here, we have chosen to save the file to the Desktop.

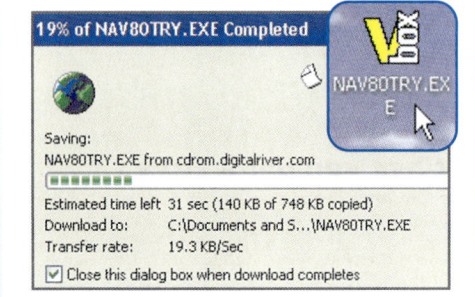

5 Once the download is complete, double-click on the program icon to install the software.

RESCUE DISK

When your PC restarts after you've downloaded Norton AntiVirus 2002, you have the option of creating a 'rescue disk' to help get your system back on track if it is damaged by a virus. This is well worth doing. Click **Create** and follow the instructions.

The program will then scan your PC and give you a virus report – this may take up to 30 minutes. Follow the instructions, then click **Close**. The program will now scan any incoming e-mails for viruses.

To change Norton's default settings, open the program and select **Options**. You can change its 'Auto-Protect' status, the varieties of files it should scan, whether it starts up immediately and how it should respond if it locates a virus.

GETTING STARTED

HOW TO: SCAN YOUR E-MAILS FOR VIRUSES

It is easy to set up a security program, such as Symantec's Norton AntiVirus 2002, to scan your incoming e-mails for any viruses. If a virus is located, an alert box will appear on screen informing you of what has been found. The alert box will also ask you what you want to do.

You can repair an infected file, 'quarantine' a suspicious item, delete an infected file, or respond to any damaging activity that may have been caused by a virus and stop it.

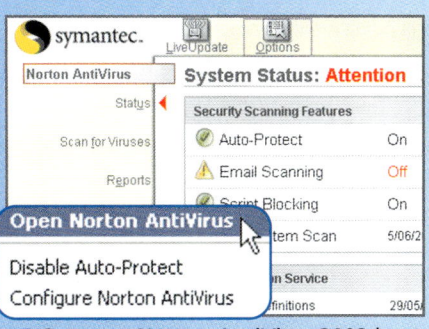

1 Open up Norton AntiVirus 2002 by right-clicking on the icon at the bottom right of your screen. Check whether 'Email Scanning' is enabled.

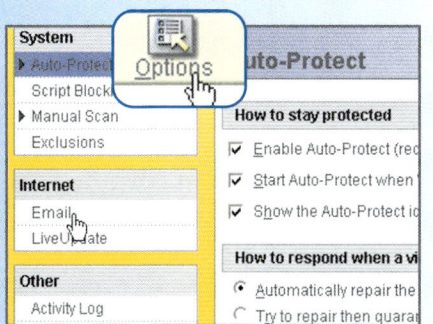

2 If it's not (as here), click the **Options** icon, which will allow you to customise all the program's features. In the 'Options' window, click on **Email**.

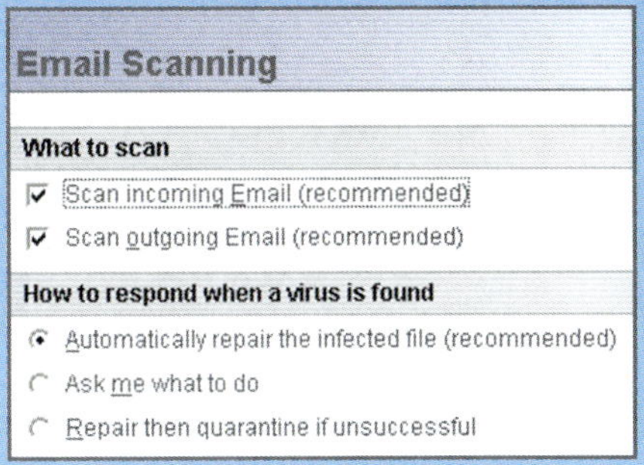

3 Now activate both boxes under 'What to scan' to ensure that Norton AntiVirus scans both incoming and outgoing e-mails automatically.

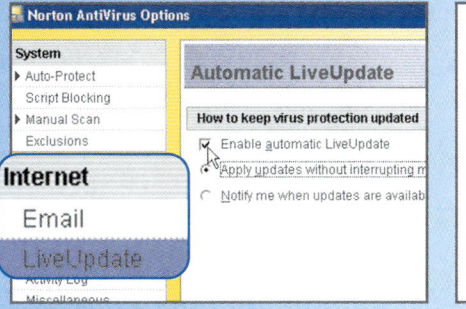

4 In the left-hand menu, click on **LiveUpdate** and then select **Enable automatic LiveUpdate**. This will ensure that the program downloads new virus definitions when they become available.

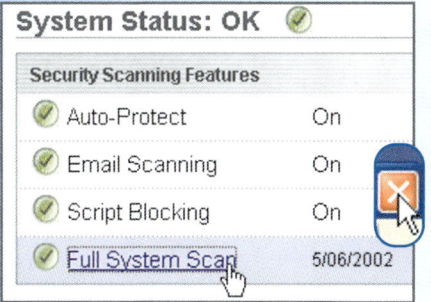

5 Click **OK** to return to the opening window, where you'll see that 'Email Scanning' has been enabled. You can now carry out other virus checks, or simply exit the program.

When you get a virus

If someone sends you an e-mail virus, either deliberately or by accident, Norton AntiVirus will detect it automatically if you have 'Scan incoming Email' enabled. Unless you instruct it otherwise, Norton will attempt to repair the infected file, and will tell you if it cannot do so. You should then allow the program to quarantine the file so you can attempt to repair it later when an appropriate new virus definition becomes available on the Internet.

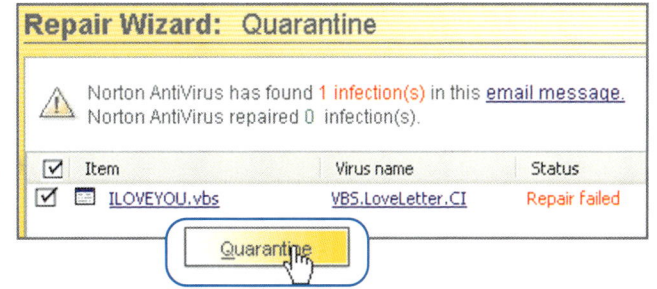

Did You Know?

If you receive a virus which Norton AntiVirus can't repair, and there is no record of it at the Symantec site, you should send the original e-mail to the Symantec anti-virus team so they can develop a fix for it.

Watch Out!

Make sure your e-mail software is not open before setting up a virus scan – otherwise the process will not work.

SEE ALSO
- Receive e-mail attachments – page 48
- Dealing with spam – page 62
- Download from the Web – page 86

Dealing with spam

Avoid **junk e-mail** and unwelcome messages

Anyone who uses e-mail is at some time likely to receive unsolicited e-mail messages and advertisements, also known as 'spam' – the Internet equivalent of junk mail. Often they take the form of 'too good to be true' offers. Like paper junk mail, such e-mails aren't harmful, just annoying. Sometimes, however, your ISP Inbox can be clogged by a deluge of spam; or the messages themselves may be offensive. Fortunately, you can take steps to filter out such material without ever seeing it.

Junk e-mailers
Unsolicited e-mail can come from a number of sources, some of which are perfectly reputable. But other junk mailers, such as pornographic sites, will send messages with personal-looking but often false e-mail addresses. These addresses serve the purpose of both preventing messages from looking like junk mail, and stopping the recipient from replying directly to the company.

Whatever else you do, never reply to spam messages asking to be taken off the mailing list. Your reply will simply confirm to the senders that their messages have got through to you, and you are likely to receive even more.

Chain e-mails
You may receive e-mails promising that you'll win a huge amount of money if you forward the letter to the first 10 people in your address book. Or the message may be a 'poison letter', threatening you with bad luck if you fail to send it on.

Such letters are generally hoaxes, designed to generate extra traffic on the Web. They are not especially dangerous, but they are malicious in that they slow down the Web. Do all Internet users a favour by deleting chain e-mails without forwarding them to your friends.

GETTING STARTED

HOW TO: DELETE SPAM AUTOMATICALLY

Outlook Express allows you to specify what should happen to e-mail messages from certain sources. You can use this to delete spam automatically and prevent it from clogging up your Inbox.

For example, you may receive an unwanted promotional e-mail from a marketing company. You may then want Outlook Express to delete any more messages that come from that source automatically.

1 Open Outlook Express and click on **Tools**. From the menu that appears, select **Message Rules**, then **Mail**.

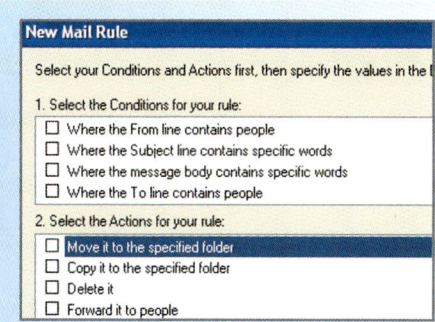

2 The 'New Mail Rule' window will open. (If the 'Message Rules' window appears, click on **New**.) This dialogue box presents a list of ways to filter your e-mail.

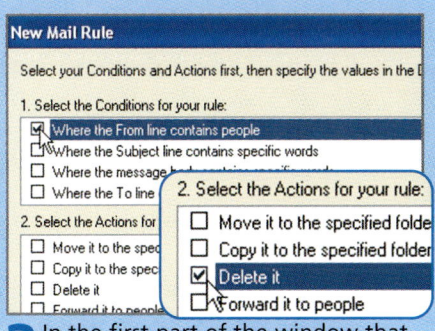

3 In the first part of the window that appears, click next to 'Where the From line contains people'. In the second part, click next to 'Delete it'.

4 In the third part of the window click on **contains people** and type in the e-mail address of the source of spam you have received. Click **Add** after each one. Then click **OK**.

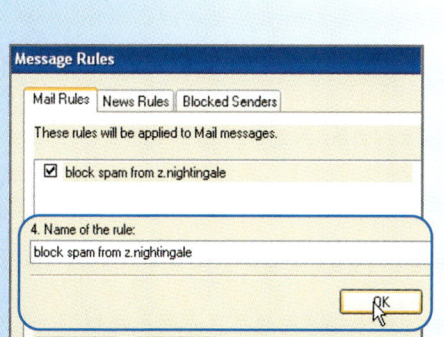

5 In the final part of the window give your message rule a name and click **OK**. It should now appear in your 'Message Rules' window. Click **OK**, then **Apply Now** to exit the 'Rules' window.

Avoiding spam – further steps

To avoid receiving spam, remember to be careful about who you give your e-mail address to, especially if it could be added to a mailing list. If you have subscribed to a mailing list, keep the e-mail which explains how to cancel the subscription.

Remember also that you are very likely to start receiving spam if you sign up to a bulletin board or newsgroup, as spammers regularly extract e-mail addresses from such sites. For advice on how to outwit them, see *Avoid junk e-mail*, page 101.

Did You Know?

You can install a commercial spam filter such as SpamBuster (http://contactplus.com) as an added safeguard against receiving spam.

Problem Solver!

If you need to register with mailing lists, you can set up an alternative e-mail address using a Web-based service such as Hotmail or Yahoo! Mail. These services offer filters that can stop most junk mail from reaching you.

SEE ALSO
- Send and receive e-mail – *page 38*
- Send e-mail attachments – *page 46*
- Avoid computer viruses – *page 58*

HAVE A GO AT SEARCHING

Search the Internet

Find what you're **looking for** on the **Web**

Finding what you want on the Internet is not always easy. But there are free tools to help you to seek out the particular piece of information you are looking for. These are known collectively as search tools or, more loosely, 'search engines' – although a search engine is in fact only one type of search tool. To make searching quicker and more profitable it is worth taking time to learn how different search tools work.

Search options
There are three main types of search tool on the Internet – search engines, search directories and search agents. You tell them to search for something by entering 'keywords' or 'search words' and they then check your words against a database of Web sites and list the results. The difference between the three is the way in which they compile their databases.

Engines
Search engines use programs to scan the Web and retrieve information on the content of as many sites as they can find. This means they can provide a thorough, regularly updated database of sites.

Directories
Search directories employ people to pick the best sites on the Web and then file them under categories and subcategories, which you can search through. They include fewer Web sites, because people cannot sort information as quickly – but they generally list better-quality ones.

Agents
Search agents look through other databases rather than creating their own – and they can search several databases at once.

GETTING STARTED

TYPES OF SEARCH TOOL

Most search tools fall into one of three main categories:

Search engines

Strictly speaking, the term 'search engine' applies to only one kind of service. These are engines which automatically produce indexes of Web sites using software that does no more than index the words on the site's homepage.

You enter some information about what you want the engine to find. It then searches its index for matches to your search terms. In a matter of seconds it returns a list of matches and you can select which sites to visit. Search engines are fast and efficient, but because they are generated 'blindly' they can turn up hundreds or even thousands of answers to a general enquiry.

Some search engines, such as Google (www.google.com), for example, have a very simple look, while other more specific search engines, such as AltaVista (http://au.altavista.com), are more complex in appearance and structure.

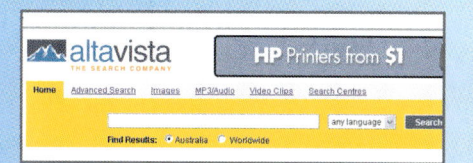

Search directories

These services generally use people to research Web sites, and to organise sites into topic groups. You can click on topics and further subheadings until you find sites suited to your specific interest. Alternatively, you can enter a keyword and search the directory for suitable sites. Examples include Yahoo! (http://au.yahoo.com) and Looksmart (www.looksmart.com.au).

Search agents

When you enter a keyword into a search agent, it employs several search engines at once to look for it. One such site, which gives you information on different search engines, and lets you choose which to search, is Netscape Search (http://search.netscape.com).

There are also comparison agents, which can search sites for much more detailed information. At 1stHeadlines (www.1stheadlines.com), for example, you can search for news stories on selected topics and in particular newspapers from all around the world, while Shopping Home (http://shopping.ninemsn.com.au) will compare prices from a range of on-line shops.

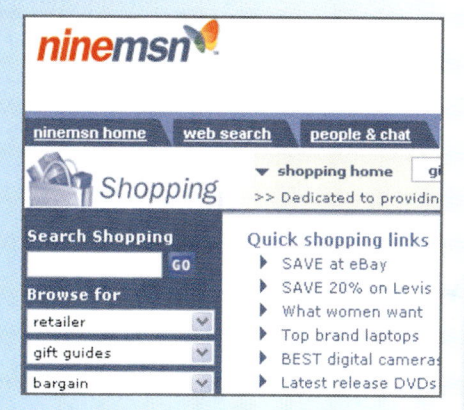

Using search tools

Search engines and search directories produce different results when carrying out the same search. If you enter 'vegetables' into the Google search engine and the Yahoo! search directory, Google will come up with approximately 1,910,000 sites and Yahoo! with 685 relevant sites.

iMac

*The iMac comes equipped with its own search agent. Go to the **File** menu and select **Search Internet**. Enter your search term and click the magnifying glass to begin searching.*

Did You Know?

Search engines contain indexes of millions of Web sites, so you should never have to wait more than a few seconds for a search to be completed.

65

HAVE A GO AT SEARCHING

CHOOSING A SEARCH TOOL

Selecting which search tool to use for any given search can be difficult. Some people try to get to know a large number of search tools, but this is not the most effective tactic.

A better option might be to try out some search tools and find a small number you really like and which are the most relevant to what you are doing. Learn how they work and how to make the best of them by reading their 'help' pages and practising with them. Using this method, you can build a small library of search tools in your 'Favorites' list that you can turn to for any eventuality. Here are some suggestions for different kinds of search tool you might want to examine as a way of starting your Favorites list:

● A search tool with country-specific site options – such as Yahoo! – which allows you to limit your search to local sites, or to expand your search globally if you so wish. This is useful as it can narrow the number of Web sites indexed in a database, ensuring that the results of a search are more specific. It also prevents you from searching for sites in countries which will obviously not include the data you require: for example, if you are looking for a shop selling designer hats in your area or city.

Many search tools have a specific Australian/New Zealand site, including:
Yahoo!: http://au.yahoo.com
AltaVista: http://au.altavista.com

● An engine which allows you to make a search by combining several terms. Many search engines let you combine terms in specific ways to get more precise results (see overleaf). One example is AOL Anywhere (http://search.aol.com).

● An engine that can find images and other specific kinds of media, for example, AltaVista (http://au.altavista.com).

● A search directory with listings within subject areas such as 'Health' or 'Recreation', such as Yahoo! (http://au.yahoo.com), can help you to search under a topic even if you are not sure precisely what you are looking for.

● A search agent that can combine a search of several different engines at once, such as Ask Jeeves (www.ask.com), is suitable for those times when you need to get a general overview quickly, and simply want a list of sites to browse through. It is also a useful way to find more unusual sites.

Time Saver!

Put any search tools you find useful into the Favorites list in your Web browser. You can make a special folder for them. Then you will be able to return to them easily whenever they are needed.

MAJOR SEARCH SITES

● **AltaVista (http://au.altavista.com)**
An excellent search engine that also offers a directory and specialist image and video clip searches.
● **Google (www.google.com)**
A simple-looking automated search engine with a vast database and quicker-than-average response time.
● **HotBot (http://hotbot.lycos.com)**
A well-designed search engine that offers simple ways to make your search more accurate.
● **Looksmart (www.looksmart.com.au)**
One of the best search directories around with top-quality sites and an exhaustive list of categories.
● **Lycos (www.lycos.com)**
Good search engine with a built-in directory. Also allows you to search more specifically within your first search results.
● **Telstra (http://telstra.com)**
Offers a search facility as well as a range of useful contents. Popularly used as a homepage.
● **WebCrawler (www.webcrawler.com)**
Gets impressive results by probing several search engines at once.
● **Yahoo! (http://au.yahoo.com)**
Excellent search directory with great breadth and depth of coverage. Often used as a homepage.

GETTING STARTED

HOW TO: SEARCH

Most search engines work in roughly the same way. On the homepage you need to enter the search terms you are interested in (see overleaf for more guidance on choosing search terms).

If you are searching for general information on a particular health condition, such as diabetes, use a search engine such as AltaVista (http://au.altavista.com) as you can click to decide whether to make a country-specific or worldwide search. In this example it makes sense to perform a worldwide search because diabetics have similar concerns the world over.

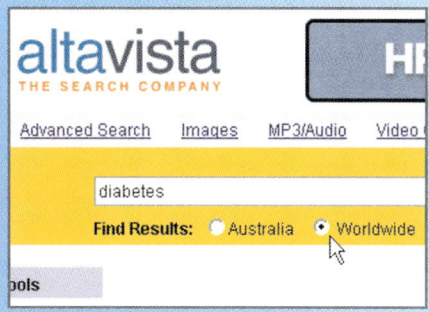

1 Go to **http://au.altavista.com** and type the subject of your search in the 'search box' – here we have chosen 'diabetes'. Then click 'Australia' or 'Worldwide' to select where to search.

2 Click on **Search** and wait a few seconds for the results. The 10 sites which best match your search terms will be listed first, and you can click the **Next>>** link to see more.

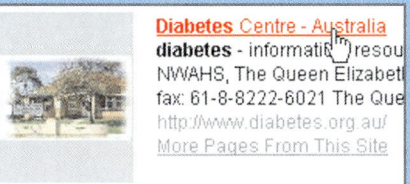

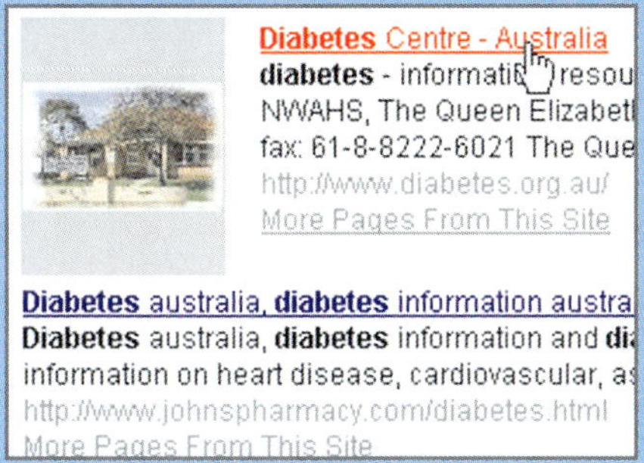

3 Each site is presented with a short description and its address. If one of the sites listed is what you want, then click the link to go to it.

4 If there are too many results, refine your search by using more specific terms, or click the **Advanced Search** link to narrow your search criteria.

5 To keep the window with your list of search results, open the link to a desired site in a new window by right-clicking on the link and choosing **Open in New Window**.

Relevancy ratings

Some search tools indicate how closely their finds match your search criteria and list the best ones first. This rating is usually expressed as a percentage. It is judged on how many of your search terms are found in the document and whether they appear in the title, the address or just in the main text.

However, assessing the relevance of a site is a difficult qualitative task for a computer to perform, so don't be surprised if a highly rated result turns out to be of limited use, or vice versa.

Watch Out!

Many search tools show the last time that each site it has found was updated. If a site has not been updated for months, it may be out of date and not worth visiting.

HAVE A GO AT SEARCHING

ENTERING THE CORRECT SEARCH TERMS

The more specific you are when using search terms, the more precise the results will be. Search engines generally have a place for you to enter search terms on their main page, but you may also find a link to an 'Advanced Search' option, or to some search tips. If you find either of these, explore them.

Advanced searches may provide a form you can fill in to give precise information about what you want to find – such as words you'd like to include or exclude or the date when the site was created.

There are also symbols you can combine with your search terms to help you to achieve greater precision. There are several ways to do this:

- Use + before a word to indicate that you want it to be in all the sites that the search engine finds. If the word does not appear in some sites, you can be sure you don't want to see them.

- Use – before a word if you want it excluded: for example, 'King Charles – Spaniel'. This command tells the search engine to find sites about the historical figure but to ignore sites about dogs.

- Use * to search for sites that include a certain word regardless of its ending. For example, if you enter 'garden*' the search engine will return sites that include the words gardening, gardens and gardeners as well as garden.

- To find an exact phrase, put it in double quotation marks – for example, "hanging gardens of Babylon". This will bring up far fewer sites and most of them should be very closely related to your chosen topic.

- Use upper-case letters only when you know you are looking for a name, or when you are using Boolean terms (see opposite). A lower-case search will find both upper and lower-case results, for example, OXFAM and oxfam.

SEARCH NATIONALLY

Some search engines, such as AltaVista (http://au.altavista.com) allow you to search for sites written in a specific language. This can be helpful if you want to narrow down the sites found to their country of origin, but it could also mean that you miss some really useful Web sites.

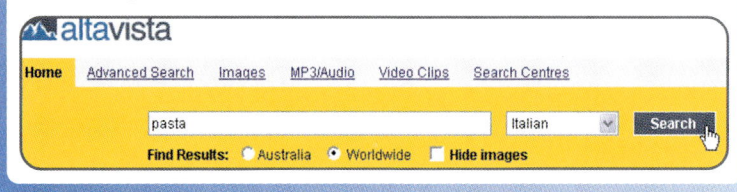

Watch Out!

Different search engines have individual ways of listing search results and are therefore useful for different reasons. For example, Google prioritises results according to how close together your search terms appear – for instance, 10 words apart – on a site.

68

GETTING STARTED

COMBINE SEARCH TERMS

You can determine how search terms combine to include and exclude each other in a search. You can use the terms AND, OR, NOT and NEAR (in capitals) to tell a search engine how to bring words together in a search. This is sometimes referred to as a 'Boolean search'.

AND
This tells the search engine to show only sites that include both terms. Type in 'Cosmetics AND allergies' to find Web sites about allergies of this specific type.

OR
Typing OR between search terms lets you look for two separate terms simultaneously and bring up results that feature either or both the terms included in the search. Type in 'Edna Everage OR Barry Humphries' and you will get a list of sites about both the Australian celebrity and her less glamorous alter ego.

NOT
This lets you search for sites that include the first term but not the second. Type 'Python NOT Monty' into the search box to rule out references to the cult comedy series from your search for snakes.

NEAR
An extension of the AND search, this lets you specify that the terms must appear close to each other on the site. For example, 'cooking NEAR5 prawn' will find sites with the word 'cooking' within five words of 'prawn'.

Boolean combinations
Many search engines allow you to combine Boolean terms using brackets. For example, 'browser AND (Microsoft OR Netscape)' will find sites which contain either the word 'Microsoft' or 'Netscape' and the word 'browser'.

CASE STUDY
Erin had been told by a friend about a plant that had purple-coloured leaves, which were light-sensitive and folded at night into a sort of pyramid shape. As someone that had recently moved into a home with a garden she was keen to find out more about plants, and maybe buy this particular one. Her friend thought the plant might be called oxalis, or perhaps sorrel, and so Erin started an Internet search.

She began with a general search engine, Google (**www.google.com**), where she entered the search term 'oxalis'. By doing this, Erin learned that while some species of oxalis are called sorrels, the genus is unrelated to the true sorrel. She also discovered that some oxalis species are edible and used in salads.

But this was all rather general botanical information, and finding it was relatively hard work as many of the sites Erin's search retrieved were for various companies called Oxalis.

What Erin needed, she decided, was the exact name of her plant. This would help her search more precisely.

Erin visited AltaVista (**http://au.altavista.com**) and chose to do an image search. As she had suspected, most of the oxalis plants had green leaves, but she found a few with purple ones. Clicking the links to go to their Web sites, she soon learned her plant's full name – *Oxalis triangularis*.

Erin then returned to Google, and searched under the plant's correct name. There were plenty of Web sites from which she could get information, and she even found sites where she could buy the plant on-line.

Did You Know?
Many search engines have their own methods to help make your search more exact. Look for a link called 'Advanced Search' or similar, which will provide this service.

HAVE A GO AT SEARCHING

Searchbots

It is possible to download special search agent programs called 'searchbots' onto your PC. You can use a search agent such as Image Wolf to search through thousands of servers for hard-to-find images. Go to www.trellian.com for more details.

Did You Know?

Because search engines use their own individual databases, a search with one engine may reveal different results from a search with another.

USING A SEARCH AGENT

Search agents are able to send queries to a number of different search engines at once and retrieve the results in a single operation. They aren't good at very precise searches, but they are excellent for helping you to get a broad idea of what is available on a given subject. One search agent that works in this way is the CitySearch site (**www.citysearch.com.au**). You fill in a simple form describing the product or service you are looking for and the search agent then looks for it across a range of possible sources.

Other search agents, such as qbSearch (**www.qbsearch.com**), allow you to make a search using several selected search engines (chosen by you), and then compare the results on the same page. You might wish to use qbSearch if you want to research a topic quickly and thoroughly.

1 First go to the qbSearch Web site (**www.qbsearch.com**) and type in the keyword (or words) that you want to search for. Here we have chosen the keyword 'roses'.

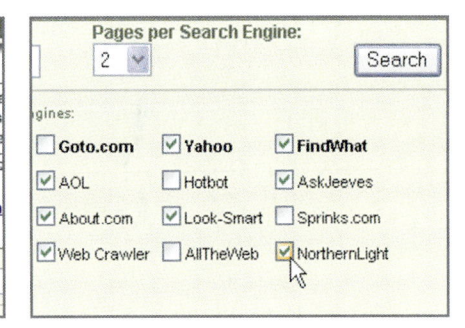

2 Select the search engines that you want qbSearch to trawl through. You can limit the number of pages returned by each engine to ensure the process does not become too slow.

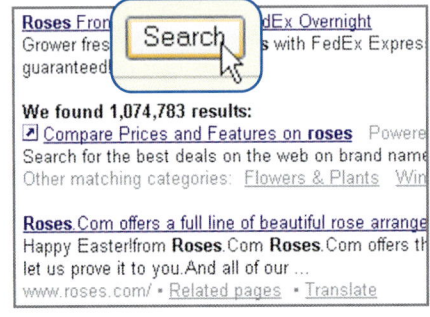

3 When you have set up the search as you want it, click the **Search** button and the results will soon start appearing on the screen as they are collected.

4 You can refine your search further, or simply click on any link that looks promising. Remember that you can open a Web page in a new window by right-clicking on its link in the list of results.

70

GETTING STARTED

HOW TO: USE SEARCH DIRECTORIES

Directories organise their Web sites into subject areas. This means they are useful if you aren't sure what you want, or want to see what the Internet has to offer on a broad topic. Directories usually offer keyword searching in addition to browsing through their subject lists.

Looksmart (**www.looksmart.com.au**) and Lycos (**www.lycos.com**) are Web directories with high-quality sites. Yahoo! (**http://au.yahoo.com**) is generally much larger than any of its competitors, and is worth using if you want to find as wide a range of Web sites as possible and don't mind spending some time browsing.

1 First, go to the Yahoo! homepage (**http://au.yahoo.com**). This is the Yahoo! site for Australia and New Zealand, but you can also use it to search across the world.

2 Choose the main subject heading you want to browse, then pick a topic from those listed. If your chosen subject is not obvious, enter it in the search box and then click **Search** to find it.

3 You may be presented with more subject divisions, and Web sites will also be listed. You can usually request the site to show Australian and New Zealand listings only if you wish.

✋ Watch Out!

If you allow younger users to use standard search engines without supervision, they may (even accidentally) retrieve material you might prefer them not to see.

YOUNGER INTERNET USERS

Many parents are concerned about protecting their children from the less desirable areas of the Internet. So it is good to know that there are search engines which cater specifically for their needs.

Many popular search engines, such as AltaVista, have a 'Family Filter' which can be used to block out certain Web sites. Such filters tend to rely on special Internet filtering software which uses keywords and lists of blocked sites to prevent access to some information (see *Filter out unsavoury sites*, page 56). This is similar to the kinds of filtering software you might use at home, and is not always totally reliable.

Another option is to choose a search directory with contents selected to be appropriate for children. Such search directories use a database of Web sites chosen by people who check their content before including them – so you can be sure that nothing undesirable can creep in. Suitable directories include, among others, KidsClick! (**http://kidsclick.org**), Yahooligans! (**www.yahooligans.com**), Ask Jeeves Kids (**www.ajkids.com**) and AOL Kids Search (**www.aol.com.au/site/aol/kids/kidsearch**).

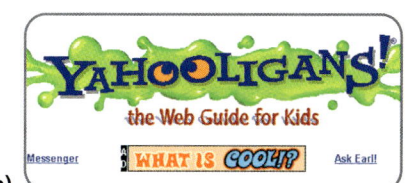

HAVE A GO AT SEARCHING

SPECIALIST SEARCHES

Some search tools allow you to search for specific items on the Web, such as images, video and news stories.

Images
Some search engines, such as AltaVista (http://au.altavista.com) and Google (www.google.com), will help you to find images on-line. In both cases, go to the site's homepage, click on the **Images** tab and enter a search term, such as 'Uluru'.

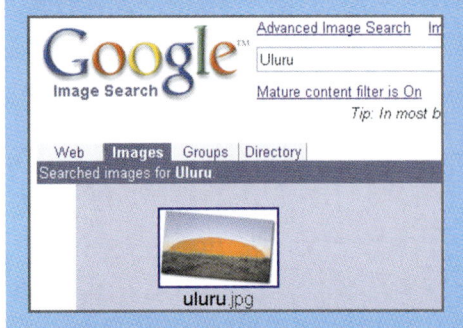

Video clips
AltaVista (http://au.altavista.com) is also a good place to start searching for a video clip. Choose **Video Clips** on the homepage, then type in what you are looking for. If you need a special type of video format, make sure that you select it before you search.

News and current affairs
There are several Web sites which gather news stories from around the world. One such service is 1stHeadlines (**www.1stheadlines.com**). This functions very much like a search engine: you can choose a subject of interest from a large list, or select a country of interest. There is also a search tool so you can look for something specific.

Usenet is a collection of more than 30,000 discussion groups, each covering a different subject. Joining these groups is mostly free, and you don't have to be a member to read the information on offer. Visit **http://groups.google.com**, where you can search the Usenet archive, and also join any groups you like.

In most areas of interest there are Web sites that act as searchable databases – as you get more familiar with using the Internet, you will find those that suit your field of interest. For example, book-lovers might like to visit abebooks (**http://abebooks.com**) and BookFinder (**www.bookfinder.com**), both comprehensive databases that collect the catalogues of a number of second-hand booksellers and allow them to be searched in one go.

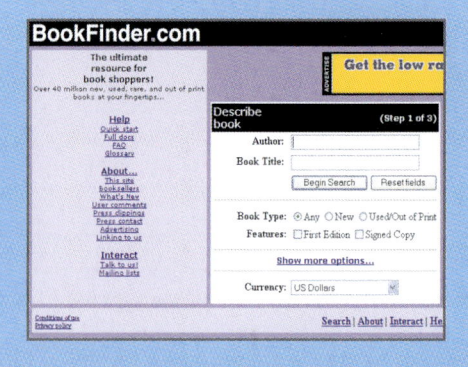

Did You Know?
There is a search facility built into Internet Explorer. Click on the **Search** button to open a search box to the left of your browser window. Enter your text and start your search.

Time Saver!
If you find a Web site with useful links, remember to put it in your Favorites list for future reference.

72

GETTING STARTED

SEARCHING THE WEB FOR A PERSON

The Internet can help you to track down an individual, and there are several tools to help you.

White Pages on-line

To search for people and household phone numbers in Australia and New Zealand, use the appropriate White Pages (**www.whitepages.com.au** OR **www.whitepages.co.nz**). Enter the name of the person you want and as much of the address as you know or can guess, and press **Search** or **Go**.

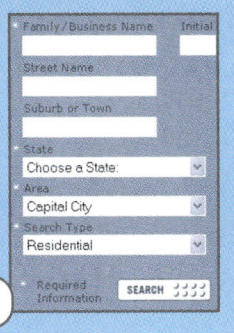

Yellow Pages on-line

To search for businesses in Australia and New Zealand, use the on-line Yellow Pages (**www.yellowpages.com.au** OR **www.yellowpages.co.nz**). You can search by name, location or both.

Postal information

Up-to-date information on postcodes, postal costs, international postal guides and parcel tracking can be obtained on-line from both Australia Post (**www.austpost.com.au**) and New Zealand Post (**www.nzpost.com**). If you want postcodes in the UK, go to Consignia (**www. consignia-online.com**) and click on **Find any UK postcode or address**.

Phone directories

If you want to find the telephone number for a person or business in another country, a good place to start is Teldir.com (**www.teldir.com**). This site has links to phone directories all over the world.

E-mail address finders

Finding someone's e-mail address is much more tricky. There is no single directory of e-mail addresses. Instead there are many sources which could prove useful. You can start by trying WhoWhere? (**www.whowhere.lycos.com**) or MESA, Meta Email Search Agent (**http://mesa.rrzn.uni-hannover.de**). Alternatively, go to My Email Address Is (**http://my.email.address.is**), or try a 'People Search' in Yahoo! (**http://people.yahoo.com**).

WEB PORTALS

A portal is a Web page that combines searching services and other information in one place. The idea behind Web portals is that you choose a site and set it as your homepage so that every time you start an Internet session your browser automatically goes there first. Then you are immediately presented with information you like to have handy.

Some search sites offer portal services. OptusNet (**http://dial.optusnet.com.au**), for example, has a range of information services on its homepage, including stock market quotes, cinema and TV listings, weather forecasts, daily news headlines, horoscopes and many useful links. To get the service, you need to register, then configure it to meet your needs.

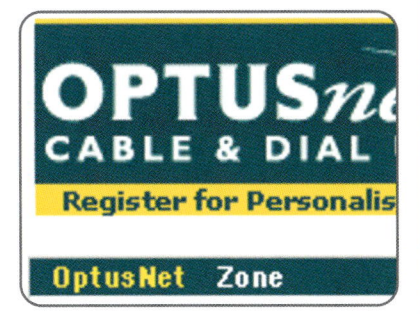

Watch Out!

People-search tools are only as good as their databases, and there is no guarantee you will be able to locate a person using the Internet. Use a combination of these tools to increase your chances of success.

Did You Know?

The first thing most people do when they try using a search engine is to enter their own name. It is fascinating to find out if you have made it onto the Web and whether you have any interesting namesakes around the world.

73

HAVE A GO AT SEARCHING

Did You Know?
If one of the links listed on a Web page doesn't work, it may be possible to report it to the search engine, which can then check the problem or remove the site from its database. Look for a link called 'Feedback' or 'Contact Us' to report a problem.

PROBLEM SOLVING
Sometimes you will find a Web site listed in a search engine and try to go to it, only to get a message saying that the site is not available. There are several reasons why this might be the case.

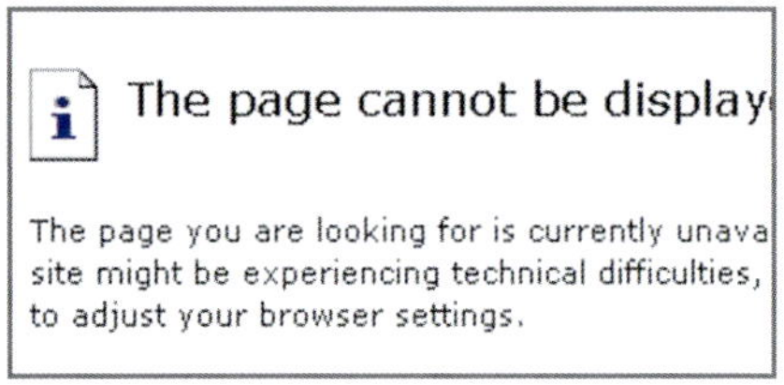

Out-of-date search engines
Web search engines regularly trawl the Internet to produce databases of sites. When you use a search engine, it is these databases – rather than the Web as it is at that instant – which are scanned. This means a search engine might not know that the site authors have changed the structure of their site, or removed it from the Web completely.

For example, if you were looking for a company that designs mapmaking software, a search engine might try to send you to **www.mapmaker.co.uk/software/downloads**. This means your browser is going to look in a folder called 'downloads', which is inside a folder called 'software' on a site called mapmaker.co.uk. If the site's author has changed the way information is filed at the site since the search engine created its index, your browser will be unable to find what it wants, even though it may not be far away.

You can still find out if the Web site is running by trying to go to the homepage. This page is generally easy to find. Simply delete everything after and including the first '/' in the site address. For example, **www.mapmaker.co.uk/software/downloads** becomes **www.mapmaker.co.uk**. If you get there, you can then look for the information you want, which may be listed under a different heading.

Problems with a server
Another possible cause of being unable to get through to a particular Web page is that the server you need to connect to is temporarily unavailable. If you get an error message to this effect, try again at a later time.

The site has moved
Alternatively, the Web site you want might still be available, but may have moved – for example, to a new ISP, giving it a new URL. If you think this might be the case, try another search engine and see if this comes up with a different site address.

Gremlins in the program
Sometimes when you click on one of the links provided by a search engine, the site doesn't appear and you don't even get a message. This may just be a glitch in your browser software. Try clicking on the **Stop** button to stop your browser's attempt to load the page, then click the link again. If it doesn't work a second time, there is more likely to be a problem with the Web page itself.

Keep looking
If all else fails, don't despair. There are millions of Web sites on the Internet, and if there are problems with the one that seems to cover the information you want, you can be sure that there will be many others that deal with similar material – and that do work.

GETTING STARTED

HOW TO: PLAN YOUR SEARCH STRATEGY

Trying to find what you want on the Internet can seem like looking for a needle in a haystack. But if you learn how search tools work and plan a search in your mind before starting it, locating information can be remarkably straightforward.

Think before you start

Decide what it is that you want to find. It might be something very precise, such as the population of a city, next week's weather forecast in Rome, a place to buy German sausage, or a map of the Moon. Or, it could be something more general – basic data on a holiday destination, some tips on using your new digital camera, or a few Web sites for your 'Favorites' list that relate to your hobby. The important thing is to have an idea of what you want.

Be specific

Tell a search engine precisely what you are looking for. If you want recipes that use chillies, type 'cooking with chillies', and not simply 'cooking'.

If a search engine doesn't locate what you're looking for, then try:

● A wider or narrower search

Perhaps you aren't being specific enough, or the words or phrase you are using are too precise – such as 'cooking with bird's eye chillies'.

● Synonyms

Maybe there are other ways to describe what you want – use a dictionary or thesaurus to find similar words and try those, for example, 'chilli', 'chilli pepper', or 'chillies'. There are on-line dictionaries and thesauruses that can help you out. Try Merriam-Webster OnLine (**www.m-w.com**) and Thesaurus.com (**www.thesaurus.com**).

● Using the appropriate search tool

Try a search agent (see *Types of search tool*, page 65) if you want to get a broad range of Web sites related to a subject, and use a single search engine if you want to find something very precise. If you are having trouble with one search engine, go to a different one and try that.

Always remember:

Think laterally about your subject, considering every single possibility, and you stand a better chance of finding exactly what you are looking for.

Refining your search

After you have completed your first search, some search engines, such as Lycos (**www.lycos.com**), allow you to conduct another search within those results. This can be a good way to narrow your search down, especially if you had not anticipated a problem with your first search. For example, an initial search for 'springbok' may bring up a lot of sites about the South African national rugby union side as well as about the species of antelope you were looking for. Searching within your initial results for 'antelope' should cut out most of the irrelevant sites.

Watch Out!

Search engines often use American wording, so for example, you may find 'coriander' under 'cilantro' or 'grilling' under 'broiling'.

SEE ALSO
● Filter out unsavoury sites – page 56
● Improve your browsing – page 76
● Learn something new – page 110

ADVANCED BROWSING

Improve your browsing

Get more out of surfing the Web

Once you have learnt the basic browsing commands, it takes only a few simple steps to build on this knowledge so that browsing on the Web becomes faster and more effective. Internet Explorer provides a variety of tools you can use to make the most of your time on the Net.

History
The 'History' tool keeps a record of the sites you have visited – for a specified length of time. This is especially useful for those sites whose addresses you have forgotten, but would like to revisit.

Favorites
The 'Favorites' tool lets you create a list of the sites that you visit most often. These can then be accessed quickly, without having to type in the address again. Using this list to store addresses also means that you can often access pages off-line. This will save time and money spent connected to the Internet.

Time savers
There are other practices which can make your browsing time more efficient, such as opening several different Web sites at the same time or checking your e-mails while downloading from the Web.

GETTING STARTED

HOW TO: USE HISTORY

Internet Explorer keeps a record of the sites you have visited most recently – a feature known as 'History'. You can use this to revisit a site when you have forgotten its address. You can also use History to keep an eye on what your children have been looking at on the Web – although this is by no means foolproof, as History is easy to edit.

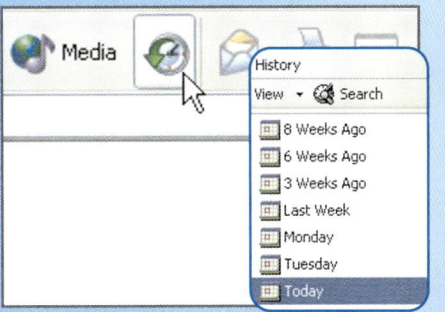

1 Click on **History**. A window will open in the left-hand column entitled 'History'. There are various folders – for today, preceding days, and others for previous weeks.

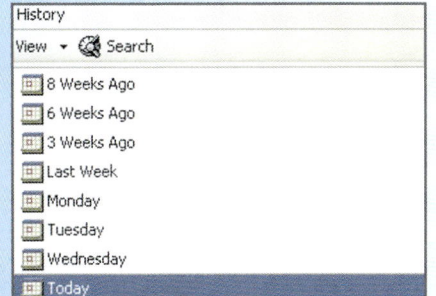

2 If you recall when you saw a site, click on the folder for that day or week. A list of sites will drop down in alphabetical order. Click on the one you want to access.

SETTING YOUR HISTORY

You can change the length of time that your browser remembers the Web sites you have visited and stores them in its History; or you can clear out everything listed in History altogether.

Click on **Tools** at the top of the screen, then select **Internet Options** from the drop-down menu. A new window will open. Towards the bottom of this is a section named 'History'. To change the number of days you want to store details for, click on the number next to 'Days to keep pages in history' and type in whatever you want. You can also empty your History, freeing up space on your hard drive, by clicking **Clear History**.

3 Another list of all the pages within that site that you visited will now drop down. Again, find the one you want, and click on it. It will then load up in the main browser window.

Using 'Search'

If you want to find a site quickly, and you know its name, click on **Search** and a box will appear enabling you to search through the whole History listing. Type what you are looking for into the 'Search for' box, then click **Search now**.

Did You Know?

You don't have to order lists of sites by date. Click on **View** *and you will be given the choice of ordering sites by name, or by the number of times you have visited them.*

77

ADVANCED BROWSING

Favorites button

An alternative way to add a site to your list of Favorites, and to recall this site later, is to click on the **Favorites** button on the toolbar. This opens a panel on the left of the screen. A button allows you to add a site. Clicking on a site name takes you to it.

⏱ Time Saver!

*There is a quick way to add any Web page to your list of Favorites. Hold down the **Ctrl** + **D** keys and the page will be stored. You may want to place it into a folder later to keep your list manageable.*

HOW TO: USE FAVORITES

Most browsers allow you to make a list of the sites that you visit most often. In Internet Explorer, this feature is called 'Favorites'. By adding a site to your Favorites list, you are storing details of its address, which you can then use to access the site more quickly. This is also a good way to ensure you don't forget a particularly useful Web site address.

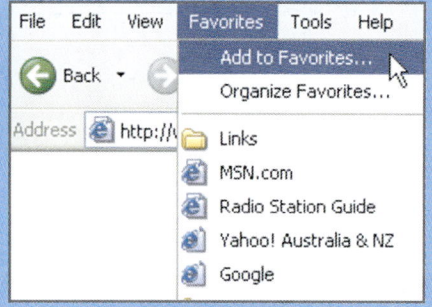

1 When you find a useful site, go to the **Favorites** menu at the top of the screen, above the toolbar; then select **Add to Favorites** from the drop-down menu.

2 A new window will appear. In the 'Name' box at the top of the screen is the name of the page you wish to store. Beneath is a list of folders in which you can store the site.

3 If you want to create a new folder, click on the button to the right marked **New Folder**.

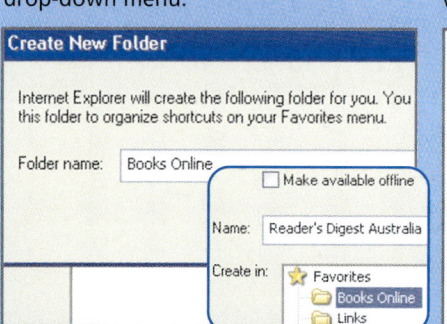

4 Name the folder and click **OK**. It will then be displayed with the others in the lower box. To store the site in here, click **OK**.

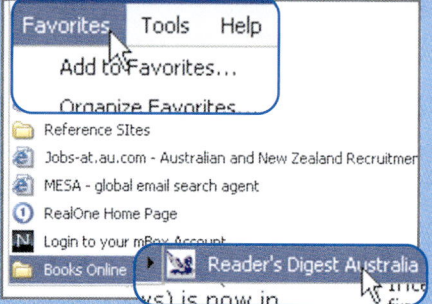

5 Go to the **Favorites** menu again. A drop-down menu will appear. Click on the folder you've created. A list will appear with the site you've just added. Click on this, and it will begin to load up.

Creating shortcuts

To create a shortcut to your most visited favourites, click on **View**, and **Toolbars**, then select **Links**. A 'Links' button will now appear on the right-hand side of your toolbar. To store a Web address there, click on the small Web page icon next to the site address in the Address Box and drag it to the Links button. You can then click on this button to get a drop-down list of favourite Web addresses; simply click on any address to go straight to its Web site.

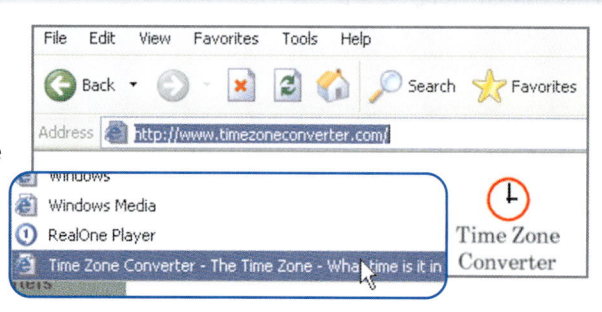

GETTING STARTED

HOW TO: BROWSE OFF-LINE

With Internet Explorer it is possible to make certain Web sites available to be viewed off-line. This means that your computer stores the site on its hard drive so that you don't have to access the Internet to view it. This can be extremely useful when looking at huge documents which would take hours to read. Not only does it allow you to access the information later, it also saves you time and money that you would otherwise have spent by being on-line.

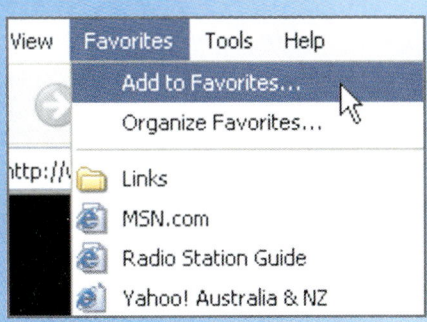

1 Find the Web site you would like to make available off-line. Now go to the **Favorites** menu, and select **Add to Favorites** from the drop-down list.

2 In the next window tick the box marked 'Make available offline'.

3 Give the page a name, and choose (or create) the folder you wish to store it in. Click **OK**, and the page will be stored for you to access later.

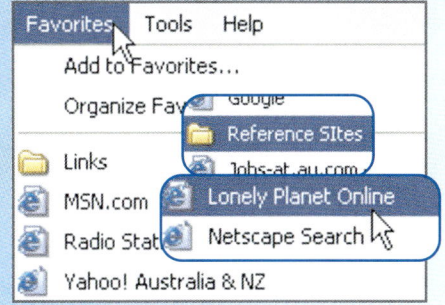

4 You can access the page through your **Favorites** menu without connecting to the Internet. However, if you click on a link, you will need to connect to retrieve more information

SAVING TO YOUR PC

An alternative way of storing a Web page to view when you are not on-line is by saving it to your computer. This is a similar process to saving any document.

Find the Web page you wish to store, go to the **File** menu, and select **Save As**. A new window will open enabling you to choose where on your computer you save the page, what name to give it and what format you save it in. If you want to retain the whole Web page, select **Web Page, complete** in the box marked 'Save as type'.

If you do not want to save pictures – so making it a smaller file – select **Web Page, HTML only**. Then click **Save**.

Links
You can make further pages available by clicking on **Customize** in the 'Add Favorite' dialog box. This shows pages linked to the one you are saving. You can then choose if you want to make any of these pages available off-line as well.

Did You Know?
*You can copy text from a Web page into a Word document by clicking the **Edit** button in the toolbar. The contents of the Web page will automatically load into Word.*

79

ADVANCED BROWSING

MAKE THE MOST OF YOUR TIME ON THE WEB
Spending time on-line means spending money, so it is a good idea to find ways of maximising your browsing efficiency.

Browse in separate windows
If you are going on-line to look at several different Web sites, why not have them all open at the same time? While you are viewing one site, your PC can load up another one or more in the background. To do this open your first Web site then go to the **File** menu and select **New**, then **Window**. Type in the address of the next site you want to see. You can then click back to the first window while the second site loads.

Check e-mail, browse and download at the same time
Whenever you are browsing the Internet, you can check your e-mail or download some files at the same time.

You can begin the download procedure and then open another browser window and continue browsing while you have to be on-line. To check your e-mail, open Outlook Express and click on **Send/Recv**; because you are already on-line, any new messages will appear in your in-box immediately.

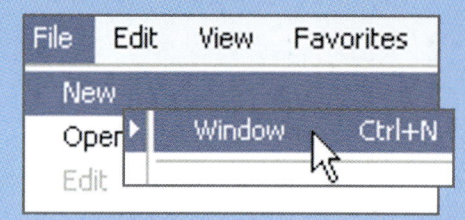

Work off-line when possible
The cheapest way to surf the Web is to save a Web site to view off-line (see *How to browse off-line*, page 79). This way you can browse through the page at your leisure. When you start up your browser, click **Work off-line** rather than **Connect** and then select the site from your Favorites list. Most sites are available off-line but some may not be.

Add particular favourites to your toolbar
Rather than accessing a favourite site through menus, you can add it directly to your toolbar. Simply drag the address from the Address Box onto the Links bar underneath (or to the right), and a button will appear.

Turn off pictures or animated GIFs
Pictures and animations take longer to load, so if you don't want to spend the time waiting for them, click on **Tools**, then **Internet Options** and select the **Advanced** tab. Scroll down to the 'Multimedia' section and untick the boxes next to 'Play animations' and/or 'Show pictures'. Click **OK**. If there are any pictures you do want to see, you can always right-click on the empty picture box and select **Show Picture**.

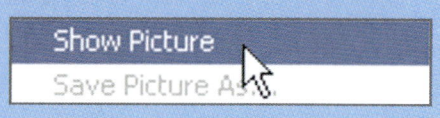

USING AUTOCOMPLETE
Save time filling in on-line registration forms by using the 'AutoComplete' facility on Internet Explorer. You can turn this facility on by clicking on **Tools**, then **Internet Options**, and clicking on the **Content** tab.

The AutoComplete section is at the bottom of the window. Click on **AutoComplete** and place a tick next to 'Forms', then click **OK**. You can also click beside 'User names and passwords on forms' to instruct your PC to remember your identity and password. The next time you have to complete a registration form, you will only need to begin typing in your name for the browser to anticipate what you are typing and offer to complete the entry for you.

Did You Know?
*If there is a Web page you like, you can send it to a friend. Click on **Mail** and choose from the list. 'Send Page' sends the whole page, while 'Send a link' generates a new e-mail with the address of the viewed page automatically included.*

GETTING STARTED

SPECIAL BROWSING FEATURES FOR MACS

The Macintosh version of Internet Explorer varies from the PC version in a number of ways:

Internet Scrapbook

This is a separate section of the browser where you can store copies of any pages, images or on-line documents that you may wish to refer to later. This is particularly useful for receipts for on-line shopping, or news articles that you might want to refer to after they have disappeared from the site where you found them. You can access this while looking at any Web page by clicking **Scrapbook** on the far left of the window.

Auction Manager

Internet Explorer for Macs also offers an 'Auction Manager' – a feature enables you to keep track of any bids you might have with on-line auctions. As well as alerting you when someone has made a higher bid, it also allows you to set a maximum bid limit and instruct it to keep bidding in pre-set increments when necessary. Find this by clicking **Tools** then **Auction Manager**.

Page Holder

Another bonus for Apple Mac users, the 'Page Holder' function enables the Internet browser to place its main page in a side window while any links that you click on open in the main window. To take full advantage of this, you need a large monitor set to a wide resolution.

Access this function by clicking **View** then **Explorer bar**, then clicking **Page Holder** on the far left of the window. To use the Page Holder function, copy the Web page whose links you want to browse to the Page Holder pane. Then, when you click a link on the page, you will see the link's destination page in the main window.

TRANSLATION

Because the Internet is a global phenomenon, there are sites in many different languages. With the help of translation Web sites such as Babel Fish you can transform them into English – giving you access to many more sites around the world.

It is worth pointing out that Babel Fish offers only a limited range of languages and the translations are often highly inaccurate. Nevertheless it is a useful resource if, for example, you wanted to get an idea of what an auction item is on the German version of Ebay (**www.ebay.de**). To translate a Web site, go to Babel Fish (**http://babelfish.altavista.com**), type the Web address of the site you wish to translate into the appropriate box, and select the languages you wish to translate from and to, from the 'Translate from:' drop-down menu. Click **Translate**. After a few moments, the translated page will appear. You can also use the facility for individual sections of text.

The Google search engine offers a similar service. When it lists a foreign language site as one of your search results, it also offers to translate the page for you. Again, the translations offered can be very flawed, and cannot be relied on.

Problem Solver!

*If you can't see a button for 'Scrapbook' to the left of your screen, go to the **View** menu and select **Explorer bar**. It will now appear.*

Did You Know?

You can change the background colour of Internet Explorer to match your iMac. Click and hold on the toolbar and a menu will appear with the different colour schemes.

SEE ALSO
- Download from the Web – page 86
- Do some research – page 113
- Buy and sell at auction – page 208

81

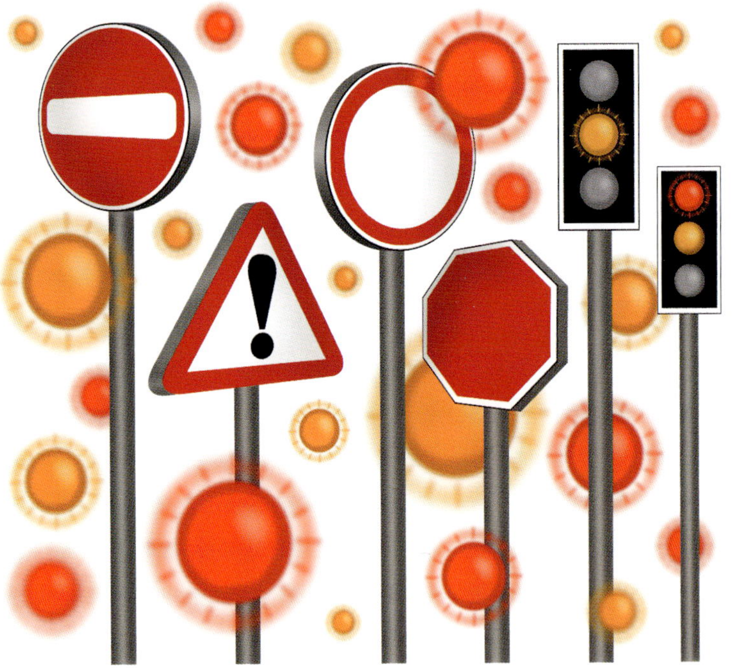

ADVANCED BROWSING

Solve browsing problems

Find **solutions** to make your time on the Internet trouble-free

Much of the time you spend surfing the Web will be completely trouble-free – your browser software is designed to view all standard Web pages without a problem. But sometimes you will come across a page that won't load, or a warning message that you haven't seen before.

This is perfectly normal and doesn't mean that there is anything wrong with your computer. Some Web pages include advanced features that your browser cannot see without some help. Other pages have programming errors or have simply been removed. In most cases, the problem is easy to resolve.

PLUG-IN PROGRAMS

Sometimes when accessing a Web page you will be told you need some extra software – or 'plug-ins' – to view it properly. These are mini-programs that work alongside your browser to allow you to view special Web site features such as animations and film, or to participate in other interactive features such as games and virtual tours.

The most common plug-ins are Macromedia Flash, Macromedia Shockwave (**www.macromedia.com/downloads**) and RealOne Player (**www.real.com**). To find out more about what these programs do, see *Software on the Web*, page 84.

You can load plug-ins onto your computer directly from the manufacturer's Web sites. All three plug-ins can be downloaded free of charge (but you can also buy a more advanced version of RealOne Player, if you need it).

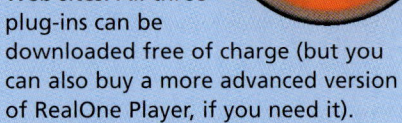

If you come across a page that needs any of these plug-ins, it is likely that you will be given a link to the manufacturer's Web site. There you can choose to download the plug-in, which can take anything from a few minutes to an hour depending on your modem speed (see *Download from the Web*, page 86). But if you want to be prepared, it is easy to visit the plug-in sites and download the software in advance.

USING COOKIES

You may receive a warning that 'Cookies need to be enabled'. Cookies are files issued by Web sites to identify you when you visit them. They are stored on your computer and contain details that the Web site can access. Users of a groceries site, for example, might be given a cookie that tells the site who they are so that their last shopping list can be displayed.

You can choose to enable all cookies automatically wherever they come from, or you can disable all cookies, or ask your computer to prompt you whenever a site offers you a cookie. Some people disable cookies so that they can choose when to give out information. Generally it is best to let your browser handle your cookies.

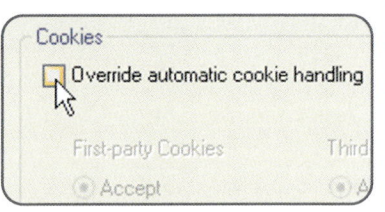

To make your choice, select **Tools**, then **Internet Options**. Click on the **Privacy** tab and the **Advanced** button, then scroll down to the 'Cookies' section.

GETTING STARTED

OTHER PROBLEMS

The page won't load
The message that tells you that a page won't load may give a clue about why this is happening. The most common message is 'Error 404 File not found', meaning that the address does not exist. Often the problem is just that you have typed the address wrongly, perhaps by leaving a space between letters. Check the Web address again, and make sure you have typed it accurately.

Other error messages include 'Host Unavailable' – meaning that there is a problem with the server that stores the page – or '401 Unauthorized', which usually means you have entered an incorrect password.

Everything has stopped
Look at the far right of the taskbar at the bottom of your desktop screen for an icon showing two computers. Click on it to open a window showing the data flow through your modem. If the numbers are changing, the page is still loading. If they are not, the page has stopped loading. In that case, click **Stop**, then **Refresh**. If that doesn't work, try restarting your PC and trying again. This clears your computer's temporary memory, which may free it up to solve the problem. If this does not work, something is wrong with the page and there is nothing you can do.

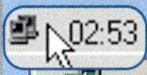

My computer is frozen
If everything has stopped and your computer is not responding to your mouse clicks, press **Ctrl** + **Alt** + **Delete** together. In the window that appears, click on **End Task**. If this doesn't get your machine going again, switch your computer off and then on again.

The wrong page has loaded
If you've accessed the page via a link, it may be that the link is wrongly set up. Try typing in the Web address directly or going via other pages or search engines.

I don't know the address
Try searching for the site using a search engine such as Google (**www.google.com**). If you are after a specific page on a site, go to that site's homepage and click through to find it. If you've visited the site before, use 'History' to find it. Click on **History** and scroll through until you locate it.

I clicked a warning and was taken to another site
Some advertisements are designed like warning messages to entice you to click them. Look closely – if they are not in a separate window, they are not genuine.

I need to enable Java
You may get an on-screen message saying you need to have Java enabled to view a page. Java allows you to play interactive games. To enable Java, open up Internet Explorer, select **Tools**, then **Internet Options**. Click **Advanced** and scroll down to 'Microsoft VM'. Three options are under this. Make sure there is a tick next to 'JIT compiler for virtual machine enabled'.

Windows 95, 98, Me
If you are running an older version of Windows, you will need to download earlier versions of both Flash and Shockwave. Go to the Downloads section of the Macromedia Web site (**www.macromedia.com/downloads**) and click on **Other Players** to find a list of players compatible with a wide range of operating systems.

Too slow
Connection speed depends on the time of day you are on-line. If your connection is always slow, check if there is a problem on your telephone line. If that is fine, then contact your ISP to report the slow connection.

Time Saver!
If you have an old computer, ensure a quick Internet connection by closing down all other programs so that you only have your Web browser open. All resources are then available for browsing the Web.

SEE ALSO
● Security on the Internet – page 52
● Search the Internet – page 64
● Improve your browsing – page 76

83

ADVANCED BROWSING

Software on the Web

Use the Internet to access different kinds of **software** for your PC

As you become a more proficient Internet user, you will find that you need more than a Web browser and some e-mail software to get things done. You may come across a site that requires special software to view its content. Or you may need a program to help you to view moving images or listen to music on-line. There is often software available on-line that can help – some of which you can acquire for free.

Once you have located some software that you want, you can load it straight from the Web site onto your computer. This is called 'downloading'.

SOFTWARE ON-LINE

On-line software is classified according to the terms by which it is made available. Some programs are free, others come with various kinds of strings attached.

What is freeware?
The term 'freeware' describes programs that you can download free of charge. But they are protected by copyright laws, which means that you can't sell or pass them on without the author's permission. If your friends are interested in the program, direct them to the source you got it from.

What is shareware?
Shareware is software that you can download and try out for a specified period – usually two or three weeks – before being asked to pay for it. Shareware usually either stops functioning after its initial 'demo' period, or continues to work with only limited features. In other cases, the software retains its functionality, but reminds you of the need to pay every time you use it.

What is demoware?
Demoware is software that is made available for evaluation purposes with some of its features switched off. There are usually enough active features for you to be able to decide if you want to buy the full version.

What is adware?
Adware is free software which contains advertisements to cover its development costs. If you like an adware program, do the developers a favour by visiting their sponsor's Web site, or see if there is an ad-free version of the program for sale.

What are updates?
These are mini-programs designed to add new features to existing software packages. They are also used to fix problems that have come to the attention of the manufacturer since the software was launched. When you run these mini-programs, they look for the existing program on your hard drive and make the required alterations. The next time you open your program, it will have all the extra features.

GETTING STARTED

WHAT SOFTWARE DO YOU NEED?

Your decision about what software to download often depends on what tasks you need to perform. The most common are listed here. But there are thousands of programs available, with functions you may never have thought of. It is often worth browsing through general download sites, such as those listed in the box below, for ideas.

Plug-in software

As you use the Web, you may be asked if you want to download a plug-in to add to your browser. Plug-ins are small programs that help your Web browser to perform different functions.

One example you may come across early is Macromedia Flash (**www.macromedia.com/downloads**), which is used to view animations. Another is RealOne Player (**www.real.com**), which allows you to listen to Internet radio and other sound files. If you need to download a plug-in to view a site, you will be told to do so and offered a link to the plug-in manufacturer's site. Otherwise, you do not need to download plug-ins until the need arises.

Compression software

If you often send or receive large files by e-mail, it is worth using compression software, which allows you to reduce (or compress) the size of your files before you send them, and to 'decompress' any compressed files that you receive yourself. Popular compression programs include WinZip (**www.winzip.com**) and StuffIt (**www.stuffit.com**), which both have to be paid for.

Adobe Acrobat Reader

This is a free program that reads PDF (Portable Document Format) files, which are designed to make it easier to share documents on-line. Since the millions of Internet users worldwide do not all have the same software, some people may not be able to view a file properly, with all the right formatting. PDF files, on the other hand, can be viewed by anyone with Acrobat Reader.

A PDF file is a read-only version of a document – effectively a snapshot that cannot be altered by the recipient. Files in this format can be greatly compressed, so they are much quicker to send over the Internet. Download a free version of Acrobat Reader from the Adobe Web site (**www.adobe.com/acrobat**). To create PDF files yourself, you will need the full version of the software.

FTP software

File Transfer Protocol (FTP) software is used to load Web pages onto the Internet. If you decide to set up your own site, you can use FTP software to upload your files. Popular FTP applications include CuteFTP (**www.globalscape.com**) and WS_FTP (**www.ipswitch.com**).

DOWNLOAD SITES

Tucows (www.tucows.com)
More than 30,000 software titles – both freeware and shareware.

CNET (http://download.com.com)
Large shareware library, with popular downloads clearly marked.

Jumbo! (www.jumbo.com)
Offers a range of software, with entertainment titles a speciality.

Microsoft (www.microsoft.com)
Software add-ons and upgrades for many Microsoft products.

ZDNet (www.zdnet.com)
Software for every aspect of using your computer and the Internet.

Did You Know?

*Windows XP has a compression facility built into it. Simply right-click on a file, select **Send to** and choose **Compressed Folder**. You will find a compressed version of the original file in that folder, ready to be e-mailed.*

SEE ALSO
- Download from the Web – *page 86*
- Tune into television – *page 148*
- Play games on-line – *page 186*

ADVANCED BROWSING

Download from the Web

Find out how to copy **computer files** from the Internet

Downloading is the process of getting software or other files from a Web site onto your own computer using an Internet connection. There is a huge range of software, images, video clips and many other resources available on the Internet, which makes it worthwhile mastering download procedures. The main drawback of downloading from the Internet is that it can take a long time, and will take even longer if you need to carry on doing other things on your computer while downloading is in progress.

What do I need?
If you use Internet Explorer or Netscape Navigator as your Web browser, downloading requires no additional software.

How long will it take?
Downloading files can take from a few seconds to several hours depending on the size of the file, the speed of your modem and the amount of activity on the Internet at the time you are connected.

Is there a risk of viruses?
It is unlikely that you will get a virus while downloading, but this can depend on the reliability of the site you are downloading from. As a precaution, always run anti-virus software to check files when they have downloaded and before they are run for the first time.

How can I check the quality of downloaded software?
Most download sites, such as CNET (**http://download.com.com**) and Tucows (**www.tucows.com**), show you how many times a program has been downloaded (a fair indication of its popularity), and even provide feedback from users or their own panel of experts.

GETTING STARTED

HOW TO: DOWNLOAD SOFTWARE

A software title that is well worth downloading is QuickTime, a media player that allows you to view a huge range of multimedia files. The program is available for both iMacs and PCs.

1 Go to Tucows (www.tucows.com) and click on the **Windows** link under 'Desktop Software'.

2 On the next page, click on the tab marked **Multi Media**; and on the following page, under 'Video Tools', select **Movie Viewers**.

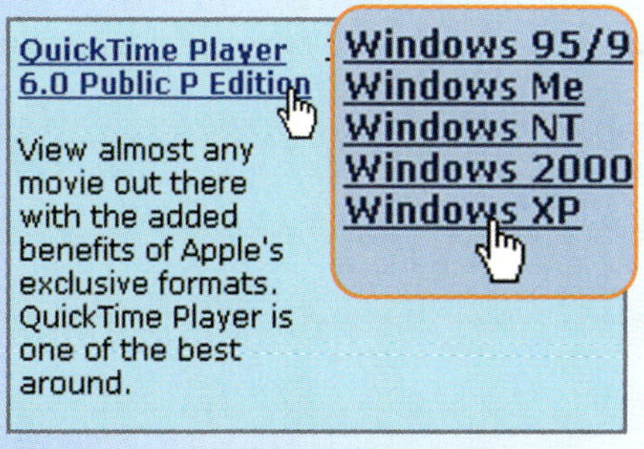

3 Now search for the latest QuickTime player and select your operating system from the choice on the right. Here we have chosen Windows XP.

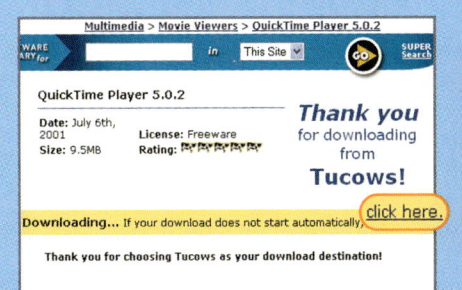

4 The download should start to run automatically. If it doesn't, then click on the link that reads **click here**.

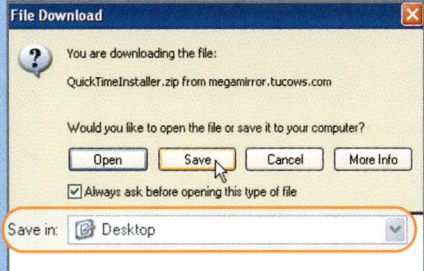

5 In the window asking if you want to save the file to your PC, click **Save**; then choose where you want the file to go (usually the Desktop).

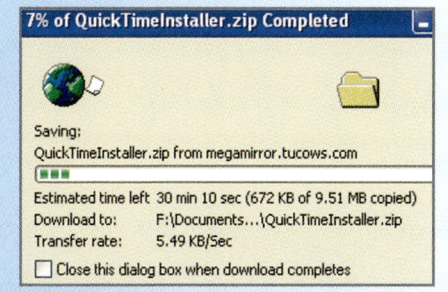

6 Wait while the software downloads. You get a visual representation of how much has been downloaded, and an estimate of the remaining time.

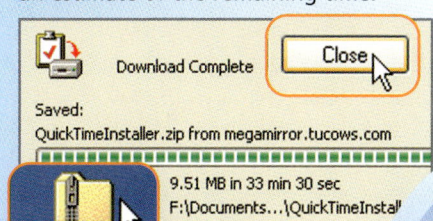

7 When the download is complete, click **Close**, then double-click on the QuickTime icon to install the program.

COMPRESSED FILES

Many downloads are compressed so that they will take less time to download. The most common compression format is called 'zip', and Windows XP has the ability to create and extract 'zipped' files. You can recognise a zip file by the distinctive zipper running down its icon, and its '.zip' file extension.

Another common compression format has '.exe' as an extension. Such files are called self-extracting archives, which means they can decompress themselves. Make sure you run a virus scanner over any .exe file you receive from the Web because they are a common means of transmitting viruses.

Watch Out!
Sometimes files are circulated illegally on the Internet. To ensure you download a legal copy of a program, ensure you obtain it from widely recognised Web sites (see Software on the Web, page 84).

Did You Know?
*If, for any reason, you want to stop the downloading process, you can click **Cancel** at any stage.*

SEE ALSO
- Avoid computer viruses – page 58
- Software on the Web – page 84
- Solve computer problems – page 133

87

OTHER OPTIONS

Other ways to connect

A standard **modem connection** is not the only way to go on-line

The most common way to access the Internet is to connect your home computer to a telephone line via a modem. While this method is good enough for most Internet users, there are quicker connections available for those who spend a lot of time on-line. There are also ways to access the Internet when you are away from home – either from publicly accessible computers or on your own mobile phone or laptop computer.

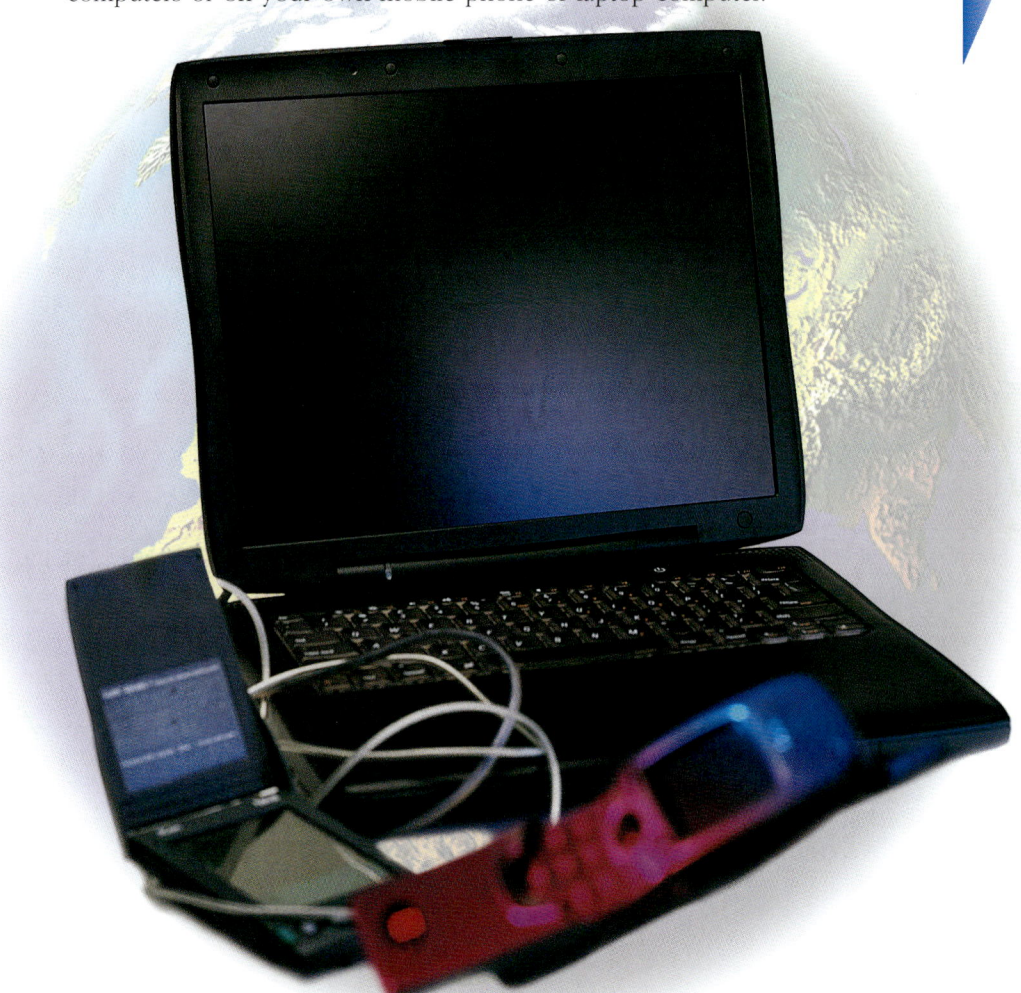

Broadband connections
A standard modem connection is the cheapest way to access the Internet, but also the slowest: Web pages can be very slow to appear on your screen, and large files can take ages to download. Various 'broadband' connections, which use cable, ADSL or satellite to access the Internet, are more expensive but many times faster than a modem connection.

Comparing costs
A typical ADSL line costs about twice as much as a dial-up service, and there is also an extra connection fee. Cable and satellite tend to be even more expensive, but prices vary widely between different suppliers.

Weighing it up
You must balance the convenience and savings offered by faster connection speed against the cost of installation and subsequent monthly subscription fees. Most home users probably don't spend enough time on-line to make broadband worthwhile – but you might need a faster connection if you play on-line games, do research, run a small business or download a lot of video and music files.

GETTING STARTED

FASTER CONNECTIONS

Cable
Many cable TV companies offer Internet access via a cable modem, using the same cables that deliver your TV signal. You do not need to be a cable TV subscriber in order to have cable Internet access, but the two services are often offered together at a discount. At present, cable connections are available only in major cities in Australia and New Zealand. To find out how to get yourself connected, use a search engine such as Google (**www.google.com**) to look for cable ISPs in your location.

Cable access can be extremely fast, but you need to check the company's charge rates, as these vary depending on how much information you need to send down the cable. Some cable providers also place a limit on the amount of data you can send and/or receive before they begin charging a premium rate. Check the precise terms offered by your cable provider to make sure that you are getting the best value package.

ADSL
A slightly slower option than cable is ADSL (Asymmetric Digital Subscriber Line). This technology is generally a little cheaper than cable, though it is still relatively expensive. It allows you to use a conventional phone line to send greater amounts of data than a modem can – and at faster speeds. To use ADSL, you need to get an ADSL modem installed. There is an initial set-up cost and then a flat monthly rate.

At present, ADSL is available only if you live within 5 km of a telephone exchange that has broadband technology. If you live in Australia, you can find out whether this applies to your area by contacting Telstra (**www.bigpond.com/broadband**). In New Zealand, you should get in touch with TelstraClear (**www.telstraclear.co.nz**).

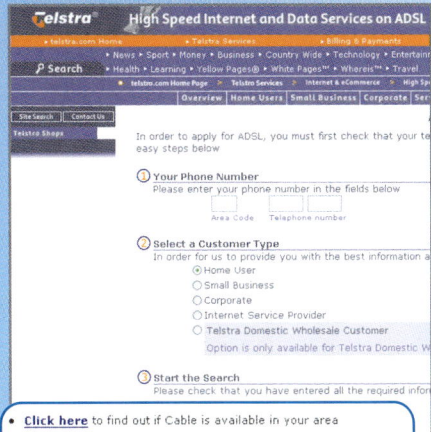

Satellite
If you live outside a major city and want a broadband connection, your best bet is probably satellite. Although this is slightly slower and a bit more expensive than ADSL, it has extremely good coverage, so it's great for the outback and other remote areas.

Satellite broadband is asynchronous, which means that your requests for Web pages travel down a standard phone line at around 33Kbps, but you receive pages and downloads from the Web at 500Kbps – more than 10 times faster. To get a satellite connection, you'll need to have a satellite dish mounted on your roof, a decoder box, a phone line and a modem, so initial installation costs can be relatively high.

There are several satellite Internet providers, among them Blast Surf in Australia (**www.blastsurf.com**) and ihug's Ultra service in New Zealand (**www.ihug.co.nz**).

Connection time
Examine your monthly phone and ISP bills to see how you use the Internet before choosing a new connection method. That way you'll find out how many times you dial in, how much time you spend on-line and how many megabytes you download in a month. Sometimes an offer that looks good may turn out to be more expensive than you first think, or vice versa.

Watch Out!
*A broadband connection may make you vulnerable to attack from hackers if you don't take steps to protect your computer. You would be advised to install 'firewall' software such as Norton Personal Firewall (**www.symantec.com**).*

89

OTHER OPTIONS

ACCESS THE INTERNET ON A HAND-HELD DEVICE

Computers and mobile phones

If you have a portable laptop or palmtop computer, it is possible to link it up to your mobile phone and access the Internet from anywhere, provided your mobile phone can get a good signal.

To do this, you need to slot a GSM (Global System for Mobile Communications) internal modem into your laptop or palmtop.

Data transfer speeds for GSM modems are currently around 9600Kbps, which is slower than standard land-line services.

Faster technology, called General Packet Radio Service (GPRS), allows quicker data transfer, but is still slower than a land-line modem. The latest wave of mobile technology, called 3G (Third Generation), has been launched, but a useful range of products is still to be developed.

Palmtop devices

Hand-held devices are making mobile computing a reality. You can now access the Web to send and receive instant messages and e-mails using a device that is also your diary, address book, notebook and mobile phone.

WAP

Wireless Application Protocol (WAP) is a way to access images and information from 'WAP-enabled' sites on the Internet on your mobile phone. However, WAP phones can only access Web sites that have been specially written in a format called WML (or WAP Markup Language), so you'll be able to see only a fraction of the sites that you can on your computer.

Popular uses for WAP are the ability to access continually updated information, such as cricket and rugby scores, surf reports and stock market data. You can also use your WAP phone to read your e-mail and access on-line shopping sites. However, the system suffers from images that are generally too small and of poor quality.

To take advantage of this new technology, you'll need a WAP-capable phone, or an even newer GPRS (General Packet Radio Service) phone that has been registered with your mobile phone network. You can find out more about WAP – and preview a number of WAP sites – by going to Yahoo! (http://au.yahoo.com) and doing a search under 'WAP'.

GETTING STARTED

METHODS OF ACCESS

Most Internet users spend the majority of their time on-line at home or at work. But there are other places you can go to get on-line:

Internet cafés
If you need access to the Internet while travelling, Internet cafés are ideal. They provide computers that you can use to access the Internet on the premises. They normally charge by the minute from the time you log in to the Internet to the time you log out – so you should be wary of using a computer with a particularly slow connection. You are free to browse and send and receive e-mail, but you may have to pay extra to print out anything. You should also ask before downloading any files from the Internet, since this could potentially leave the café open to a virus attack.

Enterprising retailers have set up Internet cafés in almost every part of the world – facilities range from huge computer-filled halls to sandwich shops with an ancient PC in the corner. Such cafés are a great way to keep in touch when you or your family are away on holiday, and they are generally far cheaper than an international telephone call.

Internet kiosks
These kiosks are rather like phone boxes, but they provide access to the Internet. In Australia and New Zealand, Internet kiosks are being set up in train stations, shopping centres, airports and service stations. They provide a keyboard or a touch-sensitive screen that enables you to browse the Web or send and receive e-mails.

At present Telstra is experimenting with a version of a kiosk called MMP (Multi-Media Phone) which incorporates a phone, keyboard, touch-sensitive screen, ATM card reader and printer.

E-MAIL ON THE MOVE
Most ISPs now allow you to access your standard e-mail account to read and write messages directly over the Web, a handy facility when you're travelling (see *Access e-mail through the Web*, page 45). You can take advantage of this on a friend's PC, or by using an Internet café or Internet kiosk anywhere in the world.

Wireless networks
It's now possible to use wireless technology in the home to access the Internet. Products such as Bluetooth, Home-RF and Apple's Airport are able to provide secure cable-free connections that are bound to become ever more popular in future.

SEE ALSO
- What is the Internet? – page 10
- Are you Net ready? – page 14
- Security on the Internet – page 52

OTHER OPTIONS

Other ways to communicate

E-mail is **not the only way** to make contact on-line

By adding some software to your computer, you can communicate in several different ways on the Internet. You can use services such as instant messaging, which allows you to see when friends are on-line and exchange messages with them instantaneously. And with appropriate hardware – such as a microphone, headphones and a Web-cam – you can use your computer to make inexpensive long-distance telephone calls, and even see live moving images of your friends as you talk to them.

Live communication
The disadvantage of e-mail is that you cannot guarantee instantaneous communication. Although you can send an e-mail message across the world in seconds, it may be hours before your recipient goes on-line and picks it up. More immediate communication is now possible.

Instant messaging
This enables you to create a private chatroom with another person on the Net. You can pass written messages to and fro as easily as if you were sitting next to each other.

Internet telephony
You can use your PC to make a phonecall across the Internet to someone else on another PC, or on a standard phone. PC-to-PC calls are free, but PC-to-phone calls vary widely in price.

Video conferencing
You can also speak to one or more people while watching live video images of them on your screen. Picture quality depends on the speed of your Internet connection.

GETTING STARTED

INSTANT MESSAGING

Instant messaging applications monitor when your family, friends and contacts are on-line and allow you to conduct text-based conversations with them.

Virtual meetings

There are already more than a billion instant messages sent worldwide every day, and instant messaging is becoming popular with businesses as a way of conducting 'virtual' meetings.

You will also find instant messaging a useful and enjoyable way to keep in contact with friends and family who use the Internet. It's especially useful if they live overseas, provided you can find a mutually convenient time to chat.

Instant messaging can also be a good way to make new friends. Many services hold events for users to meet on-line, or allow you to search for users who are interested in a particular topic.

The software is free, so all you have to pay are the connection fees charged by your ISP and telephone company.

Applications

Among the most popular instant messaging services are AOL Instant Messenger (www.aim.com), Yahoo! Messenger (http://messenger.yahoo.com) and ICQ (http://web.icq.com).

If you are using Windows XP, you should take a look at the new version of Windows Messenger, which has a number of powerful features that were not available under previous Windows operating systems. You can start Messenger from the Internet Explorer toolbar, or else go to the **Start** menu, and look for it under 'All Programs'.

In general, different messaging programs don't talk to each other, so you and your friends need to be using the same software to be able to communicate in this way.

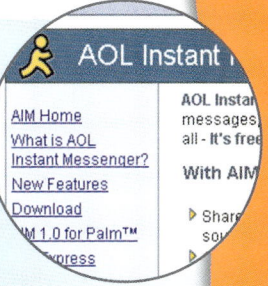

Using instant messaging

To use instant messaging in Windows XP, you can either take advantage of the built-in Windows Messenger, or you can register with another service, and download and install its software.

An instant messenger program operates in the background while you are on-line. It will include an address book of your friends and contacts, and will notify you whenever they are on-line at the same time as you. You can then exchange written messages, files and even drawings on a 'whiteboard'.

WINDOWS MESSENGER

The first time that you use Windows Messenger, a set-up wizard will guide you through the various steps and will require you to register a Hotmail account (**www.hotmail.com**) or a Microsoft .NET Passport account (**www.passport.com**).

Once you have set up the program and signed in, you can start adding the names of 'contacts' to your Messenger account. You can copy these from your e-mail address book, or search the Hotmail member directory for friends that you know use the service. When you are on-line, Windows Messenger will automatically keep track of any names in your 'Contacts' list and notify you if they also come on-line. You can then exchange messages, files, photos and other data with each other, with the transfer taking place almost instantly.

Watch Out!

To get the most out of instant messaging, you need to be on-line regularly, and for more than just a few minutes. You need to bear this in mind when you select an account with an ISP.

Time Saver!

Rather than wait for your friends to come on-line, send an e-mail well in advance to suggest a time that suits everyone. Then you can all chat together at the most economical rate.

OTHER OPTIONS

PHONECALLS AND VOICE CHAT ON THE NET

Internet telephony uses your computer to transmit and receive voice signals so that you can talk on-line just as you would over a telephone. Your PC will need a 'duplex' sound card, speakers (or headphones) and a microphone. Recent computers will probably have these supplied as standard.

If both parties also install a Web-cam, they will also be able to see each other as they talk (see opposite). However, unless you both have fast Internet connections you may be disappointed by the quality of Web-cam images.

Call quality

The process works by breaking down the sound of your voice and Web-cam images into digital 'packets' for transmission on-line. These packets are then reconstructed at the recipient's PC.

The quality of the call will depend on the quality of the Internet connection and on the amount of traffic on-line. Therefore, quality of both sound and images may suffer during busier periods, and be subject to occasional 'clipping' or 'drop-out', similar to a poor mobile-phone connection.

PC-to-PC conversations

You can use an Internet telephone program such as PC-Telephone (**www.pc-telephone.com**) to talk to another PC user as long as you are both using the same software. Aside from the cost of connecting to your ISP, the 'phone call' is free, no matter which country in the world you are calling.

PC-to-phone conversations

You can also use your PC to make a phonecall to an ordinary telephone. In this case, however, the call is not free, as you have to pay an Internet-to-phone company to route your call through its 'gateway'. Charges vary widely depending on the company used and the destination called. Some of the larger companies include Dialpad (**www.dialpad.com**), MediaRing (**www.mediaring.com**) and Net2Phone (**http://commcenter.net2phone.com**).

> ### Additional hardware
> **To take advantage of services like Internet telephony, voice chat and video conferencing (see opposite), you may need to connect additional hardware to your PC, such as a sound card, a Web-cam, a microphone and a set of speakers (or, better still, a headset that combines headphones and a microphone).**
>
> **A sound card needs to be fitted internally, so it would be best to ask for it to be installed by a technician at the shop that you buy it from. You can add the other items yourself by plugging them into the Firewire or USB sockets at the rear of your PC.**
>
> **As soon as you connect a new device to your computer, Windows XP will display an alert stating that it has 'Found New Hardware'; it will then invite you to use the 'Add Hardware Wizard' to install and set up the appropriate drivers.**

Problem Solver!

To avoid on-line echo during Internet voice calls, you – and the person you are speaking to – should listen using headphones, or have your speakers facing away from the microphone and set their volume as low as possible.

Audio chatrooms

There are a number of services that now support audio chatrooms, such as Yahoo! Chat (**http://au.chat.yahoo.com**). These are a little like a party telephone line in which anyone can dial into and join in the conversation. They are also ideal for partially sighted or blind computer users. The chats hosted at Audio-tips (**www.audio-tips.com**) are aimed at making a difference in people's lives.

GETTING STARTED

VIDEO CHATTING AND CONFERENCING

To set up your PC for a video chat or video conference, you need to have all the items required for voice chat (sound card, speakers, a microphone) as well as a Web-cam. You can then either use the latest Windows Messenger built into Windows XP, or else download and install specialist software, such as the ones mentioned below.

Video conferences are generally held between people who already know each other and want to communicate on-line. But there are also video chat forums, such as those hosted by PalTalk (www.paltalk.com), where anyone can join in.

Using the service

Once you have set everything up, you can begin your first video conversation. Apart from your Internet connection, there are no additional costs for placing a video call anywhere in the world.

PC-based video calls work best with smaller images on a low frame rate (the number of times the image is refreshed per second). Internet congestion often results in dropped frames and frozen images, creating jerky or distorted pictures and sound. It is advisable to talk slowly and clearly to minimise the effect of any line distortion.

Microsoft Messenger

The version of Messenger that comes with Windows XP has voice and video capabilities built into it. Simply right-click on the icon of one of your contacts and select whether you want to start a voice chat or a video conference.

Microsoft NetMeeting

If you're using Windows 95, 98 or Me, you should try NetMeeting, one of the most widely used conferencing tools, which comes built in to Windows. The program allows you to transfer files, share applications and exchange text messages. It also has a 'whiteboard' on which you can write, scribble or draw.

PalTalk (www.paltalk.com)

This works in a similar way to Messenger software in that it tells you when your address book contacts are on-line. It supports text, voice and video chats and conferencing between users. PalTalk also hosts video chat forums.

Using a Web-cam

A Web-cam is a small, relatively inexpensive camera that you connect to your computer so that you can send live images of yourself across the Internet. The most convenient place to put it is on top of your monitor, facing towards you. Web-cam images are not very detailed, but they do provide a unique opportunity for people to see the friends or family they're talking to.

PhoneFree (www.phonefree.com)

PhoneFree software supports free PC-to-PC voice and video calls over the Internet. It lets you participate in video calls even if you don't have a Web-cam yourself.

Video forums

Video chat forums are not nearly as popular as audio chat forums. One reason for this is the relatively poor technical quality when several people are participating. Many people also prefer the anonymity and security of standard chatrooms, where they can choose to be known by a nickname. Video chat reduces your anonymity, but it also allows you to see who you are talking to.

If you are interested in trying out an on-line video chat forum, have a look at those provided by PalTalk, or just broadcast your image alongside normal forum contributions at Yahoo! Chat (http://au.chat.yahoo.com).

Time Saver!

Time your video conferences for off-peak Internet traffic times to get the best performance and minimise possible delays and disruption.

Did You Know?

You can use your Web-cam to illustrate the subject under discussion. If you're talking about something you've made, you can put it in front of the camera.

SEE ALSO
- What is e-mail? – page 30
- Take part in a newsgroup – page 96
- Use a bulletin board – page 100
- Use a chatroom – page 102

95

SHARING INTERESTS

Take part in a newsgroup

Read and post messages on the Web

A newsgroup is like an on-line notice board generated by people with common interests. Anyone can look at the notice board, add new messages and answer current ones. Newsgroups are a great way to swap thoughts, ideas and information about topics ranging from broad subjects, such as education or gardening, to specialised interests such as boat-building, archaeological digs, Star Trek and Polish literature.

Accessing newsgroups
It costs nothing to join or access a newsgroup. You can use your Outlook Express e-mail software to find a list of groups to choose from. Or you can search for newsgroups with your Web browser, using a search engine such as Google. Go to **www.google.com**, click on the **Groups** tab and then select the category you want from the list that appears.

What to expect
A newsgroup is a place for the free exchange of ideas, queries, gossip and news. The quality of a newsgroup depends on the people that use it. When a message is posted, you may get no answers or possibly hundreds; you may receive the response you were looking for or something completely different. The lively, unpredictable nature of newsgroups is one of their main attractions for the millions of people who use them every day.

GETTING STARTED

HOW TO: ACCESS A NEWSGROUP

To set up Outlook Express to access newsgroups, you will need your ISP username and password, which was chosen when you first registered for an account with your ISP.

The address of the ISP's news server will also be asked for. To get hold of this you'll need to call your ISP's support line (this is a commonly asked question) or check their homepage.

For example, if you are registered with Telstra BigPond, use your browser to go to the BigPond homepage (**www.bigpond.com**) and click on **Support**, and then on **Configuration information**. You'll find all the information you need to access the BigPond servers.

If you used a CD-ROM to install your ISP, the newsgroup settings are very likely to have been entered already.

1 In Outlook Express, click on **Tools**, then select **Accounts** from the drop-down menu.

2 A new window will now open called 'Internet Accounts'. Click the **Add** button and select **News** from the menu that appears.

3 The Internet Connection Wizard will begin. Enter your name, e-mail address, news server, and account ID and password. Click **Next** to get to each new screen, then **Finish**.

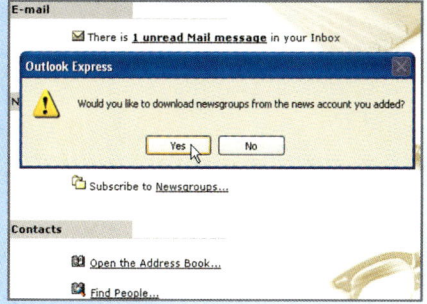

4 You now have a news account. Outlook Express will then ask you if you wish to download newsgroups to this account. Click **Yes**, then proceed as described overleaf (page 98).

Beware of spammers

Some companies use special programs to regularly trawl through newsgroups for e-mail addresses that they then add to their bulk mail databases. It's a good idea to modify your own e-mail address in an obvious way to fool the programs that the bulk mailers use, but not individual newsgroup respondents. For example, **debbie.peters@kastracosmetics.com** could become **debbie.peters@remove-thiskastracosmetics.com** to avoid receiving junk e-mail.

Browser access

Although it's convenient, you don't have to use Outlook Express to participate in a newsgroup. You can also use your browser for Web-based access to newsgroups. Take a look at the groups listed in Yahoo! (**http://au.groups.yahoo.com**) and Google (**http://groups.google.com**) for details.

Did You Know?

If you want more features and facilities for accessing newsgroups, you can get specialist software at sites such as Jumbo! (**www.jumbo.com**).

SHARING INTERESTS

Conduct
Treat other people with respect when responding to newsgroup messages. Do not reply to any offensive or inappropriate comments because this could escalate into a row, known as a 'flame war'.

Watch Out!
Most newsgroups are not censored or 'moderated', so sexually explicit language and images are very common. You may be surprise how many newsgroups are taken over by people wanting to talk about sex and nothing else, even in a newsgroup that's meant to be about politics. Use a program such as Net Nanny (*www.netnanny.com*) if you are worried about your children accessing such material.

HOW TO: FIND A NEWSGROUP TOPIC

Once you have downloaded the list of newsgroups, you are ready to take part in a discussion. The next step is to find a topic that interests you from the huge number available.

You can enter any subject you like in the window called 'Newsgroup Subscriptions', which will open automatically in Outlook Express.

1 In the 'Newsgroup Subscriptions' window, enter a topic such as 'world politics'. A list of newsgroups with this text in the title will appear. Click on the one you want and click **Go to**.

2 A new list of message titles appears. Find one that interests you and double-click on it. Just as with an e-mail, the newsgroup message will then appear in a new window.

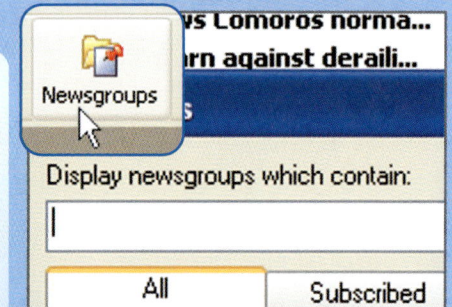

3 If at any time you want to look at different subject areas, click on **Newsgroups**, then repeat the process shown in step 1 above, choosing any other subjects that interest you.

NAMES OF NEWSGROUPS

Newsgroups are named using a convention. Each name begins with a word or an abbreviation, followed by a full stop. This describes the type of discussion the newsgroup contains, such as the following:

- **alt.** Absolutely anything and everything not included by the other groups.
- **comp.** Computers, technology and development.
- **humanities.** Fine arts, the classics, literature, music and philosophy.
- **news.** Network news topics and Usenet itself.
- **rec.** Recreational pastimes and hobbies.
- **sci.** Scientific research and the applied sciences.
- **soc.** Social issues, such as history, culture, religion and lifestyle.
- **talk.** On-line live group conversation with others.
- **misc.** Topics that don't fit into any of the above groups.

This is followed by the name of the topic; for example, 'politics'. Further sub-topics such as 'american' and 'federalism' may follow to narrow down the scope of the discussion, each separated by a full stop.

```
humanities.lit.authors....
humanities.lit.authors.y...
humanities.misc
humanities.music.com...
```

GETTING STARTED

HOW TO: READ AND POST A REPLY

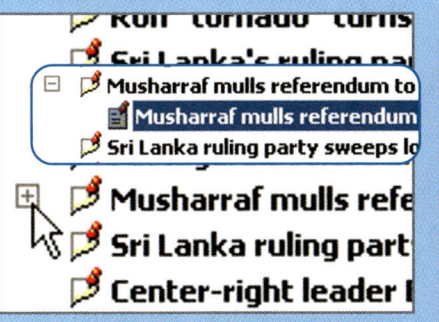

1 As well as reading newsgroup messages, you can reply to them or read others' replies. The plus sign to the left of a message indicates they have replies. Click on this sign to see them.

2 To add your own reply to a message, double-click on a message title to open the message window.

3 To reply to the author alone, click **Reply** and type a reply in the new window. Or, to send a group reply, click **Reply Group**. Either way, a new window will open for you to type your reply in.

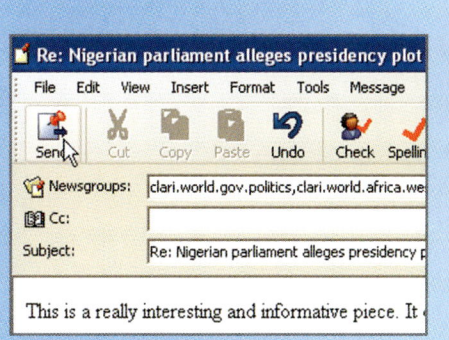

4 Once you have finished typing your message, click **Send**. It may take a short while for the message to appear in the newsgroup (if you have selected Reply Group).

5 If you close Outlook Express or try to access another newsgroup, you will be asked if you want to subscribe to the group you are leaving. Click next to 'Don't ask me this again' and make your choice.

SET UP A NEWSGROUP

It is easy to set up a newsgroup of your own. For example, if you are a keen classical music fan and can't find any suitable newsgroups, then post your idea to a USENET newsgroup called news.announce.newsgroups. Here your idea will be discussed and possibly voted on before it is accepted to go on-line.

It is a good idea to look at this newsgroup before you make any suggestions and also to check that there is definitely no newsgroup on the subject you are interested in. For more information on how to set up your own newsgroup, go to the UseNetServer site (**www.usenetserver.com**) and read the 'frequently asked questions' by clicking on **faq's**.

Did You Know?

Raising a new topic within a newsgroup is known as 'starting a thread'. Any replies to the initial message are then added to that thread.

Jargon Buster!

Subscription
Subscribing to a newsgroup does not mean paying a fee or becoming a member. It means that the address of the newsgroup will be held in Outlook Express permanently.

SEE ALSO
- Avoid computer viruses – *page 58*
- Use a chatroom – *page 102*
- Do some research – *page 113*

SHARING INTERESTS

Use a bulletin board

Swap **opinions** with other people **on-line**

A bulletin board (or BBS – Bulletin Board System) is an area on-line where you can exchange messages and opinions on a given subject. Bulletin boards work in a similar way to newsgroups, but unlike newsgroups they are Web sites, or part of Web sites. The term 'bulletin board' is now used loosely to mean any Web-based forum or message board, but when bulletin boards were devised, they were completely separate from the Internet and used different technology.

PAST AND PRESENT

Across the board
Bulletin boards include messages on topics as diverse as international trading markets, dog shows and disability groups. There are also boards where consumers can post their good and bad experiences with businesses.

Dial-up
In the 1980s, before the Web was invented, you accessed a bulletin board by dialling up to its host computer directly rather than via the Internet. There are still about 40,000 dial-up bulletin boards, which you can access in this way.

These old-fashioned bulletin boards work very differently to Web sites. For example, you cannot use your mouse to move around a bulletin board and you have to type in special commands to perform simple tasks.

For more information and a list of bulletin boards of this type, go to The Directory (www.thedirectory.org). This site also provides links to download free bulletin board dial-up software.

Telnet
Later, bulletin boards were made accessible via the Internet using a system called Telnet, which you can still use today. To access one of these message areas, you need to have some Telnet software. All Windows users should already have a program called HyperTerminal installed on their PCs.

Alternatively, you can find free Telnet programs at sites like CNET (http://download.com.com). Programs to look for include CRT, mTelnet, NetTerm and ZOC.

World Wide Web
Today you can find bulletin boards all over the Web using nothing more than your standard Web browser. Many sites, such as EZBoard (www.ezboard.com), specialise in bulletin boards. Alternatively, use a search engine and enter 'bulletin board' together with a term indicating the topic that interests you.

MESSAGE DETAILS
Most bulletin board messages are accompanied by a range of details to help you to decipher their content:
- the subject of the message
- the name of the person who posted it
- the date it was posted
- the number of people who have viewed it
- the number of people who have replied to it
- what sort of topic it is (new, active or 'hot' – a particularly popular talking point)
- an icon indicating the mood of the message, such as puzzled, amused or angry

Author	Replies	Viewed	Last Date Pos
smokey420	24	229	April 24, 2001 By: smokey
fetalcacti	3	26	April 24, 2001 By: RoxyP

GETTING STARTED

HOW TO: REGISTER WITH A BULLETIN BOARD

1 Go to Yahoo! (**http://au.yahoo.com**). Click on **Computers and Internet**, and select **Internet**, then **Chats and Forums**, and finally **Bulletin Boards System (BBS)**.

2 You will now be given a list of boards to choose from. Look for a subject or title that interests you (some also have a brief description to help you to decide). Once you've found one, click on it.

3 There may be a selection of bulletin board forums to choose from within the site. If so, find the one that suits you, and click on it.

4 You may have to register with a site. Look for **Register** and click on it. Fill out the required fields (usually your chosen username, password and e-mail address) and click **Submit**.

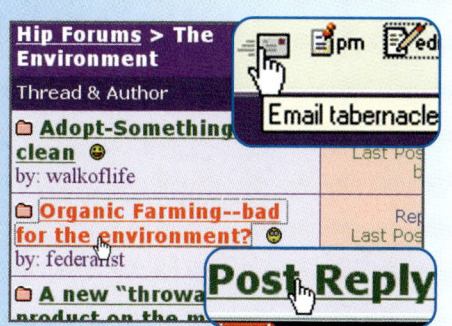

5 To read a message, click on your chosen topic. To reply, scroll to the symbols at the end of each message. You can choose to e-mail your reply directly, or post it on the bulletin board.

AVOID JUNK E-MAIL

To register with a bulletin board, you usually have to give your e-mail address. Unfortunately, many junk e-mailers send messages to addresses that they pick up from bulletin board sites. To avoid this problem, create a new e-mail address, perhaps a Hotmail one, and enter that when you register. Any junk e-mail will then be sent to that address, not to your 'everyday' mailbox.

Another way is to add a coded phrase to your address when you register with a bulletin board (e.g. turn 'michael@bigpond.com' into 'michael@removethisbitbigpond.com'). This fools junk e-mailers who rely on a computer program to extract addresses from Internet correspondence. But it is easy for a genuine correspondent to work out your address and e-mail you.

Taking part

To post a new message click on **New Thread** (or similar) to open a new blank message form. Type in your message and click on **Submit** (or similar).

If you want to reply to a message, click on it to open a window containing the message and any replies that have already been posted. You will be presented with a list of options. Click on **Post Reply** (or similar) to open a ready-addressed blank response form.

Did You Know?

It is possible to find out what every icon on a page means. If the function of an icon isn't clear, place your pointer over it and after a few seconds a box should appear giving its function (for example, 'reply to this message').

SEE ALSO
- Take part in a newsgroup – *page 96*
- Use a chatroom – *page 102*
- Make new friends – *page 169*

SHARING INTERESTS

Use a chatroom

Get **in touch** with other people who **share your interests**

Chatrooms are areas on the Web where people can exchange live messages about subjects that interest them, such as stamp collecting or a favourite sports team. They can be a stimulating way to get information and make conversation, or they can be a source of genuine help and support, as in the case of chatrooms for sufferers of a particular illness, such as multiple sclerosis.

A chatroom is only as useful as the people in it, however. You'll find many filled with teenagers exchanging in-jokes. But if you are prepared to look for the right site, chatrooms can be a great way to discuss issues of interest.

Where to start
You can chat on the Internet in three ways. You can use the latest version of Microsoft Messenger, or a Web-based service like Yahoo! Chat – neither of which needs extra software (see opposite). Or you can use Internet Relay Chat (IRC), a dedicated chatting network, for which you need to download some free software (see page 104).

Chatroom structure
Chat sites are divided into 'rooms' devoted to certain subjects. For example, people who like fly-fishing can 'talk' to others with the same interest. And if you're new to chatting, you can opt to talk to other newcomers, rather than people who've been chatting for years.

On-line personas
In a chatroom, people can be whoever they want to be. This can add to the fun, but you shouldn't always believe everything the person you're chatting to says. It might be that 21-year-old Janine from Canada is actually 50-year-old Hamish from Scotland. With this in mind, you should be very wary of meeting up with someone you've previously chatted to on-line.

GETTING STARTED

HOW TO: FIND A CHATROOM

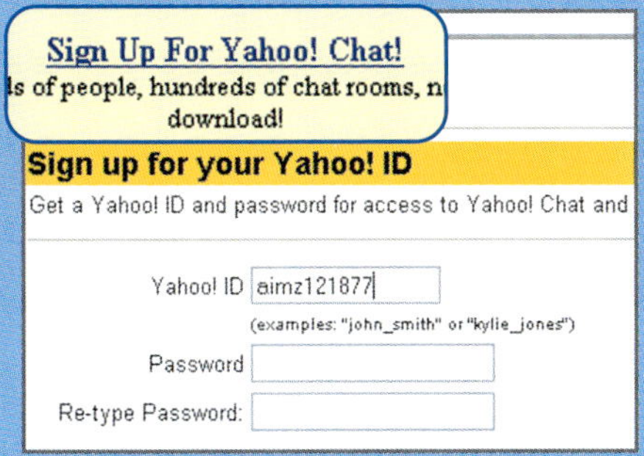

1 Go to Yahoo! Chat (**http://au.chat.yahoo.com**) and click on **Sign Up For Yahoo! Chat!** Review the 'Terms of Service' and click **I Accept**. Then fill in the next form and click **Submit This Form**.

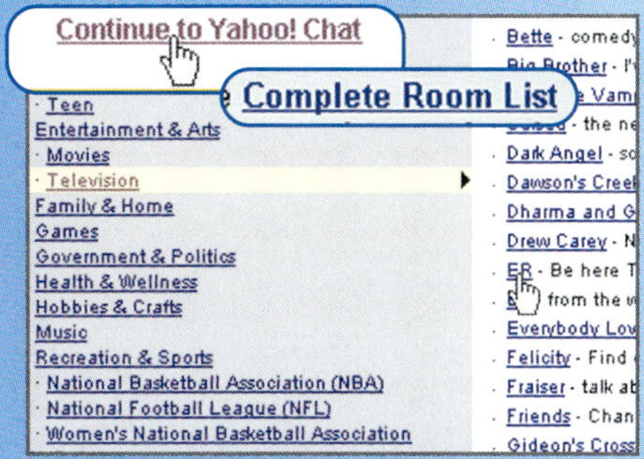

2 Click on **Continue to Yahoo! Chat** and then **Complete Room List** to see a list of categories and rooms. Click on one that interests you. A chat screen will load within a few minutes.

3 Once the screen has loaded, look at the right-hand side to see a list of other people in the room. If you are the only person in the list, click on **CHANGE ROOM** and choose another one.

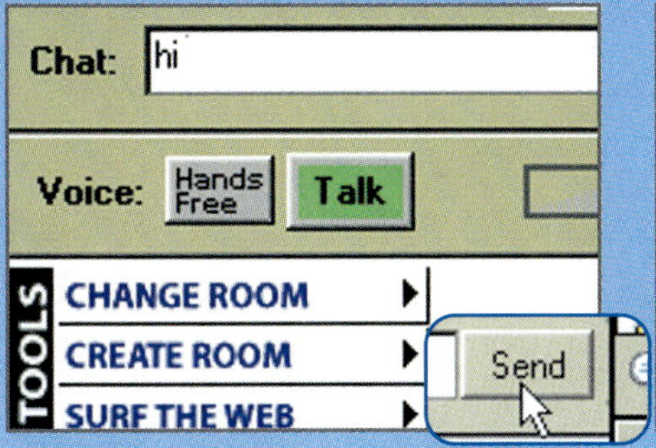

4 To begin 'speaking', type into the box marked 'Chat:'. Click on the **Send** button to submit your message.

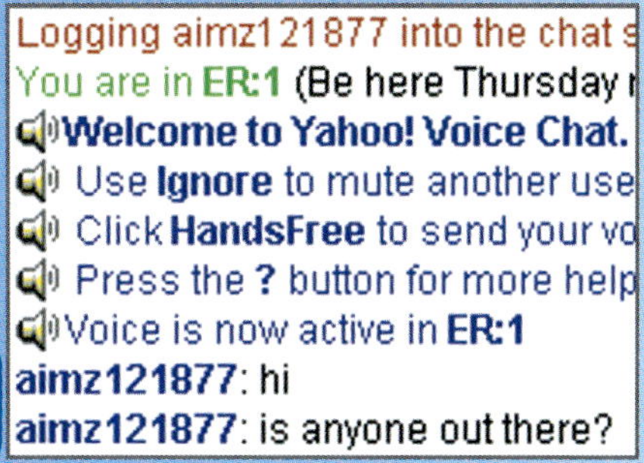

5 Your text appears on screen beside your name. Anyone viewing that page can respond. If someone does reply, carry on the conversation by typing in another message.

6 When you feel like a change of topic, click on **CHANGE ROOM**, or on **CREATE ROOM** – to make your own room. You can use it to chat to friends if you arrange a time to meet beforehand.

Windows Messenger

You can also use the latest version of Windows Messenger (see page 93) to take you straight to the MSN chatrooms. Open Messenger from your **Start** menu and click on **Go to Chat Rooms**. The next window will show you a list of Australian sites, but you can also click on **Worldwide** for a list of international chatrooms. You can also select rooms from different categories, such as 'General' or 'Teens'.

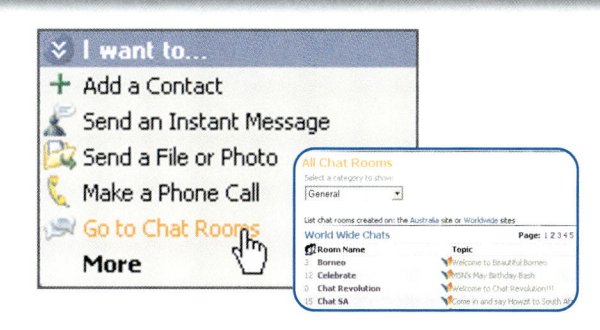

Safe chatting

Choose your chatroom carefully. You'll find a diverse range of people when you join a chatroom. Some people are only there to be provocative or abusive. Try to avoid these trouble-makers by choosing rooms devoted to a particular interest or hobby, rather than a general chatroom.

Jargon Buster!

A/S/L? stands for *Age/Sex/Location, and is commonly used as an opening question in chatrooms when people are getting to know you.*

103

SHARING INTERESTS

HOW TO: USE INTERNET RELAY CHAT

Internet Relay Chat (IRC) is a network of tens of thousands of chatrooms worldwide. The difference between IRC and Web-based chatrooms is that IRC requires additional software.

To use IRC, you'll need to download a 'client' program which connects you to an IRC network. One of the most popular is mIRC, a shareware program. Go to the mIRC site (**www.mirc.com**), click on **Download mIRC**, then on a server in your country (or a country close to you) to start the download.

Watch Out!

Some sites say they have a 'chatroom', but in fact only have a message board. You can use these to exchange messages over a period of time – but it is not the same as live chat.

1 When the file has finished downloading to your computer, double-click on the file's icon to start the mIRC set-up process.

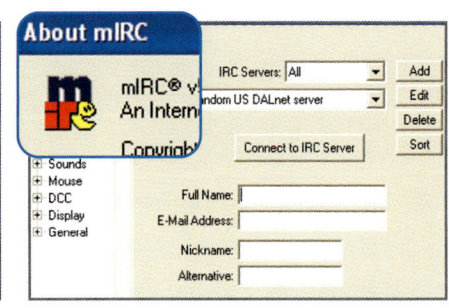

2 Close the 'About mIRC' window to open a 'mIRC Options' window.

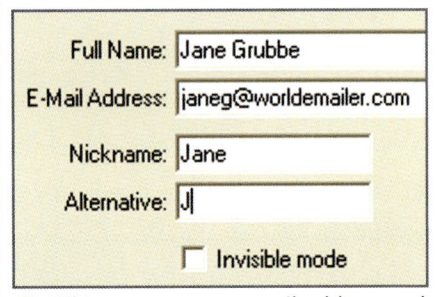

3 Fill in your name, e-mail address and nickname (the name you wish to be known by in the chatroom).

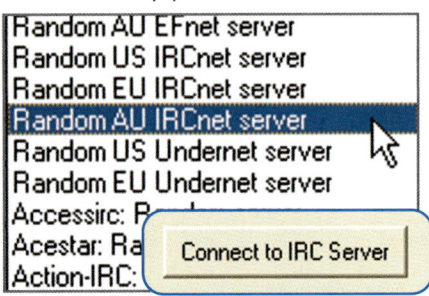

4 Click the arrow next to 'Random US DALnet server' and select a server geographically near to you – for a faster connection. Click **Connect to IRC Server**.

5 A list of chat channels (some with brief descriptions) appears. Choose one and click on **Join**. In this example, 'newbies', a newcomers room, was chosen.

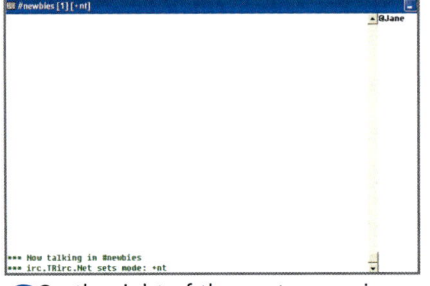

6 On the right of the next screen is a list of who is in the chatroom. The main section shows the current chat and the bottom line is for your message.

7 Type in your message and hit the return button. Your words will be displayed in the main window for everyone to see and reply to.

GETTING STARTED

CHATTING ON-LINE

Netiquette
As with any social interaction, if you're communicating in a chatroom there is a certain etiquette (or 'Netiquette') you should follow closely.

For a good on-line Netiquette guide, go to The Netiquette Home Page (www.fau.edu/netiquette/net), but meanwhile, be sure to follow these general rules.

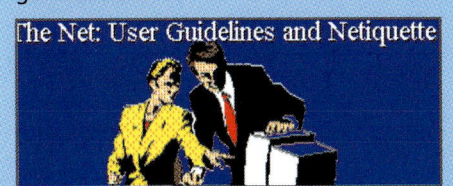

- Always know where you are on the Web. Read the introductory passage when you enter a chatroom. This will explain what the subject of the room is, and whether there are any restrictions on language or other content.

- Try not to type in capital letters. It looks like SHOUTING and is considered rude.

- Address your comments to a specific person in the room – to save confusion about who is talking to whom.

- Chatrooms are not private. Other people, even children, may be present in the room. Moderate the content of your messages accordingly.

- Blasphemous words may be considered inappropriate – depending on the chatroom you are in. If you do swear, you may find a 'moderator' gives you a warning. This is the person who monitors language in the site – and if you continue to use bad language, you may find yourself evicted.

- If someone offends you in a chatroom, ignore them and hopefully they will leave. Some chatrooms allow you to evict someone. To do this, send a chat message of complaint to the room's moderator. Avoid arguing with whoever is offending you. Your attention may be exactly what the person is seeking.

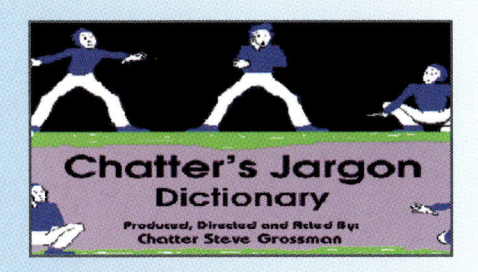

Abbreviations
There are many abbreviations and acronyms commonly used in chatrooms and other Internet message areas. For a comprehensive list, see the Chatter's Jargon Dictionary compiled by Steve Grossman (www.stevegrossman.com).

It is not necessary to use acronyms such as those shown below (many people prefer to use plain English), but they can save you a lot of time when typing messages.

ADN	Any Day Now
AFAIK	As Far As I Know
BTW	By The Way
B4N	Bye For Now
GMTA	Great Minds Think Alike
IC	I See
J/K	Just Kidding
L8R	Later
np	No Problem
TNX	Thanks

Chat for kids
Supervise your children when they use a chatroom to make sure they don't give out personal details. You can buy special filtering software, which prevents them from doing this. In addition, mIRC has filtering options which parents can set up to block their children from accessing certain channels.

EMOTICONS
'Emoticons' are combinations of letters and punctuation marks that are used to express emotion. They can add colour to a conversation, and many chat programs convert them to pictures automatically.

You do not have to use them, and may find them rather unnecessary. But for many people, they are part of the fun of on-line chatting, and are worth recognising. Try looking at the examples opposite with your head tilted to the left.

:)	a smile
;)	a wink
: (	sad
: – I	ambivalent
: P	sticking out your tongue
: – O	surprise
: *)	clowning
:–{}	blowing a kiss
(( )) : **	hugs and kisses
:O	in shock
: – &	tongue tied
: – \	undecided
> : – (	angry

SEE ALSO
- Filter out unsavoury sites – page 56
- Other ways to communicate – page 92
- Use a bulletin board – page 100
- Make new friends – page 169

SECTION TWO

Explore the Web

Explore the best sites on the Internet. Find information and inspiration on all kinds of subjects. And learn how the World Wide Web can make your life easier.

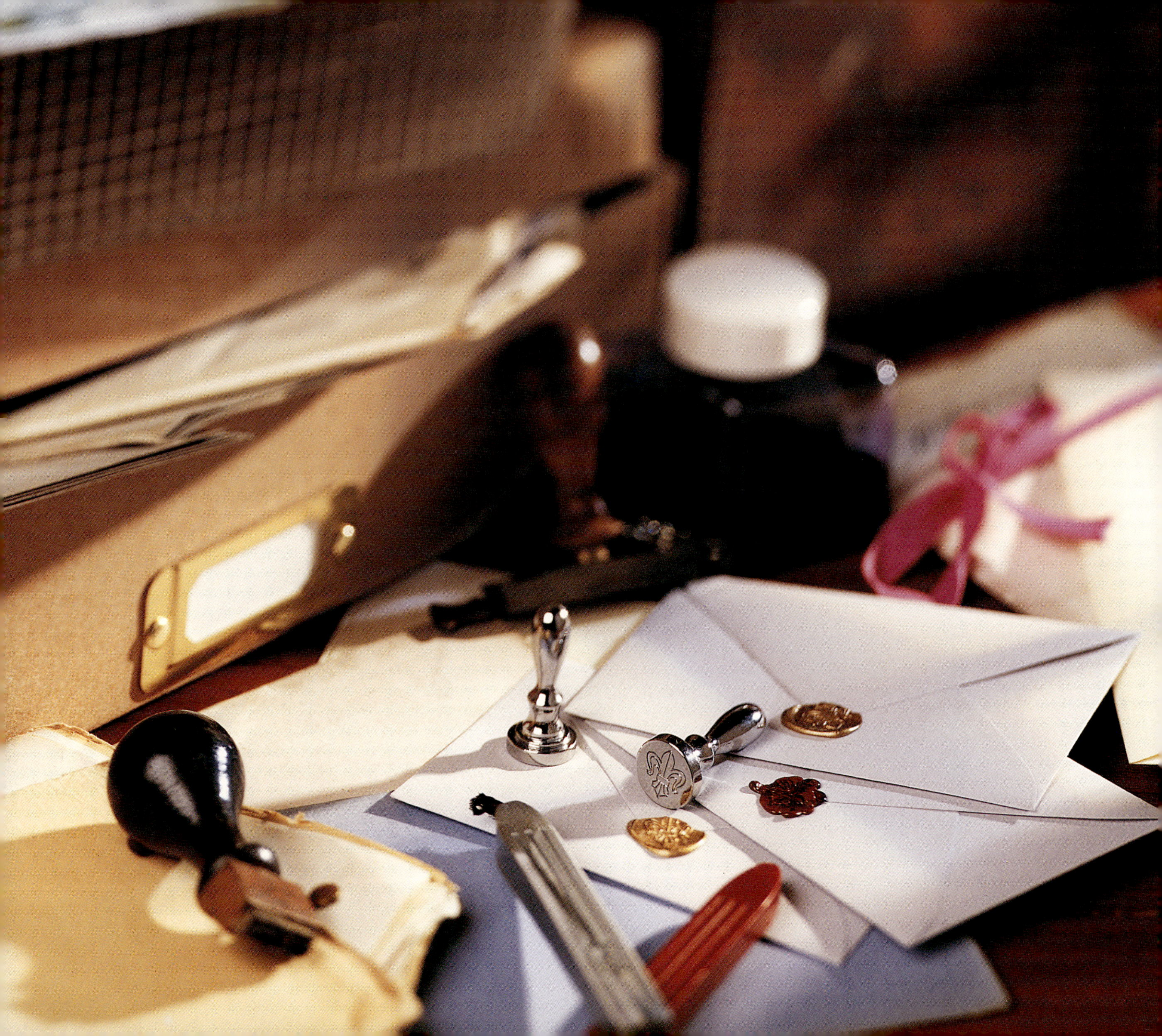

Advice and information

- **110** Learn something new
- **113** Do some research
- **116** Get the latest news on-line
- **120** Find legal advice
- **122** Look for a job
- **126** Seek medical advice
- **130** Improve your diet and fitness
- **133** Solve computer problems
- **136** Help your child to learn on-line

ADVICE AND INFORMATION

Learn something new

Use **the Internet** to further your **education**

The Web is a useful gateway to further studies. You can search for details of classes near you, or enrol for an on-line course in another country. Perhaps you want to 'go back to school' to finish your studies, get a professional qualification, or learn something just for fun. You can even do a complete university degree course. There are on-line courses in subjects ranging from accounting to wine tasting – ideal if you're tied to the home or can't travel far. Whatever you want to study, a high level of computer knowledge is not necessary; if you can use e-mail, you're ready to begin.

What is on-line learning?

Studying on-line is much like taking a traditional correspondence course. The difference is that you have far more interaction with the tutor and the other students. Students access the 'classroom' through their own personalised homepage on a Web site. This is where students 'meet' to discuss the materials and review each other's work before it is reviewed by the teacher.

To find a course, you can use the listings sites mentioned overleaf, or conduct your own research using a search engine, such as AltaVista (**http://au.altavista.com**).

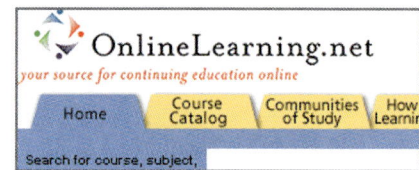

On-line colleges

You don't need to live in the same area – or even the same country – to take the class of your choice. Indeed, many on-line classes are offered by colleges in America. At Online Learning (**www.onlinelearning.net**), you can take courses from several American universities.

For a range of courses closer to home, see Open Learning Australia (**www.ola.edu.au**) and the Distance Education Association of New Zealand (**www.deanz.org.nz**).

EXPLORE THE WEB

QUESTION AND ANSWER

Before you start looking for a course, ask yourself a few questions. How much spare time do you have? Do you want a qualification at the end, or do you want to learn something without pressure? Can you afford to pay fees or are you looking for a free course? Do you want a course that offers a lot of feedback? If so, those offered by educational institutions will be better than those offered by enthusiasts.

Consider all these questions when choosing between courses. If you can't find the information you want on the college's Web site, look for a contact number or e-mail address. Admissions offices and tutors will be glad to help.

How do I organise classes?
Once you have signed up, the course centre creates a 'desk' for you – a homepage with icons that help you navigate through your classes.

Your course will usually be led by an instructor. There's a fixed start and end date, and you may use a textbook, which can be downloaded, purchased from a local shop, or ordered on-line from the course centre and mailed to your door.

At the University of Phoenix Online, for example (**www.uofphx.quinstreet.com**), classes are offered in sequence. Once you finish one course, you move on to the next, until all the degree requirements have been met.

You can begin a class at any time and work at any hour. Courses last five or six weeks.

Your weekly schedule
Typically, on the first day of the week, the instructor sends you the week's topics and sets assignments, such as writing an essay or reading from the textbook. He may also post a short lecture and provide discussion points. You can download the lecture and notes to read off-line, in your own time.

Times for conferences, when you can chat with your instructor and other students in the class, are organised through your desk. Each class shares a mailbox which serves as an 'electronic classroom'.

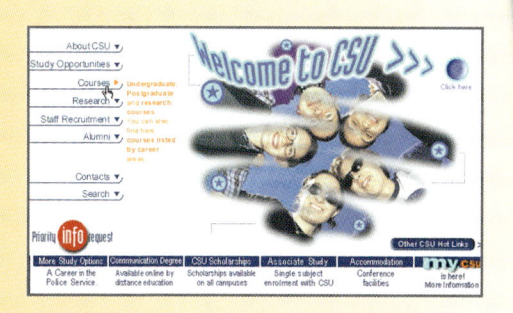

You and your instructor
When your work is due, you e-mail it to your instructor, who marks it and e-mails it back with comments. You take exams by downloading them and e-mailing them back in the specified time. Your grades are then sent to your desk.

Course fees
Many on-line courses are free, and those with fees are often cheaper than a traditional course. With most courses, you register by filling out a form on a Web site, and pay fees by credit card.

CASE STUDY

Margaret enrolled for an on-line MBA (Master of Business Administration) last year.

'I'd always wanted to go back to university and get my Masters degree, but I thought there was no way I could fit it in around my family.

'Then I was watching a TV documentary about education on the Internet and I thought I might look up a few of the larger local universities.

'They had no on-line courses that were suitable, but it occurred to me that there might be other options available. Searching with specific keywords through the Yahoo! search engine (**http://au.yahoo.com**) I ended up with the World Wide Learn site (**www.worldwidelearn.com**) and it was there that the course at the University of Southern Queensland jumped out at me. Their MBA with an emphasis on e-Business was perfect for what I wanted.'

Exams
If you are just doing a course for fun, you don't have to worry about exams. Just read, participate and learn.

Watch Out!
Check the cost of your course before you enrol. Check, too, whether you are eligible for a grant.

111

ADVICE AND INFORMATION

WHERE TO LEARN

Best place to start
Education World (www.educationworld.com)
Start your search for education with an education-oriented search engine. Education World is a database of more than 500,000 educational Web sites. Another good alternative is the Distance Learning Resource Network (**www.dlrn.org**).

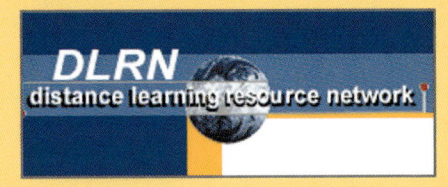

On-line education resource
World Lecture Hall (www.utexas.edu/world/lecture)
The World Lecture Hall provides links to university-level on-line courses offered by institutions around the world. The courses are divided into 83 categories, so that you can browse through the areas that interest you. Simple click on a course title to see more details. The site also offers a 'Find a Course' service, as well as advanced search utilities.

Courses around the world
World Wide Learn (www.worldwidelearn.com)
The world of on-line learning is dominated by American institutions, but sites such as World Wide Learn make it easy to find courses elsewhere. Enter 'Australia' or 'New Zealand' into the search facility and you will find links to, among others, a Master of Aviation Management at the University of Newcastle.

Virtual university
Virtual University (www.vu.org)
This is the world's largest on-line learning community, serving thousands of students in 128 countries.

Once you register, an electronic desk is created for you. From your desk, you can sign up for classes, log into classrooms and access student chat rooms, with just a few clicks of the mouse.

One modest registration fee allows you to take up to three courses each term. Most courses are for continuing education credits. That means you'll have a certificate to prove you passed the course, but it will not count towards an academic degree.

You can also take classes just for fun (in which case, you get to sit out the final exam).

Local content
The Australian Correspondence Schools (www.acs.edu.au)
Over 300 courses are offered by the ACS, in subjects areas ranging from horticulture to journalism. Course material is sent by mail, and students can submit assignments and contact their tutors by e-mail.

Watch Out!
If you are taking a course leading to a final qualification – in accounting or law, for example – check that it is accredited by the relevant local body or authority.

SEARCH IT YOURSELF

Many colleges and universities offer a range of on-line courses. If you would like to study through a specific university, try typing its name into a search engine such as Google (**www.google.com**).

If you are looking for a course in a particular subject – for example, astronomy – then try entering the subject name into a search engine. Entering 'online astronomy course' into the Google search engine, for example, retrieves a free course run by an enthusiast at **www.synapses.co.uk/astro**.

Another way is to click through the search categories at Yahoo! (**http://au.yahoo.com**). Click on **Education**, then **Distance Learning** and **Courses Online** to see a list of subjects such as History and Psychology. Click on one to see a list of courses.

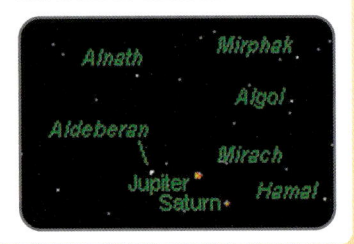

SEE ALSO
- **Do some research** – page 113
- **Help your child to learn on-line** – page 136
- **Enjoy the literary world** – page 166

EXPLORE THE WEB

Do some research

Surf the Web to **dig deeper** into a subject of interest

Unless you have unearthed a new manuscript by a famous author, or made a startling discovery in the laboratory, conducting original research is largely a matter of finding a new angle on the currently held facts, or making new connections between them. You can use the Internet to help you to find the facts, chase down leads, make contacts, exchange ideas and investigate related research in other disciplines. In the often lonely world of the researcher, it can provide you with the stimulation to make that all-important breakthrough.

Search If you are researching a particularly esoteric subject, the Web makes it easier to get in contact with the few people in the world who are working in the same field. A specific keyword search can unearth related Web pages, articles and news stories, all of which can provide leads and contacts that you can follow up. Setting up your own Web site can also attract like-minded people to your work.

Archives Many newspapers, journals and magazines have on-line archives so you can search for the article you want and pay for a copy to be e-mailed or posted to you. Try the National Library of Australia (**www.nla.gov.au**) or the National Library of New Zealand (**http://tepuna.natlib.govt.nz**), where you will find links to many local and national newspapers

Official material Much government information is now on the Web. Go to **www.gov.au** or **www.govt.nz** for access to material from all levels of government.

Multimedia You can also find text, speeches, photos, music, radio and video clips to use as source material.

Watch Out!

Use a search engine, such as AltaVista (http://au.altavista.com), that lists the most relevant sites first. Some simply list all the relevant pages on their database, which is less use to serious researchers.

113

ADVICE AND INFORMATION

New angles
A good way to shed light on your subject is to use the findings of other academic disciplines – a mathematics student may find that a discovery in astronomy provides a perfect model for his theory. Someone interested in the diaries of an 18th-century duke may find an economic study of the period helps to explain the diarist's concerns.

GOOD PLACES TO LOOK

On-line library
Librarians' Index to the Internet (www.lii.org)
For a great variety of research sources, try the Librarians' Index to the Internet. A large team of indexers has chosen and annotated Web sources on a broad range of topics – so saving you valuable searching time. The Virtual Library (**www.vlib.org**) is also worth a visit. This consists of individual subject collections from universities around the world.

Pioneering service
The Internet Public Library (www.ipl.org)
The first library designed specifically for Internet users, the IPL is run from the University of Michigan. Their aim is to find, evaluate, select, organise, describe and create information resources. Simply click on a subject area, and follow the links to find what you want.

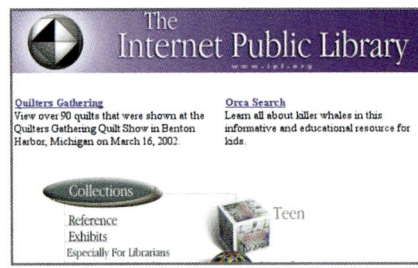

Traditional resource
National Library of Australia (www.nla.gov.au) 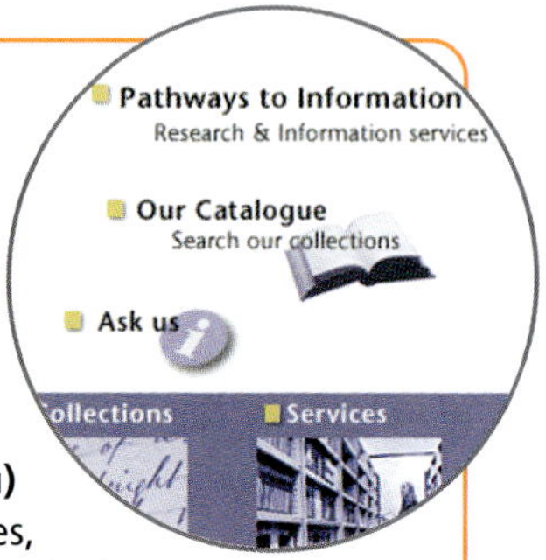
Copyright libraries, such as the National Library, have long been invaluable to researchers. Among other services, you can search the library's public catalogues by author, title or subject.

The National Library also offers a Document Delivery Service, which will arrange for items to be photocopied and sent to you by standard mail, express post or fax. All services must be prepaid by credit card.

Research advice
Expert Central (www.expertcentral.com)
If you can't find the information you're looking for, ask an expert for some help. Expert Central will link you up with a specialist who can answer questions on your subject of interest.

Ask An Expert (**www.askanexpert.com**) also lets you search its directories, which include hundreds of experts in a wide range of academic and general interest subjects. This site promotes itself as being 'kid-friendly'.

MetaCrawler
If your research topic is obscure or you want to retrieve results from a variety of search engines with a single search, try MetaCrawler (**www.metacrawler.com**). This checks many search engines simultaneously and gives you a single list of sites.

CASE STUDY

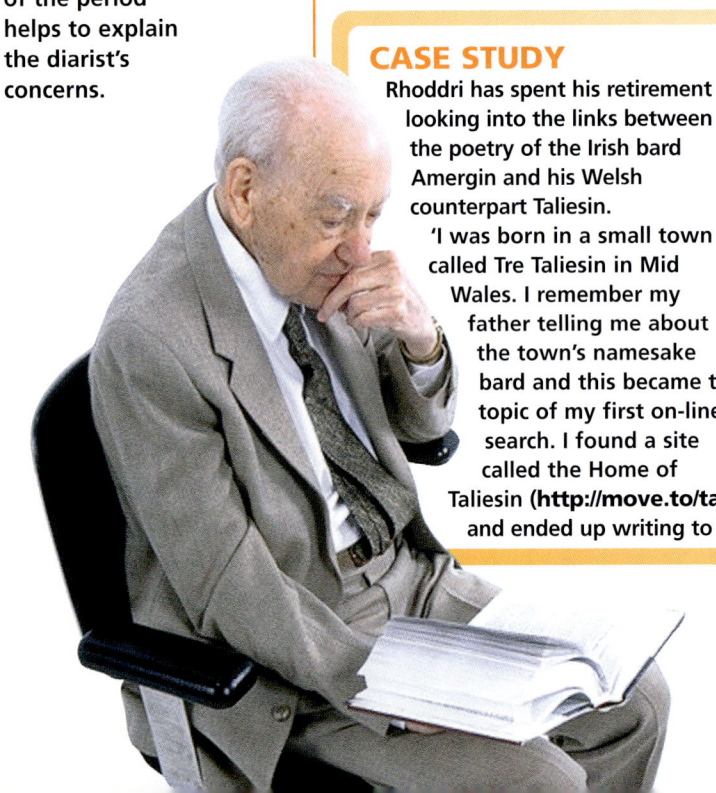

Rhoddri has spent his retirement looking into the links between the poetry of the Irish bard Amergin and his Welsh counterpart Taliesin.

'I was born in a small town called Tre Taliesin in Mid Wales. I remember my father telling me about the town's namesake bard and this became the topic of my first on-line search. I found a site called the Home of Taliesin (**http://move.to/tali**) and ended up writing to its author, who turned out to be a very nice young woman in Queensland. It was through her that I found out about Amergin, who was a druidic poet, reputed to have led an invasion of Ireland.

'When I read the Song of Amergin (**www.druidways.co.uk**), I was struck by the similarities with Taliesin's work. I'm no academic but I've since enjoyed comparing Amergin's work with other early Welsh poetry at the Index to Welsh Poetry in Manuscript (**http://maldwyn.llgc.org.uk**) and am now something of a bardic bore!'

EXPLORE THE WEB

RESEARCH METHODS

If you have hit a dead end with your research, try the following:

Keyword searching
This is the easiest type of search. Type in a word or words that relate to your subject in the search box on your search engine or portal. Make keywords as relevant to your subject as possible: the closer the word to the subject, the quicker you'll find relevant material. To get the most out of your keyword searches, turn to page 64.

Academic resources
One way to kick-start your research is to look for details of a course in the subject which will provide you with a recommended reading list. This can be a great way to widen your list of sources. If you find that a particular academic is a specialist in your field, try entering his name into a search engine. You may find references to other books, journal articles or even a Web site.

Newsgroups and bulletin boards
Although there may not be a newsgroup or bulletin board dedicated to your exact area of interest, there is likely to be one that is quite closely related. If you are looking for an answer to a particular question, it is worth posting it on a site just to generate some correspondence. This may provide you with the answer or a lead to follow up. Even just framing the question may help you to figure out a way round the problem. See *Take part in a newsgroup*, page 96 and *Use a bulletin board*, page 100.

There are also thousands of newsletters on the Internet. A search for 'genetics + newsletter', for example, reveals several on the subject.

Links and Web rings
Most good sites have a page of links to related sites, or they may be part of a 'Web ring' – a loop of sites all carrying each other's addresses. This is one way to widen your research. Even obscurely connected links may open an avenue of thought that you haven't considered. Make sure you save every useful link as one of your favourite sites.

Site owners
If you find a useful site but it doesn't have exactly what you need, you should try e-mailing the site's author. Most would be thrilled to find someone who has visited their site and is interested to find out more. Sharing and exchanging ideas can be invaluable – especially with experts in an area that touches on the main body of your research.

Physical resources
The Web can also help you to find useful off-line resources. For rare books, try BookFinder (**www.bookfinder.com**) or abebooks (**http://abebooks.com**), which both have databases of millions of second-hand and out-of-print books offered for sale by book shops around the world.

The Welsh town of Hay-on-Wye has the world's largest concentration of second-hand book shops (35 in all). Visit **www.haybooks.com** to search among the four million books stored there.

Watch Out!
Small sites run by amateurs and enthusiasts can often disappear from the Web without warning. If you find some useful information on a small site, print it out.

Set up your own Web site
If you still can't find what you want on-line, why not set up your own site to attract people who might have the information you want? There may be others with exactly your interest waiting to discover such a site.

For more details on how to do this, turn to the *Making Web sites* section, page 244.

SEE ALSO
- **Search the Internet** – page 64
- **Improve your browsing** – page 76
- **Trace your family's past** – page 159

115

ADVICE AND INFORMATION

Get the latest news on-line

Keep up to date with **current events,** expert analysis and commentary

The main advantages of the Internet over other media are that news is constantly updated, and that you can read the latest news when it suits you, rather than at times dictated by a TV or radio broadcast. Serious news addicts can even have newsflashes sent to them via e-mail or mobile phone. The other advantage of the Internet is personalisation – at many news sites you can choose to be shown only the subjects that interest you, without having to wade through screeds of irrelevant information.

Newspapers and TV
Most traditional news sources offer some sort of on-line coverage. The Internet gives newspapers and broadcasters the opportunity to provide more in-depth explanations of news stories and detailed discussions of background issues, as well as links to related Web sites. Newspaper Web sites are also useful for researching old news articles.

News links
Both Yahoo! and OptusNet have categorised directories of news links, and constantly updated stories and headlines. When you register with a portal, you can enter your preferences so that the site displays just the topics you're interested in, such as sport, entertainment or foreign news.

News tickers
Some news sites offer a ticker – a small window that sits in a corner of your screen and displays scrolling headlines as the news unfolds, provided you're connected to the Internet. Look for a 'ticker' link on a news site and follow the instructions to download the ticker program.

EXPLORE THE WEB

NEWS HEADLINERS

A daily newspaper
The Sydney Morning Herald (www.smh.com.au)
This site carries the news as printed in the daily newspaper, and much more. The homepage shows all the current top stories, with links to full reports so you can really explore the issues. You can download a pdf file of the latest *Herald* front page or subscribe to *News Alert*, a daily e-mail newsletter sent out at 3 pm every weekday. There are also sections devoted to business, technology and sport, as well as weather and TV. If you fancy yourself as a news expert, you might care to try the News Trivia Quiz.

Asian news
CNN Asia (http://asia.cnn.com)
This is CNN's portal for news in Asia and the Australia–Pacific region. You will also find links here to CNN's portals for news in Europe and the USA. Or you can access bulletins at CNN's Headline News site (**www.cnn.com/HLN**).

News without the spin
Scoop (www.scoop.co.nz)
Scoop is a Wellington-based news agency that presents both local and international events from a New Zealand perspective. Its boast is that it specialises in 'disintermediated news' – defined as 'news without a spin put on it by journalists'.

Top ticker
WorldFlash News Ticker (www.worldflash.com)
The free WorldFlash news ticker sits at the bottom of your computer screen so that it can be seen while other programs, such as Word, are active. You can configure user settings to alter the range of information that is displayed, which includes world news from a range of sources, sport, weather and stock prices. You can also change the size of the ticker and its scrolling speed (see overleaf).

News around the world
Assignment Editor (www.assignmenteditor.com)
This site provides links to a large number of newspapers and magazines from the USA and around the world. Read today's news in Moscow or look at a local weather forecast from Tokyo.

★ STAR SITE
For the most authoritative current Australian news, log on to the ABC's Web site (**www.abc.net.au/news**). Here you will find details of the top local and international stories, many of which are accompanied by audio and video. Apart from the headlines, a range of other important news stories are listed by category, under headings such as rural, business, politics, art, sport and environment. In New Zealand, a similar but less comprehensive Internet service is offered by One News (**http://onenews.nzoom.com**).

Weird world
For updates on some of the world's more peculiar news events, have a look at the Offbeat section of ABC News Online (**www.abc.gov.au/news**), or the Quirkies sections (both text and video) on the Ananova news site (**www.ananova.com**).

Did You Know?
You can get a first-hand view of debates in the Australian Parliament at Parliament's Live Broadcasting site (www.aph.gov.au/live/webcast2.asp).

117

ADVICE AND INFORMATION

HOW TO: DOWNLOAD A TICKER

Did You Know?

You can find sites for newspapers from all around the world at Yahoo! (http://au.yahoo.com). For example, click on Yahoo! UK & Ireland then News & Media then Newspapers to see links to sites such as The Scotsman (www.thescotsman.co.uk).

1 Go to WorldFlash (www.worldflash.com) and read through the information provided. This is a US site, but most of the contents can be tailored to suit users living elsewhere in the world. Click first on **Download** and then **Click Here to Install**.

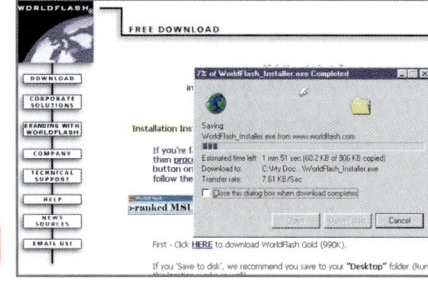

2 When the program asks you where you want it to be installed, specify the desktop. Click **OK** for the download to begin. It takes only a short time.

3 When the WorldFlash installer icon appears on your desktop, double-click on it to be guided through the installation procedure.

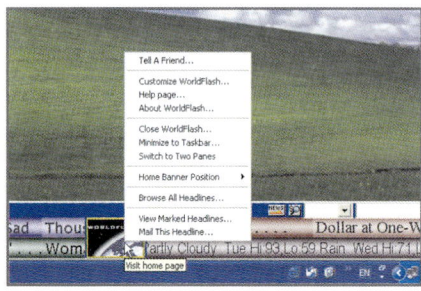

4 Once it has been successfully installed, WorldFlash will launch automatically. Right-click on the ticker to see the customisation options.

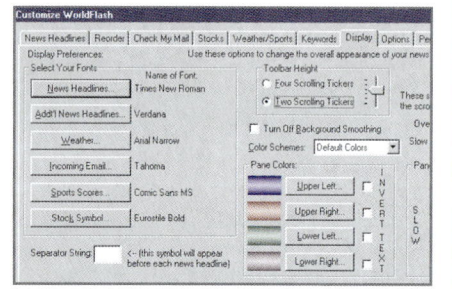

5 First of all, click on the **Display** tab to adjust the appearance of the ticker, including how many bars are shown, the scrolling speed and colours.

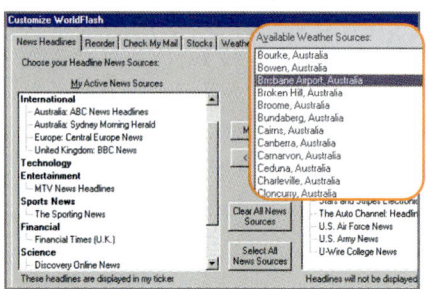

6 Next, click on the **News Headlines**, **Weather/Sports** and **Stocks** tabs to select the contents you want displayed. You can also adjust the order of display.

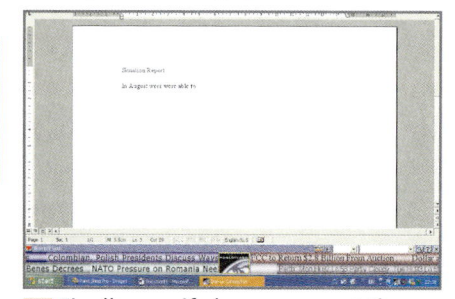

7 Finally, specify how you want the ticker to be launched at start-up. It usually sits at the bottom of the screen with active programs above it.

EXPLORE THE WEB

HOW TO: GET NEWS BULLETINS BY E-MAIL

1 Go to *The Sydney Morning Herald* Web site (**www.smh.com.au**) and browse through the different sections and news stories featured, to decide which categories of news you would like to have e-mailed to you.

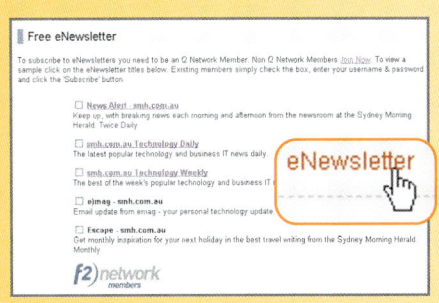

2 Click on the link for **eNewsletter**, and in the next window view any sample service – such as News Alert – by clicking on its link. You will now be asked to join the f2 Network to receive the newsletter. Click on **Join Now**.

3 In the next window, fill in all your personal details and check the box next to each news service you would like to receive.

4 Make sure you take a moment to read and accept the conditions for using this service. Then click **Join**.

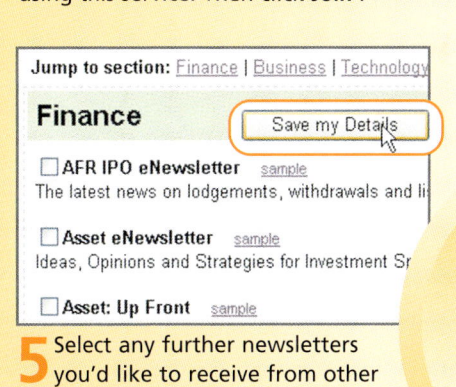

5 Select any further newsletters you'd like to receive from other sections – such as Finance – then click **Save my Details** when finished.

WATCH A NEWS BROADCAST

Several on-line news Web sites, such as the Australian Broadcasting Corporation (**www.abc.net.au/news**) and Television New Zealand (**www.tvnz.co.nz**), make it possible for you to watch video of the news, news highlights or selected news stories live on your computer screen.

To watch the broadcasts you will need to download a media player if you don't already have one on your PC. The player that is usually specified is RealOne Player from Real.com (**www.real.com.au**) – see page 150 for more details. Other media players will also work, so if you have one, give it a try.

Once you have downloaded RealOne Player, go to a news Web site and click on the link that interests you. RealOne launches automatically, and after a moment the video broadcast will start. Use the control buttons to play, pause and rewind the bulletin.

Time Saver!

You can e-mail a letter to the editor to comment on a newspaper article the day it is published. To write to The Australian, *go to **www.theaustralian.news.com.au**, click on **Contact Us** and then on **Letters**.*

SEE ALSO
- **Take part in a newsgroup** – *page 96*
- **Tune into television** – *page 148*
- **Listen to the radio** – *page 152*

119

Find legal advice

Consult the **Web** for **legal information** and **advice**

The Web can't fight court cases for you. For that you will need a 'real' lawyer. But the Internet is a great source for researching information, locating solicitors in your area, and gaining free advice on many types of legal question. It may be that you want advice on a divorce or accident claim, or are looking for the right form for a rental agreement. You'll be surprised how much the Internet can offer, and how easy this information is to access.

Before taking any advice, ensure any Web sites you use are accredited by reputable organisations, and check your information with more than one source.

Official sites

The Internet offers a wealth of sites that provide legal advice and information at all levels. If you are looking for help with a legal problem, it's a good idea to begin by finding out what the various government departments and services have to offer. In Australia, the situation is complicated by the fact that laws are enacted by both federal and state governments. Since laws vary considerably from state to state, you need to be careful that the information you find is relevant in your area. As a starting point, visit Australian Law Online (**http://law.gov.au/wotl.html**) or Courts of New Zealand (**www.courts.govt.nz**).

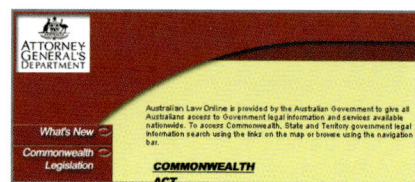

Commercial alternatives

In the USA, on-line legal information and consultations have been offered by commercial firms and individual practitioners for many years. Similar services are now increasingly available in Australia and New Zealand, but not to the same extent. To get an idea of what is on offer, have a look at FindLaw Australia (**www.findlaw.com.au**), FindLaw New Zealand (**www.findlaw.co.nz**) and Legalmart (**www.legalmart.com.au**).

EXPLORE THE WEB

LEGAL SITES

Free advice

Grassroots Community Centres
Community Legal Centres (in Australia) and Community Law Centres (in New Zealand) both exist to supply basic legal services to individuals and organisations, especially those who are in some way disadvantaged. For a directory of Australian Community Legal Centres (as well as links to legal aid and related services), visit **www.austlii.edu.au/au/other/clc**. In New Zealand, have a look at the Legal Services Agency Web site (**www.lsa.govt.nz**).

Help for young people

Lawstuff (www.lawstuff.org.au)
Young people who find themselves in trouble with the law may have difficulty getting legal advice that is easy to understand. This problem is addressed by the Lawstuff Web site – run by the National Children's and Youth Law Centre – which is aimed specifically at those under the age of 18. The site offers advice on a range of topics, including alcohol, drugs, leaving home, school, sex and driving offences. There are separate sections dealing with the law in each state and territory in Australia.

Specialised help

People in certain professions, or with particular interests or concerns, may find that their unique legal needs are addressed by Web sites specifically developed for that purpose. Artists, authors and composers, for example, can turn to several on-line resources for legal help and advice. In Australia, try the Arts Law Centre (**www.artslaw.com.au**) or the Australian Copyright Council (**www.copyright.org.au**). In New Zealand, visit the Copyright Council of New Zealand (**www.copyright.org.nz**).

Which lawyer

If you are looking for a lawyer in your area, try the free service at the Law For You site (**www.law4u.com.au**). Otherwise, visit the relevant state law society to find directories of members and practices. Links are provided by the Law Council of Australia (**www.lawcouncil.asn.au/links.html**).

In New Zealand, try the Auckland District Law Society (**www.adls.org.nz/public/lawlist.cfm**) or the Lawlink Web site (**www.lawlink.co.nz**).

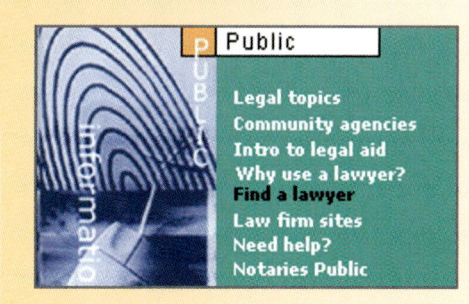

SEARCH IT YOURSELF

A number of sites have compiled extensive lists of links to help you track down law-related sites on the Internet.

Start with the Law Council of Australia (**www.lawcouncil.asn.au/links.html**), which has links to all the various state organisations as well as federal agencies and a range of community-based sites.

Another great mine of information is the Australasian Legal Information Institute (**www.austlii.edu.au**), which has links to legal resources, not only in Australia, but also New Zealand and elsewhere in the world as well. For a great collection of international legal links, go to Legal Sites on the Web (**www.ih2000.net/ira/legal.htm**).

Problem Solver!

When you ask for legal advice, make your query as detailed as you can. Also, ask if there will be any fees involved or if you are required to come in for a consultation.

Watch Out!

Before you act on any free advice received over the Internet, get a second opinion from another advice service.

SEE ALSO
- Search the Internet – page 64
- Get a mortgage quotation – page 204
- How e-commerce works – page 296

ADVICE AND INFORMATION

Look for a job

Using the Internet can make it easier to **look for work**

The Internet can play a useful part in your job search. You can search thousands of on-line listings in Australia, New Zealand and overseas – and it takes only a few minutes.

Many sites offer useful tools to help you find the best job. You can read up on the latest industry news, get advice on how to apply for a job successfully and test out your suitability for different careers.

Some sites also allow you to design your résumé on-line using their templates. You can even store your completed résumé on the site for prospective employers to view and consider.

On-line listings Companies advertise vacancies on their own sites, as well as at job listings pages. Register your job preferences with an employment site, and they'll e-mail you details of vacancies as they arise.

Applications Recruitment sites are full of advice on interview etiquette, and offer guidelines on how to write a good covering letter and résumé. Some, such as Seek (www.seek.com.au), let you post your résumé and then choose whether to classify it as Public, Anonymous or Private. You can even prevent specified companies from viewing it if you wish, so that your present employer doesn't find out that you're looking for another job!

Aptitude tests The Internet can help you to decide which career best suits your talents and personality. With on-line aptitude tests you can find out your personality type and preferred working environment. Try the free test offered by Quest (www.questcareer.com/career_assessment_resources.html).

EXPLORE THE WEB

HARD-WORKING SITES

Where to start
Monster (www.monster.com.au)
This is a comprehensive and user-friendly Web site for job-seekers, offering jobs in Australia and New Zealand and overseas. You can ask to be notified of vacancies according to your own preferences, then have the details of suitable positions e-mailed to you when they arise.

Other resources on the site include advice on writing a résumé, an Interview Centre, where you can have virtual interviews and get expert advice, and a Salary Centre, where you can find out what salary to expect. The location and category search features allow you to make targeted searches in your geographic region and area of expertise.

Official help
If you are looking for a job, don't overlook the assistance offered by official government agencies and organisations. In Australia, visit **www.fed.gov.au/KSP** for links to a range of useful sites, including JobSearch, Job Network, Indigenous Employment and Seasonal Work. The JobSearch site (**www.jobsearch.gov.au**), for example, allows you to search for a wide selection of positions in every state and territory. In New Zealand, try the KiwiCareers site (**www.careers.co.nz**) and click on **Job Vacancy Links** to see dozens of recruitment consultants and employment agency sites. Among a range of other sites is CareerPoint (**www.careers.govt.nz/c-key.htm**), which offers free information on careers and training.

Excellent advice
Mycareer (www.mycareer.com.au)
This site offers a wide range of job vacancies, which can be searched by employment sector, location and keyword. You can even sign up for the free *Get Smart* fortnightly newsletter.

The site also offers a range of additional services, such as a 'Resume Manager', which has sample résumés, as well as tips for writing effective letters and making a good impression at interviews. One particularly interesting feature offered on this site is Job Alert. Just specify you employment needs, and you will be sent regular e-mails of job advertisements that may be of interest.

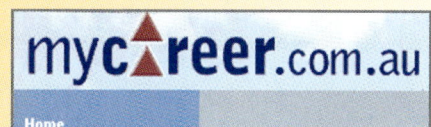

APPLYING FOR JOBS
- Set yourself a weekly target, such as sending out five applications.
- Try to tailor your letter and résumé for each application, making your skills seem as relevant as possible.
- Check your letter and résumé for mistakes. Many applications are put straight into the bin for this reason.
- Write to companies even if they have not advertised a job. If it arrives at the right time, your speculative approach may succeed.
- Adopt a personal approach. Call the company and ask for the name of the head of the department that interests you, or the Human Resources manager.
- Keep a file of all your applications. Put the ad, your letter and résumé in it. Refer to this when you receive replies.
- Don't give up. While you have applications out there, you are still in with a chance.

Watch Out!
Don't just look for work on-line: not all companies rely on the Internet. Look in industry magazines, newspapers, recruitment agencies, and wherever jobs of interest to you might appear.

Did You Know?
Many people get a job through contacts rather than through an advertisement. Be sure to ask around about jobs and let people know you are available.

ADVICE AND INFORMATION

Personal profiles
A personal profile is a summary of your skills, personality, motivation and aims. Creating one can help you to focus on what you want to get from a job and so target your job applications more effectively.

HOW TO: CREATE A PERSONAL PROFILE

1 To create a profile of your skills, go to the Big Trip (**www.thebigtrip.co.uk**) and click **Finding Yourself**, then **Yes**. Then click **Transferable Skills** (skills that are useful in a number of different jobs).

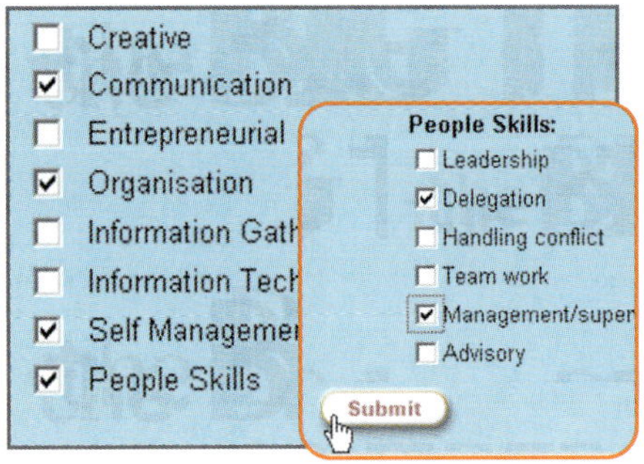

2 When the next page comes up, select four areas in which you display strengths, and click **Continue**. Select two skills in each subsection to narrow these areas further. Then click **Submit**.

3 Click **Personal Strengths** and choose the ten adjectives which best describe you. There are over 60 to choose from, so consider the subtleties carefully. Click **Submit**.

4 Click **Key Personal Values** and pick three values important to you. Click **Submit**.

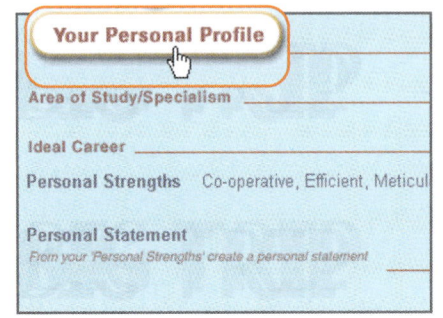

5 Click **Your Personal Profile**. Fill in the form by clicking on the red areas to type your name and other details on screen. Or, you can print out the page to fill in by hand later.

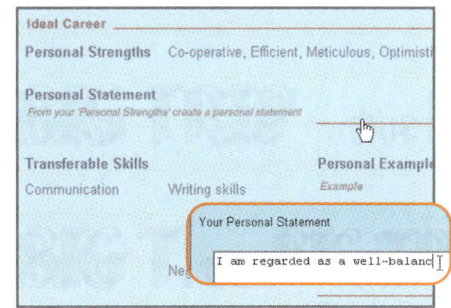

6 You can add examples as well as comments about why particular values matter to you. You can now use your profile to rewrite your résumé and to add focus to your cover letter.

Using employment sites

Some employment sites have thousands of jobs, and scrolling through an entire section can take far too long. You can speed up the search process by selecting only jobs in your region and your industry. Enter an area such as 'Australia-VIC-Regional' and an industry such as 'Banking' to narrow down the responses.

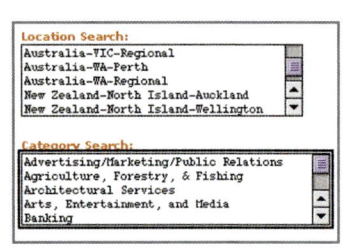

EXPLORE THE WEB

HOW TO: CREATE YOUR RÉSUMÉ ON-LINE

1 Many sites allow you to build a résumé on-line. This example uses Monster (**www.monster.com.au**). To start, click on **Resume Centre** and then **Build your Resume**.

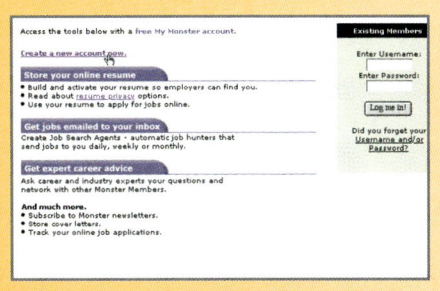

2 Signing up with Monster will not cost you anything and you can, of course, sign on with as many Internet job sites as you like. To sign on, click **Create a new account now**.

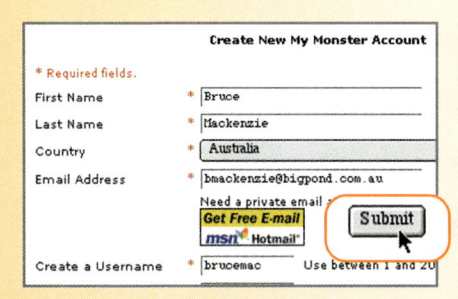

3 Fill in all the details requested. The boxes marked with an asterisk are essential and must be completed. When you are satisfied, click **Submit** to proceed.

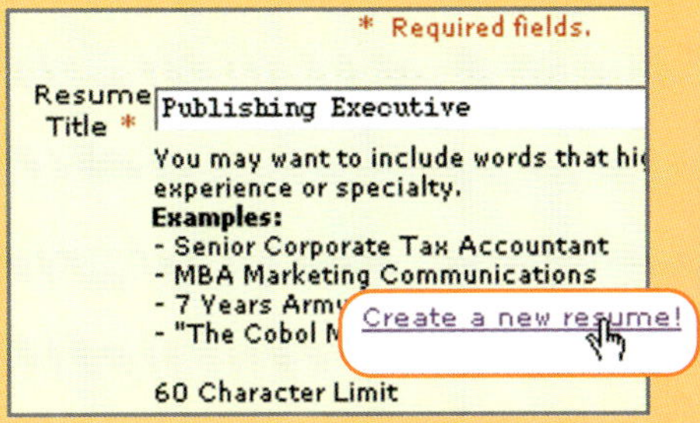

4 Once your registration has been accepted, you can access a range of resources. When you are ready, click **Create a new resume** and fill in the details on the pages that are presented.

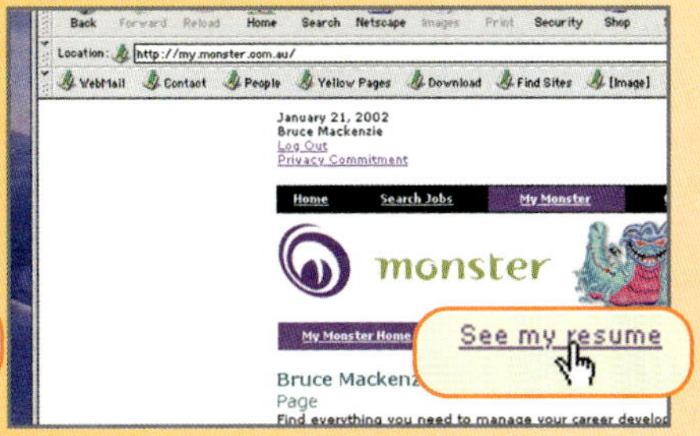

5 You can view your résumé as you add information to it by checking 'Show my resume in another window as I build it' at the start, or by clicking **See my resume** on subsequent pages.

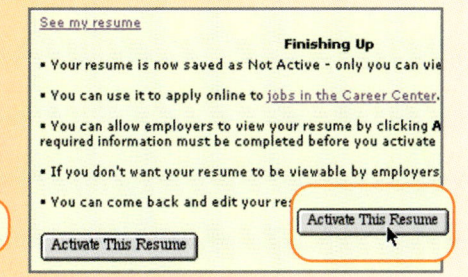

6 Your résumé can now be used to apply for jobs. You can choose whether you want it to be viewable by prospective employers, or whether you want to send it only when requested.

E-mailing your résumé

If the person you're e-mailing your résumé to has a different word-processing package, your formatting could be lost. Tell the recipient which format you used to save your résumé, or save your work in a format suitable for their software. Go to the **File** menu and select **Save As**. Under 'Save as file type', choose a format, name your résumé, and click **Save**.

Time Saver!
Type out the main points of your résumé before you go on the site, then cut and paste the information onto the form.

SEE ALSO
- **Set up Outlook Express** – page 34
- **Find legal advice** – page 120
- **File your tax return** – page 196

ADVICE AND INFORMATION

Seek medical advice

Use the Internet to **get help** on a range of health issues

Should you fall ill, nothing can take the place of a consultation with a qualified professional. But the Internet is packed full of medical data and advice. It's especially helpful for those who are housebound by illness. The Web can offer self-care advice for mild conditions, information on over-the-counter and prescription medicines, and access to support groups. Most medical Web sites also offer e-mail newsletters covering recent developments in medical research.

Health on-line
On the Internet you'll find detailed explanations of diseases and conditions, signs and symptoms, and the range of treatments available. One of the best sites for general medical health issues is the Mayo Clinic (**www.mayoclinic.com**) in the USA. The site has an A–Z of medical conditions, a first-aid and self-care guide and nutritional advice. Bear in mind that some products suggested by sites such as this may not be available in Australia or New Zealand.

Help and support
The Internet offers support for people with similar health concerns. There are on-line groups and charities for almost all conditions, from acne to yeast infection.

Health questions
If you need more specific advice, some sites have interactive questionnaires to fill in on-line. Others let you ask a professional. At eMedical (**www.emedical.com.au**), for example, you can get an on-line consultation (for a fee).

EXPLORE THE WEB

BEST OF HEALTH

Practical help
**The Patient's Guide
(www3.telus.net/me/patientsguide)**
Medical information and advice is one of the most popular Internet research topics. There are now many thousands of sites you can explore, and the number is growing daily. If all this seems a bit daunting, you may welcome some help, such as that offered by The Patient's Guide, a site with many resources, including a guide to identifying and researching medical conditions.

Advice and information
MDAdvice (www.mdadvice.com)
MDAdvice has an 'Ask An Expert' section where you can get advice from a doctor about common medical issues, such as allergies and earache, and less common ones, such as Pickwickian syndrome (hypoventilation due to obesity). You can also search through the question-and-answer archive (many questions have been asked before). There is advice and information about health issues specific to groups such as children, women, men and the elderly, plus a news section with the latest information.

Government information
Both the Australian and New Zealand governments offer advice on medical issues. In Australia, visit the HealthInsite page (**www.healthinsite.gov.au**), and remember that all state and territory governments also offer information. In New South Wales, for example, the health site **www.search.nsw.gov.au/health.asp** has links to information ranging from fitness and diet to lists of hospitals and health centres. You'll find links to all regional government sites at **www.gov.au**. In New Zealand, make a start with the Health Information Service (**www.nzhis.govt.nz/intranet/index.html**).

Medical information
**NHS Direct Online
(www.nhsdirect.nhs.uk)**
This excellent site – run by the UK National Health Service – has a range of information on almost every health issue. See 'Health features' for in-depth studies of conditions such as depression or heart disease, including a rundown of symptoms and treatments, and advice on finding support (much of it directed at UK residents).

Cautionary notes
DON'T give out your medical history on-line unless you are sure of confidentiality.
DO remember that medicines and treatments may differ in other countries.
DON'T assume that another person's experiences of the same condition will be the same as your own.
DO get a second – or even third – opinion.

SEARCH IT YOURSELF
For information about health issues, go to a search engine such as Yahoo! (**http://au.yahoo.com**), then click the **Health** option on the site's homepage.

You will see a wide range of health-related topics, such as First Aid and Women's Health. Click any one of these to get to further subdivisions, and keep clicking until you locate the precise subject you want. Australian and New Zealand sites are marked with 'au' or 'nz'.

Many collections of links can be found on the Internet, and these can make the task of searching a lot easier. Take a look at The Drs Reference Site (**www.drsref.com.au**), which is also searchable, or the BlackStump medical page (**www.blackstump.com.au/medical.htm**).

ADVICE AND INFORMATION

HOW TO: USE AN INTERACTIVE HEALTH TEST

There are lots of interactive health tests available on the Internet, ranging from diagnostic tests to reviews of your overall health, diet and fitness. You fill in your details in the spaces provided and the Web site then assesses your entries and produces a likely diagnosis, or suggestions as to how you could improve your general lifestyle.

The UK government site NHS Direct Online (www.nhsdirect.nhs.uk) has a thorough diagnostic questionnaire for you to fill in to establish the cause of your symptoms. In this example, the symptoms presented are raised, itchy areas on the skin.

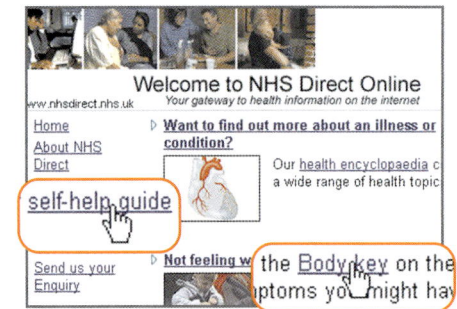

Time Saver!

The World Health Organization (www.who.int), like many other health agencies, makes leaflets available at its Web site. You can then download and print just the sections you want, saving yourself the bother of phoning or writing to the agency directly.

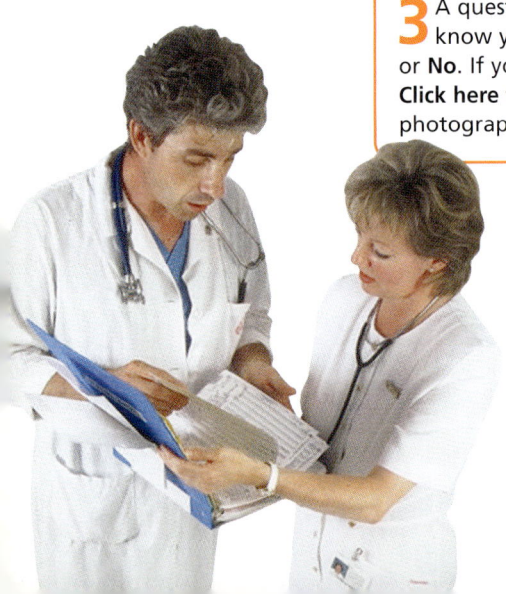

1 Go to the NHS Direct Online site (www.nhsdirect.nhs.uk), and click on **Try our self-help guide for advice**. In the next page, click on **Body key**.

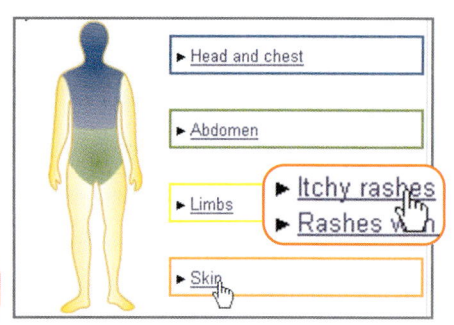

2 When the 'Body key' appears, click on the link to **Skin** disorders. Then select **Itchy rashes** from the list of conditions you are given.

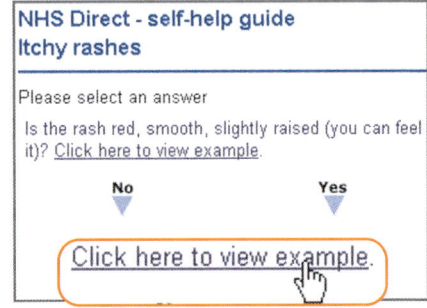

3 A question now appears. If you know your answer already, click **Yes** or **No**. If you are in any doubt, click on **Click here to view example** to see a photograph of the condition.

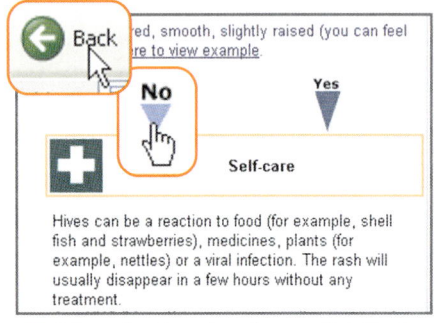

4 After viewing the photo, click **Back** to return to the initial question. Clicking **Yes** will give you your diagnosis and suggested self-care advice. Clicking **No** will bring up a further question.

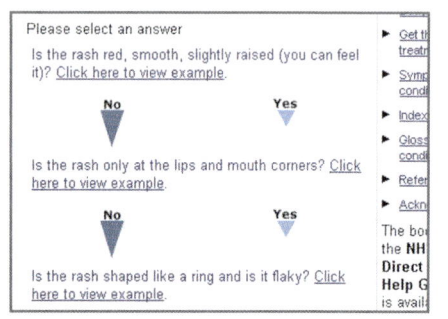

5 Continue to click **No** to get further questions which will narrow down an identification of your condition. When your answer to a question is 'Yes', click **Yes** for your diagnosis.

Consult a doctor

If you remain in any doubt about any on-line diagnosis – particularly one obtained from an overseas site, where local conditions may differ from those in Australia or New Zealand – contact your GP. A health test such as the one described above is no substitute for seeing a real doctor, and unusual conditions may require more specialised help.

EXPLORE THE WEB

HOW TO: FIND THE BEST SUPPORT GROUP

On-line support groups provide a forum for meeting people with similar health concerns to your own. They can be a good place to exchange practical information on different medicines and treatments, care equipment and techniques, and benefit entitlements. Most importantly, they offer support for individuals and their families.

This example shows a search using the HotBot search engine (**http://hotbot.lycos.com**) for support groups for hepatitis sufferers. If a search returns too many sites, you can narrow down your choices to get fewer, but more relevant, results.

1 Go to the HotBot homepage (**http://hotbot.lycos.com**) and enter the keywords you wish to search for – in this case, 'hepatitis support group'. Then click **Search**.

2 HotBot displays results from all over the world. These are listed, ten at a time, in decreasing order of relevance to the search criteria.

3 Narrow your search by checking the 'Search within these results' box, and then enter 'sydney nsw' in the search window (you don't need to use capital letters). Click **Search**.

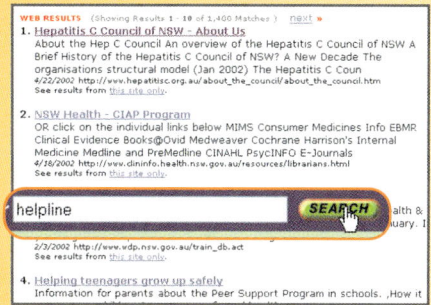

4 The results list a large number of sites, all in Sydney. If you want to narrow the results to sites that have a helpline, check the 'Search within these results' box and search for 'helpline'.

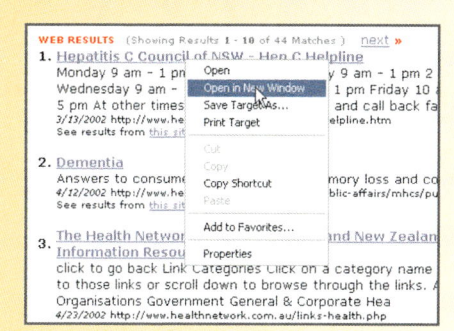

5 Browse through the list, and if you would like to see more of any site, right-click on its link and select **Open in a New Window**. You can then return more easily to the HotBot list.

Watch Out!

When looking up medicines on an overseas site, remember that generic and brand names in other countries are often different from those in Australia and New Zealand. Paracetamol, for example, is called acetaminophen in the USA.

Buying medicines from overseas

Some people buy medicines over the Internet from overseas that are not available in their home country. Always get medical advice before doing this – both for health and legal reasons. You should always check medical information against two or more independent sources, and if you still have any doubts at all, check again with a qualified doctor.

SEE ALSO
- Improve your diet and fitness – *page 130*
- Enjoy the great outdoors – *page 225*
- Live the sporting life – *page 238*

ADVICE AND INFORMATION

Improve your diet and fitness

Use the World Wide Web to organise a healthier lifestyle

The Internet cannot do the hard work of dieting and getting fit for you, but it can help you to get started and keep you on the right track. You can use the Web to check out national fitness and health programs, find a personal trainer, get nutritional advice, or look up local health clubs and sports groups. Many Web sites will help you to devise a fitness plan to suit your lifestyle and physical constitution, while forums and newsgroups allow you to share your views, and your successes and failures with other, like-minded people.

Good health
For overall health, you should eat a sensible diet and exercise regularly. There are many Web sites that can help you to do this. There are some where you can submit details of your eating habits and physical activity and receive suggestions for improving your lifestyle. Kilojoule counters can help you to monitor day-to-day eating, while body-mass calculators can help you to decide whether you are overweight or not.

Helpful programs
There are health and diet shareware programs available to download. Both Tucows (**www.tucows.com**), and Jumbo! (**www.jumbo.com**) provide software where you fill in a personal profile to track and report the items you eat and the nutrients they contain, and create a customised fitness regime. This is designed to help you to manage weight loss, diet sensibly and train effectively.

Precautions
Remember that information you find on the Internet is no substitute for a consultation with your doctor. If you are planning to lose more than a kilogram a week, or if you have a medical condition, you should consult your GP before embarking on any course of action.

EXPLORE THE WEB

BEST OF HEALTH

Fitness log
Just Move (www.justmove.org)
This site – maintained by the American Heart Association – has practical advice on maintaining a healthy heart as well as the latest health news.

The exercise diary is a useful starting point for anybody

Week	Time Goal
1	90 min
2	90 min
3	120 min
4	120 min
5	160 min

trying to get fit. The site provides specific feedback, which is based on your progress reports and statistical summaries of your fitness program.

You can also sign up to a personal trainer service, which means you will receive messages of encouragement via e-mail.

Nutrition
Dietsure (www.dietsure.com)
This site offers a guide to nutritional analysis and a healthier lifestyle. You can store details of your food intake on-line and monitor the progress of your healthy eating program from anywhere. You can also analyse your diet by completing a questionnaire about your eating habits over the past week.

Click here to analyse your diet

General health
Oxygen (www.oxygen.com)
Oxygen is a lifestyle site, oriented towards women, with a section devoted to health and fitness. You can use its facilities to calculate your energy intake and plan fitness schedules (see page 132 overleaf). If you register with the site, you'll gain access to a range of extra resources.

Dieting
Shape Up America! (www.shapeup.org)
A site that uses interactive technology to show how you can balance food with physical activity to maintain a healthy weight. There are even recipes for the suggested meals.

Fitness and health
Active Australia (www.activeaustralia.org)
Managed by the Australian Sports Commission, this is a site for anyone who always promises to get serious about exercise … some day soon! Here you will discover the benefits of exercise, how to get started, activities that might suit you and even lists of sporting and recreational clubs or fitness centres in your area.

SEARCH IT YOURSELF

Many Web-indexing services have categories that cover both health and fitness. These services organise Web sites by topic, making it easier for you to find what you need.

For example, go to Yahoo! (**http://au.yahoo.com**), and click on **Health** to see a list of subdivisions, with headings such as Fitness, Disabilities and Weight Issues. Click on any of the subdivisions and you will see a list of Web sites to visit. Note that Australian and New Zealand sites are identified by symbols containing the letters AU or NZ.

Watch Out!
If a site is making grandiose claims – for example, 'drop a dress size in under a week' – then it's probably overselling itself. In the end it is you who have to put in the effort.

Did You Know?
Sites such as Silver Hammer Publishing (http://silverhammerpub.com) and Health and Fitness Tips (www.health-fitness-tips.com) will e-mail you regular free diet and fitness newsletters.

ADVICE AND INFORMATION

HOW TO: CREATE A FITNESS PLAN

1 Go to Oxygen (www.oxygen.com), and click on **health & fitness** in the heading bar. On the next page, click on **Fitness Planner**.

2 You will be presented with a series of options according to the sort of fitness you are trying to achieve – strength, cardiovascular, flexibility etc.

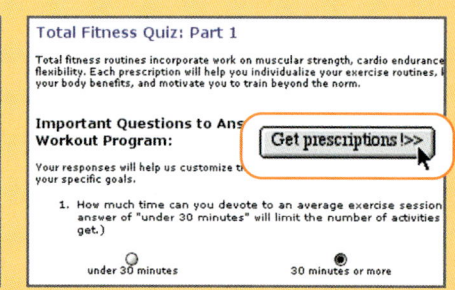

3 Now answer all the questions in the on-screen questionnaire. When you have finished, click **Get prescriptions!** to see the suggested plans.

HOW TO: CONTROL YOUR DIET

1 Go to Shape Up America! (**www.shapeup.org**) and click on **Weight Management**. When the Cyberkitchen page opens, click **Enter Here**.

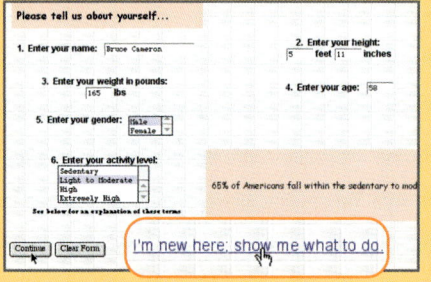

2 If this is your first visit to the site, click **I'm new here; show me what to do** and then fill in the details requested in the on-screen form.

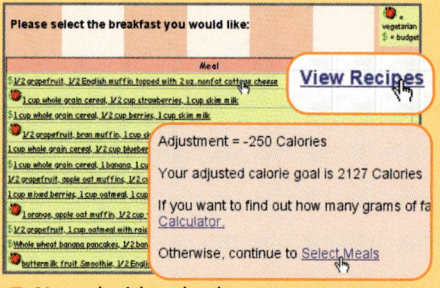

3 Now decide whether you want to lose, gain or maintain weight, and you will be shown meals and recipes to help you to achieve your goals.

Did You Know?

In Australia and New Zealand, the energy value of food is measured in kilojoules (kJ). To convert the calories used on overseas sites to kilojoules, just multiply by 4.2.

Watch Out!

Before beginning a weight-reduction diet, get advice on your individual energy needs (in kilojoules) – based on your age and lifestyle – from your GP.

Join a gym

If you are advised by your doctor or by a Web site to get more exercise, it may be worth joining a gym. Search through on-line databases, such as Ultrafit (**www.ultrafit-ozegyms.com**) or Fitness New Zealand (**www.fitnessnz.co.nz**) to find a gym that's right for you. You can search by postcode or region to find one nearby.

SEE ALSO
- **Seek medical advice** – page 126
- **Do your weekly shop** – page 192
- **Get cooking** – page 236

Solve computer problems

Enhance your PC using the Internet

One of the best places to look if you are having problems with your computer, or want to improve the way it works, is the Internet. Learning how to share problems and gain access to expertise on the Internet can help you to solve almost any computer problem – or at least tell you that the problem can't be solved.

Software bugs
Bugs are programming errors that cause your software to malfunction. It is not unusual for new versions of software to contain bugs. After the software is released, manufacturers soon learn about any bugs from their customers and some create mini-programs called 'patches' to solve them. You can download patches from the Net.

Hardware problems
Every device connected to your computer, such as a printer or scanner, needs software called a 'driver', which allows your PC to control the device. Often, when a piece of hardware isn't working properly, it is due to the driver malfunctioning.

Some drivers (for your keyboard, for example) are included in your operating system, but when you buy new hardware, such as an external Zip drive, you usually need to install a driver for it. If you don't have the right driver, or the driver is defective, your device won't work. Use the Internet to locate and download the right driver.

Identifying the problem
Often you won't even know what the problem is – you will just know that something is wrong. By sharing details of the symptoms with other Internet users, you can often diagnose the problem and take steps to solve it.

ADVICE AND INFORMATION

Did You Know?

The first computer bug was an actual bug. In 1945, Grace Hopper of Harvard University was working on an early computer, the Mark II Aiken Relay Calculator, when a moth became trapped in the machine and caused it to shut down.

Watch Out!

Make sure you have anti-virus software running to prevent any potential problems when you are downloading new software.

IMPROVING YOUR PC

Help with Windows
Microsoft (www.microsoft.com/australia)
First click on **Windows**, under 'Product Families', and then select your version of the operating system. In the case of Windows XP, click on **Using Windows XP** for a wide range of tips and How-to articles, as well as links to Windows XP newsgroups. More experienced users may like to explore the Downloads and Technical Resources links. Click on the **Support** tab to search Microsoft's extensive Knowledge Base, where you can enter one or more keywords and review articles on a variety of technical questions that may be useful.

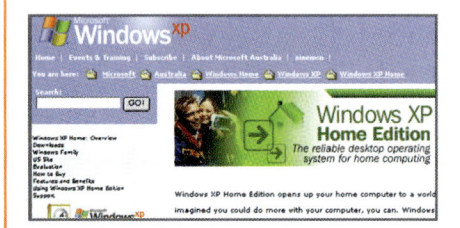

On-line help
Whatever the subject, you are likely to find a free tutorial, or the answer to a difficult question, somewhere on the Internet. Tracking it down can be a problem, however, so make a start with a site such as Intelinfo (**www.intelinfo.com**), which has gathered together links to thousands of tutorial and help sites on the Web.

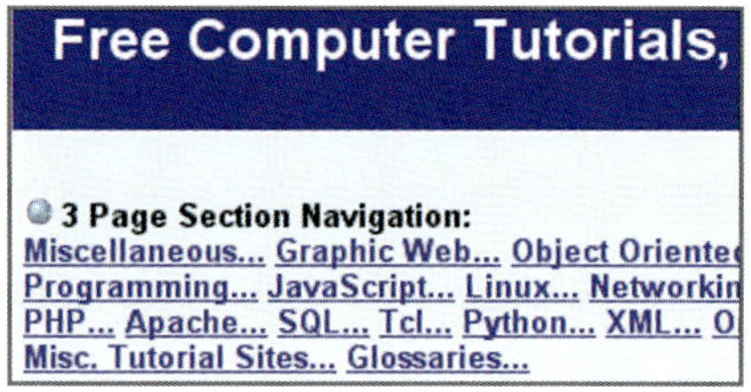

Ask an expert
Doctor Keyboard (www.drkeyboard.com)
Doctor Keyboard is a computer journalist in the UK. You can chat to the Doctor live or e-mail him questions and receive a response. Search the site for answers to previous questions and browse the Message Board – the sections include hardware, software, the Internet and Mac problems. There is a useful 'Jargon for Beginners' page and advice on what to do 'When it all goes wrong', such as looking through the program's 'help' files or checking that all the cables are connected.

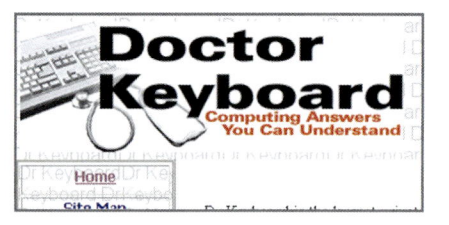

Computer newsgroups
Cyberfiber Newsgroups (www.cyberfiber.com)
This is a categorised directory of newsgroups. To find newsgroups on a computer topic, search by keyword or browse the subject listing. Click on **Computers (OS and Platforms)** if you have problems with your Windows or Mac operating system (OS), and **Computers (Not OS Specific)** for other computer problems. Click on a newsgroup name to go to it. Browse the previous posts to find an answer to your problem, or post a question for the newsgroup members to answer. Alternatively, go to Google Groups (**http://groups.google.com**) and browse through the 'comp.' newsgroups listed.

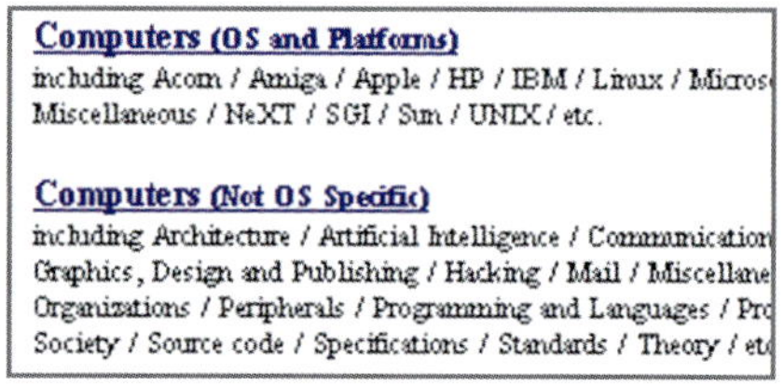

Shareware
Some programs, known as shareware (see *Software on the Web*, page 84) can really improve your PC's performance. At Jumbo! (**www.jumbo.com**), programs are compared and reviewed so you can find what would make a difference for you. See the useful 'Jumbo Guides' for help on 'PC Essentials' or uses for an ageing PC.

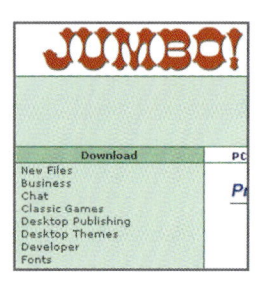

FIND THE RIGHT DRIVER

Imagine a friend has given you an old printer that works fine on his computer, but not on yours – because you haven't got the right driver. How can you find one? Here are a number of routes to finding an answer.

Search engine
Go to a search engine site such as Google (**www.google.com**) and search under the make and model of your printer and the word 'driver', for example, 'Epson stylus color 400 driver'. The results page will list a lot of relevant sites, which you can sift through to find your driver.

Manufacturer's site
The best place to find drivers is at the manufacturer's Web site. At Epson (**www.epson.com**), you can click on **Download Library** to see a list of drivers arranged by type of hardware. Click on a category, such as **Inkjet Printers**, select the model and your operating system, then click **Search** to see any relevant drivers. Click **Download** to download the driver.

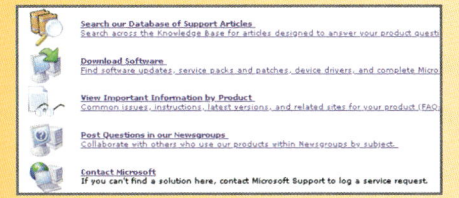

Microsoft site
Recent versions of Windows provide access to Windows Update, an on-line extension that helps you to keep your operating system and device drivers up to date. To access this service you must be running a licensed copy of Windows and a current Web browser. Alternatively, you can search Microsoft's Knowledge Base for relevant articles, using search terms such as 'Windows XP' and 'drivers'.

Bulletin boards
There are many bulletin boards where users can post and respond to computer problems, such as missing printer drivers (see *Use a bulletin board*, page 100).

Newsgroups
To search newsgroup postings for computer-related newsgroups at Google Groups (**http://groups.google.com**), click **comp.**, and look for an entry that matches what you need, such as 'comp.periphs' (peripherals). To search for your driver in that newsgroup's 135,000 postings, enter your search term, select the 'in this newsgroup only' button and click **Search**. To post a message of your own, you need to subscribe using a news reader program such as Outlook Express.

Alternatives
If you find it hard to locate the right driver for your printer, you may be able to use another one that works just as well. This will not apply in all cases, but it is worth looking up your printer model at the UK Technical Support site (**www.uktsupport.co.uk**) – a free archive of home computer help – to see if there is any alternative driver listed for it. You can read and post messages, or browse the site by manufacturer and model. Driver downloads are also available.

Frequently Asked Questions
If you want to find out something about your PC or the software you're using, one of the best ways to do this is by consulting the FAQs (Frequently Asked Questions) on the manufacturer's Web site. It's very likely that other users will have encountered the same problem as you, so – rather than e-mailing the site and then waiting for an answer – you can see what advice was handed out the last time your particular problem occurred.

Problem Solver!

If you find a site with instructions on how to solve a problem, print these out rather than saving them. Don't forget that you may need to turn your PC off in order to solve a particular problem, and then you may not be able to remember exactly what you were meant to do next!

SEE ALSO
- **Are you Net ready?** – page 14
- **Software on the Web** – page 84
- **Download from the Web** – page 86

Help your child to learn on-line

The Web offers a **whole new medium** for children to do **school work,** prepare for exams and satisfy their curiosity

There are many Internet learning facilities for children of school-going age. These include on-line dictionaries, encyclopedias, thesauruses and sites on famous explorers, artists and politicians. Children can chat to each other or ask teachers for advice, and parents can put questions to schools and the government. Some Web sites also offer educational software that you can download and use from home.

LEARNING IS FUN

The Internet can complement and support the education your child receives at school. You and your children can find out about schools around the country, visit the world's best museums and talk to teachers and students on-line.

Web resources

If your child needs a picture for a school project, there are millions of copyright-free images to choose from on the Web. If they're looking for ideas, they can read about any period in history and search through newspaper clippings from the past 30 years. They can even conduct science experiments from the safety of their PC desktop.

Homework help

Difficult homework can be tackled with the help of the Internet. There are sites that provide answers to tough questions, from information on a specific author or historical figure to facts on cities or countries. Help with English grammar and spelling is available, as well as on-line foreign language dictionaries. There are also message boards and chatrooms where children can talk to people of their own age on any subject they want.

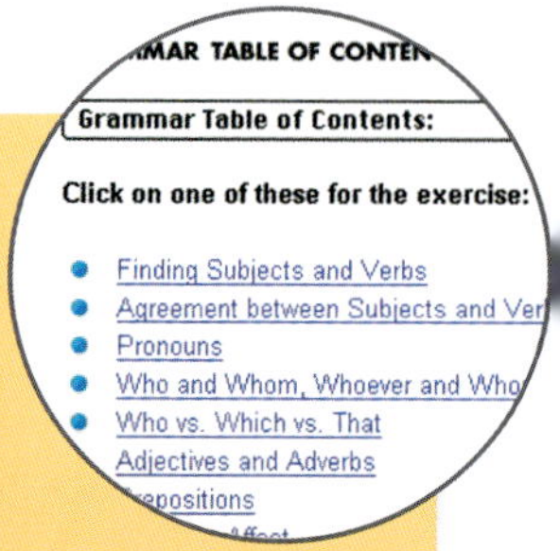

Just for kids

There are some great 'child-friendly' search sites that list a huge number of educational sites – and protect your child from finding offensive ones.

When your children are not on-line, they can benefit from educational software designed to improve their subject skills. Find the best free and commercial software at the SuperKids Educational Software Review site (**www.superkids.com**).

If you are worried about your child's education, find out exactly what's in the curriculum at the official education Web site. In Australia you will find links to all state and territory government home pages at (**www.gov.au**). In New Zealand, go to **www.minedu.govt.nz**.

EXPLORE THE WEB

THE BEST SITES

Where to begin
Ask Jeeves Kids (www.ajkids.com)
A good place to start your search for educational information. Unlike most search engines, Ask Jeeves lets you type in a question in plain English, such as 'What are the rings of Saturn made of?' It then returns a set of questions, such as 'Where can I find an astronomy page about Saturn just for kids?' that you can click on for answers. It also filters out sites that are unsuitable for children.

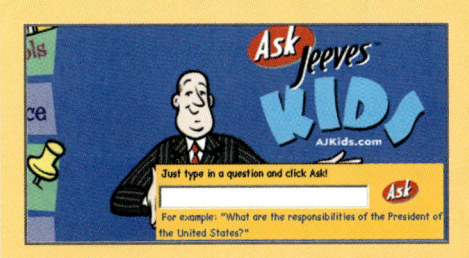

On-line learning
Education Network Australia (www.edna.edu.au)
EdNA Online promotes learning and training on the Internet for students at all levels, from school to university. The EdNA site provides a range of resources, including directories and databases that can be useful to both teachers and students alike.

Integrated resource
ABC Learn online (www.abc.net.au/learn)
The ABC's Learn Online site brings together a range of Web resources as well as access to educational programs on both radio and television. There are links to popular programs, such as 'The Science Show' and Radio National's 'Lifelong Learning'.

Educational site
US National Museum of Natural History (www.mnh.si.edu)
This Web site's educational resources include 'electronic fieldtrips' on the Galapagos Islands, dinosaurs, gemstones and messages from outer space. Each section includes fun projects and activities for kids to take part in.

Fun way to learn
Discovernet (http://amol.org.au/discovernet)
Discovernet is a gateway to museums and galleries all over Australia. You can find museums, explore fascinating new exhibitions and even play a game – 'Make your own Exhibition'. Both the National Museum of Australia (**www.nma.gov.au**) and the Museum of New Zealand (**www.tepapa.govt.nz**) also provide many resources.

SEARCH IT YOURSELF
One of the most accessible sites for finding educational resources is Looksmart (**www.looksmart.com.au**) or (**www.looksmart.co.nz**). Although it's a general search engine, it also has a directory of selected Web sites with particular focus on children and education.

On the Australian site's homepage, scroll down to 'Library' and click on **Education**. You will be presented with further options, such as 'For Teachers', 'For Parents' and 'For School Students'. Click on a category that interests you and you will be presented with a range of further options, which you can explore until you find what you want.

On the New Zealand Looksmart homepage, click on **Reference & Education**, then on **Education**, and a range of categories will appear, including, 'For Students', 'Maori Education' and 'Rural Education'.

Alternatively, you can simply use the search facility of either site. Type the subject you're looking for in the 'Search the Web' box at the top of the homepage and click on **Search**.

SITE CHECKS
There are ways to determine if a site is child-friendly:
- Look for a link to see who runs the site
- Check for a link to the site's safety policy
- Read a few pages to check the language
- Check the links page for unsuitable sites
- Look for accreditation from official organisations

ADVICE AND INFORMATION

Watch Out!

For peace of mind, use a software package such as Net Nanny to filter out any unsavoury sites your children might encounter. See page 56 for more details.

HOW TO: E-MAIL A HOMEWORK QUESTION

Some Web sites allow you to send in a question and have it answered by a team of experts. Although the best of such sites are generally based in the UK and USA, local students can still find them useful. The curricula for some subjects, such as science, biology and mathematics, can be very similar in different countries.

Time differences may mean that, in most cases, Australian and New Zealand children will not be able to take part in the 'live' sessions offered by some sites, but they will still be able to send in questions and have them answered later.

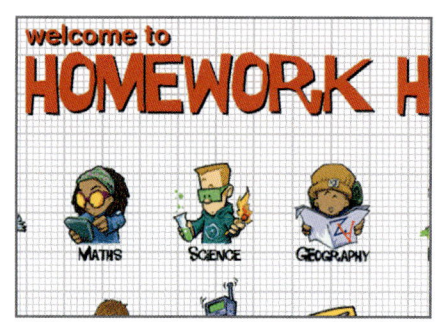

1 Go to the Homework High Web site (**www.homeworkhigh.co.uk**) and click on the subject that you wish to ask a question in; for example, Maths, English or Science.

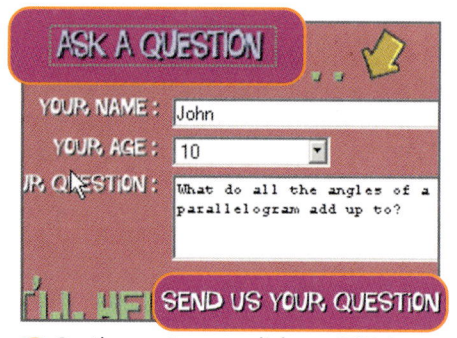

2 On the next page, click on **ASK A QUESTION**. A screen will appear asking you for your name, your age, your question, and your e-mail address. Click on **SEND US YOUR QUESTION**.

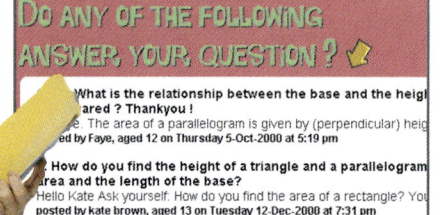

3 A list of other questions that have already been asked will appear. Check if yours is listed. If it is, click on the question for the answer. If it isn't, click **NOPE, MINE'S A NEW QUESTION**.

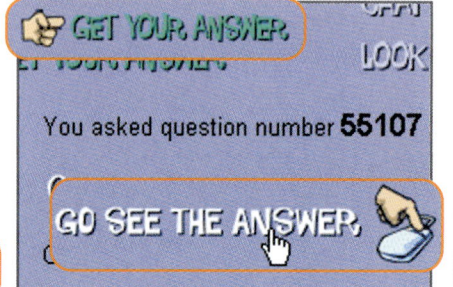

4 A message will now inform you of your question number. Write this down. Click on **GET YOUR ANSWER**, and enter your number in the box supplied. Then click on **GO SEE THE ANSWER**.

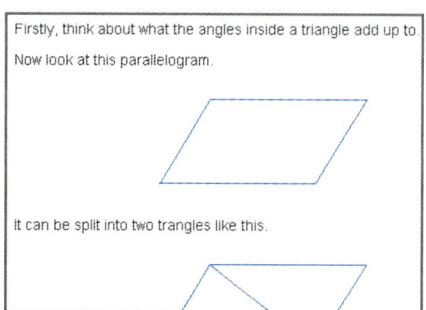

5 The answer to your question will appear and also be e-mailed to you. If there is a delay in replying, then 'PLEASE CHECK AGAIN LATER' will show. Keep a note of your question number.

Book sites

For inspiration on books to buy for children, and to get them interested in reading, look up a Web site such as Scholastic Australia (**www.scholastic.com.au**), which has book clubs for all ages, and even a games page where kids can try out the latest software.

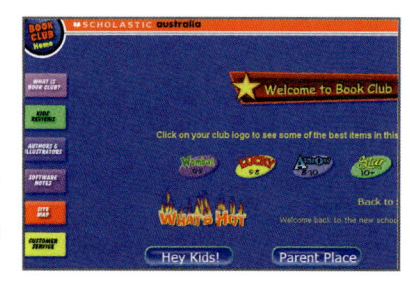

138

EXPLORE THE WEB

HOW TO: FIND USEFUL INFORMATION FOR A SCHOOL PROJECT

The Internet is excellent for finding useful information for your child's school work. A quick search using a child-friendly search engine can provide all sorts of relevant material, aimed at just the right level.

Good Web sites also provide links to sites that deal with other related questions and subjects. This can help your children to think around the subject, learn the value of creative research and get ideas and inspiration for their school work.

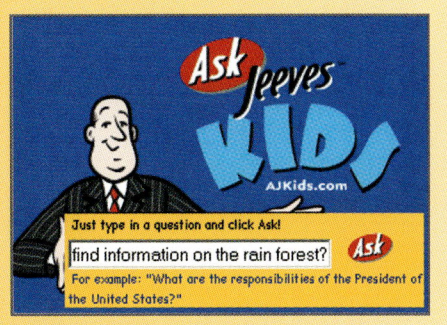

1 Go to Ask Jeeves Kids (www.ajkids.com). In the box in the centre of the page, type in a question, such as 'Where can I find information on the rain forest?', then click **Ask**.

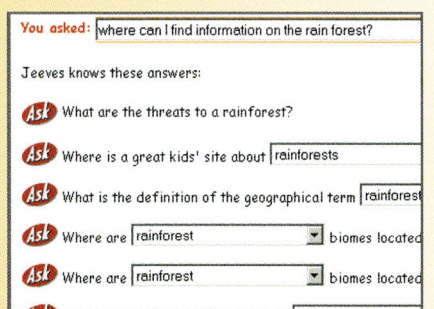

2 The site will bring up a list of questions similar to the one that you asked – 'Where is a great kids' site about rainforests?', 'What are the elements of a rainforest?', and so on.

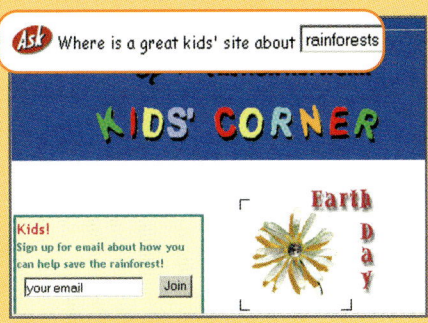

3 If you are interested in the answers to any of the questions, click on the **Ask** button next to it, and a Web site will appear. You can then click on the subject that interests you.

4 If you want to return to the original range of options your question created, click on the back arrow at the top of the page.

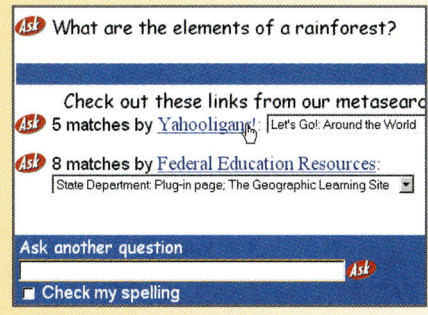

5 Scroll down to the bottom of this page for a list of other sites that will link to your question and give you more general information concerning the subject.

Watch Out!
Web sites run by fellow students are prone to error. Where possible, double-check your information against another Web site or a reference book.

Cut download time

Many sites aimed at children contain a lot of pictures. But if you don't need the pictures, you can set Internet Explorer not to show them. Click **Tools**, then **Internet Options**. Click the **Advanced** tab, scroll down to 'Multimedia', and untick the box next to 'Show pictures'. Pages will now load quicker. If you want to see a picture after all, right-click on the picture box and select **Show Picture**.

SEE ALSO
- Go into outer space – page 142
- Explore the natural world – page 156
- Keep the children entertained – page 174

139

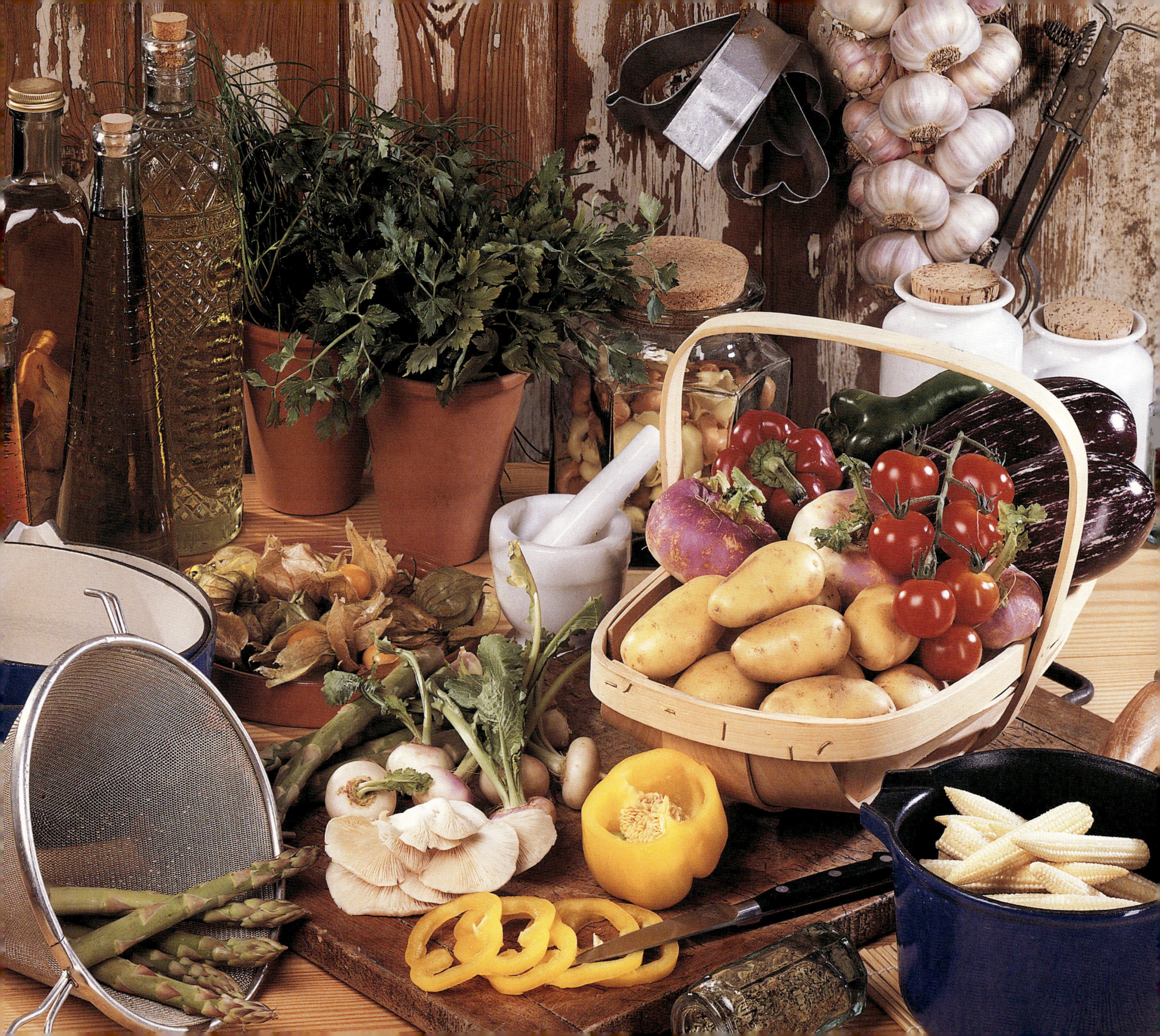

Hobbies and leisure

- 142 Go into outer space
- 145 Take a virtual tour
- 148 Tune into television
- 152 Listen to the radio
- 156 Explore the natural world
- 159 Trace your family's past
- 164 Access showbiz news
- 166 Enjoy the literary world
- 169 Make new friends
- 172 Explore painting
- 174 Keep the children entertained
- 180 Go motoring
- 183 Improve your home
- 186 Play games on-line

Go into outer space

Learn about **the Universe** on the **World Wide Web**

Thanks to the Internet, astronomy has come out of the observatory and into the sitting room. Anyone using a computer can become a space enthusiast or a witness to cosmic events such as eclipses and solar flares. Official and unofficial sites provide a mix of science, speculation, philosophy and fun. Amateurs can follow debates that previously raged in academic journals only. Does the discovery of ice on the Moon increase the chances of its colonisation? Do the marks on the surface of Mars signify an ancient civilisation?

Space travel You can catch the latest space mission news at the official sites of the National Aeronautics & Space Administration (**www.nasa.gov**) and the European Space Agency (**www.esa.int**). For news of research by local experts, visit the Australian Space Research Institute (**www.asri.org.au**).

Space images The Web is rich in exciting movies and images from space. NASA and ESA do not copyright their pictures, so they are available as free downloads.

Astronomy The study of space is well served on-line at sites such as **www.astronomyforum.net** with star-gazers discussing their hobby.

Aliens Sites about aliens are very popular. For all the latest news, explore the UFOs/Aliens Homepage (**http://ufos.about.com**). Click on the **UFOs Down Under** link for reports of sightings in Australia and New Zealand.

Simulations The Internet cannot take you into space, but you can try landing Apollo 11 on the Moon at the Apollo Project Archive site (**www.apolloarchive.com**). Click on **Lunar Lander Simulator**.

EXPLORE THE WEB

SITES FOR THE STARS

Where to start
NASA (www.nasa.gov)
This huge US government department has what must be one of the Web's most thorough, complex and rewarding sites. It contains information on space travel and astronomy as well as material about such sciences as meteorology and navigation, which rely on space research and observation.

Eclipses, meteorites, life on Mars – it's all here. From the homepage, you can access the latest space news, or click on links to historical archives, education, videos or children's pages.

You can even get an astronaut's view of the interior of the huge orbiting International Space Station by taking a virtual tour at **http://spaceflight.nasa.gov/gallery/vtour**.

Space science
Zoom Astronomy (www.enchantedlearning.com/subjects/astronomy)
This is a sensible, family-oriented site with lots of information on the Sun, stars, Moon and planets.

Subjects such as solar eclipses are explained with the aid of clear diagrams. There are also fun things to do, such as working out how much you would weigh on another planet.

Space news
Spaceflight Now (www.spaceflightnow.com)
Spaceflight Now carries news on all manned and unmanned space missions, as well as stories from the world of astronomy. Learn about the eruption on Io, one of the Jupiter's moons, and see the latest pictures from the Hubble Space Telescope. Click **Launch Schedule** for a comprehensive guide to upcoming launches throughout the world. You can even view some of the launches on live Internet broadcasts. Click **Features** then **Video Vault**, for video images from exciting rocket-based cameras.

Search for aliens
SETI Institute (www.seti-inst.edu)
The SETI Institute leads the field in the Search for Extra-Terrestrial Intelligence, analysing radio telescope data for unusual signals. The main purpose of the site is to convince you to lend the institute the power of your own computer to help to conduct this research (see overleaf).

But the site also feeds the public's voracious appetite for all things alien. You can read articles on what would happen if a signal was discovered and verified (the first person to be informed would be the secretary-general of the United Nations, in accordance with Article XI of the Treaty on Principles Governing the Activities of States in the Exploration and Use of Outer Space, Including the Moon and Other Bodies).

If you think you have spotted an alien, you can report your sighting to Project: S.E.T.L.A.B. (Study of Extra-Terrestrial Life and Answers from Beyond) (**www.setlab.org**). This site is not intended to be funny, but you may need to suspend disbelief to enjoy it.

Best site for children
SpaceKids (www.spacekids.com)
With space news and features, plus pictures, videos, games and a Solar System Tour, this site is informative, lively and lots of fun.

The 'Ask Experts' feature allows your child to find out almost everything he or she has ever wanted to know about space.

SEARCH IT YOURSELF
Go to Yahoo! (**http://au.yahoo.com**) and click on **Science**. Then click on **Space**, and then choose one of the headings, such as 'Astronauts' or 'Satellites', to see a list of relevant sites.

Alternatively, type one or more keywords, such as the following, into a search engine:

Alien	Astronomy
Astrophysics	Extraterrestrial
Mars	Observatory
Planet	Space
Space exploration	Star

Watch Out!
Scan downloaded files for viruses before you open them, especially if they are not from a trusted source such as NASA. Most anti-virus software can be set to scan downloaded files automatically.

HOBBIES AND LEISURE

HOW TO: SEARCH FOR EXTRA-TERRESTRIAL LIFE

SETI@home (http://setiathome.ssl.berkeley.edu) uses millions of home PCs to search radio telescope data for unusual signals. To volunteer, you need to download a piece of software and a chunk of data onto your PC. The software runs when your PC is idle – generating a colourful graph that makes a great screensaver. The program then sends the results over the Internet to a research institution for evaluation, and downloads another piece of data.

Your PC needs at least 32Mb of RAM to run the software. To check this, go to your **Start** menu, right-click on **My Computer**, and select **Properties**.

WATCH SPACE FOOTAGE

The Apollo Project Archive (www.apolloarchive.com) has the best collection of images, sounds and video from the historic Apollo lunar landings. Video quality is better on the later missions, but all the clips are fun to watch.
1. Click **Apollo Multimedia** in the Table of Contents, and scroll through the archive.
2. Scroll down to the Apollo 11 section and click on the link for Neil Armstrong stepping onto the Moon's surface.
3. Windows Media Player will open up and the video will play – at first, only in small chunks at a time. This is because the Media Player is playing the video faster than your computer can download it. But after your computer has fully downloaded the video, you will be able to replay it in its entirety.

1 Go to SETI (http://setiathome.ssl.berkeley.edu). Click on **Download SETI@home**. From the next page, click on the Windows version of the program. Scroll down and click on **Download**.

2 Follow the on-screen instructions to download the installation program to your PC, then double-click the program icon on your desktop to install the software.

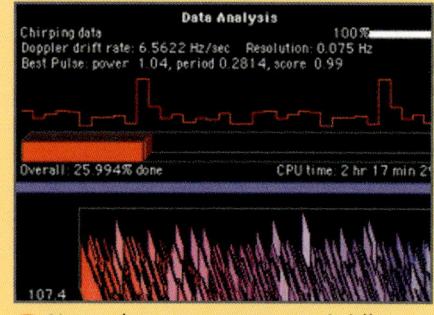

3 Now when your computer is idle, the SETI screensaver will start up, and begin analysing your chunk of data on-screen. Perhaps the first signs of alien life will be found by your computer.

Did You Know?

Apollo 13 astronaut Jack Swigert never said 'Houston, we have a problem'. In fact, the words he spoke were: 'Okay Houston, we've had a problem here'. Read NASA's full transcript of the mission at www.hq.nasa.gov/office/pao/History/Timeline/apollo13chron.html.

A dream come true

The European Space Agency is recruiting for missions taking place over the next few years. Visit **www.esa.int** and click **Frequently Asked Questions**. Scroll down to **How can I become an astronaut?** to see the selection requirements. You need to be a citizen of one of the ESA nations.

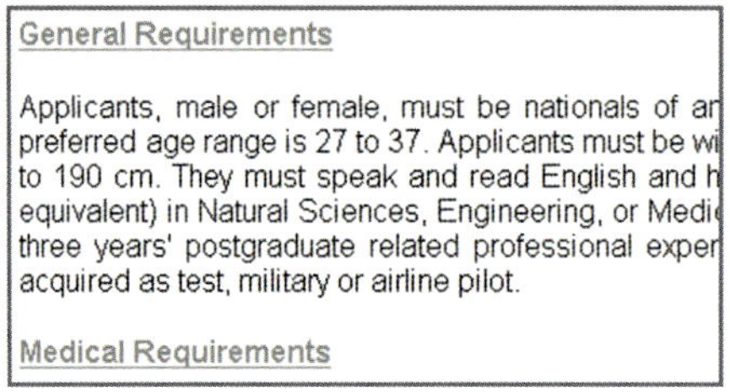

General Requirements

Applicants, male or female, must be nationals of an preferred age range is 27 to 37. Applicants must be wi to 190 cm. They must speak and read English and h equivalent) in Natural Sciences, Engineering, or Medic three years' postgraduate related professional exper acquired as test, military or airline pilot.

Medical Requirements

SEE ALSO
- **Download from the Web** – page 86
- **Explore the natural world** – page 156
- **Keep the children entertained** – page 174

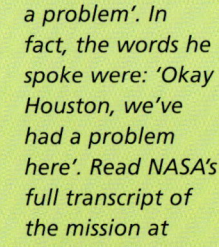

EXPLORE THE WEB

Take a virtual tour

Explore the world **from the comfort** of your own home

A virtual tour is a feature on a Web site that attempts to recreate the movement and interactivity of the real world on your computer screen. It uses sounds, pictures, maps, videos, animation and 3D images to give you 'virtual experiences' that would be far less accessible in real life – such as viewing the world's great art treasures, walking around the US Capitol building in Washington or exploring a Roman fortress.

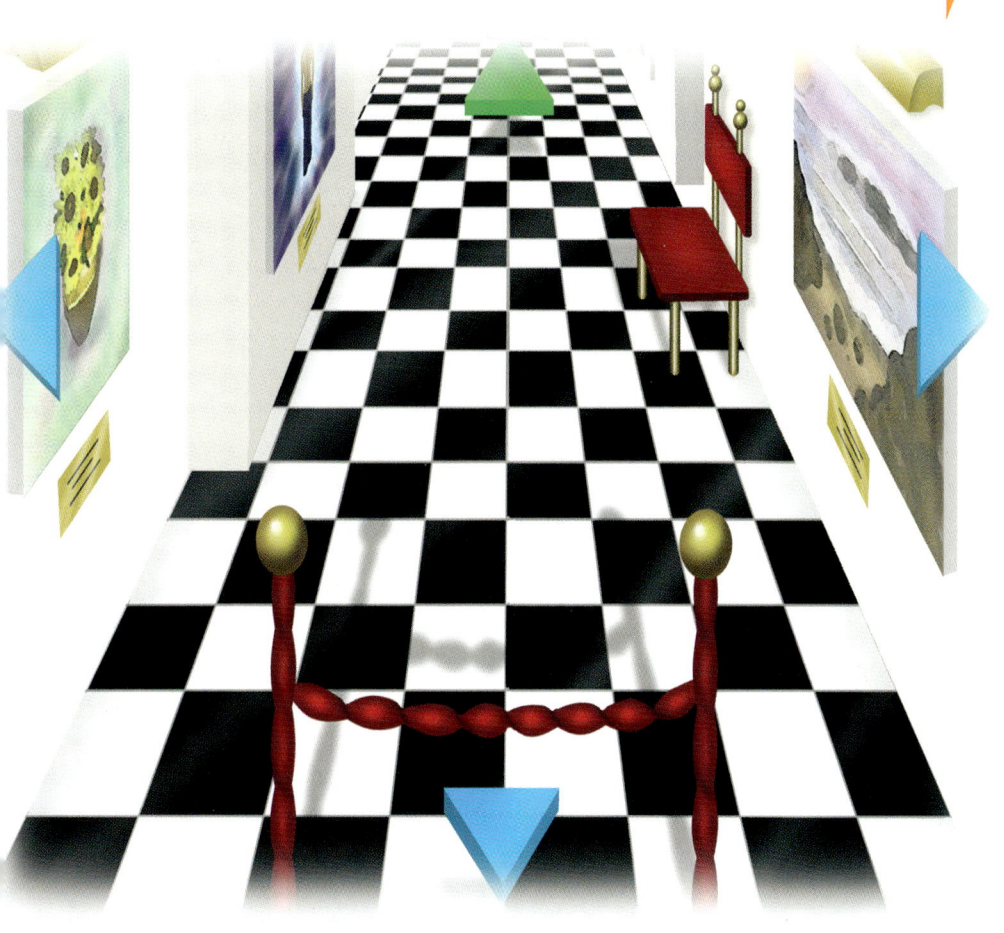

How it all works

Virtual tour sites often use video clips or panoramic images that you can 'walk' around. Some real estate agents, for example, offer virtual tours of properties for sale. These can show you the inside of a house, allowing you to use on-screen buttons to rotate your view.

Many travel sites include these virtual panoramas. To find them, search under your destination and add the word 'panorama' – for example, 'Rome panorama'.

More complex virtual tour sites include impressively realistic 3D imagery. You can walk around a 3D model of the Sydney Opera House and other famous buildings at The Great Buildings Collection (**www.greatbuildings.com**).

Most virtual tours can be viewed using your usual Internet browser, but some sites require you to download additional software.

Watch Out!

Different sites use different programs to create 3D images. This means that you cannot download one single program to view them all. Each site will provide a link to the software you require.

145

HOBBIES AND LEISURE

THE BEST SITES

Gallery tour
The Louvre (www.louvre.fr)
Take a closer look at great works of art, such as the *Mona Lisa*. Select **English** as your language, then click **Virtual Tour** and select a gallery. You'll see a list of rooms. Click the **Q** icon next to each room to see a 360-degree panorama. You need QuickTime to view the rooms. Some rooms also have a high-resolution panorama (indicated by a large 'Q'), which offers a better quality picture.

New York's Museum of Modern Art (**www.moma.org**) lets you tour an image gallery with audio commentary. Click **Collection**, then choose a department, such as **Painting and Sculpture**, to open a thumbnail gallery. Click on one of these miniature images to see a larger version and hear the accompanying commentary.

Best collection of links
Ipix (www.ipix.com) is the company that makes the software used to view most 360-degree panoramic images on the Web. Click **Gallery** for links to various panorama sites. Look under 'Transportation' for links to tours around a Boeing 777 plane or Julio Iglesias's private jet. Look under 'Events' for a link to the official site of the British Open golf championship (**www.opengolf.com**), with a video fly-by of every hole at St Andrews.

Best use of the Internet
EarthCam (www.earthcam.com) combines panoramic images with Web cams to bring you live-action video or still panoramic images which are updated every 60 seconds. Click **N.Y.C.** to wander around New York's Times Square and take your choice of nine cameras showing live still, panoramic and video images.

The EarthCam site also has an extensive directory of Web-cam links. You can browse through categories such as 'Traffic Cams', 'Space & Science Cams' or 'Metro Cams', featuring views of major cities around the world.

SEARCH IT YOURSELF
Click **Travel** at directory site About.com (**www.about.com**) for links to hundreds of travel sites. You can also use the site's internal search engine to find what you want. Searching under 'virtual south america' locates the Virtual Tour of South America, starting at Angel Falls, Venezuela.

Troubleshooting virtual tours
Some virtual tours rely on a mini-program called Java, which works as part of your Web browser. To check that Java is functioning correctly, go to the World Wide Web Test Pattern (**www.uark.edu/~wrg**), click on **Compliance Tests** and then on **applet support**. If your browser supports Java, there will be a brief pause and you will see a scrolling banner. If you cannot see the banner, you need to upgrade your browser. Contact Microsoft (**www.microsoft.com/downloads**) to update to the latest version of Internet Explorer.

Did You Know?
You can follow a yellow cab around New York City by going to the 'Cab-Cam' at **www.ny-taxi.com**. The broadcast is live between 9 am and 5 pm New York time, or about 11 pm to 7 am Sydney time (depending on the time of year).

EXPLORE THE WEB

CASE STUDY

Like many children, George and Grace were fascinated by the mysteries of ancient Egypt. Their father Mark was happy to encourage them and decided to spend some time looking for Web sites on the subject.

'I wanted to find something fun, interactive and educational, so I tried looking for a virtual tour. Once I found one, it took an hour or so to get all the right software, but I have since found a lot of other tours which use the same programs, so I think it was worth it.'

Mark started his search at About.com (**www.about.com**). 'I like the way they check the sites out first.'

1 Mark entered 'educational virtual tour Egypt' into the search box. One of the results was a which specialised in home schooling.

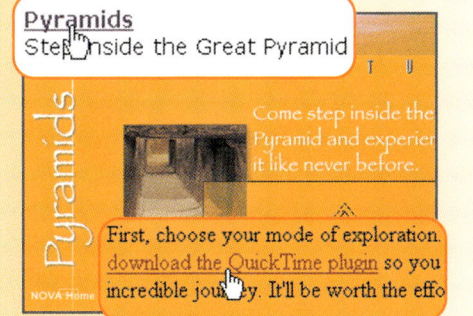

2 One of the tours on offer was a trip around a pyramid. The introductory text stated that the tour required the free QuickTime plug-in, so Mark clicked the link to go to the QuickTime site.

3 On the QuickTime site, Mark chose to download the PC version of the plug-in and spent an hour downloading the program, following the on-screen instructions to install it.

4 Returning to the pyramid site, Mark then downloaded the tour itself, which took about ten minutes. The tour was made up of a series of QuickTime virtual reality pictures.

5 Mark and his children used the mouse and keyboard to rotate the images and move through the passageways and chambers of the pyramid. George and Grace loved it.

QuickTime links

The QuickTime Web site (**www.apple.com/quicktime**) has links to many exciting sites that use Quicktime technology. Click on **Movie Trailers** for the latest movie previews, or try **What's On** for games, music or a range of virtual reality pictures of places such as New York City and Mt Everest. You could also try Neovisioni (**www.neovisioni.com**), which offers great panoramic views from high in the European Alps: click on **Gallery** and then **cubic qtvr**.

Jargon Buster!

Plug-in A mini-program, which is added to your Web browser, to open and run certain files, such as 3D images.

HOBBIES AND LEISURE

Tune into television

Find out **everything about TV** from your computer

Whatever TV programs you like, you can often use the Web to catch up on the latest plot-lines, find out the time and channel of a specific episode, or get behind-the-scenes information. You can also download shows to watch on your computer – though the size and quality of video images on the Internet is poor. Many programs, such as 'reality' TV shows, now have accompanying on-line content, including extra material not broadcast on TV, and round-the-clock coverage of events.

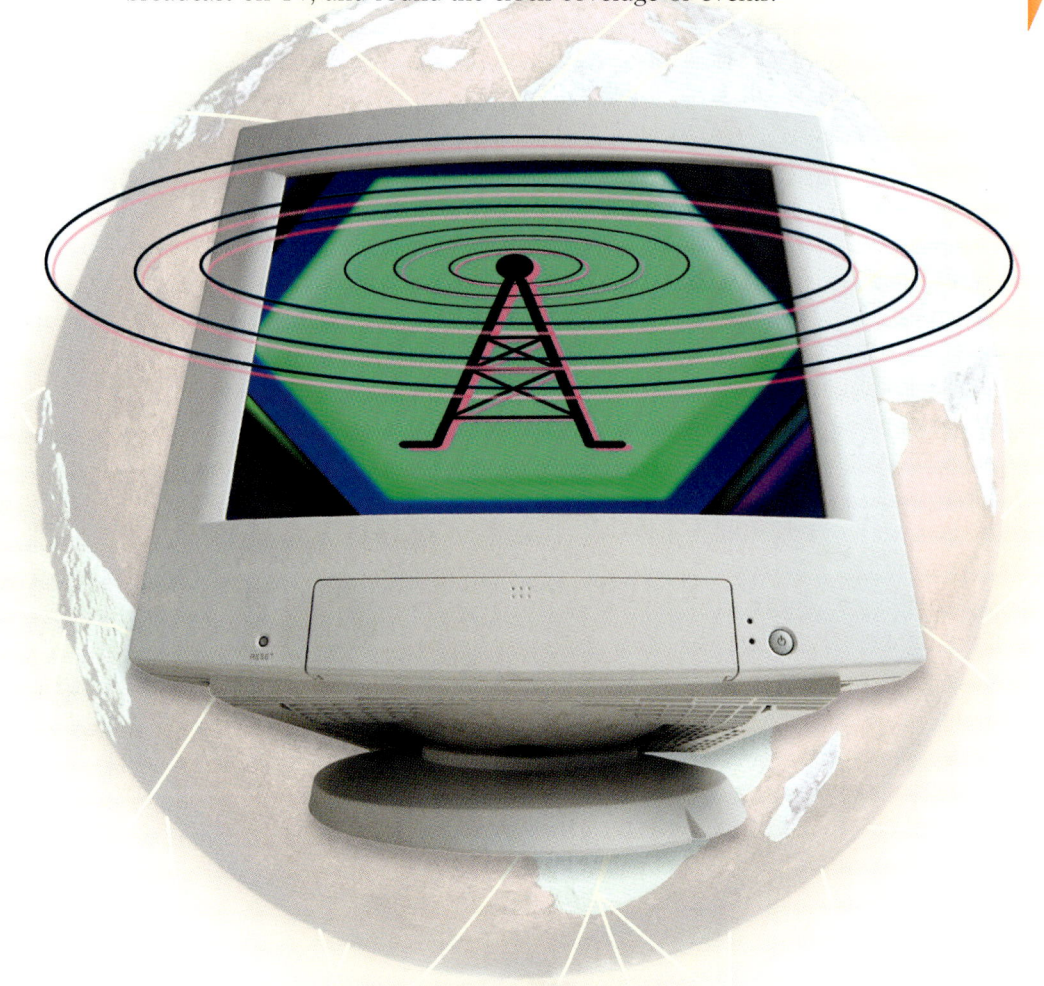

Desktop TV
You can watch a variety of live TV and Web broadcasts on your computer. You can download old series, watch live TV over the Internet or record cable programs and play them back later.

Web cams
You can also watch live footage from cameras positioned in all sorts of places around the world, from ski slopes to the Elvis wedding chapel in Los Angeles. These cameras are known as Web-cams.

The right gear
In order to watch TV or video delivered over the Internet, you must have up-to-date equipment and a fast connection. While it is possible to watch brief news broadcasts from sites such as the ABC or CNN using only a dial-up connection, the pictures will often be jerky and out of synchronisation with the sound. For satisfactory results you need a broadband link to the Internet (Cable or ADSL), a computer with a Pentium III processor or its equivalent, and a high-speed video card. See *Are you Net ready?*, page 14, and *Other ways to connect*, page 88.

EXPLORE THE WEB

PRIME-TIME SITES

Where to start
TV Show (www.tvshow.com)
This site offers schedules from almost every country in the world, and links to sites about every aspect of TV programs, news, stations and personalities, as well as sites about TV production (find out how to sell a TV script) and technology (discover how your TV works or how to fix your VCR).

TV listings
Yahoo! (http://au.tv.yahoo.com/tv)
At the Yahoo! site you can enter details of where you live in Australia, the date and time of day, and receive a listing of programs on all TV channels. For daily listings of New Zealand TV, go to NZoom.com (**http://ontv.nzoom.com/schedules**). If a TV channel has its own Web site, you may be able to find background information and articles about individual programs.

Great Web-cams
Discovery Channel (http://dsc.discovery.com/cams/cams.html)
The Discovery Channel presents a variety of Web-cams, showing live views of locations around the world and beyond. You can look in on sharks and gorillas in their natural surroundings, an active volcano in central Mexico, or even view the surface of the Sun.

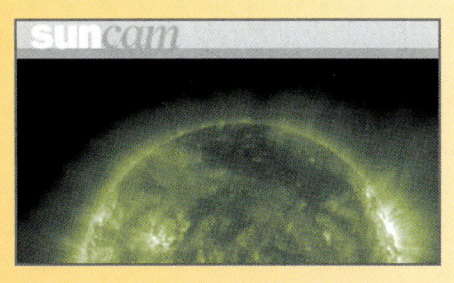

Hot gossip
TV Week (www.tvweek.com.au)
Catch up with what's happening on Australian television at this on-line version of the popular newsstand magazine. You can revel in all the gossip about stars and shows, or take part in contests and polls, with the chance to win products and tickets. Or chat about TV with fellow enthusiasts at the .auTV Forums (**www.dolphinx.org/autv**).

Classic TV
LikeTelevision (www.liketelevision.com)
This subscription site has hundreds of classic TV shows, commercials, cartoons, movies and music videos for you to watch on your PC.

All you need to do is install RealPlayer to watch shows such as *Bonanza*, *Bugs Bunny* or *Superman*, or movies featuring stars like Charlie Chaplin.

SEARCH IT YOURSELF
For links to TV-related job opportunities, chatrooms, broadcasters' addresses, and fan pages of virtually every show ever made, from *I Love Lucy* to *Bob the Builder*, try TV Show (**www.tvshow.com**) or epguides.com (**www.epguides.com**), which has episode lists for over 1800 TV shows (mostly from the USA).

Most TV stations, popular shows and networks maintain their own sites. You can quickly find most of these by entering their name into a search engine. This will work with many TV stars as well. Or, if you are really in a hurry, try simply entering the name of the show or person as a basic Web address, for example 'www.baywatch.com'. If you are looking for sites dedicated to the television shows of the past, try the links at TV Cream **http://TV.cream.org**) and Yesterdayland (**www.yesterdayland.com**).

Time Saver!
If you use a TV monitor service, you can set it to send you several mentions of your keyword at once, rather than individually. Otherwise, you may receive an almost constant flow of e-mail.

HOBBIES AND LEISURE

RealOne Player
A program that plays picture, sound and video files, RealOne Player is also used by Internet radio and live Web-casts. You can download a free version from the Real.com Web site (**www.real.com.au**).

HOW TO: DOWNLOAD REALONE PLAYER

1 Go to the Real.com Web site (**www.real.com.au**) and click on **Click Here to Download**, above the icon for the 'realONE Player'.

2 In the next window you are invited to try the Premium Player for 14 days (after which you have to pay for it). Find the link for the **Free RealOne Player**, and click on this instead.

3 Another window opens, in which you again have to click **Download the Free RealOne Player Only**. Then choose the download location nearest to you to ensure the best connection.

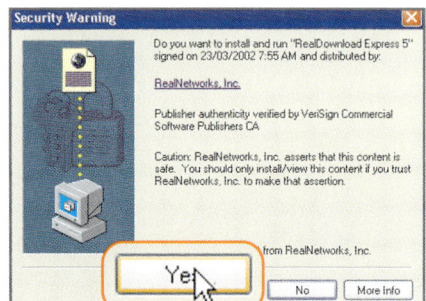

4 Give your approval to the security certificate that appears and wait for the download to start. If it does not start automatically, you can click on a link that will set it in motion manually.

5 Wait until the download program has installed the player to your PC. Once it has finished, the player is ready to use. You can look for it under **All Programs** in your **Start** menu.

EXPLORE THE WEB

HOW TO: WATCH TELEVISION ON-LINE

1 Go to a site that offers TV and movies on-line, such as LikeTelevision (**www.liketelevision.com**). Click on **LikeTelevision** in the centre of the homepage.

2 You first need to sign up to the site. Click **Subscribe**, and select the offer that interests you (note that prices are in US $). Fill out the form, including your credit card details, and submit it.

3 Go to the list at the top of the page, and click on **Classic TV**. In the next page that opens, choose the series you want to watch – for example, **The Beverly Hillbillies**.

4 A list of episodes will now come up, each with a description. Click on the episode you want to watch.

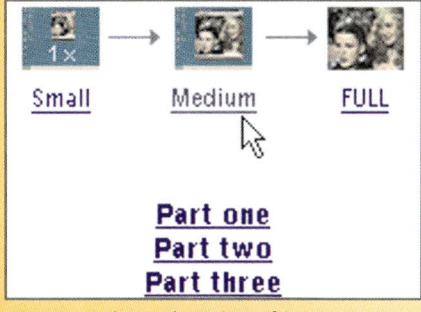

5 Now select what size of image you want to watch – 'Small', 'Medium' or 'FULL' screen size. Choosing a larger screen size will reduce the quality of the image.

6 To watch your program, click on **Part one**. When that section has finished, click on **Part two** and so on.

Software requirements

When you enter a TV or movie site, the first thing you should check is what software you need to view its material. Some items may be configured to utilise the in-built Windows Media Player, but others may be in RealPlayer or QuickTime format, with special additional plug-ins required, which you'll have to download: see *Software on the Web*, page 84, and *Download from the Web*, page 86.

iMac

Apple Macs come loaded with an alternative to RealPlayer, called QuickTime. But some sites may still require you to have RealPlayer. You can download a Mac version of the program from the RealPlayer site.

SEE ALSO
- **Listen to the radio** – *page 152*
- **Access showbiz news** – *page 164*
- **Buy a book, CD or video** – *page 201*

151

Listen to the radio

Use your PC to **tune into Internet stations**

You might think listening to the radio using a computer is unnecessary if you already own a radio. But Internet radio offers far more than the broadcasts available on a standard set. With the Internet, you can listen to diverse and stimulating broadcasts from all around the world. If you are living away from home, or have family or friends in other countries, it's easy to keep in touch with 'local' news. There are also special-interest Internet stations covering music or subjects that you cannot receive on a standard radio.

What do I need?
Most radio sites on the Web broadcast either for the RealOne Player or for the Windows Media Player. It's a good idea to make sure both are installed on your computer before you go looking for Web-casts. If you are running Windows 98 or Windows XP, you will already have Windows Media Player installed. If you have an older operating system, you may have to download the free Media Player from Microsoft's Web site: (**www.microsoft.com/windows/windowsmedia/download**). For instructions on downloading the free RealOne Player, see page 150. You can also choose a more sophisticated version for a small fee.

How do I listen?
To listen to a radio station, you need to browse the Web and click on a suitable link. This opens up RealOne Player or Windows Media Player, which starts playing the station through your computer's speakers.

What is available?
Many Internet radio stations exist only on-line. Type 'Internet radio' into your search engine to locate some of the many radio stations around the world that you can listen to on your PC.

EXPLORE THE WEB

RADIO SITES

Local stations
There are many Australian and New Zealand Internet radio stations, and new ones appear as rapidly as some existing ones close down. There is no definitive list of links to the current crop, so you will need to search to locate them all. Try international directories, such as Live Radio on the Internet (www.live-radio.net) or VirtualTuner (www.virtualtuner.com), as well as local sites, such as Median Strip (www.medianstrip.com).

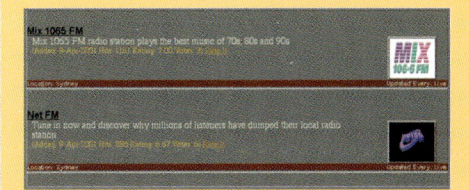

Ultimate cool
Anetstation (www.anetstation.com)
One of the more unusual Internet radio stations is run from the US McMurdo base in Antarctica. The station prides itself on broadcasting non-commercial music and has a top rating for playback quality. The site also contains a wealth of information about Antarctica.

Station listings
VirtualTuner (www.virtualtuner.com)
This site boasts that it provides links to over 6000 on-line radio sites. One particularly useful feature offered by VirtualTuner is the listing of sites by various criteria, such as by Musical Genres, Country, Player type, Language and Bandwidth. It is therefore easy to track down only those stations that use RealPlayer, for example, or those that broadcast just classical music or blues.

Unusual radio site
Book Radio (www.bookradio.com)
Book Radio is not a radio station, in the conventional sense, but it shows what can be achieved using the idea of Web-casting sounds. The site is dedicated to all things book-related, and includes extracts from books, literary discussions, and interviews with authors. Book Radio is regularly updated with feature Web-casts on the latest works of fact and fiction.

★ STAR SITE
Live Radio on the Internet (www.live-radio.net)
This popular UK site has one of the largest directories of links to radio stations broadcasting live on the Internet throughout the world. Links are monitored and updated daily, so you can be confident that you'll be able to hear all the stations listed.

The many thousands of national and international radio stations that broadcast over the Internet are grouped by world region, with each area having its own homepage, making it easy to find the country whose stations you are interested in.

Read through the Information Page before you start, then click on a world area, such as 'US Section', select a State, and then browse through the available stations, such as Beethoven.com, which broadcasts from Connecticut. When you have found a station of interest, click on the **Live Feed** button to start listening to the broadcast on your computer.

Did You Know?
You can listen to Internet radio by selecting stations from Web directories, but it's better to listen directly from their homepages, where you'll find additional news and information.

153

HOBBIES AND LEISURE

HOW TO: TUNE IN TO INTERNET RADIO STATIONS

Once you have installed RealOne Player, you can use its own built-in listings to find a radio station. Another way to find stations is to use a search directory. Here are two routes to some good music.

1 First make sure you are on-line, then open the RealOne Player and select the **Radio** icon on the lower menu bar.

2 Wait a few moments, then select the type of music you like from the list that appears. In this example, we have selected **World** music.

3 A new list appears, in which we have chosen **2FM** in Dublin, which plays 'easy-listening' music.

4 Wait while RealOne connects to the station. If there is a problem, contact your ISP to ask if you should use a 'proxy', though this is rarely the case.

5 After connecting, the radio will start playing. If you don't have a fast Internet connection you may wish to click the **Pause** or **Stop** buttons if you need to do other things on the Internet.

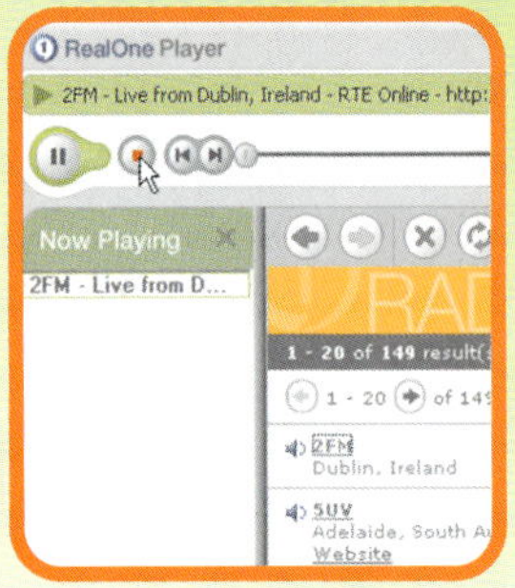

1 Go to Google and type search terms, like 'Dublin Internet radio' in the search box. Then click **Google Search**.

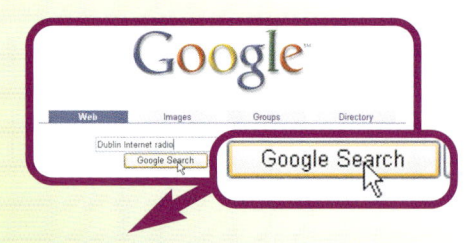

2 Click on **European Live Internet Radio Stations** and bookmark this link if you think you'll want to return to it.

3 On the next page, click on the link to **2FM** in Dublin (or any other station you fancy).

4 On the 2FM Web site, find the **Listen Here** button and click on it. This will activate RealOne, which will automatically open and play in its own sub-window.

154

EXPLORE THE WEB

HOW TO: ORGANISE STATIONS IN REALPLAYER

There are so many radio stations available on the Web that you will probably want to create a 'favourites' list. This is easy with RealOne Player. It is a bit like setting the pre-tuned stations on your car radio.

1 To add any station to your list of Favourites in RealOne Player, simply right-click on the station's name and select **Add to Favourites**.

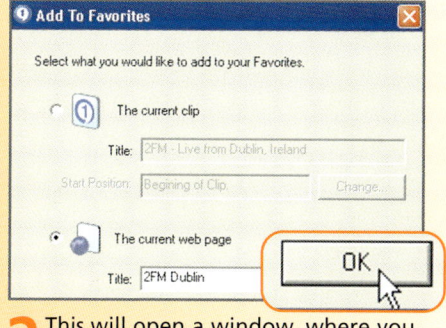

2 This will open a window, where you can give the radio station a title if one does not appear automatically. Then click **OK**.

3 When you want to return to a particular station, click on the Favourites icon (shaped like a heart), and select the station you want from the pull-down menu.

4 You can arrange your Favourites by clicking the Favourites icon and selecting **Manage Favourites**. This allows you to create folders, change station names or delete them totally.

DIGITAL RADIO

Take care not to confuse Internet radio, which is broadcast digitally via the Web, and digital radio, which is transmitted through the atmosphere like ordinary analogue radio. Digital radio is gradually replacing analogue radio around the world and there are plans to introduce the service in Australia and New Zealand in the near future.

Digital radio transmits very high quality audio – said to approach the standard achieved by domestic CD players. But you will need a special receiver to pick up the signal, or a digital radio tuner card for your PC.

Other on-line radio features

Any sounds that can be broadcast over the airwaves can be made available on-line. This means speeches, news reports and even events from space can be listened to as Internet radio broadcasts. Many radio sites have live Web-cam feeds showing the broadcast in action.

Did You Know?

While some Webcasts are live – that is, transmitted in real time – some are archived. Live and archived material are normally clearly marked and differentiated.

SEE ALSO
- **Take a virtual tour** – page 145
- **Tune into television** – page 148
- **Buy a book, CD or video** – page 201

155

HOBBIES AND LEISURE

Explore the natural world

Access **unique** nature **images** and **information**

The Internet can take you to parts of the natural world, such as the inside of a beehive or the crater of a volcano, that are inaccessible to most people. It also provides information and research findings on plants and animals from around the world, and facts about ecological issues. And, if you're interested in wildlife, there are virtual zoos at which you can learn about animals and observe them through live Web-cam images.

Animals
The Internet can provide advice on keeping animals as pets. You can even visit a Web-cam of an anthill at London's Natural History Museum site (**http://antcam.nhm.ac.uk**) – although like many such sites, it allows only a few visitors (generally up to ten) on at a time.

Plants
The Internet is also full of specialist factual information, such as the scientific (Latin) names of plants and flowers. You can get instant access to extensive databases and photos.

The environment
You can find debate on topics such as global warming, and explanations of natural phenomena, such as the Northern Lights (aurora borealis). Take a look at Virtual Finland (**http://virtual.finland.fi/finfo/english/aurora_borealis.html**).

EXPLORE THE WEB

NATURE SITES

Research and exploration

National Geographic (www.nationalgeographic.com)
This site is designed to accompany the *National Geographic* magazine and TV channel. Under 'Guides', click on **Adventure** to join a team of explorers on a virtual trek through the Congo Basin. You can read their field notes and view their photographs as they go.

Or you can watch Web-casts of intrepid explorers reporting back to the National Geographic Society. The archive of Web-casts includes lectures on subjects such as *The Inca Mummies of the Andes*, but look out for new lectures which are broadcast live on the site.

Insect life

Australian Insect Common Names (www.ento.csiro.au/aicn)
You don't need to go any further than your own back garden to explore the amazing world of insects. Identification is a constant problem for amateur naturalists, so the CSIRO's insect name site is particularly welcome. Here, you can look up insects by either their common or scientific names.

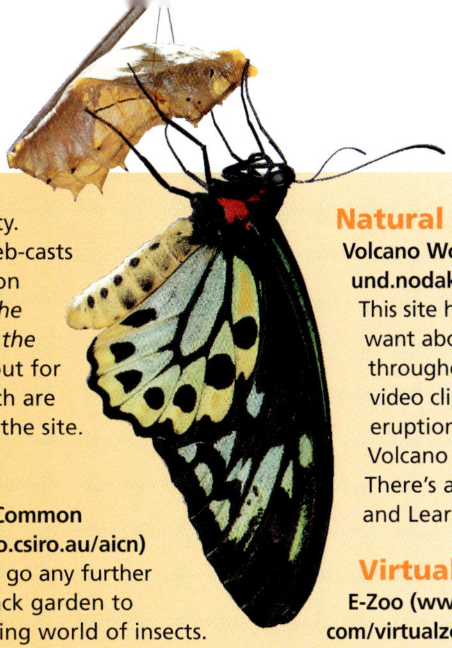

Natural phenomena

Volcano World (http://volcano.und.nodak.edu/vw.html)
This site has all you could want about volcanoes throughout the world, including video clips, links to current eruptions, and a 'Today in Volcano History' feature. There's also a useful 'Teaching and Learning' section.

Virtual zoo

E-Zoo (www.sandiegozoo.com/virtualzoo/homepage.html)
San Diego Zoo offers on-line users a wealth of resources. You can visit the polar bear and panda enclosures live via Web-cams, and view a range of videos showing major events in the lives of the zoo's inhabitants. There are also photographs and virtual tours to the Ituri Forest and the Heart of Africa.

If you enjoy animal Web-cams, pay a visit to WebCam Central (**www.camcentral.com**) and navigate their Aquariums and Zoos page: click on **CategoryCam** and then select **Aquariums & Zoos** from the list of categories. You will find links to cameras trained on everything from frogs to gorillas.

CASE STUDY

Kevin found planning his weekend birdwatching trips was much easier once he began accessing up-to-date information on the Internet. Using sites such as Birdwatching Australia (**www.ausbird.com**) and the Australian Bird Study Association (**www.absa.asn.au**), he could monitor the latest bird news. He could also provide news of his own sightings to the Atlas of Australian Birds (**www.birdsaustralia.com.au/atlas/index.html**).

Kevin is particularly interested in parrots, and is a member of the Birds Australia Parrot Association (**www.tasweb.com.au/bapa**). One of his greatest ambitions is to see a specimen of the world's largest parrot – the kakapo of New Zealand – in the wild. Having read about these unique birds on the Kakapo Recovery Program Web site (**www.kakaporecovery.org.nz**), Kevin has arranged a trip to remote Stewart Island where wild specimens are still thought to survive.

Problem Solver!

Some interactive museum sites or Web-cams require special software. The site should make it clear if you need particular software, such as QuickTime (see page 87) – and provide a direct link to a site where you can download it.

HOBBIES AND LEISURE

UNIQUE NAMES
A major difficulty with any on-line research is finding search terms that will turn up only the pages you want. With plants and animals, however, the fact that each species has a unique Latin name makes searching more predictable.

CASE STUDY

The research illustrated here had its origins in early summer, when Linda Harris was walking with friends in the Snowy Mountains. Climbing the hill above Dead Horse Gap, they came across a patch of beautiful blue flowers in the lee of a boulder.

Linda took some photos and was keen to identify the plants when she got home after her holiday. She hoped to be able to use these flowers to brighten up her own garden, if they would grow at a lower altitude, and if she could find somewhere to buy them. But first she had to be able to give them a name.

1 Linda first searched Yahoo! (**http://au.yahoo.com**) using the words 'snowy mountains flowers'. She was rewarded with a page of photos, where she recognised the flower she had seen.

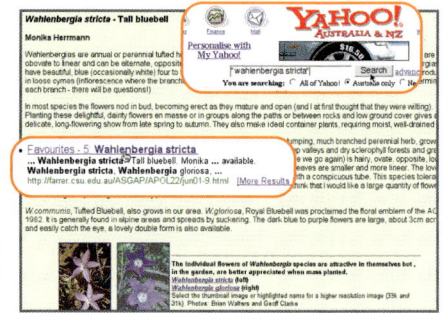

2 Once she knew the plant's scientific name, Linda was able to target her search, and she soon turned up a page that gave detailed information about the species and a clearer photo.

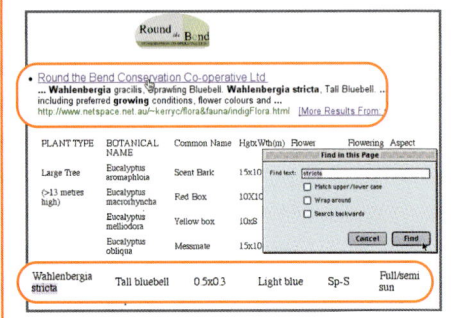

3 Linda has many native plants in her garden and she wondered whether the plant – a type of bluebell – would grow in her area. Another search found a site confirming that it would.

4 Linda then searched the Internet to find a nursery that stocked the bluebell. Although she found several that did, none was in her area. She then thought about buying seeds instead.

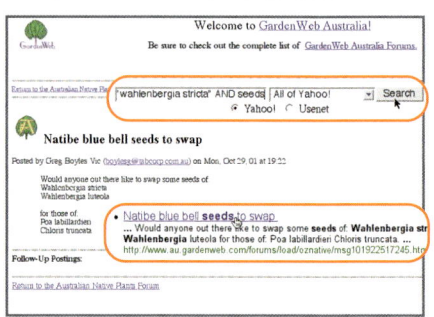

5 Linda's next search combined the plant's name with 'seeds'. This failed to locate any retailers, but did turn up a grower who was advertising to swap seeds. She'll ask if he'll sell her a few.

Search terms

It is always very important to take care with your spelling when entering search terms. This is particularly the case with the Latin names for plants and animals, most of which will be unfamiliar. If you don't get any results from a search, double-check to be sure that you have the correct spelling.

SEE ALSO
- Take a virtual tour – page 145
- Support a good cause – page 206
- Enjoy the great outdoors – page 225

EXPLORE THE WEB

Trace your family's past

Use the Internet to **find out** about your **family history**

The Internet adds a whole new dimension to family history research. Information resources, such as census data and other public records, are accessible over the Internet, minimising the time you spend tracking down resources. The Internet also makes it easier for you to share information with family members, link up with fellow researchers, track down individuals, and then publish your findings.

Genealogical societies
Organisations such as the Society of Australian Genealogists (**www.sag.org.au**) and the New Zealand Society of Genealogists (**www.genealogy.org.nz**) can help you in your search. They provide a range of resources, such as collections of research materials and databases, as well as guidance on family history research. Membership will also put you in touch with other enthusiasts.

Software
Family history software enables users to scan in pictures, record information, create Web sites and construct family trees in several different ways. Some of the best software available is Family Origins (**www.familyorigins.com**), Family Tree Maker (**www.genealogy.com**) and Genealogy for Windows (**www.deltadrive.co.uk**). For reviews of genealogy programs, go to the Genealogical Software Report Card (**www.mumford.ca/reportcard**).

Discussion groups
To exchange information, or ask others for help, try a newsgroup such as **alt.genealogy** or an e-mail-based discussion list that covers family trees, surnames or genealogy. Hundreds of discussion groups are devoted to these subjects.

Watch Out!
Don't assume your favourite family history Web resource has a record of everyone. Always use two or three different sites, and compare their results.

HOBBIES AND LEISURE

WHERE TO START

Library resources

Family history research is very popular in Australia and New Zealand, and most libraries – from national to local – offer a range of resources. Make your first port of call the National Library of Australia (**www.nla.gov.au/oz/genelist.html**) or the National Library of New Zealand (**www.natlib.govt.nz/en/collections/general/family.html**).

In Australia, most state libraries also offer valuable resources, such as the State Library of NSW's Family History Service (**www.slnsw.gov.au/family**) and the State Library of Victoria's Genealogy Centre (**www.statelibrary.vic.gov.au/slv/genealogy**).

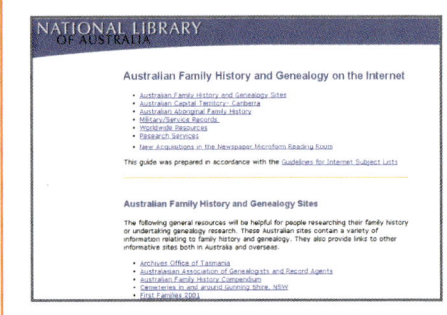

Genealogy resources

Cyndi's List (www.cyndislist.com)
Don't be put off by its informal name – Cyndi's List is an enormous Web site with more than 120,000 links to other sites. It is an excellent site to bookmark as a main research source.

If you are particularly interested in genealogy, you might want to make Cyndi's List your homepage. The resources listed at the site span the entire globe and cover all kinds of information, from census details to royal lineages, ships' passenger lists and military records. There is also a comprehensive set of Australian and New Zealand links. Scroll down the site's main page and click on **Australia & New Zealand**, or simply go to **www.cyndislist.com/austnz.htm**.

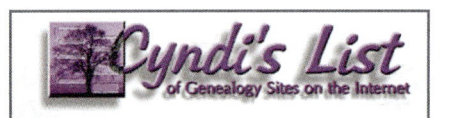

Software links

Louis Kessler's Genealogical Program Links (www.lkessler.com/gplinks.shtml)
Louis Kessler is a Canadian genealogy enthusiast, who has gathered together links to a wide range of software resources. The list covers commercial, shareware and free applications for Windows, Mac, some handheld PDAs (Personal Digital Assistants) and other operating systems. There are links to the Web sites of the software creators, so you can find out more detailed information about the different programs. There are also links for back issues of genealogical periodicals as well as to newsgroups and mailing lists.

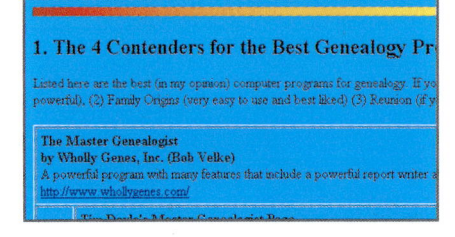

Britain and Ireland

GENUKI (www.genuki.org.uk)
For people of British or Irish descent, a good place to start is the Genealogical Information Service For the UK and Ireland (GENUKI). This site is run by volunteers as a virtual reference library to provide basic general information about family research in the British Isles, including record offices and surname lists. GENUKI provides comprehensive links to other significant Web sites which deal with British and Irish family history.

Time-saving links

When conducting a search for material on the Web, the first things to look for are up-to-date collections of links. Since most of the legwork has been done for you, a carefully compiled list of links can dramatically reduce the time you have to spend looking for information.

Lists compiled by experts also help to remove that nagging doubt that you might accidentally have missed some brilliant resource. A very useful list of miscellaneous genealogical information can be found at the Web site compiled by *Australian Family Tree Connections* magazine (**www.aftc.com.au**).

Problem Solver!

When searching by a person's name, don't use a directory, such as Yahoo!, which only looks through sites that it has already listed. Use a search engine such as Google, which looks through the entire Web.

EXPLORE THE WEB

HOW TO: USE FAMILY HISTORY SOFTWARE

There are hundreds of genealogical programs available, ranging from large (and sometimes expensive) commercial packages to more modest shareware or freeware offerings. If you want to try out one of the simpler programs to see if it suits your needs, go to the 'Software and Computers' page at Cyndi's List (www.cyndislist.com/software.htm), and browse through the descriptions that are given there. In the following example, we have used Ages!, a shareware program from DaubNET (www.daubnet.com/english.html).

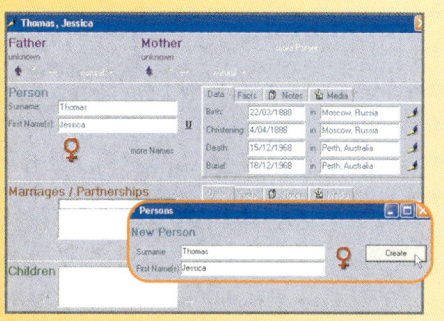

1 Download and install Ages!, then launch the program from your **Start** menu. From the **File** menu, choose **New** and enter a name in the 'Persons' box that appears. Click **Create**.

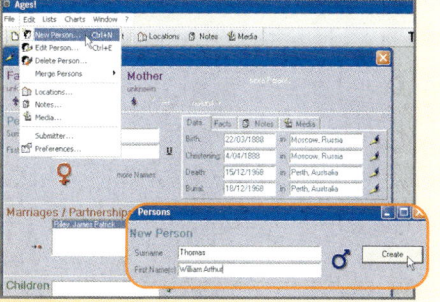

2 Fill in all the details requested. To create new entries, go to the **Edit** menu, choose **New Person**, and repeat the process to gradually build up a database of family members.

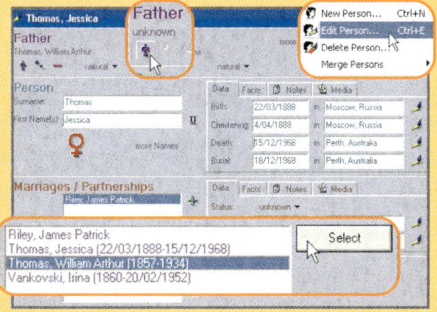

3 Every entry you create can be revised by going to the **Edit** menu and choosing **Edit Person**. In this way, if you add someone to your database, you can update the entries of all other family members to complete the 'tree'.

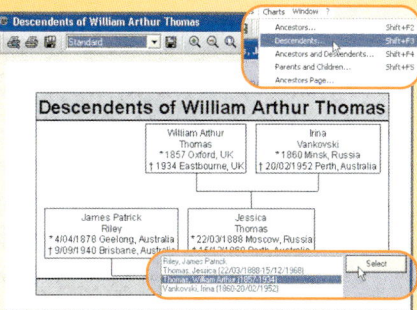

4 To review your family tree in chart form, go to the **Charts** menu and select one of the five options that appear. A chart will be displayed, which you can print out if you wish.

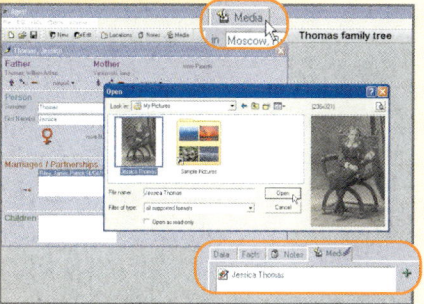

5 You can also include photographs and sound recordings in your database. Make sure they are saved in an appropriate format, then click on the **Media** tab, find the file you want, and click **Open**, then **OK**.

Try a newsgroup

The **alt.genealogy** newsgroup is the best place for answers to specific questions. Its members are enthusiasts, who are happy to offer answers to your queries. You can also try the newsgroup **soc.genealogy.britain,** which is specifically devoted to British genealogy.

Photographs and sound

For more details about preparing photographs and sound recordings for use on a computer, see pages 264–269 and 276–281. Whether you upload your sound and image files to the Web, or use them to enhance a database on your own PC, the processes are much the same.

161

HOBBIES AND LEISURE

SPECIALIST SOURCES

Indigenous Australians

Genealogical research is hard enough when written records have been kept of the major moments in a person's life – birth, marriage and death. When written records were never kept, and when oral records have been dispersed, the task of tracking down family members becomes almost impossible. This is the case for many Aboriginals.

Fortunately, there are a growing number of resources on the Web that can help with the task.

Start with the Family History Unit of the Australian Institute of Aboriginal and Torres Strait Islander Studies (**www.aiatsis.gov.au**). Also useful is the Aboriginal Genealogy & History Sources & References page (**www.standard.net.au/~jwilliams/native.htm**).

Maori family history

Maoris encounter many of the same problems as someone looking into Aboriginal family history. Yet again, however, there are resources on the Web that can help. To read about Whakapapa Maori (Maori Genealogy), go to **www.maaori.com/whakapapa**. Then begin your investigations at GENEoNZ's Maori Whakapapa Research page (**www.geocities.com/Heartland/Park/7572/mresear.htm**).

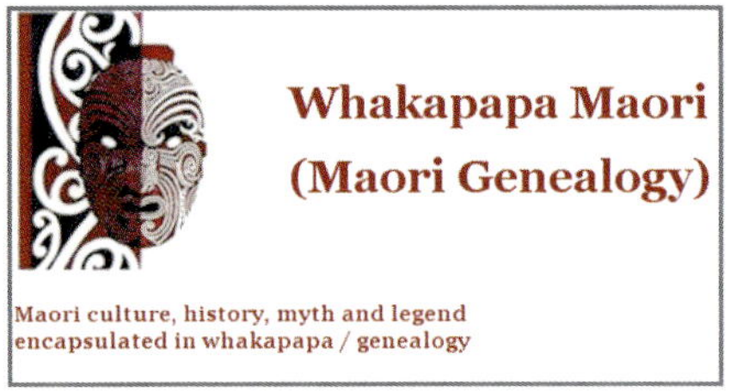

Whakapapa Maori (Maori Genealogy)
Maori culture, history, myth and legend encapsulated in whakapapa / genealogy

Military Service

Fortunately, in both Australia and New Zealand, meticulous records are kept of those who served their country in any of the armed forces, especially since the late 19th century. Australians researching their families' military history should start by visiting the Research and Family History page at the Australian War Memorial (**www.awm.gov.au/research**).

For information about relatives killed overseas, the Office of Australian War Graves (**www.dva.gov.au/commem/oawg/wargr.htm**) will be of interest. In New Zealand, the Commonwealth War Graves Commission (**www.mch.govt.nz/History/HPU/CWGC.htm**) has a lot of valuable information, as has Archives New Zealand (**www.archives.govt.nz/holdings/military_service.html**).

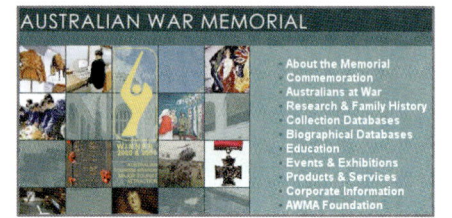

⛔ Watch Out!

When sending an e-mail to someone you have found on the Internet, be polite and don't write too much. They may not be the person you are looking for.

SEARCH IT YOURSELF

If you have a relative who died in action in the First or Second World Wars, you can search the records of the Commonwealth War Graves Commission to find out more.

1 Go to the Commonwealth War Graves Commission Web site (**www.cwgc.org**) where you will see the Debt of Honour Register.

2 Enter your relative's name, and his initials if you know them. Enter the year of his death, or if you are not sure, select either **First World War** or **Second World War**.

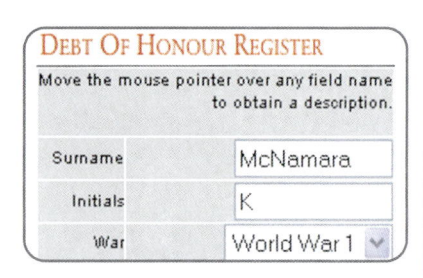

DEBT OF HONOUR REGISTER
Move the mouse pointer over any field name to obtain a description.

Surname	McNamara
Initials	K
War	World War 1

3 Enter the force your relative served in, and the nationality – of the force, not the person. For example, Australians who joined a UK regiment are listed under UK forces. Click **Search** to find records under your relative's name.

EXPLORE THE WEB

HOW TO: FIND RECORDS OF YOUR ANCESTORS

Because of its belief that ancestors can be baptised posthumously, The Church of Jesus Christ of Latter-Day Saints, also known as the Mormon Church, maintains one of the world's largest family history archives. The International Genealogical Index (IGI) has around 600 million entries dated between 1550 and 1875. Records cover baptisms, marriages and census information, as well as letters and family Bibles. The data is also available on CD-Rom.

1 Go to the Family Search Web site at **www.familysearch.org** and click on **Search for Ancestors**.

2 Enter your ancestor's first and last name and any other information you know, such as spouse's name, parents' names or country. This will help to narrow down your search.

3 If you know the date of an event such as your ancestor's birth, marriage or death, enter this. You can search within 2, 5, 10 or 20 years if you're not sure of the exact date.

4 Click **Search** to display the results. You will see a list of Web sites that could lead you to information on your ancestor. These sites may be official records, personal Web sites or message boards.

5 The Church also maintains over 3400 Family Research Centers worldwide, where you can access their extensive library resources. Click the link on the homepage to search for one near you.

Exchange information

You can buy genealogical software to help you share the findings of your family tree with other people. You should choose programs which can use the two most common family tree file formats: PAF (Personal Ancestral File), and GEDCOM (Genealogy Data Communications). Try **www.cyndislist.com/software.htm** for links to a range of software sites.

Did You Know?

*You can take genealogy classes on the Internet. Genealogy.com (**www.genealogy.com**) and Mother Hubbard's Cupboard (**www.rootsweb.com/~genclass**) offer a range of classes.*

SEE ALSO
- **Search the Internet** – *page 64*
- **Take part in a newsgroup** – *page 96*
- **Do some research** – *page 113*

163

Access showbiz news

Learn about your **favourite celebrity** on-line

The Web is a great place to find celebrity news, on-line interviews and fan club chat. It allows you to read and swap trivia and opinions on celebrities more widely and quickly than ever before. Fans have also taken the opportunity to create their own, unofficial Web sites devoted to their idols, and virtually every film, TV show and other entertainment event has at least one Web site of its own.

Specific fan sites
There are many fan sites where you can find out information about a particular celebrity – such as Janet Jackson (**http://miss-janet.com**). Some such sites are officially endorsed by the featured celebrity, but there are also unofficial sites, which offer a range of more unusual information and opinions.

General fan sites
There are also general fan sites – such as fansites.com (**www.fansites.com**) – which do not focus on any one individual.

The Internet can help you to find biographical details or a fan club address. Or to find out what the stars say about themselves, or what fashions they are wearing. You can read on-line interviews, and, for a more interactive experience, join one of the specialist fan discussions in a chatroom.

Latest news
The Internet can help you to keep up with the latest music, theatre, film and video releases so you can follow celebrity careers. Or read fanzines on-line and keep up to date with who was spotted where, and with whom.

EXPLORE THE WEB

CELEBRITY SITES

Guide to fan sites
Obsessive Fan Sites (www.ggower.com/fans)
This site provides links to hundreds of fan sites that are funny, strange and often completely ridiculous. It filters out unsuitable material and features the true fans' homages to their favourite personalities. Here you can find links to such obscure, fascinating sites as My Shrine to Kevin Costner, and The Star Wars Trilogy Bloopers Guide. This is a fanatic's guide to mistakes in all the *Star Wars* films, such as an early scene in *Return of the Jedi* where the film runs backwards for a split second.

Gossip
People News (www.peoplenews.com)
This site is filled with the very latest celebrity news and gossip. You can find out which celebrities were spotted where, when and with whom, and pick up tips on the favourite haunts of the rich and famous. The site is made up of over 1000 pages and is updated 20 times a day, making it a great place to keep yourself one step ahead of the gossip game.

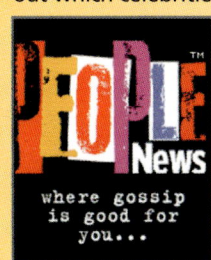

Music site
Oz Music Central Band Links (www.ozmusic-central.com.au/ozlinks.html)
There are vast numbers of fan sites on the Internet for almost every band or artist you can think of. The best places to start searching for information are sites that specialise in the particular area of music that interests you. This Oz Music Central page offers links to a huge number of Australian band sites.

Who starred in what?
The Internet Movie Database (www.us.imdb.com)
Go to this invaluable site – one of the best on the Web – to find out every film a specific actor, such as Humphrey Bogart or Jodie Foster, has appeared in. There are hundreds of entries, and more are being added all the time.

CELEBRITY INFORMATION

- To find photos of your favourite celebrity go to AltaVista (**http://au.altavista.com**), click on **Images** and key a name into the search box. AltaVista also has movie clips that you can view. Click on **Video Clips** and search using a name.
- For celebrity memorabilia such as autographs or clothing, try entering a name in the Universal Search box at AuctionWatch (**www.auctionwatch.com**), or use the specialist Startifacts site (**www.startifacts.com**).
- Celebrity merchandise such as books, videos and clothing is also available for purchase on the Internet at Celebrity Merchandise (**www.celebritymerch.com**).
- To join a fan club and get general celebrity news, gossip and reviews, go to Eonline (**www.eonline.com**) or Popstazz.co.uk (**www.popstazz.co.uk/fanclubs.htm**).
- To locate the official site of a particular celebrity, try searching with fansites.com (**www.fansites.com**) and Celebritybase.net (**www.celebritybase.net**).
- Search Yahoo!'s entertainment section for celebrity news stories (**http://au.yahoo.com**).

Watch Out!
Some Web sites use the names of celebrities to attract visitors to sites which contain unsuitable material that has nothing to do with the star in question.

SEE ALSO
- Use a chatroom – page 102
- Tune into television – page 148
- Buy a book, CD or video – page 201

HOBBIES AND LEISURE

Enjoy the literary world
Use **the Internet** to access **literature on-line**

The Internet is helping to change the way we read and think about books, literature and the printed word. Using the Internet, you can buy books at on-line stores, read books in electronic form or download texts that are out of copyright. On the Web you will find articles about books and writing, literary quotations, information about setting up or joining a book club, and details of how to publish your own work on-line.

Author, author!
If you are an unpublished writer, the Internet can help you to get your work seen by a wide audience. Sites such as Poetry.com (**www.poetry.com**) allow you to submit your own typescript to be read and evaluated by potential publishers and other writers. They also run regular competitions.

Prospective authors can also visit publishers' Web sites, which often give details about their policy regarding unsolicited manuscripts.

Literary groups
You can use the Internet to set up an on-line reading group. For ideas about books the group might like to discuss, visit booksellers' and publishers' sites, which often have reviews of new books.

Finding books
You can buy books at discount prices at book retail sites, and there are recommendations and features to read there too. You can also search the catalogues of secondhand and antiquarian booksellers to find specific old or out-of-print books.

EXPLORE THE WEB

LITERARY SITES

Booksellers
Booksellers are a valuable source of information on books and authors. National chains such as Dymocks (www.dymocks.com.au) or Angus & Robertson (www.angusrobertson.com.au) offer a range of resources for readers and buyers. You can browse through catalogues, read reviews, and order books on-line.

Talk to other enthusiasts
Book Clique Cafe (www.readinggroupsonline.com)
It's fun to discover another person who shares your passion for particular books and authors, and this is the idea behind the Book Clique Cafe. Individuals and established groups are welcome, and all groups are open to new members. Topics range from science fiction to thrillers, and if can't find what you want you can always start your own group!

Go to a library
Project Gutenberg (www.promo.net/pg)
A vast collection of electronic texts by authors who are out of copyright (because they died 50 years ago or more). Search for classic works of fiction, poetry, philosophy and reference. Download *David Copperfield* in just a few minutes; The Bible will take a while longer. All the books are in plain text format and can be read by any computer. Once you've downloaded a text, you can locate any word or phrase in it by using your word processor's search facility. This is a good way to pin down a specific quotation or reference.

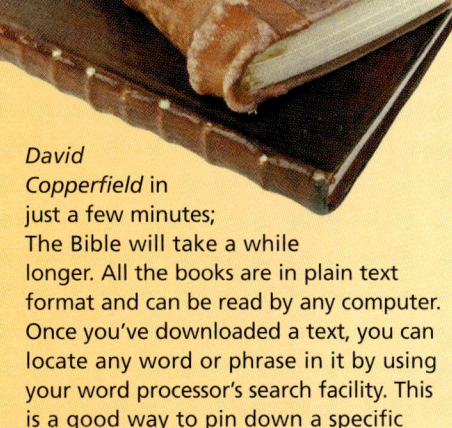

Best publisher's site
Penguin (www.penguin.com.au)
Penguin's Web site features recent publications, book summaries and reviews, in-depth author profiles and an 'author of the month' feature. You can search the entire Penguin catalogue by author, title or subject area, then find out how to order on-line. There are also useful links to a range of sites, both local and overseas. The company's UK site (www.penguin.co.uk) is very comprehensive.

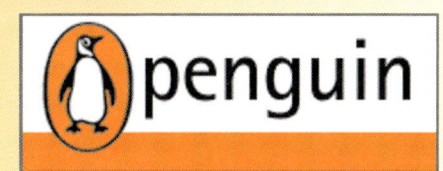

Home grown
Ozlit (http://home.vicnet.net.au/~ozlit)
Are you interested in Australian literature? If so, this is the site for you. It offers a wide range of resources, including a database of books and writers, pages devoted to poetry, lists and links for younger readers, and a free book exchange. For New Zealand literary links, try the Te Puna Web Directory (http://tepuna.natlib.govt.nz/web_directory/NZ/literature.htm).

SEARCH IT YOURSELF
Many authors have their own Web sites, and there are also a large number of 'unofficial' sites set up and maintained by fans. You can use a Web directory such as Yahoo! to find them.

Go to Yahoo! (http://au.yahoo.com) and, under 'Arts and Humanities', click on **Literature**, then **Authors**. If, for example, you are interested in Peter Carey, click on **C** and scroll down the list of authors until you come to his name.

If an author has more than one site, you will get a listing of them all, otherwise you will be taken straight to the single Web site that is available.

At any time, you can choose to click on either the **New Zealand only** or **Australia only** headings for only local sites to be displayed.

Did You Know?
You can play poetry games on-line. Go to the Fridge Magnet Poetry Boards site (www.thepixiepit.co.uk/magnets.htm) and create verses from the words given. You can also submit your efforts to the poetry 'Gallery'.

Problem Solver!
If you would like to know what books are due to be published in the near future and would like to place an order, go to the on-line bookstore BOL (www.bol.com) and click on **United Kingdom** followed by **Coming Soon**.

HOBBIES AND LEISURE

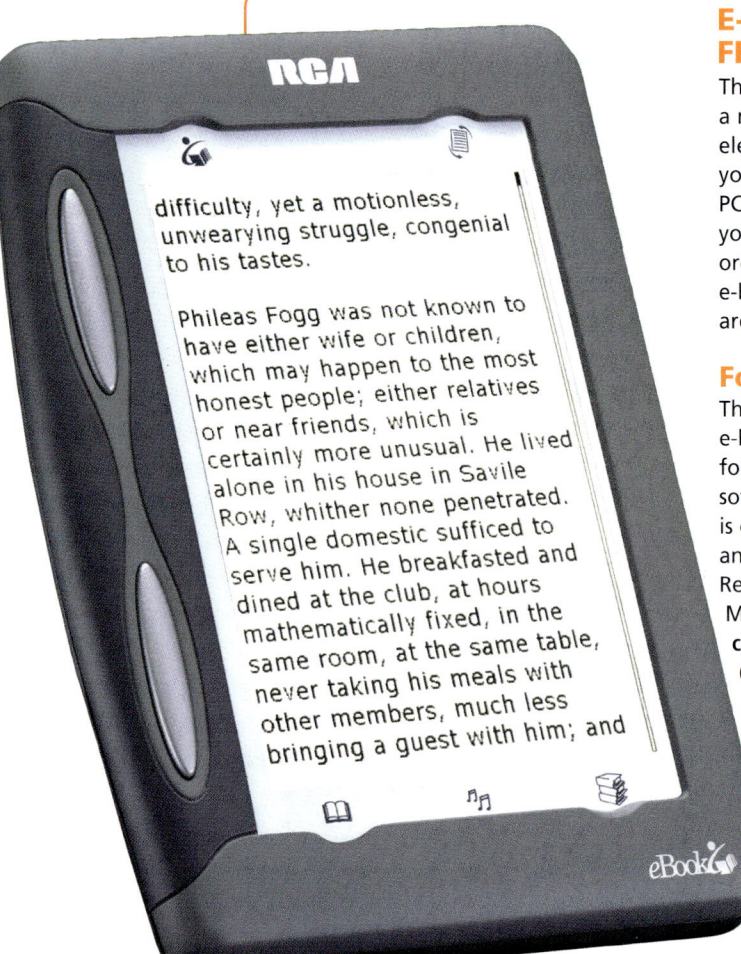

E-BOOKS – DOWNLOADED FROM THE WEB

The Internet now provides access to a revolutionary type of book – the electronic book (or e-book) – which you buy on-line and download to your PC. You can then read the e-book on your PC, laptop, pocket PC, Palm organiser, or even on a dedicated e-book reading device, of which there are already several on the market.

Formats

There are currently two major e-book formats, each one designed for a specific e-book 'reader', as the software needed to display an e-book is called. They are Microsoft Reader and Adobe Acrobat e-Book Reader, available free from Microsoft (**www.microsoft.com/reader**) and Adobe (**www.adobe.com**).

You have to download this software and register it before you can buy and download a commercial e-book. Palm organisers and dedicated e-book devices use other formats, so you need to specify your preferred format when you download an e-book. However, you can have more than one reader on your PC at a time.

Resources

You can buy e-books on-line at Amazon (**www.amazon.com**) and at many other sites, including Online Originals (**www.onlineoriginals.com**), eBooks.com (**www.ebooks.com**), eBooks N' Bytes (**www.ebooksnbytes.com**) and eBookMall (**www.ebookmall.com**). Some books are available only as e-books, and most are much cheaper than a conventional book.

At other sites, you can download e-books for free, usually texts that are out of copyright. The University of Virginia Library (**http://etext.lib.virginia.edu/ebooks**) has thousands of free e-books on its Web site, as does Free-eBooks (**www.free-ebooks.net**).

The future?

E-books are bound to become more common, especially as students embrace the technology. In the near future, students may be able to save money by downloading (and paying for) only the chapters they need from a textbook or reference work, instead of having to buy the whole book.

Did You Know?

Computer users now use the term p-book – meaning 'printed book' – to distinguish a conventional book from an e-book, which exists only in digital form.

Find out more

For more information about e-books, take a look at the excellent fact sheets available on the Amazon Web site. Go to **www.amazon.com** and click on **Books**. Then choose **E-BOOKS & DOCS** from the menu bar at the top of the page, and finally click on **e-Books FAQ**. This will open a page with many useful links. Another site with a range of informative articles is eBooks N' Bytes (**www.ebooksnbytes.com**).

SEE ALSO
- Take part in a newsgroup – page 96
- Explore painting – page 172
- Buy a book, CD or video – page 201

Make new friends

Use the Internet to find and make new friends

Although it can't replace face-to-face communication, the Internet can, if used with caution, open up new possibilities for finding friendship, rewarding long-term correspondence and even romance. You could easily come across someone interesting through a lucky encounter on a bulletin board, but you can increase your chances by making regular use of all the meeting points that the Web has to offer.

How to begin Rather than going to a site that specialises in getting people together, you could begin with a site or chatroom dedicated to your own interest, whether it's bridge, flower pressing or origami.

You can exchange friendly messages on the site's notice board or join a forum to discuss topics with like-minded individuals.

Penpal Web sites These specialise in setting up new friendships between people of similar interests from all over the world.

Dating agencies These operate in much the same way as their off-line counterparts, and have to be treated with a similar level of caution. There are also places, such as Yahoo!, where you can post personal ads. As with their newspaper equivalents, these can be a hit-and-miss affair.

Clubs and groups Use the Internet to find out about clubs, teams or groups that you can join in your area.

Revive old friendships Find long-lost school friends with one of the Internet's people-finder sites. Start by searching the White Pages (**www.whitepages.com.au**) or (**www.whitepages.co.nz**).

Did You Know?

*You can meet new friends on Internet Relay Chat (IRC), a network of live 'chatrooms' around the world (see page 104). Go to **www.irchelp.org** to learn more about how to chat, and how to look up chat groups in your area or devoted to your favourite topics.*

HOBBIES AND LEISURE

THE BEST SITES

Penfriends

International Penfriends (www.internationalpenfriends.co.uk) International Penfriends is for adults and children who want to correspond with someone from another part of the world. It has over 300,000 members from 210 different countries, and you can write in English, French, German, Spanish or Portuguese.

Enter your personal details and preferences and pay a subscription fee to receive the names and addresses of people whose age group, hobbies and interests best match your own.

Personal ads

OptusNet Personals (www.optusnet.com.au/lifestyle/personals) This free service has thousands of personal ads. You can browse to find someone with similar interests, or search for someone who will meet particular specifications regarding age, build, location etc. In order to place an advertisement of your own, you will need to join (for free). You can opt to receive the Personals newsletter, as well as a list of weekly matches, by e-mail.

Dating agencies

There are hundreds of dating agencies on the Web, all of them offering more or less the same services, although obviously some are better than others.

To find an agency, just enter a phrase such as 'dating agency', 'new friends' or 'romance' into a search engine such as Yahoo!, click **Australia** or **New Zealand**, and then review the list that appears. For an overview of some of the pitfalls you may encounter, have a look at the following site: **http://romance.live.com.au/articles/introductionAgencies.html**.

People-finder

Oz Reunion (www.ozreunion.com.au) This service aims to reunite lost families and friends through the Internet. The site offers a free Event Register where you can submit a listing for an event under a category such as 'sports club' or 'family & friends'. Alternatively, you can pay for a 100-word classified advertisement when searching for adoptees, descendants, lost contacts or missing persons.

SEARCH IT YOURSELF

To find a club, no matter what your interest, start searching through Yahoo! Groups (**http://au.groups.yahoo.com**). You could also try entering the name of your hobby into any search engine, followed by the words 'club' and 'online', as in: "fly fishing" + online + club (the double quotes ensure that "fly fishing" is treated as a complete phrase).

To find a mailing list, chat group or newsgroup on any topic, go to Topica (**www.topica.com**). For a list of the top 100 Web chat channels, go to 100hot.com (**www.100hot.com/chat**).

To search for dating sites, look through the on-line database at SingleSites (**www.singlesites.com**), which contains links to thousands of on-line dating agencies around the world. For local sites, click on **Global Regions**, and then on links for **Australia** or **New Zealand**.

EXPLORE THE WEB

HOW TO: FIND LONG-LOST FRIENDS

1 Go to WorldPages (www.worldpages.com). Click on **International**. On the next page, select a country (in this case the United Kingdom) from the drop-down list and click on **Search**.

2 A list of phone directories for that country will now appear. Here we have clicked on **British**, the link for British Telecom (BT) Directory Enquiries.

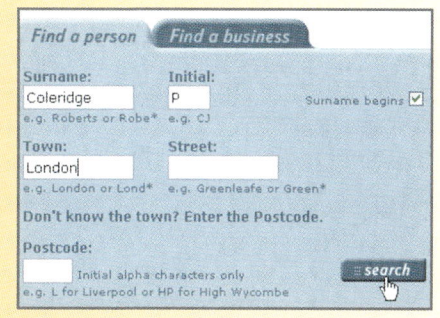

3 A new window opens to show the BT search page. Enter the name and area of the person or business you are trying to locate. Then click on **Search**.

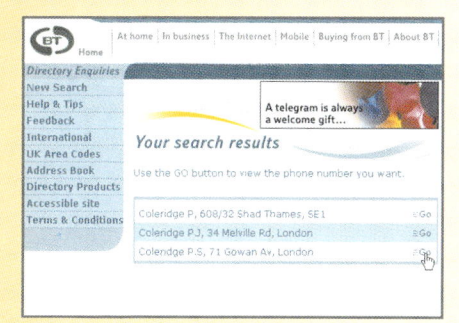

4 A results window will appear, listing the names and addresses of all individuals who fit your search criteria. Click **Go** beside any name to see the phone number of that person.

MUSICAL MATCH

Like many of the other copywriters in his advertising firm, Nick also wrote in his spare time – in his case it was song lyrics.

'For a while, I was quite happy crooning away at the piano in my rumpus room, but I reluctantly agreed to my wife's demands that I take things further.

'I didn't feel confident enough to advertise for musicians to make up a band. But I did want to get someone else to listen to the songs and find out if they were any good or not.

'A friend mentioned that there was a Web site where you could upload recordings of your songs (**www.allnoise.com**). He helped me upload a couple of songs and then I sat back to wait for the recording contracts to come flooding in.

'I didn't hear anything for weeks, but eventually a guy called Mark e-mailed me to say that he liked my lyrics but thought he could do a better job of singing them.

'We arranged to meet at a pub in Brisbane and hit it off immediately. We then recruited a drummer and a guitarist through the Musicians Online site (**www.musiciansonline.com**) and recorded the songs again. The new versions have been on-line for a few months and we're still not famous, but getting together to make music has been great fun.'

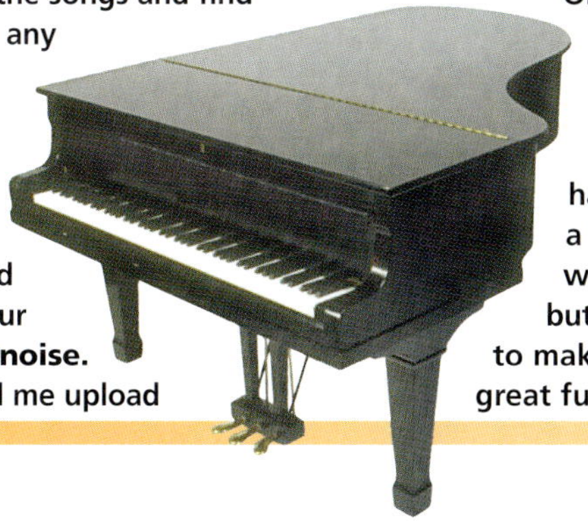

Watch Out!

Check out the dating safety precautions recommended by ninemsn (**http://aca.ninemsn.com.au/factsheets/572.asp**), such as meeting in a public place and telling a close friend what you are doing.

SEE ALSO
- **Use a chatroom** – page 102
- **Do some research** – page 113
- **Trace your family's past** – page 159

171

HOBBIES AND LEISURE

Explore painting

Get creative **through the Web**

If you've always wanted to wield a paintbrush, palette and easel but have never known how to get started, why not take advantage of the Web to learn more about painting? You can look at works of art over the Internet, and access art supplies and tuition. You can also use computer programs to 'paint' on the screen instead of on canvas.

If you are an artist, you can post your paintings on a Web site so that other people can see your work. You can even put your paintings up for sale through an on-line gallery.

View art
Most museums have their own Web sites, displaying paintings and providing information on the artists and their work. There are also sites dedicated to the history of art, such as Art History Search (**www.arthistorysearch.com**), which offer specialist insights into art theory, history and techniques.

Art courses
There are free on-line art courses that offer tuition to people of all ability levels who may not have the time or money for conventional classes. But if you prefer a mouse to a paintbrush, you can try a painting program for free at a software site such as Corel (**www3.corel.com**).

Art lovers
The Internet can also help you to research painting holidays and workshops. Or, if you're an art lover and aspiring collector, The Art Connection Inc. (**www.art connection.net**) connects you to painters, and paintings for sale.

EXPLORE THE WEB

PAINTING SITES

On-line tutorials
WetCanvas! (www.wetcanvas.com)
This site sets out to bring 'art education to the masses'. Offering free on-line courses, catering for children and adults of all abilities, WetCanvas! also includes a virtual museum, information on art supplies and services, and an on-line shop where you can purchase fine art.

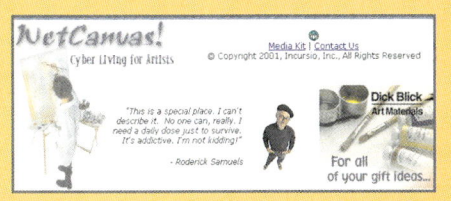

Art supplies
ArtResource (www.artresource.com)
Head to ArtResource for a huge range of art supplies and useful links. To buy equipment and materials, visit one of the Web's many on-line suppliers, such as The Art Scene (**www.artscene.com.au**) or Art Supplies Online (**www.artsupplies.co.nz**). Check prices carefully, as local stores may be cheaper.

Art history resources
The Mother of All Art History Links (www.art-design.umich.edu/mother)
This award-winning site, put together by a university art history department, contains links to museums, on-line art, fine art schools, research resources and image collections.

Go to Artserve at the Australian National University (**http://rubens.anu.edu.au**) for surveys of great artists, especially from the Mediterranean.

On-line gallery
Art Gallery Online (www.art-gallery-online.org)
This is a private, non-profit-making virtual art gallery devoted to showcasing the work of contemporary international artists. Browse artist portfolios and an on-line gallery.

SEARCH IT YOURSELF
To find out who painted what and when, look at the art database at ArtCyclopedia (**http://artcyclopedia.com**). Another site with a wide range of information is World Wide Arts Resources (**http://wwar.com**). This site also has many helpful links to museums and galleries, as does the International Council of Museums (**www.icom.org/vlmp/world.html**).

EXHIBITING ART ON-LINE

There are many options for painters (amateur or professional) who want to show their work over the Internet. One way is to create your own Web site and place your images there.

To do this, you need to convert your painting into a digital image using a scanner. If your paintings are too big or delicate to fit on a scanner, you can get slides or photos made of them. Or, if you own a digital camera, you can take a picture of your work and then download it onto your PC.

Selling Your Art Online (**http://1x.com/advisor**) offers a range of useful advice on selling your art via the Web. World Wide Arts Resources (**http://wwar.com**) invites submissions of art work. If you e-mail photos of your creations to them, they will create an on-line portfolio of your art for free.

Exhibiting your work on-line ensures that your work gets seen by people around the world and saves you having to find a gallery. You can also correspond and receive feedback from the people who view your work, who would never have been able to view it in a conventional gallery. You never know who will come across your paintings on the Internet.

Problem Solver
*If you're doing research, you may want to subscribe to the comprehensive reference work, The Grove Dictionary of Art Online (**www.groveart.com**). You can register for a free trial to see what the site has to offer you.*

SEE ALSO
- Use a chatroom – page 102
- Enjoy the literary world – page 166
- Buy a book, CD or video – page 201

173

HOBBIES AND LEISURE

Keep the children entertained

Discover Web sites **specifically for children**

At its best, the Internet is a useful educational tool as well as a playground. Most children will enjoy it both for learning and for fun. They can use it to play games on-line, download stories or read reviews of books. They can also get help with homework or set up an e-mail penfriend anywhere in the world. The Net will yield suggestions for activities to do in the holidays and chatrooms specifically for children. With good supervision and proper use of filtering software, children can spend time on the Internet safely and productively.

Before you start

- When you start an on-line session, use specialist children's portals – sites with extensive editorial content and a large collection of links, such as Zeeks (**www.zeeks.com**). These bring together a useful range of resources for younger users.

- Use child-friendly search engines such as Yahooligans! (**www.yahooligans.com**).

- There are sites, such as Kids Domain (**www.kidsdomain.com**), that provide detailed advice for parents and carers on how to ensure that their children surf the Web safely.

- With Windows XP, you can create a separate user identity, activated by a password, for each child who uses the computer; or simply set up a single user identity for all your children. You can then set up filtering software and browser security (see pages 52 and 56) that become active whenever your children log on to the computer.

EXPLORE THE WEB

FUN SITES FOR CHILDREN

Where to start
Kids Domain (www.kidsdomain.com)
Intended mainly for primary school-aged children, Kids Domain is a great Web site with thousands of pages of 'childsafe Internet content'. The site includes reviews of commercial software by parents, safe surfing information, suggestions for holiday activities, interactive games and more than 3000 downloads for both PC and Mac. The range of contents is huge, from colouring-in competitions to monthly story-writing contests and a variety of quizzes and puzzles that are both challenging and entertaining.

There are separate areas for adults and children, with the adults section offering, among other things, useful guidelines to help younger users to get the most from their computers and the Internet.

Children's shareware
Tucows (www.tucows.com)
This site has a huge library of shareware – both educational and entertaining – for downloading. Many programs are written specifically for children, and you can find these by going to the Tucows homepage and clicking on **Windows**. Then select **Home & Education** and you'll see a range of kids' categories, including 'Coloring and Painting', 'History', 'Math', 'Science', 'Teaching and Testing' and 'Writing and Reading'. Click on any of these for a list of associated software.

Alternatively, type 'kids' and any other relevant search term in the search window and click **Go**. You may find additional software in this way. Every item of software is priced, described and rated, so you can see what you are getting before you download it.

Internet communications
Kidlink (www.kidlink.org)
This site offers an immediate way to interact with children from all over the world. There are e-mail discussion groups in the Kidcafé area. If you prefer live on-line chat then head for the Kidcafé conferences section. There is also a gallery of computer art where children can submit their own work.

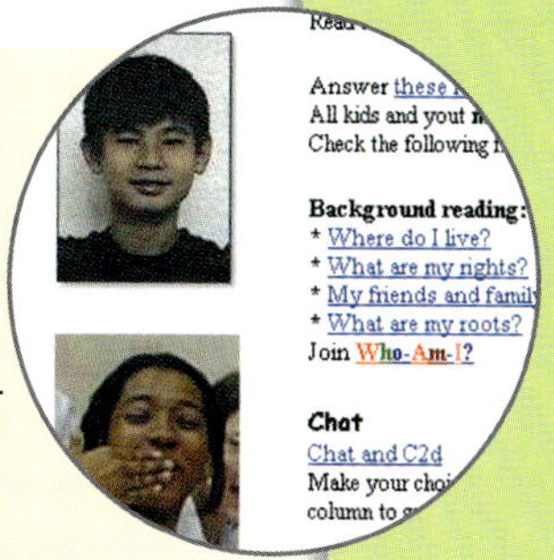

Start writing
Kidnews.com (www.kidnews.com)
This site gives children around the world the chance to get their work published on-line. Participants send in their stories, poems, opinions and reviews, and these are checked for language and content before being posted on the site. Teachers are encouraged to get entire school classes involved.

There is also a penpal section which is carefully vetted to exclude anything undesirable. Parents or teachers must sign a consent form before a child's e-mail address will be posted on the site.

Swap messages
Bulletin boards are an alternative to live on-line chat. You leave messages here to be commented on by other bulletin board members later. For a selection of bulletin boards for children, which they can contribute to, visit Zeeks (**www.zeeks.com**).

Did You Know?
*You can copy text from a Web page into a Word document. To do this, highlight the text, go to the **Edit** menu and select **Copy**. Then open a blank Word document, go to the **Edit** menu and select **Paste**.*

175

HOBBIES AND LEISURE

MORE KIDS' SITES

On-line activities
Crayola (www.crayola.com)
Crayola make colouring pens, crayons and other art materials. They run an excellent art activity Web site full of creative ideas and fun things to do, such as the Idea Generator, which creates silly sentences to set the imagination in motion. There are many pictures and craft projects which you can print out and complete off-line, and an Inspiring Ideas section. This has a changing range of activities which you can view by topic, target age, and length of time the activity will take. There is also a section for creating printed cards and e-cards.

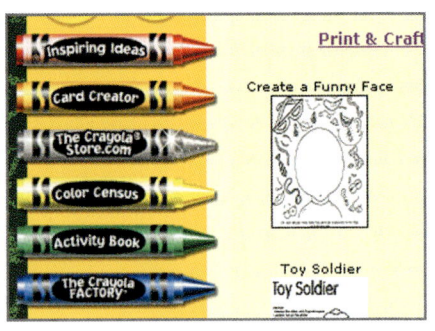

TV tie-in
Bob the Builder (www.bobthebuilder.org)
Many children's TV shows have tie-in Web sites that offer activities and information related to the show. The Bob the Builder site is particularly well thought out. It offers exciting on-line activities for younger users, featuring characters from the show. There are jigsaws, on-line drawing and colouring exercises, and various other activities which encourage skills such as co-ordination. For example, you can help fix the jug that Pilchard has broken by dragging the mouse over each piece, or assist with spelling in Mrs Percival's lesson. This is a good site for children to use with an adult. It will help younger users to get familiar with computers and the Internet.

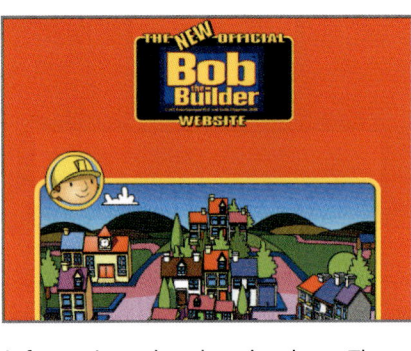

Fun for all ages
The Playground (www.abc.net.au/children)
The Australian ABC children's site offers a huge range of material for kids of all ages. There are links to dozens of popular children's TV shows, many of which have their own Web sites containing cartoons, games, contests, songs and a range of activities.

The ABC site also provides links to the new digital ABC Kids channel, which broadcasts programs throughout the day.

Time Saver!

Bookmark your favourite children's Web sites and organise the bookmarks in a folder in your Web browser. This makes it easy to return to them at a later date.

EXPLORE THE WEB

HOW TO: COLOUR IN A PICTURE THEN E-MAIL IT TO A FRIEND

There are many Web sites, such as UpToTen (**www.uptoten.org**), which provide pictures for children to colour in on-line, or to print out and colour in. Some also allow you to send images that have been coloured in on-line to friends and family, or to point those people to the Web site where the images are stored.

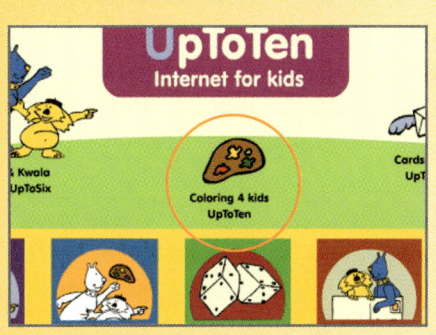

1 First go to the UpToTen homepage (**www.uptoten.org**). Then click on the icon **Coloring 4 kids UpToTen**.

2 A new window will open, offering a range of colouring choices. You can either print out one of the projects on the page, or click on **Index** and choose a project to colour-in on-line.

3 Choose an image and colour it in using the palette and paintbrush that will appear. Drag the paintbrush onto a colour and then click on the part of the picture you wish to colour in.

4 When you have finished, click the paper aeroplane icon on the menu at the top and fill in the next form with your name, e-mail address and your friend's e-mail address. Then click **Send**.

5 A short animation will let you know that the e-mail has been sent to your friend. Now wait for the response from the recipient.

Sounds like fun

Make your PC more enjoyable for children to use by setting it up to play sounds when it performs various tasks, such as opening a folder or receiving an e-mail.
   Go to the Windows XP **Start** menu, click **Control Panel** then **Sounds, Speech and Audio Devices**. Click **Change the sound scheme** to bring up a dialogue box where you will see a list of events to which you can assign sounds. To apply a sound to a specific event, select the event and then click **Browse** to search for a suitable sound. You can create a separate sound scheme for each person who uses the computer.

Money Saver!

*If a phone call to your ISP is charged by the amount of time you spend connected, then it is worth making sure that you and your children keep on-line activity within the cheap-rate times as much as possible. To save money, you can also print out Web pages and read them off-line. To do this, go to the **File** menu and select **Print**, or click on the **Print** button on the toolbar.*

HOBBIES AND LEISURE

Ask around
Don't just use the Internet to find an e-pal for your child. Ask your family, friends and colleagues if they know anyone with a child of a similar age. Having some common ground may help the children when they begin to correspond.

Did You Know?
Many Web sites can help with school work. For example, the Australian ABC's Lab Notes pages (www.abc.net.au/labnotes) is ideal for science projects. There are also encyclopedias on-line which may be helpful.

HOW TO: FIND E-PALS

Children have always enjoyed having penfriends, and with the Internet it is now also possible to have e-friends, or e-pals – contacts around the globe who can be e-mailed rather than written to using conventional pen and paper. Corresponding with an e-pal is much faster than posting a letter overseas, and the reply can come back much sooner too.

Selecting an e-pal Web site
It's easy to make new e-pals, as there are many Web sites offering contacts. Some adults are concerned about the kinds of contacts children might make on the Internet. However, you can minimise the risk by selecting the site for them.

What to look for
- Try to find sites that are aimed specifically at children, rather than those for all age groups.
- Look for a site that is regulated by an official body, such as the Children's Online Privacy Protection Rule (COPPR).
- Find a Web site with a wide and varied selection of prospective e-pals on offer – preferably from different countries around the world. Help your child choose one.

1 Go to Kidnews.com (**www.kidnews.com**) and click on the **Penpal** icon, which is on the lower left-hand side of the circle of links.

2 Read the Welcome! screen and click on the **permission form** link. You will need to fill in this form and post it off before you will be allowed to put your e-mail address on the site.

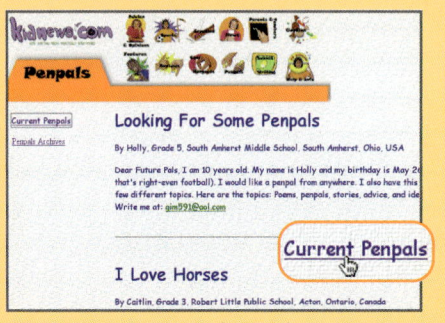

3 Now go back to the Welcome! page and click on the **Current Penpals** link to see messages from children who are looking for someone to write to.

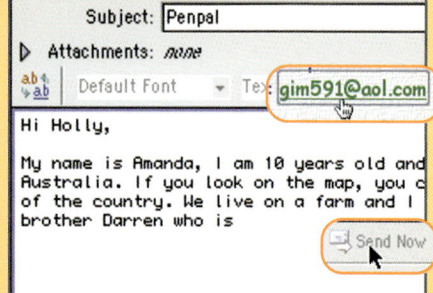

4 Click on any e-mail address and Outlook Express will automatically launch a new e-mail form. Write your e-mail and click **Send Now** to post it off.

Learn a language
If your child is learning a new language, such as French or Spanish, encourage them to get an e-pal in a country where that language is spoken, and start corresponding. This will make learning the language much more enjoyable.

EXPLORE THE WEB

ORGANISE A CHILDREN'S PARTY ON-LINE

The Internet can be extremely useful when it comes to organising children's parties. In fact, it can provide everything you require without the bother of trailing around the shops. If you need inspiration or to buy presents, decorations, games or food for a kids party, here's how the Web can help.

Presents
Many Web sites provide gifts for children's parties. On-line stores such as PeeDee Toys (**http://store.yahoo.com/peedeetoys**) have sites from which you can order birthday presents. These will then be delivered directly to your house.

Decorations
You can order simple balloons or elaborate bouquets of balloons at Balloons Online (**www.balloonsonline.com.au**).

Themes
Get inspiration for party themes, ranging from a Dinosaur Dig to a Pirate Party at Amazingmoms (**www.amazingmoms.com**).

You can also book an entertainer, such as a clown or a magician. Many entertainers have their own sites, where you can book them directly. If you don't know of any entertainers in your area, try the directory at EntertainOz (**www.entertainoz.com.au**).

PARTY CAKES
You can get a unique cake designed by specialists at The Cake Whole Web site (**www.cakewhole.com.au**). Make a selection from one of the cakes illustrated in the on-line catalogue or, if you have an idea for an original cake, you can ask the designers to make it specially for you.

Entertainment
For games and other entertainment ideas to keep the partygoers happy, visit The Party Games Ideas Resource Page (**http://freespace.virgin.net/ken.tew/party/list.html**). Here you will find an extensive list of party games for young children, teenagers and adults.

Design your cards
If your child would like to design an original invitation, why not use an on-line drawing or colouring site, such as Cory's PaintBox (**www.corypaints.com**). Print out the drawn or coloured picture, and use that as the basis of a printed invitation.

Party venues
Many sites have lists of venues where you can hold a party – for instance, Sydney's Child (**www.sydneychild.com.au**). Click on the **directory of products** link, then choose **Party** from the list that comes up.

SEE ALSO
- **Download from the Web** – page 86
- **Help your child to learn on-line** – page 136
- **Play games on-line** – page 186

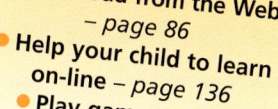

HOBBIES AND LEISURE

Go motoring

Get on the road with the information superhighway

On the Internet, you can find any number of official and unofficial sites devoted to every aspect of motoring. If you like to get your hands dirty, there are tips and guides for maintenance checks to help to get your car through its annual registration check, and bigger jobs such as fitting new brake pads. Or you can find local mechanics to handle the servicing for you. Anyone who wants to buy a car will find reviews and dealers for all the latest models, and classified advertisements for second-hand vehicles. You can also use the Internet to advertise that your own car is for sale.

Buying and selling Checking on-line classifieds is far more convenient than poring over magazine ads. You can search for the exact model and year you want, and view only offers in your local area and your preferred price range. When selling a car, on-line ads also allow you to reach a huge potential audience, free of charge or at low cost.

You can also get an approximate value for any make or model of used car, which will help with your purchase or sale.

Mechanical advice Use the Web to find test reports, repair guides and checklists to deal with all types of DIY work. If you own an older model, you can also search for that elusive chrome wing mirror or a set of original hubcaps.

Other enthusiasts You can join a car club and meet new people at motoring events, or you can take part in on-line discussion boards to swap tips and gossip with fellow experts and amateurs.

EXPLORE THE WEB

TOP VEHICLE SITES

Where to start
Yahoo! Australia & NZ Cars (http://au.cars.yahoo.com/au/car) The Yahoo! site has done a lot of the hard work for you. Search experts have sorted through many of the most useful local Web sites and organised them by category to make searching easier. The categories include Insurance, Car Parts, Dealers, Clubs and Car Makes.

Impartial advice
Glass's Guide (www.glassguide.com.au) Glass's Guide has always been thought of as the pricing authority when it comes to buying and selling second-hand vehicles in Australia. Their independent valuations, based on age and condition, are used by most car dealers in their calculations. Glass's boast that they can supply market values for 48,000 car models, dating back to 1960. Their database includes passenger vehicles, commercial vehicles, motorcycles, boats and caravans.

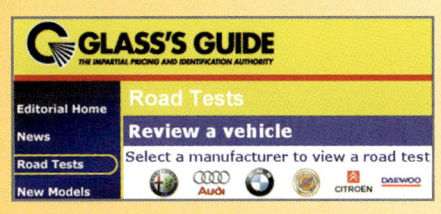

To get an on-line valuation, simply click on **Glass's Values** and follow the steps that are laid out in the next pages. You will receive a valuation by e-mail in less that five minutes, for a small fee.

Car DIY advice
Car Care Clinic (www.carcareclinic.com) This is the place to go for advice on any repairs you are undertaking. You can pick the problem you are trying to solve from an alphabetical list or e-mail your question to the site. There is also a forum where you can swap tips with other car enthusiasts.

Buyer beware!
If you buy a second-hand vehicle from a private seller with money owing on it, you could end up having it repossessed. So it's worth doing a free on-line search of the Register of Encumbered Vehicles, or REVS, (**www.revs.nsw.gov.au**), a database linked to similar registers across Australia. A small fee gets you written confirmation.

In New Zealand, you need to check two registers: the Motor Vehicle Securities Register at the Companies Office (**www.companies.govt.nz**) and the Personal Property Securities Register (**www.ppsr.govt.nz**) at the Ministry of Economic Development.

Selling a car on-line
- First get your car valued. Go to a site such as Glass's (see above) or The Red Book (**www.redbook.com.au**) and enter your car's details.
- Check the listings at a site such as Drive.com (**www.drive.com.au**) or Car.co (**www.car.co.nz**) for similar cars to see if the price is realistic.
- Now choose a price, giving yourself room for negotiation by adding 'or nearest offer' (ono).
- Take a digital photo of the car or get a normal photograph scanned in to use when advertising your car.
- Advertise your car on-line (see overleaf) as well as in local newspapers and trade magazines.
- E-mail the details of your car to your friends and colleagues, and ask them to circulate these.
- Read the advice in the 'Guide to Selling your Car' at Autotrader (**www.autotrader.com.au/selling.asp**), for the advantages and pitfalls of selling by auction, privately or through a dealer.

Time Saver!
You can get free maintenance tips e-mailed to you. Sign up to Car Adviser (*http://caradviser.cars.com*).

Watch Out!
When searching US sites, use American English. Try 'auto parts' rather than 'car parts', 'hood' instead of 'bonnet', 'tire' rather than 'tyre' and 'trunk' in place of 'boot'.

HOBBIES AND LEISURE

HOW TO: ADVERTISE YOUR CAR FOR SALE

1 Go to a car site, such as Car Sales (www.carsales.com.au), and start by checking how much the car you are selling is actually worth.

2 If you decide to continue, return to the homepage and click on **sell your car**, then click **Create Now** to start assembling your advertisement.

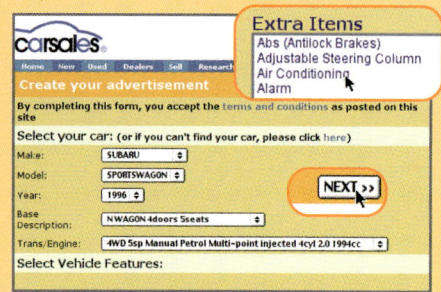

3 Fill in your car's details, adding any extra features, such as a CD player, from the drop-down menu provided. Click **Next** when you have finished.

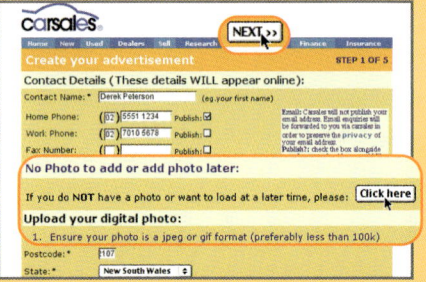

4 Now fill in your contact details, including a 'Username' so you can alter the advert later if necessary. You can also upload photos if you wish.

5 You can then view your finished ad as it will appear, both as a brief item in 'Search Results' and with full details showing. Click **next** if you are satisfied.

6 Now decide how you want to pay for the advertisement, and then provide the information requested. Confirm the details and click **Process Payment**.

Problem Solver!

If you are unsure about how to create images that are suitable for the Internet, read the information on preparing and uploading digital images on pages 264–269.

Did You Know?

You can pick the brains of other car owners through a newsgroup. In Outlook Express, click on **Tools** and **Newsgroups**. Enter the make and model of your car to bring up a list of relevant groups.

CASE STUDY

John recently retired and finally had the time to devote to his beloved MGB TF Midget, which had languished unused in his garage for many years.

He also used his new-found free time to improve his PC skills, and soon found that his two hobbies coincided when he came across the MG Club (www.mgcarclub.org.nz). 'I saw the site and joined my local club in Auckland on-line right away,' said John. 'I was able to get advice on repairing the gearbox that really helped me get my TF back on the road. Now I'm working hard on the bodywork because I'm planning to take part in the next Pre 56 Rally.'

SEE ALSO
- Send e-mail attachments – page 46
- Take part in a newsgroup – page 96
- Buy and sell at auction – page 208

EXPLORE THE WEB

Improve your home

Plan a new look for your house and garden

The Internet is a great place to find inspiration for maintaining your home, inside and out. You'll find a vast range of DIY instructions, home decorating hints and horticultural tips. Explore the Web to find just the right plants for your location and type of garden, buy home accessories, tools and garden furniture locally or interstate, or locate a recommended builder in your area.

Do-it-yourself You can get advice on every type of job around the house. There are step-by-step guides for you to print out and guides on what products to use.

DIY supplies Browse the Web for all your DIY and home furnishing supplies – tools, paintbrushes, kitchen units, lighting and more. See what's available before you head for the shops, or order specialist or professional goods on-line directly from the supplier.

Gardening tips Consult local horticultural societies for advice and information about growing various plants, whether natives or exotics. You can also look up on-line plant encyclopedias for details on different plants and the best ways to care for them.

Garden supplies Many sites offer specialised plant finders to locate exactly the right plant for the climate, light availability and size of your garden. You can then order delivery of the appropriate plants.

the magic of **australian plants** *native*

Did You Know?

Find out how to glue almost anything to just about anything else at the This to That site (www.thistothat.com). Although many of the proprietary products listed on this US site are not available locally, it is generally possible to find good substitutes.

183

HOBBIES AND LEISURE

SITES TO HOME IN ON

Home improvements
Mitre 10 (www.mitre10.com.au)
This is a good place to start your home improvement research. Go to this site to view the latest Mitre 10 catalogue, to find your closest store, or to get detailed instructions for carrying out a wide range of DIY projects, from building a fence and caring for a lawn to tiling a floor and repairing a fuse. The site also has an advice service, where you can either e-mail or phone in your questions and get expert help for free.

DIY solutions
DIY-Online (www.diy-online.co.nz)
This site will help you to choose the best materials for the job you want to undertake, and you can then go ahead and order them on-line at the same time. DIY-Online also offers a 'How To' section, where you can read articles on a wide range of topics, including 'Building', 'Design', 'Tools' and 'Painting'.

Great garden advice
Garden UK (www.garden-uk.org.uk)
Click on **Reference** for an invaluable compilation of gardening links and reference sites, including Botany.com's 'Encyclopedia of Plants' – which can be searched by both common and botanical names – and 'Gardener's Guru', with advice on growing organic produce.

Native plants
Association of Societies for Growing Australian Plants (http://farrer.riv.csu.edu.au/ASGAP)
This is the site for you if you want to create a garden using Australian native species. There is a wealth of information which will help you to select, buy and grow a wide range of natives.

Garden shopping
There are literally thousands of on-line gardening superstores to choose from, of which the following are typical: GardensOnLine (**www.gardensonline.com.au**) and Bestgardening (**www.bestgardening.co.nz**). The best of these sites generally offer a wide selection of plants, gardening tools and other products for purchase, together with a range of information that will be useful to gardeners. This often includes articles and planting calendars, as well as links to other gardening sites on the Internet. Some sites – such as Bestgardening – will also e-mail you a free newsletter to keep you in touch with seasonal tasks and any special offers they may have.

SEARCH IT YOURSELF

For specific advice, look for a specialist site. The Kitchen Specialists Association (**www.ksa.co.uk**) is a great place to get a range of ideas and information for planning a new kitchen.

To create a 3D plan of your new kitchen before going shopping, visit KitchenWeb (**www.kitchenweb.com**).

If you are after that elusive finishing touch, the Internet is a great way to track down items and information. A quick search at Yahoo! (**http://au.yahoo.com**) for 'heritage colours' reveals a wealth of sites. Not only can you read about the colours that were popular in the late-19th century, you can place an order for the right amount of paint for the effect you are after.

If you draw a blank in your search, post a query on a forum at a lifestyle site, such as iVillage (**www.ivillage.com**).

Did You Know?

Horticultural therapists have developed tools and techniques to help you to avoid getting back pain in the garden. Go to Fredshed (*www.fredshed.co.uk*) for details.

EXPLORE THE WEB

HOW TO: USE AN ON-LINE PLANT SELECTOR

The Savewater site (**www.savewater.com.au**) has a unique plant selector that not only allows you to choose plants that are attractive, but also those that will survive with little or no water in the type of climate where you live. This can be very useful if you live in an arid area or are concerned about water conservation issues generally.

Once you know which plants are appropriate, it is a simple matter to go on-line and find a local nursery where you can buy seeds or seedlings.

1 Go to Savewater (**www.savewater.com.au**) and click on the box labelled **Click here to make your garden Grow**.

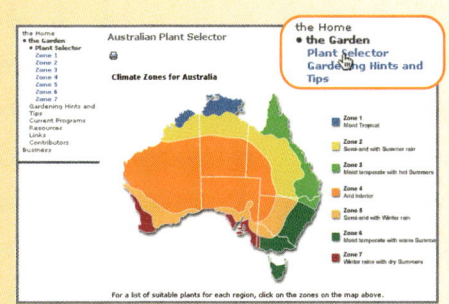

2 Click on **the Garden** and read the article that comes up. Then click on the **Plant Selector** link. When the map page opens, read the accompanying text.

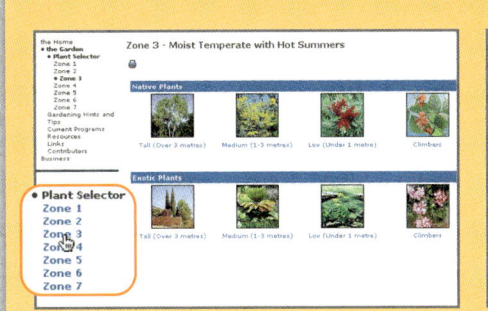

3 Now click on the link for your climate zone, based on the data supplied. You will be presented with four categories of both native and exotic plants.

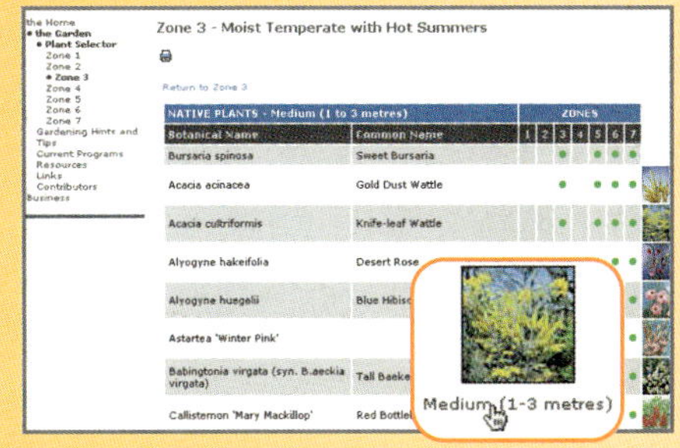

4 Click on each category in turn – **Tall**, **Medium**, **Low** and **Climbers** – and make a selection as you go. Draw up a list based on the scheme you have in mind.

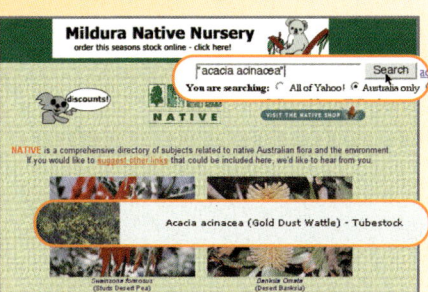

5 Now go to a search engine such as Yahoo! (**http://au.yahoo.com**) and enter a species name. Once you track down a local supplier, you will probably find that most of your other choices are available there as well.

AS SEEN ON TV

Most of the home and garden improvement programs have an on-line presence. Go to ninemsn (**http://lifestyle.ninemsn.com.au/ourhouse**) to visit the Our House site. Here you can download fact sheets, visit the 'Resource Centre' to join the DIY Club, or click links to visit sites such as Burke's Backyard.

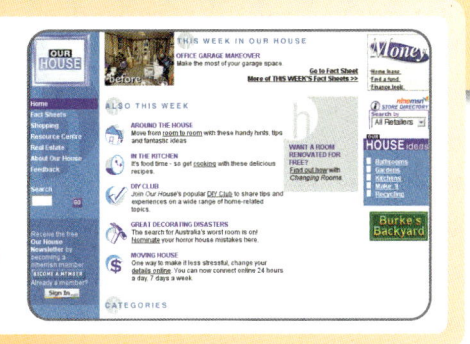

Don't forget
There is always a risk in buying plants by post because you can't check whether they are healthy or not.

Watch Out!

Avoid botched jobs! Make sure any tradespeople you use are properly licensed. Check on-line with your regional builders association or with the builders registration authority in your state.

SEE ALSO
- **Shop safely on the Web** – page 54
- **Get a mortgage quotation** – page 204
- **Buy and sell at auction** – page 208

HOBBIES AND LEISURE

Play games on-line

Use the Web to play almost any game imaginable

Whatever games you like to play, the chances are you can play them on the Web. You can play virtually every video game, sport or board game, either alone or against other players – and even chat to them while you're doing so. There are also trivia quizzes and puzzles for you to ponder. There is plenty for children too, including sites with child-safe games for them to enjoy.

Play on-line
Most games work with your normal Web browser, but some may require you to download a small program. Many games can be played for free, but some charge subscription fees.

Types of games
On-line games include solitaire, crossword puzzles and arcade games such as pinball – with sound effects and flashing lights – as well as classic video games such as Space Invaders and driving games. There is also a range of simulation games, where you manage a city or build a civilisation from scratch.

Playing off-line
If you're worried about the expense of your Internet connection, you don't have to play games on-line. There are free downloadable games, such as blackjack, to play off-line, many with high-quality 3D graphics.

EXPLORE THE WEB

GAMES SITES

Best place to start
About.com's Internet Games section (http://internetgames.about.com)
This site provides an introduction to games sites. Categories include cards, action and role-playing games. Most can be played free, and there are also free games to download and play off-line.

Games to play off-line
Freeware Gaming (www.freewaregaming.com)
Choose from hundreds of free downloadable games in categories such as Puzzle/Logic, Sport, Card/Casino and Action/Arcade. Games are rated and reviewed, and each listing shows the file size and system requirements.

Even more games
Free Games Online (www.freegamesonline.com)
Yet another site that boasts thousands of free games. These are organised into categories that include Freeware, Shareware, WebTV (games that are WebTV compatible) and Online.

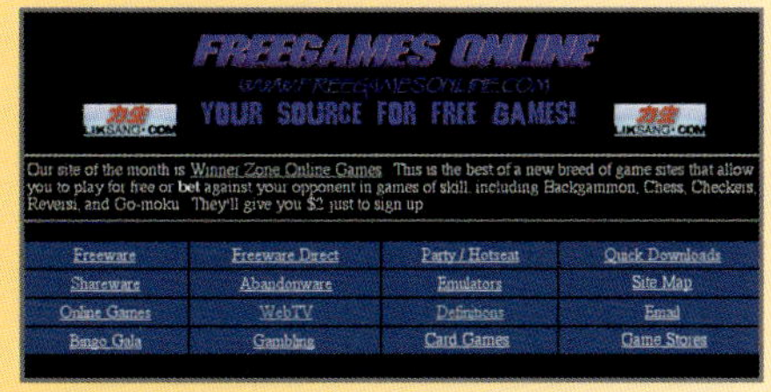

Playing against other people
MSN Games (http://zone.msn.com)
Hundreds of games you can play with others on-line are offered by MSN. To play bridge, for example, click **Card & Board** then **Bridge** and enter one of the listed game rooms, divided into Social or Competitive. Pick a social room to start with: you'll find that the locals are friendly. In all the games, you can chat to each other as you play. Each game's homepage has a 'Getting Started' guide, plus tips, strategies, and technical help.

Games for children
Rainy Day Playhouse (www.pen-web.com/rainyday)
This site offers fun, easy-to-play games. Click **Alex Warp** to bend the faces of famous celebrities, such as Leonardo Di Caprio, into bizarre new shapes. Or choose from arcade and puzzle games and send an electronic postcard.

SEARCH IT YOURSELF

SimCity is a computer simulation game that allows you to become the ruler of existing cities or create a dream city from scratch. To play, go to a search engine such as Google (**www.google.com**) and search for 'SimCity'. Some hits will be articles containing the word SimCity, but most will relate to the game.

The rules of SimCity are based on city planning, resource management, human factors, strategic planning, unemployment, crime and pollution.

Your city is populated by Sims – Simulated Citizens – and to keep your city running profitably you must keep the Sims happy.

For a guide to the latest computer simulation games, go to About.com (**www.about.com**) and click on **Hobbies & Games** and then **Computer Simulation Games**.

Problem Solver!
If a game won't load, your browser may be unable to read the script language used by the makers of the game. Go to **Tools** *and* **Internet Options**, *select the* **Security** *tab and click* **Custom Level**. *Under both 'Active scripting' and 'Scripting of Java applets', click* **Enable**, *then* **OK**.

HOBBIES AND LEISURE

HOW TO: PLAY A SINGLE-PLAYER GAME ON-LINE

Many games can be played on-line by single players. At various sites on the Web you can play against computer opponents – card games such as hearts or euchre, or board games such as chess, Othello and backgammon. You can also try your hand at trivia quizzes and puzzles such as crosswords and word-searches.

FUTURE ON-LINE GAMES

On-line games are as old as the Internet. Researchers began playing simple on-line strategy games in the 1970s, and millions of gamers now play on-line. There is even a professional league – the Cyberathlete Professional League.

At present, most on-line gamers are American, because Internet connections are cheap or free in the USA. However, as Internet access becomes faster and cheaper in other parts of the world, many more people will be able to take part in on-line games.

1 To play games at MSN Games (**http://zone.msn.com**), click **All Games**, and a list will appear showing which are suitable for single players. Click on any game; here we have chosen **Blender**.

2 When the page loads up, click on **click to start**. The picture squares will then scramble. You have a set length of time to put it back into order, depending on the puzzle's difficulty.

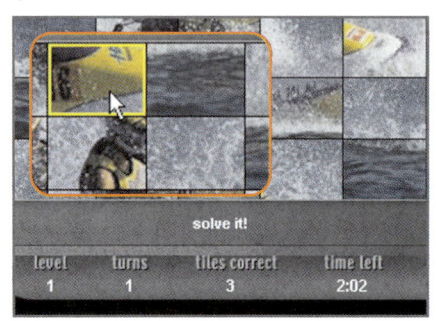

3 To solve the puzzle, click on the square you wish to move, then on the square where you want to position it. Monitor your progress by checking the details at the bottom of the window.

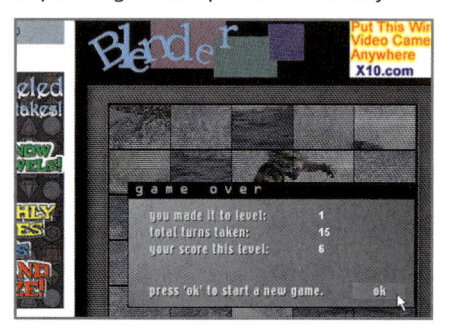

4 Repeat the process until the puzzle is completed. If you don't succeed before the time limit runs out, you will get a message saying 'game over' and the option of starting a new puzzle.

EXPLORE THE WEB

HOW TO: PLAY A MULTI-PLAYER GAME ON-LINE

At station.com (**www2.station.sony.com**) you can play a number of on-line games against other players, including the popular TV favourite, Jeopardy!

When you join up to play Jeopardy!, you will be asked whether you are a beginner, intermediate or advanced player. It is better to be honest, since you will then find yourself playing against others of the same level. Once you get the hang of the rules of the game, you can play against more seasoned opponents. You can either join an existing game when a place becomes available, or you can start your own game. Since there are three players to each game, you may have to wait a while for the other places to fill.

Most players are English-speaking, although they can be from anywhere in the world. You can see only the character names of your opponents, not their real names. However, there is a chat window on the page which lets you speak to the other players, and you can make your character smile or frown, as appropriate, while you chat.

1 Go to station.com (**www2.station.sony.com**) and click on **Jeopardy! Classic**. Then choose **Sign In** if you are a member, or **click here to JOIN, Free!** to register as a new user.

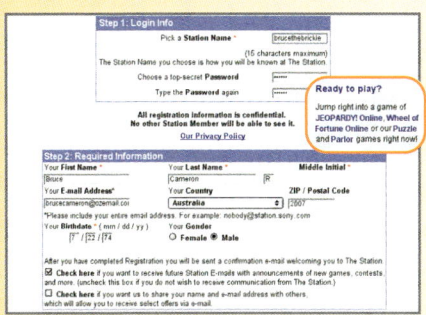

2 Choose a 'Station Name' and password, complete the panel of 'Required Information' and confirm that you accept the 'Terms of Service'. Click on the **Jeopardy!** link to start playing.

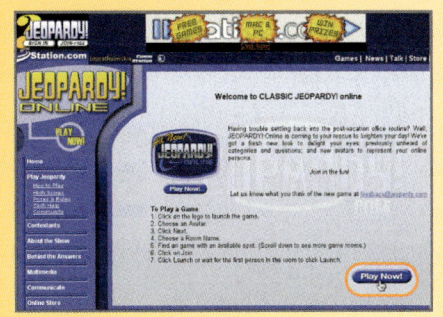

3 Read the rules of the game – you may want to print them out – and, when you are ready, click **Play Now**. You will have to wait a few minutes for the game to download to your computer.

4 Now choose an 'Avatar' – a figure to represent you – as well as a level of play. Finally, select a room to play in, or choose **Quick Start Multiplayer** to set up your own room that others can join.

Did You Know?

At chessKIDS academy (**www.chesskids.com**), young chess players can take free lessons, chat with other users of the site or play against a computer opponent.

SEE ALSO
- Search the Internet – page 64
- Download from the Web – page 86
- Keep the children entertained – page 174

189

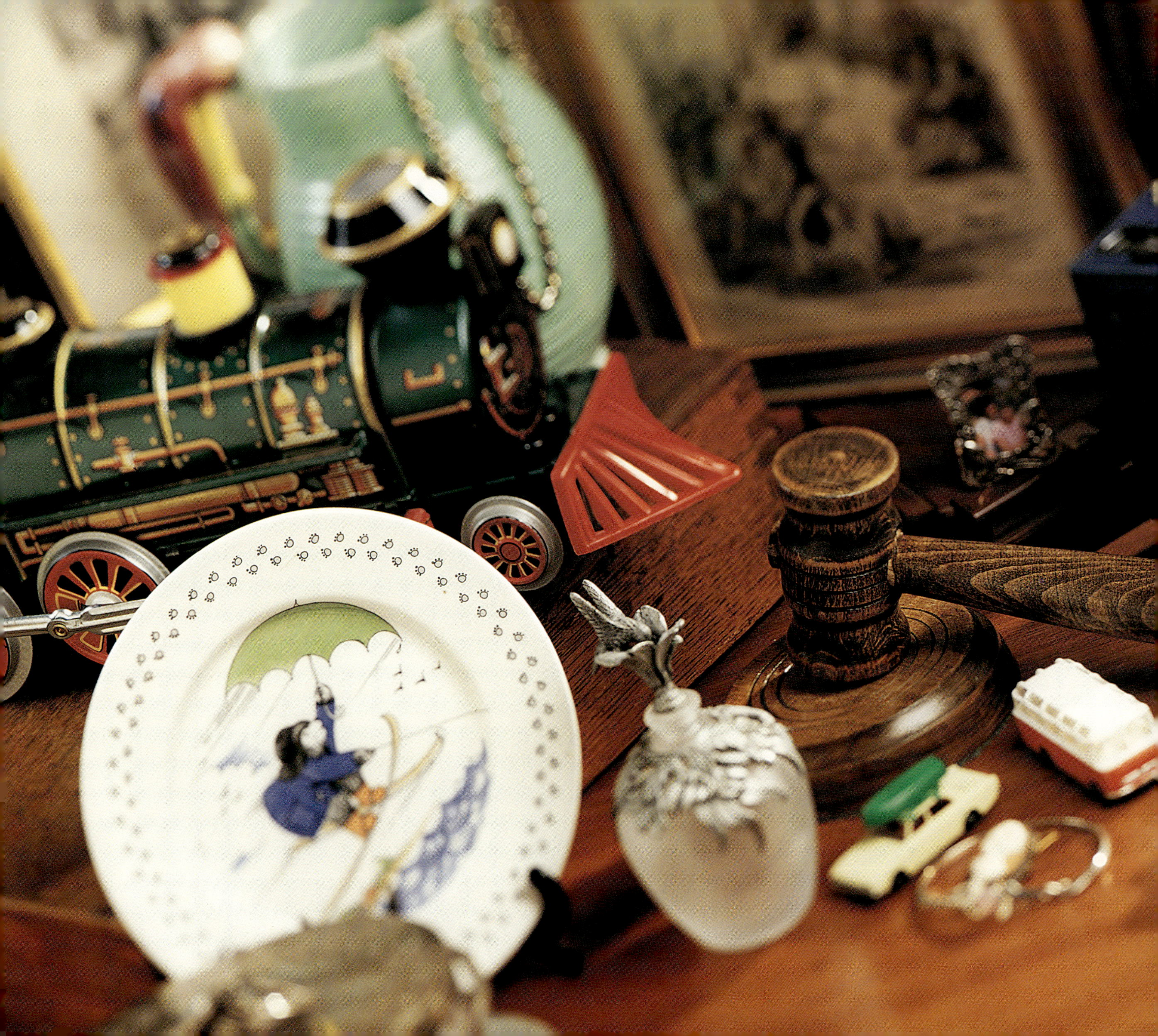

Money and shopping

- **192** Do your weekly shop
- **196** File your tax return
- **198** Become a share trader
- **201** Buy a book, CD or video
- **204** Get a mortgage quotation
- **206** Support a good cause
- **208** Buy and sell at auction
- **212** Open an on-line bank account

Do your weekly shop

Order your groceries **from home** and get them **delivered** to your doorstep

More and more people are saving valuable time by using the Internet to have their weekly shopping delivered to their door – especially heavy goods that can be bought in bulk, such as canned and dried food.

At present, on-line shopping in Australia and New Zealand is still in its infancy and is restricted to the most densely populated areas surrounding the major cities. No stores – not even the largest ones – service all the state capitals.

SITES TO TRY

Woolworths Australia
(www.woolworths.com.au)
Woolworths Internet HomeShop serves greater Sydney and Canberra, with plans to expand countrywide. Registered customers can access their Master List – a list of all the products they have purchased from the on-line store, or any particular previous order. Using these features, routine shopping for stock items becomes much less of a chore. The site also offers recipes and nutrition advice.

Woolworths New Zealand
(www.woolworths.co.nz)
This New Zealand on-line store is a separate operation from Woolworths Australia, but offers many of the same features, including access to previous shopping lists. At present the store delivers throughout much of the South Island and to many centres in the North Island.

GreenGrocer
(www.greengrocer.com.au)
As its name implies, GreenGrocer specialises in selling fresh fruit and vegetables, as well as a range of other perishable goods, such as meat and seafood. Orders placed on the GreenGrocer Web site by midnight are purchased at markets early the following morning and delivered to customers on the afternoon of the same day. Deliveries are currently limited, however, to greater Sydney and Melbourne as well as parts of regional Victoria.

shop online
Shop online and experience a value added shop. We'll be making sure you are the first to know about our special offers available only online.
MORE >>

EXOTIC TASTES

Grocery shopping on the Web need not be restricted to those run-of-the-mill items found in every supermarket trolley. You can also buy a wide range of exotic and specialist foods on-line.

Indulge yourself with some Bush Tomato Chutney or Kakadu Plum Jelly from Blue Gum Fine Foods **(www.bluegumfinefoods.com)**, for example. Or perhaps you have special dietary needs, but don't see why you shouldn't eat well. If so, you will find a variety of products – ranging from gluten-free pastas to salt-free potato chips – at Freedom Foods **(www.freedomfoods.com.au)**. And what about rounding off a meal with a cup of fine coffee. There are dozens to try at Danes Gourmet Coffee **(www.danes.com.au)**.

EXPLORE THE WEB

YOUR SHOPPING GUIDE

Several well-known supermarkets offer on-line shopping, including Woolworths in Australia and New Zealand (see left). But their services are not available in every part of the country, so this is the first thing you should check. You can do this by entering your postcode in the appropriate section of the site.

You should also look at the services offered. Woolworths in Australia, for example, only accepts orders of $60 or over, with a service fee of $12.50 per order. Coles has a $13.69 service fee, but no minumum order value.

Registration
All the major supermarkets' registration systems are similar. They request your name, address and a contact telephone number, and then you get to choose a password or PIN number to help to protect your account details.

Range of goods
On-line supermarkets offer almost everything that you would find on their shelves – fruit, vegetables, canned food and smallgoods. If you find products you want are routinely missing from your site, try another supermarket chain.

What to buy
Many people choose not to buy goods that are easily damaged, such as eggs or biscuits. Some also prefer to choose their own fresh fruit and vegetables, rather than rely on the choice of a supermarket employee. However, most on-line supermarkets do indicate the quality of each line of produce, and undertake to deliver the best available.

Buying bulk items such as canned food, pasta, pet food or nappies is a great way to save money, both in special deals and by cutting down on the number of times you need goods to be delivered.

Substitute items
Most on-line supermarkets give you the chance to say what should happen if one of your items is not available. You can choose to accept the nearest substitute or simply not to receive the item or any replacement.

The choice of a suitable substitute item is in the hands of the supermarket, which can create problems. You have to be prepared to receive a lesser brand of chicken-liver pâté in place of the special duck-liver pâté that you ordered.

Bargain-hunting
Most sites alert you to cut-price goods that you might overlook in the bustle of a supermarket. So while you might miss out on the fun of spying them in the aisles, you won't miss out on any good bargains.

Shopping lists
You can save your shopping lists and use them to place repeat orders. It is also possible to save your order halfway through and come back to it later. So, while your first shopping trip may take some time, the next one will be quicker.

Booking delivery
As you can't always be in to receive your groceries, supermarkets let you pick the time of the delivery (usually, a two-hour slot). If you're not in when the truck arrives, you may incur extra fees for a rescheduled delivery.

Dealing with problems
If you do not receive the expected quantity and quality of goods, you should contact the shop by e-mail or on a helpline to get a refund or replacement goods. The charge to your card is normally made on the day the goods are sent out rather than when you ordered them. This allows for changes in availability and price. You will be charged only for the available items at their price on the day of delivery. Again, contact the shop if this causes you problems.

Time Saver!
When you go back to a shopping site after you have registered, it will recognise who you are. This means that you don't have to re-enter all your details – you just have to enter a password or PIN number.

MONEY AND SHOPPING

Shopping account
The process of setting up an account is similar for all on-line supermarkets. Here we have set up an account with Woolworths.

HOW TO: SET UP AN ACCOUNT

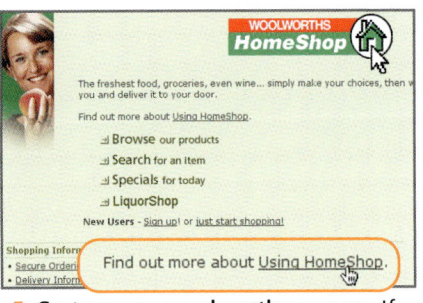

1 Go to **www.woolworths.com.au**. If this is your first visit, click on **Find out more about Using Homeshop** to see how the site operates and what it has to offer.

2 Once you have read the instructions, you can return to the homepage and click **Browse our products**. If you decide to give on-line shopping a go, click **Sign up!**

3 First of all, choose your 'User name', which is what you will be known by on the Woolworths site. Select a secondary name if your first choice is already taken; also, choose a password.

4 Now fill in your delivery details, including any special instructions for the driver – such as advice for negotiating a difficult access road or driveway.

5 Select your preferred 'Automated Emails' options, and finally choose what the store should do regarding substitution. When you have finished, click **Signup for HomeShop**.

6 Read carefully through the details on the confirmation form that appears next, to make sure they are all correct. When you are satisfied, click **Start Shopping**.

Organic groceries

Most of the major on-line supermarkets offer some organic produce. For a more specialised service, try a local supplier such as the Organic Grocer (**www.theorganicgrocer.com.au**), which supplies Sydney. An Auckland company, iE produce (**www.organicfresh.co.nz**), boasts that it can supply over 2000 organic products, both dry goods and fresh fruit and vegetables.

EXPLORE THE WEB

HOW TO: CHOOSE AND PLACE AN ORDER

1 Go to Woolworths Australia (**www.woolworths.com.au**) and enter your 'Username' and password in the boxes provided. Click **Login** to start shopping.

2 There are several ways to find items. You can choose **Browse all** and click on headings and subheadings until you reach the product you want. Click **Add to Trolley** if you want to buy an item.

3 Alternatively, you can choose **Product Search**, enter an item's name in the box that appears, and click **Search**. Again, click **Add to Trolley** to select any item you want to buy.

4 Once you have finished making your selection, click on **My Trolley** to review your purchases and their costs. Click **Copy Trolley To Master List** if you want the items to be recorded for future reference.

5 When you have finished shopping, click on **Proceed To The Checkout**. Read through the confirmation screen that now appears, and enter any new information. Click **Next Step** when you are ready.

6 Finally, choose a delivery time from the available slots shown in the list that appears next. To finalise the transaction, click **Purchase** and the goods will be dispatched. You will be billed on delivery.

Problem Solver!

If you have difficulty using a shopping site, consult its help section, where you will find answers to all the most common questions.

Weighty problem

At first you may find it disconcerting to shop without being able to view the products properly. Most sites offer pictures of some of their goods, but it can still be hard to visualise quite how much 500g of margarine is.

One solution is to save the supermarket receipt (which shows all the weights) from your last shopping trip and use it to compose your first on-line shopping list. You can then save this and refer to it every time you go shopping.

SEE ALSO
- **Shop safely on the Web** – page 54
- **Improve your diet and fitness** – page 130
- **Get cooking** – page 236

195

File your tax return

Get **advice** and fill in and **lodge** your personal **tax return** on the Internet

Filing your tax return is an obligation that no Australian or New Zealand citizen can afford to ignore. The Web has made the task of getting up-to-date information and advice much easier, and now the Australian Taxation Office has provided a special Web site for those who would like to file their annual returns online (see opposite). An equivalent service is not, however, yet available to individuals in New Zealand.

TAXING MATTERS

Official sites
Australian Taxation Office (ATO) (www.ato.gov.au)
New Zealand Inland Revenue (IRD) (www.ird.govt.nz)
Wherever you live, the best place to start your search for information on taxation is the official government

Web site. Both the ATO and the IRD offer a wide range of information on taxation matters, designed to help both individuals and businesses. However, only the ATO allows you to fill in and submit your annual tax return on-line (see opposite).

Help from the experts
If your tax affairs are complicated, or you feel unsure about how to go about claiming all that you are legally entitled to, then it may be in your best interests to get help from a tax professional. Several professional bodies in both Australia and New Zealand have Web sites that will help you track down a qualified adviser, including the Institute of Chartered Accountants in Australia **(www.icaa.org.au)** and the Taxation Institute of New Zealand **(www.tinz.co.nz)**.

Staying informed
Australian Taxation Index (http://commerce.flinders.edu.au/tax)
If you need detailed information on any aspect of tax in Australia then this site provides a great starting point. Assembled and maintained by the School of Commerce at Flinders University, it provides a wide range of links to sites dealing with everything connected with taxation – from ATO Case Judgments to a legal dictionary.

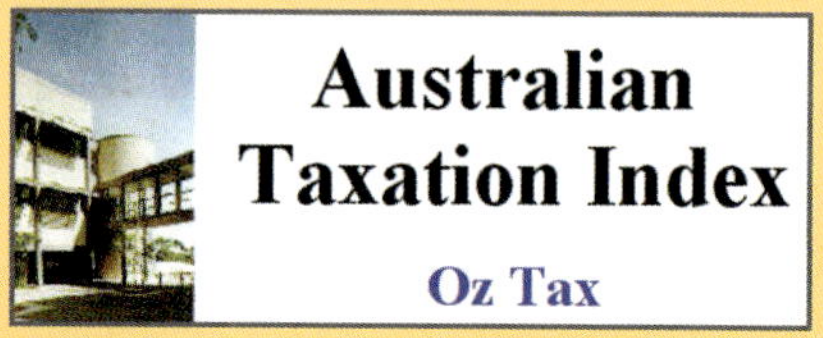

Mind your accounts
Accurate figures are what you need most when tax time comes around each year. Although accounting software is most often used by businesses, there are programs that can be used by individual and families as well. Some of the best known are made by MYOB **(www.myob.com.au** and **www.myob.co.nz)** and Quicken **(www.quicken.com.au** and **www.quicken.co.nz)**. Your local retailer will be able to advise you about programs made by smaller software firms.

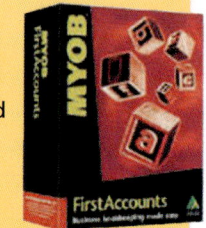

EXPLORE THE WEB

HOW TO: FILE YOUR TAX RETURN ON-LINE

Australian taxpayers can lodge their individual tax returns electronically using *e-tax*, a user-friendly software package that can be downloaded free from the ATO Web site (as shown here).

The service is available from the start of each new financial year (1 July) until December of that year. The process is very easy, and is like being interviewed by your computer while the tax return is completed in the background. Several members of a household can use the program to complete their respective tax returns.

1 Go to the main ATO Web site (**www.ato.gov.au**), click **For Individuals** and then navigate your way to the *e-tax* site. Read any relevant information on the way that you think may assist you.

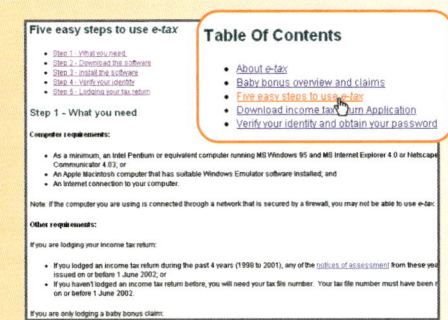

2 When you reach the *e-tax* site, read the sections that may be relevant to you, especially the one entitled **Five easy steps to use *e-tax***, which outlines the entire procedure.

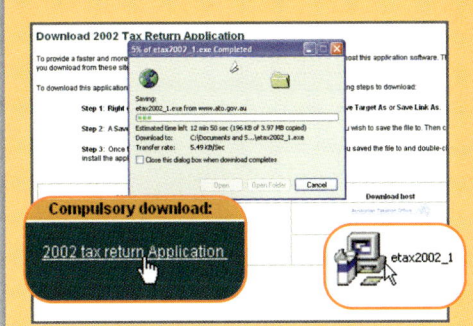

3 When you are ready, click to get your **Tax Return Application**. This will take about 20 minutes to download. When finished, double-click the icon to install the program on your computer.

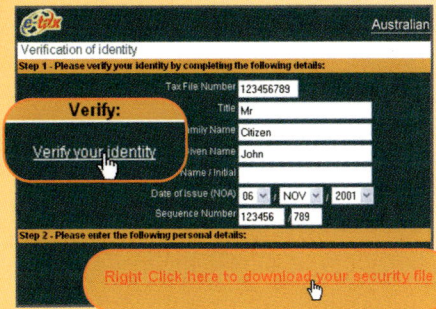

4 Now you will have to download your security file. To do this you must verify your identity with the ATO. You may need to consult your last Notice of Assessment – if you have one.

5 Once the file has been downloaded, you can go off-line to complete your return. Double-click on the desktop icon and follow the instructions to complete and then submit the form.

Other useful sites

A number of general sites also provide useful information on taxation, especially when it is needed most, at the end of each financial year. The Yahoo! Finance Tax Centre (**http://au.pfinance.yahoo.com/tax**) has some good features, as has the Tax section of the Quicken site (**www.quicken.com.au/tax**).

Taxing!
Madonna pays some £32,800 (A$86,300) in tax a day! Check out the Celebrity tax meter at Digita TaxCentral (**www.digita.com/taxcentral/home/break time/celebrity taxmeter**) for some light relief from those boring forms.

Time Saver!
Keep all your financial papers together and have them close to hand. This will save you time when filling in the form on-line.

SEE ALSO
● **Become a share trader** – *page 198*
● **Get a mortgage quotation** – *page 204*
● **How e-commerce works** – *page 298*

MONEY AND SHOPPING

Become a share trader

Own and **manage shares** using the **Internet**

Stocks and shares information was once the exclusive property of brokers and stock market traders. But the Internet has opened up the possibility of share trading for everyone. Many Web sites give you straightforward answers to basic questions such as which shares can be traded and how the actual purchasing process works. These sites also provide key information for first-time traders, such as how to reduce risks, trading tips, plus guides to the current performance of shares to help you to make investment decisions.

Where to begin
You can either register with an on-line broker who will deal with shares for you or – to cut out the middle man – register with a share trading site to start researching share performances yourself.

Choosing investments
Most Web sites will warn you about risky investments. The usual advice for beginners is to invest in shares from reliable companies on which you have current information.

Reduce risks
You can put your money into a variety of shares or join an on-line collective fund – made up of a group of people who invest together, contributing a certain, set amount each month.

Trial run
There are Web sites that let you practise trading on-line. These offer 'fantasy' share buying and selling facilities where you can find out how good you are at spotting potential stock market winners without spending any money.

EXPLORE THE WEB

SHARE TRADER SITES

Pre-trading site

The Motley Fool (www.fool.com) Before you begin share trading, it is wise to do some research. Motley Fool is a US site which provides information and advice on all aspects of financial management, including on-line share trading. The articles at the site are written in a clear, easy-to-understand language. Motley Fool also has a site in the UK (**www.fool.co.uk**), where you can get information on UK markets.

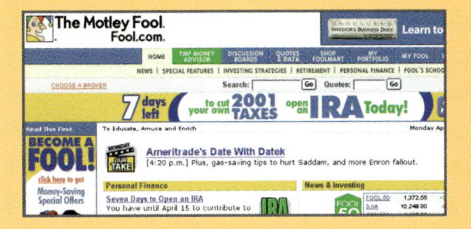

The exchange

The local stock exchange is a great place to start your exploration of the world of share trading. Both the Australian Stock Exchange (**www.asx.com.au**) and the New Zealand Stock Exchange (**www.nzse.co.nz**) offer an extensive range of information as well as advice for novice traders. The Australian exchange even offers on-line courses – some free and some for a fee – for investors who wish to develop their skills.

Trial run

If you are nervous about the idea of buying and selling shares on-line, there is one way of finding out what it's all about without risking a cent. The Australian Stock Exchange runs both a Charity Sharemarket Game and a Schools' Sharemarket Game. Go to **www.asx.com.au** and click on **Investor Education**; then on **ASX games**.

The New Zealand Stock Exchange runs a similar game called Stockmarket Challenge (**www.nzse.co.nz/links/challenge.html**), and an international version of the same idea can be found at Fantasy Stock Market (**www.fantasystockmarket.com**).

Share news

One of the keys to successful share trading is keeping up with financial news. One of the best ways to do this is to join one of the larger on-line share trading sites. There is generally no fee for joining, and once you have done so you'll have access to as much information as you could possibly need.

Most traders offer a tour for non-members, so try exploring E*TRADE Australia (**www.etrade.com.au**) or NZIJ Stockbrokers (**www.stockbroker.co.nz**).

SEARCH IT YOURSELF

To find out more information about the variety of share dealing services available, try using a search engine – especially one that lets you specify whether you want to search sites in Australia, New Zealand or the whole world.

1 For example, go to Yahoo! (**http://au.yahoo.com**).
2 Type in 'share trading sites' if you want to begin researching share information yourself. This will give a list of trading sites with advice and information for the private investor.
3 Alternatively, if you would prefer a share broker to deal for you, then type in 'share broker', which will give you a list of on-line brokers.

Did You Know?

Short-term investment is risky and if you want to get out in a hurry you may not get a good price. It is better to invest over a period of at least five years to minimise the effect of fluctuating share prices.

Money Saver!

Make sure you know the costs of share trading. In Australia, go to Brokerchoice, which compares the services and charges of on-line brokers: **www.brokerchoice.com.au**.

199

MONEY AND SHOPPING

HOW TO: LEARN TO TRADE

Before signing up with an on-line share dealer, try one of the sites that allows you to trade with make-believe money. Both the Australian and New Zealand stock exchanges have on-line trading competitions in which players are 'given' $50,000 to trade with, but these are only run at certain times of the year (see page 199).

A few trading sites around the world – mostly in the USA – also offer practice portfolios, but no local companies do so. However, it is still worth trying one of the overseas sites, which will give you the feel of what it's like to trade on-line. Whatever the outcome, you can at least be certain that your lack of experience will not cost you a cent.

1 Go to a stock market game site, such as that run by Lycos Finance (**http://finance.lycos.com/home/maxinvest/game.asp**), and sign up as a member. This does not commit you to anything.

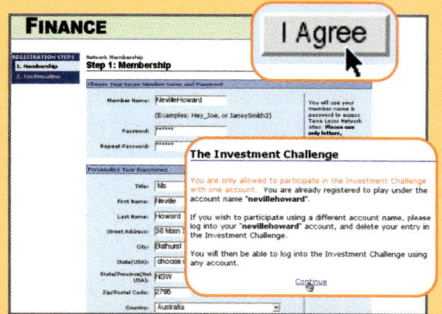

2 Fill in a few personal details on the form provided and click **I Agree**. Acknowledge the confirmation that appears next, and then click to start playing the Investment Challenge.

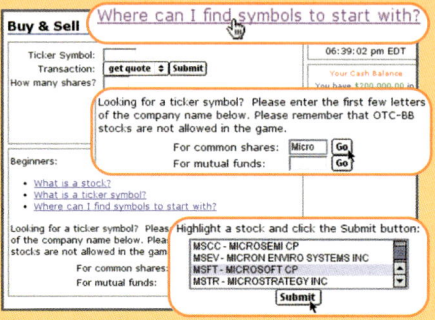

3 To get a quote on a stock you are interested in, enter its code in the box provided (click on **Explanations of terms** if you need to); then click **Submit** to see current details.

4 To buy a stock, enter the number of shares you want and click **Submit**. You are asked to confirm the order and are shown your updated cash balance. Now try to make the total grow!

THE REAL WORLD

When you sign up to do business with an on-line broker, you will have to set up a trading account. Requirements vary from broker to broker, with some requiring you to deposit an initial amount of money. Other brokers may permit you to buy stocks in the top 150 companies on credit.

In some cases, a broker will require you to set up a trust or cash management account with an initial deposit of up to $5000. If you do have to set up such an account, check to see whether you will be paid a good rate of interest on the balance.

Watch Out!

When buying shares on-line, always make sure to double-check any information you enter into forms. An extra zero accidentally added to a figure, for example, could end up being very expensive.

SEE ALSO
- **Do some research** – page 113
- **Find legal advice** – page 120
- **Open an on-line bank account** – page 212

EXPLORE THE WEB

Buy a book, CD or video

Access searches, information and previews before **buying on-line**

The Internet gives you fast and convenient access to the largest selection of books, music and videos available to buy anywhere in the world. There is no longer any need to spend time and money telephoning or travelling to shops. You can do it all from home. You can find shops which specialise in out-of-print books, textbooks, foreign books, CDs, old vinyl records, and virtually every film ever made both on video and DVD. There are also on-line shops which have reviews, links, samples, ratings and news to help you decide what to buy – this service is also a great way to get inspiration for gifts for people of all ages.

Most wanted
New and recent titles are easy to find on the Net, but where the Web really comes into its own is with obscure or out-of-print books and records. You can scour the world in an instant to find that first edition of *Brighton Rock*, or some German pressing of early Beatles hits. You can also access Web sites with information and prices on converting old film to video.

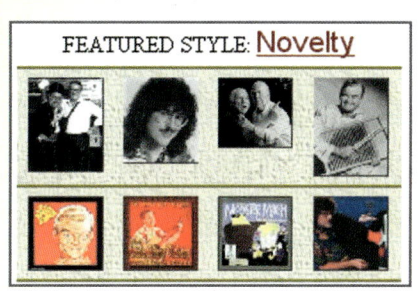

Previews
Some on-line video and DVD shops offer small preview clips of films, so you can see what to expect before you buy. Many on-line bookshops offer sample chapters on-line.

FEATURED STYLE: Novelty

MONEY AND SHOPPING

Money Saver!

Shopping on-line can save you money, but the postal costs can easily add up. The best way to maximise your savings is to wait until you need several items and then order them to be sent at the same time. Alternatively, club together with friends and put in a joint order.

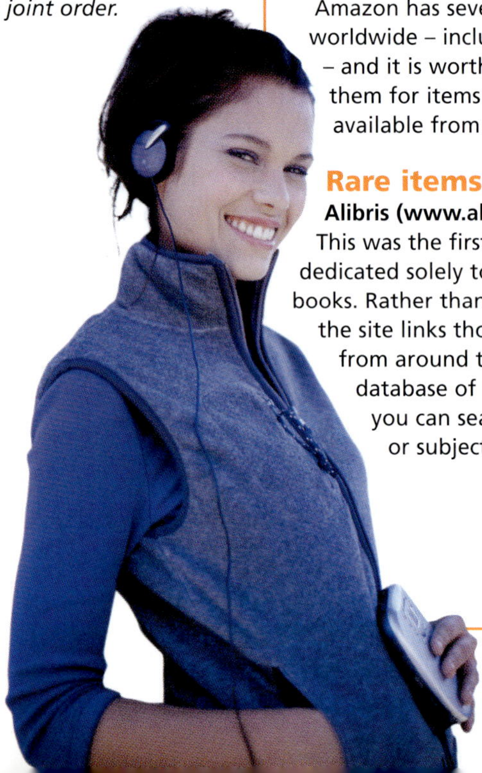

THE BEST SITES

Overall shopping
Amazon (www.amazon.com)
For the world's largest on-line store for books, music and films, go to Amazon. This US site has many innovative options: for example, it will generate a list of titles it thinks you will like (based on previous purchases). It can be quite an eye-opener to discover the kind of reader Amazon's computer thinks you are.

Amazon has several stores worldwide – including one in the UK – and it is worth checking with them for items that may not be available from the main US site.

Rare items
Alibris (www.alibris.com)
This was the first on-line site dedicated solely to selling hard-to-find books. Rather than storing the books, the site links thousands of sellers from around the world. With a database of millions of books, you can search by title, author or subject area.

The best price
BuyGuide Australia (www.buyguide.com.au)
This site does not stock any items itself, but will help you to search 250 on-line stores in Australia for the products you are after. BuyGuide claims to offer impartial advice, as well as a price comparison service that will help you to track down the best possible deal.

Vinyl site
GEMM – The Global Electronic Music Marketplace (http://gemm.com)
Although vinyl records are becoming more rare in the shops, they are easily available on the Internet. At this site you can search through the world's largest catalogue of music with listings of over 11 million new and used records for sale. Supply your own 'Want List' or browse the selection on offer by artist, category or era.

Movie site
The Internet Movie Database (www.imdb.com)
Virtually everything you want to know about any film or actor can be found on this site. Film buffs can also create a personalised database to help them keep track of when favourite films are to be released on video or DVD.

SEARCH IT YOURSELF

If you can't find what you're looking for at one of the large, international shops, try searching through speciality database sites. For a worldwide list of booksellers, try BookWeb (**www.bookweb. org/bookstores**), or take a look at Bookfayre (**www.bookfayre.com**), which has a searchable database of rare books.

For on-line bookshops in Australia and New Zealand, take a look at Dymocks (**www.dymocks. com.au**), the Co-op Online Bookshop (**www. coop-bookshop.com.au**) and New Zealand Books (**http://newzealandbooks.co.nz**).

If you're after an exhaustive music database, try the All Music Guide (**www.allmusicguide.com**).

EXPLORE THE WEB

HOW TO: BUY SECOND-HAND BOOKS ON-LINE

There are many second-hand book sites accessible via the Internet. BookFinder (www.bookfinder.com) is one of the best. This site is linked to booksellers and book search sites around the world, and can provide immediate access to millions of rare, used and out-of-print books, as well as more recent publications.

You can search by title and author or, if you don't know or can't remember those, by keywords. Because the titles are found internationally, always check where the book is being shipped from and how much that will cost.

1 Go to BookFinder (www.bookfinder.com). Type the title and/or author of the book, or any keywords, in the search box. Specify any special features and the type of book you are after.

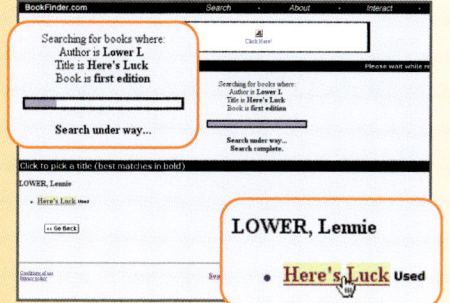

2 There is usually a brief pause while a search is made for your request. When the results are displayed, click on any that interest you (there is only one on offer in this example).

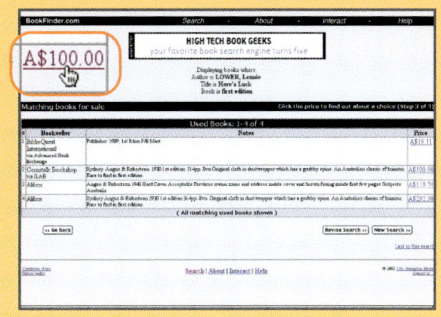

3 You will now see a list of books you can buy, ranging from the cheapest to the most expensive (in whichever currency you chose on the opening page). Click on one to see more details.

4 You will now be taken to the Web site of the dealer who has the book for sale. If you wish to proceed with the purchase, click on the appropriate link – here **Add to Shopping cart**.

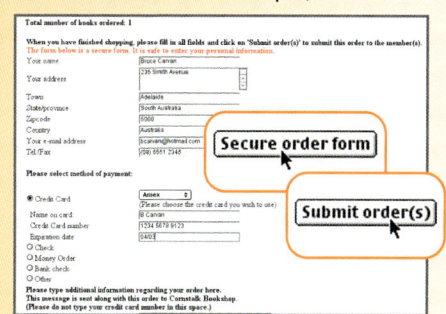

5 Before completing the payment form with details of your identity, address and credit card, check that the site is secure (look for a locked padlock symbol in the bottom left corner).

Time Saver!

Some Web shops boast huge catalogues, but in fact they only order an item from a supplier once you have purchased it. This can slow down your order. The better on-line shops, such as Amazon (www.amazon.com), will check their stock levels before confirming your order.

SEE ALSO
- **Shop safely on the Web** – page 54
- **Do some research** – page 113
- **Enjoy the literary world** – page 166

MONEY AND SHOPPING

Get a mortgage quotation

Use **the Internet** to get the finance for your move

Most building societies and banks advertise their mortgage products on-line, so if you are looking for the best deal, it makes sense to try the Web. It will be quicker and simpler than traipsing up and down the street or sending off for brochures. You can use the information you find as a basis for discussion with brokers or financial advisers. Some lenders even allow you to make your application on-line.

Find out about a mortgage
At most lenders' Web sites you can view details of the policies on offer and, if you find one that suits you, make an initial application on-line. By answering the questions on the on-line form, you'll get an instant reply informing you of your eligibility. On-line applications can save you time and trouble. An application form is sent to you by post with your details filled in. All you need to do is read, check and sign it.

Choose a mortgage
When choosing a mortgage, you don't have to search through all the lenders' sites. Use an independent site such as Right Loan (**www.RightLoan.com.au**) or E-Loan (**www.eloan.co.nz**) to compare rates and products. Most mortgage sites let you specify your exact requirements and then search their database for suitable mortgages.

Calculate your mortgage
Many sites let you enter details of your mortgage and then calculate what your monthly payment will be. Or, you can enter the monthly amount you want to pay, and find what you can afford to borrow.

EXPLORE THE WEB

TOP MORTGAGE SITES

On-line magazine
**Your Mortgage
(www.yourmortgage.com.au)**
This Web site is the electronic arm of *Your Mortgage* magazine, which is published bi-monthly. Here you can compare mortgage rates, read about various types of loans, their advantages and disadvantages, and even subscribe to a free on-line weekly newsletter.

Mortgage comparisons
eChoice (www.echoice.com.au)
According to the eChoice Web site, 'it takes the average Australian 28 hours, spread over eight weeks, to hunt down a suitable mortgage'. To save you time, eChoice offers an easy alternative: all you do is fill in a single form giving your particulars, and then eChoice identifies the best choice of lender and loan. You can choose to have eChoice call you back to discuss your options, and if you decide to proceed, you will be put in touch with the lender of your choice. eChoice does not lend money itself, but acts on behalf of several mortgage providers, including Westpac and St George among others.

Time-saver
**Mortgage Australia
(www.mortgageaustralia.com.au)**
As with eChoice (above), Mortgage Australia offers a brokering service that is free to the borrower. The site includes a home-loan calculator and a borrowing guide, as well as answers to a range of commonly asked home-loan questions.

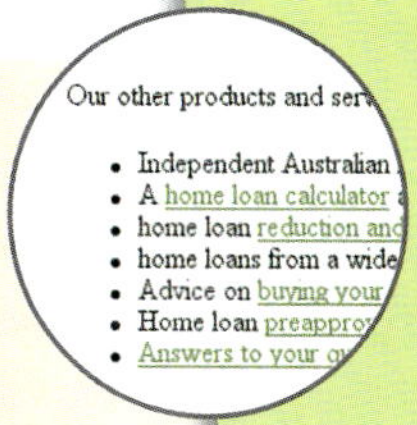

New Zealand broker
Loansurf (www.loansurf.co.nz)
Loansurf's Mortgage Tender System collects information from you and forwards it to several participating financial institutions. These are given one working day to respond with an expression of interest, after which Loansurf collates all the offers that have come in and forwards them to you to make a decision.

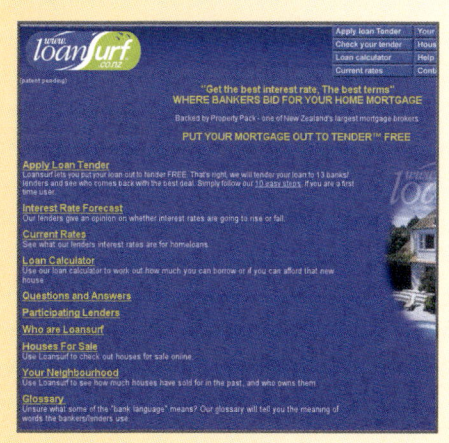

SEARCH IT YOURSELF
Yahoo! (**http://au.yahoo.com**) has links to most financial institutions in Australia and New Zealand.

Open the Yahoo! homepage and identify the Yahoo! Finance box. Here you will find headings that include Mortgages, Personal Loans, Business Loans and Bank Accounts.

For mortgage information, click on **Personal Finance**. Try the Yahoo! Loan Selector, or check the loan rate summary for your area.

The links under the 'Categories' section will take you to individual bank, credit union and mortgage provider Web sites.

Problem Solver!
*Still wondering if you're paying too much for that house? Ask an on-line valuer, such as Property Value (**www.propertyvalue.com.au**) or QV (**www.quotable.co.nz**), for an estimate, which they will provide for a fee.*

SEE ALSO
- **Find legal advice** – *page 120*
- **Improve your home** – *page 183*
- **Open an on-line bank account** – *page 212*

205

MONEY AND SHOPPING

Support a good cause
Find out how you can help using the Web

The Internet has opened up new ways of putting your time or money to work in a good cause. The Web has made it easier than ever before to find out about organisations that need your help. On-line fund-raising also means that charities can spend less time and money campaigning and more time applying their funds where they are most needed.

Shop and click to donate
One of the best ways to donate money over the Internet is through shopping. Each time you purchase from a retailer listed with a charity on the Internet, that retailer will donate a percentage of the sale to the charity. At other sites, such as The Rainforest Site (**www.therainforestsite.com**), you can click on a button to have a donation made for you by the site's sponsors – making it easy for you to help a cause.

Getting involved
All the international community organisations such as Greenpeace (**www.greenpeace.org**), Amnesty International (**www.amnesty.org**) and the World Wide Fund for Nature (**www.wwf.org**) have Web sites – with links to their own Australian and New Zealand sites – where you can find out how to get involved in worthwhile projects by donating either your time or your money.

EXPLORE THE WEB

CHARITY SITES

Research
United Devices (http://members.ud.com/projects/cancer)
To participate in scientific research that may eventually help to cure cancer, you can download a screensaver from United Devices for the National Foundation for Cancer Research. The screensaver will process scientific research data while your computer is idle. The technology, pioneered by the Seti@home project (see *Go into outer space*, page 142), uses the program to link up millions of home computers, creating a virtual super-computer. This then screens millions of chemicals for their usefulness in fighting cancer by using the vast amounts of unused computing power in your PC.

Shopping
Charity Mall (www.charitymall.org.nz)
This is a shopping portal with a directory of links to on-line retailers. Shoppers can select which non-profit organisation or charity will receive up to 30 per cent of the value of their on-line purchases. The directory includes a number of New Zealand charities, and a selection of local and international retailers.

Giving
Donations (www.donations.com.au)
The Donations Web site provides a central point from which you can make donations to your favourite charities. All you need to do is select the organisation you wish to support, select the amount, complete your details and donate. The organisers claim that this procedure streamlines the process of giving, thus ensuring that as much money as possible reaches the intended recipients.

Auctions
Yahoo! charity auctions
Charity auctions are a popular way of raising funds for a variety of worthy causes. New events are constantly appearing, so to find out what's currently available, visit the Auctions section of Yahoo! (http://au.sold.yahoo.com) and click on any of the listed auctions, or on **All Charity Auctions**.

MAKE A CHARITY SITE YOUR HOMEPAGE
You can use a charity site – such as World Vision (**www.worldvision.org.au**) or The Hunger Site (**www.thehungersite.com**) – as your homepage. Open Internet Explorer and click on the **Tools** menu. Select **Internet Options**. Type the charity site's address in the address box, then click **OK**.

Volunteering your help
One of the most effective ways you can help others is to donate some of your time. Charitable and community organisations always need extra hands to help with work or fund-raising. To find out how you can participate, visit Australian Volunteer Search (**www.volunteersearch.gov.au**) or Seek Volunteer (**www.volunteer.com.au**). If you want to help further afield, check out the Global Volunteer Network (**www.volunteer.org.nz**).

Watch Out!
The Internet is home to many frauds, with new ones appearing all the time. For news of all the latest scams, check out the Commonwealth Government's Consumers Online site (www.consumersonline.gov.au).

SEE ALSO
- Security on the Internet – *page 52*
- Shop safely on the Web – *page 54*
- Buy and sell at auction – *page 208*

Buy and sell at auction

Find out how you can **bid for almost anything** over the Internet

One person's trash is another person's treasure. No matter what it is, you can be sure there's someone out there who collects it. The Internet has made auctions open to anyone. If there is something you want, you can probably find it, and often at a bargain price. Equally, you can sell virtually anything at an Internet auction site – perhaps an antique figurine or a pile of old comics. Transactions need not involve money, since the Internet can also be a useful 'swap shop'.

HOW IT ALL WORKS

On an auction site such as eBay (www.ebay.com.au), a seller places an ad for an item, listing a minimum bid and a closing date for the auction. Buyers enter their bids by filling in a form on-screen and the highest bidder at the close of the auction wins. At this point the auction site notifies the winner and the seller by e-mail and the two parties make arrangements to complete the transaction.

Other ways to bid Some sites, such as Safetender (www.safetender.co.nz), let you state how much you want to pay for an item, and then notify you if anyone accepts your offer. Other sites conduct 'reverse auctions', where a buyer states a price and sellers then compete to undercut each other. At this stage there are few such sites in Australia and New Zealand, but this approach is popular in the USA.

You can also use a service, such as eSnipe (www.esnipe.com), which places your bid in the last seconds before an auction closes – a process known as 'sniping'. This keeps prices down by masking your interest in an item and so avoiding bidding wars. Buyers have sniped for years, but eSnipe automates the process and increases your chances of success.

There are many specialised exchange sites on the Web, such as The CDexchange (www.thecdexchange.com) and On-Line Swap Market (www.swapmarket.com.au), which deals in cars and car parts.

HOW TO PAY SAFELY

You would normally pay for goods bought on the Internet by cheque or credit card. Paying by credit card gives you more rights as a consumer, but a private seller may only accept a cheque or cash.

Most sellers are reliable but there are always a few dishonest traders. Regardless of how you pay, the best way to ensure that you are not defrauded is to use a payment company that acts as an intermediary between you and the seller. These are known as Escrow companies (after a legal term for a fund held in trust).

Instead of paying the seller at once, you pay the agreed amount to an Escrow company such as Secure-Commerce (www.secure-commerce.com.au). The seller then ships the goods to you and, if you're satisfied, you inform the Escrow company to pay the seller. Such companies charge around 4 per cent of the transaction price for this service.

EXPLORE THE WEB

TOP AUCTION SITES

eBay
www.ebay.com.au
http://pages.ebay.com/nz
Of the hundreds of on-line auction sites, eBay is the biggest – think of it as the world's largest flea market. Coins, toys, books or gems, even cars, boats and houses – they're all here. Buyers and sellers can register for free. Items can be put up for sale for a small fee plus a percentage of the final sales price.

One of the best things about eBay is its feedback system, which rates sellers according to the number of positive comments posted by buyers. Most sellers are in the USA, but eBay's country-specific sites (such as those for Australia and New Zealand) indicate which items are available locally.

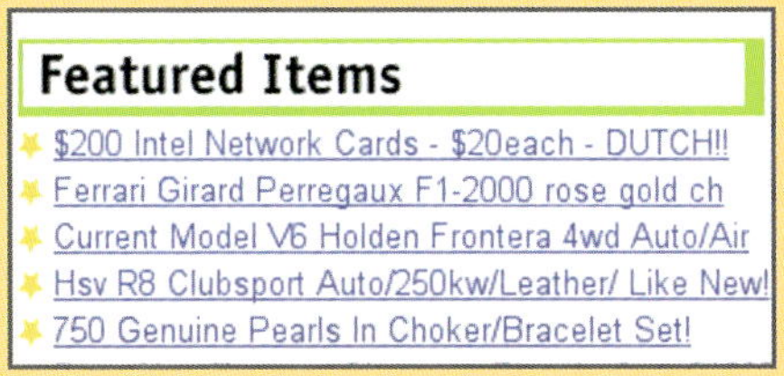

Sold.com
http://au.sold.yahoo.com
If you are looking for a particular item, the bigger the auction house the better. Sold.com, which is affiliated to Yahoo!, lists more than 17 major categories containing over 150,000 items for sale.

To see what else may be available, go to the Yahoo! homepage (**http://au.yahoo.com**). At the bottom, click on one of the overseas Yahoo! sites, and then on **Auctions**.

Sold.com also hosts auctions on behalf of charities, such as the Salvation Army. Make a successful bid and your money goes to a good cause. Click on the **All Charity Auctions** link to see what charities are available at any one time.

AuctionWatch
www.auctionwatch.com
If you're looking for something very specific – a program from an old Ashes test match, say – try this site, which will search through all on-line auction sites and let you know as soon as the item you want has been found. Similar services are offered by other sites, including Bidfind (**www.bidfind.com**).

AuctionGuide
www.auctionguide.com
Full of handy explanations of auction procedures and terminology, this is a great site for learning auction basics. If you have any doubts about auction pitfalls, such as hidden costs, consult the 'Tips 'n Hints' section.

Built-in help
The latest iMac version of Internet Explorer has a feature called Auction Manager, which monitors the status of auctions that you are interested in, and notifies you when someone places a higher bid than you and when the auction closes.

To find out more, go to the **Tools** menu, select **Auction Manager** and then click on the **Help** button for an on-screen tutorial.

Did You Know?
eBay set up the first on-line auction in 1995. Electronic auctions now generate annual profits in excess of A$100 billion.

SOLD TO THE HIGHEST BIDDER!
Auction sites can be a good way to get the best possible price for any items you want to sell.

Be it the watch worn by grandad in the trenches, or a newspaper from the 1880s, someone, somewhere, will want it. For an object you know to be genuinely precious, consider contacting Sotheby's (**www.sothebys.com**) for a valuation and also to browse their on-line auctions to check the prices of other similar objects.

If you are selling an item that seems to defy the categories of most auction sites, you can search for a speciality auction by typing 'auction' and your subject (such as 'thimbles', 'stamps' or 'railways') into a search engine.

Bidfind (**www.bidfind.com**) and Bidville (**www.bidville.com**) also offer a range of speciality auctions that you can try.

MONEY AND SHOPPING

HOW TO: TAKE PART IN AN ON-LINE AUCTION

Most auction sites let you browse through the listings without registering. You can also check the bidding on an item you're interested in. Bookmark the page and return to it periodically to see what the highest bid is and how much time is left in the auction. You need only register with the site when you want to place a bid or to put an item up for sale.

All the auction Web sites operate on largely the same principles. Here we have shown how to register with eBay, locate an item and bid for it.

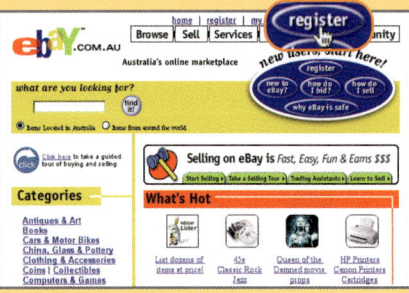

1 Go to **www.ebay.com.au** and click on **Register**. Select your country of residence and click **Continue**.

2 Type your personal details in the form that appears next and click **Continue**. You must then read and accept the User Agreement.

3 You will then be sent an e-mail with your identity code. Click on the link in the e-mail and you will be returned to eBay for the final stage.

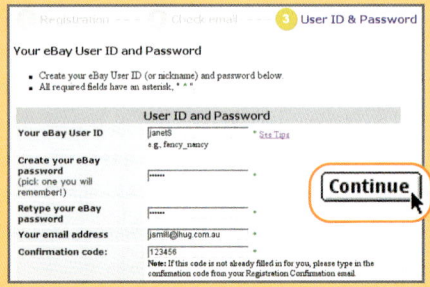

4 Enter a User ID and password in the form provided, and create a secret question and answer. Click **Continue** and you'll be welcomed as a member.

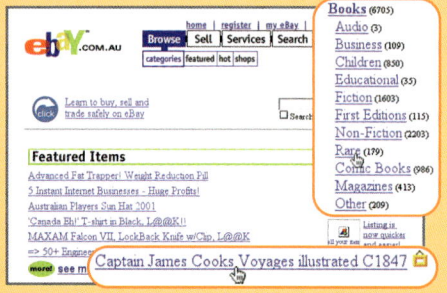

5 To bid for an item, click on **Browse** and look through the categories. Here we have chosen an early account of Captain Cook's voyages.

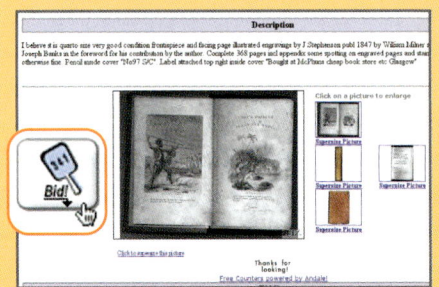

6 You are now shown details of the item, including a picture if there is one, the price and the name of the seller. To make an offer, click **Bid**.

7 Now enter the maximum amount you are willing to bid (here in Australian dollars) and click **Review bid**. Check your details and click **Place bid**.

8 You will immediately receive a message telling you whether you are the highest bidder – if you are not, you can reconsider your offer.

You will then receive an e-mail every day until the auction closes, telling you whether you are still the highest bidder – and finally whether you have been successful with your bid.

If you have, you are bound by contract to contact the seller (using the details given on the site) and arrange payment and delivery of the item.

Auction aficionados

It is possible to make a living by selling at auction. But finding items to sell, organising lot descriptions and photos, posting auctions, handling queries, notifying winners, taking payment and shipping the goods will make it a full-time job. Successful sellers work 10 to 16 hours a day.

✋ Watch Out!

If a seller does not deliver an item as arranged, contact the auction site. Some will try to resolve the dispute for you. Many sites also offer some form of guarantee.

210

EXPLORE THE WEB

AUCTION TIPS

Every auction site offers a guide to its own bidding system – both for sellers and buyers. You should always refer to this for specific help and advice. But there are several useful tips worth bearing in mind:

DO watch an auction before joining one yourself. This way, you can get a feel for how they work without having to bid.

DO make sure you know the shipping costs before you make a bid, by checking the auction house's FAQ page. Shipping fees vary widely, even though all auction houses use standard courier services. Shipping costs and insurance can vastly increase the price.

DON'T bid for a product before investigating its retail price. A search through retail sites such as Yahoo! Shopping (http://au.shopping.yahoo.com) or BuyGuide (www.buyguide.com.au) will help you to check.

DO pay taxes on your auction earnings. If you earn a substantial income from your on-line trading, you will have to declare it. Check with the Australian Tax Office (www.ato.gov.au) or the Inland Revenue Department (www.ird.govt.nz).

DON'T sell an item at auction without first setting a reserve price at the minimum amount you want to get. Bids that don't reach the reserve price are rejected. That protects you against being forced to sell an item if the highest bid is very low. Remember, an agreement between a buyer and seller is a legally binding contract.

DO learn how to spot and protect yourself against auction scams. See the tips offered by AuctionGuide (www.auctionguide.com/tips).

DON'T buy any item you feel has been poorly described. You want to be sure you know exactly what you are getting. A photo is helpful.

DO check the site for feedback left by previous buyers to see if the seller is honest.

DO ask for help if you are a victim of auction fraud. eBay, for example, offers a free Fraud Protection Program, with a maximum reimbursement of $400 to all its members.

GOING, GOING...

It is no exaggeration to say that just about anything you can think of can be bought at an Internet auction.

One of the most bizarre items ever sold through eBay was a Second orld War submarine, put up for sale by a small town in New England that decided it no longer needed it.

Someone once tried to sell a missile through eBay. Although the auction company thought the sale was only a prank, the federal authorities in Washington, DC, advised them to keep the sale open, then made the winning bid themselves and arrested the would-be arms merchant.

Perhaps the strangest item ever put up for auction was a soul. eBay eventually cancelled the sale when they could not decide how the winning bidder would take delivery.

Money Saver!

Compare prices for similar items at different auction sites before you bid, or you might waste money paying more than you need to.

SEE ALSO
- Security on the Internet – page 52
- Shop safely on the Web – page 54
- File your tax return – page 196

MONEY AND SHOPPING

Open an on-line bank account

Do your **banking** business **whenever** it suits you on the Web

Most major banks and building societies now offer instant on-line access to your finances at any hour of the day. On-line banking services range from checking your balance to making transfers, payments and managing your investments. You can apply for loans, new accounts, credit cards and even a mortgage on-line. You can move money electronically between any of the various accounts you have at a particular bank, and transfer it back again. With some on-line accounts, you can also move money between different banks by simply logging on to the Internet.

On-line banks
There are two kinds of Internet bank: those with bricks-and-mortar branches, such as Westpac, that allow you to access your accounts on-line; and Internet-only banks, such as ING, which have no physical branches.

With some Internet-only banks, you can obtain cash through ATMs; others only allow you to pay bills and transfer funds to another bank, from which you can access your money.

Is it free?
Both kinds of Internet bank may charge for their services. How fees are applied varies from bank to bank, so this is one of the first things you should check when shopping around for an Internet account.

What banking can you do?
You can check your balance, transfer funds between accounts (generally at the same bank), pay bills, view and print out transaction summaries, and set up automatic monthly payments, such as your rent.

Most Internet accounts offered by the major Australian banks also let you use the BPay system to settle accounts, where this is an option.

EXPLORE THE WEB

THE KEY QUESTIONS

How do you bank on-line?
If you have an account with one of the traditional banks and have registered for telephone banking (so that you already have your own customer number and password), you can usually access Internet banking by going to the bank's Web site; if you are unsure of the address, you will probably find it on a recent statement.

If you have not registered for phone banking, call your bank for advice; you may be able to register for phone and Internet banking with the same call.

How do you take cash out?
Despite the popularity of credit cards and Internet bank accounts, most of us still need cash for everyday transactions. This can be a problem with some Internet-only banks. If your Internet-only account does not have cash-out facilities, you will probably need to have another account with a bank that does provide this service.

Some Internet-only banks, such as BankDirect (www.bankdirect.co.nz), provide access to cash through ATMs.

How do you pay money in?
If you have on-line access to an account at one of the traditional banks, you can still

> **Easy Deposits.**
> You can do virtually all your banking transactions via the phone or the Internet.
> - To deposit cash in your BankDirect account, simply visit any bank branch or ASB Bank ATM machine with a deposit facility.
> - To deposit a cheque, you can also post it in to us in the Freepost envelopes we can provide you.
> - Of course you can also deposit money into your BankDirect accounts via direct credit or automatic payments.

pay in cheques or cash by going to your branch, or using the post or the deposit facilities at an appropriate ATM.

With an Internet-only account, you either have to post your cheques to the bank using the Freepost envelopes provided, or pay your money into another bank (one that is affiliated with, or approved by, your on-line bank), from where you can transfer the funds into your Internet-only account.

One of the simplest ways of getting money into an Internet-only account – especially a savings account – is to have part of your salary paid directly into it.

What are the interest rates?
Because Internet-only banks have lower overheads, they can often offer better rates on savings accounts, loans and overdrafts. Together with ease of access, this is the biggest advantage of such accounts.

What if I have a problem?
All banks that offer on-line facilities also provide a comprehensive telephone help service for customers – often for 24 hours a day, seven days a week.

Will my account be secure?
All banks offer a secure service. There is a rigorous system of passwords and access criteria to establish your identity. And all the personal data sent to and from your computer is encrypted, making it virtually impossible for anyone to gain unauthorised access to your account.

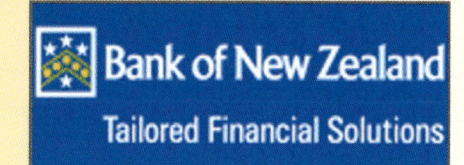

CASE STUDY

Grant, a self-employed property developer, has just come back from his first holiday in five years.

'I'm a control freak. I need to know if all the rents have come in, and the contractors have been paid. I simply didn't feel I could take a holiday.

'In the end my wife made me get on-line access to my Wespac accounts and then took me to an Internet café in town. She made me sit in front of a computer, whipped a straw hat out of her bag, stuck it on my head and said "Just pretend you're on holiday".

'I gave it a try and found that I could be a control freak anywhere in the world! In fact we spent the next hour or two browsing for a holiday and booked one there and then!'

INTERNET-ONLY ACCOUNTS

Pros
- Savings rates often better than average
- Some fees and charges may be lower
- Instant access to your account and balance information
- 24-hour access, seven days a week
- Automatic payments easily viewed and amended

Cons
- No face-to-face assistance
- Some services may not be available
- Withdrawing money may involve more effort

213

MONEY AND SHOPPING

Time Saver!
Make your on-line banking or Internet account site one of your Internet Explorer Favorites and add it to your toolbar for fast access.

Watch Out!
Keep all your passwords in a safe place or, better still, memorise them and destroy any hard copies.

EASY-TO-USE SITES

Westpac
www.westpac.com.au
This site provides clear instructions for accessing all the on-line banking services offered by Westpac. If you want to find out what is involved in Internet banking, click on **Online Banking**, then **active demonstrations**. There are also instructions on using a WAP-compatible mobile phone to access the site.

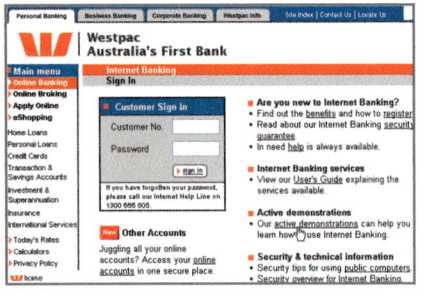

As with all Internet banking sites, there is a button that you should click to check whether your browser is up to the task. Older browsers can be unsafe for financial transactions on-line.

The National Bank of New Zealand
www.nationalbank.co.nz
The National Bank offers many of the same on-line services as other major banks for both personal and business customers. Click on **CAN WE SHOW YOU AROUND?** or **Online Services** to be shown the key features available.

As with other on-line banks, you can access your account from anywhere in the world if the browser you are using meets the bank's encryption standards.

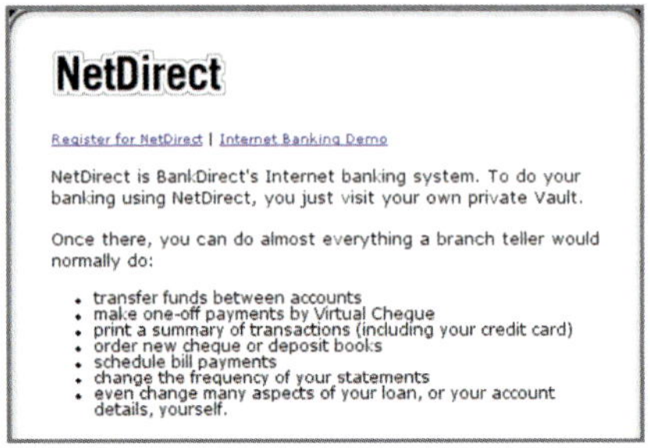

BankDirect
www.bankdirect.co.nz
BankDirect provides a phone- and Internet-only banking service (the latter known as NetDirect), which means it has no physical branches. However, you can make withdrawals from, and deposit money at, a country-wide network of affiliated ATMs.

Because this bank has no branches, its overheads are lower than those of conventional banks, and so too, it claims, are its fees and charges. You can take the usual on-line guided tour, and if you want personal assistance there is a 24-hour telephone service.

Moneymanager
www.moneymanager.com.au
To find out which institutions provide Internet banking services in Australia – together with a brief summary of what they offer – visit the Moneymanager site. Go to the homepage and click on **Banking**, then **Internet Banking**.

This useful site also offers a vast amount of information on a range of other financial topics, such as mortgages, personal finance, insurance and investments.

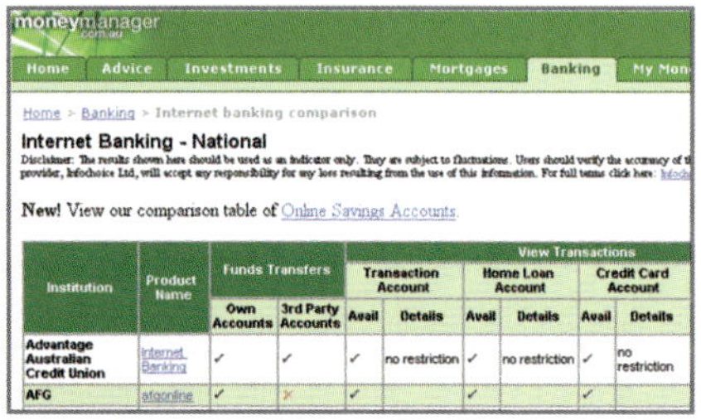

SEARCH IT YOURSELF
A basic keyword search such as 'Internet banking' will bring up thousands of sites. It's better to start with a well-known banking name, such as:

ANZ: **www.anz.com**

Bank of New Zealand: **www.bnz.co.nz**

ING Direct: **www.ingdirect.com.au**

HSBC: **www.hsbc.co.nz**

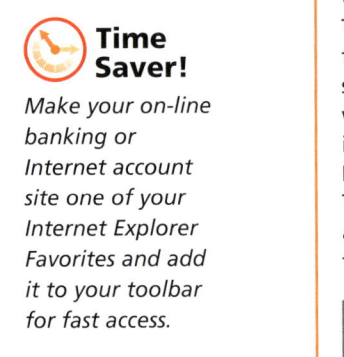

EXPLORE THE WEB

HOW TO: GET ACCESS TO YOUR ACCOUNT ON-LINE

If you have a cheque, savings or credit card account at a major bank – say, Westpac, as here – you can register for on-line access to your funds.

First, however, you need to register for phone banking to obtain a customer number and banking access code (a form of password or PIN number). Some banks will let you do this over the phone, but others require you to register in person.

Most banks will let you access their services using a standard browser, such as Internet Explorer, but a few – such as the Bank of New Zealand – require you to download special software.

1 Once you have registered for phone banking with Westpac, go to the bank's homepage (**www.westpac.com.au**) and click on **Online Banking**.

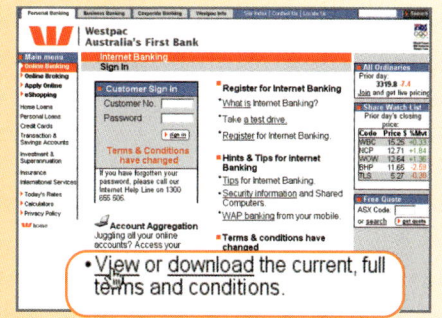

2 The first thing you should do is take a look at the 'Terms & conditions' of Internet banking. Click on the **View** link to see what you will be signing up for.

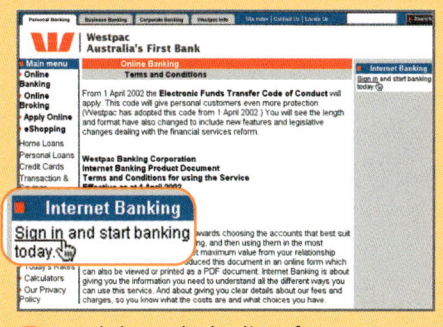

3 Read through the list of 'Terms & conditions', and when you're satisfied click **Sign in and start banking today** at the top right of the page.

4 You will return to the 'Sign In' page, where you need to click **Register for Internet Banking**. Read the instructions that appear next and then click **Register for Internet Banking Online**.

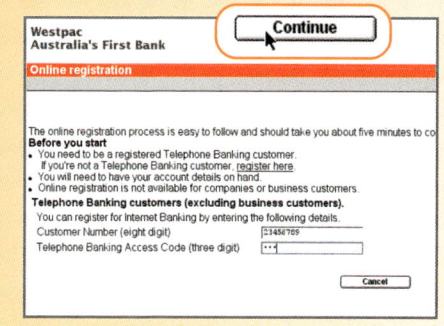

5 Enter your customer number and access code on the form and click **Continue**. The entire process takes about five minutes to complete.

Get it in print

Make sure you print copies of Web pages to record any on-line transactions you make. Many sites provide a **Print** button for this purpose. This ensures that you have hard-copy evidence of your account activity should any problems arise later. These documents also act as a handy back-up should your PC's hard disk ever suffer a fatal crash.

Money Saver!

To help you choose between accounts, create a table in Word or Excel to compare the features and interest rates of all the accounts you are interested in. Alternatively, take a look at the comparative charts in Yahoo! Finance (http://au.pfinance.yahoo.com), under 'Banking Centre'.

Watch Out!

If you log on in a public place, such as a Web café, make sure no one can see you type in your password.

SEE ALSO
- Security on the Internet – *page 52*
- File your tax return – *page 196*
- Get a mortgage quotation – *page 204*

215

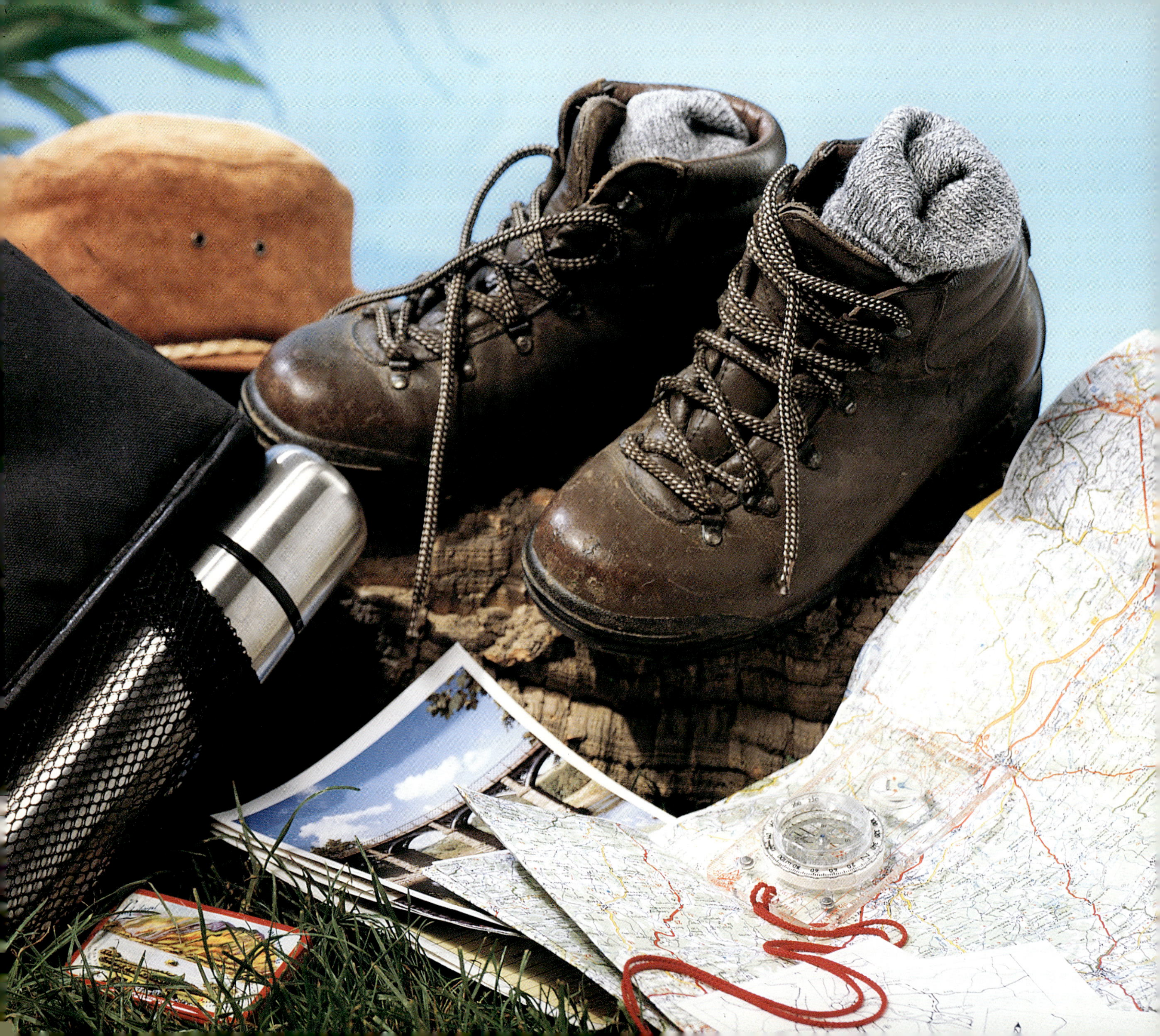

Great days

- **218** Mark a special occasion
- **222** Find a fun night out
- **225** Enjoy the great outdoors
- **228** Book a perfect holiday
- **232** Plan your overseas trip
- **236** Get cooking
- **238** Live the sporting life
- **241** Plan a wedding

GREAT DAYS

Mark a special occasion

Find the **perfect way to celebrate** every type of event

Sending a card over the Internet is a great idea. It's usually free, you can choose from thousands of musical and animated designs, and you can do it at the very last minute and still not miss the big day. If you tend to forget birthdays and anniversaries, there are Internet services to remind you. You can also buy gifts on-line and find other ways to mark a special day. You can have balloons, flowers, chocolate, food and all sorts of novelty items delivered to almost anywhere in the world.

E-cards
Many sites offer free Internet greetings cards, known as 'e-cards'. You can choose a card, add your message, enter the e-mail address of the recipient, and the e-card will show up in their inbox a few minutes later. Sending an e-card is an easy and immediate way to keep in touch with friends and relatives in other countries.

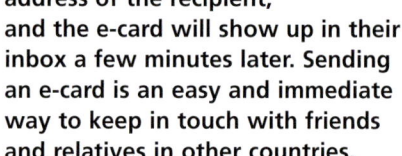

Real cards
If you'd prefer to send a real card, there are organisations on the Web that will do this for you as well. Select a card and a message and they will put it in the post for you.

Gifts
The Internet is also the place to track down gifts. You have to pay for the item and for delivery, but this can still be worthwhile for convenience alone. What's more, Web sites often offer real bargains because the overheads involved in running a Web business are much lower than those of a bricks-and-mortar shop.

EXPLORE THE WEB

CELEBRATE IN STYLE

Best e-card sites
Yahoo! Greetings (http://au.greetings.yahoo.com) This site offers a huge range of colourful and entertaining e-cards, and enables you to send them very easily. There is something for every occasion, from Halloween to retirement.

Another good free card site is The Postcards Network (**www.postcards.net**), where you can send, not only e-cards, but also virtual flowers and virtual presents. Send your best friend a virtual elephant, Porsche or Caribbean holiday – money no object!

Real card Web site
WCardz (www.wcardz.com.au) If an e-card does not feel personal enough, you can still order 'real' cards over the Internet. A good local Web site for sending cards anywhere in the world is WCardz. This site lets you create your own customised cards and then posts them for you. Once registered at the site, you simply have to choose a card design from the on-line catalogues, write your own message and supply the address of the recipient.

There is, of course, a charge for the service, but bear in mind that you won't have to leave your computer.

Reminder services
If you have a hard time remembering important dates, there are sites on the Web that offer help. An international site is Candor's Birthday and Anniversary Reminder Service (**www.candor.com/reminder**), but there are also local services, often run by florists. Typical sites are the Petals Network (**www.petals.com.au/reminder.htm**) and Auckland Flowers and Gifts (**www.nzflower.co.nz**). You can enter as many dates as you want and specify when to be reminded.

Unusual gift ideas
International Star Registry (www.starregistry.com.au) For a really unusual gift, go to this site to have a star officially named after a person of your choice. The star name will then be copyrighted and authenticated, and your recipient will be provided with a certificate and precise co-ordinates for locating the star in the sky.

That special gift
Sometimes an e-card or a bunch of flowers (see page 221) just won't do the job. But don't despair – the Web offers many more possibilities.

Among the options you could try are chocolates from Chocolate Boutique Cafe (**www.chocolateboutique.co.nz**); a hamper from M&A Hampers Online (**www.hampersonline.com.au**); a piece of jewellery from the Gift-Arcade (**www.gift-arcade.com.au**); some scent from Perfume Express (**www.perfumeexpress.co.nz**); or even some lingerie from Beautydirect (**www.beautydirect.co.nz**). The possibilities are limited only by your imagination.

Delivery times
When ordering a delivery of a gift or flowers on-line, check with the company to find out when it will be delivered. Even the fastest deliveries can take up to eight to ten hours. If you are trying to surprise someone with flowers or a gift at work, it is best to order the day before to ensure delivery on time.

Money Saver!
You can send an e-card to as many people as you like. This makes it a cheap way to make a special announcement, such as 'We've had a baby girl'.

Watch Out!
Before sending an e-card, double-check that you have typed the recipient's e-mail address correctly. Otherwise the card might be sent to the wrong person, or returned to you undelivered.

GREAT DAYS

HOW TO: SEND AN E-CARD

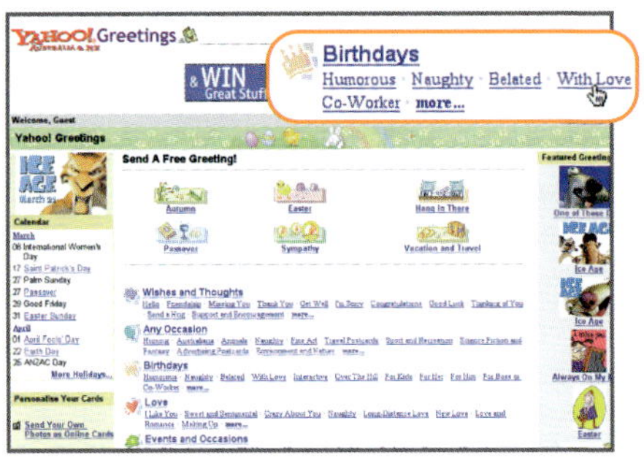

Watch Out!

Remember that an e-card will arrive instantaneously. There is no need to send the card ahead of time.

1 Go to Yahoo! Greetings (**http://au.greetings.yahoo.com**), find the appropriate category – in this case, 'Birthday' – and click on a subcategory.

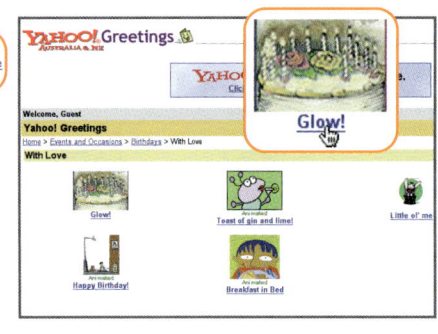

2 A new page opens, showing the selection of cards available in the subcategory you have chosen. Click on any card that you consider suitable.

3 Review the card and, if you like it, click on the link marked **Personalise & send this greeting**. Otherwise you can review other cards if you wish to.

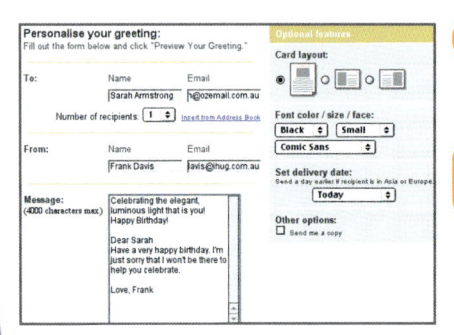

4 Fill in the information requested to personalise your greeting. You can choose a layout, change the font style, size and colour, and also specify a day when the card should be delivered.

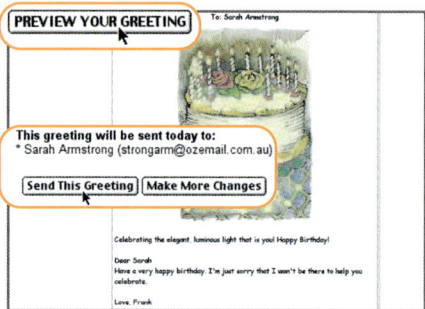

5 Click **Preview Your Greeting** to see how the card will look when it is delivered. Keep making changes until you are happy with the result, and finally click **Send This Greeting**.

Receiving an e-card

When your card arrives at its destination, the recipient will either see it in an e-mail or there will be an e-mail message from the card company announcing that you have sent a card. This e-mail will supply a Web address link which the recipient can then click on in order to view the card.

If the recipient wants someone else to see an e-card, they can send the address to them. After viewing the card, they can also click on a link to reply with an e-card of their own.

EXPLORE THE WEB

HOW TO: USE A REMINDER SERVICE

1 Go to Candor's Birthday and Anniversary Reminder Service (**www.candor.com/reminder**). Reminders are sent out at 00.30GMT, so check that you will receive yours in time.

2 Go to the top of the page and either log in if you are an existing user, or enter your e-mail address and password (with confirmation) if you are a new user on this site.

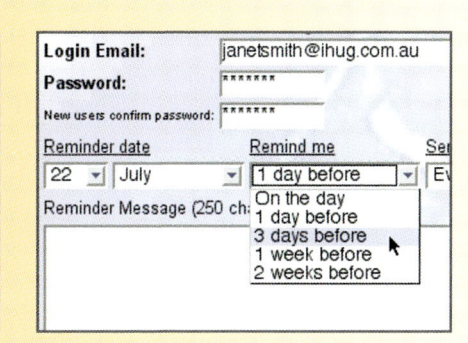

3 Now fill in the details of the date you want to be reminded about, together with how long before the event, and how often, you want to receive the reminder e-mail.

4 Finally, type in the message you want to receive and click **Add Reminder**. If you have any problems, the site has a Help Page where most issues are dealt with.

SEARCH IT YOURSELF

On-line florists
There are literally hundreds of on-line flower delivery services, and you should be able to find one in your area for local deliveries. If you have any difficulties try a national service such as the Petals Network (**www.petals.com.au**), which has over 700 florists in Australia, or Teleflora (**www.teleflora.co.nz**) with its network of 200 New Zealand florists.

While both the Petals Network and Teleflora deliver overseas, the best known international service is Interflora (**www.interflora.com**), which has outlets in more than 150 countries. As a result, Interflora can offer same-day deliveries to distant places such as Benin or Guatemala.

E-greetings cards
Posty City (**http://postycity.net**) saves you time by searching greetings cards sites until it finds a card that matches the specifications that you enter. For a personalised photo card, visit CardStore (**www.cardstore.com**); you upload photos and they make cards and mail them for you.

Watch Out!
When using a Web-based reminder service, remember to check for possible time differences. If your Internet service is based in California in the USA, for example, your reminder could arrive a day late.

Did You Know?
*There are card and gift shops on the Web which give their profits to charity. For charity e-greetings, go to say-it-with-ease.com (**www.say-it-with-ease.com**).*

SEE ALSO
- **Shop safely on the Web** – page 54
- **Buy and sell at auction** – page 208
- **Find a fun night out** – page 222

GREAT DAYS

Find a fun night out

Use the **World Wide Web** to find out what's on where

When you are stuck for ideas for a place to meet friends, where to go on a special occasion, or a last-minute evening out, you can find all the information – and usually book the tickets – on-line. Forget about buying listings magazines and restaurant guides. All the tools you need are on the Internet.

On-line guides

If you are not sure what you want to do, a good place to start is an on-line guide. In Australia and New Zealand, most of the major cities and tourist regions have their own local guides in which you can search for events and venues. The larger centres may have several guides, which can vary in quality and scope.

Big night out

To plan an evening out in Sydney, for example, go to Discoversydney (**www.discoversydney.com.au**) and CitySearch (**http://sydney.citysearch.com.au**). If you don't have a car with you – or you'd prefer to leave it behind – you can plan your journey by ferry, bus or train at Jumpstation (**www.sydneytransport.net.au**).

Foreign breaks

Most popular tourist destinations overseas have Web sites where you can quickly find out what's on. At Time Out (**www.timeout.com**), for example, you can find information about theatres, cinemas, restaurants, clubs, pubs and bars in London and other major capitals around the world. For more details, go to local sources, such as the Paris tourist office site (**www.parisbienvenue.com**).

EXPLORE THE WEB

NIGHT LIFE

All-round entertainment information

CitySearch (www.citysearch.com.au)
CitySearch offers leisure, entertainment and events guides to all of the state capitals (excluding Darwin and Hobart, which are included in regional guides to the Northern Territory and Tasmania respectively), in addition to Cairns, Townsville, the Central Coast, the Gold Coast and the Sunshine Coast.

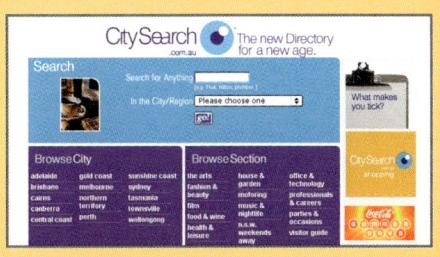

Out and about

Xtra (http://xtra.co.nz)
The Xtra site provides guides to nine of New Zealand's largest cities – Auckland, Hamilton, Tauranga, Rotorua, Napier/Hastings, Palmerston North, Wellington, Christchurch and Dunedin. Click on the Out & About link and then on the city that interests you. The site's categories include movies, restaurants, takeaways, events, pubs, clubs, gigs, things to do and resources.

Gig guides

Whatever your taste in music, you can get up-to-date information from the Web. A good first stop is the Yahoo! music page (**http://au.music.yahoo.com/music**), which has news and reviews as well as an extensive gig guide. Similar guides are offered on a range of other sites, including GrooveOn (**www.grooveon.com.au**) and the Australian Music Web Site (**www.amws.com.au**). In New Zealand, try Re:Action (**www.reaction.co.nz/nzmusic**) or Bandwave (**www.bandwave.com**).

Classical music fans can get information from The Australian Music Centre (**www.amcoz.com.au**) or from the Centre for New Zealand Music (**www.sounz.org.nz**).

Eating out

At this stage, there are no really comprehensive national restaurant guides for either Australia or New Zealand on the Web, but take a look at de Groots Best Restaurants of Australia (**www.bestrestaurants.com.au**) and Menus.co.nz (**www.menus.co.nz**). The best eating guides are all regional; just type the word 'restaurants' and a locality name into your favourite search engine.

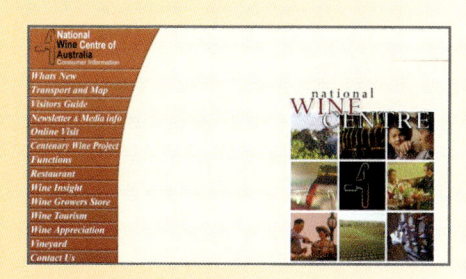

Drinker's guides

To explore the world of wine, visit the National Wine Centre of Autralia (**www.wineaustralia.com.au**) or Wine Online (**www.finewineonline.co.nz**).

Beer drinkers should head for the Australian Good Beer Directory (**www.ecn.net.au/~dilbert/agbd.htm**) or Realbeer (**http://realbeer.co.nz**).

SEARCH IT YOURSELF

Many theatres, performances, clubs and restaurants now have their own Web sites. So, if you already have an idea of where you would like to go – for example, the Sydney Opera House – try entering the venue name, preceded by 'www' and followed by '.com.au' or '.co.nz'. In many cases this strategy will find a venue straight away, but if that does not work, you can always use a search engine.

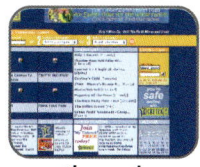

Good sources of information on most areas of entertainment – including music, dance and theatre – are the major national ticket agencies. To see what's on, visit Ticketmaster 7 (**www.ticketmaster7.com**), or Ticketek (**http://premier.ticketek.com.au**) and (**http://premier.ticketek.co.nz**).

Watch Out!

As with paying for anything on-line, make sure you are buying tickets on a secure site. Look for the padlock in the Status Bar at the bottom of your browser window and make sure the site has a refund policy.

GREAT DAYS

HOW TO: BOOK A NIGHT OUT ON-LINE

1 Go to one of the national ticket purchase sites. The best ones – such as Ticketek (**http://premier.ticketek.com.au**), shown here – list hundreds of events and shows.

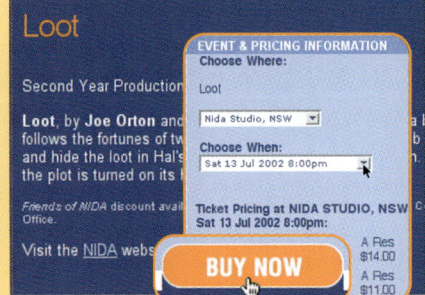

2 Read on-line descriptions of shows and, once you have found one that you are interested in attending, choose a date and click **Buy Now** to see what seats are available.

3 If you are already a member of the ticket site, you will be asked to sign in, otherwise you will have to join. Now choose the type of tickets you want and click the **Go** button.

4 You will now receive a ticket offer and have 10 minutes to make a decision. View the seating plan, and if you are satisfied, click **Continue** to complete the transaction.

FINDING A FILM

One great feature of the Internet is being able to find out what films are on in your area. There are several sites that will help you to do this, wherever you live.

For any place in Australia, simply go to Yahoo! Movies (**http://au.movies.yahoo.com/movies**), choose your location from the drop-down menu, as well as a movie name, and you can then check complete details of screening locations and times. Alternatively, you can browse a list of currently screening movies. In New Zealand, go to Xtra (**http://xtra.co.nz/out_and_about**), click on a city name and then on the **Movies** link. Both sites offer film reviews, and you can also watch some movie trailers on Yahoo!

For more details on particular films and their stars, try one of the international sites, such as The Internet Movie Database (**www.imdb.com**). Many films also have their own Web sites, such as *The Lord of the Rings* (**www.lordoftherings.net**).

Time Saver!

Many sites have graphics that are time-consuming to download to your browser if you don't need to see all the images. Find a 'low graphics' or 'text only' version of a page, or turn the graphics off in your browser's Preferences.

SEE ALSO
- Access showbiz news – page 164
- Mark a special occasion – page 218
- Book a perfect holiday – page 228

224

EXPLORE THE WEB

Enjoy the great outdoors

Look on the Internet for inspiring holidays and days out

The Internet makes planning an outdoor activity less difficult and time-consuming. It can also help you decide where to go if you are running low on ideas. There are enough dedicated travel sites on it to inspire a year of trips. And you can find information on virtually any place you want to visit around the world.

Tourist sites

Begin your research at general sites, such as the one maintained by the Australian Tourist Commission (**www.australia.com**) or Destination New Zealand (**www.purenz.com**). Here you'll find details about each country and its various regions, as well as information on things to do and places to stay. For more detail on particular locations, use a search engine such as Yahoo! (**http://au.yahoo.com**). Organisations such as walking clubs are also a great source of information.

Finding accommodation

To find what you need, search by town and type of accommodation – bed and breakfasts, farmstays and self-catering accommodation are all available, and you are not limited to Australia or New Zealand. Numerous tour operators offer walking and activity holidays worldwide. Book a guided trek in the Himalayas on-line, or a kayaking trip in Belize, an exotic tropical destination. Consult official and unofficial sites in each country for more information.

GREAT DAYS

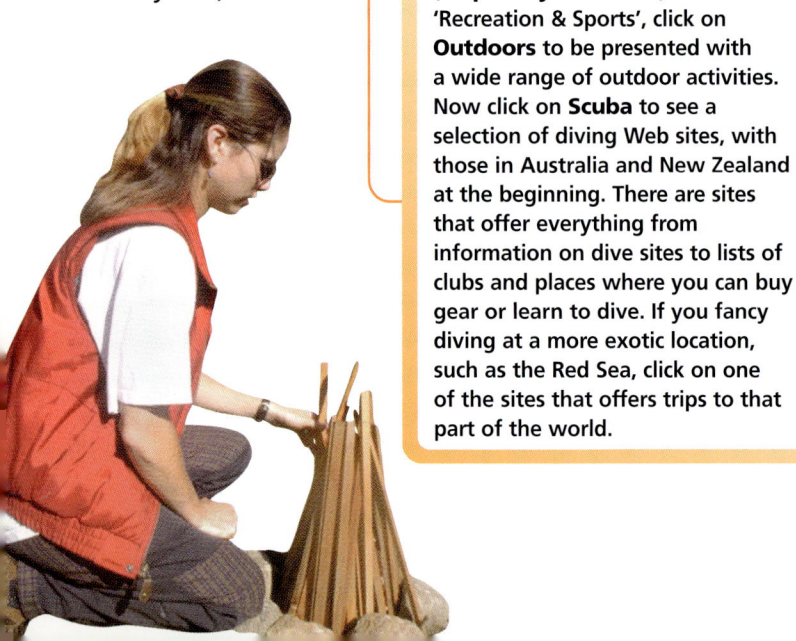

OUTDOOR SITES

On foot
Bushwalking in Australia (www.bushwalking.org.au)
Packed with useful information, this site offers guides to walks everywhere in Australia, as well as articles on a range of subjects, such as 'Safety in the Bush', the 'Bushwalkers Code' and 'Things to Watch out for in the Bush'. There are also links to many other useful sites.

For a wealth of links to New Zealand tramping sites, visit eNZed (**www.enzed.com/tramp.html**).

Adventure travel
The Adventure Travel Company (www.adventure-travel.com.au)
This company specialises in selling adventure holidays to Australians and New Zealanders. While the company does not run its own trips, it does bring together a wide range of international suppliers on the one site. The activities on offer include cycling, kayaking, scuba diving, skiing and walking; and the destinations include every continent on Earth. Sign up for the company's free newsletter if you are looking for inspiration.

Equipment shops
Whether you are interested in climbing, skiing, camping or just walking, you can purchase the full range of outdoor gear from Paddy Pallin in Australia (**www.paddypallin.com.au**) or the Outdoor Store in New Zealand (**http://outdoorstore.co.nz**). Both sites are designed specifically for Internet shopping. If you can't find what you're looking for, use a search engine to track down a specific manufacturer or some of the big on-line stores in the USA or Europe.

Camping site
Campsites in Europe (www.interhike.com)
If you are planning to go camping or backpacking in Europe, take a look at this handy site. It's a guide to camping and hiking throughout Europe, with details of campsites from the Czech Republic to the Canary Islands. Visit the Camping Forum where travellers exchange advice and information.

National Parks
Both Australia and New Zealand have set aside vast areas of their very best scenery in National Parks, where it can be enjoyed by everyone. If you are looking for helpful information about Australia's National Parks, the Australian Tourism Net (**www.atn.com.au/parks**) is a good place to start.

For New Zealand parks, go to the Department of Conservation Web site (**www.doc.govt.nz**) and click on **Explore**; then choose **National Parks** or **Tracks and Walks** from the links on the next page.

Problem Solver

*Even experienced outdoor travellers forget things from time to time. That is why checklists are so invaluable. As a starting point, download a ready-made food, equipment or first-aid list from Safety in the Bush (**www.bushwalking.org.au/safety.html**).*

SEARCH IT YOURSELF

If you are looking for places to go scuba diving, first go to Yahoo! (**http://au.yahoo.com**). Under 'Recreation & Sports', click on **Outdoors** to be presented with a wide range of outdoor activities. Now click on **Scuba** to see a selection of diving Web sites, with those in Australia and New Zealand at the beginning. There are sites that offer everything from information on dive sites to lists of clubs and places where you can buy gear or learn to dive. If you fancy diving at a more exotic location, such as the Red Sea, click on one of the sites that offers trips to that part of the world.

EXPLORE THE WEB

HOW TO: PLAN A WALK

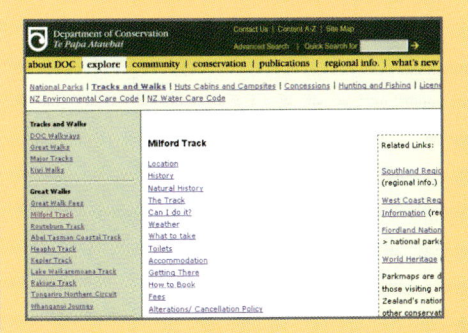

1. Go to New Zealand's Department of Conservation site (**www.doc.govt.nz**) and look for a walk that interests you. Full details of all walks are given, including how difficult they are.

2. Some walks, including the splendid Milford Track, are so popular during the summer that visitor numbers are controlled and booking is essential. Application forms can be downloaded.

3. The Department of Conservation publishes detailed maps of all the most popular tracks, and these can also be ordered on-line.

CASE STUDY

Both Clive and his wife, Robyn, had thought for some years about visiting Central Australia, but neither wanted to drive so far and both felt that a coach tour would cut them off from experiencing the country at first hand.

The answer was provided by Clive's brother, Darren, who had booked a cycling tour of France on the Internet. Clive decided to look for something similar in Australia and discovered Remote Outback Cycle Tours (**www.cycletours.com.au**). After checking out the various trips on offer, Clive and Robyn signed up for the six-day Great Victoria Desert Ride, which included a visit to Uluru and Kata Tjuta.

Their tour consisted of a combination of four-wheel-driving and cycling, with the support vehicle taking care of baggage during the cycling stints. When Robyn felt a bit stiff on the third day, she simply rode in the support vehicle and joined Clive at the lunch stop. The experience of cycling through the desert so impressed Clive and Robyn that they are planning a longer trip next year.

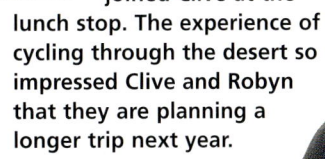

4. Walkers who prefer to be guided will find several companies – such as Ultimate Hikes (**www.ultimatehikes.co.nz**) – on the Internet.

Did You Know?

Mount Everest is beyond the reach of most amateur climbers, but you can enjoy an interactive journey from base camp to the summit at The Tech Museum of Innovation (www.thetech.org/exhibits_events/online/everest).

SEE ALSO
- Explore the natural world – page 156
- Book a perfect holiday – page 228
- Plan your overseas trip – page 232

GREAT DAYS

Book a perfect holiday

Plan your break away on **the Internet**

You can use the Internet to research and book a holiday – it is great for both last-minute deals and pre-arranged breaks at home and overseas. The Internet can help you to book a flight, find out about the best places to see, hire a car, check up on the local cuisine and language, and investigate exchange rates. Using the Internet can be much faster than ploughing through brochures, and when you have found what you want, you can book and pay for your holiday on-line.

On-line travel

It's easy to book a holiday on-line. Travel agents such as travel.com.au (**www.travel.com.au**) and Travel Online (**www.travelonline.co.nz**) offer flights, accommodation, insurance, car hire and travel guides. Or you can find and book a flight directly from an airline's Web site.

Guides

The Internet offers travel guides from official tourist agencies such as the Tourist Authority of Thailand (**www.tourismthailand.org**), independent organisations, and even individuals who publish their holiday experiences on the Web.

Passports and visas

Australian citizens must apply in person for a passport (for details, see **www.passports.gov.au**), but New Zealand citizens can apply by post using a downloaded form (**www.passports.govt.nz**). To check on visa requirements, contact the local diplomatic representative of the country you plan to visit, or consult the Lonely Planet site (**www.lonelyplanet.com**). First click on **worldguide**, then choose a region or country and click **go**; then click on **Facts for the Traveler**.

EXPLORE THE WEB

HOLIDAY SITES

Destination Europe
European Travel Commission (www.etc-europe-travel.org)
If you are planning a European holiday, this is a good place to start. The role of the European Travel Commission is to promote Europe as a holiday destination worldwide, and their site provides a central hub from which you can link to the official travel sites of participating countries. More than 30 countries are involved in the initiative.

Accommodation
The Travel Mall (www.oztravel.com.au)
The Travel Mall site enables you to search for places to stay in Australia and New Zealand by region. The operators of the site claim to provide the best rates, and they undertake to try to match any lower price that you find advertised on the Internet for the same product. Try the 'Top 10' categories for recommendations on places to go and things to see.

Cheap air fares
Flight Centre (www.flightcentre.com.au) (www.flightcentre.co.nz)
Enter details of the trip you want to make and press **Go!** to get a quote. Flight Centre boasts that, as a global player, it can negotiate better deals with the airlines than any other travel retailer. The claim on the company's Web site states 'We guarantee to BEAT any genuine current quoted airfare!' Click **Frequently Asked Questions** for the company's terms and conditions.

Last minute holidays
lastminute.com (www.au.lastminute.com)
As the name implies, this is a great site if you've left your holiday plans to the last minute. It offers a range of services: not only holidays, but also hotels and entertainment. If you suddenly find yourself with a free weekend, click **Next Weekend** for a selection of exciting ideas and offers.

Car hire
Most on-line travel agents offer a car hire service, but it may be cheaper and easier to go about organising it yourself. Leading car rental companies such as Budget (**www.budget.com.au** or **www.budget.co.nz**), Hertz (**www.hertz.com**) and Avis (**www.avis.com**) allow you to book and pay for car rental on-line.

Tourist information
Lonely Planet (www.lonelyplanet.com)
Here you can find detailed information on a wide range of destinations around the world. Browse the site by city or country, or use the search tool. Enter a destination or keyword to see entries from the relevant Lonely Planet guide, or check out the extensive bulletin board by clicking on **the thorn tree**.

SEARCH IT YOURSELF
At Looksmart (**www.looksmart.com.au** or **www.looksmart.co.nz**), click on one of the options under 'Travel' (for Australia) or 'Travel & Holidays' (for New Zealand) to see a selection of sites that have been selected by the site's editors. Alternatively, search the Web by entering one or more keywords into the 'Search the Web' window, and click **Go!** or **Search**.

Watch Out!
It is sometimes hard to know on the Web whether you are dealing with a backyard operator or a large company. Membership of a professional association can be a measure of reliability. Check that Australian agents are members of the Australian Federation of Travel Agents (AFTA), and that New Zealand agents belong to the Travel Agents Association of New Zealand (TAANZ).

GREAT DAYS

HOW TO: FIND AND BOOK A FLIGHT ON-LINE

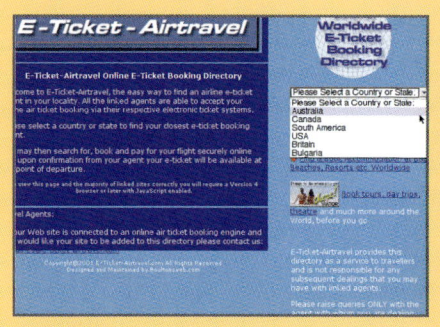

1 Go to a site where you can compare prices and book flights. In this example, we use E-Ticket-Airtravel (www.e-ticket-airtravel.com). First, choose the country where you live.

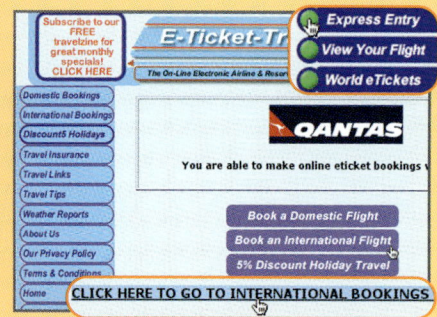

2 On the next page, click **Express Entry**, and then choose between domestic and international bookings. On the International Bookings page, click on the link indicated to enter.

3 Enter details of your planned trip in the form that appears next. If you can be flexible about departure and return dates, you will stand a better chance of finding the cheapest fare.

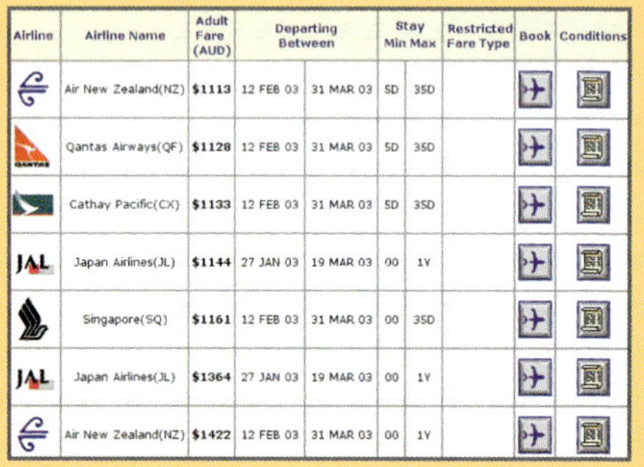

4 A list of flights will now appear. Scroll through it to see if you can find something suitable. Your choice of airline may be important if you are a member of a frequent flyer program.

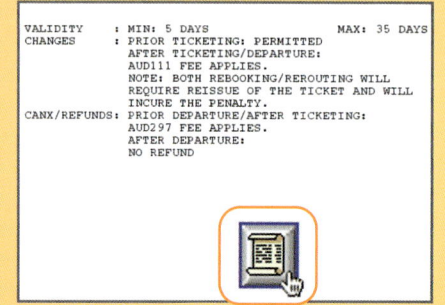

5 Click on the **Conditions** icon beside flights that you are considering. Some bookings cannot be changed, while others can be changed provided you pay a penalty fee.

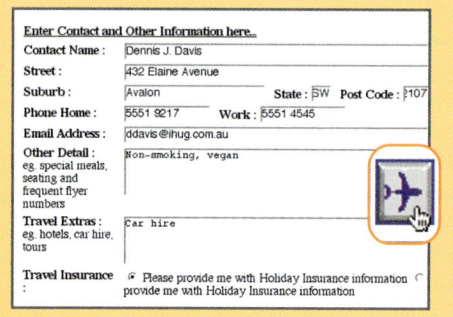

6 When you have made a choice, click **Book** and fill in the details on the form provided. Finally, click **Request Booking**; you will be notified by e-mail when everything has been processed.

Weather check

Check the weather at your selected destination before you depart. Try WeatherOnline (www.weatheronline.co.uk), which provides global coverage. Just click on the region of the world that interests you. For weather forecasts in Australia, visit the Bureau of Meteorology (www.bom.gov.au); for New Zealand, go to the MetService (www.metservice.co.nz).

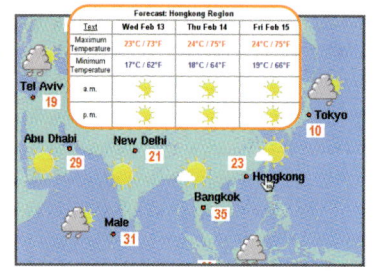

Watch Out!

Discount flights may not go to city centre airports and may arrive at unsociable hours. If you arrive at London Stansted at 2 am, you won't be able to get a train into central London for hours.

Time Saver!

Many travel retailers have their own Web sites with timetables and direct booking. Book trains from London to Paris at Eurostar (www3.eurostar.co.uk) and coach journeys in North America at Greyhound (www.greyhound.com).

230

EXPLORE THE WEB

CASE STUDY

When Dave Bartlett and his wife Helen received an invitation to a wedding in Perth, one of their first thoughts was that it would be a great opportunity to get back into diving. Dave and Helen had met in the Caribbean, where they had both learned to dive when in their twenties. Over the years, however, they had become bored with the run-of-the-mill holidays offered by most dive operators. What they really wanted was a diving holiday with a bit of a challenge – and, ideally, one that could be combined with Helen's life-long fascination with history.

1 The Bartletts began their search with Yahoo! (http://au.yahoo.com), typing in various combinations of 'diving', 'scuba', 'holiday' and the like, and limiting their search to Australian sites.

2 Among the hundreds of Web pages they looked at, the one that caught their interest was run by the Earthwatch Institute (www.earthwatch.org), which has volunteer projects around the world.

3 There were six 'Scuba and Snorkel Projects' on offer, with two of them in Australia. At first, the most attractive option looked like an expedition to Lizard Island on the Great Barrier Reef – one of their dream dive sites.

4 However, it was the second that proved to be the great find – an expedition investigating two shipwrecks quite close to Perth. This looked like the perfect option, so Dave went on-line and booked straight away.

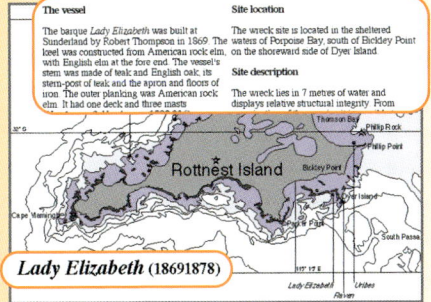

5 Dave and Helen were even able to research the wrecks on-line, finding a wealth of information, with maps, at the Western Australian Maritime Museum site (www.mm.wa.gov.au).

Counting the cost of knowledge

Hard work and wrinkled skin aren't the only costs of volunteering – it can also be expensive. Apart from air fares to faraway locations, volunteers must also pay a fee to cover food, accommodation and training. To get more for your money, look for projects that offer courses and lectures, which in some cases can be counted towards a university degree.

Did You Know?

Activity holidays are increasingly popular. You can choose from an amazing array of activities, such as walking, cycling, trekking, cross-country skiing, birdwatching, painting and gourmet eating, among others, all around the world. Type the words 'activity holiday' in any search engine and see what comes up.

GREAT DAYS

Plan your overseas trip

Surf the Web for **inspiration** as well as **information**

A large part of the fun of a long-anticipated big trip lies in the planning you do in the months before leaving. Now, with the help of the Internet, you can explore even more possibilities. Can we get a ferry to that remote island? Will we be able to change money on Friday? Does anyone there speak English? It is amazing how much local information you can uncover – information that will help you get the most from any journey. In this section we'll imagine you're planning a trip to the UK.

Where to start
All the traditional sources of travel information – tourist offices, guide books and travel agents – can be found on the Web. But the best place to start is a general travel site (see opposite).

Travel sites
The advantage of such sites is that they are moderated: that is, someone has taken the trouble to trawl the vastness of the Web, and assess and organise the many thousands of travel-related sites – so you don't have to.

A good travel site is like an all-knowing librarian: it will lead you quickly to the information you want.

KEW PALACE
The smallest royal palace
A hidden treasure in the
Royal Botanic Gardens, Kew

EXPLORE THE WEB

WHERE TO START

Official site
**VisitBritain
(www.visitbritain.com)**
An official site is one that is set up and run by an authoritative organisation. For example, there is an official British Museum site, though you will find a lot of other sites about the museum – both good and bad – by people who have no actual connection with it.

Official sites can usually be relied on to provide correct factual information, but since they are in the business of promoting their organisation, they are not necessarily the place to look for a 'warts-and-all' assessment.

VisitBritain is the official site of the British Tourist Authority. It is comprehensive, reliable and easy to navigate. It has many useful links to other sites, and a good search engine which makes it a fine starting point if you have only a rough idea of what you are looking for.

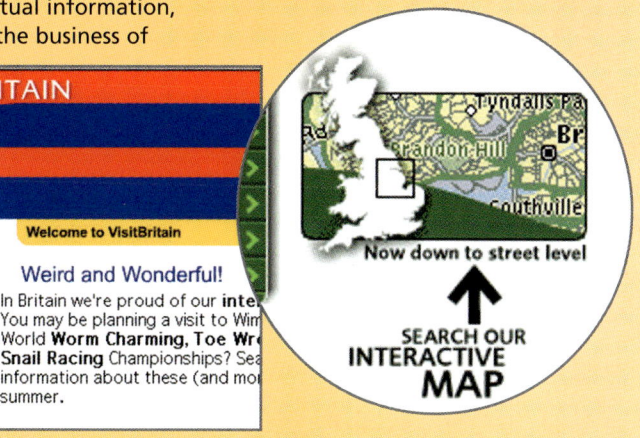

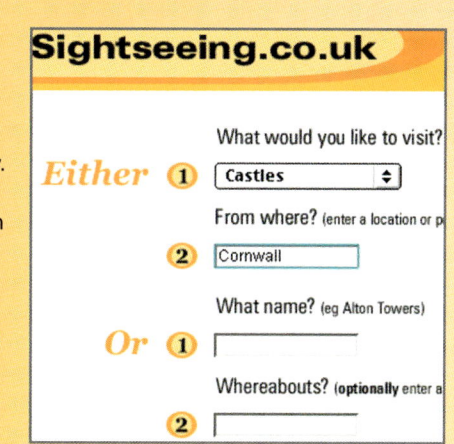

A second opinion
**The UK Travel Guide
(www.ukguide.org)**
When you are planning to visit a place you have never been to before, it is a good idea to get a view from an independent source. This is a no-nonsense site with very few graphic or pictorial elements – but is is full of good content including maps and links. The site has basic information designed to be helpful to visitors from abroad.

Best of the rest
Association of Leading Visitor Attractions (www.alva.org.uk)
This site provides links to a selection of Britain's most popular tourist sites, with separate sections on 'Museums & Galleries', 'Heritage', 'Cathedrals', 'Leisure Attractions' and 'Gardens & Conservation'.

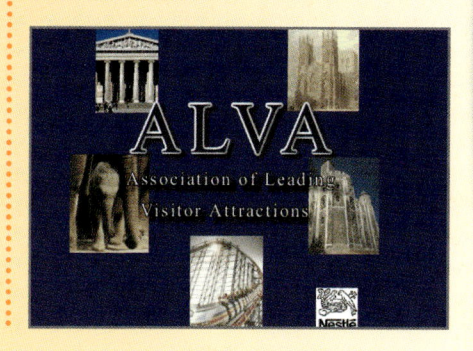

Practical help
**Sightseeing.co.uk
(www.sightseeing.co.uk)**
This site allows you to search for destinations in a natural, user-friendly way.

You specify the part of the country and the type of attraction you are interested in (for example, castles or gardens), and it creates a list of possible trips within easy travelling distance.

With each suggestion come contact and location details, admission prices, maps and travel tips. There are also links to other sites devoted to each attraction.

Problem Solver!
*Forgotten the address of a site you visited earlier? Click on the **History** button at the top of the Explorer window. This shows you a complete list of all the pages you have visited. Click on the page you want and you will go straight to it.*

Watch Out!
Many good Web sites state the last time they were updated. It is a good idea to check this before using any information you find on the site.

233

GREAT DAYS

WHERE TO GO: START WITH YAHOO!

All the sites on the British Yahoo! Web site (http://uk.yahoo.com) are organised into a vast directory or family tree. You narrow your search by clicking down through the levels. There is no right way to find your way to the specific site you need, but here are two possible approaches to finding somewhere interesting to go.

1 One of the main headings on the Yahoo! homepage is 'Art & Humanities'. That might lead to an interesting museum to visit.

2 First, limit the choice by clicking **UK Listings Only**. Now click on the most likely heading in the revised list – **Museums, Galleries, and Centres**.

3 This yields both Web site addresses and more categories. The @ symbol after a name indicates that a site is listed in several Yahoo! categories.

4 Under Web site listings is MuseumNet, which provides a comprehensive guide to museums across the UK.

1 If you know that what you want is a day by the sea, you can start your search by specifying the city or town you want to visit. Click on **Regional** and then **UK Cities and Towns**.

2 There are over 2000 cities and towns listed, so first click on a letter in the A–Z list and then make a choice: Bournemouth is a popular resort.

3 There are several dozen sites divided into categories such as 'News and Media' and 'Recreation and Sport'. Click on **Travel and Transportation**.

4 In the 'Local Guides' section there are several sites that provide information about Bournemouth: where to stay, where to eat and what to see.

234

EXPLORE THE WEB

CASE STUDY

The Johnson family were staying in central London and wanted a day in the fresh air – somewhere they could explore and have a picnic. They thought it might be good to search for inspiration on-line.

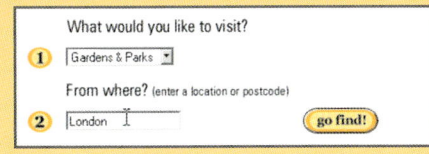

1 They began by browsing at **www.sightseeing.co.uk**, looking for interesting gardens and parks in and around London; the children wanted more than nice scenery.

2 Third on the list of results was Kew Gardens, which looked the kind of thing they wanted. They thought that Kew Palace in the grounds would be worth seeing.

3 There was no Web site listed for Kew Palace. The Johnsons wanted to be sure it was open, so they did a search for 'Kew Palace' at Lycos.co.uk (**www.lycos.co.uk**).

4 There was a page on Kew at the official site for Historic Royal Palaces. It said that there was renovation going on – so they decided to look at another of the palaces featured on the site.

5 When they saw the Hampton Court site, they knew it was the right place to go. The maze would keep the kids happy, and the gardens looked fantastic.

Homes and gardens

Britain has many historic and well-known homes and gardens which are open to the public. Plan a day out to one with Historic Homes of Britain (**www.specialtytraveluk.com**). They organise tours for groups and individuals with special private visits to houses that are not open for general public viewing.

Time Saver!

*If you want to find information about a particular town in the UK, it is worth starting at the relevant local authority's site. The address will usually take the form: **www.town.gov.uk** (replace the word 'town' in the address with the name of the place in question).*

Get cooking

Find **good food** information on the **Internet**

The Internet offers facts and advice about food and drink that would be difficult to find anywhere else. Find out how to prepare a traditional Maori hangi (food cooked over hot stones in an earth oven), perhaps, or join a recipe and food-related newsgroup. Or, find out where you can buy some gumleaf oil for that special dish you're planning to make at the weekend. However much you know about culinary matters, you will always be able to learn a lot more on the Web.

Recipe sites
Many Web sites offer a unique way to choose from a selection of recipes without having to open a single book. You can look up a recipe site that will suggest a meal you can make from leftover ingredients in your cupboard, or browse through hundreds of recipes at ucook.com (**www.ucook.com**).

Food from overseas
The Internet also gives you instant access to food you cannot buy in local shops. However, if you're ordering from overseas, you'll need to check whether any quarantine restrictions apply. In Australia, try **www.affa.gov.au**; in New Zealand, go to **www.quarantine.govt.nz**.

Cooking courses
Whether you are an experienced cook or not, you can benefit from on-line cooking courses and instructional videos – for both everyday and entertaining ideas.

There are dedicated sites for vegetarians and vegans, wine buffs, curry fans and Italophiles.

EXPLORE THE WEB

DISHES OF THE DAY

Food and drink
Epicurious (http://eat.epicurious.com) This online magazine is full of culinary articles, from advice on outdoor entertaining to tips on how to keep steaks from curling, as well as step-by-step on-line cooking demonstrations.

There are thousands of recipes, each one with a feedback and ratings section so that people who have cooked the dishes can comment on them. The site has numerous useful links, and articles on subjects as diverse as choosing the right wine glass for a dinner party and locating the best places to eat in many parts of the world.

Traditional food
Indigenous foods and flavours are becoming increasingly popular in both Australia and New Zealand. If you would like to try adding the authentic flavours of the Australian bush to your culinary repertoire, pay a visit to Cherikoff Rare Spices (**www.bushtucker.com.au**), where you can find out how to use traditional foods and where to buy them. And for an extensive database of traditional Maori recipes, pay a visit to The Modern Maori Cookbook (**www.culture.co.nz/recipes**).

Alternatively, if you have a yearning for the sort of food the pioneers ate, such as damper and kangaroo tail soup, then browse through the collection of traditional and contemporary Australian recipes (including Pavlova) at the Kavenga Publishing Web site (**www.kavenga.com.au**).

Food demonstrations
The Food Network (www.foodnetwork.com) Learn all the techniques and tips you need for fabulous cooking at The Food Network – a site devoted to teaching you how to cook. Once you have RealPlayer or Quicktime (which you can download via links on this site), you can watch film clips and learn cooking techniques from the experts. You can also save the clips to your computer and keep them for reference.

Recipe tips
The Cook's Thesaurus (www.foodsubs.com) This site is a cooking encyclopedia which offers information on thousands of everyday and unusual ingredients, as well as advice on the kitchen tools you need to cook them with. You can also find substitutes for fatty, expensive or hard-to-find ingredients.

SEARCH IT YOURSELF
For a comprehensive database with more than 10,000 food- and drink-related sites, try The Kitchen Link (**www.kitchenlink.com**). Site links are also provided at Seasoned Cooking (**www.seasoned.com**); look out for those with a Five-Star rating – granted only to the best.

To find out about vegetarian food in all its manifestations, try The Vegetarian Resource Group (**www.vrg.org**) or Veggies Unite! (**http://vegweb.com**). To find vegetarian restaurants, go to VegDining (**www.vegdining.com**) or Happy Cow (**www.happycow.net**).

If it is unusual kitchen utensils and equipment you require, search at The Cooks Kitchen (**www.kitchenware.co.uk**) or Lakeland Limited (**www.lakelandlimited.com**). At these sites you can order items such as 'Aquatronic' weighing scales (which measure liquids and solids), a hachoir set, or a blowtorch for finishing off those crèmes brûlées.

Did You Know?
If you love spicy food, you can find out everything you've ever wanted to know about chillies, such as why they are hot and which is the hottest. Use a search engine to search the term 'chile-head' to find many chilli enthusiasts' sites.

SEE ALSO
- Improve your diet and fitness – page 130
- Do your weekly shop – page 192
- Find a fun night out – page 222

Live the sporting life

Use the **World Wide Web** to find out almost anything about sports

With up-to-the-minute results, plus facts and figures from the archives, the Internet will help to satisfy your sporting cravings, whether you're a keen player or a committed armchair enthusiast. Most sports on earth – even tug-of-war and camel racing – have dedicated Web sites, created by participants and fans as well as official governing bodies. Or if you want to take up a sport as a player or official, the Web is useful for learning rules of games or finding local coaching sessions.

Footy fever
Soccer is the world's most popular sport and there are thousands of sites devoted to it. At the official sites of the top local and overseas clubs you will find news, match reports and fixture lists, along with multimedia elements such as panoramic tours and live Web-casts.

Sport for all
Browse through any Web directory and you'll find sites on every conceivable sport and quite a few you've probably never heard of, such as tchoukball (a little like basketball but with two small square net goals on the floor) or yukigassen (an organised snowball fighting game popular in Finland, Norway and Japan).

Events
For sports trivia buffs, there are challenging quiz sites, such as that offered by BBC Radio Five (**www.bbc.co.uk/fivelive/sportonfive**), where you can try out a new set of questions every day.

And if you want to attend a sporting event locally or overseas, you can often use the Web to buy tickets on-line.

EXPLORE THE WEB

SPORTING GREATS

Best national source
ABC Sport (www.abc.net.au/sport)
ABC Sport probably provides the best national coverage of Australian sport on the Net. The homepage lists all the current top stories within each sport, from AFL to WNBL. There are also special feature articles, as well as transcripts, reports and interviews from the various ABC television and radio programs that deal with sporting issues.

In addition, each major sport has its own special site, where more detailed information, including audio and video match reports, can be found. If you feel strongly about an issue, join an on-line forum to exchange views with others.

Latest sports news
Almost all major Australian and New Zealand TV stations and newspapers have their own sports Web sites. Content varies – often according to commercial interests – so you will need to experiment to discover the sites that you like best.

In Australia, try *The Sydney Morning Herald* site (**www.smh.com.au/sport**), News Limited (**http://sport.news.com.au**) and ninemsn (**http://sports.ninemsn.com.au**).

In New Zealand, go to *The New Zealand Herald* (**www.nzherald.co.nz/sports**), One Sport (**http://onesport.nzoom.com**) or Xtramsn (**http://xtramsn.co.nz/sport**).

Footy heaven
For many Australians and New Zealanders, too much footy is barely enough – and this is confirmed by the sheer number of football Web sites. Make a start with the official offerings of the Australian Football League (**http://afl.com.au**), the National Rugby League (**www.nrl.com.au**), the Rugby Union (**www.rugby.com.au**) and Soccer Australia (**www.socceraustralia.com.au**).

In New Zealand, take a look at NZ Rugby League (**www.rugbyleague.co.nz**), NZ Rugby Union (**www.nzrugby.co.nz**) and New Zealand Soccer (**www.soccernz.co.nz**).

Cricket in paradise
As is the case with the various forms of football, cricket also generates enormous interest among sports lovers in Australia and New Zealand. A simple search for cricket sites produces tens of thousands of hits. A good place to start is CricInfo.com (**www.cricinfo.com**), an international site with links to cricket's official governing bodies in numerous countries.

Click on **Australia** or **New Zealand** (or any other country link) to find news, details of current and upcoming matches, and links to many regional cricketing authorities.

SEARCH IT YOURSELF
If you want to participate in a sport, good places to start are sites such as SportSelect (**www.sportselect.com.au**) or Sport NZ (**www.sportnz.co.nz**), which provide links to various sporting organisations and bodies.

Say, for example, that you have just moved to Canberra and would like to take up cycling. Begin by going to SportSelect and clicking on **Cycling** in the directory. Scan the list of clubs to see if there is one in your area, which there is – the Canberra Cycling Club. But perhaps, first of all, you need some advice on buying a bike to get started? A quick browse turns up Bicycles Network Australia, which has a useful guide to 'Online Shopping for Bicycles and parts'.

Did You Know?
*To search for local sports information go to a search engine such as Google (**www.google.com**) and enter the sport you are interested in and your home town or suburb. For example, 'hockey+Manly'.*

GREAT DAYS

Did You Know?

Sports news can be tailored to your interests and e-mailed directly to your computer, or sent to your WAP phone, as it happens. Visit a general sport site and look for an 'e-mail alerts' link.

HOW TO: FOLLOW A LIVE SPORTS EVENT

Many sport sites let you follow the action with a live audio or video Web-cast. Look for a link that says something like 'Internet Radio' or 'Live Matches'. The procedure is broadly similar for all sites that offer this facility. You may be asked to download QuickTime or the RealOne Player before you can access these services (see page 150). If your audio broadcasts skip from time to time, try closing your browser window and listening just using the RealOne Player, which takes up less memory.

This example shows the site for the Wimbledon tennis tournament, which, during the competition fortnight, offers live audio and video features, virtual tours, archived video clips and a Web-cam ('Slamcam') with a choice of robotic camera angles that you can control.

1 To see the latest scores, go to www.wimbledon.org, click on **Interactive** and choose **IBM Real-Time Scoreboard**. Download the **'Lite Version'** if you are connected to the Internet by modem.

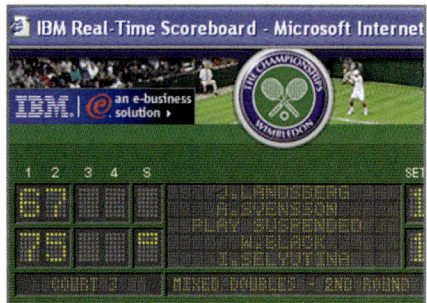

2 When the scoreboard has loaded, you'll be able to view the latest scores. These are updated frequently, though not instantaneously.

3 To listen to a live match commentary, return to the homepage and click **Radio Wimbledon**. The Media Console appears, and within a few seconds you will hear the broadcast begin.

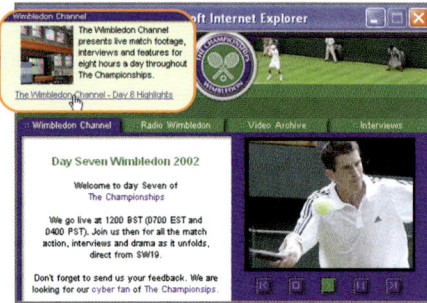

4 To watch a broadcast, return to the homepage and click **Wimbledon Channel**. Again, the Media Console appears and you can watch the live action or view videos from the archive.

Web-cast limitations

Although you can watch and listen to 'live' video and audio broadcasts from sport Web sites, the technical limitations of the Internet mean that the broadcasts may be jumpy and 'live' scoreboards may take a while to update. The quality and immediacy of standard radio or television broadcasts remain higher. However, sports coverage on the Internet is more interactive – for example, you can control camera angles. The quality is also likely to improve as connections to the Net become more efficient.

SEE ALSO
- Improve your diet and fitness – *page 130*
- Tune into television – *page 148*
- Play games on-line – *page 186*

EXPLORE THE WEB

Plan a wedding

Make **the big day** go with a bang

Arranging a wedding is stressful and time-consuming, but the Internet can help to ease the burden. On the Web you can seek inspiration for music, flowers, cakes and speeches, research venues and organise gifts. Specialist wedding Web sites provide many of these services and are a great place to go for information and advice.

World Wide Wed
The Internet provides a single convenient point for finding caterers, photographers, printers, dressmakers and musicians – even poets who will write a few special verses for your big day. You can also get help on choosing venues, managing money and meeting important deadlines.

Some sites even allow you to store all your notes and plans on-line for easy reference.

Australian Weddings - www.ozlines.com.au
- I-do Wedding Net
- Kiss The Bride
- Local Wedding Guide
- Marriage Maintenance
- Melbourne Weddings
- Oz Wedding Planner

Helpful advice
There are sites to help you to produce and circulate your wedding list and others that offer advice on speechmaking or writing your own vows. A good place to start your research is Australian Weddings **(www.ozlines.com.au/wedd.htm)**, which has links to a range of sites.

Time Saver!
If you circulate your gift list on-line you can manage it so that friends and relatives see what they each have given and don't duplicate gifts.

Did You Know?
*If you are unsure about the role of the best man or how to seat divorced parents of the bride or groom, you can get advice on etiquette at i-do.com (**www.i-do.com.au**); or go to Yahoo! (**http://au.yahoo.com**) and click on **Society & Culture**, and then on **Weddings**.*

GREAT DAYS

PLAN THE PERFECT DAY

Finding wedding services

Hundreds of sites on the Internet offer directories of wedding services. Simply click on a category – such as caterers or photographers – followed by your postcode, and you will be shown an extensive range of suppliers. Be aware, however, that few sites offer a national or even a statewide service. The best directories are very regional, often concentrating on a single city.

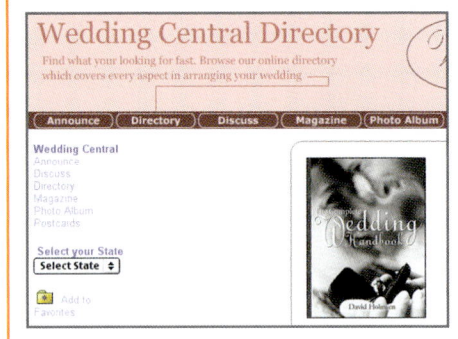

You can nevertheless get ideas and sample possibilities at sites such as Wedding Central (**www.weddingcentral.com.au**), Your Local Wedding Guide (**www.weddingguide.com.au**) or New Zealand Weddings (**www.newzealandweddings.co.nz**).

Alternatively, type the words 'wedding directory' and the name of your city into your favourite search engine to find guides to services in your particular area.

On-line planners

Who speaks at a wedding, and in what order? Everyone involved in planning a wedding puzzles over questions of etiquette and procedure such as this. Fortunately, almost all wedding sites offer help. Visit the enormous i-do wedding site (**www.i-do.com.au**) for planning tips, advice and articles on subjects ranging from 'Toasts & Speeches' to 'Entertainment and MCs'. Planning checklists are also offered by many sites, such as Your Wedding Plan (**www.yourweddingplan.com.au**).

Gift registries

Many sites offer on-line gift registries – where the happy couple can choose a range of gifts they would like to receive, and then guests can visit the site, browse through items on the list, make a choice, pay on-line and have the gift wrapped and delivered for them.

Some sites limit the choice to gifts from participating retailers or a pre-prepared catalogue, but the larger ones allow the bride and groom to select items from sources they choose. As a start, check out The Wedding Gift Company (**www.weddinggift.com.au**), Wedding Wishes (**www.weddingwishes.com.au**) or Bridal Gift Registry Online (**www.bridalgiftregistry.co.nz**).

A wedding to remember

If you are not excited by the thought of a traditional white wedding with all the trappings, perhaps you'd prefer to be married on a mountain top or in a hot-air balloon? New Zealand Wedding Services (**www.nzweddingservices.co.nz**) can arrange both for you.

If these suggestions still sound a bit ho-hum, how about getting married beneath the waves? To find out more go to Underwater Weddings (**www.underwaterweddings.com**).

Or if you want to find a special location far away from everything that's familiar, try Weddings Away (**www.weddingsaway.com.au**).

Wine

If you supply your own wine for the reception, you can save a lot of money – especially if you buy it in bulk – rather than paying a caterer to provide it. But remember, if your reception is in a hotel, you may be charged a fee for corkage.

SEARCH IT YOURSELF

When looking for wedding-related Web sites, there are so many to choose from that it pays to be specific when using a search engine. For example, if you are looking for some ideas for wedding cakes, use 'wedding cakes' as your search term, rather than just 'wedding', to narrow down the subject area.

EXPLORE THE WEB

CREATING AN ON-LINE WEDDING LIST

There are many on-line wedding gift services. Wedding Wishes (**www.weddingwishes.com.au**) is easy to use and does not require that everyone buying a gift has access to the Internet.

The bride and groom will need to register with Wedding Wishes, where they can create their wedding list from an on-line catalogue or from any other source they care to choose.

To make a purchase, family and friends can use the Internet, or get details by phone, fax or post from Wedding Wishes. The site will buy the gift and also take care of wrapping and delivery.

1 Go to Wedding Wishes (**www.weddingwishes.com.au**) and click on **Couples**. On the next page, click **Start** to begin the registration process.

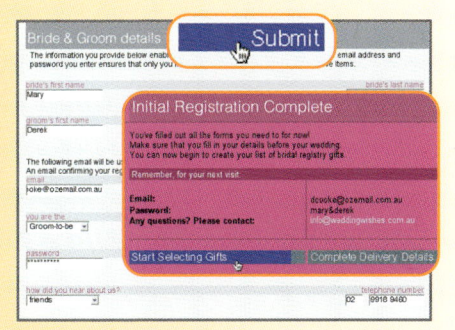

2 Fill in the Bride and Groom details as requested and, once the initial registration is complete, click **Start selecting gifts** to create your own list.

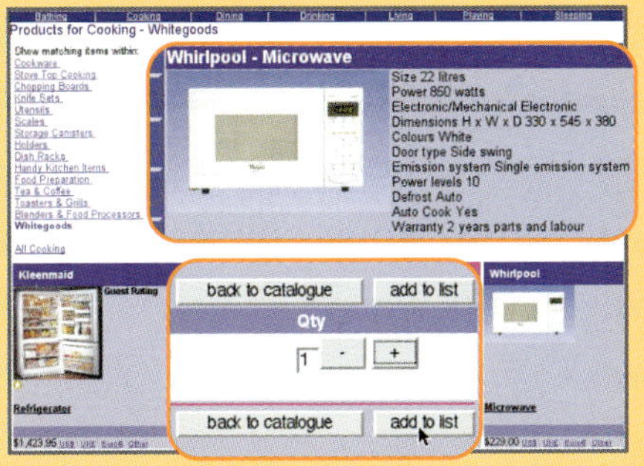

3 Work your way through the gifts offered in the site's catalogue, clicking on **details** for more information on particular items. To add something, specify quantity and click on **add to list**.

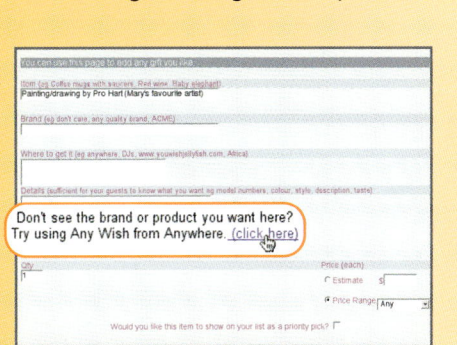

4 You can also add items that are not in the site's on-line catalogue. Click the **Any Wish from Anywhere** link and fill in as many details as possible on the form that appears.

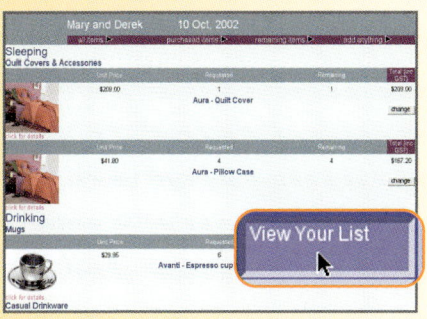

5 To review progress, click **View Your List**. You can always return later to alter your list or add to it if necessary. Once started, the list can be viewed by any guests who wish to make a purchase.

How guests can access your list

Once you've set up a gift list, send the site address and your wedding number to all your guests who have Internet access. To see your list, they need to click on the **Guests** link, enter the last names of the bride and groom in the boxes supplied and then confirm the identity of the couple from a list. When the correct gift list appears, guests select an item to buy and are then taken to a secure site to enter their payment details.

Did You Know?

After the big day you can make an on-line wedding album using personal Web space provided by your Internet Service Provider. Scan in your photographs so anyone who was unable to attend can see the event (see Add a picture to your page, page 264).

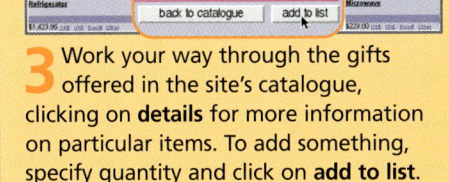

SEE ALSO
- Mark a special occasion – *page 218*
- Book a perfect holiday – *page 228*
- Plan your overseas trip – *page 232*

243

SECTION THREE
Making Web sites

Design and set up your own Web site and make sure people see it. Add sound, pictures and home movie clips, to make it stand out. And learn how to create an on-line business.

INTRODUCTION

What is a Web site?

Find out how **Web sites** and **Web pages** work

Look at any newspaper or magazine advertisement, or watch almost any television commercial, and you are likely to see references to Web sites. A presence on the Web has become an essential part of most companies' marketing strategies, and they're keen to make sure you know where to find them. But the Web isn't just for big companies. Most sites are actually run by individuals to promote an interest or hobby, or to keep in touch with their families. If you've got something to say or share, why not start your own site?

How the Web works

The World Wide Web is a huge network of Web sites, each made up of one or more Web pages. A Web page is a document stored on a computer (known as a 'server') that is permanently connected to the Internet, so that it can be viewed by anyone at any time.

Web pages are written in a computer language called HTML (HyperText Markup Language) that allows separate documents to be linked together. A collection of linked pages forms a Web site, which in turn can be linked to other sites around the world – forming the World Wide Web itself.

Creating your own site

You don't need to know how to write HTML in order to make your own Web site. You can use a good word-processing package such as Microsoft Word, or an on-line authoring program, to create the HTML for you (see *Build a Web page in Word*, page 256; and *Design a Web page on-line*, page 288).

Whether you build your site on your PC and upload it to the Web, or build it directly on the Web, it will be hosted on a Web site server, so you don't always have to be on-line for your site to be seen.

MAKING WEB SITES

Time Saver!
Learn from other sites as you surf the Web. If you see a design feature or idea that you like, think how you could do something similar.

HOW TO: ANALYSE A WEB SITE

Think of a Web site as being like a magazine. A good magazine has interesting stories or articles displayed over a number of pages using text and graphics. A good Web site delivers a similar product, but its pages are stored on a computer connected to the Internet.

Like magazines, Web sites are generally dedicated to exploring a specific theme or a related group of themes. Both can be 'browsed' rather than read from beginning to end and both hope to capture the interest of the reader so that they return again in the future.

The pages that make up a Web site are either created on, or loaded onto, an Internet server computer (see *Upload your site*, page 262). The pages are then available to anyone who enters the appropriate file address into their Web browser (see *Start browsing*, page 26).

Web pages have greater flexibility than printed pages because you can include moving images, links to related Web sites and interactive features such as bulletin boards. You can also print the page out, copy and paste useful text into a word-processing document or e-mail the page to a friend.

Designing your own site

If you are considering making your own Web site, the most important thing to think about is its content. Who is the site for? What will a visitor to your site want to get from it? What is the most important information you want to provide? Even interesting content is not necessarily enough. It also needs to be accurate and up to date. Visitors to your site will soon notice if your material is stale and may not visit again. You should expect to have to update your site regularly – or use material that will not go out of date.

Once you have settled on your content, you then need to create a design that suits your needs. For information on how to create a well-designed Web site, see *Web design basics*, page 254).

HOME OF THE McKAY FAMILY

Sign My GuestBook | View My GuestBook

Hello, and welcome to the McKay family homepage, we decided to build this homepage for something to leave our childeren, grandchildren, and greatgrandchildren. We will be including many family photographs taken over the years with some stories attached to them, we hope that this homepage will be added to in future years by those mentioned above, in a way it will be a family tree, my wife and I would like to include some of our personal stories about where we were born, what we accomplished in our lifetime, and what we are doing now. We sincerely hope you enjoy this homepage, and I hope it will be added to in the many years to come.

Why have a Web page?

If you have an extended family, you could use your site to keep in touch by publishing photographs and family news. If you're a collector or have a lot of knowledge about a particular subject, you could use a Web site to share your experience with the world, making new contacts and friends along the way. If you run a small business or have a freelance or part-time career, you could use a Web site to promote yourself.

SEE ALSO
- **What is the Internet?**
  – *page 10*
- **Web design basics**
  – *page 254*
- **How e-commerce works**
  – *page 298*

INTRODUCTION

How are Web sites made?

The **nuts and bolts** of Web design

To create your own Web site, all you need is a software package that will help you to design your site, and Web space that will ensure the Web pages are available to the rest of the Internet. You then need to think about the plan and layout of the site, how people will navigate their way around it, and the look of your site – which involves deciding on what kinds of text, graphics and colour to use.

Web design software
You can use a word-processing program such as Microsoft Word to design your Web site, so if you can use Word you're halfway there already (see *Build a Web page in Word*, page 256). If you feel inspired to create a more intricate Web site, you can buy a more complex program such as FrontPage (see *Other design programs*, page 294).

Design your page on-line
You can also use software on specialist Web sites – or Web space providers – to design your own Web site on-line. Some sites boast that it can take as little as 10 minutes to create your own site (see *Design a Web page on-line*, page 288). Some of these sites charge for their services, but others are free provided you allow them to place advertisements on your Web site.

Web space
Whether you design your Web site on-line or by using a program on your PC and then uploading it to the Web later, it will have to take up some space on a host server. That space is known as Web space (see opposite) and it is from there that your site can be accessed by other users of the Internet.

MAKING WEB SITES

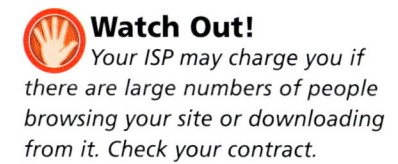

Watch Out!
Your ISP may charge you if there are large numbers of people browsing your site or downloading from it. Check your contract.

HOW TO: FIND WEB SPACE

Your ISP
You may already have some Web space allocated to you by your current Internet Service Provider (ISP) as part of your Internet access agreement. This could be a few megabytes (more than enough for an average homepage) or several hundred megabytes. If you want to create a commercial site, check whether your ISP will let you use the space for business.

Other sources of space
If your ISP does not provide Web space, there are many other host companies to choose from. Go to HostSearch (**www.hostsearch.com**) for a list – and reviews – of these. A few companies provide free Web space while others charge significant amounts. Choosing the right host for your Web site will depend on the level of service you require. If you need guaranteed availability, fast response times and security, for example, in order to support a business, one of the subscription companies with clear service levels will be appropriate. If your pages are not commercial and access times and availability are less important to you, one of the free services might be acceptable. But some of these free hosting companies will automatically add advertising to your site in return for the service.

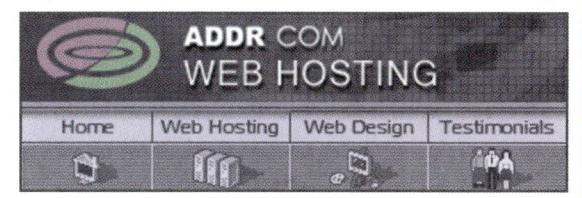

The amount of Web space you can obtain with a specialist host varies from a few to several hundred megabytes (Mb). You need a lot of Web space only if you want to enhance your site with high-quality graphics, video or other large files, which use up a lot of computer memory. For most personal homepages, 5Mb is more than enough.

USING PHOTOGRAPHS ON YOUR SITE

If you want to use your own images, you'll need to have them available as computer graphic files. A scanner or a digital camera will be useful if you'll be making a site that uses a lot of images.

Scanners
A scanner copies images from paper and converts them into computer graphic files, which you can later enhance on your PC. Some scanners can also copy slides and negatives. Scanner quality is measured in terms of 'dpi' (dots per inch), which indicates its 'resolution'. A scanner of 1200 dpi will be better than one of 600 dpi, but the latter will be more than adequate for the Web.

Digital cameras
These cameras take photographs without using any film and store them as graphic files, which you can transfer onto your computer. Camera quality is determined by its resolution, which is measured in megapixels. For Web sites, a 1.5–2 megapixel camera provides ample quality.

Other options
You can get your standard camera film transferred to CD-ROM when it is developed, or have pictures scanned at a shop specialising in copying and reproduction.

SEE ALSO
- Upload your site – *page 262*
- Link to more pages – *page 270*
- Set up a business site – *page 300*

249

INTRODUCTION

Web site ingredients

Discover ways to make your **Web site** exciting and unique

There are many useful resources on the Internet, such as images, sounds, animations and Web page builders, which you can use when designing your site. Some are protected by copyright, which means that you have to pay for them or get permission to use them; others are available free of charge; and almost all can easily be added to your site. Remember: the more interesting your site, the more likely it is that people will return to it and recommend it to others. But don't go overboard – a well-designed Web page won't need more than one or two special features to impress visitors.

Sound
Adding a spoken commentary, background music or just an interesting sound effect to your site is easy and adds impact (see *Add sound to your page*, page 276).

Animated images and text
The easiest way of adding some movement to your page is to include an animated GIF image. This is a series of pictures saved into a single file that are shown in quick succession to create the impression of a moving image. There are thousands of such animations available free of charge on-line (see *Add a picture to your page*, page 264).

Streaming video
With the faster Internet connections now available, you can add video clips to your site without slowing up or crashing your visitors' computers. By connecting your video camera to your computer, you can save your own video clips, edit them and put them on-line (*Add a video to your page*, page 282).

250

MAKING WEB SITES

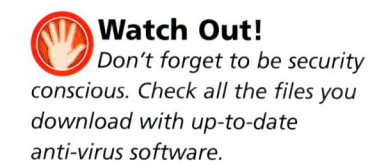

Watch Out!
Don't forget to be security conscious. Check all the files you download with up-to-date anti-virus software.

HOW TO: FIND IMAGES ON-LINE

General multimedia
Photographs, sounds, animated icons, streaming video, desktop wallpaper, screensavers, music files and ClipArt are all available on the Web. The quality is often excellent and the best sites are those that have broken their content down by theme so that you can quickly find the subject matter you need.

WorldAtlas.com (www.worldatlas.com/clipart.htm)
An excellent site for free ClipArt graphics of world maps and flags.

Art by Cheryl.com (www.artbycheryl.com)
Thousands of themed hand-drawn images are available at this site. They are free as long as you follow the site's Acceptable Use policy.

Google's image search
Google (http://images.google.com) has indexed more than 330 million images on the Web. By typing in a name or a description, you are likely to find an image of almost anything you might want. However, there is no guarantee that any particular image is free, so make sure you check the copyright or trademark details of an image before using it on your own Web page.

American Memory (http://memory.loc.gov/ammem/amhome.html)
This site has several million historical and cultural images from the USA – including photographs, manuscripts, maps, recordings and moving images – most of which have no copyright restrictions.

Free Graphics (www.freegraphics.com)
An index of dozens of sites which have a variety of free image resources.

NASA (www.nasa.gov/gallery/photo)
NASA's Web site provides a vast collection of space exploration images which are free to use for educational and non-commercial purposes.

Web design elements
Many sites offer buttons, borders and backgrounds designed specifically for use on Web pages. Some sites offer packages of these features all designed to complement each other.

ABC Giant (www.abcgiant.com)
An excellent site for free graphics, ClipArt, animation, buttons, bullets, borders, fonts and other Web graphics.

Backgrounds Archive (www.backgroundsarchive.com)
This site provides small images that can be used repeatedly across the screen to create attractive textured backgrounds.

Free Buttons.com (www.freebuttons.com)
Find themed buttons for all Web page purposes at this site. The buttons are free, but you have to provide a link to this site on your Web page.

Technical resources
For more advanced Web page design, you can find programming generators for HTML and JavaScript. You'll also find Flash and Shockwave animations, but remember that your visitors will need to have the Flash viewer plug-in installed.

Flash Kit (www.flashkit.com/movies)
Try this site for hundreds of Flash animations, movies and tutorials.

Webmonkey (http://hotwired.lycos.com/webmonkey)
Go to the Webmonkey site for an enormous collection of examples and tutorials on all aspects of Web scripting. The site covers HTML, DHTML, Javascript, PHP CGI and more.

INTRODUCTION

> ## HOW TO: FIND INTERACTIVE FEATURES
> There are many lists of Web resources on the Internet, but a good place to start looking for additional features for your Web page is the CNET download service (**http://download.com.com**), where you'll find files and links to sites providing tools for all the ideas listed here, plus many other possibilities: click on **Web Developer** and then on **Web Design Utilities**.
>
> Before you choose any particular on-line service to add to your site, see what it looks like on a few existing sites and be sure that you can make it work with your overall design. Also check if the service uses pop-up advertising and decide whether it'll be appropriate for the people who'll visit your site.

Bulletin boards
World Crossing (www.worldcrossing.com)
You can make your site interactive by adding a feature like a bulletin board – a place for visitors to place notices, ask questions and generally discuss the subject matter of the site. World crossing is a provider of free message boards, which are easy to customise to your own design.

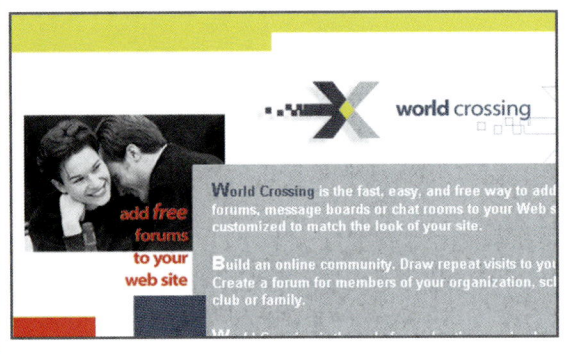

Guest books
Sign my Guestbook (www.signmyguestbook.com)
Invite people to comment on how interesting or useful they found your site by adding a guest book. This free site allows you to choose the appearance and contents of your guest book. Click on **F.A.Q.** to find out how it works.

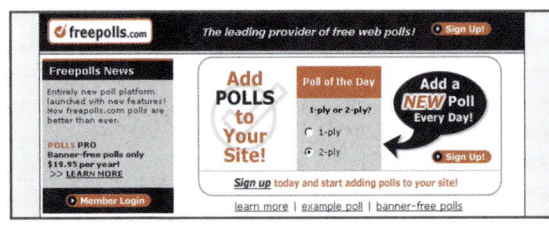

Opinion polls
Freepolls (www.freepolls.com)
If you want a quick snapshot of what visitors want, and what they think of your site, consider using an opinion poll. This offers a set of questions, usually in a multiple-choice checkbox format, which can be completed quickly. The feedback will not be as comprehensive, however, as in a bulletin board.

Hit counters
WebCounter (www.digits.com)
A hit counter can tell you an enormous amount about the visitors who are browsing your site, such as how many there are, where they come from and what browsers they are using. To add a counter you need to register with a service and add a bit of HTML code to your Web page. Some services, such as GeoCities (**http://au.geocities.yahoo.com**), offer free counters to their customers.

> ### Sound advice
> Sound files can be very large, making a site slow and frustrating to use. Unexpected sounds or music can also be annoying or unwelcome. Make your sounds optional by providing a button to turn them on if visitors would like to hear them.

252

MAKING WEB SITES

Problem Solver!
If your visitors can't access your video or audio clips it's probably because they haven't got the right player software installed on their PC. Always provide your visitors with a link to the supplier's site so that they can download the appropriate player software.

HOW TO: GET ADVICE ABOUT YOUR SITE

Ask an expert
If you need advice on designing your Web page, the Internet provides forums and expert sites on most subjects. However, you should proceed with caution when following this advice. Many of the contributors to these sites are fellow Web-users who, however well intentioned, may not always possess all the expertise you need.

Pose a problem
BigNoseBird (**www.bignosebird.com**) is a site that helps people to learn about a wide range of Web page design issues. It includes many free resources and a popular bulletin board where you can post questions asking for feedback and advice on a range of topics, such as HTML, graphics, JavaScript and issues relating to managing your own server.

For a wealth of further resources and handy hints about setting up your own Web site, take a look at Webmonkey (**http://hotwired.lycos.com/webmonkey**) and the Web design pages at About.com (**http://webdesign.about.com**). You can search for examples or explore the different subject categories. Often the writer of an article will leave an e-mail address, so you can write asking for further advice.

Ask for feedback
Another useful place to visit is SiteCritique (**www.sitecritique.net**). Once you register (for free), you can submit your own site for criticism by other members, according to categories such as 'usability', 'graphics' and 'navigation'. Awards are given out each month to the sites that receive the best reviews.

HOW *NOT* TO DESIGN YOUR SITE
Vincent Flanders' Web Pages That Suck (**www.webpagesthatsuck.com**) is all about badly designed sites. You can learn a lot about Web page design from other people's mistakes, and Vincent Flanders has scoured the Net for them.

The examples are all commercial sites, since Flanders considers personal Web pages too subjective to criticise. There is a 'Daily Sucker' feature highlighting a different site every day, as well as countless examples of sites which are hard to read or use because of jarring combinations of over-elaborate fonts, colourful graphics or unnecessary features.

The site isn't simply negative, though. Flanders uses examples to show how you can fix similar problems with your own site. You can also submit suggestions for sites to be considered, although you can't get feedback on the design of your site.

SEE ALSO
- Avoid computer viruses – *page 58*
- Download from the Web – *page 86*
- Solve computer problems – *page 133*

253

Web design basics

Find the **most appropriate way** to present your site's content

In Web design, as in any kind of graphic design, it is important that the visual elements enhance the message rather than hinder it. If your site is about flower arranging, for example, you should avoid spinning graphics, sound effects and flashing text. The design of the site should always highlight its main features and make it easy for the visitor to use.

Before you begin designing your site, take time to consider its main aims, the material that is going to be on it and how it will be organised.

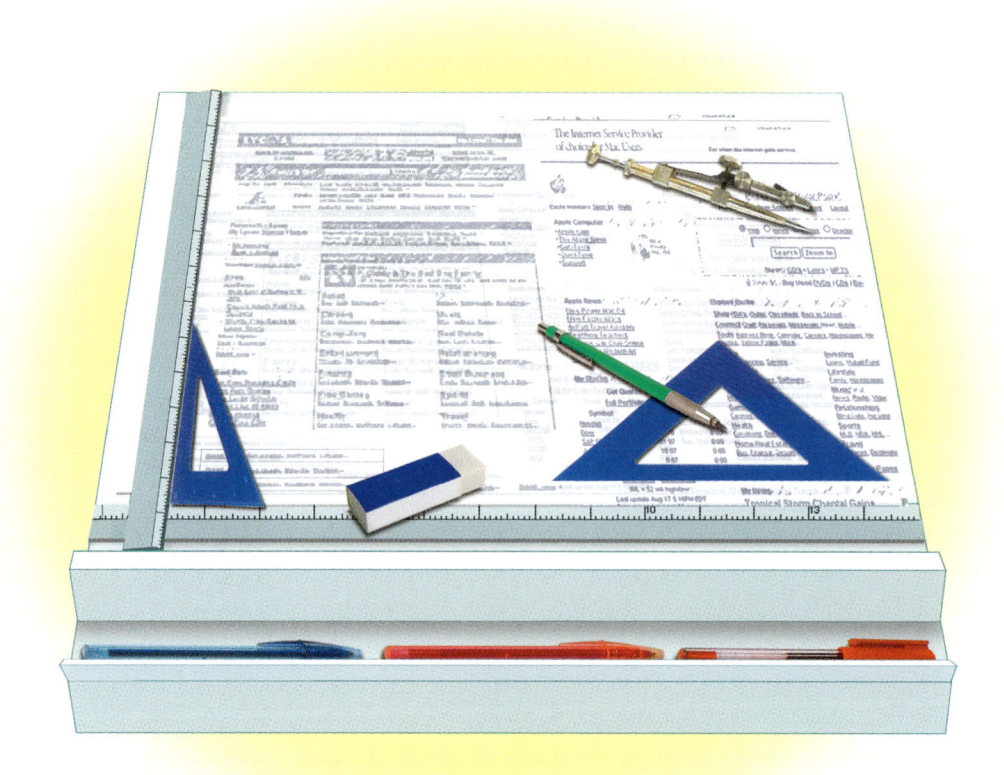

The golden rule
Don't overcomplicate. This applies to every aspect of your design – fonts (typefaces), colours, effects. Too many competing visual items can put the user off.

Colour
Make your site easier on the eye by limiting the number of colours you use to three or four. You should also use colour consistently – one colour for links, one for headings, one for text. This gives the user a visual sense of how your site works.

Backgrounds
Keep the background simple. For example, a patterned background often makes it difficult to read the text. Research has shown that the human eye is most comfortable reading green text on a black background, whereas white text on a colour is hardest to read.

Fonts
Use only two or three fonts on your page. Any more will make it look messy. You should also choose fonts that other computer users are likely to have on their computers, such as Verdana and Helvetica. If you use an unusual font, it may not display correctly on all computers.

MAKING WEB SITES

> **Did You Know?**
> If you're feeling confident, you can put up your site for a Web design award, which can help attract more visitors. For details on how to apply, go to Website Awards (*http://websiteawards.xe.net*).

FIRST STEPS IN WEB DESIGN

Before you start designing your pages on a computer, you should first draw sketches of what you are aiming to achieve. This forces you to work out how each page will be structured, what will appear where, and the numbers of words and images you will need.

Draw a table
When you create a Web page in Word, it is best to create a 'table', which acts as a framework for everything you want to include on the page (see *Build a Web page in Word*, page 256). Without a table, the position of text and pictures on your Word document may change once your page is on-line. A table keeps everything between fixed boundaries.

Once you have drawn a sketch of your Web page, divide each element into different segments (marked in red on the sketch shown). This will form the basis of your table. Now count the number of columns and rows the table will need and keep this information to hand before beginning to design your page in Word.

Make it easy for the visitor
When sketching out your site, ensure that you create distinct 'signposts'. Include a clear title and unambiguous explanation of what your page is about. Give some space to a list of contents to direct visitors around the site – this will be especially useful when you start to create additional pages (see *Link to more pages*, page 270).

Keep it interesting
Provide one or two attractive images to add visual interest to the page. But don't overdo it: too many pictures will make the page load slowly. If you can find an image that is informative as well as appealing (for example, a picture of the stamp collection that your site is about), use that.

Always try to provide links to other sites of interest. It can be annoying for visitors to find that your site is a cul-de-sac. But don't overdo this; a few useful links are better than an endless list of them.

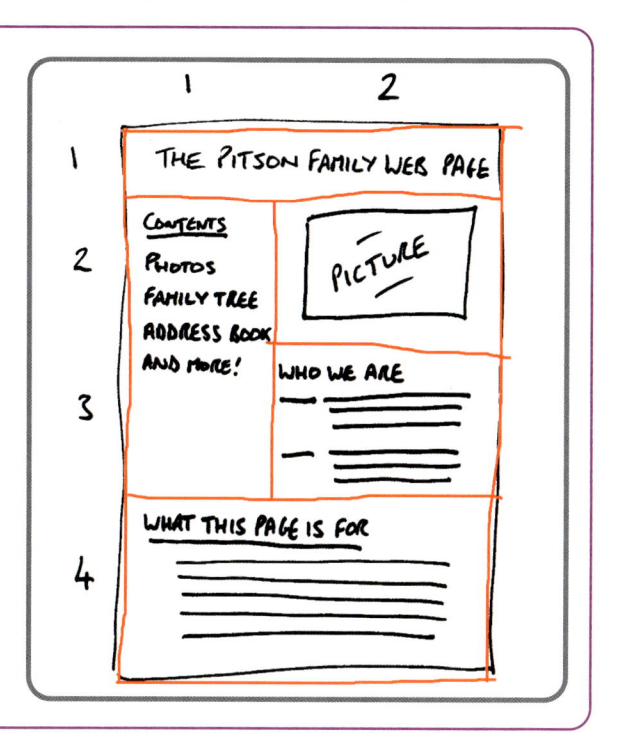

HINTS AND TIPS

DON'T have long lists of links, as they are not user-friendly. If you want to offer many links, split them into smaller groups by theme.

DO consider adding a site map. This is a visual representation of how the pages on your site link together. It can be a great help to the visitor.

DON'T use yellow for text. It doesn't display well on many monitors and is almost always difficult to read.

DO design your pages so that as much as possible can be seen on screen at once. Your site users will quickly tire of scrolling down or across to see the rest of your page.

DON'T give large blocks of text a central alignment. Such text can be hard to read.

DON'T try to fit too much on a page, especially in a small type size. Dense pages are off-putting. If you want to include a lot of material, split it into separate pages, then link them.

SEE ALSO
- Build a Web page in Word – page 256
- Add a picture to your page – page 264
- Add sound to your page – page 276

YOUR FIRST WEB PAGE

Build a Web page in Word

Creating your own pages is easier than you might think

Microsoft Word is ideal for creating your own simple Web pages. If you already use Word for creating your paper documents, you will be familiar with its general menus and options. Word also includes some powerful tools that simplify putting together Web pages. You can do it all just by keying in text and pointing and clicking with your mouse. There is no need to learn any complicated programming techniques. Shown here is Word 2002, but the instructions will also work with earlier versions of the program.

Using Word
Creating a Web page in Microsoft Word is very similar to creating a normal printed paper document. You position all your text and images manually using the standard document editing menus. Word then translates your page into HTML automatically.

Before you start
It is worth taking a few minutes to sketch out on paper a brief design of what you want your page to look like before you start up your software. This will be a useful reference point when you start creating the electronic version. See *Web design basics*, page 254, for more details on how to do this.

Options in Word
Word allows you to save a document as a Web page (the method illustrated in the step-by-step instructions following). Alternatively, you can use the program's own 'Web Page Wizard' or its 'Web page template'. For more information on using the wizard and the template, go to the 'Word Help' search bar in the top-right hand corner, type 'Web Page' and hit the **Return** (or **Enter**) key. Choose **About creating a web page** and read the information that comes up.

MAKING WEB SITES

✋ Watch Out!
Don't use more than three or four colours, and use colours consistently – one colour for text, another for links, and so on. That will make your page easier to read.

HOW TO: STRUCTURE YOUR WEB PAGE

When you are preparing a document for the Internet, rather than for printing out, you need to take extra care to ensure that all the elements of the page are correctly positioned. Otherwise they will not be properly displayed on other people's Web browsers.

The easiest way to do this is to place all the text and images in a table, using the table's rows and columns to act as boundaries, and set the position of each item. You can use your sketch to work out the number of rows and columns you need, though you can always add more later if you need to.

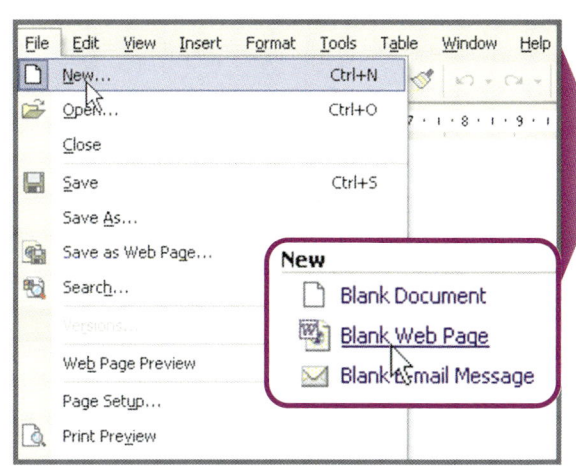

1 Open Microsoft Word. Go to the **File** menu and select **New**. In the 'New Document' window that opens on the right, select **New Blank Web Page** and then click **OK**.

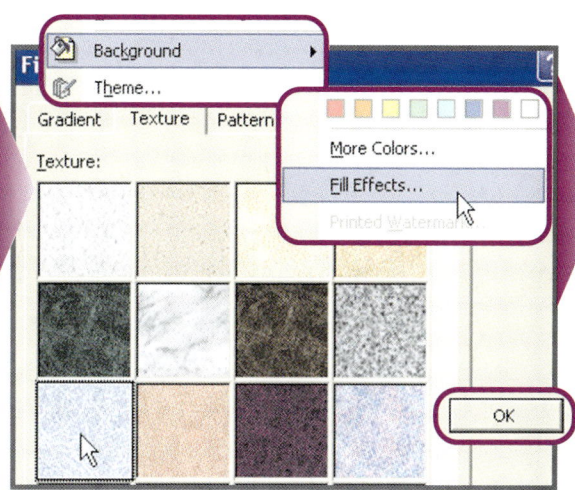

2 Begin by adding a background to your page. Go to the **Format** menu and select **Background** then **Fill Effects**. Click on the **Texture** tab, then select a texture that you like and click **OK**.

Using Word's Web Page Wizard
To find the Web Page Wizard, go to **File** and select **New**; a 'New Document' window will appear on the right of the screen with a list of options. Under 'New from template', click on **General Templates**, then choose the **Web pages** tab, and in the next window double-click on the **Web Page Wizard** icon.

YOUR FIRST WEB PAGE

Problem Solver!
*If you want to add a row to your table, click in the row above where you want to insert it, go to the **Table** menu and select **Insert** and then **Rows Below**. You can insert a column using the same principle.*

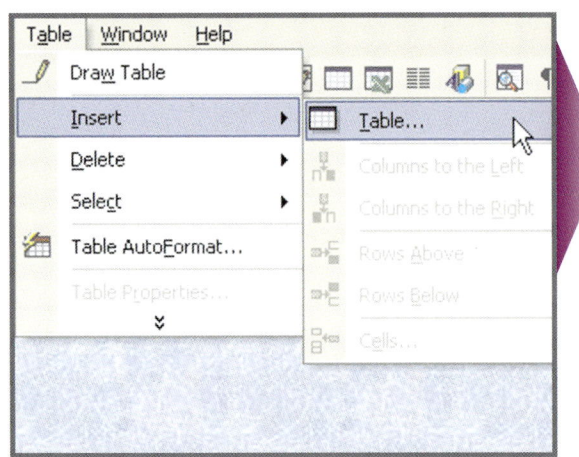

3 Now insert your table to help to position the various items that will appear on your page. Go to the **Table** menu and select **Insert** and then **Table**.

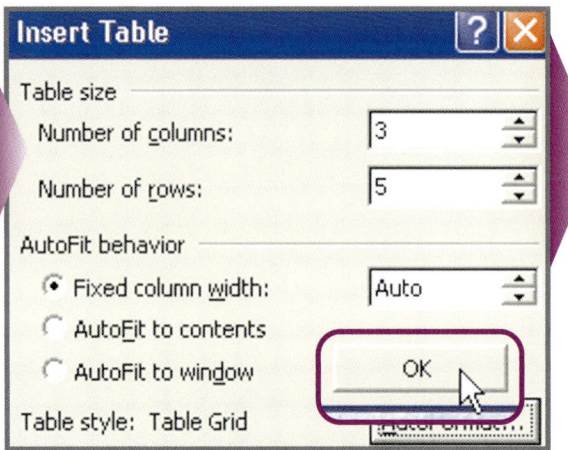

4 Then select the number of columns and rows you require, and click **OK**.

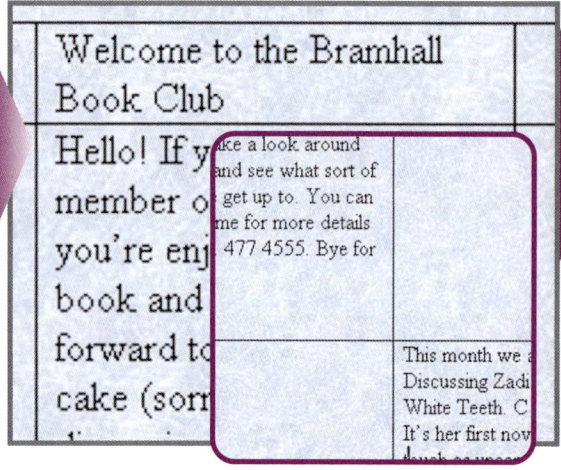

5 Now click in the first section of the table in which you want to write some text, and type it in. The height of the row increases to accommodate the text. Type in the text for each section of the table.

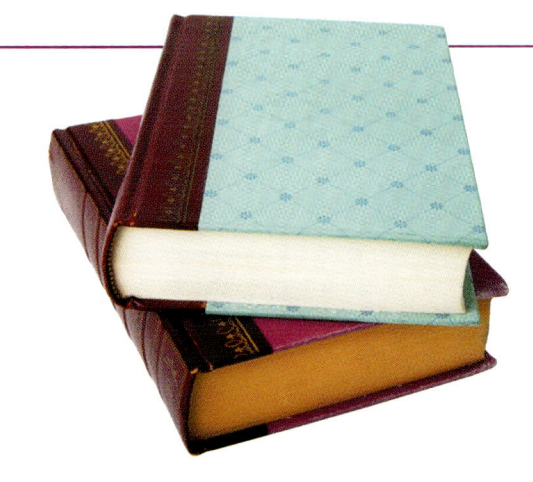

MAKING WEB SITES

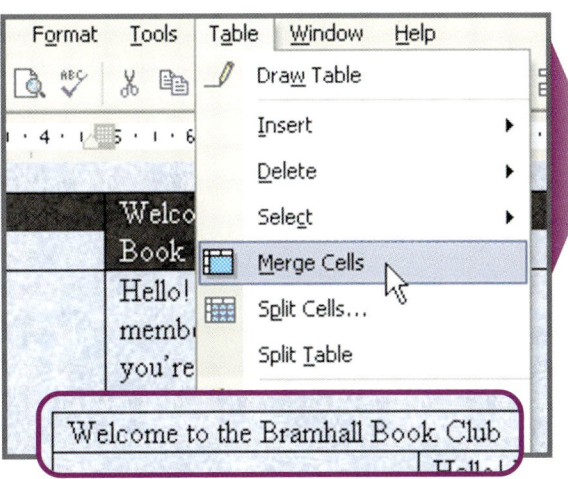

Did You Know?
*You can find free site building resources, including ClipArt, sounds and other add-ons, at Reallybig.com (**www.reallybig.com**).*

6 You can remove the divisions between parts of the table to allow text to run right across. To do this, highlight the top three cells by clicking and dragging across them. Go to the **Table** menu and select **Merge Cells**. Then do the same for the second row.

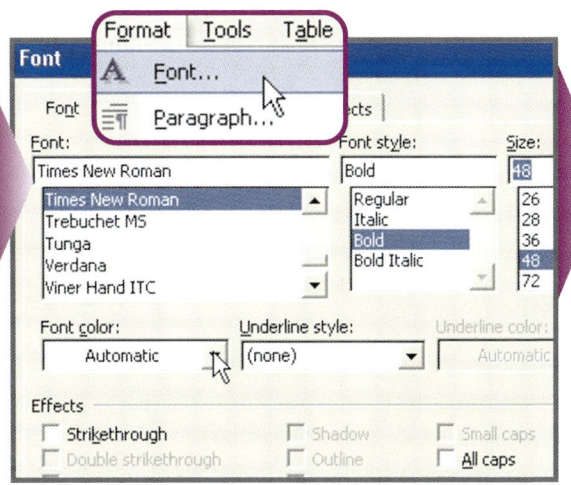

7 You are now ready to style your text. Highlight the text in the first section of the table. Go to the **Format** menu and select **Font**. In the next window, select a font, style, size and effect. Then click on the arrow beneath 'Font color'.

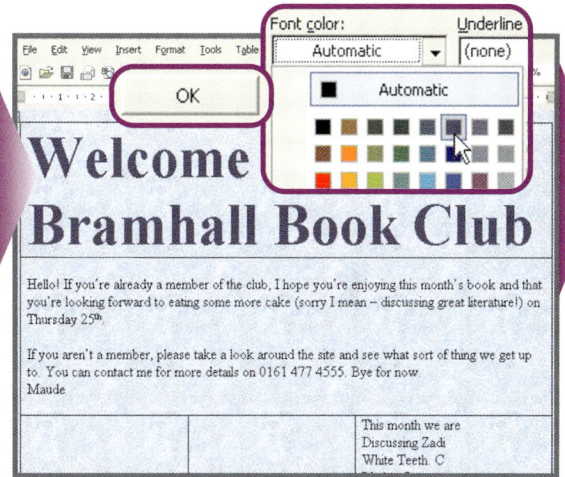

8 Click on a colour from the pop-up menu that appears. Then click **OK** to apply your changes to the highlighted text.

Themes

Instead of using a background colour, you can apply any of a number of pre-set themes to your page. Go to the Format menu and select Theme. Then click on a few of the options from the list to see the available effects. You cannot use a theme and a background colour together.

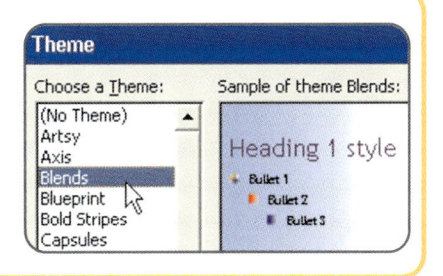

259

YOUR FIRST WEB PAGE

Problem Solver!
If you can't find an appropriate piece of ClipArt in the Word gallery, have a look at some of the sites mentioned in Web site ingredients, *page 250, or search the Web yourself using the terms 'Clips' or 'ClipArt'.*

9 Now align your text, choosing between left, right centred or justified formats. Highlight a block of text and then click on the appropriate button on the toolbar. Repeat steps 8 and 9 to style and then align each block of text on your page.

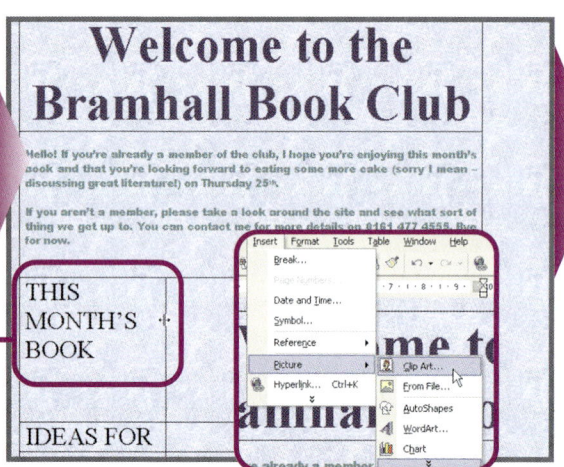

10 Once all the text is prepared, you can add some images to liven up the page. Word has a gallery that you can pick from. Click in the appropriate section of the table, go to the **Insert** menu and select **Picture** and then **Clip Art**.

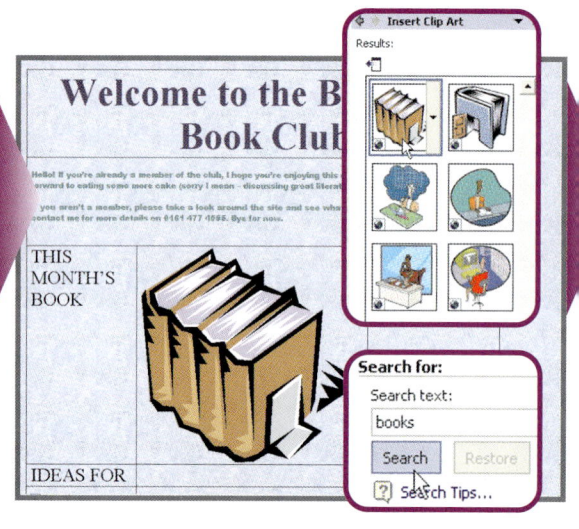

11 In the window that pops up, type in a word describing what you're looking for and click **Search**. Scroll through the results and double-click on the image of your choice to insert it in your document. Close the Clip Art window when finished.

You can also change the width and height of each row and column of the table to suit your text. To do this, hover the cursor over the border-line between sections. When a set of parallel lines with a double-headed arrow appears, click and drag the cursor to move the border.

MAKING WEB SITES

> **Watch Out!**
> *If you double-click on your saved Web page, it will open in your Web browser. To open it in Word, you need to go to Word's **File** menu and select **Open**.*

12 The picture will now appear in the table. To re-size it, click on it and then click and drag one of the corner handles which appear.

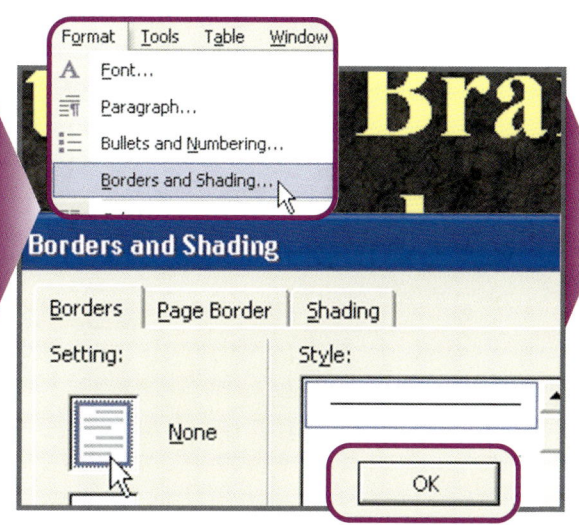

13 Now make your table invisible so that it won't appear on your Web page. Highlight the table by dragging across it and then go to the **Format** menu and select **Borders and Shading**. In the next window, click the icon next to 'None' and click **OK**.

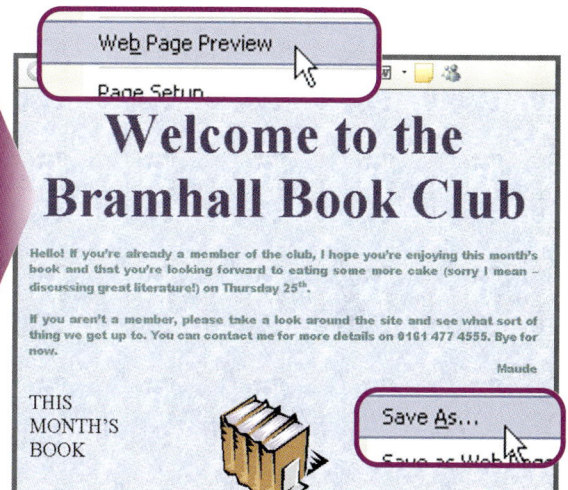

14 Go to the **File** menu and select **Web Page Preview** to check your page in your browser. If you are not happy, close the browser window and make changes to the Word file. When you are ready, go to the **File** menu and save your page (see below).

SAVING YOUR HOMEPAGE

When you save your page, call it 'index'. The main page of your site should always be named in this way, because browsers automatically look for (and open) the 'index' page when they go to a site address. You could then call your site, for example, **www.geocities.com/bramhall-bookclub**. If you call the page something else, you will have to add that name to your basic Web address. For example, if you call your first page 'welcome', your address would need to be something like **www.geocities.com/bramhall-bookclub/welcome.htm**.

SEE ALSO
- **Upload your site** – *page 262*
- **Design a Web page on-line** – *page 288*
- **Ensure your site is seen** – *page 306*

261

YOUR FIRST WEB PAGE

Upload your site

Get your **Web site on-line** for all to see

Once you have created your Web page you can upload your site onto the Internet. This process uses specialist software to transfer copies of your Web page files from your computer to the Internet server you have chosen to host your pages. Windows XP comes with a Web Publishing Wizard that allows you to upload your files easily, either to your own ISP (the process shown opposite) or any other suitable Web host site.

Getting your Web site on-line is straightforward, but it is critical to prepare your page carefully. You also need to have accurate notes of the names and locations of all the files required to make your site complete.

Preparation
You will find it is much easier to upload your site, and to maintain it, if you ensure that all the files comprising your site are stored in the same folder. Keep this folder exclusively for your Web site files so that you can upload the entire contents of the folder to publish your site.

If your site contains images, store these in a sub-folder within your main Web site folder so that they can be easily located.

File names
It is good practice not to use spaces or upper-case (capital) letters in your file names – some browsers and servers are case-sensitive and will not find a file if the wrong case is used.

Web host information
When you sign up with an ISP you should be provided with a 'host address' or the URL of an FTP server. This is a computer that is always connected to the Internet and it's where your Web pages will be stored. You will need the URL for this server to access your Web site. You will also need the username and password you chose when you logged in. Keep this information safe as you will need it if you ever want to make changes to your site.

MAKING WEB SITES

Time Saver!
Different Web hosts have different procedures for uploading pages. Always read the 'help' pages provided by your Web host.

Jargon Buster!
FTP (File Transfer Protocol) is a method for copying files between computers. It is most commonly used for transferring Web site files from your PC to an Internet server.

HOW TO: PUBLISH YOUR SITE ON THE WEB

1 To create a shortcut to the ISP server you want to upload your files to, go to your **Start** menu, click on **My Network Places** and in the next window choose **Add a network place**. When the Wizard starts up, click on **Next**.

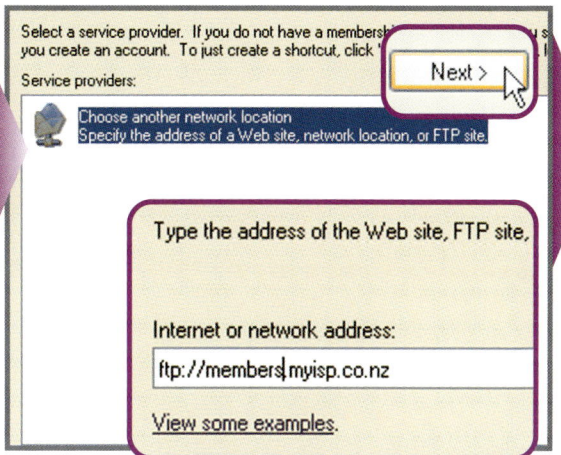

2 Now select **Choose another network location** and click **Next**. Then enter the URL of the ISP server you will upload your Web pages to, and click **Next** again. You'll need to get this information from your ISP if you don't already have it.

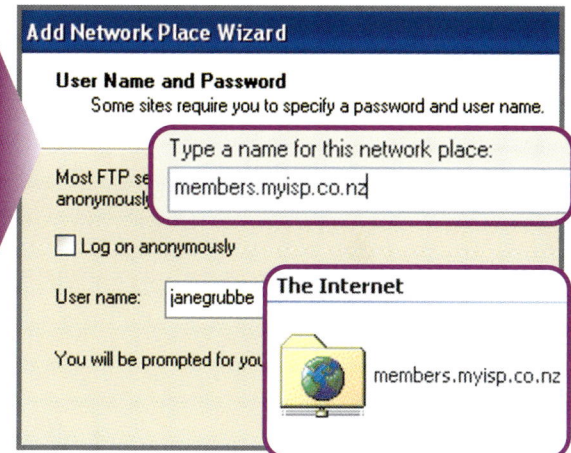

3 De-select the 'Log on anonymously' option, enter your 'User name' and click **Next**. Then type a name for this connection, click **Next** again and then **Finish**. You can now drag and drop your Web site into the resulting folder to publish it.

CHECK YOUR WEB SITE
Once you have finished uploading your page, you should check that it looks correct and that all the elements have been properly published. Open your Web browser and enter the URL of your Web page. Then click on the **Refresh** button in case the browser is loading an earlier copy of the page from your computer's memory.

Updating your site
To update your site, make the changes you want to the original Word file and save it. If you have used new sound or picture files, get rid of any that are defunct. Then drag and drop the updated files, including the complete Word file, onto the folder of your ISP Web host listed under **My Network Places**. Any existing files will be automatically overwritten by the new ones. Open your Web browser and check that the process has been successful.

SEE ALSO
• Link to more pages – *page 270*
• Design a Web page on-line – *page 288*
• Set up a business site – *page 300*

263

BUILDING ON YOUR SITE

Add a picture to your page

Enhance your Web site with the images of your choice

Once you have created your own Web site, you can add pictures to it. These can be images of your own – family photographs or drawings, for example – or pictures downloaded from a library of Web resources. Using a scanner makes it easy to add images from printed sources, though you should make sure you don't infringe the owner's copyright.

Preparing an image
Once you have an image that you want to use on your page, you need to prepare it so that it is suitable for use on the Web. This involves 'optimising' the image – that is, balancing its size and quality – by compressing it to reduce its file size. You then need to save it in a format that is appropriate for the Web (see pages 266–267).

Image size
The optimising process is necessary to ensure that your pictures load as quickly as possible. Graphics that are not optimised can take a long time to load, making your site tedious to view. This may result in visitors to your site losing patience and going elsewhere before they have seen what you have to say.

Copyright
Most printed material is covered by copyright laws, and is not freely available for you to scan in and use without the permission of the copyright owner. You should always check up on this, and seek the owner's permission, before scanning in images from books, magazines or newspapers.

MAKING WEB SITES

Did You Know?
A number of Web sites let you download images for free. You can then use these on your own site. For more details, see page 251.

HOW TO: GET YOUR IMAGE ONTO YOUR COMPUTER

Scanning
Scanners are ideal for turning your favourite pictures into images you can use on your Web page. A scanner takes a digital copy of an image and then displays it on your computer screen This means you can transfer photographs, or pictures from newspapers or books, to your own computer.

There are two main varieties: flat-bed scanners, which are best for images on paper, and film scanners, used for slides and negatives. Some flat-bed scanners will also scan film, but the results are rarely as good as with a specialised film scanner.

Using image editing software (see below), you can then manipulate a picture in various ways – changing its size, colours and other properties to create a new and different image.

You can also decide at which image resolution you wish to make your scan. Resolution describes picture quality and is measured by the number of dots per inch (dpi) that make up an image. The greater the dpi, the better the quality of the picture and the larger the size of the file will be.

Digital cameras
A digital camera takes photographs without using film. Instead it stores images as graphic files, such as JPG (see *Image file formats*, page 266), which you can transfer directly to your PC. You can then edit these images and prepare them for the Web using any graphics package.

The main advantage of digital cameras is their immediacy. There is no need to wait around to finish a film and then develop it. You can see your photos immediately and use them as soon as you connect your camera up to your computer.

Windows XP makes it easy to store and use digital images. It even has a folder, called 'My Pictures', prepared for you. Go to the **Start** menu and you will see it in the list on the right-hand side.

IMAGE EDITING SOFTWARE
There is a variety of specialist and general graphics tools you can use to prepare pictures for your Web site; some are inexpensive, but others are very costly. In the case of the more expensive programs, such as Paint Shop Pro and Adobe Photoshop, it is worthwhile downloading a trial version before investing in the complete package.

Microsoft Paint
Paint is the image editor that comes with Windows XP. You can find it by going to the **Start** menu, clicking **All Programs** and then **Accessories**. Although not as powerful as the other two graphics editors listed here, it is completely free.

Paint Shop Pro
This is a popular graphics program that includes all the tools you'll need to optimise images for the Web. It is good value and suitable for people who don't have previous photo-editing experience. Go to **www.jasc.com/products/psp** to download the 30-day trial version.

Adobe Photoshop
This is a top-of-the-range program, with a huge variety of controls, more suited to professionals than beginners. There is also a simpler version called Photoshop Elements. Trial versions of both programs can be found at **www.adobe.com/products/tryadobe**.

BUILDING ON YOUR SITE

Problem Solver!
If you are not sure how much to compress your image, put several different versions onto your Web page and look at them in your browser. The one that has been compressed the least will look the best, but you should choose the one that has been compressed and yet still looks acceptable.

HOW TO: PREPARE AN IMAGE FOR A WEB SITE

1 Download Paint Shop Pro from the maker's Web site (**www.jasc.com/products/psp**). Install and start the program, then open the image you want to use. This photograph, a JPG file of 2.3Mb measuring 1400x1300 pixels, is too large for Web use.

2 First you need to crop the image to discard any unwanted sections of the picture. Click on the **Crop** tool in the left-hand toolbar, and click and drag your mouse across the area you want to keep. From the top menu, select **Image** and **Crop to Selection**.

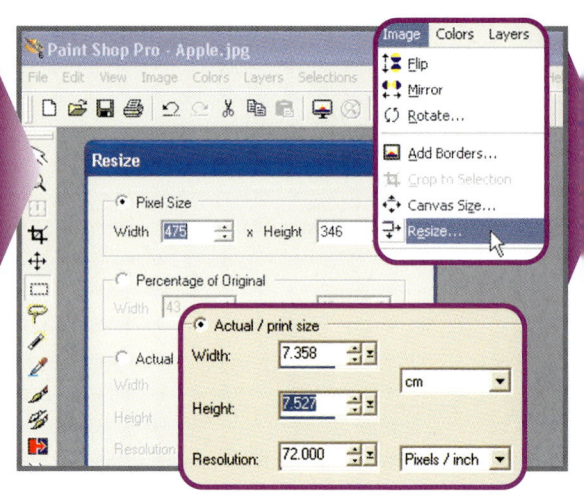

3 Now resize the image. From the menu bar, select **Image** then **Resize**. Make sure the resolution in the 'Actual/print size' section is set to 72 Pixels/inch. Click on the 'Pixel Size' section and select a width of about 475 (the height will adjust automatically).

IMAGE FILE FORMATS

When you save your image, you are offered a number of different file formats. The one you choose depends on the kind of image you have and what you will be using it for.

GIF (.gif) – Limited to 256 colours or less and so suitable for buttons or simple graphics on a Web site. Other features include transparency (the ability to add a see-through background) and animation.

JPG/JPEG (.jpg) – Ideal for photographs, it produces a compact file, up to 100 times smaller than the original, by merging similar colours into a single tone to save space. Unsuitable for images with few colours.

PNG (.png) – A relatively new format not yet widely used on Web pages. It aims to eventually replace the GIF format. However, some older browsers do not display PNG images correctly.

MAKING WEB SITES

Jargon Buster!
Optimising Balancing the size and quality of a file to make it suitable for use on a Web site.

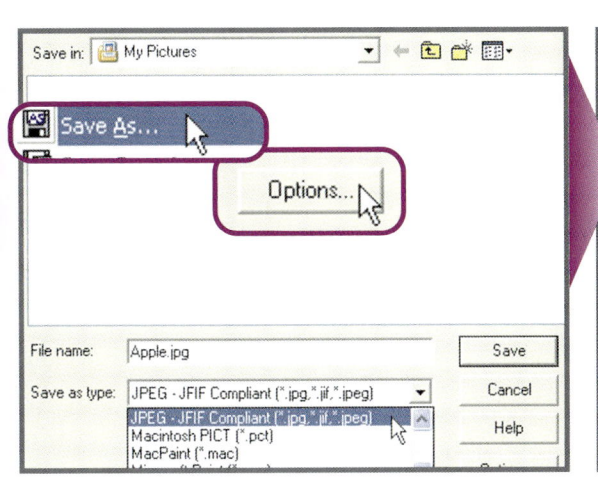

4 Now go to the **File** menu and choose **Save As**. In the 'Save As' window, go to the 'Save as type:' section and choose 'JPEG' from the pull down menu. Then click **Options** at the bottom right.

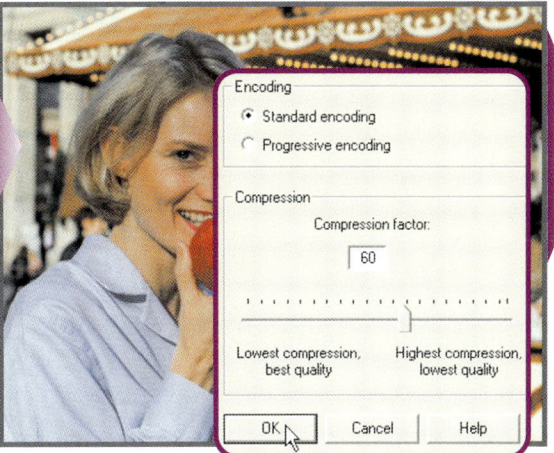

5 In the 'Save Options' window, move the slider to give the image a compression factor of about 60. You can compress the file even more, but the quality may deteriorate to a level that is unacceptable. When you're satisfied, click **OK**.

6 You will return to the 'Save As' window. Go to the 'Save in' section at the top and select the Web page folder you created earlier (see below). Then click on the **Save** button to place your new, optimised JPEG image in that location.

STORING YOUR IMAGES

It's a good idea to keep a copy of your original image in a separate folder from the one where your final, optimised version is stored. If your Web page has a lot of images, store all the optimised versions together in an 'images' folder created within your main Web page folder. This will make things much easier later when you come to upload your site.

BUILDING ON YOUR SITE

Did You Know?
Only minor sizing adjustments should be made to your image at this stage, as major changes can lead to a poorer quality image. It is best to get the size right (or as close as possible) in your image editing program (see page 266).

HOW TO: INSERT YOUR IMAGE

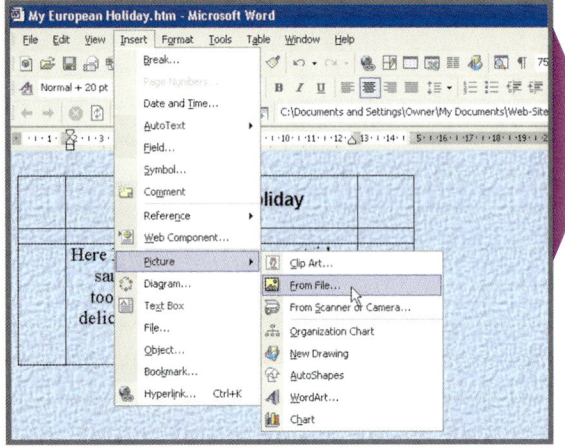

1 First open Microsoft Word, and then open the Web page you created in that program. Click in the part of the table where you want to place the image, then go to the **Insert** menu and choose **Picture** and then **From File**.

2 Locate the image and click **Insert** to add it to your Web page. A copy of the picture will also be made in your Web page files directory (which Word creates when you first save your page), and it is this copy that is displayed on your page.

3 You can now make minor adjustments to the size of the image so that it fits the design of your page. To do this, first click on the image, then click on a corner and drag it to the size you want. The entire page will adjust automatically.

SETTING YOUR DESKTOP
A great way to personalise your computer is to scan in your favourite picture and use it as Desktop wallpaper. Go to the Start menu and select Control Panel, then Appearance and Themes and finally Change the desktop background. Click on Browse and locate your scanned-in image. Then choose whether you want it to appear as a single image (Center), repeated many times (Tile) or magnified (Stretch). Check the preview and click OK to activate your choice.

MAKING WEB SITES

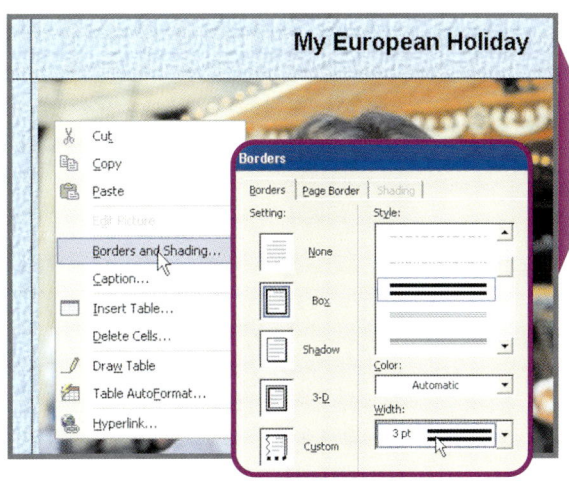

Did You Know?
An optimised image is also perfect for sending by e-mail. Just enclose it as an attachment with an e-mail message (see Send e-mail attachments, *page 46).*

4 You can now add a frame to your picture. To do this, right-click on your picture and choose **Borders and Shading** from the menu that appears. In the next window, select your border style by clicking on one of the options available.

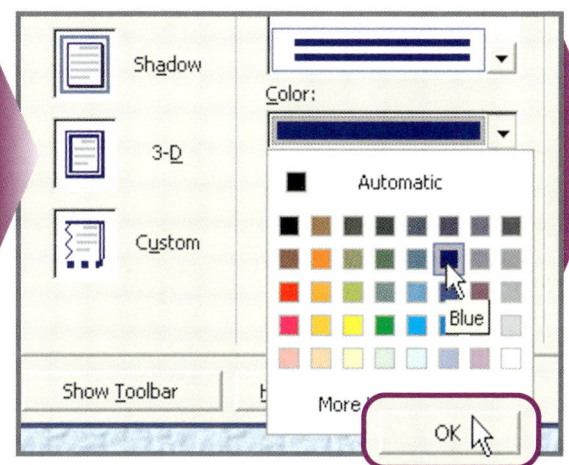

5 In the same window, choose a colour for your border, and specify its width. You can also choose a style such as **Shadow**, which gives the illusion that the picture is sitting slightly above the level of the page. Click **OK** to apply your selections.

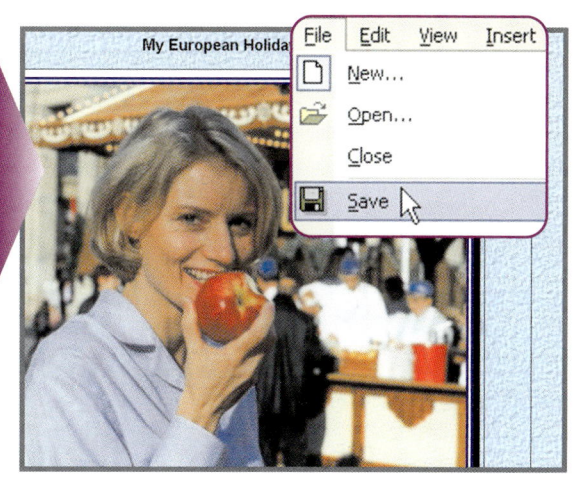

6 To save your document, go to the **File** menu and select **Save**. If you want to, you can go back later to edit any of the new features you have added.

SEE ALSO
- **Web site ingredients**
  – page 250
- **Link to more pages**
  – page 270
- **Ensure your site is seen**
  – page 306

Link to more pages

Connecting your **Web page** to other sites on the Internet makes your page more **useful** and **fun to visit**. It also means that you are **adding** to the **accessibility** of the Web

A link, or 'hyperlink', is an item on a Web page which, when you click on it, takes you directly to another page anywhere else on the Internet. The World Wide Web is a huge collection of interconnected sites, and links are the basis of how they are all joined together. Following links is a great way to access related information on a subject. Using Word, you can link your page to other useful sites elsewhere on the Web, and also create links between several of your own Web pages to form one integrated site.

HOW TO: ADD A LIST OF LINKS TO OTHER WEB SITES

One of the most common features on most Web sites is a list of links to other, related sites. These could be your favourite sites or sites that cover similar material to your own.

Once you have decided which sites you want to put on your list and have their Web addresses to hand, the first step is to add a list of their names to your Web page.

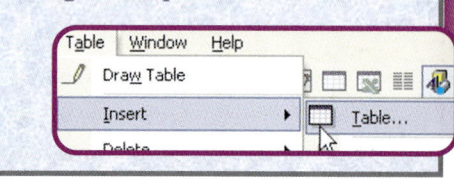

1 Open your Web page in Word. Click on the page at the point where you want to insert your list of links. Then go to the **Table** menu and click **Insert** and then **Table**.

MAKING WEB SITES

Watch Out!
When you make the table grid invisible, you will still be able to see the table in thin grey outline. Don't worry – this will not appear on your Web page.

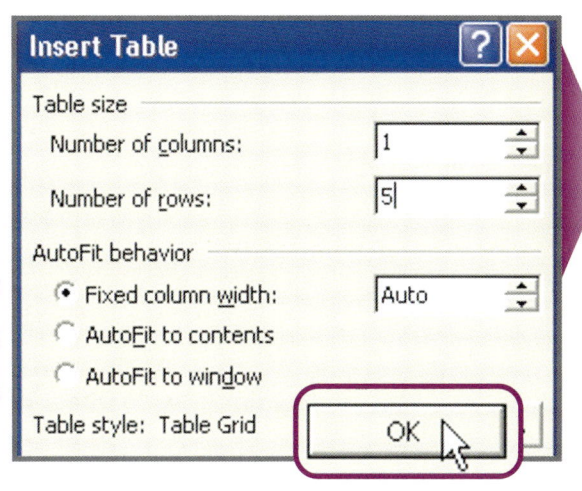

2 In the 'Insert Table' dialogue box, specify one column for the site name, and as many rows as you have sites to include. Then click **OK**.

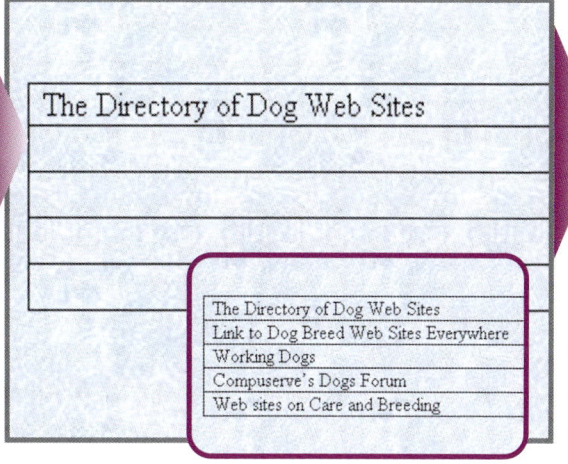

3 A table now appears on your page. Click in the first section and type in the name (not the address) of the first site you want to include. Then add the other site names to the other sections.

4 Now make the table grid invisible. Highlight the table by dragging across it, then go to the **Format** menu and select **Borders and Shading**. Click on the icon next to 'None' and then click **OK**.

ADDING EXTRA ROWS

If you decide to add more rows to your table (to add more sites, or to provide a description for each one you mention), click in the row above where you want to insert a new one. Then go to the **Table** menu and select **Insert** and then **Rows Below**.

BUILDING ON YOUR SITE

Did You Know?
You don't have to place your links in a separate table. You can name another site within a paragraph of text, highlight the reference and turn that into a link.

5 You can move the table anywhere on the page by hovering your cursor over the table until a four-way arrow appears at its top left-hand corner. Click on the arrow and drag the table to where you want it to be.

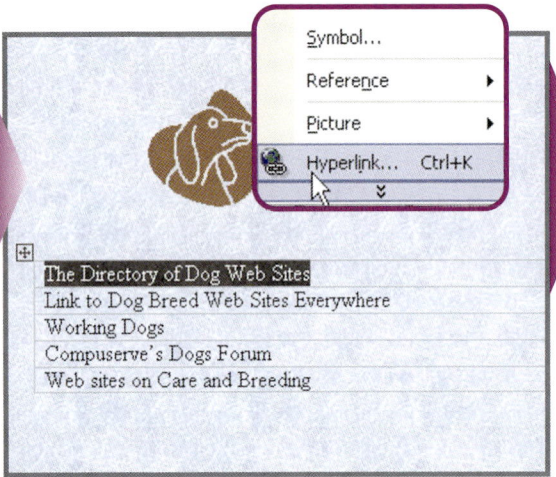

6 Now highlight the name of your first entry, go to the **Insert** menu and select **Hyperlink**. This opens up the 'Insert Hyperlink' dialogue box.

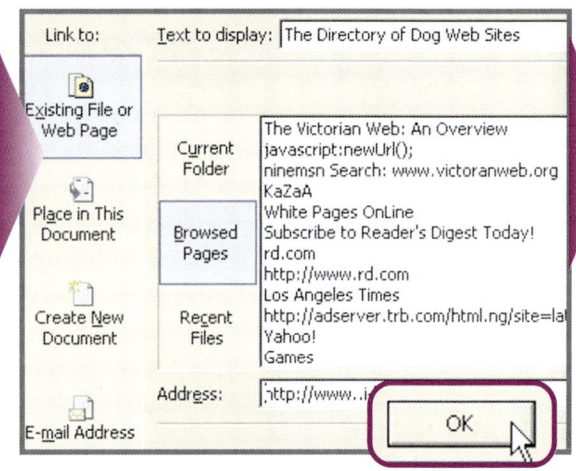

7 Enter the full Web address of the site you want the link to go to. Alternatively, if you have visited the relevant site recently, click on **Existing File or Web Page**, then on **Browsed Pages**, and choose the site from the list that appears. Then click **OK**.

Create links automatically
Word can be set up to automatically recognise a Web address and turn it into a link – colouring and underlining it accordingly. This is a quick way to create a list of links. To activate this function go to the **Tools** menu and select **AutoCorrect**, then click **AutoFormat As You Type**. In the 'Replace as you type' section, tick next to 'Internet and network paths with hyperlinks' and then click **OK**. Then type the addresses of your links in the table rather than the site names.

MAKING WEB SITES

🕐 Time Saver!
*A quicker way to insert a hyperlink is to highlight the text, then hold down the **Ctrl** key and press the **K** key.*

✋ Watch Out!
Once you have uploaded your updated Web page, it is worth checking it on-line using your browser. This is how visitors will see it, and it's always possible that you might spot a problem that was not obvious before.

8 The name of your site now appears in blue underlined type. When you move your cursor over it, the cursor will change into a pointing finger indicating that it has found a link.

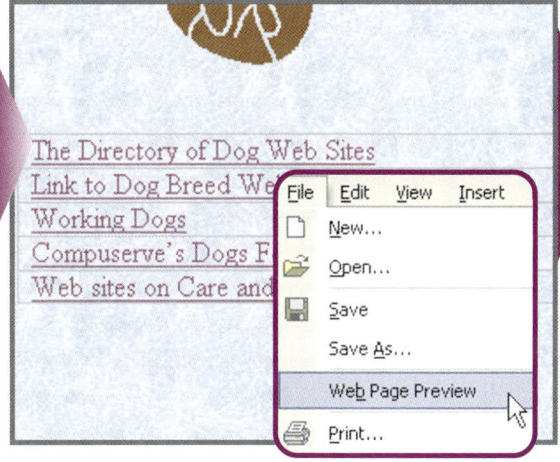

9 Repeat the process for each Web site in your list and then save your page. To test that your new links are working, go to the **File** menu and select **Web Page Preview**.

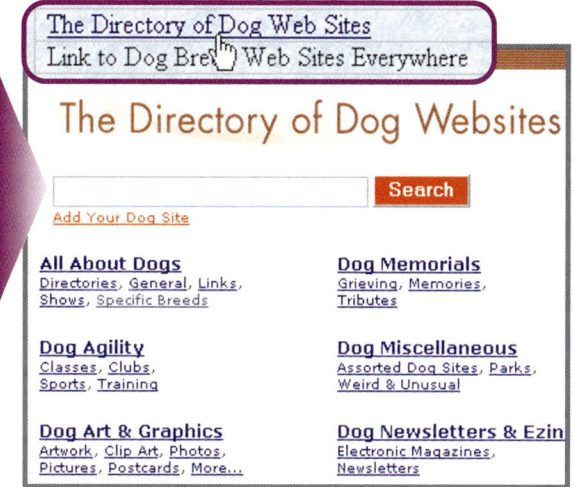

10 Now click on a link – and your browser should display the relevant page. If it does not, check the address that you typed in the 'Insert Hyperlink' dialogue box. When satisfied, you can upload your new page (see *Upload your site*, page 262).

Change the colour of a link
Word automatically displays links in blue underlined type. If you don't want them to appear this way, highlight the text, go to the **Format** menu and select **Font**. Then choose the colour and underline style you want. Be careful though – people expect to see links as blue underlined text and may not notice the link if you change its appearance.

BUILDING ON YOUR SITE

Did You Know?
You don't always have to make it clear that a word or graphic is a link. Sometimes it's fun to create a secret link for the sharp-eyed visitor to find when they move their mouse over it.

HOW TO: LINK PAGES TOGETHER

You can also create links between Web pages that you have created yourself. Say you have a homepage on dog breeding – you could then create another page about grooming, and a third about dog showing, then link them all together to make a more interactive and useful Web site.

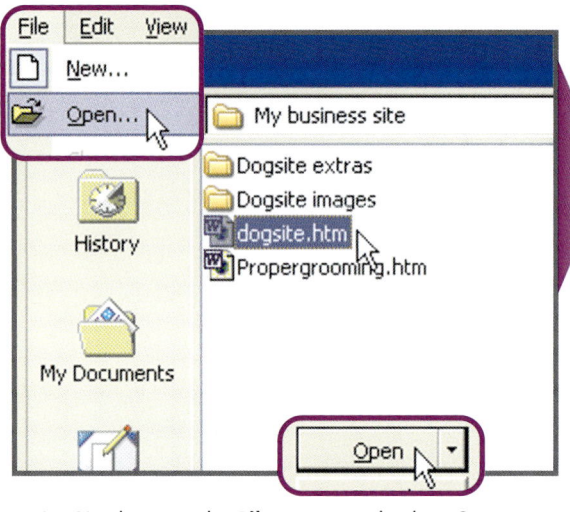

1 In Word, go to the **File** menu and select **Open**. Use the window that appears to locate your original Web page file and click **Open**.

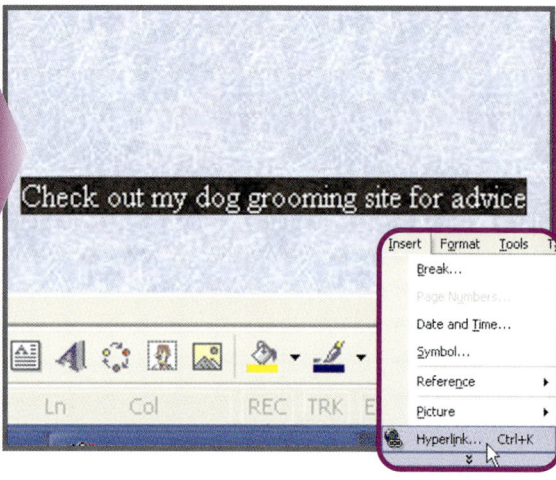

2 At the bottom of the Web page, type some text inviting the reader to visit your second page. Next highlight the text, go to the **Insert** menu and click on **Hyperlink**.

TURNING OBJECTS INTO LINKS

You can also turn images and graphics into links. Right-click on the image on your page and select **Hyperlink**. The 'Insert Hyperlink' window will appear. Now enter the location of the Web page you want to link to – just as you did to link your two Web pages above.

Images that look like buttons can look particularly effective. Take a look at the ClipArt gallery offered by Word, and the huge range available on-line at Free Buttons.com (**www.freebuttons.com**).

MAKING WEB SITES

Did You Know?
You can edit a hyperlink (to change the Web address) by right-clicking on it and then clicking **Edit Hyperlink**.

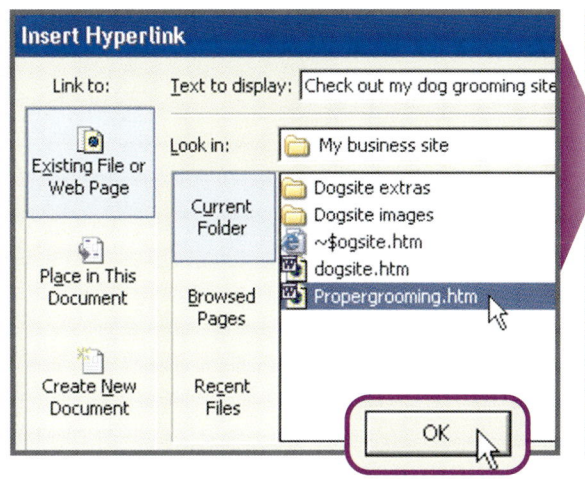

3 Now locate your second Web page on your hard drive. Ideally it should be in the same folder as your first page, but you may have stored it in a separate folder. When you've found it, click on it and then click **OK**.

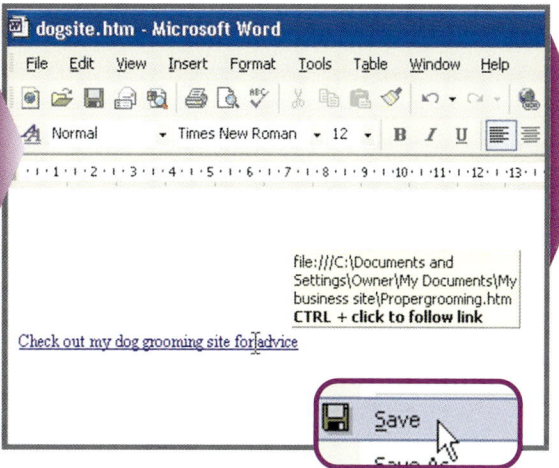

4 The line of text you highlighted on your first page will now turn blue and be underlined, indicating that it serves as a link. Place your cursor over the text and a box will appear confirming the link. Save your Web page and then close it.

5 Now open your second Web page and follow the same procedure to add a link from there back to your first page so that visitors can move between the two. Finally, save your second page and close it.

Taking it further

If you have enjoyed and mastered the process of creating links, you can now make more Web pages and expand your site. You could create pages for every member of the family, a page of photographs or links to sites run by other relatives. You will find your ISP has provided plenty of space.

SEE ALSO
- Build a Web page in Word – page 256
- Add sound to your page – page 276
- Design a Web page on-line – page 288

275

BUILDING ON YOUR SITE

Add sound to your page

Enhance your Web site by **creating audio** features

A few well-chosen sound effects can enhance the appeal of your Web site. If you have pictures of a new family member on your site, for example, you could have happy baby noises to accompany them. Or, if your site is more serious, you could add some music appropriate to its tone. You can find all sorts of audio effects and music clips on the Internet, many of which are free to download and use on your Web site. You can also create sounds of your own using your PC's Sound Recorder facility.

Different set-ups
There are two different ways in which you can set up sound files for your Web site. The first is to have them play automatically as soon as someone visits your site or moves from one page to another. The second is to add the sound files as links. This means that visitors can hear any particular sound by clicking on the designated link, such as a picture or a line of text.

Etiquette
The second method is considered the more considerate among Internet users, because it allows visitors to choose whether or not they want to hear the sounds. A sound that plays automatically can be quite annoying for unsuspecting visitors – especially if they are listening to music of their own, or trying not to disturb other people in their home or office, or in an Internet café.

MAKING WEB SITES

Problem Solver!
*If you can't hear sound when you click on a link, check your volume settings by going to your **Start** menu and clicking on **Control Panel**, then **Sounds, Speech, and Audio Devices**, and finally **Adjust the System Volume**.*

The text on many Web sites is never proofread. As a result, you will find that, as here, words are often spelt wrongly or inconsistently – sometimes within the same Web page.

HOW TO: FIND A SOUND FILE ON-LINE

1 Go to Yahoo! (http://au.yahoo.com) and click on **Computers & Internet**. On the following pages, click on **Multimedia**, then **Audio** and finally on **Archives** for a list of sound sample files.

2 Take a look at what is on offer. Here we have chosen **Audio Browser Sound Files** and then **Sunsite Sound Effects** – just one of many sites offering sound files to the public.

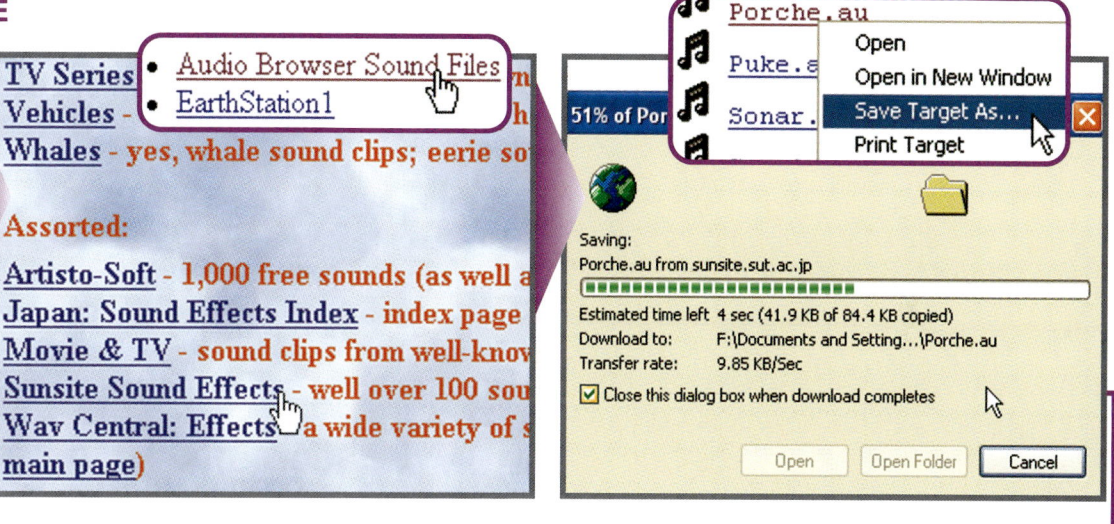

3 Right-click on a sound and download it to your PC by selecting **Save Target As…** Now save it to the folder in which you are storing the elements of your Web site. Here we have chosen **Porsche.au**.

SITES FOR SOUND
Among the many thousands of sites on the Web from which you can download sound files of all kinds, here are a few:

Partners in Rhyme	(www.partnersinrhyme.com)
Sounddogs.com	(www.sounddogs.com)
Sound Effects	(www.stonewashed.net/sfx.html)
Ultimyate Sound & Music Archive	(www.ultimatesoundarchive.com)

Listening to a sound
You can hear what a sound file sounds like before downloading it. Simply left-click on it in your Web browser. This will cause Media Player to open automatically and start playing the sound. Hence the need to right-click on a file if you wish to download it.

BUILDING ON YOUR SITE

Jargon Buster!
Plug-in A mini-program that adds extra functions to a Web browser. It allows visitors to a Web site to play sounds or see videos, for example.

HOW TO: ADD A LINK TO A SOUND FILE

1 Open your Web page in Word. Click on the item that will act as the link. Here, a picture of a car has been selected.

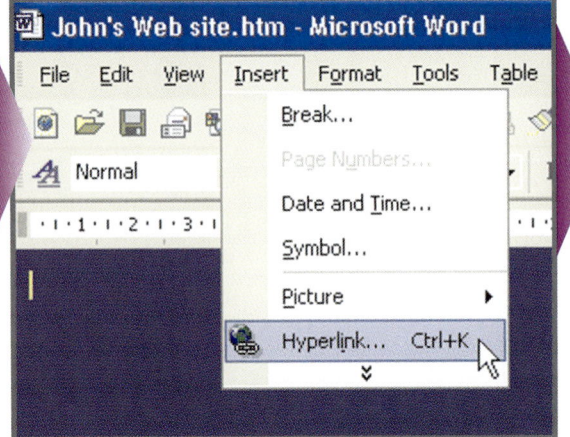

2 Go to the **Insert** menu and select **Hyperlink**. If you want to use some text as a link, rather than a picture, highlight the text and do the same.

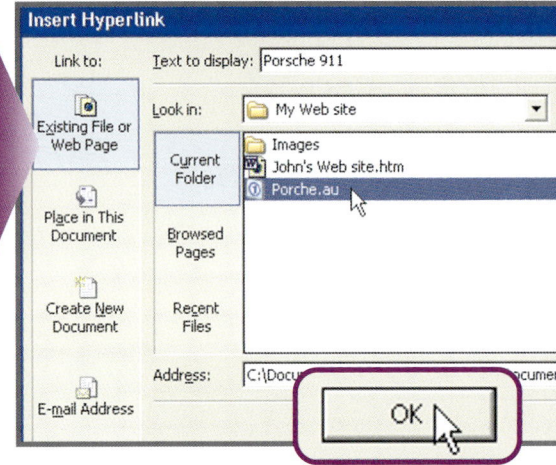

3 In the 'Insert Hyperlink' window that appears, go to the 'Look in:' panel, click on the downward-pointing arrow on the right and locate your Web site folder. Click on the sound file itself, and then click **OK**. Finally, save your Web page and close it.

No sound?
If people browsing the Web don't have the correct plug-in installed on their computers, they won't be able to hear the sounds on your site. However, when they click on the link you created, their Web browser will automatically offer them the option to visit a suitable site, from where they can download the necessary plug-in.

MAKING WEB SITES

Did You Know?
If you are using RealPlayer components on your site, you'll need Helix Producer Basic, which can be downloaded for free (*www.realnetworks.com/products/producer/basic.html*) to convert a variety of different sound files to the RealAudio format.

HOW TO: ADD A SOUND THAT PLAYS AUTOMATICALLY

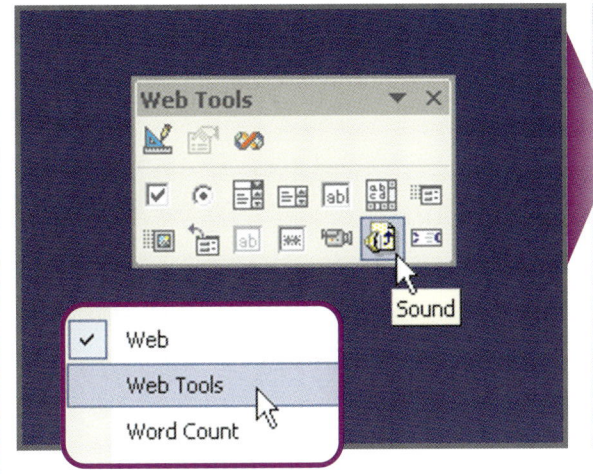

1 Open your Web page in Word, go to the **View** menu, select **Toolbars** and click on **Web Tools**. When the toolbar appears, click on the **Sound** button.

2 When the 'Background Sound' window appears, click on **Browse**. Look through your hard drive to locate the sound file you wish to use (it should be in your Web site folder), click on it and then click **Open**.

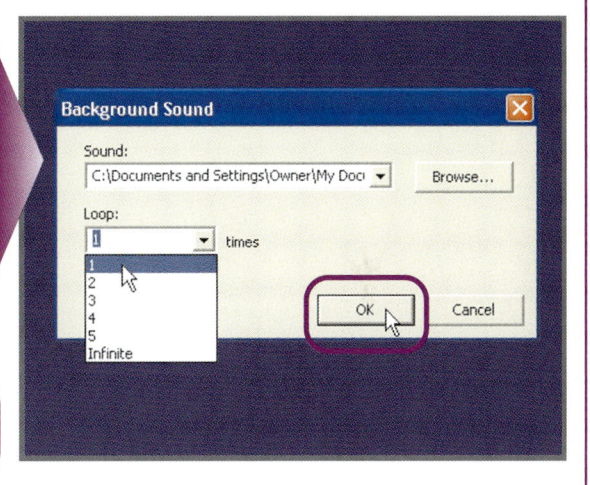

3 Click in the 'Loop' box and select the number of times you want the sound to play. Finally, click **OK**. Save your Web page and then close it.

TESTING YOUR SOUND

Double-click on your Web page to open it in your browser. If you added an automatic sound, it should play as soon as the page appears. If you added a link, click on it and the sound should start playing.

You are now ready to upload your updated Web page onto the Internet. See the box on *Updating your site*, page 263, for more information.

BUILDING ON YOUR SITE

HOW TO: CREATE SOUNDS

You can also record your own words and other sounds using your computer. This can be good for adding a personal touch to your Web site, such as a welcome in your own voice, or a tune played by one of your children.

Before you start
Make sure you have plugged your microphone into the appropriate socket at the rear of your computer. The microphone socket will be marked 'mic' or perhaps it will have a picture of a microphone next to it. Remember to switch the microphone on, and check that it has a battery if it needs one.

SOUND FORMATS

There are many digital sound formats available for use on your computer. You can tell the format of a sound file by looking at the 'file extension' – the last section of the file name:

.au (Audio) – is widely used on the Web.

.mid (MIDI) – tells your computer to re-create a tune using instrument sounds stored in its own hardware.

.mp3 (MP3) – provides high quality, and is now the most common format for sound files.

.ra (RealAudio) – is the best format for longer excerpts of recorded music.

.wav (Wave) – is used for a PC's everyday sounds. It's perfect for short sounds on Web pages and is compatible with most browsers.

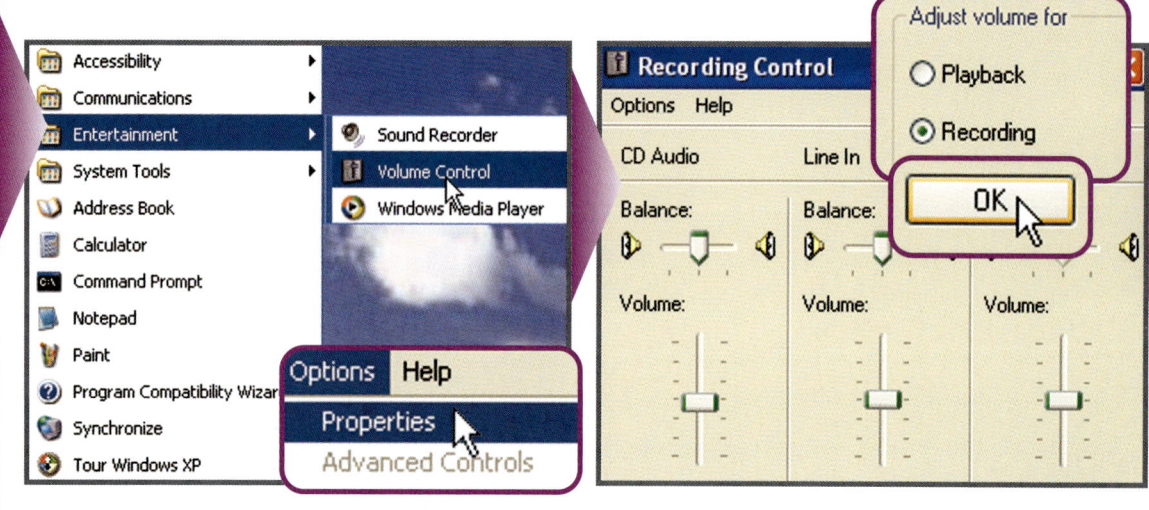

1 Go to the **Start** menu and select **All Programs**, **Accessories**, **Entertainment** and then **Volume Control**. When the 'Master Volume' window appears, click on **Options** and select **Properties**.

2 In the 'Properties' window, click the **Recording** option and then **OK**. Make sure the 'Select' box beneath 'Microphone' in the 'Recording Control' window is ticked. Now Windows knows you will be using a microphone.

MAKING WEB SITES

What you need
To record your own sounds on your computer, you need a sound card inside your system unit (if you have speakers, then you have a sound card). You also need a microphone and the Sound Recorder software, which comes as a standard feature of Windows.

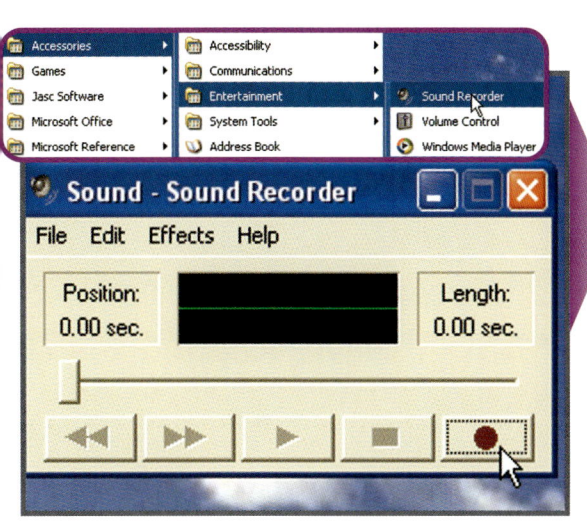

3 Go to the **Start** menu and select **All Programs**, then **Accessories**, **Entertainment** and finally **Sound Recorder**. Your computer is now ready to record any sound you wish.

4 Click the **Record** button (marked with a red dot) and speak into the microphone, or start a CD. The green line in the sound recorder changes, giving a visual image of the sound. Click the **Stop** button (marked with a black rectangle) when done.

5 To hear your sound, click the **Play** button. If you are happy with it, go to the **File** menu, click **Save As** and save it. You can now use the sound file in your Web page. To re-record, go to the **File** menu, select **New** and click **No** to delete and start again.

GET THE EQUIPMENT
You can buy microphones from most electronics or computer retailers. Expect to pay about A$10–20 for a suitable model. Take a look at Dick Smith Electronics (**www.dse.com.au**) or Harris Technology (**www.ht.com.au**).

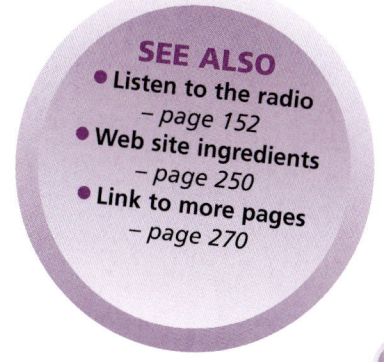

SEE ALSO
- Listen to the radio – page 152
- Web site ingredients – page 250
- Link to more pages – page 270

281

BUILDING ON YOUR SITE

Add a video to your page

A movie clip can add **a whole new dimension** to your site

Adding a video clip to your Web site can be a great way to personalise your page. It is not possible to upload a long full-screen video, but many sites now include short clips that play in a small window on your computer's Desktop – everything from home movies of the family to a product demonstration. To add a video clip, all you need is a digital camcorder, a reasonably fast computer, the right plugs and cables and the Movie Maker program that is a standard part of Windows XP.

Transferring digital video
To transfer video from a digital camcorder to your computer, you will need a cable and the appropriate input socket on the back of your computer. Camcorder connections are usually USB or Firewire, and if you don't have a suitable input already, it's a simple matter to buy an internal card that slots inside your PC's system unit to provide the necessary socket.

Many digital camcorders will also allow you to transfer analogue video – such as that from a VHS tape – into a digital format. If you don't have a digital camcorder, you will need to buy a video capture card instead to transfer analogue video to your computer.

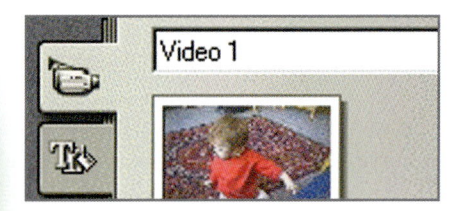

Video capture cards
Video capture cards, such as the popular Studio DC10 from Pinnacle, take the output from a VHS video recorder or an analogue camcorder and convert it into digital format so you can save and edit it on your computer. Before buying one, make sure that your computer, paricularly its hard disk, is fast enough for the job. Once the video has been digitised, you can import it into Windows Movie Maker.

MAKING WEB SITES

HOW TO: LOAD AND SAVE YOUR VIDEO

The following procedure will help you to transfer a short film from your video camera onto your computer, then prepare it so you can add it to your Web page. For this example we used Windows Movie Maker and a digital camcorder. With other hardware and software, the process may vary slightly. Always check the appropriate manuals for clarification before you start.

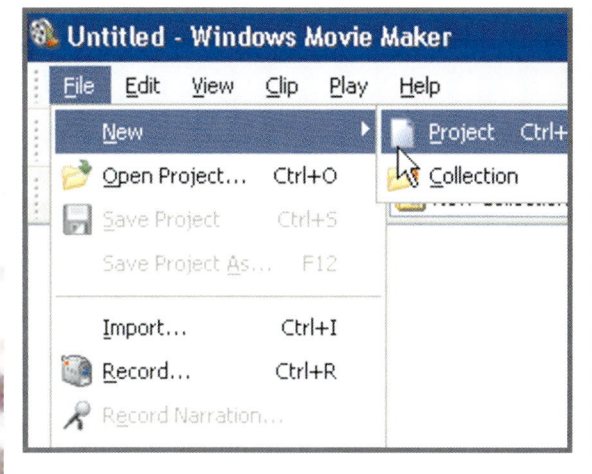

Watch Out!
Be careful when loading video onto your PC. Even a few minutes of high-resolution video can consume many megabytes of disk space – so make sure you have sufficient space free. If you are likely to work with video regularly, it may be worth investing in a second (fast) hard drive.

1 Connect your digital camcorder to your computer using the cables provided. Go to your **Start** menu and click on **All Programs**, then **Accessories**, then **Windows Movie Maker**. Now click on the **File** menu, and choose **New**, then **Project**.

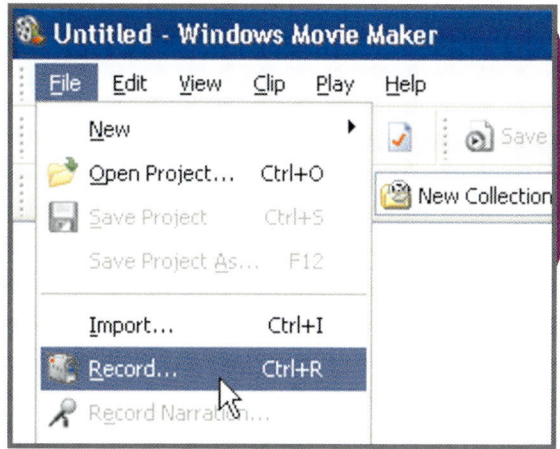

2 Go to the **File** menu, click **Record** and the 'Record' window will open. Switch your camera on and turn it to VCR. The program should recognise your camera automatically, and its name will appear beside 'Video device' at the top of the window.

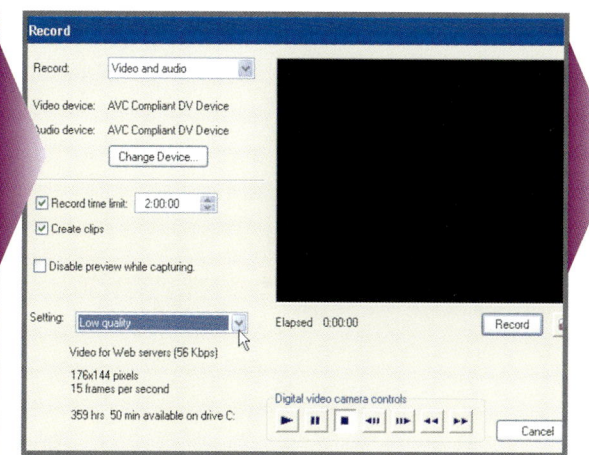

3 Set the 'Record time' limit to two minutes, check the 'Create clips' box and select either **Low** or **Medium quality** in the 'Setting' box. Low quality is recommended for viewing by those who are connected to the Internet via a 56K modem.

PREPARING YOUR VIDEO

Windows Movie Maker automatically prepares your video for the Web. In the process it resizes it and compresses it so that it takes up less disk space. This means it can be downloaded by visitors to your site in less time. Resizing means altering the dimensions of the size of the window the video will play in. Compressing reduces the file size of the video still further by saving it in a different way.

BUILDING ON YOUR SITE

Jargon Buster!
Pixel An individual dot on a computer screen. All images on the screen are made up of these dots.

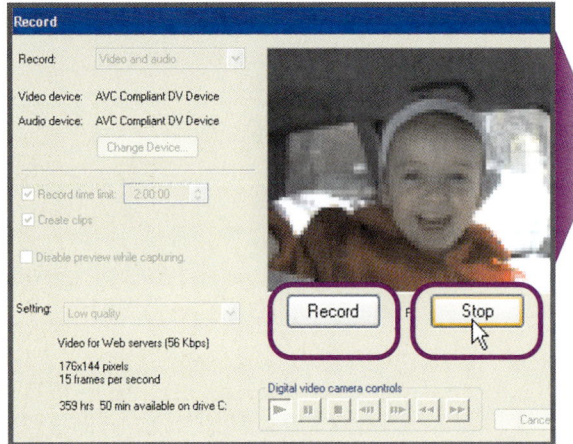

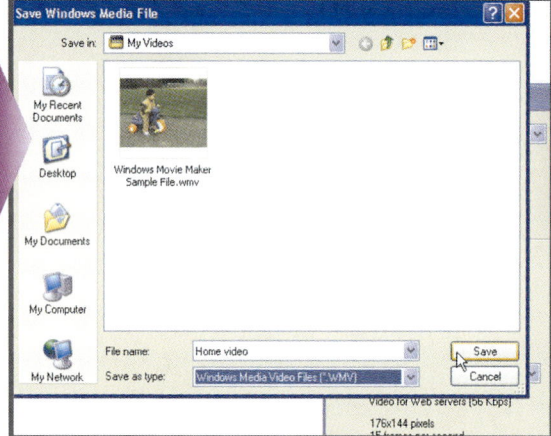

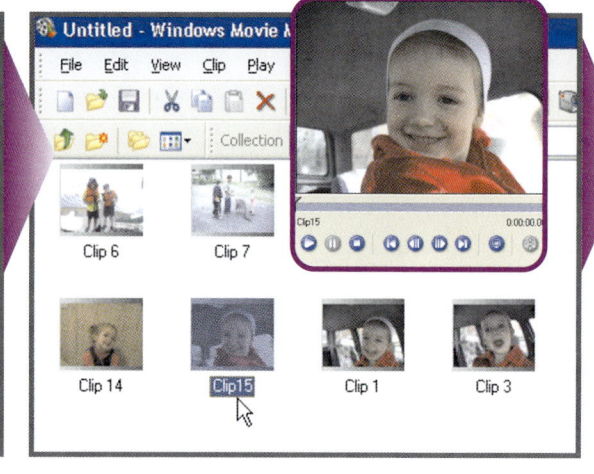

4 Under 'Digital video camera controls', click the 'play' button (shaped like an arrow) to start the camera playing, and then click **Record** when you reach the segment you want to capture. Click **Stop** to end the capture process.

5 Choose a name for the video you have captured, and choose a folder to save it in (Windows will automatically take you to the 'My Videos' folder). Now click **Save**. A progress bar will appear while the video is saved to your hard disk.

6 Every section of film you capture will be shown as a numbered 'clip' by Windows Movie Maker. To play a clip, double-click on it and it will appear in the video window, where it can be edited.

File formats
The standard video format for PCs is AVI (.avi), but files in a variety of other formats can be imported into Windows Movie Maker, including the following: video (.asf, .avi, .wmv); movie (.mpeg, .mpg, .m1v, .mp2, .mpa, .mpe); audio (.wav, .snd, .au, .aif, .aifc, .aiff, .wma, .mp3); Windows Media (.asf, .wm, .wma, .wmv); and still images (.bmp, .jpg, .jpeg, .jpe, .jfif, .gif, .dib).

MAKING WEB SITES

Watch Out!
Try to keep your video file below 2Mb in size. If most of your visitors have a standard 56K modem, a video clip of this size should take less than 10 minutes to download.

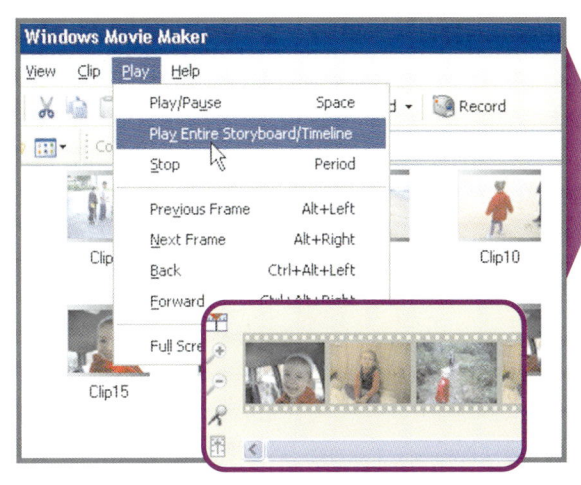

7 To arrange clips in order, drag them onto the 'storyboard' (which looks like a film strip) located at the bottom of the Movie Maker window. Once you have arranged the clips, click **Play**, then **Play Entire Storyboard/Timeline** to view your creation.

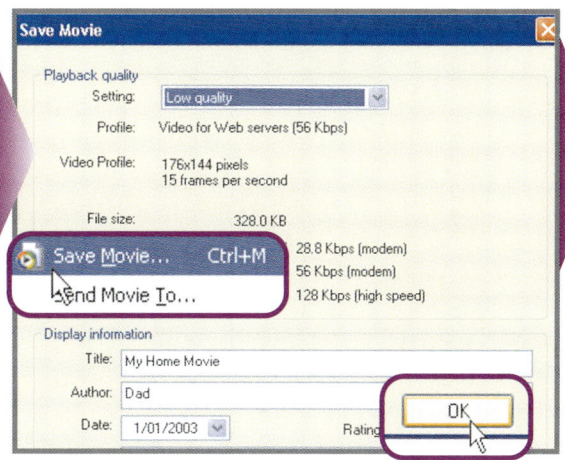

8 Finally, record a narration if you wish, using a microphone. To do so, click on **File**, then **Record Narration**. When satisfied, go to the **File** menu and click **Save Movie**. Choose the appropriate quality in the 'Setting' box, enter other details and click **OK**.

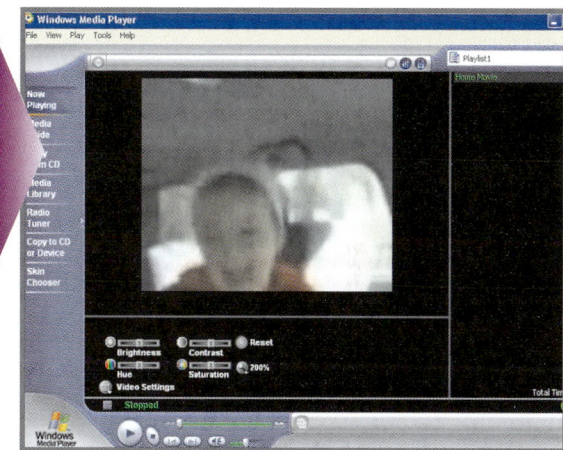

9 Now choose a file name for your movie and click **Save**. Movie Maker will ask you if you want to watch a preview of your masterpiece in the Media Player window (shown above).

COMPRESSION SOFTWARE

When you save your movie, you can choose from a range of Windows media settings, according to how you think it will be viewed. It is important that anyone who wishes to view your movie has the latest version of Windows Media Player, which can be downloaded for free from the Microsoft site (**www.microsoft.com**).

BUILDING ON YOUR SITE

HOW TO: ADD YOUR MOVIE TO YOUR PAGE
Now that you have prepared your movie, you can add it to your Web page. This works in much the same way as inserting a static image, but Word provides a special toolbar for working with movie files. Note that you may need the latest version of Word to carry out this operation.

Problem Solver!
To ensure that you are getting the most out of your hard disk space, go to the **Start** menu and select **All Programs**, then **Accessories**, **System Tools** and finally **Disk Defragmenter**. Click **OK** to get your computer to reorganise the way it stores all your files.

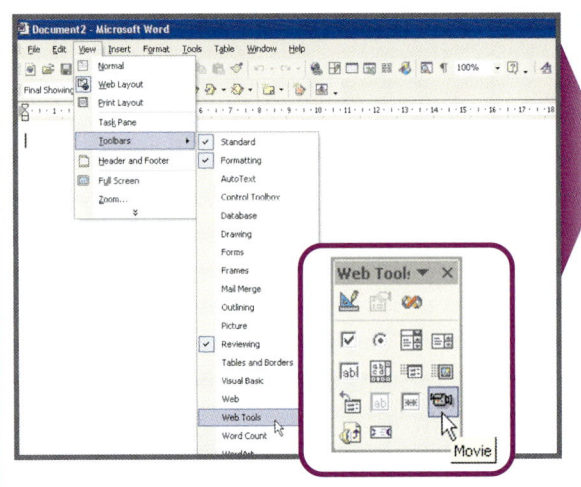

1 Open your Web page in Word. Go to the **View** menu and select **Toolbars**, then **Web Tools**. Now position your cursor where you want your movie to appear and then click on the **Movie** icon in the Web Tools toolbar.

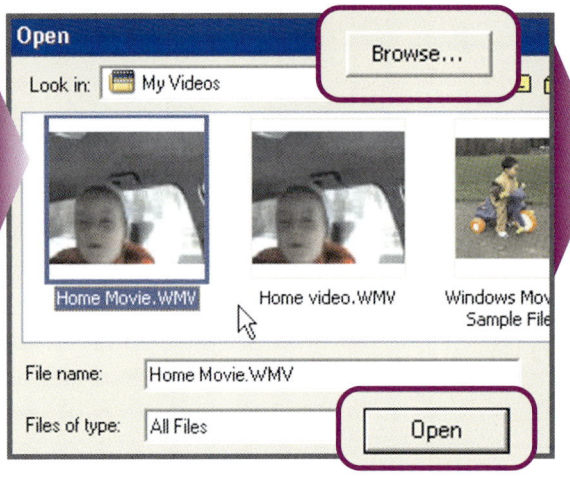

2 When the 'Movie Clip' dialogue box appears, click on **Browse**. This will bring up a new window asking you to identify the movie file you wish to play. Locate the appropriate file and click **Open**.

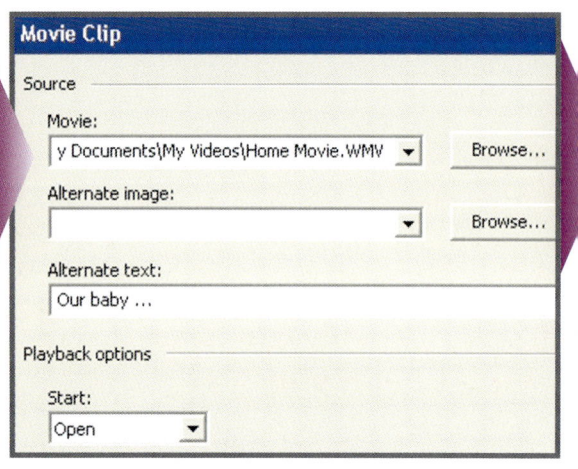

3 In the 'Alternate image' and 'Alternate text' boxes, you can select a single image and a message to display if the visitor's browser can't play movies (see below for more details).

Entering a graphic image
Not everyone may be able to view your movie, so you can use the 'Alternate image' and 'Alternate text' boxes to display a picture or text instead. Simply write your message into the 'Alternate text' box or click on **Browse** to select an image file from your Web folder (don't forget to upload this picture too).

MAKING WEB SITES

Watch Out!
It is polite Web etiquette not to set your film to play as soon as a visitor opens your site. It is better to inform visitors of the size of your video file, its length and its content, so that they can decide if they want to play it or not.

Placing movies or photos on the Web
You don't have to place movies (or photos) in your Web pages for them to be seen on-line. You can also simply upload movies or images to the Web space provided by your ISP, and then give friends the necessary log-on details to view them. However, this is a little more cumbersome than updating your Web site, which anyone can visit without being given special access rights.

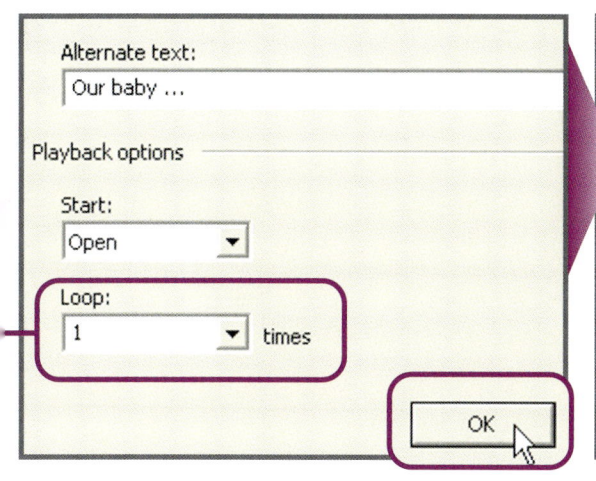

4 In the 'Start' section, select how the movie will be played – either **Open** so that the movie plays as soon as someone opens the page, or **Mouse-over** which allows your visitors to decide whether to view the movie (see *Watch Out!* above). Then click **OK**.

5 You can preview your video by right-clicking on the movie panel and selecting **Play**. When you are satisfied with the changes you have made to your page, save it and close Word.

6 You can now upload your modified page to the Web (see *Upload your site*, page 262), or you can place the movie itself on the Web, so that friends can view it (see above). From the **Start** menu, locate your movie, and click **Publish this file to the Web**.

The 'Loop' section allows you to specify how many times you want the movie clip to play. Once is normally enough.

SEE ALSO
• **Upload your site** – page 262
• **Add a picture to your page** – page 264
• **Link to more pages** – page 270
• **Add sound to your page** – page 276

OTHER DESIGN TOOLS

Design a Web page on-line

Use the Internet to **design your own** site in a **matter of minutes**

There are many on-line services that help you to create your own Web site without the need for Web-authoring software. The GeoCities site (**http://au.geocities.yahoo.com**) provides all the tools and Web space you need to create your own site. There is also plenty of help and support available, and a huge community of existing users, many of whom have developed sophisticated Web sites from which you can learn many helpful tips and tricks.

Get started
GeoCities is part of Yahoo!. It provides an on-line community where you can design and post your Web pages. The service is free, but in return you have to carry advertising on your site. The ads appear in small, pop-up windows on your Web site.

Design your site
Once you've signed up, you will be provided with 15Mb of disk space (plenty for the average user), which you can develop in a number of ways. GeoCities provides a simple Web page generator called PageWizard, and a version for making more complex sites called PageBuilder. It also offers template designs you can alter to suit your needs. You can also use this service to publish pages developed off-line, so if you have already created your page with Microsoft Word, for instance, you can still use GeoCities as your host.

Develop your site
Once you have got your basic page together, GeoCities provides several easily added tools, including search boxes, forms, clocks, visitor counters, menus, news headlines and weather forecasts.

MAKING WEB SITES

Time Saver!
When deciding what to put on your Web page, go to the GeoCities Members Directory to see other members' sites and how they have used their pages.

HOW TO: SIGN UP TO GEOCITIES

Registering with GeoCities only takes a few minutes and you can begin designing your site immediately afterwards. So before you go on-line, save yourself time and money by making a few preparations.

First, decide what you want to appear on your Web site. Then create a Word document containing any text that you want to include. You can save time by copying and pasting the text in during the on-line design stage.

Finally, save any pictures you want to use in their appropriate formats. For more information on this, see page 264.

1 Go to GeoCities (**http://au.geocities.yahoo.com**) and sign in using your Yahoo! ID if you have one. If you are not registered with Yahoo! you need to set up an ID for yourself. To do this, click on **Sign in**.

2 In the next page, click on **Sign up now**, then review the Yahoo! 'Terms of Service' and click **I Accept** at the bottom of the page.

Other on-line Web site providers

There are several places on the Internet that offer free Web space, site building tools and links to other free providers.

FreeWebspace.net   (**www.freewebspace.net**)
Tripod   (**www.tripod.lycos.com**)
FortuneCity   (**www.fortunecity.com**)

OTHER DESIGN TOOLS

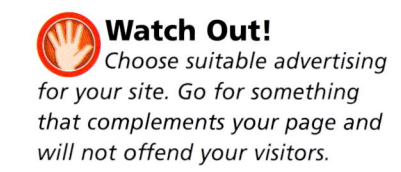

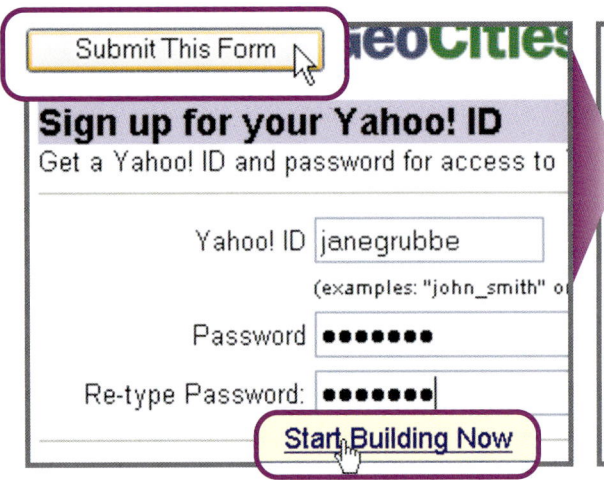

Watch Out!
Choose suitable advertising for your site. Go for something that complements your page and will not offend your visitors.

3 Now create a name for yourself, choose a password and fill in the other details required (make a note of these for when you next sign in). Then click **Submit This Form**. On the next page, click on **Start Building Now**.

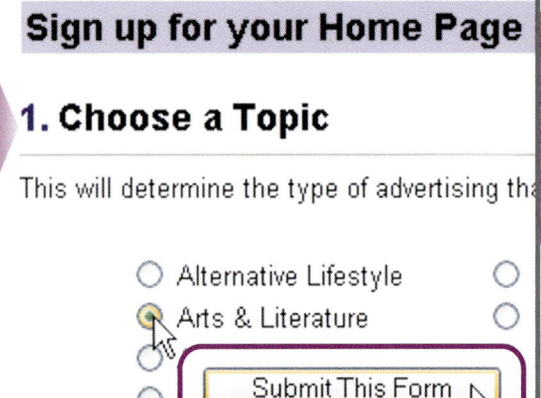

4 This opens up a form asking you to specify what type of advertising you want to appear on your site. Choose one or more categories, follow the remaining on-screen instructions and then click **Submit This Form**.

5 Now make a note of the Web address (URL) of your Web page. Then click **Build your page now!** to get started.

YAHOO! DIRECTORY

To include your site in the Yahoo! directory, so it can be found by anyone in the world, go to **http://au.yahoo.com** and choose a directory category. At the bottom of the page, click on **Suggest a Site** and follow the instructions. You will then have to wait for your site to be reviewed and selected by Yahoo! before your listing appears.

290

MAKING WEB SITES

Did You Know?
If you design your site at GeoCities or another on-line site provider, you can have it ready and on-line in about 20 minutes.

Time Saver!
Add the GeoCities site and your own Web page to your 'Favorites' list for easy access. Go to each site, then go to the **Favorites** menu and click on **Add to Favorites**.

HOW TO: CREATE A SITE ON-LINE

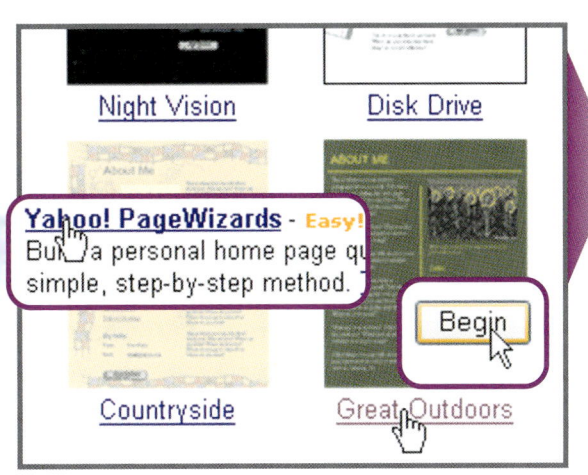

6 Click on **Yahoo! PageWizards** to see a selection of template designs. (For more designs, go to the main GeoCities site: **http://geocities.yahoo.com**.) Click on the design of your choice, then click **Begin** and a Web page design wizard will open.

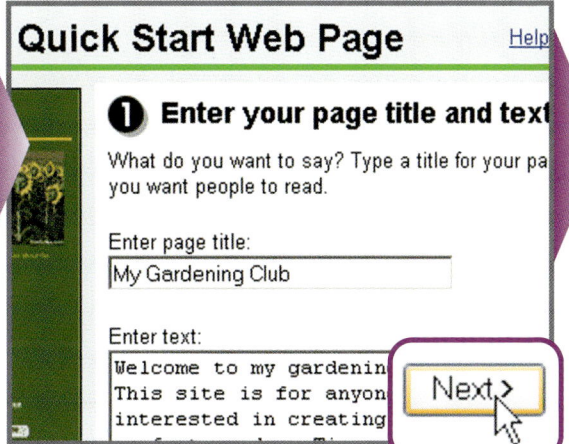

7 Choose the style of your page and click **Next**. Now enter the title of your Web page as you want it to appear on screen, and then, under 'Enter text', paste in your prepared text for the page. When you've finished, click **Next**.

8 Select a picture to illustrate your page. Simply click **Next** to use the one already on the template (as here). Alternatively, click **Use your picture**, then **Upload new picture** then, in the next window, **Browse** to find an image stored on your PC.

Editing your site
To make changes to your site once you have created it, re-run the GeoCities Wizard and select **Edit existing page**, rather than 'Create new page'. Select the page you want to edit from the drop-down list and go through the original creation steps, making any alterations you require.

291

OTHER DESIGN TOOLS

✋ Watch Out!
Think before you place your contact details on your Web site. You may prefer to withhold these details in order to protect your privacy.

List your site
To list your site for other GeoCities members to see, first sign in at GeoCities, then click on **or list your own** under 'Member Pages'. Enter a keyword that describes your site, then select a category in which it will be listed, write a short description of your page and finally, click **List Page**.

9 Now enter the links that you wish to appear on your site. Click **Next** and then, if you wish, enter your contact details so that visitors can send you e-mail messages. Then click **Next** to continue.

10 Finally, give your page a name. This will be used in its Web address. Click on **Preview** to check the design of your page. You can click **Back** to return to any previous stage to modify your choices. When satisfied, click **Done** to exit the design wizard.

11 The Web address of your new page will now be confirmed. Make a note of it and e-mail it to your friends so that they can look at it.

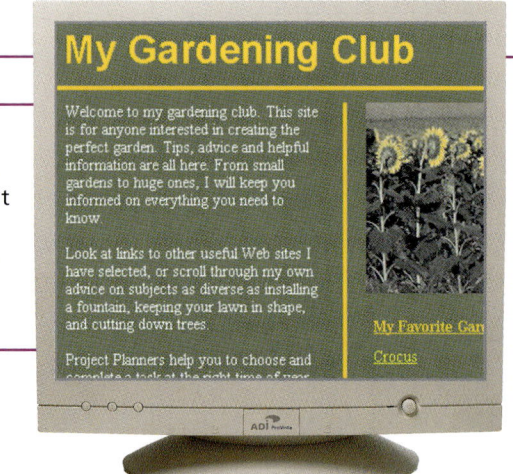

12 Your finished Web page is now available for all to see. Click on the link provided to view it yourself. If you spot anything you want to change, you can edit your page using the Web page design wizard as described previously.

MAKING WEB SITES

HOW TO: ADD EXTRA FEATURES

One advantage of using an on-line Web page creation service is that there are usually many extra interactive features you can easily add to your page. In GeoCities, you can use the Yahoo! PageBuilder to edit your page and add any extra features. This makes editing your site very easy.

To use PageBuilder, go to the GeoCities homepage and click on the links provided. The program will load onto your hard drive, a process that may take several minutes.

Watch Out!
Don't add extra features to your Web site just because it is easy. They should be relevant to your page and not distract from its main themes.

1 Log onto the GeoCities site and click on **Yahoo! PageBuilder**, then **Launch PageBuilder**. Once the program has loaded, click on the **Open** icon, and in the window that appears select the Web site that you would like to modify and click **Open**.

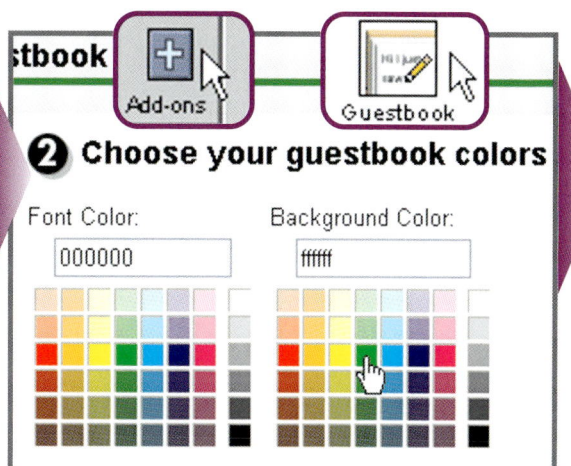

2 Now click on the **Add-ons** icon, and in the next window click on a category in the left-hand menu, such as **Interactive**. Then click on one of the add-ons displayed, such as **Guestbook**. Select the text style and colour of the guest book and click **Next**.

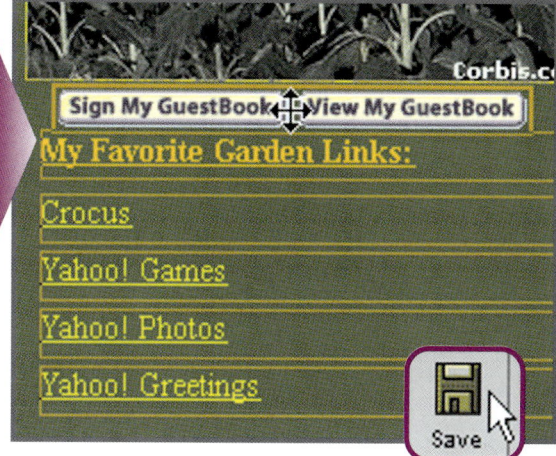

3 The Guestbook icon will now appear on your page. Click on it and drag it to wherever you want it to lie. Then click the **Save** icon to save and publish your changes. You can now view your altered page and then make more changes if you want.

Extra features
You can use the process shown above to use all sorts of add-on features, including a counter to show how many visitors you have had to your site, a weather forecast or an opinion poll. Some you can drag straight onto your page without going through the second step above. For others, follow the on-screen instructions.

SEE ALSO
- What is a Web site? – page 246
- Build a Web page in Word – page 256
- Ensure your site is seen – page 306

293

OTHER DESIGN TOOLS

Other design programs

Use **Web-authoring** software to **create** a site with more features

You can make a great Web site using Word or free on-line software, but the most stylish sites on the Web are made with specialist Web-authoring programs. These offer features not found elsewhere, such as buttons that change shape when you click on them. They are more complicated to use, as most require some understanding of HTML, the programming language of the Internet. Some programs are designed for professionals, but there are also inexpensive or free programs written for amateurs. So, if you are serious about Web design, you may want to try some of them out.

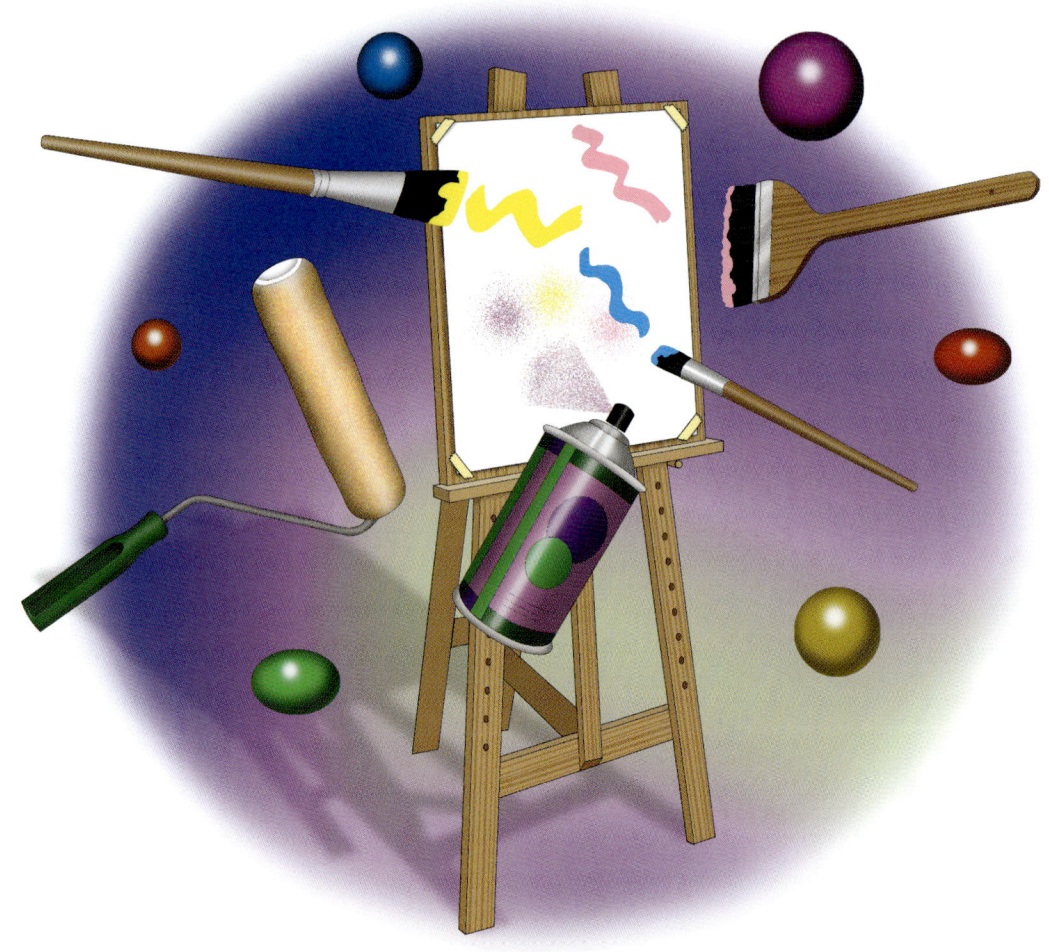

Learning HTML
You don't need to know any HTML code to work with most features offered in Web-authoring programs. But the more complex you want your site to be, the more likely it is that you will need to learn something about the underlying language. Perhaps you will have some faulty HTML code that needs to be edited out, or you need to ensure that a page element can be viewed by all browsers. In such cases, you may need to edit the HTML code manually.

HTML help
Web-authoring programs can help you to learn HTML by giving you an instant preview of what the page will look like, as you make your changes in the code. For an on-line tutorial in basic HTML, consult 'A Beginners Guide to HTML' offered by the National Centre for Supercomputing Applications (**http://archive.ncsa.uiuc.edu/General/Internet/WWW**).

MAKING WEB SITES

WEB DESIGN PROGRAMS

Microsoft FrontPage
(www.microsoft.com/frontpage)
FrontPage is aimed at beginners and advanced users alike. Because it is a Microsoft program, the layout and buttons should be largely familiar to you. It is also easy to drop in tables and other elements from related programs such as Word and Excel. It costs about A$400 and can be purchased from a computer retailer or on-line.

Netscape Composer
(http://browsers.netscape.com)
Users of Netscape Communicator or Netscape 6.2 (both of which include the Navigator browser) will already have this program. It is a simple HTML editor that is suitable for beginners and offers more features than Word – such as automatic conversion of images into Web format.

You can get Netscape Composer for free by downloading the latest Netscape package from the Netscape Web site.

Evrsoft 1stPage 2000
(www.evrsoft.com)
This is a professional Web-authoring program that is free to download. You can edit HTML text and preview the results in a built-in Internet Explorer browser window, or in three other browsers. Features include an image viewer and layout and design tools.

Sausage HotDog PageWiz
(www.sausagetools.com)
HotDog PageWiz is an HTML editing program that is aimed at beginners and intermediate Web authors. Whether you need to correct mistakes in your site's code, or you just want to experiment with HTML, this program makes it easy. You can preview the results of your HTML changes as you make them. Features include the ability to download an entire Web site, make changes and upload it again. You can download a free 30-day trial from the Sausage Web site.

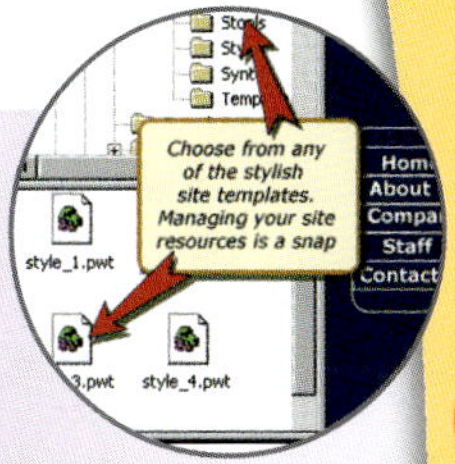

Macromedia Dreamweaver
(www.macromedia.com)
Dreamweaver is an HTML editing program aimed at serious designers, but is not difficult to use – especially if you follow the built-in tutorials. The program is especially good for such tricky elements as tables, forms, rollovers and animation, and includes the basic tools required for editing images.

The program costs about A$650, but you can also download a free 30-day trial version from the Macromedia site.

Deciding on a program
For further advice on Web software, go to CNET's 'Spotlight on production tools' page (**http://builder.cnet.com/webbuilding/pages/Authoring/ProdTools**). You can read a selection of useful reviews and product comparisons.

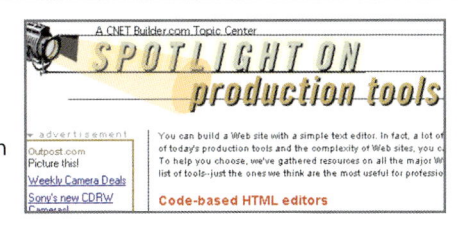

Jargon Buster!

HTML Editor
Another name for a Web design program. When you make a change to your design, the program makes the relevant changes to the underlying HTML code.

Money Saver!

Using free trials of programs is a good way to evaluate them. Once you know what you will be getting, you can then decide whether it's worth paying for the full version of the program or not.

SEE ALSO
- Build a Web page in Word – *page 256*
- Add a picture to your page – *page 264*
- Add sound to your page – *page 276*

OTHER DESIGN TOOLS

Advanced Web design tools

Use **plug-ins and codes** to make your site more **sophisticated**

Once you've mastered the basics of Web design, you may feel tempted to make your Web site more memorable by setting up interactive features, such as animations, competitions or a message board, where visitors can give you comments and feedback. There are several ways of doing this, with varying degrees of complexity. You may never use the programs or scripting languages described here, but you're bound to come across references to them and should at least know what they are.

Scripting
None of the languages or programs described opposite is as complex as computer programming, which is why they are known as 'scripting'.

On-line help
Don't be put off by the thought of learning more advanced Web site building techniques. There are many thousands of people on the Web who are keen to share their knowledge with others. The on-line communities that evolve around problem solving can be some of the most open and friendly on the Web.

Best resources
The best places to look for scripting resources are Webmonkey (**http://hotwired.lycos.com/webmonkey**) and CNET (**http://download.com.com**). There are also many books on the subject, and if you want more personal help, try searching the Web for a support group (usually functioning as a message board), or just search for any particular question you may have.

You may even find that someone who has solved a particular problem has posted the code for anyone to download. In time you may be posting your own codes for other Web authors to use!

MAKING WEB SITES

Did You Know?
*If you've ever wondered what the secret is behind an interactive Web site, you can find out what code has been used by selecting **View**, then **Source** in your browser.*

DIFFERENT TYPES OF TOOLS

Macromedia ColdFusion MX
ColdFusion is one of the simplest applications you can find for creating Web pages with on-line message boards, shopping trolleys and animated buttons, making it a favourite among designers of business sites. The program is not free, so the amount of on-line support is not quite as good as for the other tools mentioned here, but resources are available, as at **www.forta.com**.

You can download a trial version, or buy the full program, from the Macromedia Web site (**www.macromedia.com/software/coldfusion**).

Macromedia Flash MX
Flash is another easy-to-use program with which you can add a range of interactive features to your Web site. To buy and download a copy of Flash, go to the Macromedia site (**www.macromedia.com/software/flash**). The program creates Flash plug-ins – such as animations, games and multimedia enhancers, which play automatically when someone visits your site.

You can also pick up ready-made plug-ins from the Macromedia site (**www.macromedia.com/desdev/mx/flash/sample_files**), or from other developers, drop them into the folder containing all your site files, and then create links to your Web page.

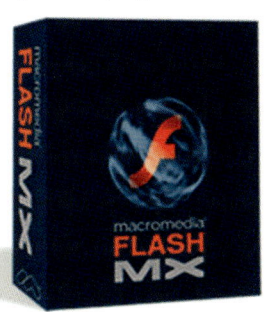

PHP
PHP is a very popular scripting language for which there is a huge amount of help and advice to be found on the Web, such as the tutorial at the PHP site (**www.php.net**).

Unlike ColdFusion and Flash, PHP needs to be written as code, which you would need to learn. PHP is the power behind thousands of on-line shopping sites and databases, yet it remains accessible to the amateur Web page writer.

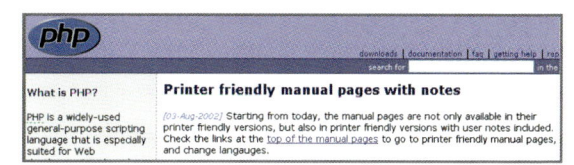

JavaScript
JavaScript is another widely used programming language, which is written as code in Web pages opened in HTML format (see page 308). There are numerous JavaScript resources on the Web, including libraries of code from which you can download for free, such as the one at Webmonkey (**http://hotwired.lycos.com/webmonkey**).

The best thing about JavaScript is how much you can do with only a basic understanding and very little scripting. All you need is a word-processing program and a browser. You can even test your code on your desktop computer, to see what your animations and personal touches will look like before placing your site on the Web.

Perl
Perl (**www.activestate.com/Products/ActivePerl**) is one of the most widely used scripting languages on the Web. Writing Perl is almost like writing English, and there is no shortage of support sites, including some, like Tripod (**www.tripod.lycos.com**), that will allow you to upload Perl scripts to your Web site. A good place to start looking for help is the Perl Mongers site (**www.perl.org**). An extremely versatile language, Perl is ideal for, among other things, setting up a message board where visitors can leave comments about your site.

SEE ALSO
- Web site ingredients – page 250
- Other design programs – page 294
- Ensure your site is seen – page 306

GETTING PROFESSIONAL

How e-commerce works

Turn the **Internet** into a source of **profit**

The collapse of the 'Dot Com' boom has shown that it's not nearly as easy to make money out of the Internet as some people thought it would be. Businesses that are successful on the Internet are usually those that use the Web as an additional means of reaching customers, alongside more conventional channels such as walk-in shops and mail order. If you want to make money out of the Web, there are ways of doing so – but they almost certainly won't make you a millionaire overnight.

What is e-commerce?
E-commerce is no different from everyday commerce: it just means using the Internet as part of your business strategy.

How do I start?
Your first step should be to create a business plan setting out the nature of your enterprise, how much money you need to invest, and the target revenues you hope to attract. Identify your potential customer base and the unique selling points of your business.

Many commercial sites have failed because their expectations of visitor traffic and sales were unrealistic. They ended up paying more to run the business and attract visitors than they earned from sales to those visitors.

On-line business advice
Before you start, you should take a look at sites such as E-Commerce Labs (Australia) (**www.ecla.com.au**), the E-Commerce Times (**www.ecommercetimes.com**) and ZDNet's 'eBusiness' section (**http://techupdate.zdnet.com**) for news and advice on the latest trends and developments in on-line business practices.

MAKING WEB SITES

Jargon Buster!
Click-through When you see an on-line advertisement and click on it to be taken to the advertiser's site, you are said to 'click-through'. Click-through rates are falling, so advertisers are paying less to place ads on other people's sites.

E-COMMERCE MODELS
You will need to think about the nature of your business before you decide how to present it on the Net. Is it a 'hobby' enterprise intended to generate a small amount of extra money. Or, will it be your main source of income, which would need to cover your living expenses and possibly pay staff salaries?

A successful e-commerce site will probably develop revenue from a combination of the models below.

Specialist product sales
Develop a niche market for selling unique products on-line – for example, rare collectible items. Use the Web to promote and handle orders and deliveries. Unique products give your business the best chance of success in a crowded marketplace.

General product sales
It may be difficult to use the Internet to sell general goods cheaply if it means competing with large, established companies. But remember that you can also use the Web to promote a service. Selling your abilities as a reliable mechanic or furniture removalist can be as lucrative as selling physical goods.

On-line services
If you're suitably qualified, you could choose to offer your expertise in a certain area on-line, perhaps by answering questions, doing research or offering advice on anything from gardening to the share market.

Advertising
Design a site which will appeal to people around the world, and then sell advertising space to other firms wishing to reach a wider audience.

Affiliate model
Provide links on your site to other on-line retailers and receive a commission for any sales they make to customers who have come from your site. If you have a specialist site on astronomy, for example, you could provide affiliated links to Amazon (www.amazon.com) for visitors to buy books recommended by your site, and receive a small commission for doing so.

On-line subscription service
If you are offering specialist information, such as financial data or reference material, you could make this available to customers who pay a subscription fee, which gives them access for a certain period.

Customer data model
A specialist site can collect detailed information about its visitors, and then sell that on to other businesses targeting the same market. Any site that presents you with a registration questionnaire is probably intending to generate some income in this way.

BUSINESS TIPS
- The Internet is not a magic money maker. Products that won't sell in shops are unlikely to sell any better on-line.
- Ask yourself if your business would work if it relied on printed catalogues and telephone orders? If not, why would it do better on-line?
- Set targets that will keep you in profit, and monitor your success against them. Be prepared to make changes and look at a range of ways of promoting your site.
- Many consumers don't like buying certain products on-line. Sales that rely on trying things on, such as footwear, don't work well.
- Some consumers are reluctant to buy expensive goods, such as jewellery, because of the danger of fraud or counterfeiting.
- Conversely, low-cost goods may not be economically viable on the Web, once delivery and credit card commissions have been met.
- Always seek professional financial and legal advice at every stage.

SEE ALSO
- Shop safely on the Web – page 54
- Find legal advice – page 120
- File your tax return – page 196

GETTING PROFESSIONAL

Set up a business site

Use **the Web** to improve your company

Having considered the pros and cons of e-commerce, you may decide to take your business onto the Web. To do this, you need to decide how best to reach your market through the design and publicity of your site. The worldwide accessibility of the Web means that an on-line business has the potential to reach a huge international market, whether it is selling a service, a product or information.

Design your own site

The Internet can be used to sell a service such as plumbing or joinery, and to sell goods such as homemade fudge or fresh flower arrangements. If your product or service can be effectively promoted and illustrated with basic text and pictures, then the cheapest option would be to design a site yourself (see *Design a Web page on-line*, page 288). Otherwise you may need to hire a Web designer or consultant to help you to create a more complex design.

Business software

There are a number of Web sites offering basic Web design templates with easy-to-follow instructions on how you can insert your own product pictures and text to produce customised Web pages. These sites can also help you to establish a secure way for customers to complete transactions on-line. However, you have to pay for this part of the service, so if sales volumes are likely to be low, you may prefer to take orders over the telephone instead.

MAKING WEB SITES

> **Watch Out!**
> *Only promise what you know you can deliver. Reputation is important on the Web, and if you let your customers down, word will quickly get around through newsgroups and forums.*

BUSINESS ADVICE

Get your product right

In recent years, a number of companies that were confident of making a profit from the Internet have gone out of business. There are several lessons you can learn from these failures.

In the rush to get on-line, many businesses failed to realise that their ideas were not viable for a Web-based business. It has been found, for example, that people are often reluctant to buy tactile items – such as clothes and furniture – over the Internet, preferring to see them and try them for size in the shops before making a purchase.

It has also been difficult for some businesses to persuade people to order expensive items, such as handmade jewellery, over the Internet. This is partly the result of a 'must see' shopping preference, as well as the fear of fraud or counterfeiting. While well-known shopping brands can rely on being recognised and trusted by consumers, new Web-based shops have to earn this trust (see *Shop safely on the Web*, page 54).

Don't expect miracles

Some companies have set up an on-line presence as an attempt to address marketing and profitability problems in their main, off-line business.

It is important to ask why your business might be more successful on the Internet if it is not working well in its current format. Who are the customers that will come to you over the Web that don't come to you already? Can you actually deliver the goods or service you are offering, and how quickly?

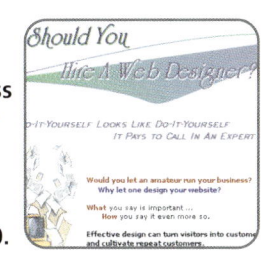

Don't overdo the design

Web site design has been a clear factor in the success or failure of some ventures. An ambitious interactive multimedia presentation might look great on a test machine, but your potential customers aren't going to hang around wasting time and money while huge graphics and animations download.

Some companies have attempted to provide a virtual equivalent of the 'touch' experience by offering interactive 3D animations of their products. However, because these images and animations required powerful hardware in order to be viewed properly, the sites could not be used efficiently by many customers, and the companies concerned struggled to make a success of their business.

When designing a site, take a good look at what's on the Web, especially in the area that your business will be in, and try to work out what works well for you.

You can also learn from others' mistakes by reading the comments of Vincent Flanders, a professional Web designer, who runs a site devoted to showing how **not** to design a Web site (**www.webpagesthatsuck.com**).

Hire a designer

If you don't have the time or expertise to design your own business Web site, you can employ a company or designer to build a unique site for you. However, this is usually a fairly expensive solution and even a small site can cost from upwards of A$1000.

GETTING PROFESSIONAL

PLANNING YOUR SITE

A business site needs to be organised so that visitors can find their way around it easily, locate services or goods that interest them, and place orders or make appointments simply and with confidence. You will need to attract people to your site and be able to gather information about them and their interests while they're visiting. Many of the issues you need to address are the same as if you were opening a physical shop.

Did You Know?
You can find impartial advice about on-line and off-line business at Business Review Weekly (www.brw.com.au).

Designing the site

Your site, and in particular your opening homepage, needs to be welcoming, clear and helpful.

Keep it simple. Don't use huge graphics or animations that slow things down. Get your message across quickly and have a clear navigation system that can be easily understood. Try to have a short statement that clearly sets out your site's objective, and choose a memorable Web address.

For instance, a name such as 'Flowersthatlast' tells you pretty much all you need to know. More esoteric names are likely to need a bigger budget to get brand recognition. Would you associate Amazon with books if you had not seen their adverts?

Attracting customers

It is important that you decide at an early stage how customers will be able to place orders for your products so that both you and they can conduct the transfer of goods and money with ease and confidence. Customers often appreciate being given a choice of ways to order and pay.

You can subscribe to a secure credit card service for on-line payments, but you might also want to arrange facilities for telephone, fax and mail orders as well – particularly if your on-line business has an off-line counterpart.

Orders and deliveries

Once you've made a sale, you need to ensure you can deliver the goods. Consider whether or not you can cope with worldwide orders, how the delivery charges will be calculated and included in the overall costs, and what delivery times you can promise.

How any business fulfills its orders is critical for customer satisfaction. People want to know how quickly their items will be delivered, and they want to be confident that they can check on the progress of an order if it seems to be delayed.

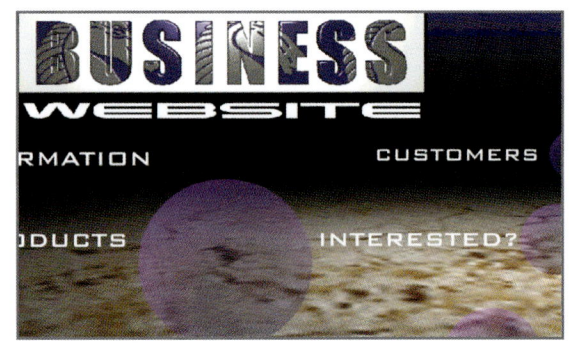

You also need to arrange insurance so that customers can be compensated for the non-delivery of an order, or for the delivery of damaged goods.

Promoting the site

Publicity is very important. You should include all the 'tags' that will help to get your site listed by search engines (see *Ensure your site is seen*, page 306), and spend time registering it with as many search engines as you can.

Payment

To accept credit card and cheque orders through your Web site you need a secure Internet Payment Gateway and an Internet Merchant Account. On-line shopping malls (see opposite) offer links and sometimes free access to this service.

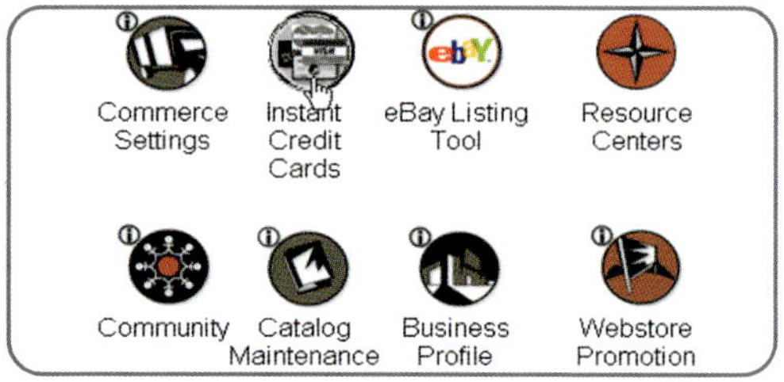

MAKING WEB SITES

HOW TO: USE WEB DESIGN SITES
One way to simplify the Web site design process is to join an on-line shopping mall such as Bigstep, FreeMerchant or Bizhosting (see below). These sites will get your shop or service on-line for the minimum amount of money and trouble.

While these services offer free start-up packages to get your Web site on-line, if you want your business site to be able to receive secure payments on-line you will need to start paying a monthly fee.

Jargon Buster!
Shopping cart The program that tracks customers' orders as they move around a shopping site, then allows them to 'check out' through a payment-and-delivery module, ensuring the transaction is both complete and secure.

Bigstep
www.bigstep.com
This site offers an excellent step-by-step Web-building module that allows you to create an attractive-looking Web site to your specifications. Or, you can ask a Bigstep consultant to do it for you (for a fee). You can have your own URL attached to the site and register your shop or service with the major search engines. You can also have an e-mail database to keep in touch with your customers.

If you need a sales section on your site, you can use the shopping cart function whereby you can have payments made though a secure server with on-line order tracking. You can also receive detailed breakdowns of user activity on your site, so you can see which parts are most successful.

FreeMerchant
www.freemerchant.com
Working in a similar way to Bigstep, FreeMerchant's Web page design tools are also easy to use. However, unlike Bigstep, you will need to make your own arrangements for customers' credit cards to be accepted on your site.

Two advantages of using this service is that your FreeMerchant shop can be listed at InternetMall (**www.internetmall.com**) – a site which promotes FreeMerchant stores, and you can also use a link to the eBay auction site to list your goods or services for auction there. This will help to promote your site and increase sales.

Bizhosting
www.bizhosting.com
Providing a full range of point-and-click design tools, Bizhosting helps you to build a free site for selling goods and services by phone and mail. You can upload an existing site into your Bizhosting Web space, rather than designing a new one on-line.

Bizhosting offers a range of hosting services, including a free basic package. You can also upgrade your site to accept credit cards from either your own Merchant Account or through the Bizhosting service, though this may involve higher transaction charges.

LEGAL ISSUES
Before trading on-line, you will need to check the terms of service associated with your Web host, since you are obliged to comply with local laws regarding employee and stock conditions. Also, international copyright laws need to be considered if your trade is in music or books.

There are consumer groups concerned about how e-commerce companies use information about visitors and shoppers, and this may lead to stronger legislation to protect the rights of customers. If you are in any doubt, seek legal advice on the Web. The E-Commerce Law Source (**www.e-commercelawsource.com**) is a very useful starting point.

GETTING PROFESSIONAL

Watch Out!
Consult your bank manager or financial adviser before creating a business site. Find out how much you can afford to invest and what terms and conditions are involved.

HOW TO: REGISTER FOR A FREEMERCHANT STORE

Use the process shown here to register with FreeMerchant. You can then start building a simple on-line shop. It is worth remembering, however, that you may not be able to accept orders on-line with some trial services. And if you upgrade to a membership package, you may need to make arrangements for accepting credit card transactions.

All the services mentioned in this section have similar procedures, so you could experiment with several free trial offers before making a final choice about which of them is suitable for hosting your business.

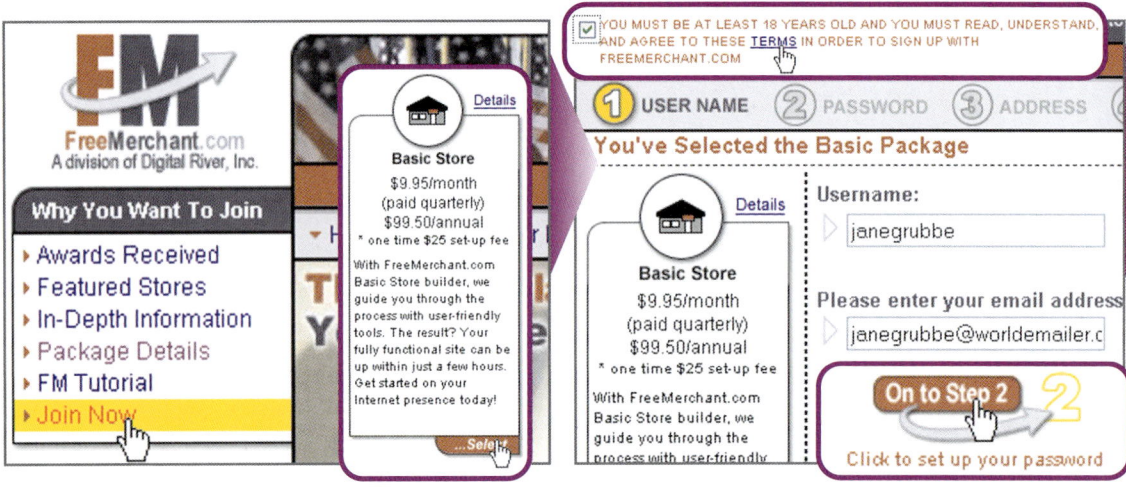

1 Go to the FreeMerchant Web site (**www.freemerchant.com**) and click on **Join Now**. Look over the deals that are on offer and choose one by clicking on **Select** at its base (here, we've chosen the 'Basic Store' package).

2 Review the terms and conditions of the service and click in the box indicating that you accept them. Then choose a 'Username', enter your e-mail address, and click **On to Step 2**.

Be prepared
In the world of e-commerce, computer problems are also business problems and need to be solved fast. Make sure that you know where you are going to get help before you need it – whether it concerns Web design, hosting or performance. Have a fall-back position ready for each of your service providers in case things break down irretrievably.

MAKING WEB SITES

> **Money Saver!**
> Don't forget that many of the extras offered by hosting firms will come at a price. Check the potential total cost for all your requirements in advance and allow for different volumes of transactions to see which service offers the best deal for your business.

3 Type in your password and security-related details and click **On to Step 3**. On the next page, enter your personal information, the name and address of your business and click **On to Step 4**.

4 Complete and submit the credit card payment form and click **Process Secure Payment**. You will then be offered a variety of additional choices, including how you would like your customers to pay.

5 Finally, confirm that you are registering for the 30-day free trial – you will be charged US$99.95 a year after the trial period. Remove the tick from the PowerTools check-box, and click on **Enroll!**. You are now registered with FreeMerchant.

Using different currencies

If you are paying over the Internet by credit card, it does not matter what currency the product has been priced in. Your bank will simply deduct the equivalent amount of Australian or New Zealand dollars from your account. Equally, if you are selling an item, you can price it in any currency – the appropriate amount will be credited to your account once the transaction is complete.

SEE ALSO
- **Find legal advice** – page 120
- **Become a share trader** – page 198
- **Link to more pages** – page 270

GETTING PROFESSIONAL

Ensure your site is seen

Get your **site noticed** by **registering** with a **search engine**

When you register your site with a search engine, you are alerting the search engine to the existence of your Web page and its contents. Then, if someone uses that search engine to look for the type of content you offer, your site will be one of the ones listed among the search results. Most search engines do not charge you to register with them. Registration is straightforward; however, owing to the volume of sites on the Web, it can take a month before your site is catalogued and starts appearing in searches.

HOW TO: REGISTER YOUR SITE WITH ALTAVISTA

Submitting a site to a search engine such as AltaVista is straightforward. When you register, your URL is added to the list of sites for the AltaVista 'Web spider' to visit right away. A Web spider is an automated program that records the information and links on Web pages. As millions of pages are visited each day, it can take a while for the content to be indexed and catalogued into the AltaVista database.

1 Go to AltaVista (**http://au.altavista.com**). Scroll down towards the bottom of the page and click on **Submit a Site** within the 'Services' section in the left-hand menu. Then click on **Basic Submit** near the bottom of the next page.

MAKING WEB SITES

Jargon Buster!
URL stands for Uniform Resource Locator – the technical name for a Web address.

2 You will be given a unique submission code, which you need to type into the appropriate box. Then enter your Web site address and click **Submit**. Your address will be confirmed and your site will be registered with AltaVista.

3 AltaVista also provides a directory service, though this requires you to pay a subscription fee. To get your site listed, return to the 'Submit a Site' page and click on **Express Inclusion**.

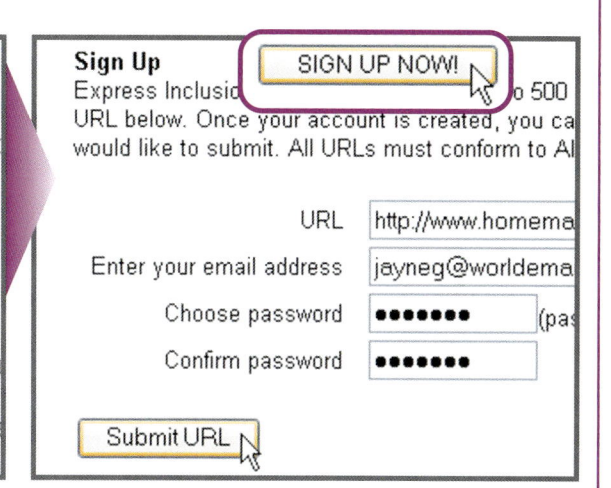

4 After reading though the description of the service, click **Sign Up Now!** On the next page, review the conditions and charges, fill in your URL and other requested details and click **Submit URL**. Finally, fill in and submit your payment details.

MULTI-REGISTRATION WEB SITES

Many Web-based and software application services specialise in automating the submission of sites to search engines.

Ineedhits.com (**www.ineedhits.com**) will submit your site to over 25 search engines, including Google and Lycos, free of charge.

Microsoft's Submit It! service (**www.submit-it.com**) provides a subscription-based service which registers your site with hundreds of search engines from a single form and includes tools to check that your keywords are the best ones to use.

GETTING PROFESSIONAL

Jargon Buster!
Directories Lists of Web sites, organised into groups by subject matter, such as 'Hobbies & Interests'. Locate the area most suited to your site and ask for it to be added.

HOW TO: MAKE SURE YOUR SITE GETS LISTED

Once you have registered with a search engine, you can take steps to ensure your site appears higher than other sites on the list of results when someone enters a relevant search term.

To do this, you need to add a brief description and a list of keywords to your site. These words will be invisible to someone viewing your site, but can be read by the search engine. However, you can only do this by manipulating the HTML code underlying your page. This may turn out to be the only HTML work you ever do, or it may whet your appetite to try some more. Either way, it is well worth doing so that your Web site gets as much prominence as possible.

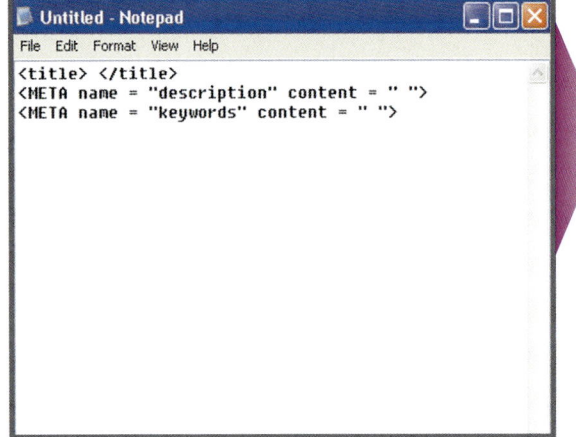

1 First open your Notepad program by going to the **Start** menu and selecting **All Programs**, then **Accessories** and **Notepad**. Type in the text shown above. The items enclosed in < > are known as 'tags'. They are the building blocks of HTML (see below).

2 Now type the name of your Web site between the two <title> tags. For example, type: <title>Homemade Fudge</title>. Make sure that the title clearly describes what your site offers.

HOW HTML WORKS

All HTML instructions are enclosed within markers called 'tags'. There are many types of tag, each referring to different areas of the page. Most tags come in pairs and are positioned before and after the text or item that they are referring to. For example, the first title tag would look like this: <title> and the second like this: </title>. The forward slash indicates that it is the second, or closing, tag.

MAKING WEB SITES

Problem Solver!
*In order to come up with every keyword someone might use to locate your site, go to **www.thesaurus.com** and get a list of every variant on each word you use.*

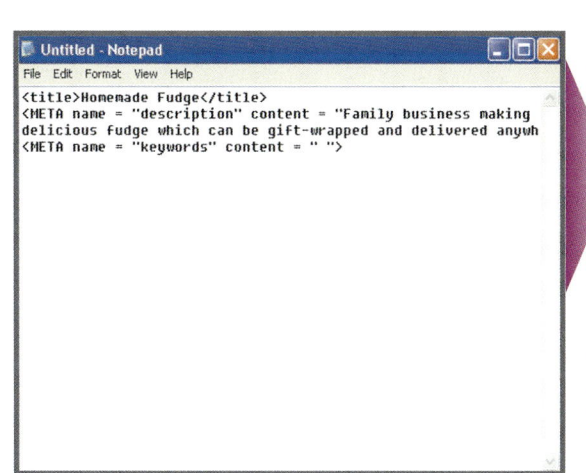

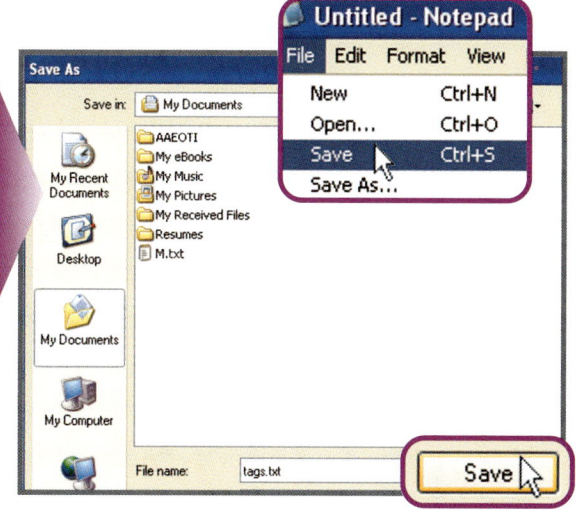

3 Then, between the inverted commas of the first <META> tag, enter a description of your site. This text summarises the content of your site and appears beneath your site name in the search result list, so use this text to attract visitors to your site.

4 Between the inverted commas of the second <META> tag, enter a list of keywords associated with your Web site. Separate each by a comma. Try to anticipate what keywords someone might put into a search engine and type them in.

5 Now go to the **File** menu, and click on **Save**. Save the Notepad file as 'tags.txt'. You are now ready to insert these tags within the rest of the HTML that makes up your Web page.

Choosing keywords
The main keywords should directly reflect your site content. If you sell homemade chocolates, your list would start with 'chocolates' and perhaps be followed by 'fudge', 'truffles', 'milk', 'dark', 'white', 'confectionery', 'sweets' and so on. Do not repeat words, but do include plurals, such as 'chocolate, chocolates', and other variations to cover all the combinations people might search for.

GETTING PROFESSIONAL

> **iMac**
> *The equivalent of Notepad on an iMac is SimpleText. To open this, double-click on your **Hard Drive** icon, then on the **Applications** folder and finally on **SimpleText**.*

HOW TO: ADD THE TAGS TO YOUR HTML PAGE

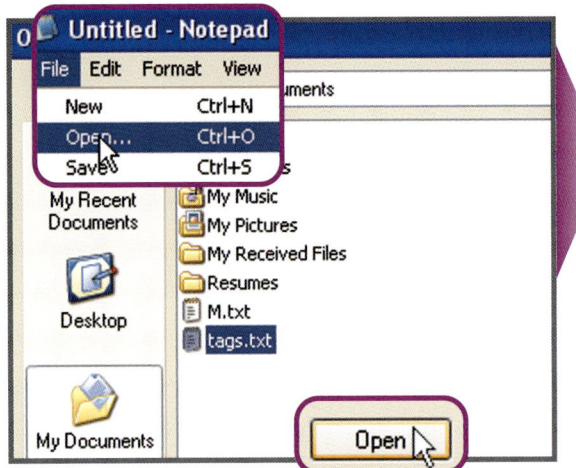

1 Open your tags.txt file in Notepad by going to the **File** menu and selecting **Open**. Choose **All Files** from the 'Files of type' menu, locate your file in the folder you saved it to, and click **Open**.

2 Next, open a second Notepad Window. Once you have used Notepad, you should find the program in the **Start** menu. Otherwise, select **All Programs**, then **Accessories** and finally **Notepad**.

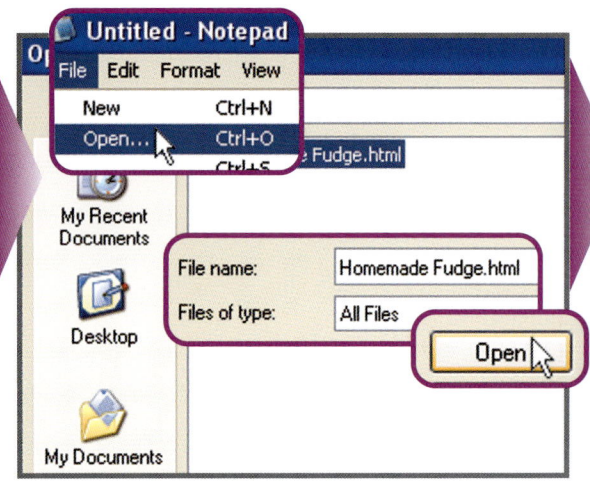

3 Now open your homepage in the new Notepad window. Go to the **File** menu and click **Open**. Choose **All Files** in the 'Files of type' menu, and locate your homepage. Click **Open**.

Publicise your site

Search engines are only one way to publicise your site. You should also consider placing an advertisement in a local or national newspaper – for example, by going to the Fairfax Advertising Centre (**www.adcentre.fairfax.com.au**). Or you could e-mail a Web site you like and ask its owner if it would be possible to set up a link to your site. If you run a business from your Web site, you should be prepared to pay a fee for this service, but some small business sites may not charge you at all.

MAKING WEB SITES

Did You Know?
If you want to find out more about HTML and how it works, there is an excellent site on the subject called WEBalley (*www.weballey.net*).

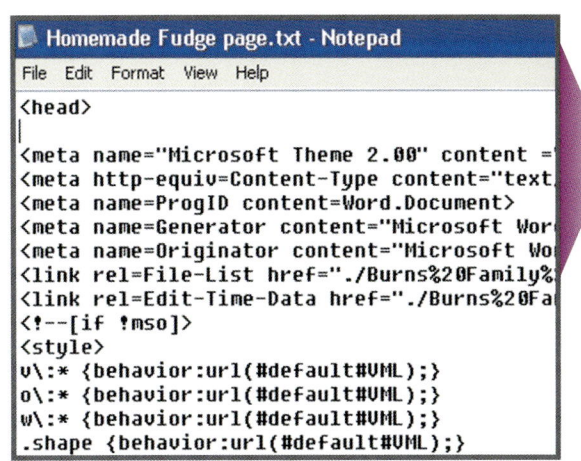

4 Scroll down to the tag that marks the beginning of the 'head' section (it will look like: **<head>**). Click after the tag and press the **Return** key to add a blank line beneath it.

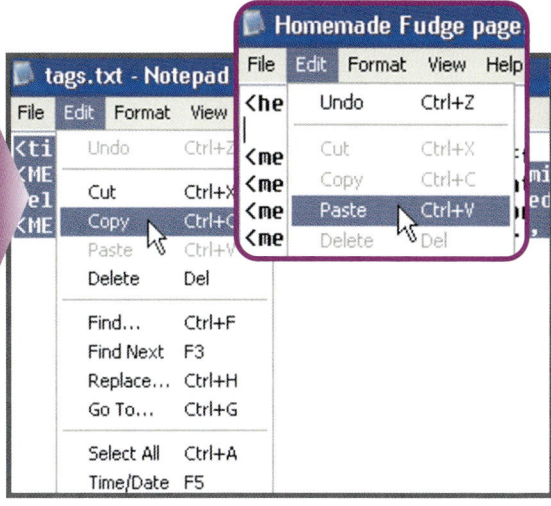

5 Then, switch back to your tags.txt document and copy all the text. Return to your homepage document and paste the text into the blank space under the **<head>** tag.

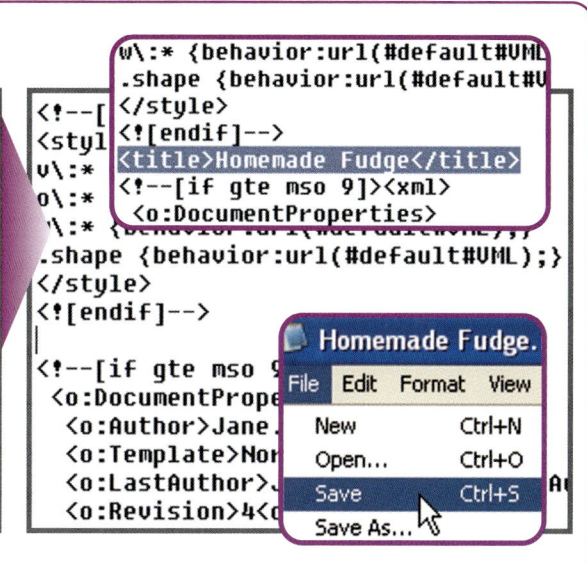

6 Word will already have inserted a 'title' tag, which you now need to delete. Scroll down the document until you see **<title>...</title>**. Delete the tags and anything between them. Then save your Web page, ready to upload it to the Web.

SEE ALSO
- Build a Web page in Word – *page 256*
- Upload your site – *page 262*
- Add a video to your page – *page 282*

Web Directory

Advertising 313
Classifieds
Personal

Art 313
Architecture
Artists
Arts & crafts
Fine art
Galleries
Guides
Supplies
Virtual images

Bizarre 314
Paranormal
Stupid
Weird

Books 314
Authors
Book buying
Children's
Classics
Poetry
Publishers
Writing

Children 315
Babies
Celebrations/parties
Early learning
On-line activities
Penfriends
Search engines
Toys

Computers 316
E-mail, conferencing & instant messaging
Games
Hardware
Help
Macs
News

PCs
Sales
Shareware
Software
Viruses

Education 318
Adult
Children
Finding schools
Libraries
On-line courses
Revision
Schools
Universities

Employment 319
Careers advice
Listings
Psychological profiles
Résumés

Entertainment 319
Celebrities
Children
Cinema
Dance
Gossip
Listings
Music
Opera
Radio
Theatre
Web-cams

Finance 320
Advice
Economics
Insurance
News
Pensions
Savings & loans
Share trading
Tax

Food & Drink 321
Dieting
Drink
Eating in
Eating out

Health 322
Alternative medicine
Diagnosis
Fitness
Information
Institutions
Mental
Nutrition
Pharmacies

History 323
Ancient
Australia & New Zealand
General
Medieval & Renaissance
Modern
Pre-history
World

Home & Garden 324
Design & furnishing
DIY
Gardening
House buying

Humour 324
Cartoons
Comedians & shows
Jokes & satire

Internet 325
Advice
Broadband
Chatrooms & communication
ISPs
News

Search engines
Security
Web design
Web design – business
Web hosting

Leisure & Hobbies 327
Collectibles
Genealogy
Museums
Outdoor pursuits
Photography

Lifestyle 328
Beauty & fashion
Weddings

Motoring 329
Automobiles
Brands
Buying & selling
Classic
Importing
Maintenance
Motorcycles

Music 330
Blues
Classical
Country
Downloads
Folk
Jazz
MP3
News
Pop
Rock
World

Natural World 331
Animals & birds
Environment
Exploration
Web-cams

News 331
Local sources
Tickers
World

Reference 332
Children's
Dictionaries & grammar
Encyclopedias
Maps
Miscellaneous
Thesauruses

Relationships 333
People-finders
Romance

Science 333
Discovery
News
Scientists

Shopping 334
Antiques
Auctions
Books
CDs & records
DVDs
E-commerce
Florists
Furniture & houseware
General shopping sites
Gifts
Greetings
Major stores

Society 336
Charity
Government
Law
Politics
Pressure groups

Space 337
Aliens
Astronomy
Travel

Sport 338
Adventure
Boxing
Cricket
Cycling
Fishing
Football
General
Golf
Horse racing
Martial arts
News
Racquet sports
Water sports
Winter sports

Television 340
Broadcasters
Children's
Classic
Listings
Programs
Web-cams
World

Travel 341
Attractions
Car rental
City guides
Guides
Health
Holidays
Maps
Timetables
Travel tips

Weather 343
Forecasts

DIRECTORY

All the Web sites mentioned in the book are listed here with an accompanying page number so that you can refer to them for additional detail. Remember that Web site addresses change frequently and without warning.

A
Advertising
Classifieds
Autotrader
www.autotrader.com.au/selling.asp 181
Car Sales
www.carsales.com.au 182
Drive.com
www.drive.com.au 181
eBay Australia
www.ebay.com.au 208, 209, 210
eBay New Zealand
http://pages.ebay.com/nz 209
Fairfax Advertising Centre
www.adcentre.fairfax.com.au 310
Sold.com
http://au.sold.yahoo.com 209
Trading Post
www.tradingpost.com.au
Buy or sell just about anything at this Internet bazaar – you'll be amazed at what's available.

Personal
100hot.com
www.100hot.com/chat 170
OptusNet Personals
www.optusnet.com.au/lifestyle/personals 170
Oz Reunion
www.ozreunion.com.au 170
SingleSites
www.singlesites.com 170
Yahoo! Groups
http://au.groups.yahoo.com 170
NZ Connections
www.nzc.co.nz
Meet other single Kiwis or make friends further afield.
RSVP
www.rsvp.com.au
Billed as Australia's largest singles site, where you can find like-minded people and chat with them on-line.

Art
Architecture
The Great Buildings Collection
www.greatbuildings.com 145
Guggenheim Bilbao
www.guggenheim-bilbao.es
The shape of this building is fabulous.
Westminster Abbey
www.westminster-abbey.org
Conduct your own virtual tour of this magnificent building.

Artists
Art Gallery Online
www.art-gallery-online.org 173
Selling Your Art Online
http://1x.com/advisor 173
Art Advocate
www.artadvocate.com
Gallery of new art for sale.
Artchive
www.artchive.com
More than 2000 scans from over 200 artists. Also has reviews and gallery links.
Artist-Show
www.artist-show.com
Add your own site to this huge list of art links.
Artshow.com
www.artshow.com
Artists' portfolios and resources for artists in many media.

Arts & crafts
The Art Connection Inc.
www.artconnection.net 172
Corel
www3.corel.com 172
About.com – Arts and Crafts
http://artsandcrafts.about.com/hobbies/artsandcrafts
A site that tells you how to start up a crafts business.
Art Links
www.4artlinks.com
A Web site with a variety of links to other useful sites devoted to arts and crafts.
Artnet
www.artnet.com
Estimate the value of an artwork by comparing it to similar auctioned works.
The Australian Arts & Crafts search engine
www.artstralia.com.au
Promotes Australian and New Zealand arts and crafts and provides an on-line resource for all creative people.
Craft Site Directory
www.craftsitedirectory.com
Get a helping hand with your beadwork, quilting or even gourd art.
Porcelain Painters International
www.porcelainpainters.com
The site offers two free on-line lessons on the art of painting porcelain or china.
Rittners School of Floral Design
www.floralschool.com
Loads of information about floral design from a school of professionals.
SoapTeacher
www.soapteacher.com
Discover how to make soap that looks and smells just like a slice of apple pie.

Fine art
Art History Search
www.arthistorysearch.com 172
Artserve
http://rubens.anu.edu.au 173
The Mother of All Art History Links
www.art-design.umich.edu/mother 173
The Getty Provenance Index
http://piedi.getty.edu
Multiple databases of books and CD-ROMs for tracing the past ownership of works of art.

Galleries
Art Gallery Online
www.art-gallery-online.org 173
The Louvre
www.louvre.fr 146
Museum of Modern Art, New York
www.moma.org 146
The Getty
www.getty.edu
Find out more about the J. Paul Getty Museum in Los Angeles, with its huge collection of manuscripts, paintings, ceramics and sculptures.

313

ART

National Gallery, London
www.nationalgallery.org.uk
Guide to the collection and current exhibitions of London's famous art gallery.

National Gallery of Australia
www.nga.gov.au
Guide to the collections and exhibitions, as well as news and information on opening times.

Prado Museum
http://museoprado.mcu.es
Take a guided tour and learn how to look at paintings and analyse them in detail.

Tate Gallery
www.tate.org.uk
Explore the four Tate galleries in the UK through the 50,000 images from the collections.

Van Gogh Museum
www.vangoghmuseum.nl
Includes a virtual tour and many fascinating facts about Van Gogh's life and times.

Guides

ArtCyclopedia
http://artcyclopedia.com 173

The Grove Dictionary of Art Online
www.groveart.com 173

Art Holidays
www.art-holidays.co.uk
UK site offering painting and craft holidays for all levels of ability worldwide.

Supplies

ArtResource
www.artresource.com 173

The Art Scene
www.artscene.com.au 173

Art Supplies Online
www.artsupplies.co.nz 173

WetCanvas!
www.wetcanvas.com 173

World Wide Arts Resources
http://wwar.com 173

MisterArt
www.misterart.com
The world's largest on-line art supply store – everything from tempera to gold leaf.

Virtual images

American Memory
http://memory.loc.gov/ammem/amhome.html 251

Art by Cheryl.com
www.artbycheryl.com 251

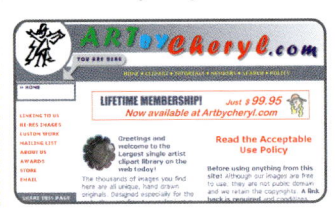

Backgrounds Archive
www.backgroundsarchive.com 251

Free Graphics
www.freegraphics.com 251

Google's Image Search
http://images.google.com 251

Ipix
www.ipix.com 146

NASA Photo Gallery
www.nasa.gov/gallery/photo 251

Neovisioni
www.neovisioni.com 147

QuickTime
www.apple.com/quicktime 147

WorldAtlas.com
www.worldatlas.com/clipart.htm 251

World Wide Web Test Pattern
www.uark.edu/~wrg 146

AllFreeArt.com
www.allfreeart.com
Free ClipArt paintings and sketches.

Animagic GIF Animator
www.rtlsoft.com/animagic
Create your own animations with this shareware program.

Animation Factory
www.animfactory.com
Thousands of humorous free animations for your Web site.

FreeStuffFactory
www.freestufffactory.com
A huge collection of free art, browser skins and screen savers.

2Cool Animations
www.gifanimations.com
Great cartoon animations.

B
Bizarre
Paranormal

Circlemakers
www.circlemakers.org
Created by aliens – or, as this site suggests, the formations of a dedicated band of artists.

Fortean Times
www.forteantimes.com
The on-line edition of this journal of 'strange phenomena and experiences, curiosities, prodigies and portents'.

Ghostcam
www.knoxstudio.com/ghostcam/ghost
Take a virtual tour of 'haunted' buildings.

Stupid

The Smoking Gun
www.thesmokinggun.com
Mad, bad or stupid acts committed by police officers, rock groups and the public.

Wait all day
www.waitallday.com
Go to this site and see what happens!

Weird

Allnoise
www.allnoise.com 171

Aliens, Aliens, Aliens
http://aliensaliensaliens.com
'Serving our Alien Overlords since December 18, 1995'.

Luna
www.mufor.org/moon.html
Photos of alien fortresses on the Moon.

Skeptic.com
www.skeptic.com
Web site of the Sceptics Society, dedicated to questioning humanity's weird beliefs.

UFO Casebook
http://bjbooth.topcities.com/alientypes.html
How to tell a Grey Type A alien from a Grey Type B.

Books
Authors

Stephen King
www.stephenking.com
The official Web presence of the master of horror novels.

Book buying

Abebooks
http://abebooks.com 72, 115

Alibris
www.alibris.com 202

Amazon
www.amazon.com 168, 202, 203

Angus & Robertson
www.angusrobertson.com.au 167

BOL
www.bol.com 167

Book Clique Cafe
www.readinggroupsonline.com 167

Bookfayre.com
www.bookfayre.com 202

BookFinder
www.bookfinder.com 72, 115, 203

BookWeb
www.bookweb.org/bookstores 202

BuyGuide Australia
www.buyguide.com.au 202

Co-op Online Bookshop
www.coop-bookshop.com.au 202

Dymocks
www.dymocks.com.au 167, 202

eBookMall
www.ebookmall.com 168

eBooks.com
www.ebooks.com 168

eBooks N' Bytes
www.ebooksnbytes.com 168

Free-eBooks
www.free-ebooks.net 168

Haybooks
www.haybooks.com 115

New Zealand Books
http://newzealandbooks.co.nz 202

Online Originals
www.onlineoriginals.com 168

Ozlit
http://home.vicnet.net.au/~ozlit 167

Te Puna Web Directory
http://tepuna.natlib.govt.nz/web_directory/NZ/literature.htm 167

University of Virginia's E-Book Library
http://etext.lib.virginia.edu/ebooks 168

CHILDREN

Bibliofind
www.bibliofind.com
Search on-line for new, second-hand, out-of-print and rare books around the world.

BookChat!
www.4-lane.com/bookchat
Chat to fellow book readers and writers live.

Messrs Berkelouw
www.berkelouw.com.au
Search for books on-line.

MysteryNet
www.mysterynet.com
Classic and modern mysteries investigated and cases to solve.

The New York Review of Books
www.nybooks.com
On-line edition of the venerable literary magazine.

Palm Digital Media
www.peanutpress.com
Electronic books for hand-held and desktop computers.

Children's

Scholastic Australia
www.scholastic.com.au 138

Beatrix Potter
http://wiredforbooks.org/kids.htm
Enter the delightful world of Peter Rabbit, Squirrel Nutkin and Jemima Puddleduck.

Harry Potter Books
www.bloomsburymagazine.com/harrypotter
Reader's club for aspiring witches and wizards everywhere.

Roald Dahl Fans.com
www.roalddahlfans.com
Find out about his life, books and poems, and play games – lots of fun stuff.

Seussville
www.seussville.com/seussville
The crazy world of Dr Seuss complete with recipes for green eggs and ham.

Classics

Project Gutenberg
www.promo.net/pg 167

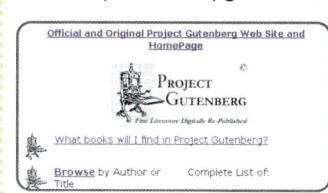

Concordances of Great Books
www.concordance.com
Search for words and phrases in the works of over 150 great authors.

The Dickens Project
http://humwww.ucsc.edu/dickens/index.html
Scholarly site devoted to Charles Dickens, with links to further study and on-line editions.

Mr. William Shakespeare and the Internet
http://shakespeare.palomar.edu
Good for revision, this site has a guide to hundreds of Web sites, plus a biography of the bard.

The Online Books Page
http://digital.library.upenn.edu/books
The full texts of over 17,000 classics of English literature.

Poetry

The Fridge Magnet Poetry Boards
www.thepixiepit.co.uk/magnets.htm 167

Poetry.com
www.poetry.com 166

About.com – Poetry
http://classicpoetry.about.com
Busy poetry site, with analysis, discussion, reviews and history.

Academy of American Poets
www.poets.org
Resources for poets, students and teachers, with a poetry archive.

Interviews with Poets
www.interviews-with-poets.com
Interviews with contemporary poets such as Seamus Heaney.

The Poetry Society
www.poetrysociety.org.uk
Reviews, competitions, events calendar and books for sale.

Vers Libre
www.nth-dimension.co.uk/vl
Classic poetry searchable by author or first line.

Publishers

Penguin Books
www.penguin.com.au 167

Penguin UK
www.penguin.co.uk 167

Virago
www.virago.co.uk
Try the 'reading guides' for helpful information.

Writing

The New Zealand Writers' Website
www.nzwriters.co.nz
Provides encouragement, information and support to New Zealand writers.

NSW Writers' Centre
www.nswwriterscentre.org.au
A resource and information site for professional writers and anyone aspiring to become one.

Quotez
www.quotations.co.uk
Archive of ancient and modern quotes.

Xlibris
www.xlibris.com
Get your book into print with this self-publishing service.

C
Children
Babies

BabyCentre
www.babycentre.co.uk
Childcare advice from the professionals and tips from parents who know the score.

Coles Baby Club
www.babyclub.coles.com.au
Useful advice and a membership program that offers a free magazine and discounts.

Parenting Bookmark
www.parentingbookmark.com
Parenting and education advice on issues such as discipline.

Celebrations/parties

Amazingmoms
www.amazingmoms.com 179

Balloons Online
www.balloonsonline.com.au 179

The Cake Whole
www.cakewhole.com.au 179

EntertainOz
www.entertainoz.com.au 179

The Party Games Ideas Resource Page
http://freespace.virgin.net/ken.tew/party/list.html 179

Sydney's Child
www.sydneyschild.com.au 179

Early Learning

Cory's PaintBox
www.corypaints.com 179

Scholastic Australia
www.scholastic.com.au 138

On-line activities

Bob the Builder
www.bobthebuilder.org 176

Crayola
www.crayola.com 176

The Playground
www.abc.net.au/children 176

SpaceKids
www.spacekids.com 143

UpToTen
www.uptoten.org 177

BBC Nature Animals page
www.bbc.co.uk/nature/animals
Cuddly koalas, rampant rhinos and cheeky chimps all profiled.

BBC Science
www.bbc.co.uk/science
Build your own robot or find out about solar-powered pizza.

Cool Science for Curious Kids
www.hhmi.org/coolscience
Explore biology the fun way through cartoons and sounds.

Disney.com
http://disney.go.com
Visit Kids Island to play games with Tarzan, the Little Mermaid and other Disney characters.

CHILDREN

ExploreScience.com
www.explorescience.com
Multimedia experiments that illustrate the principles of optics, sound and astronomy.

Idea Box
www.theideabox.com
Art, music, cooking and other activities to keep kids busy.

Kids' Space
www.kids-space.org
International children's art gallery – open for submissions.

National Geographic Kids
www.nationalgeographic.com/kids
Find out about the bottle-nosed dolphin or brown bear, play a game or test your geography.

The Observatory
www.exploratorium.edu/observatory
Calculate your weight on other planets and find facts about sunspots, eclipses and auroras.

Reeko's Mad Scientist Lab
www.spartechsoftware.com/reeko
Fun science experiments for parents, teachers and children.

SurfMonkey
www.surfmonkey.com
Kid-safe browser with recommended fun sites, e-mail and instant messaging.

The Yuckiest Site on the Internet
http://yucky.kids.discovery.com
Worms, mud and more – all in the interests of science.

Penfriends

International Penfriends
www.internationalpenfriends.co.uk   170

Kidlink
www.kidlink.org   175

Kidnews.com
www.kidnews.com   175, 178

Search engines

AOL Kids Search
www.aol.com.au/site/aol/kids/kidsearch   71

Ask Jeeves Kids
www.ajkids.com   71

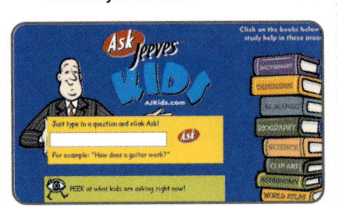

KidsClick!
http://kidsclick.org   71

Yahooligans!
www.yahooligans.com   57, 71, 174

Bonus.com
www.bonus.com
Loads of links and site summaries.

CompuServe.com Kids
www.compuserve.com/gateway/kids/default.asp
Games, movies, music, sport and lots of cool links.

Cybersmart Kids Online
www.cybersmartkids.com.au
Smart net surfing tips – for kids and parents.

Internet Watch Foundation Safe Surfing Guide
www.internetwatch.org.uk/safe
Tips on safe surfing for kids.

Toys

PeeDee Toys
http://store.yahoo.com/peedeetoys   179

Action Man
www.actionman.com
See how well you do on one of Action Man's secret missions.

Barbie
www.barbie.com
Dress Barbie for a fashion show or colour in pictures on-line.

Lego MindStorms
http://mindstorms.lego.com
Build Lego robots and program them to do what you want.

Computers

E-mail, conferencing & instant messaging

AOL Instant Messenger
www.aim.com   93

Dialpad
www.dialpad.com   94

Eudora
www.eudora.com   33

Hotmail
www.hotmail.com   93

ICQ
http://web.icq.com   93

MediaRing
www.mediaring.com   94

Meta Email Search Agent MESA
http://mesa.rrzn.uni-hannover.de   73

Microsoft.Net Passport
www.passport.com   93

My Email Address Is
http://my.email.address.is   73

Nameplanet
www.nameplanet.com   33

Netscape Download
http://wp.netscape.com/download   26, 33

Net2Phone
http://commcenter.net2phone.com   94

PC-Telephone
www.pc-telephone.com   94

Pegasus
www.pmail.com   33

SpamBuster
http://contactplus.com   63

Yahoo! Messenger
http://messenger.yahoo.com   93

Bigfoot
www.bigfoot.com
Get an e-mail address for life, even if you change ISP, with this e-mail forwarding service.

Coalition Against Unsolicited Commercial Email
www.cauce.org
Campaigning group dedicated to stamping out spam.

The Curse of a Thousand Chain Letters
http://chainletters.org
An e-mail house of horrors – threatening chain letters and bogus virus warnings.

FreeBox
www.freebox.com
A free e-mail address accessible from a browser or mobile phone.

Junk Email Resource Page
www.junkemail.org
Find out how laws are changing to regulate unsolicited mail.

Microsoft Messenger
http://messenger.microsoft.com
Download the latest updates for this popular program.

Games

About.com – Internet Games
http://internetgames.about.com   187

ChessKIDS Academy
www.chesskids.com   189

Free Games Online
www.freegamesonline.com   187

Freeware Gaming
www.freewaregaming.com   187

MSN Games
http://zone.msn.com   187, 188

Rainy Day Playhouse
www.pen-web.com/rainyday   187

Station.com
http://www2.station.sony.com   189

Hardware

Hardware Central
www.hardwarecentral.com
In-depth news and reviews of every type of hardware.

ZDNet Reviews
www.zdnet.com/reviews
Long-established and up-to-date reviews section, covering everything from digital cameras to speakers.

Help

CNET – Spotlight on Production Tools
http://builder.cnet.com/webbuilding/pages/Authoring/ProdTools   295

Cyberfiber Newsgroups
www.cyberfiber.com   134

Doctor Keyboard
www.drkeyboard.com   134

Epson
www.epson.com   135

Forta.com
www.forta.com   297

Google Groups
http://groups.google.com   134, 135

Intelinfo
www.intelinfo.com   134

Jumbo!
www.jumbo.com   134

Microsoft
www.microsoft.com/australia   134

COMPUTERS

NCSA Beginner's Guide to HTML
http://archive.ncsa.uiuc.edu/General/Internet/WWW   294

Perl Mongers
www.perl.org   297

UK Technical Support
www.uktsupport.co.uk   135

Australian Seniors Computer Clubs Association
www.seniorcomputing.org
The FAQ section is easy to understand and has links to other related Web sites in each topic.

Jargon File Resources
http://tuxedo.org/jargon
A comprehensive dictionary of hacker language.

Webopedia
www.webopedia.com
Dictionary of Internet and computer terms.

ZDNet – Help & How-To
www.zdnet.com/filters/zdhelp
Read the headline articles or search for help on viruses, worms, software and more.

Macs

Apple
www.apple.com
Product information, support and jobs from the Mac people.

MacAddict
www.macaddict.com
On-line version of the Mac magazine, with news and features, archives and resources such as Mac Web links.

MacInTouch
www.macintouch.com
Serious information for those who know their UNIX from their LINUX.

News

Australian IT
http://australianit.news.com.au
Daily updates of IT-related events. Also has reviews of new technology and job listings.

Wired News
www.wired.com
The techno generation's bible, with the latest techie news.

ZDNet News
www.zdnet.com/news
Net and tech news, fast and detailed, with a page for you to air your views.

PCs

The PC Guide
www.pcguide.com
Help and repair advice, systems and components reference guide and discussion forums.

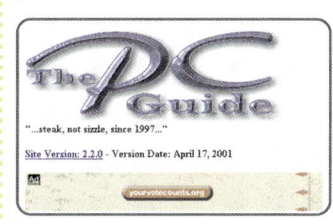

PC Pick-Me-Ups
www.users.bigpond.com/billimetzke
Troubleshooting, upgrading, installation guides and tips for PCs and peripherals.

What's In That Box?
http://members.aol.com/wbox/wbox.htm
Introduction to basic PC functions and components.

Sales

Dick Smith Electronics
www.dse.com.au   281

Harris Technology
www.ht.com.au   281

Buy.com
www.buy.com
Buy computers and related equipment on the Web.

Dell Australia
www.ap.dell.com
Choose your country and then select, customise and buy your computer system on-line.

Outpost.com
http://shop.outpost.com
PCs, Macs, peripherals, cameras and electronics, with fast international delivery.

Shareware

CNET Download
http://download.com.com   85

Jumbo!
www.jumbo.com   85, 97, 134

Tucows
www.tucows.com   85, 130, 175

Galt Download Zone
www.galttech.com
Amazing wallpapers and more.

Pass the Shareware
www.passtheshareware.com
Thousands of freeware and shareware programs to download in a range of categories.

Software

Adobe
www.adobe.com   168

Adobe Acrobat
www.adobe.com/acrobat   85

Adobe Photoshop
www.adobe.com/products/tryadobe   265

Ages!
www.daubnet.com/english.html   161

Cyndi's List Software & Computer
www.cyndislist.com/software.htm   161, 163

CNET Download
http://download.com.com   85, 86, 100

Corel
www3.corel.com   172

Cute FTP
www.globalscape.com   85

CyberPatrol
www.cyberpatrol.com   56

CYBERsitter
www.cybersitter.com   56, 57

Evrsoft 1stPage 2000
www.evrsoft.com   295

Family Origins
www.familyorigins.com   159

Family Tree Maker
www.genealogy.com   159

Genealogical Software Report Card
www.mumford.ca/reportcard   159

Genealogy for Windows
www.deltadrive.co.uk   159

Internet Watcher
www.internetwatcher.com   57

Ipix
www.ipix.com   146

Jasc Paint Shop Pro
www.jasc.com/products/psp   265, 267

Jumbo!
www.jumbo.com   85, 97, 134

Macromedia Downloads
www.macromedia.com/downloads   82, 83, 85

Macromedia Dreamweaver
www.macromedia.com   295

Microsoft
www.microsoft.com   85, 285

Microsoft Download Center
www.microsoft.com/downloads   146

Microsoft FrontPage
www.microsoft.com/frontpage   295

Microsoft Reader
www.microsoft.com/reader   168

Neovisioni
www.neovisioni.com   147

Net Nanny
www.netnanny.com   56, 98

Netscape Composer
http://browsers.netscape.com   295

Netscape Download
http://wp.netscape.com/download   26, 33

Norton Personal Firewall
www.symantec.com   89

QuickTime
www.apple.com/quicktime   147

Real.com
www.real.com   82, 85, 119
www.real.com.au   150

RealNetworks Helix Producer
www.realnetworks.com/products/producer   279

Sausage HotDog PageWiz
www.sausagetools.com   295

SpamBuster
http://contactplus.com   63

StuffIt
www.stuffit.com   47, 49, 85

Trellian
www.trellian.com   70

Tucows
www.tucows.com   85, 87, 130, 175

Windows Media Player
www.microsoft.com/windows/windowsmedia/download   152

Winzip
www.winzip.com   47, 85

317

COMPUTERS

World Wide Web Test Pattern
www.uark.edu/~wrg 146

WS_FTP
www.ipswitch.com 85

ZDNet
www.zdnet.com 85

A1 JavaScripts
www.a1javascripts.com
Enhance your site with a range of sophisticated effects, such as rollovers and backgrounds.

Java-Scripts
www.java-scripts.net
Free JavaScripts for your site, and a script-writing tutorial.

The JavaScript Source
http://javascript.internet.com
JavaScript downloads and tutorials, plus latest additions such as a calculator or metasearch.

Viruses

Symantec
www.symantec.com 58, 60

V-Buster
www.v-buster.com 60

Vmyths.com
www.vmyths.com 59

About.com – Antivirus Software
http://antivirus.about.com
Loads of information on recent virus outbreaks and how to protect your computer against future attacks.

How Computer Viruses Work
www.howstuffworks.com/virus.htm
Offers an insight into how viruses work and what you can do to avoid them.

McAfee.com
www.mcafee.com
Download VirusScan anti-virus software and subscribe to a free newsletter on the latest outbreaks.

E
Education
Adult

Adult Community Education
www.edna.edu.au/ace.html
A wide range of information for adults wanting to 'go back to school'.

Universities of the Third Age
www.u3aonline.org.au
Short on-line courses, for self-study or study in small groups, covering a wide range of recreational interests.

Children

ABC Learn online
www.abc.net.au/learn 137

Ask Jeeves Kids
www.ajkids.com 137, 139

Discovernet
http://amol.org.au/discovernet 137

Education Network Australia
www.edna.edu.au 137

Homework High
www.homeworkhigh.co.uk 138

Lab Notes
www.abc.net.au/labnotes 178

Looksmart Australia
www.looksmart.com.au 137

Looksmart New Zealand
www.looksmart.co.nz 137

Ministry of Education
www.minedu.govt.nz 136

Museum of New Zealand
www.tepapa.govt.nz 137

National Museum of Australia
www.nma.gov.au 137

Scholastic Australia
www.scholastic.com.au 138

SpaceKids
www.spacekids.com 143

SuperKids Educational Software Review
www.superkids.com 136

US National Museum of Natural History
www.mnh.si.edu 137

Ask Dr. Math
http://mathforum.com/dr.math
Browse the maths questions and answers, or ask Dr. Math a question of your own.

DaisyMaths
www.daisymaths.com.au
A site that makes maths fun.

Microsoft Encarta
http://encarta.msn.com
Integrated learning resource offering help and advice; an extensive reference source for students, teachers and parents.

Finding schools

Education Providers in New Zealand
www.nzeil.co.nz/providers/frameset_providers.htm
Information and contact details of tertiary, secondary and English language institutions – by region and type of institute.

NMIT Education and Training Online
http://online.nmit.vic.edu.au
Site with a huge database of Australian education links.

Libraries

The Internet Public Library
www.ipl.org 114

National Library of Australia
www.nla.gov.au 114

Virtual Library
www.vlib.org 114

On-line courses

Distance Learning Resource Network
www.dlrn.org 112

Education World
www.educationworld.com 112

World Lecture Hall
www.utexas.edu/world/lecture 112

World Wide Learn
www.worldwidelearn.com 111, 112

4Courses.com
http://4courses.4anything.com
Advice on how to study as well as what courses to choose.

Globewide Network Academy
www.gnacademy.org
List of more than 30,000 courses from all over the world.

The International Distance Learning Course Finder
www.dlcoursefinder.com
Information on more than 50,000 distance learning courses in over 100 different countries.

The Le@rning Federation
www.thelearningfederation.edu.au
A site specialising in on-line interactive curriculum content specifically developed for Australian and New Zealand schools.

Teaching & Learning on the Web
www.mcli.dist.maricopa.edu/tl
On-line courses plus class support materials via the Web.

Revision

Ask An Expert
www.askanexpert.com 114

Expert Central
www.expertcentral.com 114

Librarians' Index to the Internet
www.lii.org 114

Virtual Library
www.vlib.org 114

Yahoo! France
http://fr.yahoo.com
All the familiar Yahoo! services in French. Or try other Yahoo! sites in other languages.

Schools

The Australian Correspondence Schools
www.acs.edu.au 112

DiscoverySchool.com
http://school.discovery.com
US site offering homework help and advice for students, and related features for teachers and parents.

Universities

Distance Education Association of New Zealand
www.deanz.org.nz 110

OnlineLearning
www.onlinelearning.net 110

Open Learning Australia
www.ola.edu.au 110

University of Phoenix Online
www.uofphx.quinstreet.com 111

Virtual University
www.vu.org 112

Charles Sturt University
http://csu.edu.au
Information about courses, scholarships, and everything that the University offers.

ENTERTAINMENT

New School Online University
www.dialnsa.edu
New York-based virtual university with courses in media and technology.

New York Institute of Technology
www.nyit.edu/olc/olcmain.html
On-line education in arts, humanities, sciences and management.

Studylink
www.studylink.com.au
Find and apply for courses in Australia and overseas.

Universities.com
www.universities.com
Listings and links to universities in the USA and worldwide.

Which Course, Which University?
www.detya.gov.au/tenfields
Information about courses and contact details of Australian universities. Also discover how previous graduates rated courses and how many got jobs.

Yahoo! Education
http://au.dir.yahoo.com/education
Hundreds of links to a wide range of education sites.

Employment
Careers advice

Mycareer
www.mycareer.com.au   123

Career Information Products, Department of Education, Science and Training
www.dest.gov.au/archive/ty/careers/ciproducts.htm
Downloadable booklets on choosing an occupation, job searching and career planning.

Listings

Australian Commonwealth Government Information
www.fed.gov.au/KSP   123

Australian JobSearch
www.jobsearch.gov.au   123

CareerPoint
www.careers.govt.nz/c-key.htm   123

KiwiCareers
www.careers.co.nz   123

Monster
www.monster.com.au   123

Mycareer
www.mycareer.com.au   123

Seek
www.seek.com.au   122

CareerOne
www.careerone.com.au
Search for jobs in Australia and New Zealand.

Graduate.career.com.au
www.graduate.career.com.au
Graduates and soon-to-be graduates can search for jobs, and get course information and interview technique tips.

Holden
www.holden.com.au
Explore career opportunities with this company – perfect for the Holden car enthusiast.

Virgin Blue
www.virginblue.com.au
Apply on-line to become part of the Virgin cabin crew – or take a look at what other jobs are on offer.

Yahoo! Careers
http://yahoocareers.seek.com.au
Job search by work type, location or industry.

Psychological profiles

The Big Trip
www.thebigtrip.co.uk   124

Quest
www.questcareer.com/career_assessment_resources.html   122

Résumés

Monster
www.monster.com.au   125

Entertainment
Celebrities

Celebritybase.net
www.celebritybase.net   165

Celebrity Merchandise
www.celebritymerch.com   165

EOnline
www.eonline.com   165

Fansites.com
www.fansites.com   165

The Internet Movie Database
www.imdb.com   165

Obsessive Fan Sites
www.ggower.com/fans   165

Oz Music Central Band Links
www.ozmusic-central.com.au/ozlinks.html   165

People News
www.peoplenews.com   165

Popstazz.co.uk
www.popstazz.co.uk/fanclubs.htm   165

asSeenonScreen
www.asseenonscreen.com
Buy clothes and accessories worn by the stars. If you can get Jennifer Aniston's dress, Brad Pitt will surely follow.

The Celebrity Cafe
www.thecelebritycafe.com
Archive of interviews with a host of celebrities.

Stars Online
www.stars.com
'The official portal of the Stars Foundation' – news, gossip, fashion advice and more.

Children

Amazingmoms
www.amazingmoms.com   179

Balloons Online
www.balloonsonline.com.au   179

Bob the Builder
www.bobthebuilder.org   176

The Cake Whole
www.cakewhole.com.au   179

ChessKIDS Academy
www.chesskids.com   189

Cory's PaintBox
www.corypaints.com   179

Crayola
www.crayola.com   176

EntertainOz
www.entertainoz.com.au   179

Kidlink
www.kidlink.org   175

Kidnews.com
www.kidnews.com   175, 178

Kids Domain
www.kidsdomain.com   174, 175

The Party Games Ideas Resource Page
http://freespace.virgin.net/ken.tew/party/list.html   179

PeeDee Toys
http://store.yahoo.com/peedeetoys   179

The Playground
www.abc.net.au/children   176

Rainy Day Playhouse
www.pen-web.com/rainyday   187

Sydney's Child
www.sydneyschild.com.au   179

Tucows
www.tucows.com   175

UpToTen
www.uptoten.org   177

Yahooligans!
www.yahooligans.com   57, 71, 174

Zeeks
www.zeeks.com   174, 175

Cinema

The Internet Movie Database
www.imdb.com   165, 202, 224

Xtra
http://xtra.co.nz/out_and_about   224

Yahoo! Movies
http://au.movies.yahoo.com/movies   224

Classic Films
www.moderntimes.com
A site for fans of Hollywood's golden era. Style matters here – you are even told which fonts you should have on your computer to view the site!

Drew's Script-O-Rama
www.script-o-rama.com
The complete scripts of hundreds of Hollywood films and TV shows.

The Movie Quote Quiz
www.moviequotequiz.com
'You looking at me?' Test your knowledge of movie quotes, all with sound files. Answers too – but no cheating!

The Nitpickers Site
www.nitpickers.com
Cinema and TV mistakes, plot inconsistencies, technical glitches and continuity errors – and you can add any you spot!

ENTERTAINMENT

Oscar.com
www.oscar.com
The official Academy Awards site, with every sequin and trembling lip reproduced in glorious Technicolor.

Rotten Tomatoes
www.rottentomatoes.com
The 'Tomatometer' collates the reviews of hundreds of films and gives each movie a reading – from 'fresh' to 'rotten'.

ScreenSound Australia
www.screensound.gov.au
Explore Australia's moving image and sound recording collection.

Studio Creations
www.studiocreations.com
Follow the instructions to make your very own Star Wars stormtrooper costume.

Tribute to Humphrey Bogart
http://bogart-tribute.net
Discover what brand of cigarettes the great man smoked and relive your favourite moments with film and audio clips.

Dance

Australian Dance Network
www.australiandancenet.com.au
A wealth of information on the world of dance for students, parents and teachers.

DANZ
www.danz.org.nz
Terrific starting point for information on dance in New Zealand.

Gossip

E!Online
www.eonline.com
The stars! The scandals! The fashion faux pas!

The Hollywood Reporter
www.hollywoodreporter.com
Daily news from the heart of the multi-million dollar movie industry.

Star Magazine Online
www.starmagazine.com
Get the very latest film, music and television stories.

Listings

CitySearch Australia
www.citysearch.com.au   223

CitySearch Sydney
http://sydney.citysearch.com.au   222

Discoversydney
www.discoversydney.com.au   222

GrooveOn
www.grooveon.com.au   223

Re:Action
www.reaction.co.nz/nzmusic   223

Ticketek Australia
http://premier.ticketek.com.au   223, 224

Ticketek New Zealand
http://premier.ticketek.co.nz   223

Ticketmaster 7
www.ticketmaster7.com   223

Time Out
www.timeout.com   222

Xtra
http://xtra.co.nz   223

CultureFinder
www.culturefinder.com
American cultural and performing arts listings.

Event Locator
www.eventlocator.co.uk
Find a concert, class or festival anywhere in the UK.

New Zealand Arts Resources
http://url.co.nz/arts/nzarts.html
A resource site second to none – hundreds of New Zealand arts sites in categories such as craft, dance, music, festivals, photography, theatre.

Whatsonwhen
www.whatsonwhen.com
Search and buy tickets for every kind of festival or event almost anywhere in the world.

Music

The Australian Music Centre
www.amcoz.com.au   223

Australian Music Web Site
www.amws.com.au   223

Bandwave
www.bandwave.com   223

Centre for New Zealand Music
www.sounz.org.nz   223

Yahoo! Music
http://au.music.yahoo.com/music   223

Festival Finder
www.festivalfinder.com
Guide to more than 2500 music festivals in North America. You can choose between different types of music, including rock, classical, bluegrass and reggae.

Opera

New Zealand Opera
www.nzopera.com
*Find out what's on and what's coming up, or simply find out more about opera in general by clicking on **Education**. Consider yourself an opera buff? Take a look at the quiz to see how much you really know.*

Opera Magazine
www.opera.co.uk
News, reviews and a terrific links page to all things opera.

Sydney Opera House
www.soh.nsw.gov.au
Book tickets, learn about the building and even if you never manage to get there, you can take a virtual tour.

Radio

Anetstation
www.anetstation.com   153

Book Radio
www.bookradio.com   153

Live Radio in the Internet
www.live-radio.net   153

Median Strip
www.medianstrip.com   153

VirtualTuner
www.virtualtuner.com   153

Windows Media Player
www.microsoft.com/windows/windowsmedia/download   152

Theatre

The Big Idea
www.thebigidea.co.nz
On-line community site with information on all things creative – including theatre.

State of the Arts
www.stateart.com.au/sota/performing
Interesting performing arts section of this e-Zine dedicated to all things arty.

Web-cams

Cab-Cam
www.ny-taxi.com   146

BBC Webcams
www.bbc.co.uk/webcams
A portal site that takes you to hundreds of cameras around Britain – and the world.

WebCam World
http://webcamworld.com
Loads of Web-cam-related content, including links to Web-cams around the world.

F
Finance

Advice

Australian Stock Exchange
www.asx.com.au   199

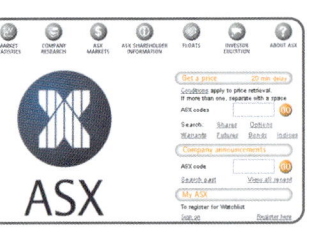

Business Review Weekly
www.brw.com.au   302

Moneymanager
www.moneymanager.com.au   214

New Zealand Stock Exchange
www.nzse.co.nz   199

Financial Planning Association of Australia
www.fpa.asn.au
Confirm that your financial planner is a FPA member or search for a company near you.

National Information Centre on Retirement Investments
www.nicri.org.au
Investment information to help people saving for retirement or facing redundancy make informed decisions.

Economics

E-commerce Times
www.ecommercetimes.com   298

ZDNet's eBusiness section
http://techupdate.zdnet.com   298

FOOD & DRINK

Briefing.com
www.briefing.com
Live analysis of the US stocks and shares markets.

Insurance

Australian Securities & Investments Commission
http://fido.asic.gov.au/fido/fido.nsf
An on-line practical guide to investments and insurance. Also, information on consumer rights and scam warnings.

NZ Ministry of Consumer Affairs
www.consumer-ministry.govt.nz/insuranc.html
Useful information about insurance, with links to other sites.

News

Moneymanager
www.moneymanager.com.au 214

Yahoo! Finance
http://au.finance.yahoo.com
Stock Exchange updates, plus breaking financial news and links to a multitude of sites, both local and international.

Pensions

Centrelink
www.centrelink.gov.au
Benefit payment advice from the Government.

Work and Income NZ
www.winz.govt.nz
Official information on retirement benefits.

Savings & loans

BankDirect
www.bankdirect.co.nz 214

Moneymanager
www.moneymanager.com.au 214

The National Bank of New Zealand
www.nationalbank.co.nz 214

Westpac
www.westpac.com.au 214, 215

Yahoo! Personal Finance
http://au.pfinance.yahoo.com 215

ANZ Banking Group
www.anz.com
or
www.anz.co.nz
On-line banking and loan applications, product information and useful investment tools.

Bank of New Zealand
www.bnz.co.nz
On-line banking services and handy calculators for life insurance, investment returns and buying a home.

BankWest
www.bankwest.com.au
Many on-line services, including links to traffic and surfing Web-cams around Perth!

Commonwealth Bank
www.commbank.com.au
On-line banking and links to other Commonwealth Bank companies.

Fintrack Financial Services
www.fintrack.com.au
Here's a way of avoiding the stress and hassle of finding a home loan – let this site do all the comparisons for you.

Infochoice
www.infochoice.com.au
Compare mortgage rates, savings rates, accounts, credit cards ... in fact, anything to do with banking.

Mortgage House of Australia
www.mortgagehouse.com.au
Check out how much you can borrow on-line.

National Australia Bank
www.national.com.au
The usual on-line services plus some useful life-event information guides.

St George Bank
www.stgeorge.com.au
Do your Internet banking or share trading, or apply on-line for a credit card or a loan.

Share trading

Australian Stock Exchange
www.asx.com.au 199

Brokerchoice
www.brokerchoice.com.au 199

E*Trade Australia
www.etradeaustralia.com.au 199

Fantasy Stock Market
www.fantasystockmarket.com 199

Lycos Finance
http://finance.lycos.com/home/maxinvest/game.asp 200

The Motley Fool
www.fool.com 199

New Zealand Stock Exchange
www.nzse.co.nz 199

NZIJ Stockbrokers
www.stockbroker.co.nz 199

Commonwealth Securities
www.comsec.com.au
On-line trading and a range of educational downloads.

Tax

Australian Taxation Index
http://commerce.flinders.edu.au/tax 196

Australian Taxation Office
www.ato.gov.au 196, 197

Digita TaxCentral
www.digita.com/taxcentral/home/breaktime/celebritytaxmeter 197

Institute of Chartered Accountants in Australia
www.icaa.org.au 196

MYOB Australia
www.myob.com.au 196

MYOB New Zealand
www.myob.co.nz 196

New Zealand Inland Revenue
www.ird.govt.nz 196

Quicken Australia / NZ
www.quicken.com.au 196
www.quicken.co.nz 196

Quicken Tax page
www.quicken.com.au/tax 197

Taxation Institute of New Zealand
www.tinz.co.nz 196

Yahoo! Tax Centre
http://au.pfinance.yahoo.com/tax 197

Food & Drink

Dieting

Dietsure
www.dietsure.com 131

Shape Up America!
www.shapeup.org 131, 132

Drink

The Australian Good Beer Directory
www.ecn.net.au/~dilbert/agbd.htm 223

National Wine Centre of Australia
www.wineaustralia.com.au 223

Realbeer Australia & New Zealand
http://realbeer.co.nz 223

Wine Online
www.finewineonline.co.nz 223

Aussie Pubs
www.aussiepubs.com.au
A listing of over 600 Australian hotels, bars and bistros, searchable by state.

Realbeer.com
www.realbeer.com
More than 150,000 Web pages about beer – try the Fun section and choose a toast to suit your beer drinking activities.

VinoSearch
www.vinosearch.com
Database of wine-related sites around the world.

Vintage Cellars
www.vintagecellars.com.au
Buy on-line from a huge range of wines, spirits and beers.

The Webtender
www.webtender.com
Bartender's companion, with recipes and histories of more cocktails than you ever knew existed – 'olle goop' anyone?

Wine Lovers' Page
www.wine-lovers-page.com
An amazing repository of information about wines worldwide.

321

FOOD & DRINK

Eating In

Australian Recipes – Kavenga Publishing
www.kavenga.com.au 237

Blue Gum Fine Foods
www.bluegumfinefoods.com 192

Cherikoff Rare Spices
www.bushtucker.com.au 237

The Cooks Kitchen
www.kitchenware.co.uk 237

The Cook's Thesaurus
www.foodsubs.com 237

Danes Gourmet Coffee
www.danes.com.au 192

Epicurious
www.epicurious.com 237

The Food Network
www.foodnetwork.com 237

Freedom Foods
www.freedomfoods.com.au 192

GreenGrocer
www.greengrocer.com.au 192

IEproduce
www.organicfresh.co.nz 194

The Kitchen Link
www.kitchenlink.com 237

Lakeland Limited
www.lakelandlimited.com 237

The Modern Maori Cookbook
www.culture.co.nz/recipes 237

Organic Grocer
www.theorganicgrocer.com.au 194

Seasoned Cooking
www.seasoned.com 237

Ucook.com
www.ucook.com 236

The Vegetarian Resource Group
www.vrg.org 237

Veggies Unite!
http://vegweb.com 237

Woolworths Australia
www.woolworths.com.au 192, 194, 195

Woolworths New Zealand
www.woolworths.co.nz 192

Family Food Zone
www.familyfoodzone.com
Nutrition for all the family, plus a database of simple recipes for children to cook.

Joyofbaking.com
www.joyofbaking.com
Apple tart, scones or tiramisu – bake your family a special treat.

RecipeXchange
www.recipexchange.com
A site where people share their best family recipes. Browse the recipes or post your own favourite.

Top Secret Recipes
www.topsecretrecipes.com
Kitchen versions of 'secret recipe' commercial foods, such as McDonald's Big Mac sauce.

Eating Out

De Groots Best Restaurants of Australia
www.bestrestaurants.com.au 223

Happy Cow
www.happycow.net 237

Menus.co.nz
www.menus.co.nz 223

VegDining
www.vegdining.com 237

H
Health

Alternative medicine

Australian Traditional-Medicine Society
www.atms.com.au
Look for a practitioner and locate information about a range of therapies.

New Zealand Charter Of Health Practitioners
www.healthcharter.org.nz
Search for complementary health practitioners throughout New Zealand by treatment type or region.

Diagnosis

The DrsReference Site
www.drsref.com.au 127

eMedical
www.emedical.com.au 126

Mayo Clinic
www.mayoclinic.com 126

MDAdvice
www.mdadvice.com 127

The Patient's Guide
www3.telus.net/me/patientsguide 127

Fitness

Active Australia
www.activeaustralia.org 131

Fitness New Zealand
www.fitnessnz.co.nz 132

Health & Fitness Tips
www.health-fitness-tips.com 131

JustMove
www.justmove.org 131

Oxygen
www.oxygen.com 131, 132

Shape Up America!
www.shapeup.org 131, 132

Ultrafit
www.ultrafit-ozegyms.com 132

New Zealand Sports Drug Agency
www.nzsda.co.nz
Information and resources relating to removing drugs from sport.

Information

BlackStump Medical & Health
www.blackstump.com.au/medical.htm 127

The DrsReference Site
www.drsref.com.au 127

HealthInsite
www.healthinsite.gov.au 127

New South Wales Health
www.search.nsw.gov.au/health.asp 127

New Zealand Health Information Service
www.nzhis.govt.nz/intranet/index.html 127

NHS Direct Online
www.nhsdirect.nhs.uk 127, 128

Silver Hammer Publishing
http://silverhammerpub.com 131

Arthritis Foundation of NSW
www.arthritisnsw.org.au
Loads of useful information about arthritis and how to deal with it.

Childbirth.org
www.childbirth.org
Find answers to your pregnancy and childbirth questions, or e-mail a question to a health professional.

The Consumer Health Information Centre
www.chic.org.uk
On-line advice service to help you understand, treat and avoid minor ailments, plus a useful link to finding the right treatment for your symptoms.

Everybody
www.everybody.co.nz
Easy-to-understand health information, and links to institutions and support groups.

Food and Drug Administration
www.fda.gov
US government site, useful for its fact sheets on food, dietary supplements and drugs.

HealthWorld Online
www.healthy.net
Advice, news and discussion on a range of subjects, such as nutrition and fitness.

Medicdirect
www.medicdirect.co.uk
Medical advice from UK healthcare professionals, plus an A–Z of diseases and a Virtual Body Tour.

myDr
www.mydr.com.au
Comprehensive information – from finding a GP or support group to medical definitions.

Quackwatch
www.quackwatch.com
A site run by an individual doctor exposing health scams and questionable medical treatments.

Institutions

World Health Organization
www.who.int 128

MedNets
www.mednets.net
Provides details of hospitals and medical practitioners throughout Australia.

Mental

Beyondblue
www.beyondblue.org.au
Australia's national depression-fighting initiative.

HISTORY

Mental Health Foundation of New Zealand.
www.mentalhealth.org.nz
Provides educational materials about mental health.

SANE Australia
www.sane.org
Loads of information to help anyone who is affected by mental illness.

Nutrition

Dietsure
www.dietsure.com   131

Shape Up America!
www.shapeup.org   131, 132

Ask the Dietitian
www.dietitian.com
Diet and nutrition questions answered, under topic headings from Alcohol to Zinc.

Food Standards Australia New Zealand
www.foodstandards.gov.au
Information from the agency that protects our health by monitoring the food supply – 'from paddock to plate'.

Nutrition Australia
www.nutritionaustralia.org
Nutrition information based on scientific fact.

Pharmacies

ePharmacy
www.epharmacy.com.au
Shop on-line for general medicines, health products, medical aids and personal care and beauty products.

HomePharmacy.com.au
www.homepharmacy.com.au
Loads of health-related information, 24-hour ordering and competitively priced medicines and prescriptions.

Online pharmacy
www.onlinepharmacy.co.nz
A pharmacy dispensing competitively priced products.

OnLine Pharmacy.com.au
www.onlinepharmacy.com.au
Secure on-line shopping, prescriptions filled and useful health information.

Pharmaceutical Benefits Scheme
www.health.gov.au/pbs
Consumer information about the scheme.

Pharmacy Express
www.pharmacyexpress.co.nz
On-line since 1997, this site dispenses prescriptions as well as offering an extensive range of pharmacy, beauty, vitamin and healthcare products.

History
Ancient

About.com – Ancient/Classical History
http://ancienthistory.about.com
Articles and links relating to the ancient world and notable figures, such as Homer and Alexander the Great.

Celtic Art and Cultures
www.unc.edu/courses/art111/celtic
Illustrated introduction to the design and origin of Celtic art and artefacts.

De Imperatoribus Romanis
www.roman-emperors.org
Biographies of every Roman emperor, with historical contexts, an atlas and Roman history links.

Exploring Ancient World Cultures
http://eawc.evansville.edu
Fascinating account of eight ancient cultures and literary traditions.

Australia & New Zealand

Convict Creations
www.convictcreations.com
Looks at – and celebrates – the convict contribution to the foundation of Australia.

Dictionary of New Zealand Biography
www.dnzb.govt.nz
Discover which worthy New Zealander was 'born on this day' – and heaps more about them – at this user-friendly site.

National Centre for Australian Studies
www.arts.monash.edu.au/ncas
Useful resources to help with the study of Australian history. The Australian Places project is fun to browse.

NZHistory.net.nz
www.nzhistory.net.nz
This site should be your first port of call when you search for information about the history of New Zealand.

Papers Past
http://paperspast.natlib.govt.nz
Images of over 400,000 pages from 25 19th-century New Zealand newspapers and periodicals.

Treasures of the State Library of Victoria
www.statelibrary.vic.gov.au/slv/exhibitions/treasures
Loads of information about, and images of, the library's treasures – including Ned Kelly's 'manifesto' and armour.

The Treaty of Waitangi
www.govt.nz/aboutnz/treaty.php3
Translations and images of this founding document of the nation of New Zealand.

Visit Gallipoli
www.anzacsite.gov.au
All about the ANZAC landing at Gallipoli.

General

BBCi History
www.bbc.co.uk/history
Visit London in the 1500s or find yourself in a World War I trench via detailed 3D models.

Britannia – British History
http://britannia.com/history
Articles on every aspect of British history, from the stories of King Arthur to the design of Sussex churches.

History Today
www.historytoday.com
On-line edition of the leading history magazine, with extra news stories and features.

Medieval & Renaissance

The Crusades
http://crusades.boisestate.edu/contents.html
The stories of each of the seven Crusades retold.

The Domesday Book
www.domesdaybook.co.uk
Find out what life was like in 11th-century England.

Life in a Medieval Castle
www.castlewales.com/life.html
A colourful description of daily life inside a medieval castle.

Palladio's Italian Villas
www.boglewood.com/palladio
Analysis of the work of architect Andrea Palladio, with illustrations and biography.

The Vikings
http://viking.no/e
Introduction to the Vikings with ideas for school projects.

Modern

AP 20th Century Timeline
http://wire.ap.org/APpackages/20thcentury/timeline.html
Stories from every year of the 20th century, in the words and pictures of the Associated Press.

Australians at War
www.awm.gov.au/atwar
Information from the Australian War Memorial in Canberra.

BBCi World War II
www.bbc.co.uk/history/war/wwtwo
Discover the stories behind key moments of World War II through news clips and personal accounts from men and women who were there.

HISTORY

Internet Modern History Sourcebook
www.fordham.edu/halsall/mod/modsbook.html
From the discovery of America to today's pop culture – aimed at US students and teachers.

Pre-history

The Cave of Lascaux
www.culture.fr/culture/arcnat/lascaux/fr
Virtual tour of the famous palaeolithic rock paintings of Lascaux in France.

Neanderthals: A Cyber Perspective
http://sapphire.indstate.edu/~ramanank
Could Neanderthals converse and are their art objects the earliest ever made? Plenty of questions raised and discussed.

Stone Pages
www.stonepages.com
A guide to European megaliths, including British sites such as Stonehenge and Avebury.

World

Any day in history
www.anydayinhistory.com
Enter a day and month to see who was born or died on that day in history, and what major events happened.

HistoryWiz
www.historywiz.com
Photographs and images tell of significant moments in history, from ancient civilisations to current affairs.

HistoryWorld
www.historyworld.net
Choose an era and a topic to explore – such as religion in the 19th century – to see a timeline of relevant events.

Home & Garden
Design & furnishing

DIY-Online
www.diy-online.co.nz 184

The Kitchen Specialists Association
www.ksa.co.uk 184

KitchenWeb
www.kitchenweb.com 184

Ninemsn Our House
http://lifestyle.ninemsn.com.au/ourhouse 185

Freedom Furniture
www.freedom.com.au
or
www.freedomfurniture.co.nz
Get free advice on designing or renovating your home, or just browse for some great ideas on decorating or entertaining.

Ikea
www.ikea.com
Room-by-room design guide, full list of products and contact details of your nearest store.

Interior Internet
www.interiorinternet.com
Stylish furniture site. Move each of your chosen items to a mood board to see the overall effect.

DIY

DIY-Online
www.diy-online.co.nz 184

Mitre 10
www.mitre10.com.au 184

This to That
www.thistothat.com 183

Bunnings
www.bunnings.com.au
Find store locations and check out the latest bargains.

Diyfixit
www.diyfixit.co.uk
Browse under room type or click on a task – such as wallpapering – for detailed step-by-step instructions.

DoItYourself.com
www.doityourself.com
American site covering home improvements, building projects, appliance repair and car maintenance.

The Family Handyman
www.familyhandyman.com
The searchable Home Improvements Library has a wealth of DIY projects from this US magazine to help you maintain your home.

The Natural Handyman
www.naturalhandyman.com
Select a home repair project from the menu to get instant expert advice.

PlaceMakers
www.placemakers.co.nz
Download one of the many 'How To' booklets for step-by-step project information. The site claims you can't go wrong with these instructions.

Gardening

Association of Societies for Growing Australian Plants
http://farrer.riv.csu.edu.au/ASGAP 184

Bestgardening
www.bestgardening.co.nz 184

Fredshed
www.fredshed.co.uk 184

GardensOnLine
www.gardensonline.com.au 184

Garden UK
www.garden-uk.org.uk 184

Savewater
www.savewater.com.au 185

Ground Force
http://ground-force.com.au
Great ideas about all aspects of gardening from the team of this TV show.

Kidsgardening
www.kidsgardening.com
Inspire children to learn about gardening by planning and designing their own gardens.

Plants for a Future
www.scs.leeds.ac.uk/pfaf
Directory of over 7000 'useful' plants – all edible or with medicinal or other uses.

The Telegarden
http://telegarden.aec.at
A 'tele-robotic installation' that allows Web users to view, water and monitor a living garden.

3D Garden Composer
www.gardencomposer.com.au
A site that lets you create and view a virtual garden at different times of the year.

Yates
http://yates.com.au
or
http://yates.co.nz
Problem solver, product guide, monthly gardening suggestions – great tips for your garden.

House buying

eChoice
www.echoice.com.au 205

E-Loan
www.eloan.co.nz 204

Loansurf
www.loansurf.co.nz 205

Moneymanager
www.moneymanager.com.au 214

Mortgage Australia
www.mortgageaustralia.com.au 205

Property Value
www.propertyvalue.com.au 205

QV – Quotable Value New Zealand
www.quotable.co.nz 205

Right Loan
www.RightLoan.com.au 204

Your Mortgage
www.yourmortgage.com.au 205

Domain.com.au
www.domain.com.au
Properties to buy, sell or rent, searchable by state, as well as house-related advice.

Propertystuff
www.propertystuff.co.nz
Register with Dream Home Alert and receive e-mails if your perfect home comes up for sale.

Humour
Cartoons

Aardman Animations
www.aardman.com
Clips, news, a fascinating archive – even a virtual tour of the offices – from the makers of Wallace and Gromit, Morph and The Chicken Run.

INTERNET

Doonesbury Electronic Townhall
www.doonesbury.com
Today's strip, an archive going back 30 years and complete character biographies.

Looney Tunes
http://looneytunes.warnerbros.co.uk
Official site, with new cartoons, games, history and advice on how to draw the characters.

South Park Studios
www.southparkstudios.com
Find out why Kenny always dies and help Cartman defeat Evil Cartman.

Comedians & shows

MontyPython.net
www.montypython.net
Huge Python archive, with more than 1000 sound files and 500 complete scripts.

New Zealand Comedy Guild
www.nzcomedyguild.org.nz
News, information and links to NZ comedians with Web sites.

Petercook.net
www.petercook.net
Tribute to the life and comedy of the infamous Peter Cook.

Roll on Floor Laughing
www.geocities.com/fiona_rohana
Portal to profiles and articles on comedians and comedy shows, mostly in Australia.

Jokes & satire

Comedy Zone
www.comedy-zone.net
Jokes, quotes, trivia, TV comedy and links.

Engrish
www.engrish.com
Smile-raising images of flawed Japanese English.

Humor Database
www.humordatabase.com
Vote for the funniest joke or cheer up a friend with a comedy card.

Joke Post!
www.jokepost.com
Post your favourite jokes, select a funny screensaver or browse the silly pictures.

The Onion
www.theonion.com
Oddball, satirical takes on the latest news stories in the USA – some serious, some strange.

Private Eye
www.private-eye.co.uk
Laugh at jokes and cartoons from the current issue of this witty UK magazine.

Internet
Advice

Internet Society
www.isoc.org/internet   12

World Wide Web Consortium
www.w3.org   12

CNET Help
www.help.com
Find information on hardware, software and numerous Internet-related issues.

HowStuffWorks
www.howstuffworks.com
Find out how absolutely everything works at this site – car engines, mobile phones, the Internet and more.

Broadband

Blast Surf
www.blastsurf.com   89

Ihug Ultra
www.ihug.co.nz   89

Telstra BigPond Broadband
www.bigpond.com/broadband   89

TelstraClear
www.telstraclear.co.nz   89

Chatrooms & communication

Audio-tips
www.audio-tips.com   94

Chatter's Jargon Dictionary
www.stevesgrossman.com   105

The Directory
www.thedirectory.org   100

EZBoard
www.ezboard.com   100

Google Groups
http://groups.google.com   72, 97

Internet Relay Chat IRC
www.irchelp.org   169

Jumbo!
www.jumbo.com   97

mIRC
www.mirc.com   104

The Net: User Guidelines and Netiquette
www.fau.edu/netiquette/net   105

100hot.com
www.100hot.com/chat   170

PalTalk
www.paltalk.com   95

PhoneFree
www.phonefree.com   95

Topica
www.topica.com   170

UseNetServer
www.usenetserver.com   99

Yahoo!
http://au.yahoo.com   101

Yahoo! Chat
http://au.chat.yahoo.com   94, 103

Yahoo! Groups
http://au.groups.yahoo.com   97

MedChat
http://community.medchat.com/commun_v3/scripts/directory.pl
Message boards and chatrooms on a range of health issues.

NewzBot
www.newzbot.com
Database of free public access newsgroup servers worldwide.

Internet Service Providers

Australian ISP List
www.cynosure.com.au/isp   20

The List of ISPs
http://thelist.internet.com   21

NetGuideWeb Australia
www.netguide.com.au/useful_stuff/isp_watch   20

NetGuideWeb New Zealand
www.netguide.co.nz/isp_directory   20

OzEmail
http://au.ozemail.yahoo.com/home   20

Quik Internet
www.quik.co.nz   20

WebWombat
www.webwombat.com.au/magazines/listings/computingau.htm   21

Wired Kiwis Web
www.wiredkiwis.co.nz/isps   20

News

CNET News.com
http://news.com.com
Portal from CNET, covering personal computing and hi-tech business information.

Internetnews.com
www.internetnews.com
The latest technology and Internet business stories, updated daily.

The Standard
www.thestandard.com
On-line edition of the leading Internet business weekly.

Search engines

About.com
www.about.com   146, 147

AltaVista
http://au.altavista.com   65, 66, 67, 68, 72

AOL Kids Search
www.aol.com.au/site/aol/kids/kidsearch   71

AOL Search
http://search.aol.com   66

Ask Jeeves
www.ask.com   66

Ask Jeeves Kids
www.ajkids.com   71, 137, 139

Babel Fish
http://babelfish.altavista.com   81

CitySearch
www.citysearch.com.au   70

ExtSearch
http://extsearch.com   49

Google
www.google.com   65, 66, 72

HotBot
http://hotbot.lycos.com   66, 129

KidsClick!
http://kidsclick.org   71

Looksmart Australia
www.looksmart.com.au   65, 66, 71, 137

Looksmart New Zealand
www.looksmart.co.nz   137

INTERNET

Lycos
www.lycos.com 66, 71, 75
MetaCrawler
www.metacrawler.com 114
Meta Email Search Agent MESA
http://mesa.rrzn.uni-hannover.de 73
My Yahoo!
http://au.my.yahoo.com 29
Netscape Search
http://search.netscape.com 65
OptusNet
http://dial.optusnet.com.au 73
QbSearch
www.qbsearch.com 70
Telstra
http://telstra.com 66
Webcrawler
www.webcrawler.com 66
Yahoo!
http://au.yahoo.com 65, 66, 71
Yahooligans!
www.yahooligans.com 57, 71, 174

ANZwers
www.answers.com.au
A useful site if you want to search for particularly Aussie or Kiwi subjects.

GOeureka
www.goeureka.com.au
This search engine favours Australian sites.

Search Engine Watch
www.searchenginewatch.com
Searching tips and help on registering your site with all the major search engines.

Search Guide Australia
www.searchguide.com.au
An index of over 100 Australian search engines. Browse by the categories listed, or use the site's search tool.

Search66
www.search66.com
This meta search engine – one that checks lots of search engines at the same time – lists its results according to their relevance to your search.

SiQit.com
www.siqit.com
Enter your search terms to use five search engines or directories at once.

Spyonit
www.spyonit.com
Enter your preferences and the site will monitor the Internet and alert you whenever a new reference is made to your topic of interest.

Virtual Sites
www.virtualfreesites.com/search.html
Over 1000 specialised search engines in 50 categories to help find what you're looking for.

Security

Australian Competition and Consumer Commission
www.accc.gov.au/ecomm/access1b.htm 55
CyberPatrol
www.cyberpatrol.com 56
CYBERsitter
www.cybersitter.com 56, 57
Econsumer
www.econsumer.gov 55
eTick
www.etick.com 55
Internet Watcher
www.internetwatcher.com 57
Net Nanny
www.netnanny.com 56, 98
TRUSTe
www.truste.com 55
VeriSign
www.verisign.com 55
Cybersmart Kids Online
www.cybersmartkids.com.au
Get the lowdown on safe and secure net surfing – for kids and parents.

PrivacyX
www.privacyx.com
Free encrypted anonymous e-mail service.

Web design

ABC Giant
www.abcgiant.com 251
About.com – Web Design
http://webdesign.about.com 253
Adobe Photoshop
www.adobe.com/products/tryadobe 265
AltaVista
http://au.altavista.com 306
BigNoseBird
www.bignosebird.com 253
CNET Download
http://download.com.com 252, 296
CNET – Spotlight on Production Tools
http://builder.cnet.com/webbuilding/pages/Authoring/ProdTools 295
Evrsoft 1stPage 2000
www.evrsoft.com 295
Flash Kit
www.flashkit.com/movies 251
Free Buttons.com
www.freebuttons.com 251, 274
Freepolls
www.freepolls.com 252
FreeWebspace.net
www.freewebspace.net 289
Ineedhits.com
www.ineedhits.com 307
Jasc Paint Shop Pro
www.jasc.com/products/psp 265, 267
Macromedia ColdFusion MX
www.macromedia.com/software/coldfusion 297
Macromedia Dreamweaver
www.macromedia.com 295
Macromedia Flash MX
www.macromedia.com/software/flash 297
Microsoft Download Center
www.microsoft.com/downloads 146
Microsoft FrontPage
www.microsoft.com/frontpage 295
Microsoft Submit It!
www.submit-it.com 307
NCSA Beginner's Guide to HTML
http://archive.ncsa.uiuc.edu/General/Internet/WWW 294
Neovisioni
www.neovisioni.com 147
Netscape Composer
http://browsers.netscape.com 295
Partners in Rhyme
www.partnersinrhyme.com 277
Perl
www.activestate.com/Products/ActivePerl 297
PHP
www.php.net 297
QuickTime
www.apple.com/quicktime 147

Reallybig.com
www.reallybig.com 259
RealNetworks Helix Producer
www.realnetworks.com/products/producer 279
Sausage HotDog PageWiz
www.sausagetools.com 295
Sign my Guestbook
www.signmyguestbook.com 252
SiteCritique
www.sitecritique.net 253
Sounddogs.com
www.sounddogs.com 277
Sound Effects
www.stonewashed.net/sfx.html 277
Thesaurus.com
www.thesaurus.com 309
Tripod
www.tripod.lycos.com 289, 297
Ultimate Sound & Music Archive
www.ultimatesoundarchive.com 277
WEBalley
www.weballey.net 311
WebCounter
www.digits.com 252
Webmonkey
http://hotwired.lycos.com/webmonkey 251, 253, 296, 297
Web Pages That Suck
www.webpagesthatsuck.com 253
Website Awards
http://websiteawards.xe.net 255
World Crossing
www.worldcrossing.com 252
World Wide Web Test Pattern
www.uark.edu/~wrg 146
Yahoo! GeoCities
http://au.geocities.yahoo.com 252, 288, 289

LEISURE & HOBBIES

Academy of Web Specialists
www.academywebspecialists.com
Make your site stand out from the crowd with the help of this on-line course.

MyComputer.com
www.mycomputer.com
Company that monitors site traffic to help you to judge the success of your Web site.

PageResource.com
www.pageresource.com
Tutorials, graphics, tools and articles on creating your own Web pages.

2Cool Animations
www.gifanimations.com
20,000 animations, ClipArt items and backgrounds.

Ulead GIF Animator
www.ulead.com/ga/runme.htm
Downloadable software for creating animations.

Web design – business

Bigstep
www.bigstep.com   303

Bizhosting
www.bizhosting.com   303

Business Review Weekly
www.brw.com.au   302

FreeMerchant
www.freemerchant.com   303, 304

InternetMall
www.internetmall.com   303

Web hosting

FortuneCity
www.fortunecity.com   289

Host Search
www.hostsearch.com   249

HostOne
www.host1.com.au
A site offering a range of web,

e-mail and domain name hosting services.

Net-Central
www.net-central.com.au
A selection of hosting packages to choose from – and there is a Web site design service too.

Website Hosting Australia
http://websitehostingaustralia.com
Ready-made Web sites and hosting plans at various prices so you can get your own Internet presence.

L
Leisure & Hobbies
Collectibles

Auction Watch
www.auctionwatch.com   165

Celebrity Merchandise
www.celebritymerch.com   165

Startifacts
www.startifacts.com   165

Collectiques
www.collectiques.co.uk
Directory of Web sites for collectors of almost anything.

Starsigned
www.starsigned.com
Locate and buy the autographs of famous actors, politicians, musicians and models.

Genealogy

Aboriginal Genealogy & History Sources & References
www.standard.net.au/~jwilliams/native.htm   162

Ages!
www.daubnet.com/english.html   161

Archives New Zealand
www.archives.govt.nz/holdings/military_service.html   162

Australian Family Tree Connections Magazine
www.aftc.com.au   160

Australian Institute of Aboriginal and Torres Strait Studies
www.aiatsis.gov.au   162

Australian War Memorial Research & Family History
www.awm.gov.au/research   162

Commonwealth War Graves Commission
www.cwgc.org   162

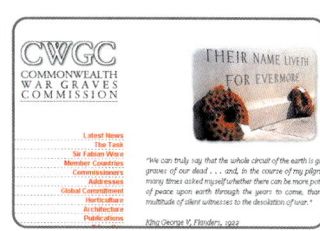

Cyndi's List
www.cyndislist.com   160, 161, 163

Family Origins
www.familyorigins.com   159

Family Search
www.familysearch.org   163

Family Tree Maker
www.genealogy.com   159

Genealogical Software Report Card
www.mumford.ca/reportcard   159

Genealogy.com
www.genealogy.com   163

Genealogy for Windows
www.deltadrive.co.uk   159

GENUKI
www.genuki.org.uk   160

Louis Kessler's Genealogical Program Links
www.lkessler.com/gplinks.shtml   160

Maori Genealogy
www.maaori.com/whakapapa   162

Maori Whakapapa Research
www.geocities.com/Heartland/Park/7572/mresear.htm   162

Mother Hubbard's Cupboard
www.rootsweb.com/~genclass   163

National Library of Australia Family History & Genealogy
www.nla.gov.au/oz/genelist.html   160

National Library of New Zealand Family History Collection
www.natlib.govt.nz/en/collections/general/family.html   160

New Zealand and the Commonwealth War Graves Commission
www.mch.govt.nz/History/HPU/CWGC.htm   162

New Zealand Society of Genealogists
www.genealogy.org.nz   159

Office of the Australian War Graves
www.dva.gov.au/commem/oawg/wargr.htm   162

Society of Australian Genealogists
www.sag.org.au   159

State Library of NSW Family History Service
www.slnsw.gov.au/family   160

State Library of Victoria Genealogy Centre
www.statelibrary.vic.gov.au/slv/genealogy   160

Genealogy.com
http://genforum.genealogy.com
Site with surname search and tutorials on how to get started.

Genealogy Online's chatroom
http://chat.genealogy.org
Chat to other family researchers for tried and tested tips.

PeopleSite
www.peoplesite.com
Use the message boards to make contact with other people researching your surname.

RootsWeb
www.rootsweb.com
One of the oldest genealogy sites on the Web, packed with tips and worldwide links.

Museums

International Council of Museums
www.icom.org/vlmp/world.html   173

The Louvre
www.louvre.fr   146

Museum of Modern Art, New York
www.moma.org   146

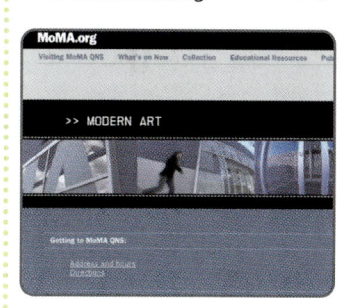

Museum of New Zealand
www.tepapa.govt.nz   137

National Museum of Australia
www.nma.gov.au   137

US National Museum of Natural History
www.mnh.si.edu   137

Western Australian Maritime Museum
www.mm.wa.gov.au   231

Australian Museums & Galleries Online
http://amol.org.au
An on-line guide to museums, their collections and travelling exhibitions in Australia.

327

LEISURE & HOBBIES

Australian National Maritime Museum
www.anmm.gov.au
Take a virtual tour of the museum or its floating fleet – and dream of the high seas.

The British Museum
www.thebritishmuseum.ac.uk
A taste of the museum's exhibits with advice on conducting your own research.

Kunsthistorisches Museum Wien
www.khm.at
An amazing site, giving on-line access to one of the world's great museums of art and antiquities.

MuseumStuff
www.museumstuff.com
Thousands of links to museums around the world, plus a 'virtual exhibit' section featuring interactive exhibits.

New Zealand Museums On Line
www.nzmuseums.co.nz
Search by region, collection theme or name.

Rijksmuseum Amsterdam
www.rijksmuseum.nl
Take the virtual tour through some of the 150 rooms of Amsterdam's premier museum – and gain insight into some fabulous artwork.

Science Museum, London
www.sciencemuseum.org.uk
Tour the Apollo 10 command module, a dinosaur gallery, or a range of interactive exhibits.

Scienceworks Museum
http://scienceworks.museum.vic.gov.au
The 'Activities at Home' section tells you how to use simple household materials to create marvellous experiments.

Smithsonian Institution
www.si.edu
Be one of the 19 million visitors to the on-line site of America's attic. There is so much to explore and learn.

Outdoor pursuits

The Adventure Travel Company
www.adventure-travel.com.au   226

Bushwalking in Australia
www.bushwalking.org.au   226

Campsites in Europe
www.interhike.com   226

eNZed
www.enzed.com/tramp.html   226

Guide to Australia's National Parks
www.atn.com.au/parks   226

New Zealand Department of Conservation
www.doc.govt.nz   226, 227

Outdoor Store
http://outdoorstore.co.nz   226

Paddy Pallin
www.paddypallin.com.au   226

Remote Outback Cycle Tours
www.cycletours.com.au   227

Ultimate Hikes
www.ultimatehikes.co.nz   227

Australian Camping Association
www.auscamps.asn.au
Directory of residential campsites that are available for groups and families – and some useful links too.

Royal Australian Navy
www.navy.gov.au
Always dreamt of going to sea? Take a virtual tour of the ships of the Australian Navy.

Youth Hostel Association
www.yha.org.au
or
www.yha.org.nz
Find budget accommodation, get travel info or take out YHA membership on-line – you don't have to be a youth to join!

Photography

American Museum of Photography
www.photographymuseum.com
On-line exhibition, specialising in the early experimental years of photography.

Behind the Viewfinder
www.digitalstoryteller.com/YITL
Illustrated diaries from 11 photojournalists give you an insight into their work.

Life Magazine
www.life.com/Life
The most famous picture magazine of all, with a must-see archive of Classic Pictures.

National Museum of Photography, Film & Television
www.nmsi.ac.uk/nmpft
Charting the history of photographic technology from the early experiments of Sir John Herschel to the modern-day IMAX 3D system.

Lifestyle
Beauty & fashion

BeautyLink
www.beautylink.com
Make-up tips from the experts, and how to create that movie star look.

Beautynet.com
www.beautynet.com
Advice on skin care, hair care, tanning and many other beauty issues. Includes a lively bulletin board where you can share advice and get feedback.

Fashion Net
www.fashion.net
Includes designer biographies and career opportunities.

firstVIEW
www.firstview.com
Photos and videos of the top designer collections around the world.

Smallflower
www.smallflower.com
US-based natural beauty and cosmetics shopping site, worth visiting for information on natural products.

Style.com
www.style.com
Packed site from Vogue and W magazines, with the latest must-have fashion trends.

Vogue
www.vogue.com.au
Read the latest beauty advice or join the chatroom to exchange views with other members.

Worldwide Beauty Store
www.worldwidebeautystore.com
Huge site, with more than 25,000 brand name cosmetics, hair and beauty products.

Weddings

Bridal Gift Registry
www.bridalgiftregistry.co.nz   242

i-do
www.i-do.com.au   241, 242

New Zealand Weddings
www.newzealandweddings.co.nz   242

New Zealand Wedding Services
www.nzweddingservices.co.nz   242

Underwater Weddings
www.underwaterweddings.com   242

Wedding Australia
www.ozlines.com.au/wedd.htm   241

Wedding Central
www.weddingcentral.com.au   242

The Wedding Gift Company
www.weddinggift.com.au   242

Weddings Away
www.weddingsaway.com.au   242

Wedding Wishes
www.weddingwishes.com.au   242, 243

Your Local Wedding Guide
www.weddingguide.com.au   242

Your Wedding Plan
www.yourweddingplan.com.au   242

UltimateWedding.com
www.ultimatewedding.com
Planning checklists, music, poetry and etiquette advice.

MOTORING

Vegas.com Weddings
www.vegas.com/weddings
Elvis and Priscilla or Antony and Cleopatra? Book your Las Vegas wedding here.

World Weddings
www.world-weddings.net
The site that allows you to plan and book a wedding in any of a number of exotic locations around the world.

M Motoring
Automobiles

Australian Automobile Association
www.aaa.asn.au
Petrol price monitoring, crash test results, driver surveys and touring information – as well as links to local (NRMA, RACV, etc.) and international motoring organisations.

BumpStop
www.BumpStop.com
Lively site for lowriders, custom cars and classic trucks.

Howsafeisyourcar.com.au
www.howsafeisyourcar.com.au
Find out how your car or 4WD rates for safety. The site claims to have figures for 80 per cent of cars on Australian roads.

New Zealand Automobile Association
www.nzaa.co.nz
Buying advice, car valuations and insurance quotes, highway reports and touring information for the whole country.

Yahoo! Automotive
http://au.dir.yahoo.com/recreation/automotive
A good place to start for car enthusiasts or anyone looking for parts and maintenance tips.

Brands

BMW
www.bmw.com.au
or
www.bmw.co.nz
Compare models, select and configure your ideal car and locate a dealership.

Ferrari World
www.ferrari.com
Cars, games, photographs, an on-line shop, screensavers, Grand Prix information – pure heaven for the Ferrari fanatic.

Ford
www.ford.com.au
or
www.ford.co.nz
Take a virtual tour of the latest model, locate a dealer, arrange a test drive – or download a screensaver or wallpaper for your computer.

Holden
www.holden.com.au
or
www.holden.co.nz
Current model information, history, local dealer locator and special offers.

Lamborghini
www.lamborghini.com
Dream on … get close to the Lamborghini driving experience with these stylish graphics and exciting sounds.

Mini
www.mini.com.au
or
www.mini.co.nz
Good graphics, games, photos and information about the new-generation Minis and their classic forebears.

Buying & selling

Autotrader
www.autotrader.com.au/selling.asp 181

Car.co.nz
www.car.co.nz 181

Car Sales
www.carsales.com.au 182

Drive.com
www.drive.com.au 181

Glass's Guide
www.glassguide.com.au 181

New Zealand Companies Office
www.companies.govt.nz 181

Personal Property Securities Register
www.ppsr.govt.nz 181

The Red Book
www.redbook.com.au 181

Register of Encumbered Vehicles
www.revs.nsw.gov.au 181

Yahoo! Cars
http://au.cars.yahoo.com/au/car 181

Collectors Car Auction
www.collectorscarauction.com
Bid on-line for collectible cars and motorbikes – in Australia, the USA and UK.

eBay Cars, Bikes and Boats
http://pages.ebay.com.au/motors-index.html
On-line auctions of all things motoring – from vehicles to replacement parts to manuals, badges and number plates.

Trade Me
www.trademe.co.nz
A large selection of vehicles for sale – and listing for an auction sale is free.

Classic

MG in New Zealand
www.mgcarclub.org.nz 182

1 in a Million Cars
www.1inamillion.com
American site with classic US and foreign cars for sale. If you're not in the US, you can still look – and drool.

Scions of Lucas
www.team.net/sol
Entertaining site devoted to classic British cars, parts, maintenance and clubs.

Vanishing Point Car
www.vanishingpointcar.com
Enthusiasts' homepage about the 1970 Dodge Challenger, as featured in the cult car chase film Vanishing Point.

Importing

Australiatrade
www.australiatrade.com.au/Shipping/Import/Vehicles/Customs.htm
Essential information about importing a vehicle into Australia.

Land Transport Safety Authority
www.ltsa.govt.nz/vehicle_ownership/import.html
Invaluable information about bringing a car into New Zealand

Maintenance

Car Adviser
http://caradviser.cars.com 181

Car Care Clinic
www.carcareclinic.com 181

About.com – Auto Repair
http://autorepair.about.com
Think you could be a professional mechanic? Try out the quiz and see if you pass.

eHow
www.ehow.com
Under 'Automotive' there are guides to all the essential tasks of car care.

Under the Hood
http://library.thinkquest.org/19199
Troubleshooting diagnosis tool, repair guides and lessons in the basics of motor mechanics.

Motorcycles

BikePoint
http://bikepoint.ninemsn.com.au
Read about the latest bike tests – and loads of other bike-related stuff too.

BikeWeb
www.bikeweb.com
Motorcycle portal with discussion boards on topics such as new bike designs.

Ducati
www.ducati.com
Visit the on-line museum for a pictorial history of this classic marque.

MUSIC

Harley-Davidson
www.harley-davidson.com
Products, dealers, a company history and information about tours – the perfect way to experience a H-D.

Honda
www.hondampe.com.au
Join the Honda Rider's Club to stay up to date with the latest news and events, receive discounts and other benefits.

MicaPeak
www.micapeak.com
A must-view site for motorcycle enthusiasts.

Triumph Motorcycles
www.triumph.co.uk
Details of every model, a dealer directory, maintenance advice, accessories and clothing.

Yamaha
www.yamaha-motor.com.au
Send in your suggestions and you may be contributing to the next generation of Yamaha motorcycles.

Music
Blues

Electric Blues
www.electricblues.com 28

Big Road Blues
www.bigroadblues.com
Blues portal with Internet radio links and slide guitar lessons.

Blue Flame Cafe
www.blueflamecafe.com
Interactive biographical encyclopedia of the greats of blues, with sound clips.

Classical

The Australian Music Centre
www.amcoz.com.au 223

Centre for New Zealand Music
www.sounz.org.nz 223

ABC Classic FM
www.abc.net.au/classic
Event listings, program details, archive information and you can listen on-line to interviews, performances and features.

Andante
www.andante.com
Record company site and portal. News, profiles, concert calendar, reference section and exclusive Web-casts.

Classical Music UK
www.classicalmusic.co.uk
Site for classical musicians as well as fans. You can find out about job vacancies and buy scores on-line.

Gramophone
www.gramophone.co.uk
News, features and interviews and – this is the best bit – a searchable archive of classical music CD reviews.

OrchestraNet
www.orchestranet.co.uk
Gateway to orchestras, with Web-casts, scores, CDs and MP3 music files.

Country

Australian Country On-Line
www.countrymusic.asn.au
Everything you need to know about country music in Australia – with a really comprehensive links page too.

CMT
www.cmt.com
Recording and concert news, artist profiles, Internet radio, MP3 and video files.

The Country Music Search Engine
http://country-music-club.com
A search engine and a directory with hundreds of country music links arranged by categories.

Country Western Song Machine
www.outofservice.com/country
Site containing computer-generated country-and-western song lyrics. Opening lines include "I met her at a truck stop wrestlin' gators"!

IFCO
www.ifco.org
Web site of the International Fan Club Organization. Has links to over 300 country artists.

New Zealand Country Music Machine
www.nzcountrymusic.org.nz
Comprehensive event listings, news and an address list to help you find your nearest country music club.

Downloads

Partners in Rhyme
www.partnersinrhyme.com 277

Real.com
www.real.com 119
www.real.com.au 150

Sounddogs.com
www.sounddogs.com 277

Sound Effects
www.stonewashed.net/sfx.html 277

Ultimate Sound & Music Archive
www.ultimatesoundarchive.com 277

Folk

Celtic Music NZ
www.celticmusic.co.nz
Interested in Celtic music? Visit this site for NZ information and resources.

Fol-de-rol
www.piper-kj.demon.co.uk
English, Irish, Scottish and Welsh folk music recordings, performers and national events.

Folk & Acoustic Music Exchange
www.acousticmusic.com/fame/famehome.htm
Reviews of new releases in contemporary and traditional folk, Celtic and bluegrass.

Jazz

A Passion for Jazz!
www.apassion4jazz.net
History and commentary, MIDI files, music theory and the Virtual Piano Chord tutor for budding musicians.

Blue Note Records
www.bluenote.com
Listen to tracks, check out new releases, search for a special pressing and read about featured artists on this stylish site – as good looking as the company's famous album covers.

Jazze.com
www.jazze.com
New releases, artist profiles, a jazz jukebox and a global jazz performance calendar.

WNUR-FM JazzWeb
www.wnur.org/jazz
US radio station site offering a 24-hour Web-cast, information on jazz artists and styles and a jazz links page.

MP3

Amplifier
www.amplifier.co.nz
Listen to and download the latest tracks, catch the latest news and shop for music and gear.

Epitonic.com
www.epitonic.com
Free MP3 source, specialising in cutting-edge rock, electronica, hip-hop, experimental and contemporary.

MP3.com
www.mp3.com
Thousands of MP3s. Musicians can register to submit their own songs to the site.

News

All Music Guide
www.allmusicguide.com 202

BuyGuide Australia
www.buyguide.com.au 202

GEMM – The Global Electronic Music Marketplace
http://gemm.com 202

Musicians Online
www.musiciansonline.com 171

Oz Music Central Band Links
www.ozmusic-central.com.au/ozlinks.html 165

Popstazz.co.uk
www.popstazz.co.uk/fanclubs.htm 165

Yahoo! Music
http://au.music.yahoo.com/music 223

Billboard
www.billboard-online.com
On-line edition of the record industry's trade magazine. Test your trivia knowledge with the interactive music crossword each day.

NEWS

MTV
www.mtv.com
Concert Web-casts and exclusive music videos from the people who made the pop video as important as the song.

VH1.com
www.vh1.com
Browse by artist or genre for biographies and links, and register to receive e-mail news of your favourite artists.

Pop

ABBA – The Site
www.abbasite.com
Official site of the Swedish supergroup – with trivia, news, music, links and much more.

andPOP
www.andpop.com
US portal for Top 40 news and artists, with photo galleries and video interviews.

BBC Eurovision Song Contest
www.bbc.co.uk/eurovision
Everything that you could ever want to know about the annual Eurovision Song Contest – includes trivia and classic clips.

The Girl Groups Fan Club
http://surf.to/girlgroups
Site devoted to pop and soul girl groups from the heady '60s and '70s.

Pop-Music.com
www.pop-music.com
All the latest news and charts of the pop music scene, as well as a searchable database of MP3s and music videos.

Rock

Elvis.com
www.elvis.com
Sadly, no word of the King's whereabouts but you can take a virtual tour of Graceland.

NME.com
www.nme.com
Music downloads, screensavers, chatrooms, as well as news, charts, reviews and features.

Rock and Roll Hall of Fame and Museum
www.rockhall.com
Beautifully designed Web site, includes a guide to the Museum and biographies of all the legends of rock.

Rockmine
www.rockmine.music.co.uk
Includes an alphabetical listing of virtually every rock band and musician – great and otherwise.

RollingStone.com
www.rollingstone.com
Watch the latest pop videos with this on-line edition of the top US rock magazine.

World

WOMAD
www.womad.org
Information on artists and details of world music festivals around the planet.

World Music Network
www.worldmusic.net
Produced by Rough Guides, the site includes a world music catalogue, sound clips and a range of MP3s to download.

N
Natural World
Animals & birds

The Atlas of Australian Birds
www.birdsaustralia.com.au/atlas/index.html 157

Australian Bird Study Association
www.absa.asn.au 157

Australian Insect Common Names
www.ento.csiro.au/aicn 157

Birds Australia Parrot Association
www.tasweb.com.au/bapa 157

Birdwatching Australia
www.ausbird.com 157

Kakapo Recovery Programme
www.kakaporecovery.org.nz 157

Animal Diversity Web
http://animaldiversity.ummz.umich.edu
Learn about the physical characteristics and behaviour of many species of animal at this University of Michigan site.

BBCi Nature
www.bbc.co.uk/nature
Look up your favourite animal in 'Wildfacts' or find out more about some amazing creatures under 'Weird Nature'.

Kingsnake
www.kingsnake.com
News stories and hundreds of links make this the largest snake-related portal on the Internet.

World Wildlife Fund
www.wwf.org/au
Join the Fund, adopt an endangered animal and find out how else you can make a difference from your desk.

ZooWeb
www.zooweb.com
Watch live Web-cam broadcasts of lions, polar bears and giant pandas, and find out how to take great wildlife pictures at the zoo.

Environment

Earthwatch Institute
www.earthwatch.org 231

National Geographic
www.nationalgeographic.com 157

The Northern Lights at Virtual Finland
http://virtual.finland.fi/finfo/english/aurora_borealis.html 156

Volcano World
www.volcanoworld.org 157

Yosemite Online
www.yosemite.org
Visit a live view of Yosemite Valley with scenic views of waterfalls or flora and fauna.

Exploration

National Geographic
www.nationalgeographic.com 157

Antarctica Online
www.aad.gov.au
Take a virtual reality tour of Australia's Antarctic Territory – all that ice and snow without getting cold!

Earth From Space
http://earth.jsc.nasa.gov
Database of Earth images taken by the NASA Space Shuttle, with sections on world weather, cities and geographical regions.

Web-cams

Anthill Web-cam at The Natural History Museum
http://antcam.nhm.ac.uk 156

EarthCam
www.earthcam.com 146

E-Zoo
www.sandiegozoo.com/virtualzoo/homepage.html 157

WebCam Central
www.camcentral.com 157

Africam
www.africam.com
View animals at several waterholes as they emerge from the bush to drink.

Eclipse Cam
http://eclipse.span.ch/liveshow.htm
Watch eclipses by Web-cam: it's almost as good as being there.

Howletts Zoo
www.howletts.net
Control the Web-cams at the elephant and tiger enclosures.

News
Local sources

ABC NewsOnline
www.abc.net.au/news 117, 119

The Australian
www.theaustralian.news.com.au 119

National Library of Australia
www.nla.gov.au 113

National Library of New Zealand
http://tepuna.natlib.govt.nz 113

NEWS

NZoom One News
http://onenews.nzoom.com   117

Parliament of Australia Live Broadcasting
www.aph.gov.au/live/webcast2.asp   117

Scoop
www.scoop.co.nz   117

The Sydney Morning Herald
www.smh.com.au   117, 119

Television New Zealand
www.tvnz.co.nz   119

Australian Newspapers on the Internet
www.nla.gov.au/oz/npapers.html
A huge list of links to the Australian newspapers that publish Internet editions.

Crikey
www.crikey.com.au
Read the hypocrisy-busting scoops that mainstream media dare not mention – until they're published here!

News.com.au
www.news.com.au
Links to the News Ltd stable of papers such as The Advertiser, The Australian *and* The Mercury. *Register with 'news pulse' to receive free news headlines by e-mail.*

NewsRoom
www.newsroom.co.nz
Breaking news stories constantly updated.

Ninemsn news
http://news.ninemsn.com.au
The latest news from Australia and around the world. Some stories have audio and video.

SBS – The World News
www.theworldnews.com.au
Fantastic coverage from SBS about what's going on around the world.

Tickers

WorldFlash News Ticker
www.worldflash.com   117, 118

BBC Newsline
www.bbc.co.uk/newsline
Easy to install and customise to display headlines in the news categories of your choice.

Infogate
www.entrypoint.com
Get the headlines from a variety of industries at this US-based news source.

WorldFlash
www.scroller.com
Colourful news ticker that can display headlines relating to the topics of your choice.

World

Ananova
www.ananova.com   117

Assignment Editor
www.assignmenteditor.com   117

CNN Asia
http://asia.cnn.com   117

CNN's Headline News
www.cnn.com/HLN   117

1stHeadlines
www.1stheadlines.com   65, 72

The Scotsman
www.thescotsman.co.uk   118

BBC News
http://news.bbc.co.uk
News and sports from one of the world's most respected broadcasters.

Drudge Report
www.drudgereport.com
A world-shattering scandal may be about to break – read about it first here.

ForeignWire.com
www.foreignwire.com
A comprehensive site with an intelligent angle on world current affairs.

Institute for War & Peace Reporting
www.iwpr.net
Unbiased analysis of wars across the globe.

Moreover
www.moreover.com/news
Brings you news headlines from hundreds of sources such as the BBC, New York Times *and* Middle East Newsline.

M2
www.m2.com
An electronic newsletter service sent straight to your Inbox.

Newsweek
www.newsweek.com
Breaking news and informative in-depth analysis from the on-line version of this respected news magazine.

Reuters
www.reuters.com
The international news agency that the other media rely on.

Washington Post
www.washingtonpost.com
Renowned US broadsheet, good on politics and world news as well as US stories.

World Health News
www.worldhealthnews.harvard.edu
Focusing mainly on American health news with plenty of opinions and articles.

World News
www.worldnews.com
News directory with topical international stories, including environmental updates.

R
Reference
Children's

AOL Kids Search
www.aol.com.au/site/aol/kids/kidsearch   71

Ask Jeeves Kids
www.ajkids.com   71

KidsClick!
http://kidsclick.org   71

Yahooligans!
www.yahooligans.com   57, 71

Fact Monster
www.factmonster.com
Dictionary, encyclopedia, atlas and almanac – plus fun facts on every subject.

Dictionaries & grammar

Merriam-Webster OnLine
www.m-w.com   75

The Chicago Manual of Style FAQ
www.press.uchicago.edu/Misc/Chicago/cmosfaq.html
The editors of a leading style manual answer your questions about grammar.

Dictionary.com
www.dictionary.com
Dictionary and language site, including foreign language dictionaries and word games.

LangToLang
www.langtolang.com
Multilingual dictionary translating between any combination of English, Turkish, French, Spanish, German, Russian and Italian.

Macquarie Dictionary
www.macquariedictionary.com.au
Search for definitions, contribute to the Australian word map, unravel some Aussie slang or just marvel at the peculiarity of the weekly word.

YourDictionary.com
www.yourdictionary.com
Dictionary and thesaurus, plus links for learning a language.

Encyclopedias

ArtCyclopedia
http://artcyclopedia.com   173

The Grove Dictionary of Art
www.groveart.com   173

Biography.com
www.biography.com
25,000 biographies of people past and present.

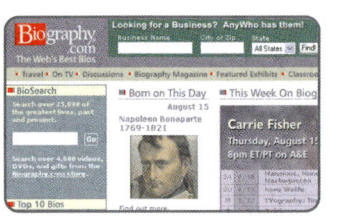

Encyclopaedia Britannica
www.britannica.com
Enter a subject to see related entries, magazine articles and Web links.

Encyclopedia Mythica
www.pantheon.org/mythica.html
Documenting myths of cultures around the world from Polynesia to ancient Egypt.

SCIENCE

Refdesk.com
www.refdesk.com
Search out facts from medical and law dictionaries.

Wikipedia
www.wikipedia.com
Help build this encyclopedia by writing entries of your own, or by editing those of other contributors.

Xrefer
http://w1.xrefer.com
Look up 50 reference books at once, including the Oxford Dictionary of Medicines and the Penguin Dictionary of Women.

Maps

Geoscience Australia – National Mapping
www.auslig.gov.au
Search for a place name and get a map, find out how far it is for the cocky to fly between two places, or just marvel at some beautiful satellite images.

Getmapping
www2.getmapping.com
Aerial photos of every square metre of Britain, by postcode.

Mapquest
www.mapquest.com
Find road maps of anywhere in the world at this US site.

National Geographic Map Machine
http://plasma.nationalgeographic.com/mapmachine
Political, historical, physical and other maps all available to download and print out at a range of scales.

Ordnance Survey
www.ordnancesurvey.co.uk
The official mapping agency for the entire UK.

Russian Subway, Railway and Tram Maps
http://parovoz.com/maps/index-e.html
Fascinating tips on navigating your way around Russia.

Miscellaneous

Australian Federal, State & Territory Governments
www.gov.au 113

Australia Post
www.auspost.com.au 73

Consignia
www.consignia-online.com 73

National Library of Australia
www.nla.gov.au 114

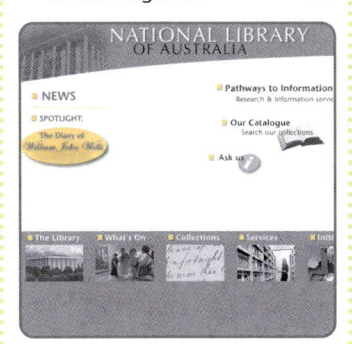

National Library of New Zealand
http://tepuna.natlib.govt.nz 113

New Zealand Government
www.govt.nz 113

New Zealand Post
www.nzpost.com 73

Teldir.com
www.teldir.com 73

White Pages Australia
www.whitepages.com.au 73

White Pages New Zealand
www.whitepages.co.nz 73

Yellow Pages Australia
www.yellowpages.com.au 73

Yellow Pages New Zealand
www.yellowpages.co.nz 73

Thesauruses

Thesaurus.com
www.thesaurus.com 75

Dictionary.com
www.dictionary.com
Access to Roget's Thesaurus for synonyms and antonyms.

The Phrase Finder
http://phrases.shu.ac.uk
Look up the meaning and origins of hundreds of phrases. Or subscribe to the service that allows you to search for related phrases and sayings.

Relationships
People-finders

Oz Reunion
www.ozreunion.com.au 170

WhoWhere?
www.whowhere.lycos.com 73

Yahoo! Groups
http://au.groups.yahoo.com 170

Yahoo! People Search
http://people.yahoo.com 73

OldFriends
www.oldfriends.co.nz
Use the free listing to get back in touch with old school friends, workmates or club members.

SchoolFriends.com.au
www.schoolfriends.com.au
Reunite with old school friends throughout Australia and New Zealand using the database of over 10,000 schools, universities and colleges.

Romance

Introduction Agency Scams
http://romance.live.com.au/articles/introductionAgencies.html 170

Ninemsn Dos & Don'ts of Internet Dating Factsheet
http://aca.ninemsn.com.au/factsheets/572.asp 171

OptusNet Personals
www.optusnet.com.au/lifestyle/personals 170

SingleSites
www.singlesites.com 170

IPCH
www.ipch.com
Offers a variety of ways to meet people on the Internet, such as chatrooms or profile sites.

Kiss.com
www.kiss.com
Use the Romance Wizard to help you find your ideal mate.

RSVP
www.rsvp.com.au
Australia's largest singles site, where you can find like-minded people and chat on-line.

S
Science
Discovery

Apollo Project Archive
www.apolloarchive.com 142, 144

Australian Space Research Institute
www.asri.org.au 142

Detailed Chronology of Events Surrounding the Apollo 13 Accident
www.hq.nasa.gov/office/pao/History/Timeline/apollo13chron.html 144

European Space Agency
www.esa.int 144

NASA Human Spaceflight
http://spaceflight.nasa.gov/gallery/vtour 143

NASA National Aeronautics & Space Administration
www.nasa.gov 142, 143

SETI@home
http://setiathome.ssl.berkeley.edu 144

SETI Institute
www.seti-inst.edu 143

S.E.T.L.A.B. Project
www.setlab.org 143

Spaceflight Now
www.spaceflightnow.com 143

SpaceKids
www.spacekids.com 143

The Astronaut Connection
www.nauts.com
Biographies of the world's astronauts, with a space exploration timeline and guide to space vehicles.

CERN – European Organization for Nuclear Research
http://public.web.cern.ch/Public
Everything you ever wanted to know about anti-matter. The people at CERN just happen to have invented the World Wide Web too.

Space Exploration Merit Badge
http://my.execpc.com/~culp/space/space.html
Earn a Space Exploration Merit Badge by completing the range of on-line tasks.

News

Discovery Channel
http://dsc.discovery.com/cams/cams.html 149

333

SCIENCE

Discover
www.discover.com
Keep up to date with topical issues such as allergies or genetic research.

Institute of Biology
www.iob.org
News on recent advances in biological research.

NewScientist.com
www.newscientist.com
Subscribe to this on-line magazine and gain access to a huge archive of scientific articles.

Popular Science
www.popsci.com
Follow the search for life on Mars and discover the world of virtual sport.

Scientists

Albert Einstein Online
www.westegg.com/einstein
List of links to other Web sites with Einstein-related material.

Darwin and Evolution Overview
http://65.107.211.206/darwin/darwinov.html
Text-based site which avoids academic jargon.

Federation of American Scientists
www.fas.org
A site that monitors and reports on the development and sale of weapons and armaments around the world.

The Nobel Prize Internet Archive
http://nobelprizes.com
Find out about prize winners in all the different categories and check the links to related sites.

Shopping

Antiques

Antiques World
www.antiquesworld.co.uk
UK directory of antique organisations, events and publications.

Collectiques
www.collectiques.co.uk
Includes a database of gold and silver hallmarks.

World Collectors Net
www.worldcollectorsnet.com
If you fancy starting an unusual collection have a look at what this site has to offer.

Auctions

AuctionGuide
www.auctionguide.com   209, 211

AuctionWatch
www.auctionwatch.com   165, 209

Bidfind
www.bidfind.com   209

Bidville
www.bidville.com   209

The CDexchange
www.thecdexchange.com   208

Celebrity Merchandise
www.celebritymerch.com   165

eBay Australia
www.ebay.com.au   208, 209, 210

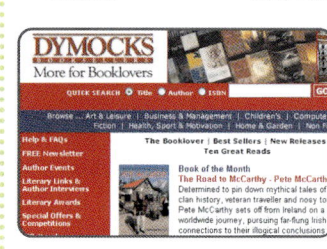

eBay New Zealand
http://pages.ebay.com/nz   209

eSnipe
www.esnipe.com   208

On-Line Swap Market
www.swapmarket.com.au   208

Safetender
www.safetender.co.nz   208

Secure-Commerce
www.secure-commerce.com.au   208

Sold.com
http://au.sold.yahoo.com   209

Sotheby's
www.sothebys.com   209

Startifacts
www.startifacts.com   165

eBay Live Auctions
www.ebayliveauctions.com
Participate in sales at some of the world's top auction houses.

Books

Abebooks
http://abebooks.com   72, 115

Alibris
www.alibris.com   202

Amazon
www.amazon.com   168, 202, 203

Angus & Robertson
www.angusrobertson.com.au   167

BOL
www.bol.com   167

Book Clique Cafe
www.readinggroupsonline.com   167

Bookfayre.com
www.bookfayre.com   202

BookFinder
www.bookfinder.com   72, 115, 203

BookWeb
www.bookweb.org/bookstores   202

BuyGuide Australia
www.buyguide.com.au   202

Co-op Online Bookshop
www.coop-bookshop.com.au   202

Dymocks
www.dymocks.com.au   167, 202

eBookMall
www.ebookmall.com   168

eBooks.com
www.ebooks.com   168

eBooks N' Bytes
www.ebooksnbytes.com   168

Free-eBooks
www.free-ebooks.net   168

Haybooks
www.haybooks.com   115

New Zealand Books
http://newzealandbooks.co.nz   202

Online Originals
www.onlineoriginals.com   168

Ozlit
http://home.vicnet.net.au/~ozlit   167

Te Puna Web Directory
http://tepuna.natlib.govt.nz/web_directory/NZ/literature.htm   167

University of Virginia's E-Book Library
http://etext.lib.virginia.edu/books   167

Bibliofind
www.bibliofind.com
Search for millions of rare and used books worldwide.

Dee Why Books
www.deewhybooks.com.au
Try this site for second-hand and antiquarian books.

Messrs Berkelouw
www.berkelouw.com.au
Seller of new, second-hand, rare and out-of-print books.

nzbooks.com
www.nzbooks.com
An independent bookstore selling New Zealand and Pacific books over the Internet.

CDs & records

The CDexchange
www.thecdexchange.com   208

CDNow
www.cdnow.com
US CD shopping site, with sound clips and gift certificates.

Hard To Find Records
www.htfr.com
UK site that includes a specialist record-finding service, easing the process of tracking down those hard-to-find favourites.

HMV Australia Online
www.hmv.com.au
Find and buy on-line the latest releases. Also chart information, a pre-order facility, reviews and a newsletter.

Sanity
www.sanity.com.au
Shop on-line, view the latest music charts, use the store locator or just download some free music.

Wonderland Records
www.wlr.co.nz
Shop for rare records, CDs, cassettes, videos, posters and memorabilia on-line.

SHOPPING

DVDs

Blockbuster
www.blockbuster.com.au
Rental and sales of DVDs, games and videos.

I love DVD
www.ilovedvd.co.nz
All you need to know about DVDs – the different region codes, pan & scan, widescreen and much more.

Planet.DVD
www.planetdvd.com.au
An under-A$20 section can help build up your collection without breaking the bank.

E-commerce

Australian Competition and Consumer Commission
www.accc.gov.au/ecomm/access1b.htm 55

E-Commerce Labs (Australia)
www.ecla.com.au 298

E-Commerce Law Source
www.e-commercelawsource.com 303

E-Commerce Times
www.ecommercetimes.com 298

Econsumer
www.econsumer.gov 55

eTick
www.etick.com 55

TRUSTe
www.truste.com 55

VeriSign
www.verisign.com 55

ZDNet's eBusiness section
http://techupdate.zdnet.com 298

About.com – Electronic Commerce
http://ecommerce.about.com
Directory of links and resources, including the 'Beginner's Guide to E-Commerce'.

Florists

Auckland Flowers and Gifts
www.nzflower.co.nz 219

Interflora
www.interflora.com 221

Petals Network
www.petals.com.au 221

Teleflora
www.teleflora.co.nz 221

Flowerbasket.com.au
www.flowerbasket.com.au
Beautiful arrangements for all occasions – and they will take international orders too.

The Flowershop.co.nz
www.theflowershop.co.nz
Offers fresh and artificial flowers, special gifts and gift baskets for all occasions.

Roses Only
www.rosesonly.com
More than roses – flowers for all occasions and champagne and chocolates too.

Wild poppies
www.wildpoppies.co.nz
Select your flowers, gifts or a combination package by mood, occasion, style or value.

Furniture & houseware

DIY-Online
www.diy-online.co.nz 184

Mitre 10
www.mitre10.com.au 184

David Jones Online
www.davidjones.com.au
On-line shopping at Australia's oldest department store. Check out the special offers, the wine club and more.

Peter's of Kensington
www.petersofkensington.com.au
An enormous selection of homewares – and extra services such as bridal registry, corporate gifts and hampers.

General shopping sites

BuyGuide Australia
www.buyguide.com.au 202

eBay Australia
www.ebay.com.au 208, 209, 210

GoodShoppingGuide.com.au
http://goodshoppingguide.com.au
On-line shopping made easy – sites are grouped into categories, and they have secure transaction procedures and regular on-line specials.

Mobile Tool Kit
http://toolkit.aca.gov.au
The Australian Communications Authority compares mobile phone packages to help you choose the best deal to meet your needs.

Not Good Enough
www.notgoodenough.org
Coordinated consumer complaints; there is greater power in a group complaining rather than just one person.

Gifts

Beautydirect
www.beautydirect.co.nz 219

BuyGuide Australia
www.buyguide.com.au 202

Chocolate Boutique Cafe
www.chocolateboutique.co.nz 219

Gift-Arcade
www.gift-arcade.com.au 219

International Star Registry
www.starregistry.com.au 219

M&A Hampers Online
www.hampersonline.com.au 219

PeeDee Toys
http://store.yahoo.com/peedeetoys 179

Perfume Express
www.perfumeexpress.co.nz 219

Hard2Buy4
www.hard2buy4.co.uk
A site with gift ideas for people who have everything.

Reader's Digest
www.readersdigest.com.au
Popular books, magazines, music and video products – and you could win a prize by shopping on-line.

www.Giftshopper
www.giftshopper.co.nz
Register to use the occasion reminder service or just check out (and buy!) a gift idea.

Greetings

Candor Reminder Service
www.candor.com/reminder 219, 221

CardStore
www.cardstore.com 221

Petals Network
www.petals.com.au/reminder.htm 219

Postcards.Net
www.postcards.net 219

Posty City
http://postycity.net 221

Say-it-with-ease
www.say-it-with-ease.com 221

WCardz
www.wcardz.com.au 219

Yahoo! Greetings
http://au.greetings.yahoo.com 219, 220

American Greetings
www.Americangreetings.com
Check out the largest selection of free greetings cards on the World Wide Web.

Egreetings
www.egreetings.com
On-line cards in categories such as weddings, kids and family or movies and TV.

123 Greetings
www.123greetings.com/general/getwell
Great selection of free e-cards – particularly strong in the 'get well' section.

Major stores

Mitre 10
www.mitre10.com.au 184

Woolworths Australia
www.woolworths.com.au 192, 194, 195

Woolworths New Zealand
www.woolworths.co.nz 192

Coles Myer Ltd
www.colesmyer.com
Portal site for access to Grace Bros, Myer, Kmart, Officeworks, Coles, Vintage Cellars and Harris Technology on-line stores.

335

SOCIETY

David Jones Online
www.davidjones.com.au
On-line shopping at Australia's oldest department store. Find gifts for any occasion or person, have a look at special offers, the wine club and more.

Farmers
www.farmers.co.nz
Shop on-line for special bargains, join the Beauty Club for member-only events, and register special dates for an e-mail reminder.

Westfield.com
www.westfield.com/au
or
www.westfield.com/nz
Use the store locator to find the centre nearest you.

Society
Charity

Amnesty International
www.amnesty.org 206

Australian Volunteer Search
www.volunteersearch.gov.au 207

Charity Mall
www.charitymall.org.nz 207

Consumers Online
www.consumersonline.gov.au 207

Donations
www.donations.com.au 207

Global Volunteer Network
www.volunteer.org.nz 207

Greenpeace
www.greenpeace.org 206

The Hunger Site
www.thehungersite.com 29, 207

The Rainforest Site
www.therainforestsite.com 206

Say-it-with-ease
www.say-it-with-ease.com 221

Seek Volunteer
www.volunteer.com.au 207

Sold.com
http://au.sold.yahoo.com 207

United Devices
http://members.ud.com/projects/cancer 207

World Vision
www.worldvision.org.au 207

World Wide Fund for Nature
www.wwf.org 206

Australian Charities
www.auscharity.org
Portal site for information on, and links to, Australian charities.

Barnardos New Zealand
www.barnardos.org.nz
Find out more about New Zealand's largest and most trusted organisation dedicated to child welfare.

Charitynet
www.charitynet.org
A quick way to access Web sites of non-profit organisations.

Disaster Relief
www.disasterrelief.org
Learn how you can do your bit for disaster relief.

GuideStar
www.guidestar.com
This US national database has information on more than 850,000 non-profit organisations.

Internet Nonprofit Centre
www.nonprofits.org
Up-to-date information about non-profit organisations around the world.

National Association for Prevention of Child Abuse & Neglect (NAPCAN)
www.napcan.org.au
Make an on-line donation to help reduce child abuse and neglect in Australia.

New Zealand Trust for Conservation Volunteers
www.conservationvolunteers.org.nz
Take action to help restore and protect the environment.

Ourcommunity.com.au
www.ourcommunity.com.au
Donate on-line or find out about Australia's 700,000 community, education and non-profit groups.

Red Cross
www.redcross.org.au
or
www.redcross.org.nz
Find out about the Red Cross at home and overseas, check out job opportunities or just make a donation.

Royal Flying Doctor Service of Australia
www.rfds.org.au
The story of this vital service to the Australian Outback – and information about its bases and visitor centres.

RSPCA
www.rspca.org.au
or
www.rspca.org.nz
Membership, news, animal advice, shopping and a special section for children.

The Salvation Army
www.salvationarmy.org.au
or
www.salvationarmy.org.nz
Find out about the work of The Salvation Army and how to get in touch.

UNICEF
www.unicef.org
Loads of facts and statistics about the work done by UNICEF, as well as opportunities for on-line shopping and donations.

Government

Australian Commonwealth Government Information
www.fed.gov.au/KSP 123

Australian Competition and Consumer Commission
www.accc.gov.au/ecomm/access1b.htm 55

Australian Federal, State & Territory Governments
www.gov.au 113

Australian Taxation Office
www.ato.gov.au 211

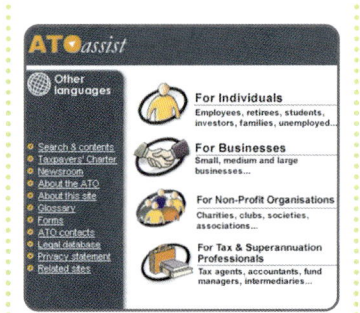

Department of Agriculture, Fisheries and Forestry – Australia
www.affa.gov.au 236

Inland Revenue Department
www.ird.govt.nz 211

New Zealand Department of Conservation
www.doc.govt.nz 226

New Zealand Government
www.govt.nz 113

New Zealand MAF Quarantine Service
www.quarantine.govt.nz 236

New Zealand Ministry of Consumer Affairs
www.consumer-ministry.govt.nz/advice.html 55

New Zealand Passports Office
www.passports.govt.nz 228

Passports Australia
www.passports.gov.au 228

The British Monarchy
www.royal.gov.uk
Visit the official Web site of the British Monarchy for profiles of kings and queens and information about the royal residences and the treasures inside them!

The Governor-General of New Zealand
www.gov-gen.govt.nz
Learn about the role and functions of New Zealand's G-G, and take a peek inside the rooms of Government House, Wellington.

National Anthems
www.gergo.com/home/midi/anthems.htm
Listen to the national anthems of more than 180 countries.

Parliament of Australia
www.aph.gov.au
All the information you may want to know about the Australian Parliament, including who's who and live broadcasts.

10 Downing Street
www.number-10.gov.uk
The history of this famous building, its past and present occupants and details of current government policy.

SPACE

Law

Arts Law Centre
www.artslaw.com.au 121

Auckland District Law Society
www.adls.org.nz/public/lawlist.cfm 121

Australasian Legal Information Institute
www.austlii.edu.au 121

Australian Copyright Council
www.copyright.org.au 121

Australian Law Online
http://law.gov.au/wotl.html 120

Copyright Council of New Zealand
www.copyright.org.nz 121

Courts of New Zealand
www.courts.govt.nz 120

Directory of Australian community legal centres
www.austlii.edu.au/au/other/clc 121

E-commerce Law Source
www.e-commercelawsource.com 303

FindLaw Australia / New Zealand
www.findlaw.com.au 120
www.findlaw.co.nz 120

Law Council of Australia
www.lawcouncil.asn.au/links.html 121

Law For You
www.law4u.com.au 121

Lawlink
www.lawlink.co.nz 121

Lawstuff
www.lawstuff.org.au 121

Legalmart
www.legalmart.com.au 120

Legal Services Agency
www.lsa.govt.nz 121

Legal Sites on the Web
www.ih2000.net/ira/legal.htm 121

APB News
www.apbnews.com
A US site providing news, data and information on crime, justice and safety.

Crimespider
www.crimespider.com
Search the Web for the most interesting crime and law enforcement sites.

Cybercrime.gov
www.cybercrime.gov
US site devoted to combating nefarious Internet or computer-related activity.

Dumb Laws
www.dumblaws.com
Entertaining look at laws which make no sense.

PursuitWatch.com
www.pursuitwatch.com
View live high-speed car chases on television.

What is Copyright Protection?
http://whatiscopyright.org
What copyright is, and how you can go about protecting your intellectual property.

Politics

Australian Federal, State & Territory Governments
www.gov.au 113

New Zealand Government
www.govt.nz 113

Parliament of Australia Live Broadcasting
www.aph.gov.au/live/webcast2.asp 117

ACT New Zealand
www.act.org.nz
Information on the party's campaigns and MPs, and how you can help.

Alliance New Zealand
www.alliance.org.nz
The social democratic, left-of-centre party's Web presence.

Australian Democrats
www.democrats.org.au
Log-on to get regular news and information.

Australian Electoral Commission
www.aec.gov.au
The ins and outs of the Australian voting system.

Australian Greens
www.greens.org.au
Keep up to date with the party and its politicians.

Australian Labor Party
www.alp.org.au
Links to state branches, information on the party's history, policies and other news.

Green Party of Aotearoa New Zealand
www.greens.org.nz
A party dedicated to caring for the earth and its people.

Liberal Party of Australia
www.liberal.org.au
All the latest media releases, speeches and interviews.

National Party of Australia
www.nationalparty.org
Information on policies and campaigns, contact details and links to state branches.

National Party of New Zealand
www.national.org.nz
Loads of information about candidates and policies.

New Zealand First
www.nzfirst.org.nz
Policy statements, information about MPs, speeches and press releases are all here.

New Zealand Labour Party
www.labour.org.nz
The official Web site of the New Zealand Labour Party.

United Party
www.united.org.nz
Information about candidates, policies and how you can help the party.

The White House
www.whitehouse.gov
Take an on-line tour of the White House, and read transcripts of the current President's speeches.

Pressure groups

Amnesty International
www.amnesty.org
Campaigning for human rights around the world.

Friends of the Earth
www.foe.org
Essential environmental information at international, national and local levels.

Greenpeace
www.greenpeace.org
Covers topics such as genetic engineering, greenhouse gases, oil drilling in the Arctic and nuclear waste disposal.

Space
Aliens

About.com – UFOs/Aliens
http://ufos.about.com 142

SETI Institute
www.seti-inst.edu 143

S.E.T.L.A.B. Project
www.setlab.org 143

Alien Abductions, How to Prevent
www.abductions-alien.com
No-nonsense advice on what you should do to avoid being abducted by aliens, and what to do if you actually find yourself being abducted!

Robots and Space Toys
www.alphadrome.com
Collectible flying saucers and space station toys from the 1940s to the present.

Astronomy

Astronomy Discussion Page
www.astronomyforum.net 142

Science Explained
www.synapses.co.uk/astro 112

Zoom Astronomy
www.enchantedlearning.com/subjects/astronomy 143

Astronomy.com
www.astronomy.com
The on-line version of the popular magazine Astronomy.

Astronomy Online
www.astronomyonline.com.au
Astronomy news, observing tips for amateurs and an on-line store for telescopes and other accessories.

Bad Astronomy
www.badastronomy.com
Corrects common mistakes and misconceptions about astronomy.

SPACE

LyngSat
www.lyngsat.com
Get the technical low-down on satellite launches, frequencies and flight paths.

Mars Network
http://marsnet.jpl.nasa.gov
Taking the Internet to Mars.

Siding Spring Exploratory
www.sidingspringexploratory.com.au
Official site of Australia's largest optical telescopes, packed with information about these devices and what they see.

Sydney Observatory
www.phm.gov.au/observe
Facts about historic Sydney Observatory and panoramic views both inside and outside.

Travel

Apollo Project Archive
www.apolloarchive.com   142, 144

Detailed Chronology of Events Surrounding the Apollo 13 Accident
www.hq.nasa.gov/office/pao/History/Timeline/apollo13chron.html   144

European Space Agency
www.esa.int   142, 144

NASA Human Spaceflight
http://spaceflight.nasa.gov/gallery/vtour   143

NASA National Aeronautics & Space Administration
www.nasa.gov   142, 143

SETI@home
http://setiathome.ssl.berkeley.edu   144

SETI Institute
www.seti-inst.edu   143

Spaceflight Now
www.spaceflightnow.com   143

SpaceKids
www.spacekids.com   143

Ambit – The Web Waystation
www.ambitweb.com
Live Web-cams showing views from NASA shuttles.

Kennedy Space Center
www.ksc.nasa.gov
Interactive information about the famous Kennedy Space Center. Gain a merit badge by completing on-line tasks.

NASA Human Spaceflight
http://spaceflight.nasa.gov/station
Up-to-date news of events and experiments on the International Space Station.

Sport
Adventure

ExtremeSports.com
www.extremesports.com
Background information and star interviews covering adventure sports from surfing to street luge.

GravityDex
http://gravitydex.com
Adventure sports portal with news, links to participants, retailers and manufacturers.

Trails.com
www.trails.com
Resources for planning, booking and equipping your next adventure.

Boxing

Boxing.net
www.boxing.net
Boxing news headlines as they happen, 24 hours a day.

Boxing Records Archive
www.boxrec.com
A comprehensive record of more than 60,000 boxers and their bouts, updated daily by a dedicated group of enthusiasts.

SecondsOut.com
www.secondsout.com
News about boxing in the US, the UK and the rest of the world. Also contains the Queensbury rules and a look at great fighters of the past.

Cricket

CricInfo.com
www.cricinfo.com   239

Australian Cricket Board
www.acb.com.au
Takes you to the Baggy Green site – loaded with cricketing info. Have a go at playing 'Team Tiles' – it's addictive!

Cricket 4
www.cricket4.com
Guide to every Test match, plus a statistics archive, which you can use to compare the records of players from every era.

England's Barmy Army
www.cricket.org/link_to_database/NATIONAL/ENG/CLUBS/barmy-army
A riot of fun and nonsense about the die-hard fans who follow England's cricketers.

New Zealand Cricket
www.nzcricket.co.nz
Heaps of cricketing info and you can download memorable images to use as wallpaper on your computer.

Wisden
www.wisden.com
Well-written feature articles, oodles of statistics and a busy bulletin board.

Cycling

Bikezone
www.bikezone.com
Cycling equipment is reviewed, compared and rated in the 'GearZone'.

Cycling Australia
www.cycling.org.au
The Web site for competitive road, track and mountain bike cycling in Australia.

Cyclingnews
www.cyclingnews.com
News, events information and rider profiles from the self-styled world centre of cycling.

CyclingNZ
www.cyclingnz.com
Product reviews, on-line chat, terrific photos and maps and trail information to help you get out and about.

Marin
www.marinbikes.com
Technical support plus the chance to share experiences with other enthusiasts.

Le Tour de France
www.letour.fr
The whole story about this world-famous event.

Trek
www.trekbikes.com
Includes a bike-finder section where you can find the exact model you want.

Fishing

FishNZ
www.fishnz.co.nz
Comprehensive links to New Zealand fishing sites. Register to get e-mailed newsletters, discounts and special offers.

Fishweb
www.dpi.qld.gov.au/fishweb
The 'Species information' section has the low-down on a wide variety of recreational, protected and noxious fish.

Game Fishing Association Australia
www.gfaa.asn.au
Game fishing records, useful links, an identification database and tournament lists.

Football

Australian Football League
http://afl.com.au   239

Australian Rugby Union
www.rugby.com.au   239

National Rugby League
www.nrl.com.au   239

New Zealand Rugby League
www.rugbyleague.co.nz   239

New Zealand Rugby Union
www.nzrugby.co.nz   239

New Zealand Soccer
www.soccernz.co.nz   239

Soccer Australia
www.socceraustralia.com.au   239

Association of Football Statisticians
www.11v11.co.uk
Includes upcoming match previews and a gallery of UK soccer's memorable matches and stars.

SPORT

The Rugby Football League
www.rfl.uk.com
Check out the hall of fame in this official rugby site.

Rugby Heaven
http://rugbyheaven.smh.com.au/
For those convinced that this is the game played by the angels!

Scrum.com
www.scrum.com
Argue the toss with fans from both hemispheres and read regular columns by stars such as Wallaby lock David Giffin.

TEAMtalk.com
www.teamtalk.com
Live soccer commentary.

UEFA.com
www.uefa.com
Join the legendary UEFA Champions League Fantasy Football game.

ZoomSoccer.com
www.zoomsoccer.com
All the European soccer gossip and news.

General

Sport NZ
www.sportnz.co.nz   239

SportSelect
www.sportselect.com.au   239

About.com – Sports Medicine
http://sportsmedicine.about.com
Excellent database on the subject of good health in sport.

Australian Commonwealth Games Association
www.ausport.gov.au/acga
Quick facts, past champions, links to completed and forthcoming Games sites and connected sporting associations.

Australian Sports Web
www.ausport.gov.au
Find out more about your particular sport through the 'Sport Information' area.

Chat Sports
www.chattown.com/chatsports
Chat to people about your favourite sport.

The Olympic Movement
www.olympic.org
Everything you could ever want to know about the modern Olympic Games.

Golf

The Open Championship
www.opengolf.com   146

Ausgolf
www.ausgolf.com.au
Latest news, golf course ratings and listings and a real estate section to help you find your dream home on an Australian golf course.

New Zealand Golf Association
www.nzga.co.nz
Info on NZGA golf clubs, news and events calendar or test yourself on the rules of golf.

New Zealand Golf Guide
www.golfguide.co.nz
Use the map to find a course and its contact details.

19thHole.com
www.19thhole.com
A light-hearted look at the game of golf.

Ozgolf
www.ozgolf.com.au
Subscribe to receive a free monthly e-mail featuring news and trends in the golf industry. You can also get a free '@ozgolf' e-mail address!

The Royal & Ancient Golf Club of St Andrews
www.randa.org
Video clips, worldwide golf news, the rules of golf and much more.

Horse racing

Aintree Racecourse
www.aintree.co.uk
Delve into the history of one of the world's most famous races – the Grand National.

Australian Racing Board
www.australian-racing.net.au
A wealth of information about all things racing, and a useful guide to owning a racehorse.

New Zealand Racing Industry Board
www.racenz.co.nz
Coverage of the thoroughbred, harness and greyhound racing industries, with news and race meeting information.

Oz Horse Racing
www.ozhoseracing.com
A–Z of Australian racing news and information

Racing Chronicle
www.racing-chronicle.co.uk
Some of the best racing photography on the Web.

Racing Pages
www.racingpages.com.au
Terrific pictures to download, as well as racing information, and local and international links.

Martial arts

The Aikido FAQ
www.aikidofaq.com
Introduction to Aikido, its ethics, principles and moves.

Black Belt
www.blackbeltmag.com
Self-defence tips for the serious martial arts enthusiast.

International TaeKwon-Do Association
www.itatkd.com
Innovative use of animation and a large archive of step patterns and articles.

Martialinfo.com
www.martialinfo.com
Covers all aspects of martial arts, from finding instructors to magazine subscriptions.

News

ABC Sport
www.abc.net.au/sport   239

BBC Radio Five Live Sport
www.bbc.co.uk/fivelive/sportonfive   238

News Limited Sport page
http://sport.news.com.au   239

The New Zealand Herald Sports News
www.nzherald.co.nz/sports   239

NZoom One Sport
http://onesport.nzoom.com   239

The Sydney Morning Herald Sport page
www.smh.com.au/sport   239

Xtramsn Sport
http://xtramsn.co.nz/sport   239

talkSPORT
www.talksport.net
Listen to the latest sports news on this Internet radio station.

Racquet sports

The Wimbledon Championships
www.wimbledon.org   240

International Badminton Federation
www.intbadfed.org
Offers a regular badminton news bulletin by e-mail.

New Zealand Tennis
www.tennis.org.nz
News and information about tennis in New Zealand.

Tennis Australia
www.tennisaustralia.com.au
Subscribe to Tennis Australia's weekly newsletter or just visit the site to read the latest news.

Tennis.com
http://tennis.com
Tennis tips and news from around the world.

World Squash
www.squash.org
Coaching tips and a friendly guide for beginners.

Water sports

Aquaskier.com
www.aquaskier.com
Photo contests, interviews with champions and information on courses around the country.

PADI – Professional Association of Diving Instructors
www.padi.com
Find out where you can learn to dive with the largest and most recognised diving organisation around the world.

Surfing Australia
www.surfingaustralia.com.au
Check out the surf at beaches around Australia, New Zealand and Indonesia on Web-cams.

339

SPORT

SurfNZ
www.surfnz.com
Subscribe to the newsletter – or surf the site (groan!) for surf reports, news, info on boards and links to many other useful surfing-related sites.

Tracks magazine
www.tracksmag.com
The surfer's bible – who'd have thought there was so much to read about surfing.

Winter sports

Board the World
www.boardtheworld.com
A snowboarding site with equipment and resort reviews.

GoSki
www.goski.com
Read other skiers' accounts of resorts and package holidays to help you plan your trip.

Perisher Blue
www.perisherblue.com.au/winter
The latest information from Australia's biggest ski resort.

Ski Central
www.skicentral.com
Links to hundreds of Web sites covering everything from snowboarding equipment to helicopter skiing trips.

Skidirectory.com
www.skidirectory.com
Read the latest weather reports from resorts around the world, plus links to clothing, chat and competition sites.

Snowco
www.snow.co.nz
New Zealand ski area locator, snow reports, accommodation and travel packages and a fantastic photo gallery.

Snowlink.com
www.snowlink.com
Filled with tips for beginners on how to ski, what equipment you need, the rules of the slopes and much more.

Television
Broadcasters

ABC TV Online
http://abc.net.au/tv
The Web site of Australia's national broadcaster, with information on programs.

Channel 7
http://i7.aol.com.au
Portal site with links to the shows aired on Channel 7.

Channel 9
http://ninemsn.com.au/tvshows
TV show highlights – and their links – from Channel 9.

Network Ten
www.ten.com.au
Breaking news stories, program guides and show information.

SBS Online
www.sbs.com.au
Register for e-mail updates, explore their news section or find out what's on when. Plus links to the SBS shop, language services and more.

TV One
http://tvone.nzoom.com
Broadcast schedule, program links and personality profiles. The site also has a search engine, so it can be used as a homepage.

TV2
http://tv2.nzoom.com
The stars, screensavers, a kids' zone with games – all related to TV2 programs.

TV3
www.tv3.co.nz
What's on and what's hot with a great colour-coded listing key to give you an overview of your favourite TV3 program.

Children's

The Playground
www.abc.net.au/children 176

Disney Channel
www.disney.com.au/DisneyChannel
Games and the opportunity to explore different parts of a make-believe Disney studio.

Hi-5
http://ninemsn.com.au/kids/hi5
Join a sing-a-long with the gang, play games or download Hi-5 wallpapers or a screensaver.

The Simpsons
www.thesimpsons.com
Find out Chief Wiggum's first name and learn about Moe's murky past as a child actor.

The Wiggles
www.thewiggles.com
Games, music, colouring-in and all you need to know about the skivvied ones.

Classic

LikeTelevision
www.liketelevision.com 149, 151

TV Cream
http://TV.cream.org 149

Yesterdayland
www.yesterdayland.com 149

ShowGuide
www.tvguide.com/showguide
Invaluable summaries of every episode of classic shows such as M*A*S*H.

Starfleet
www.sfi.org
International Star Trek Fan Association site, with fan club listings worldwide.

TV Land
www.tvland.com
Actor bios, character profiles, episode guides and you can listen to some catchy theme songs to popular shows.

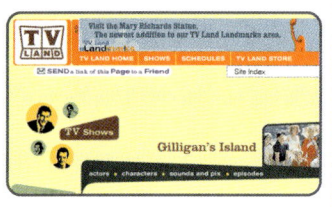

Listings

NZoom.com
http://ontv.nzoom.com/schedules 149

TV Week
www.tvweek.com.au 149

Yahoo! TV Coverage
http://au.tv.yahoo.com/tv 149

Gist TV Listings
www.gist.com
American site with soap opera updates, the latest news and gossip, funny video clips and links to fan clubs.

Programs

.auTV Forums
www.dolphinx.org/autv 149

Discovery Channel
http://dsc.discovery.com/cams/cams.html 149

Epguides.com
www.epguides.com 149

The Bill
www.thebill.com
Look up information about characters, episodes or e-mail your own questions to the show's production team.

Dawson's Creek
www.dawsonscreek.com
A picture-led companion to the self-obsessed US soap.

ER
www.ertv.com
Find out about the staff, take a look at what happens behind the scenes and try your hand at a trivia quiz.

Neighbours.com
www.neighbours.com
Behind-the-scenes features, cast photos and contact with the stars via e-mail.

Shortland Street
http://shortlandstreet.nzoom.com
All the gossip – and a behind-the-scenes look at the sets.

Yahoo! TV
http://TV.yahoo.com
Catch up on your favourite soap and read interviews with actors.

Web-cams

Discovery Channel
http://dsc.discovery.com/cams/cams.html 149

TRAVEL

EarthCam
www.earthcam.com 146

WebCam Central
www.camcentral.com 157

Camscape.com
www.camscape.com
Choose from over 2500 live Web-cams worldwide.

LochNess Live!
www.lochness.scotland.net
Use this Web-cam on the lake shore to spot the monster.

Webcamsearch.com
www.webcamsearch.com
A directory of Web-cams around the world, with tutorials on setting up and using your own.

World

TV Show
www.tvshow.com 149

BBC Television
www.bbc.co.uk/tv
Listings of all programs on BBC TV as well as an A–Z set of links to individual program Web sites, and more.

LyngSat
www.lyngsat.com
Satellite TV frequencies around the world, as well as links to satellite TV and radio stations.

Television Without Pity
www.televisionwithoutpity.com
Tongue-in-cheek look at the latest happenings in popular American TV shows.

Travel
Attractions

Association of Leading Visitor Attractions
www.alva.org.uk 233

Grand Canyon National Park
www.nps.gov/grca
The best places to stay and tips on planning your trip.

Great Barrier Reef
www.great-barrier-reef.com
Educational content plus on-line booking facilities.

Lake-district.com
www.lake-district.com
Comprehensive guide to this beautiful area of England, including weather reports.

NYCtourist.com
www.nyctourist.com
Streetwise advice plus guides to places such as Central Park and the Statue of Liberty.

The Tower of Pisa
http://torre.duomo.pisa.it
Tourist guide but also a serious research tool.

Car rental

Avis
www.avis.com 229

Budget Australia / New Zealand
www.budget.com.au 229
or
www.budget.co.nz 229

Hertz
www.hertz.com 229

Alamo
www.alamo.com
Plan a road trip across the USA with competitive hire rates.

Car Hire 4 Less
www.carhire4less.com
Offering discounts at a huge number of locations worldwide.

Maui
www.maui.co.nz
Explore Australia, New Zealand or southern Africa in a Maui motorhome.

Thrifty Car Rental
www.thrifty.com.au
or
www.thrifty.co.nz
Select the car type, get prices and book on-line.

City guides

CitySearch Australia
www.citysearch.com.au 223

CitySearch Sydney
http://sydney.citysearch.com.au 222

Discoversydney
www.discoversydney.com.au 222

Time Out
www.timeout.com 222

Amsterdam Channels
www.channels.nl
A fascinating tour through the streets of Amsterdam.

Citysearch
www.citysearch.com
Portal with links to citysearch sites from the US to Australia.

Florence by Net
www.florence.ala.it
Tour Florence's restaurants, art galleries, shops and hotels, or find a travel agent.

Wcities
www.wcities.com
Interactive guide to a selection of cities worldwide.

Guides

Campsites in Europe
www.interhike.com 226

European Travel Commission
www.etc-europe-travel.org 229

Guide to Australia's National Parks
www.atn.com.au/parks 226

Historic Homes of Britain
www.specialtytraveluk.com 235

Lonely Planet
www.lonelyplanet.com 228, 229

New Zealand Department of Conservation
www.doc.govt.nz 226, 227

Paris Convention and Visitors Centre
www.parisbienvenue.com 222

Safety in the Bush
www.bushwalking.org.au/safety.html 226

Tourist Authority of Thailand
www.tourismthailand.org 228

The UK Travel Guide
www.ukguide.org 233

Concierge.com
www.concierge.com
Daily travel deals, insider guides, maps, photos and booking information.

Department of Primary Industries, Water and Environment
www.dpiwe.tas.gov.au
The Visitors' Guides in the 'Parks & Wildlife' section are invaluable if you plan to visit any of Tasmania's national parks or World Heritage Areas.

DMOZ open directory project
http://dmoz.org/Recreation/Travel
Web directory with a selection of links, plus virtual tours of budget holidays.

Environment ACT
www.environment.act.gov.au/general
Site dedicated to the ACT environment, with a page on bush parks and reserves.

Let's Go
www.letsgo.com
Budget travel – especially good for students.

NatureBase
www.calm.wa.gov.au
Visit the 'Park of the Month' and be transported to a uniquely beautiful part of Western Australia.

NSW National Parks & Wildlife Service
www.npws.nsw.gov.au
Information on parks and wildlife – and a great area to help kids with school projects.

Parks and Wildlife Commission of the Northern Territory
www.nt.gov.au/ipe/paw
Explore the rich wildlife and scenery of the Northern Territory through this site.

Parks Victoria
www.parkweb.vic.gov.au
All the information you need on the parks, rivers, marine areas and heritage properties managed by Parks Victoria.

ParksWeb
www.environment.sa.gov.au/parks/visitors.html
All you need to know about national parks and conservation reserves in South Australia.

TRAVEL

Queensland Parks and Wildlife Service
www.epa.qld.gov.au/environment/park
Download a visitor information sheet of the park you want to visit. It will help you get the most out of your trip.

Rough Guides – Travel
http://travel.roughguides.com
Share your own travel tips and read a Rough Guide on-line.

Tourism Offices Worldwide Directory
www.towd.com
Listings of places worldwide that provide free travel information.

VirtualTourist
www.virtualtourist.com
A site where travellers can exchange information.

Walkabout
www.walkabout.fairfax.com.au
A range of travel information and 'The definitive traveller's guide to 1500 Australian cities and towns'.

Health

Healthy Flying
www.flyana.com
Information on everything from pressurised air to fear of flying.

International travel and health
www.who.int/ith
All you need to know from the World Health Organization.

The Travel Doctor (TMVC)
www.tmvc.com.au
A vaccination guide and health planner to help you stay healthy on your overseas trip.

Travel Health Online
www.tripprep.com
Everything from altitude sickness to yellow fever.

TravHealth
www.travhealth.com
Advice on health problems worldwide, and many useful services if you subscribe.

Holidays

The Adventure Travel Company
www.adventure-travel.com.au   226

Australian Tourist Commission
www.australia.com   225

Campsites in Europe
www.interhike.com   226

Destination New Zealand
www.purenz.com   225

Earthwatch Institute
www.earthwatch.org   231

E-Ticket-Airtravel
www.e-ticket-airtravel.com   230

Flight Centre Australia / New Zealand
www.flightcentre.com.au   229
www.flightcentre.co.nz   229

Greyhound
www.greyhound.com   230

Lastminute.com
www.lastminute.com   229

Remote Outback Cycle Tours
www.cycletours.com.au   227

Travel.com.au
www.travel.com.au   228

The Travel Mall
www.oztravel.com.au   229

Travel Online
www.travelonline.co.nz   228

Air New Zealand
www.airnewzealand.com
Fast fare finder, and if you book on-line, you'll save.

British Airways
www.britishairways.com
Book on-line and check out the special offers.

Countrylink
www.countrylink.nsw.gov.au
Why drive when you can catch the train?

Discover Tasmania
www.discovertasmania.com.au
Explore your holiday options in this island state.

Elderhostel
www.elderhostel.org
An American educational and travel organisation providing learning adventures for people 55 and over, world-wide.

Fodors.com
www.fodors.com
Information on world destinations with additional sections on news and hotels.

Freedom Air
www.freedom.co.nz
On-line fare and flight information – but if you can't get away you can take a virtual tour of one of their Boeings, even going into the cockpit.

Global Village Escapes
www.escapes.com.au
Their travel features – Senior Leisure or Wildlife Viewing for example – take you quickly to loads of holiday options.

GORP
http://gorp.com
Wide-ranging US site full of ideas for outdoor recreation.

Harvey World Travel
www.harveyworld.com.au
Check their special offers for Australian and international holidays, as well as cruises and exclusive escapes.

Intrepid Travel
www.intrepidtravel.com
For the traveller with a yearning for adventure, a sense of fun and a wish to escape the humdrum of mainstream tours.

Need It Now
www.needitnow.com.au
Select your destination, choose the accommodation that suits you, then book and pay on-line.

Odyssey Travel
www.odysseytravel.com.au
A not-for-profit organisation that arranges educational travel experiences for seniors in Australia, NZ and overseas.

Qantas
www.qantas.com.au
Special Internet-only fares – and you can subscribe to receive the latest specials.

STA Travel
www.statravel.com.au
or
www.statravel.co.nz
Take one of their Inspiration suggestions for your next trip.

Tranz Scenic
www.tranzscenic.co.nz
Travel on some of the most breathtaking railways in the world – in New Zealand.

Travelmate.com.au
www.Travelmate.com.au
Register to receive information on travel bargains, touring ideas and accommodation.

WEATHER

Virgin Blue
www.virginblue.com.au
Look up flight schedules, get advance notice of special offers, book on-line to receive discounted fares and check out their holiday suggestions.

Webjet
www.webjet.com.au
Save time and money by booking your entire holiday over the Net – flights, accommodation and car hire.

Yahoo! Travel
http://au.travel.yahoo.com
Great starting point for those planning a holiday. Links to specialist holiday companies, destination guides, luggage shops and much more.

Maps

Geoscience Australia – National Mapping
www.auslig.gov.au
Find the map that covers your area using the Place Name Search facility.

Multimap
www.multimap.com
Street maps and aerial photos of cities in the UK.

Stanfords
www.stanfords.co.uk
Well-stocked travel bookstore, specialising in maps for every part of the globe – including maps for astronomy, coastal navigation, hiking and mountaineering.

Terraserver.com
www.terraserver.com
Library of aerial shots of famous landmarks and streets all over the world.

Whereis OnLine
www.whereis.com.au
Type in your departure and arrival points, select the mode of transport and Hey, presto! your route, with instructions, is there for you.

Timetables

Eurostar
www.eurostar.co.uk 230

Greyhound
www.greyhound.com 230

The Sydney Transport Jumpstation
www.sydneytransport.net.au 222

a2btravel.com
www.a2b.com
Listing of UK rail, bus, ferry and other travel timetables. The site also has links to all the major rail networks of Europe.

Australian Rail Maps
www.railpage.org.au/railmaps
Maps of passenger rail services in Australia. Click on a region for more detailed maps and timetables.

SBB Online
www.rail.ch
Timetable and fare information on the Swiss rail network – you can set your watch by it!

Thetrainline.com
www.thetrainline.com
Plan your route anywhere in the UK, find the best fare and purchase your ticket on-line.

Travel tips

Adventure Travel Tips
www.adventuretraveltips.com
From animal treks to whale watching, you'll find all you need to know at this site.

The Bathroom Diaries
www.thebathroomdiaries.com
Where to find clean, free restrooms around the world – the winner of the 'Golden Plunger' award for best restroom is in Kawakawa, New Zealand.

Britannia.com
http://britannia.com
Portal aimed primarily at US tourists planning a trip to the UK. Includes virtual tours and city guides.

The National Public Toilet Map
www.toiletmap.gov.au
The location of more than 13,000 public toilet facilities in Australian towns and cities, rural areas and along major travel routes.

1000 Tips 4 Trips
www.tips4trips.com
Tips on everything from travelling with an animal to the weather in foreign destinations.

1000 Traveltips
www.1000traveltips.org
Useful information based on people's experiences: what to do, where to go and – perhaps most important – what to avoid.

RAC Route Planner
http://rp.rac.co.uk
Key in your departure and destination points and the RAC will find the fastest route. Works for all major towns and cities in continental Europe and the UK.

Travel Experiences
www.travel-experiences.net
Backpackers should go to 'Travelogues' to share advice and information.

W
Weather
Forecasts

Bureau of Meteorology Australia
www.bom.gov.au 230

MetService
www.metservice.co.nz 230

WeatherOnline
www.weatheronline.co.uk 230

BBC Weather Centre
www.bbc.co.uk/weather
Weather information around the world, including regional five-day forecasts, ski reports and weather facts.

National Climatic Data Center
http://lwf.ncdc.noaa.gov
The world's largest archive of weather data. Pages on climate change and El Niño.

Weather.com
www.weather.com
Weather reports for all the US states as well as cities around the world.

Weather Site.com
www.weathersite.com
A comprehensive US site, which also allows you to search by country.

Yahoo! Weather
http://weather.yahoo.com
Five-day forecasts and weather records for towns and cities around the world, plus features on weather phenomena.

INDEX

A

ABC (Australian Broadcasting Corporation) 119, 137
actors *see* celebrities
addresses, finding 39, 73
Adobe Acrobat Reader 85
ADSL (Asymmetrical Digital Subscriber Line) *see* Internet connections: broadband
adware 84
aliens, sites dedicated to 142, 143, 144
AltaVista *see* searching: search engines
Ananova *see* e-mail: news
animals 156, 157
animations 15, 80, 250
anniversaries *see* celebrations
AOL 66, 71, 93
Apple Mac *see* iMac
architecture: virtual tours 145
ARPANET 11
art
  collecting 172
  courses 172
  dictionaries/encyclopedias 173
  exhibiting on-line 173
  galleries 172, 173
  history 172, 173
  supplies 173
  virtual 173
  virtual tours 145, 146
  see also painting
Ask Jeeves 66
  for Kids 71, 137, 139
astronomy 142–4
attachments *see* e-mail: attachments
auctions, on-line 207, 208–11
  Auction Manager (iMac) 81
  charity 207

B

banking 212–15
  fees 212
  interest rates 213
  Internet-only 212, 213, 214
  mortgages 204–5
  on-line accounts 216
  security 213, 214, 215
  sites 214
birds 157
birthdays *see* celebrations
Bluetooth 91
books 166–8
  authors 167
  Book Radio 153
  buying 166, 167, 201–3
    rare/second-hand 72, 115, 166, 201, 202, 203
  catalogues 167
  children's 138, 174
  e-books 166, 168
  libraries *see main entry*
  literary groups 166, 167
  poetry 166, 167
  Project Gutenberg 167
  publishing 166, 167
  reading groups 166, 167
  reviews 167
  writing 166, 167
Boolean search 69
  see also searching
Bpay 212
broadband *see* Internet connections: broadband
browsers, browsing 15, 26–9, 76–84
  cookies 82
  Favorites 27, 66, 76, 78, 79
  History 76, 77
  homepages 29
  images 80, 139
  Internet Explorer 26, 27–9, 76–9
    addresses, finding 28
    commands/tools 27
      animations/images, cancelling 80, 139
      AutoComplete 80
      Favorites 27, 76, 78, 80
      History 27, 76, 77
      Refresh 27, 83
      Search 27, 77
    connecting/disconnecting 27, 28
    copying text from 79, 175
    downloading *see main entry*
    e-mailing pages/links 80
    error messages 83
    filters 53
    iMac features 81, 209
    Java, enabling 83, 146
    links 78, 79, 80
    off-line browsing 79, 80, 175
    problems 82–3
    saving to computer 79
    shortcuts/timesavers 78, 80
  Java 83, 146
  Netscape Navigator 26, 86
  plug-ins 82
  searching *see main entry*
  security *see* security: filters
building societies 204–5, 212
bulletin boards 100–1, 115, 135, 169
  children's 175
  creating 247, 252
  junk mail, avoiding 101
  registering with 101
business *see* e-commerce
buying and selling *see* auctions; books: buying; cars; e-commerce; shopping

C

cable, access by *see* Internet connections
cafés, Internet 91
cakes, ordering 179, 241, 242
cameras *see* images: photographs; Web-cams
camping 226
cancer research 207
cards 218, 219
  designing on-line 179
  e-cards 218, 219–20, 221
careers *see* job-hunting
cars 180–2
  buying/selling 180, 181, 182
  clubs 180, 182
  hiring 228, 229
  newsgroups 182
  repair services 180, 181
celebrations 218–21
  cards *see main entry*
  gifts 218, 219, 221
  invitations, children's 179
  reminder services 218, 219, 221
  weddings *see main entry*
celebrities 164–5, 197, 202
censorware *see* security: filters
champagne *see* shopping: wine
charities *see* good causes
chatrooms 13, 102–5, 169
  abbreviations 103, 105
  audio 95
  children 105, 174, 175
  'emoticons' 105
  finding 103, 170
  Netiquette 105
  security 55, 102, 103, 105
  software for 102, 104
  subjects 102
  video forums 95

children 174–9
    activities 174, 175–6
    art and craft 176, 177, 179
    bulletin boards 175
    chatrooms 105, 174, 175
    downloading 175
    education *see main entry*
    e-mail 138, 174, 175, 177
    games 174, 175, 186, 187, 189
    parties 179
    penpals 174, 175, 178
    protecting 52, 53, 56–7, 137, 138, 174
    search tools 57, 71, 112, 137, 174
    TV program tie-ins 176
chocolates, ordering on-line 218, 219, 221
cinema *see* films
climbing 226, 227
ClipArt 251, 260
clubs 169, 170
    car 180, 182
    fan 164–5
    health 130
    night 223
    walking 225, 226
CNN 117
colleges *see* education: universities/colleges
communication, non-e-mail 92–5
compression tools 47, 49, 85, 87, 267, 285
computers 14–15
    bugs 133, 134
    drivers 133, 135
    hard disk space 286
    hardware 14
        modems *see main entry*
        monitors 14
    problems 133
        Web-cams 92, 94, 95
    improving 133, 134
    portable 90
    problems 83, 133–5
        advice 134
        FAQs 135
        hardware 133
        identifying 133
        newsgroups dedicated to 134
    software *see main entry*
    sounds *see main entry*
    tutorials 134
    TV on *see* television
    viruses *see main entry*
cookery 236–7
cookies 82
courses, on-line 110–12, 134, 163
    see also education
credit cards *see* security: shopping
current affairs *see* news
CV *see* résumés

D

dance guides 223
dating agencies 169, 170, 171
demoware *see* downloading
dictionaries
    art 173
    children's 136
diet 130–2
discussion groups *see* newsgroups
diving holidays 231
DIY
    cars 180, 181
    house 183, 184
domain names 38
    see also e-mail: addresses

downloading 15, 80, 84–7, 175
    e-books 168
    images 265
    music 13, 84, 88
    search agents 70
    software 84–7
        Adobe Acrobat Reader 85
        adware 84
        chatrooms, for 102, 104
        compression 47, 49, 85, 87
        demoware 84
        drivers 133, 135
        freeware 84
        FTP 15, 85
        Helix Producer Basic 279
        patches 129
        plug-ins 82, 85, 296–7
            Macromedia Flash 15, 82, 83, 85, 297
            QuickTime 147, 157
            RealOne Player 15, 82, 85, 119, 150, 151, 152, 154–5
            Shockwave 82, 83
        news tickers 118
        search agents 70
        shareware 84, 85, 134
        updates 84, 85
        video 88, 148
        viruses 86, 143
drink *see* food and drink
drivers *see* downloading: software

E

eBay 208
e-books *see* books: e-books
e-cards 218, 219–20, 221
ecology 156
e-commerce 13, 247, 298–311
    advertising 299

    computer problems 303
    copyright 303
    customer data 299
    deliveries 302
    design 300, 301, 302, 303
    finance 304, 305
    FreeMerchant 304–5
    hosts/ISPs 305
    law and 121, 303
    links 299, 310
    ordering 302, 303
    payment 302
        currencies 305
    products 299, 301
    publicity 302, 306–11
    search tools, registering with 306–11
    security 300, 302
    subscription services 299
    see also shopping
education
    adult 110–12 *see also* reference/research work *and* specific subjects
    Australian Correspondence Schools 112
    children 136–9
    primary school 136–9
        books 138
        educational sites 137
        homework 136, 137, 138, 174, 175, 178
        learning support 137
        projects/research 136, 139
        search directories 137
        software 136, 175
    universities/colleges
        on-line courses 110, 111, 112
e-etiquette 47, 276
    see also Netiquette

INDEX

e-mail 11, 13, 30–51
  abbreviations 105
  accounts 30, 34–5
    multiple 50–1
  address book 40–1
    contacts, adding 40
    groups 41
  addresses 31, 35, 38, 50
    acquiring 21, 24, 30, 34, 35
    finding 39, 73
  attachments 46–9
    compressed 47, 49, 85
    file sizes 47
    filing 49
    receiving 48–9
    sending 46–7
    viruses *see* viruses: e-mail
  chain letters 43, 59, 62
  children 138, 174, 175, 177
  confidentiality *see* security
  contacts *see* address book;
    addresses *above*
  drafts folder 39
  'emoticons' 105
  hoaxes *see* chain letters *above*
  junk mail *see* spam *below*
  mail servers 35
  mobile phones, via 33, 90
  Netiquette 105
    'flame war' 98
  news 116, 119
  newsgroups *see main entry*
  newsletters 126, 131
  petitions 43
  rules, creating 42
  security *see main entry*
  software 15, 30, 32–51
    Eudora 32, 33
    Netscape 32, 33
    Outlook Express 15, 30, 32, 34–51

    address book 40–1
    attachments 46–9
    automatic actions 42
    commands 36–7, 39, 42–5
    deleting messages 42, 44, 45
    folders 39, 42, 44
    forwarding messages 42, 43, 47
    identities, multiple-user 50–1
    newsgroups, accessing 96, 97–9
    rules, creating 42, 51, 63
    sending/receiving 38–9
    setting up 34–5
    spam, dealing with 63
    testing 34
    toolbar icons 36, 37
  Pegasus 32, 33, 38
  spam 62–3, 97, 101
  speed 31, 92
  TV, monitoring what's on 149
  usernames 24
  viruses *see main entry*
  WAP phones 33, 90
  Web-based 11, 13, 45, 91
  Web pages/links, sending 80
  WebTV 151
'emoticons' 105
employment *see* job-hunting
encyclopedias, children's 136, 178
entertainment 222–4
  see also celebrities
environment
  helping, learning about 156, 157
Eudora *see* e-mail: software

F

family history, researching 159–63
  genealogical societies 159
  newsgroups 159, 161
  resources 160, 162–3
  software 159, 160, 161
fan sites, fanzines
  entertainment 164–5
  sport 239
FAQs 135
films 164, 202
  cinema guides 224
  stars 164, 165, 202
  videos and DVDs, buying 201, 202
filters *see* security: filters
finance *see* money
firewalls 52, 89
fitness 130–2
  see also health
'flame war' 98
Flash *see* Macromedia Flash
flowers, sending 218, 219, 221
food and drink 236–7
  buying 192–5, 236
  cooking 236–7
  restaurants 222, 223
football 238, 239
freeware *see* downloading
friends
  making 169–71
  tracing *see* people, tracing
FTP *see* software

G

games
  on-line 186–9
    children's 174, 175, 186, 187
    multiple players 187, 189

    poetry 167
    simulation 186, 187
    single-player 188
    video 186, 187
gardening *see* homes and gardens
gardens, visiting 233, 235
genealogy 161–3
  see also family history
gifts, buying 218, 219, 221
  wedding lists 241, 242, 243
good causes 206–7
  auctions 207
  donations 13, 206, 207
    e-cards 221
    shopping 206, 207, 221
  getting involved 206, 207
  health 126, 207
  homepage, setting as a 207
  research 207
government sites 113, 117, 121
GPRS (General Packet Radio Service) mobile phones 90
gyms, health clubs 130, 132
  see also health

H

hackers 52, 53
hand-held devices 90
hardware *see* computers
health 126–32
  advice and information 126, 127
  back pain, avoiding 184
  clubs 130, 132
  conditions 126, 127
  diet 130, 131, 132
  diseases 126, 127
    cancer research 207
  exercise 131, 132

first aid 126
fitness 130–2
government information 127
hospitals 127
kilojoule counters 130, 132
medicines 129
NHS Direct 127, 128
nutrition 130–2
questionnaires 126, 127, 128
search engines 127
self-care 126
support groups 126, 129
symptoms 126, 127, 128
tests 128
treatments 127
weight, losing 130, 131, 132
World Health Organization (WHO) 128
help, on-line 196
history
   family 161–3
   historical sites, visiting 231–3
   virtual tours 145, 147
hobbies and leisure 140–89
holidays *see* tourism and travel
homepage, setting 29
homes and gardens 183–5
   DIY 184
   gardening 183, 184
   home improvement 183, 184
   house buying
      mortgages 204–5
      virtual tours 145
   kitchens 184
   plants 183, 184, 185
   TV program sites 185
hospitals *see* health
Hotmail *see* e-mail: Web-based
houses *see* homes and gardens
HTML 246, 294, 295, 308–11
   see also Web design

I

iMac 27, 33, 53, 65, 81, 151
images
   animations *see main entry*
   ClipArt 251, 260
   downloading 265
   finding 66, 72, 251
   photographs 243, 247, 249
      digital 249, 265
      scanning 249, 264, 265
   research, for 113
   video *see main entry*
   virtual tours 145–7
   Web-cams *see main entry*
   Web sites, on *see* Web design
income tax return
   completing on-line 196–7
insects 156, 157
instant messaging 92, 93, 94
Internet cafés 88, 91
   see also Webmail
Internet connections 10, 24–5, 88–91
   broadband 21, 88–9
      ADSL 22, 88, 89
      cable 89
      satellite 88, 89
   configuring ISP account 24–5
      manually 25
      with CD-ROM 24
   cost 12, 20, 177
   GPRS (General Packet Radio Service) mobile phones 90
   hand-held devices 90
   Internet cafés *see main entry*
   laptops/palmtops 88, 90
   mobile phones 33, 88, 90
   modems *see main entry*
   software *see main entry and* browsers
   speed of 12, 83
   WAP (Wireless Application Protocol) mobile phones 90
   WebTV 151
   see also Internet Service Providers (ISPs)
Internet Explorer *see* browsers
Internet kiosks 91
Internet Relay Chat (IRC) 104
Internet security *see* security
Internet Service Providers (ISPs) 20–1
   choosing 21
   configuring an ISP account 24–5
   cost 20, 177
   e-mail *see main entry*
   passwords 24
   Web space 248, 249, 290–3
Internet Society 12
Internet telephony 92, 94, 95
investments 198–200

J, K, L

Java 83, 146
   JavaScript 297
job-hunting 122–5
   applications 122, 123
   aptitude tests 122
   personal profile 124
   résumé 122, 123, 125
   training courses 125
   vacancies 122, 123, 149
kiosks, Internet (Multi-Media Phones) 91
languages
   penpals 178
   search engines, and 68, 81
   translators 81
law and legal issues 120–1, 303
learning *see* courses, on-line
leisure activities 140–89
libraries 114, 167
links *see* browsers; Web, World Wide: links
literature *see* books
Looksmart *see* searching: search directories

M

Macromedia
   ColdFusion MX 297
   Flash 15, 82, 85, 297
Media Player *see* Windows Media Player
medicine *see* health
MetaCrawler 114
Microsoft Word
   creating a Web site in 246, 248, 255, 256–61
minority rights 120
modems 14, 21, 22–3, 24, 25
   cable 89
   choosing 22
   external 14, 22, 23
   installing 23
   internal 14, 22, 23
      portable PCs, for 22, 90
   speed 22, 23, 88
   upgrading 22
money 192–215
   bank accounts 212–15
   charities *see* good causes
   income tax returns 196–7, 211
   investments 198–200
   mortgages 204–5
   shopping *see main entry*
   stocks and shares 198–200
mortgages 204–5
motoring 180–2
movies *see* films

INDEX

multimedia 12, 113
  see also radio; television; video; Web-cams
museums 172
music 202
  buying (CDs, vinyl) 201, 202
  concerts 223
  downloading 13, 84, 88
  musicians 165, 171
  research, for 113
  uploading 171
  see also sound

N

natural world 156–8
Netiquette 47, 98, 105
Netscape *see* e-mail: software
Netscape Navigator *see* browsers
news 13, 72, 116–19
  Australian 117, 119
  CNN 117
  e-mail, via 117, 119
  headlines 72, 73, 116, 117, 118
  mobile phones 90, 116
  newspapers 116, 117, 118
  parliament 117
  portals 73, 116, 117
  sports 238, 239, 240
  tickers 116, 117, 118
  TV 119
  see also newspapers: online
newsgroups 11, 15, 72, 96–9, 115, 134, 170
  accessing 96, 97–8
  directories 97, 98, 134
  names 98
  replies 99
  setting up 99
  software 97
    news readers 15

spam 97
subscribing 99
topics 98, 134
newspapers
  archives 113, 116
  letters to 119
  on-line 116, 117, 118
night life 222, 223
  booking 223, 224
  finding a film 224
Ninemsn 65
nutrition 130–2

O, P

operating systems 7, 15
  see also Windows Operating System
OptusNet 73
outdoor activities 225–7
  see also sports; tourism and travel: holidays
Outlook Express *see* e-mail: software
painting 172–3
  see also art
palmtop devices 90
Parliament, Australian 117
parties, children's 179
  see also celebrations
passport applications 228
passwords 24
PDF files 85
Pegasus *see* e-mail: software
penfriends 169, 170
  children's 174, 175, 178
people, tracing 73, 169, 170–1
photographs, pictures *see* images
plants 69, 156, 158
  garden 183, 184

plug-ins 82, 85, 296–7
  see also downloading
poetry *see* books
pornography, avoiding *see* e-mail: spam; security: filters
portals 73, 116, 117
postal information 73
postcodes, finding 73
Project Gutenberg 167
publishing *see* books

Q, R

QuickTime 87, 147, 151, 157
quotations, mortgage 204–5
radio 152–5
  digital 155
  Internet radio stations 85, 152, 153–5
  news 155
  RealOne Player 85, 150, 152, 154–5
  Windows Media Player 152
RealOne Player 82
  downloading 85, 119, 150, 152, 154–5
  radio 15, 85, 150, 152, 154–5
  RealAudio 279
  sound 85, 150, 152, 154, 155
  TV 119, 150
  video 85, 119, 150
recipes, on-line 236–7
reference/research work 13, 113–15
  academic 114, 115
  archives 113
  books, rare/second-hand 72, 115
  bulletin boards 115
  children's 136, 139
  experts, finding 114

government 113, 117, 121
libraries 114
links 115
methods 115
newsgroups 115
search engines, using 113, 114
Web rings, Web sites 115
  see also education *and specific subjects*
restaurants 222, 223
résumés: preparing, submitting on-line 122, 124

S

safety *see* security
sampleware *see* downloading
scanners 249, 264, 265
scripting 296, 297
searching 64–75
  advanced 68, 69
  Boolean 69
  Favorites 66
  images 72
  keywords and terms 64, 68, 69, 75, 115, 309
  languages 68, 81
  person, for a 73
  problems 74
  search tools 64–7
    search agents 64, 65, 66, 70, 75
    'searchbots' 70
    search directories 64, 65, 66, 71, 308
      children's 137
      registering with 307, 308
    search engines 12, 64, 65, 66–9, 70, 73–5, 112, 113
      children's 57, 71, 137
      filters 71

languages 68, 81
reference/research work 113
MetaCrawler 114
registering with 306–11
reliability 74
Web portals 73, 116
symbols 68
video 72
see also specific subjects
security 52–63, 292
auctions 208
banks 213
browsing 52–3
chatrooms 102, 103, 105
children see main entry
e-mail 52, 55, 61
encryption 54
filters 52, 53, 56–7, 63, 71, 105, 138, 174
firewalls 52
hackers 52, 53
holiday bookings 229
on-line dating 171
shopping 52, 54–5
viruses see main entry
selling online see auctions; cars; shares
shares 198–200
trader sites 199, 200
shareware see downloading: shareware
shopping 13, 54–5, 65, 92–5, 194
auctions 208–11
books see main entry
CDs 201, 202
charities, aiding 206, 207, 221
chocolates 218, 219, 221
flowers 218, 219, 221
food 192–5
organic 194

gifts 218, 219, 221
kitchen equipment 237
music 201, 202
ordering on-line 195
outdoor equipment 226
search agents, using 65, 70
secure sites 54–5, 223, 300
supermarkets 192–5
tickets 223, 224, 228, 230, 238
travel equipment 226
videos and DVDs 201, 202
wine 242
see also e-commerce
show business 164–5
software 14, 15
anti-virus see viruses
browsers see main entry
bugs 133
chatrooms 102, 104
compression 47, 49, 85, 87
downloading see main entry
drivers 133, 135
e-mail see main entry
FTP 15, 85, 263
installing 134
instant messaging see main entry
Internet Relay Chat (IRC) 102, 104
news reader 15
patches 133
plug-ins 82, 85, 296–7
protective see security: filters; viruses: anti-virus software
video 282–7
conferencing 95
Web site
design 248, 294–5, 300
uploading 262–3
see also specific names

sound
cards 14, 94, 95
creating 280–1
for computer tasks 177
formats 280
Internet telephony 92, 94
microphones 92, 94, 95, 281
music see main entry
on Web sites see Web, World Wide; Web design
radio 15, 85
RealOne Player 15, 85, 150, 152, 154, 155
Helix Producer Basic 279
space science/travel 142–4
spam see e-mail: spam
sports 169, 238–40
live coverage 239, 240
news 239, 240
participation 226–7, 238, 239
quizzes 238
results 238, 239, 240
tickets, buying 238
stocks and shares 198–200
studying see courses, on-line
StuffIt Expander 49
surfing see browsers, browsing

T

tax returns 196–7, 211
telephones 11
Internet kiosks (Multi-Media Phones) 91
Internet telephony 92, 94, 95
mobile 33, 88, 90
numbers, finding 73, 171
video 92, 94, 95
WAP-enabled 33, 90, 116
see also Internet connections; modems

television 148–51
downloading old programs 148
films on 202
guides/listings 149
news 119
palmtops, on 90
QuickTime 147, 151
RealOne Player 119, 150
show sites 164
children's 176
watching live 148, 149, 151
Web-cams 148, 149
see also video
Telnet 100
tennis 240
theatre
guides 222, 223
tickets, buying 223, 224
see also celebrities
tickers see news: tickers
tickets, buying see shopping
tourism and travel 90, 228–31, 232–5
accommodation 225, 229
agents 228, 230
booking 228, 230
car hire 229
guides 228, 233
holidays 228–35
official sites 229, 233
outdoor activities 225–7
overseas 222, 228–31, 232–5
camping 226
Eurostar trains 230
flights/fares 228, 229, 230
Greyhound coaches 230
passport applications 228
security 229
travel sites 229, 232, 233
UK 232–5

INDEX

virtual tours 145–7
visas 228
walking 225, 226, 227
weather forecasts 230

U, V

universities *see* education
updates *see* downloading
URLs *see* Web, World Wide: addresses
USENET 72, 99
video
  chat forums 95
  conferencing 92, 95
  downloading 88, 148
  films, buying 201, 202
  finding 72
  formats 284
  games 186, 187
  RealOne Player 15, 82, 85, 119, 150, 151
  telephony 92, 94, 95
  virtual tours 145–7
  Web-cams 92, 94, 95
  Web sites, on 250, 282–7
  see also television
violence, avoiding *see* security: filters
virtual
  meetings 93
  tours 145–7
  university 112
viruses 58–60, 86, 143
  anti-virus software 52, 58, 59, 62, 134, 143
  effects 58
  e-mail 47, 48, 58, 60, 61–2
  hoaxes 59
visas 228
volcano sites 157

W

walking 225, 226, 227
WAP (Wireless Application Protocol) mobile phones 90
weather forecasts 230
Web, World Wide 11, 13, 246
  addresses 28, 262, 307
  Consortium 12
  portals 73
  rings 115
  servers 74, 248, 262, 263
  sites 11, 13, 246–61
    accuracy of 12, 139, 262
    advertising on 290, 299
    cookies 82
    copying text from 79
    creating and modifying 13, 17, 115, 244–311
    extra features 252, 296–7
    FAQs 135
    hosts 248, 262, 263, 303
    links 11, 12, 28, 29, 74, 115
    opinion polls 252
    providers 288, 289
    saving to computer 79
  Web space, 248, 249, 289
  see also browsers, browsing; searching; Web design
Web-cams 92, 94, 95, 156, 157
  radio sites 155
  TV sites 148, 149
WebCrawler *see* searching: search engines
Web design 247, 248–61
  advanced tools 296–7
  advice 253
  analysing 247
  animation 250
  builders 289, 303
  colours, appropriate 254, 255, 257, 273
  content 247, 250–2, 289, 302
  copyright 250, 264
  e-commerce, for 300, 301, 302, 303
  guest books 252
  hit counters 252
  homepage 261
  HTML 246, 294, 295, 308–11
  images 249, 250, 251, 255, 260–1
  interactive features 252, 293, 296
  links 255, 257, 270–5, 278, 292
  Microsoft Word, using 246, 255, 256–61
  on-line design 248, 288–93
  registering 306–311
  security 292
  sites 288–93, 303
  software 248, 294–5, 296–7
  sounds 250, 252, 259, 276–81
  structure 257
  tables, using 257–61
  text 254, 255, 256, 257, 258, 259–60, 286
  themes 259
  updating 263
  uploading 262–3
  video 250, 282–7
Webmail 45, 91
WebTV 151
weddings, planning 241–3
  wedding list, on-line 243
weight, losing 130, 131, 132
wildlife 156, 157
wireless networks 91
Windows Media Player 152, 277
Windows Messenger 93, 95, 103
Windows Movie Maker 282–7
Windows Operating System
  basics 16
  compression facility 47, 87
  configuration wizards 16
  for children 174
  older versions 7, 15, 16
  passwords 16
  user accounts 16–19
    changing 16, 19
    guest 18
    setting up 17, 18
    types of 17
  Windows XP 7, 15, 16–19, 32, 47
wine 242
WinZip 47, 49, 85, 87
Word *see* Microsoft Word
World Health Organization (WHO) 128
writing *see* books
WWW *see* Web, World Wide

Y

Yahoo! 57, 71, 234
  bulletin boards 101
  chatrooms 95, 102, 103
  directory 65, 71, 234
    inclusion in 290
  e-mail, web-based 33, 91
  GeoCities 288–93
  instant messaging 93
  Internet telephony 94
  news 116, 118
  portals 116
  search tools 65, 66, 167
    children's 57, 71, 112, 174
  ticker 118

Z

zip 47, 49, 85, 87
  see also compression tools

How to do *just about* anything on the INTERNET

Published by Reader's Digest (Australia) Pty Limited
26–32 Waterloo Street, Surry Hills, NSW 2010
www.readersdigest.com.au

Project Editor David Scott-Macnab • **Designers** Alex Stafford, Kylie Mulquin
Research Editor Alistair McDermott • **Assistant Editor** Françoise Toman
Proofreader Bronwyn Sweeney • **Rights & Permissions** Robyn Hudson
Indexer Nancy Sibtain • **Production Controller** Janelle Garside

Contributors
Edwin Barnard • Paul Bradshaw • Bill Dawes • Stephen Dunthorne • Lewis Lyons
Lisa Magloff • Barry Plows • Patrick Taylor • Guy Vella • Sandra Vogel • Kevin Wiltshire

Illustrator Nancy Dunkerley

Reader's Digest General Books
Editorial Director Carol Natsis • **Art Director** Mark Thacker
Executive Editor Elaine Russell

Based on the UK edition, edited and designed for
The Reader's Digest Association Limited, London
by Planet Three Publishing Network
Northburgh House, 10 Northburgh Street, London EC1V 0AT

We are interested in receiving your comments on the content of this book.
Write to: The Editor, General Books Editorial, Reader's Digest (Australia) Pty Limited,
26-32 Waterloo Street, Surry Hills, NSW 2010 or e-mail us at bookeditors.au@readersdigest.com

To order additional copies of *How to do Just About Anything on the Internet*
call 1300 303 210 (Australia)
or 0800 540 032 (New Zealand)
or e-mail us at customerservice.au@readersdigest.com

Picture Credits
p.11 (c) John K.Humble/Stone/Getty Images; p.13 (tl) Reader's Digest Assoc. Inc./GID; p.16 (tl) PhotoDisc;
p.28 (photo in step 2) Robert Knight; p.45 (b) PhotoDisc; p.69 (br) Doug Menuez/PhotoDisc/Getty Images; p.122 (bl) PhotoDisc;
p.147 (br) Jim Bastardo/ Stone/Getty Images; p.148 (bl) image100 Ltd & PhotoDisc; p.150 (bl) PhotoDisc; p.157 (t) Gary Lewis/Photolibrary.com;
p.184 (bl) Reader's Digest Assoc. Inc./GID; p.188 (bl) Andreas Pollok/Stone/Getty Images; p.202 (bl) Jason Homa/The Image Bank/Getty Images;
p.213 (br) PhotoDisc; p.231 (br) Stephen Frink/Corbis/Australian Picture Library; p.232 (bl foreground) ImageState,
(bl background) Wilfried Krecichwost/Stone/Getty Images; p.233 (tc) mapping with permission of the Controller of HMSO, Crown copyright, all rights reserved
(licence No. 100018100); p.235 (br foreground) Stock Market/Corbis, (br background) Pictor International; p.276 (br) Jeff Foott/Bruce Coleman Collection;
p.296 image100 Ltd, PhotoDisc, Reader's Digest Assoc. Inc./GID & Stockbyte; p.301 (br) Reader's Digest Assoc. Inc./GID.
All other photography: Karl Adamson

First Australian and New Zealand edition 2003

Copyright © Reader's Digest (Australia) Pty Limited 2003
Copyright © Reader's Digest Association Far East Limited 2003
Philippines Copyright © Reader's Digest Association Far East Limited 2003

All rights reserved. No part of this book may be reproduced, stored in a retrieval system, or transmitted in any form or by any means, electronic, electrostatic, magnetic tape, mechanical, photocopying, recording or otherwise, without permission in writing from the publishers.

® Reader's Digest, The Digest and the Pegasus logo are registered trademarks of The Reader's Digest Association, Inc., of Pleasantville, New York, USA.

Microsoft® Word, Microsoft® Internet Explorer and Microsoft® Outlook Express are registered trademarks of Microsoft Corporation in the United States and/or other countries.

Limit of Liability/Disclaimer of Warranty: The Publisher has used its best efforts in preparing this book and makes no representation or warranties with respect to the accuracy or completeness of its contents. The publisher specifically disclaims any implied warranties of merchantability or fitness for any particular purpose and shall in no event be liable for any loss of profit or any other commercial damage, including but not limited to special, incidental, consequential, or other damages.

Web site addresses and the contents of Web sites change constantly; Web sites may disappear without warning. The publisher accepts no responsibility for the accuracy of any of the information given in this book concerning Web sites, their contents, or any of the views expressed in them. Inclusion of Web sites in this book does not imply endorsement by Reader's Digest.

Every effort has been made to establish ownership of copyright material depicted in this book. All queries regarding copyright issues should be directed to bookeditors.au@readersdigest.com

Reader's Digest How To Do Just About Anything™ is a trademark of The Readers Digest Association Ltd.

National Library of Australia Cataloguing-in-Publication data:
How to do just about anything on the Internet

Includes index.
ISBN 1 876689 32 3.

1. Internet. 2. World Wide Web. I. Reader's Digest (Australia)
II. Title: Reader's digest how to do just about anything on the Internet.
004.678

Printed and bound by Tien Wah Press (Pte) Ltd, Singapore

Product code 0412567   Concept code UK1426/IC